America's Church

America's Church

*The National Shrine and Catholic
Presence in the Nation's Capital*

Thomas A. Tweed

OXFORD
UNIVERSITY PRESS

OXFORD
UNIVERSITY PRESS

Oxford University Press, Inc., publishes works that further
Oxford University's objective of excellence
in research, scholarship, and education.

Oxford   New York
Auckland   Cape Town   Dar es Salaam   Hong Kong   Karachi
Kuala Lumpur   Madrid   Melbourne   Mexico City   Nairobi
New Delhi   Shanghai   Taipei   Toronto

With offices in
Argentina   Austria   Brazil   Chile   Czech Republic   France   Greece
Guatemala   Hungary   Italy   Japan   Poland   Portugal   Singapore
South Korea   Switzerland   Thailand   Turkey   Ukraine   Vietnam

Published by Oxford University Press, Inc.
198 Madison Avenue, New York, New York 10016

www.oup.com

Oxford is a registered trademark of Oxford University Press

Library of Congress Cataloging-in-Publication Data
Tweed, Thomas A.
America's church : the National Shrine and Catholic Presence in the
Nation's Capitol / Thomas A. Tweed.
p. cm.
Includes bibliographical references and index.
ISBN 978-0-19-978298-7
1. National Shrine of the Immaculate Conception (Washington, D.C.)—
History—20th century.   2. Washington (D.C.)—Church history—
20th century.   I. Title.
BX4603.W32N345 2011
282'.7530904—dc22   2010041242

1 3 5 7 9 8 6 4 2
Printed in the United States of America
on acid-free paper

For my grandmother,
Gertrude Fitzmaurice Wurster (1895–1978),
A Roman Catholic from the generation that built the Shrine

CONTENTS

Illustrations, ix
Abbreviations, xi

Introduction: A Threshold to Catholic America, *3*

1. LAYING CATHOLICISM'S FOUNDATION: Clerical Aims and Diverse Devotees, 1909–1959, *22*

2. MOBILIZING "AMERICA'S MARYS": Women, Fundraising, and the Mary Memorial Altar, 1913–1938, *59*

3. ENGAGING CATHOLIC CHILDREN: Agency, Prescriptions, and Constraints in the Catholic Institutional Network, 1920–1959, *93*

4. CONTESTING PROTESTANT INTERPRETATIONS: The Virgin Mary, the Crypt Church, and the Incorporeal Other, 1913–1932, *123*

5. CLAIMING CIVIC SPACE: The National Shrine, the Subjunctive Mood, and the Nation's Capital, 1913–1959, *157*

6. INCORPORATING CATHOLIC IMMIGRANTS: Diversity, Migration, and the Shrine's Columns and Chapels, 1913–1997, *192*

Conclusion, *229*

Appendices: A Social Profile of Selected Pilgrims and Donors, 1916–1959, 247
Notes, 283
Illustration Credits, 357
Acknowledgments, 361
Index, 367

ILLUSTRATIONS

I.1. Basilica of the Shrine of the Immaculate Conception, *4*

I.2. Bishop Shahan, Bernard McKenna, and two lay leaders
      in front of the Mary Altar commemorative plaque, *9*

I.3. Sarcophagus of Bishop Shahan, *11*

1.1. Foundation stone ceremony, 1920, *23*

1.2. Dedication mass for the Shrine, November 20, 1959, *40*

1.3. Lower Church under construction in 1925, *42*

1.4. Shahan, McKenna, and lay devotees with the mosaic of Murillo's
      Immaculate Conception, *50*

2.1. The Mary Memorial Altar, *60*

2.2. Mary Memorial Altar presentation ceremony,
      December 8, 1928, *63*

2.3. Mary Downs and siblings, *71*

2.4. Children posing in front of *Mary, Mother of Mankind*, *78*

3.1. "The Shrine You Can Build", *94*

3.2. Eighth-grade class of St. Thomas Aquinas School, 1938, *95*

3.3. Representation of the Catholic Educational Network, 1926, *104*

3.4. May Procession, Holy Child Church, Philadelphia,
      May 5, 1940, *109*

3.5. Students and teachers from an Ursuline school in New York
      with the Shrine's director, Patrick J. O'Connor, 1953, *121*

4.1. The Crypt Church's north apse in 1926, *124*

4.2. Ku Klux Klan parade, Washington, D.C., September 13, 1926, *134*

4.3. Monsignor Russell, President Taft, and First Lady Nellie Taft,
      Pan American Thanksgiving Day Mass, 1912, *136*

4.4. Fragment of Fresco of Madonna and child, Catacomb of
      St. Priscilla, *144*

4.5. The Crypt Church, *149*

5.1. Raphael Pfisterer, OSB, *Mary Immaculate, Patroness of the United States*, *158*

5.2. President Taft and Cardinal Gibbons, Catholic Summer School of America, 1909, *161*

5.3. Francis J. Spellman, Corporal George T. Robinson, and U.S. airmen at a base in Tunisia, 1943, *163*

5.4. Father Bernard McKenna, the Sisters of Charity, and children from the nearby orphanage, St. Vincent's, 1923, *167*

5.5. President Coolidge addressing Catholics at Holy Name Society Parade, 1924, *170*

5.6. Washington National Cathedral, *172*

5.7. Dedication of the Nuns of the Battlefield Memorial, 1924, *177*

5.8. National Shrine of the Immaculate Conception, *183*

5.9. Composite photograph U.S. Capitol and National Cathedral, *187*

5.10. Postcard. "Washington, D.C.," 1993, *190*

6.1. Our Lady of Peace and Good Voyage Oratory, *193*

6.2. "Civics Catechism." 1927, *197*

6.3. Mosaic: *Descent of the Holy Spirit*, *208*

6.4. Yearbook cover, St. John's Indian School, Laveen, Arizona, 1953, *210*

6.5. Construction workers at the site, September 12, 1923, *212*

6.6. The Crypt Church's marble columns, *216*

6.7. A Latina devotee kneels in prayer at the Our Lady of Guadalupe Chapel, *219*

ABBREVIATIONS

AC   Gregory W. Tucker, *America's Church* (Huntington, IN: Our Sunday Visitor, 2000).

ACUA   American Catholic History Research Center and University Archives, The Catholic University of America

BNSIC   Basilica of the National Shrine of the Immaculate Conception

CUA   Catholic University of America, Washington, D.C.

GTB   *Basilica of the National Shrine of the Immaculate Conception: Guide and Tour Book* (Washington, DC: BNSIC, 2007).

IFCA   International Federation of Catholic Alumnae

LAAOH   Ladies Auxiliary of the Ancient Order of Hibernians

MEM   Bernard A. McKenna, *Memoirs of the First Director of the National Shrine of the Immaculate Conception, Washington, D.C.* (n.p.: n.p., 1959).

MS   *Mary's Shrine*, official publication of the BNSIC (successor of *SR*)

NOCW   National Organization of Catholic Women

NCWC   National Catholic Welfare Conference ("Council," 1919–21); succeeded the National Catholic War Council, founded 1917.

NS   William P. Kennedy, *National Shrine of the Immaculate Conception*, bk. 1, *The Story of the Crypt* (Washington, D.C.: Salve Regina Press, 1927).

PAHRC   Philadelphia Archdiocesan Historical Records Center

SR   *Salve Regina*, the official publication of the BNSIC

America's Church

Introduction

A Threshold to Catholic America

Looking out the window of my small rented room in the Theological College, a national diocesan seminary on the grounds of Washington's Catholic University of America (CUA), I glanced across the street at the enormous Byzantine-Romanesque shrine where I'd spent that long June day (fig. I.1). That morning I'd crossed the street and climbed the steep steps of the Basilica of the National Shrine of the Immaculate Conception (BNSIC) to again pause and pivot at the main doors to look down the long nave and out toward the urban landscape—an invented ritual I repeated each visit. Then I spent the rest of that day alternating between long periods in the archives thumbing through boxes of brittle documents and—when my eyes strained and my back stiffened—strolling through the building, snacking in the cafeteria, and chatting with pilgrims.

That day was memorable, though not because I unearthed any project-altering historical sources in the archives. It was contemporary Catholics' wildly divergent assessments of the building's design and purpose that stayed with me. Before heading to the archives, I ate breakfast in the first-floor cafeteria with a member of the World Apostolate of Fatima's "Blue Army." She gushed about the building's "beautiful" architecture and emphasized her devotion to the Virgin Mary, our only hope in an uncertain world. During my midmorning coffee I chatted with a CUA graduate student who, to my surprise, indicated he came there only because it was "convenient" and, when I asked about the Shrine, gleefully described the

Figure I.1. Basilica of the Shrine of the Immaculate Conception, Washington, D.C.

building as "neo-ugly." I heard very different judgments over lunch as I interviewed two devout Filipino Catholics who had led the campaign to construct an oratory enshrining an image of Mary that was beloved back in the Philippines. Those lay devotees fought back tears as they told me how important their place of prayer would be for those displaced from their homeland, and I felt like I was back in Miami, where I'd studied popular piety at a Cuban shrine for a previous book and where almost every pilgrim I interviewed grinned broadly or teared up as they talked about the significance of the site.[1]

After three more hours of eye-straining archival research, I went back to the Shrine's central doors and descended the steps to meet a colleague who was in town. Unlike the conservative pilgrim I'd met at breakfast, a woman who is more likely to subscribe to *Soul*, the Blue Army's official periodical, and order the "John Paul II Rosary Beads" sold on Eternal Word Broadcasting Network's online catalog, my friend, a "progressive" Catholic, is more likely to read "NCR Today," the *National Catholic Reporter*'s blog, and buy a "Bread for the World" T-shirt from *Commonweal*'s website. After small talk, that self-described progressive mentioned the Shrine. He'd told a Catholic colleague that the building was the focus of my next book, and the scholar had responded with a question and an assertion: "Why? It's just about bishops." My friend, who seemed to agree, went on to complain that bishops had led the "top-down" construction efforts, which had diverted funds and labor from the Church's more important business, like feeding the poor and working for peace. He then sniped about the Shrine's "Disneyland" architecture. His comment reminded me of another contemporary Catholic's remarks. Alluding to its polychromatic dome, the Catholic novelist and former Paulist priest James Carroll dismissed the building, which he had visited regularly as a child, as a "towering Byzantine beach ball." He contrasted its "garishness" with the Gothic "elegance" of the National Cathedral. As our dinner conversation drew to a close, my friend told a joke that Carroll also mentioned and one I'd hear several more times during more than a decade of research there in "Little Rome," the area of Washington that includes the offices of the United States Conference of Catholic Bishops and dozens of other Catholic institutions. It's a joke that's been circulating since the 1960s and assumes the listener knows about the tradition of Marian apparitions: one day the Virgin appeared on the Shrine's top step and, clarifying her wishes, offered a new command to her devotees: "No, I meant build me a *beautiful* church on this spot."[2]

After I returned to my sparely furnished room, I looked out the window at the Shrine and tried to make sense of all I'd heard. I had already done enough research to know that the progressive's dismissive proclamation—"it's just about bishops"—wasn't exactly right, since archived donor letters and visitor logs showed that plenty of lay Catholics had supported the building project before 1959 and many, like the Blue Army devotee and the Filipino migrants, continued to do so. I also sensed that contemporary Catholics at both extremes got it wrong in other ways—by assuming that Catholics in the earlier period were equally divided, that their divisions mirrored current splits between liberals and conservatives, and that the Shrine's early promoters were unqualified conservatives. Today's passionately polarized interpretations disclose much more about the present than the past, however. The building, I began to realize, is a sort of spiritual Rorschach test, an inkblot that reveals the viewer's beliefs, feelings, and values. If you're Catholic, tell me what you think about this building—whether you hate it, love it, or just don't care—and I bet I can make a good guess about where you stand on the continuum of contemporary Catholicism. Yet however useful the building is as a tool for discerning present-day piety, that was not what I'd set out to do. I was writing a history that attended to the recently built ethnic chapels but focused on the period between the building's founding and dedication, 1913–1959.[3]

For that purpose, I learned, contemporary reactions didn't help, since things had changed over the course of the twentieth century. An era of consolidation had given way to an era of fragmentation. The Shrine was founded at a time when the Catholic institutional network was becoming increasingly centralized and unified, a process clearly signaled in 1917 by the Vatican codification of ecclesiastical law and the U.S. bishops' formation of the umbrella organization that came to be called the National Catholic Welfare Conference (NCWC). Meanwhile, the view that the pope's authority was supreme and extended beyond Rome and "over the mountains" won the day. That view, ultramontanism, strengthened the papacy. The fortified papacy championed a single theological framework based on the philosophy of St. Thomas Aquinas (1225–1274) and condemned movements that claimed to "adapt" or "accommodate" national cultures and modern scholarship—heresies the Vatican called "Americanism" and "Modernism." Those developments abroad—and the Oath against Modernism that all clergy swore between 1910 and 1967—had a "chilling" effect at home by suppressing dissent in an American Catholic Church that, in addition, began to become somewhat more linguistically and ethnically homogenous after the number of first-generation immigrants began to decline in 1924, when Congress restricted transnational migration. By the time the Shrine was dedicated in 1959, the year Pope John XXIII announced the Second Vatican Council, consolidated Catholicism had peaked. Although no one could see the changes coming, secular and ecclesiastical forces at home and abroad soon would divide and diversify the American Church. Within the transnational Church, heated debates erupted at Vatican II between two parties: the minority, the 15 percent of the twenty-two hundred bishops who favored a reaffirmation of the Vatican-centered Thomistic worldview, and the majority, sometimes called "progressives," who favored ecclesiastical "updating" (*aggiornamento* in Italian), though they always insisted their position harmonized with Catholic tradition. After the Council ended in 1965, the issues that had stirred controversy in Rome—and topics purposely *not* addressed, like birth control and clerical marriage—divided U.S. Catholics in the decades ahead. Those who remained uncomfortable with Vatican II's "updating" seemed to have more in common with Orthodox Jews and Evangelical Protestants on many issues that split late-twentieth-century Americans, including homosexuality, feminism, and abortion. Americans, especially those in the pews of Catholic churches, also looked more like the ethnically and linguistically diverse nineteenth-century immigrant nation after Congress revised federal law in 1965 and allowed more migrants from Latin America, Africa, and Asia to enter the country. So by the end of the twentieth century, a few years after the

Filipino oratory's 1997 dedication, many observers were bemoaning the Church's internal diversity and divisions, a fragmentation reflected in the divergent views I heard at the Washington Shrine.[4]

THE BOOK'S ARGUMENT AND ORGANIZATION

As I try to show in this book, the extreme contemporary reactions to that building aptly signal the divisiveness of post-1960s American culture and the fragmentation of postconciliar U.S. Catholicism, but they conceal the qualified countermodernism and recalibrated Americanism of the Shrine's promoters. Most important, present-day assessments obscure the ways that, between the 1920s and 1950s, the building both attracted varied Marian devotees and expressed common clerical hopes. The clergy's aims, which met with mixed success, elicited minimal resistance in part because they reflected a widely shared Catholic worldview that esteemed central-ized authority, revered historical tradition, and promoted ecclesiastical unity. The Shrine, in other words, was a monument to the consolidated Church's diverse membership, clerical agenda, and shared values—just as after 1959 it became a more contested site where the wider cultural issues of the day and the divisions within the fragmented Church found expres-sion. The Shrine's advocates helped to create an important impulse in American religious practice—to claim civic space in the nation's capital—but they didn't initiate other major changes. Further, that building isn't the only ecclesiastical site that reveals the decisive shifts in Catholic life. I'm not suggesting it's uniquely important. Still, it provides an illuminating angle of vision on the history of twentieth-century Catholicism. In its ability to reveal both the consolidating impulses of earlier decades and the fragmenting forces of the later period, I argue, the Shrine has functioned as a threshold to Catholic America. A threshold is the space at a doorway, a boundary between coming and going, and much that defined American Catholic life in both periods passed through the Shrine's central portal. For all its idiosyncrasies—and nothing is quite like that massive church—the distinctive building reflects broader patterns.

That Shrine is an especially interesting vantage from which to observe those broader patterns not only because it attracted pilgrims and donors from all regions of the country and because it was built on the grounds of America's pontifical university, a site linked with the Vatican, but also because it venerates the national patroness and stands in the nation's capital. It's dedicated to Mary Immaculate, whom the U.S. bishops named the official patroness of the United States in 1846, although Protestants at the time neither noticed nor challenged the bishops' claim on American terrain and national identity. Since the 1990s, the promotional literature has called the Washington Shrine "America's Church"—or, in slightly different phrasing, "America's Catholic Church" or "America's Patronal Church." Those phrases might be more recent, but the idea is not. Even if spiritual and aesthetic concerns were primary, from the start the planners also imagined the site as a national center. That was how Bishop Thomas J. Shahan (1837–1932), rector of Catholic University, successfully pitched the idea to Pope Pius X in a private audience in 1913. After the pope granted his apostolic benediction, the planning and fundraising began. Fundraising was necessary because as a shrine it received no diocesan support, and that campaign was successful enough that construction could begin. In 1920, with eleven flags waving from the wooden speaker's platform and more encircling the recently cleared ground, ten thousand Catholics gathered on September 23 to watch James Cardinal Gibbons (1834–1921), the most important U.S. Catholic leader of his generation, lay the foundation stone. Four years later, clerical and lay devotees of Mary attended the first mass in the building—although the Crypt Church's main altar, the Mary Memorial Altar, would not be installed until 1926, and the lower level would not be finished until 1931 (see fig. I.2). The Great Depression, Bishop Shahan's death, and World War II delayed further progress, but the U.S. bishops voted in 1946 to renew efforts to finish the Shrine. The big push to construct the Great Upper Church, however, only began in 1953, just before the official Marian Year and the centennial celebration of Pope Pius IX's proclamation of the doctrine of the Immaculate Conception, the belief that Mary was conceived without sin. The renewed appeal, which reached out to dioceses, parishes, and schools starting in the fall of 1953, raised enough money by 1959 to finish the Great Upper Church, although decoration of the interior—including the addition of chapels, sculpture, and mosaics—has continued for decades.[5]

During that half century of planning and construction, Catholics of all sorts had a presence, even if some present-day critics might assume the BNSIC was "just about bishops." That's the first major point I try to make as I look beyond the misleading contemporary perceptions. According to the dictionary, the term *presence* refers to claims about whether a thing or person is actually there or not. In political usage, it can mean influence in a region—as in "the United States maintains a presence in the Middle East." In religious usage—and this was decisive for the Shrine's episcopal founder and its lay architect, Charles Donagh Maginnis (1867–1955)—it refers to the Catholic doctrine about "the manner in which Christ is held to be present in the Eucharist," as in Jesus' "real presence" in the bread and wine of

Figure I.2. Bishop Shahan, the founder, and Reverend Bernard McKenna, the first director, pose in front of a commemorative plaque after the Mary Altar dedication in 1928 with lay leaders, including Clara Sheeran, third from the left.

the sacrament. And, in this sense, the term can point to an "incorporeal being or influence felt or conceived as present"—as in "she sensed a presence in the room." Further, the term can refer not only to claims about reality but also to states of mind: we can talk about "presence of mind" and, just as important, "absence of mind," as in "inattention to what is going on." In other words, presence is cognitively and affectively generated—it's produced by how we think and feel. In turn, a failure to recognize presence might be due to errors by the observer or defects in the observation. It's our fault if we fail to notice things that are there. In this book, I try to be attentive to all those who've been present at the Shrine through ritual practice or material culture—and in all these different ways, corporeally or incorporeally. As another scholar also has suggested, I've found that the theme of "presence is central to the study of lived Catholic practice—the study of Catholicism in everyday life is about the mutual engagement of men, women, children, and holy figures present to each other."[6]

And holy figures of all sorts have had a presence at the BNSIC. No visitor to the Great Upper Church could miss the enormous Byzantine-inspired

mosaic *Christ in Majesty*, from which Jesus looks down on pilgrims, remind-
ing them of the final judgment. Images of more than 155 saints—from
Adalbert to Zita—adorn the walls and chapels. Most important, Mary,
queen of the saints, also has secured herself a prominent place throughout
the building, from the sculpted image of the Virgin on the North façade to
the statue on the South façade, from the Marian symbols on the dome to
the Mary Memorial Altar in the Crypt Church.[7]

So those who cared about the building encountered Jesus, Mary, and the
saints—especially Mary—but at first glance it might seem that that contemporary critic was right and only male ecclesiastical leaders had a
presence before 1959. After all, the U.S. bishops started visiting the Shrine
even before construction began, and they have returned during their
annual meetings each year since 1919. The next year eleven archbishops
and fifty-six bishops attended the foundation stone ceremony. More were
there for the 1959 dedication, which the Shrine's fifth director, Monsignor
(later Bishop) Thomas J. Grady (1914–2002), planned to coincide with the
dates for the U.S. bishops' annual gathering in the capital. Over the years,
there was a significant episcopal presence, including Bishop Shahan and
Cardinal Gibbons in the 1910s and 1920s; Archbishop John F. Noll (1875–
1956), chair of the Episcopal Committee for the Shrine, and Patrick Cardinal
O'Boyle (1896–1987), archbishop of Washington, D.C., in the 1940s and
1950s. Noll's presence, for example, is also inscribed on one of the black
marble piers that stand in the lower church's Memorial Hall, where the
names of the dead, clergy and laity, cover the columns and the walls. Etched
into that pier is a "testimonial" to Noll, "first chairman of the Episcopal
Committee for the National Shrine, benefactor of the Shrine, and Mary's
devoted son." Shahan was Mary's "devoted son," too, and he has had even
more of a presence than Noll and the other bishops, since his body was
interred there in 1932. The reclining marble figure on the sarcophagus,
with his hands folded in eternal prayer, assures Bishop Shahan a lasting
presence there in the lower church's Founder's Chapel (fig. I.3).[8]

To focus only on episcopal presence—however vivid, even corporeal—
would mean returning to older patterns in scholarship, which tended to
highlight bishops and their dioceses, and would fail to notice many men,
women, and children who had a presence at the BNSIC through pilgrimages
and donations, or, like Noll and Shahan, by being memorialized in stone
and marble. Parish priests, members of women's and men's religious orders,
and lay Catholics—even non-Catholics—all had a presence, I'll try to show,
though episcopal presence was somewhat more decisive in the later fundraising and construction period, from 1946 to 1959, than it was in the earlier phase, from 1909 to 1931.

Figure I.3. The sarcophagus of Bishop Shahan, with Celtic crucifix above, in the Founder's Chapel.

So in both phases varied Catholics had a presence, more or less tangible. For some locals that devotion meant regular confessions and masses at the Shrine, but for those outside Washington it involved primarily pilgrimage and donation, which was—I came to realize during my study—an important component of piety for many devotees. That piety was not always and only top down, although there was some change in lay-clergy interactions during that half-century era of increasing consolidation. Between 1909, when a Detroit priest sent the first donation, and 1931, when the lower church's exterior was completed, there was somewhat more voluntary engagement and direct influence from lay devotees, women religious, and diocesan priests than later. Diocesan priests continued to lead pilgrimages and raise funds during the 1950s, but they felt increasing pressure to do so

between 1953 and 1959 as the Episcopal Committee for the Shrine set diocesan fundraising quotas that their bishops tried to meet. Leaders of religious
orders also made fundraising promises to episcopal promoters during the
later period, and that meant convents and monasteries sometimes struggled
to raise funds, even though they often had little say about the Shrine's ornamentation. As the decades passed, the laity continued to express their devotion to Mary by donating money and making journeys, yet elite laywomen
from Catholic organizations had more of a presence in the early years, the
1910s and the 1920s, when they interacted more regularly and influentially
with the Shrine's leaders, than they did after 1953, when the centralization
of fundraising that had begun earlier in the century had more fully taken
hold. Still, as I will show, in intriguing ways women and children continued
to make their presence felt throughout those five decades.[9]

The consolidated Catholicism affirmed by those diverse devotees between
1909 and 1959 was founded on a shared worldview that was sanctioned by
the Vatican, affirmed by the bishops, and reinforced by priests in the parish
and nuns in the schools. Some of the laity, nuns, and clergy dissented—as
they have in every era—but in that period of uncommon consensus the pre-
dominant spiritual framework was circulated to the faithful in catechisms,
parish bulletins, and advice manuals and transmitted to the next generation
in the textbooks, curricula, and practices of the vast Catholic school system.
That's the second main point I make in this book: even if our vantage from
the contentious present might lead us to presuppose dissent and highlight
squabbles, the evidence suggests there was much more agreement among
Catholics, including between those who planned the Shrine and those who
supported it, than some contemporaries might imagine.

There is no single term that fully describes that shared intellectual framework; the labels change as our focus does. In ecclesiology, the worldview was
ultramontane, emphasizing the authority of the papacy and the importance
of Rome. The more egalitarian language of Vatican II—the Church as "the
people of God"—or even the midcentury talk about the Church as "the body
of Christ"—did not win the day before 1959, and most in the pulpit and in
the pews accepted—or at least did not regularly or publicly challenge—the
top-down ecclesiology. In philosophy, the worldview was unapologetically
neo-scholastic, emphasizing the comprehensive reach of Aquinas's intricate
doctrinal system and its balancing of faith and reason. In religious practice,
the framework was centered on the sacraments and the parish but also
emphasized the importance of devotion to the Virgin Mary, as spiritual intercessor in everyday concerns and world politics. In its approach to the political
state and the modern world, this regnant system of beliefs and values
affirmed—to coin new terms—a *triumphalist Americanism* and a *selective*

countermodernism. After the papal condemnations of 1899 and 1907, no good Catholic could openly strive to accommodate American culture or Western modernity. In imagining the Church's relation to the nation, accommodationist Americanism—the controversial stance that favored "adapting" to the nation's democratic politics, capitalist economy, and individualist values—had been ruled out. Yet there was still room for Catholic patriotism and for a more nuanced, even assertive, form of Americanism. The Shrine's early planners and promoters—including Cardinal Gibbons, Bishop Shahan, and Charles Maginnis—voiced this triumphalist Americanism, and it later found material expression in the Shrine's mosaics, stained glass, and sculptural program. That recalibrated Americanism asserted the chronological priority and practical superiority of Catholicism. In this triumphalist historical narrative of the United States and the Western Hemisphere, Catholics argued that they had arrived first and had established America's treasured heritage: for example, Maryland's colonial Catholics first modeled the separation of church and state. Catholics did not need to adapt their faith to America, in this view, since the nation and its traditions already were Catholic.[10]

In the same way, as the papal denunciations made clear, Americans were not free to "adapt" Catholicism to the modern world. Appealing to "an open and progressive form of Neoscholasticism," Shahan and Monsignor Edward A. Pace (1861–1938), who later supervised the woman's organization that funded the Mary Memorial Altar, managed to find their way to a more moderate view that neither completely ignored nor unconditionally endorsed modernity. Those two CUA scholars, who encountered Catholic and Protestant modernism during their European training and displayed that erudition as they coedited the multivolume *Catholic Encyclopedia*, believed that Catholicism was the best hope for the modern world. In the medieval period, they proposed, Catholicism had proven itself superior as a cultural framework; it also provided the best chance for addressing the problems of the present. The selective countermodernism affirmed by key leaders during the Shrine's early period was strategic, flexible, and eclectic, retrieving from the past what helped in the present. Less intransient than the table-pounding naysaying of leaders who nostalgically yearned for the way things had been, this approach recognized that you couldn't expect modern secular America to return to the medieval Catholic past. Some effort to restate traditional principles in contemporary idiom was required. This countermodernism also didn't condemn everything that had happened since Aquinas penned the last line of his magisterial *Summa Theologica* and an anonymous mason placed the final stone in the monumental Gothic cathedral at Chartres. This somewhat qualified stance against modernism acknowledged the social conditions usually associated with "modernity"—including migration, urbanization, industrialization, and accelerated communication and travel technology. The countermodernists who supported the Shrine in its early years even critically appropriated some things "modern," from automobiles to advertising, even if they stood ready to proclaim the cultural triumphs of the medieval European past and asserted that only a flexible reformulated Thomism—and *not* Freudian depth psychology, Darwinian evolutionary biology, Marxist political economy, or Jamesian pragmatic philosophy—could redeem American secular modernity.[11]

Not every Catholic devotee of Mary was as troubled by secular modernity, of course, and few of the faithful could recount Aquinas's proofs for the existence of God, just as few had pondered the implications of the papal condemnations of Americanism and modernism. Yet that worldview—with its commitments to authority, tradition, and universality and its complicated stance toward America and modernity—was widely shared. It permeated sermons from the pulpit, advice in the confessional, instruction in catechisms—and, later, messages broadcast on Catholic radio and television programs. It informed what Catholics read, what they heard, and what they did. Whether the laity gave it much thought or not—and most, presumably, didn't—few devotees in the pews challenged that way of seeing the world, the nation, and themselves. The Shrine's construction drew widespread support for many reasons, including the fact that the laity often—but not always—did what church leaders told them to do. But this surprising level of support was more than just the efficacy of top-down institutional authority. The archival sources also suggest a deceptively simple explanation, one that those who don't believe in the historical power of religious motives won't accept: many American Catholics of the era loved Mary and accepted the shared countermodernist worldview that buttressed Marian devotion. As spiritual intercessor, moral confidant, role model, and miracle worker, the Virgin Mary helped with the pressing problems of ordinary life. Lay adherents simply did not find much to disagree with when the Shrine's clerical promoters, who also loved Mary, requested donations and encouraged pilgrimage. They shared a sensibility and an outlook.

That common framework informed clerical hopes for the Shrine. Even before workers cleared the ground, some clerical advocates had begun to make extraordinary claims for the building: Monsignor Peter K. Guilday (1884–1947), CUA's leading church historian, predicted in 1916 that it would become, "like the Temple of Jerusalem, the pivot of the Catholic Church in this new Land of Promise." Not even the Shrine's most vigorous contemporary supporters might claim it has been the "pivot," the center around which all of Catholic America has turned. United States Catholicism has had many centers, most would acknowledge. But the BNSIC is illuminating—and not only because at that site we can notice the presence of all sorts of Catholics and trace the impact of consolidated Catholicism's shared worldview. It's illuminating in another way, and this is my third main point: the ordained men who planned and supported the Shrine between 1913 and 1959 didn't agree on everything, but most endorsed several primary aims that were distinctive but not unique. Those aims emerged at a crossing point, a juncture where localized hopes about the National Shrine flowed out and widespread concerns about American Catholicism flowed in. Clergy who supported the project were attempting what many other ecclesiastical leaders were trying to do at other sites, from small local parishes to large urban cathedrals. To the extent that these six defining aims reflected broader patterns, in this way, too, the Shrine functioned—to use my metaphor instead of Guilday's—as a threshold. It's not just that famous Catholics passed through its doors, though they did, including Dorothy Day, John Ryan, and Fulton Sheen before 1959 and Mother Theresa, Pope John Paul II, and Pope Benedict XVI after that. Rather, the fullness of Catholic America crossed its threshold during the half century between its founding and dedication, and it provides an especially useful angle of vision on six clerical interests that characterized the consolidated Church. Even though priests and bishops at the Shrine often highlighted other spiritual or aesthetic purposes—to promote Marian devotion or enjoy beautiful architecture—we also can observe there the clergy's concern to build institutions, contest Protestants, mobilize women, engage children, incorporate immigrants, and claim civic space. As I also trace the presence of diverse devotees and note the impact of the shared worldview, in each chapter of this thematically organized book I consider one of those six clerical concerns as they were expressed in verbal representations, ritual practice, and material culture at the BNSIC. In the conclusion I consider the implications of all this for thinking about Catholic history, American culture, and religious practice. I show how my approach points toward translocative histories that consider intersecting scales—the local, national, and transnational—and combine the tools of social history, cultural history, and intellectual history to attend more fully to the complex interactions of all the diverse devotees, clerical and lay, who have had a presence at this religious site.[12]

SOURCES AND METHODS

Making these three main points—about diverse devotees, shared worldview, and clerical aims—presented daunting methodological challenges, and it might help to say a bit about the approach I took and the sources I used. My approach began with the straightforward observation that the

Shrine is a building, so I developed and applied an approach to the study of religious architecture. As I see it, there are ten factors to consider in the interpretation of a religious site and the rituals conducted there: the building's name, location, appearance, context, relations, representations, makers, donors, users, and functions. What this approach entails has been hinted at in what I already have said and will become clearer in the pages that follow, but let me explain it briefly here.[13]

A building's *name* sometimes offers little help—as with the ubiquitous steel and glass structures in downtowns everywhere—but, as in this case, a name can reveal a great deal. Since Pope John Paul II conferred the honor in 1990, it has been a "basilica," so we know it came to be seen as an important building. Other words in the full title—Basilica of the National Shrine of the Immaculate Conception—also tell us much. Most important, it's a shrine, a structure that attracts pilgrims who make round-trip journeys to a site where they venerate human or suprahuman figures they consider special or sacred. Many religious traditions have established shrines, including Hinduism, Buddhism, and Islam, and they vary in origin. Some Roman Catholic shrines commemorate the site of an important event, while others mark the spot where Mary appeared—and, as the name indicates, the National Shrine of the Immaculate Conception is a Marian shrine. Devotees also have built shrines when a holy relic or image is brought from another place or when an object already on the site proves to have miraculous powers. The BNSIC and a small proportion of other Catholic shrines are devotional shrines, a site that someone, usually clergy, marks off as sacred, even though no miracles and—despite the joke—no apparitions have occurred there.[14]

Shrines also vary in scope, ranging from the purely local to the fully international. United States Catholicism always has been more or less transnational—America was a missionary territory until 1908—as the faithful have worked out their piety in relation to the formal prescriptions of Rome and, for migrants and their children, the cultural inheritance of the homeland. Still, as the building's name also indicates, the National Shrine of the Immaculate Conception was imagined primarily as a national site, even if it has attracted local devotes and has reached beyond national borders. In part, that is because of its *location* in the nation's capital. The Shrine's position in the city has remained the same, though the immediate built environment and the neighborhood's demographic profile has changed, with implications for interpretations of the building and its artifacts. For example, the 1997 dedication of a chapel to Our Mother of Africa took on new meanings in what is now a predominantly African-American section of D.C. Further, as the Shrine's architects, planners, and spokesmen emphasized, its *appearance*—with a dome that evokes not only the churches of Europe but the civic architecture of Washington—also signals something important about the Romanesque-Byzantine building. It aligns it with both ancient Catholic tradition and contemporary American democracy.[15]

The historical *context* matters, too—and not only the changes in the surrounding neighborhood and built environment. Women were the Shrine's leading fundraisers during the early period, and Cardinal Gibbons laid the foundation stone only thirty-six days after women won the right to vote. It was a time when working-class immigrants and their descendants still filled the pews of the predominantly urban parishes and—along with those who prayed mostly in their homes and in the streets—endured increased anti-Catholic and anti-immigrant sentiment. Differences in language, heritage, and viewpoint—especially conflicts about how much to accept Irish clerical authority and how much to endorse American cultural norms— divided Catholics in 1920. Yet they showed surprising solidarity as they employed the institutional network's increasingly consolidated ecclesiastical resources, not only to counter Protestant hostility but also to build and staff schools, hospitals, orphanages, and churches.[16]

As I've already emphasized, "context" changed over time, both during the era of consolidation, which I focus on, and after the Shrine was dedicated in 1959. Between 1920 and 1959, Catholicism achieved a robust presence in America. More and more Americans moved from the cities to the suburbs—one-third lived there by 1960—and many Catholics were among them. Fifties Catholics, who were farther removed from the immigrant generations but who still worked out their piety in relation to Rome, also had higher incomes and better education. Even many poor Catholics who stayed in the cities or moved to working-class neighborhoods in suburbia, which was more economically and ethnically diverse than most observers have assumed, could aspire to mass consumption and economic mobility. They also could take some satisfaction in their tradition's rising political clout. After 1959—the year of the dedication ceremony—things changed even more. In 1960, the nation would elect its first Catholic president, and Catholics soon would have proportional representation in Congress. By 1968, the Vietnam War, the civil rights movement, and revised immigration law had begun to transform American society, just as intensified migration, Vatican II's documents, and *Humanae Vitae*, the encyclical banning birth control, were transforming ecclesiastical life. The historical context for the consecrations of the Filipino oratory and African chapel in 1997 was very different from that of the acculturated (though hardly homogenous) community that had dedicated the Shrine in 1959. The faithful that gathered in Washington to venerate Mary at the end of

the twentieth century more closely resembled the transnational generation
that had laid the Shrine's foundation stone in 1920. And attending to all
those contextual shifts is important for making sense of what the Shrine
means and what it does.[17]

The BNSIC's proximity to civic structures and other national denominational centers helps to define its context and meaning, and its real or imagined *relations* with other buildings—European churches and Washington
architecture—also is an important factor to consider. Comparing it with
some of those buildings—the U.S. Capitol or the National Cathedral—helps
to make sense of the site and the practices conducted there.

Those practices constituted the multiple meanings and functions of the
BNSIC. The solitary prayers and the collective rituals, the piety of devotees
who established a presence there by giving and going, all determined what
the building meant and what it did. Those meanings and functions, in other
words, were not limited to what the clerical planners intended or the lay
architects imagined. Meaning and function emerged from the confluence
of many, sometimes competing, responses to the building. They were fashioned, in part, by reception. In other words, verbal and visual *representations*, whether in architectural drawings, donor letters, or comic books, are
relevant. A variety of persons offered those representations, including
makers, who designed and constructed the building, *donors*, who provided
funds and volunteered time, and *users*, who played a role in the creation of
the building's complex and shifting meanings and functions by engaging in
all sorts of religious practices in their homes or at the Shrine.

How then did all these factors inform the Shrine's multiple and competing *functions*? I have suggested that the BNSIC is a threshold to Catholic
America. It is a threshold in another sense, too. Religion is about crossing
and dwelling, about finding a place and moving through space, as I argued
in a theory of religion that emerged from my study of another Catholic
shrine. In other words, religions situate devotees in the body, the home,
the homeland, and the cosmos, and they enable and constrain crossings of
all sorts—terrestrial, corporeal, and cosmic—as the religious appeal to
suprahuman beings to confront suffering, intensify joy, and map and cross
the ultimate horizon of human life, which most Christians have imagined
as heaven. In a similar way, between the 1920s and 1950s the Marian
shrine in Washington functioned as a threshold, a place of crossing and
dwelling, where devotees oriented themselves in time and space, fashioned
individual and collective identities, and negotiated ecclesiastical and social
power. As threshold, the BNSIC was a site where the transcendent drew
near and devotees were lifted up—petitioning Jesus, Mary, and the saints
and remembering loved ones in purgatory and heaven. There was not only

this vertical movement, however, for artifacts and practices at the Shrine also propelled devotees out toward the built environment and into social space, where they contested Protestants and defined Catholicism, incorporated immigrants and imagined ethnic identity, mobilized women and negotiated gender roles, engaged children and enforced religious authority, built institutions and—especially important for the Washington shrine—claimed civic space.[18]

To investigate these ten factors and get some sense of the Shrine's meanings and functions, I used a wide range of sources. To understand devotion before 1959 and compare it with practices in subsequent decades, I analyzed material culture. I considered the building and the artifacts that adorn it and also objects sold in the gift shop (from holy cards to statues), artifacts mailed to devotees (from prayer booklets to donation requests), and media aimed at wider audiences (from television programs to websites). In fact, each of the book's six chapters highlights one element of the Shrine's material culture: the foundation stone, the Mary Altar, a comic book image, the Crypt Church, the Great Dome, and an ethnic chapel. A number of published texts also helped. There is no scholarly study of the BNSIC, but over the years its staff have produced a great deal of printed material: histories, memoirs, guidebooks, pamphlets, and books, including a 1927 history published by the Shrine, a 1959 memoir by its first director, a coffee-table book by the communications specialist in 2000, and a photographic history by the archivist in 2009. An especially important published source is the Shrine's official periodical, *Salve Regina*, later called *Mary's Shrine*. In the early years, that periodical not only printed news of pilgrimages but also excerpted donor letters, and as long as we keep in mind that clerical promoters selected and edited the letters, those sources can be useful, too.[19]

I also consulted unpublished archival sources. Many archivists associated with religious orders, Catholic colleges, and U.S. dioceses helped me find biographical information on donors and pilgrims, and I searched collections that hold important materials about the BNSIC, including those at the CUA, the Archdiocese of Philadelphia, the University of Notre Dame, and the Shrine itself. The BNSIC did not really have an archive when I began this project in the mid-1990s, as I was told when I first called to say I wanted to write this book; records were housed in unlabeled boxes in a small crypt-level room. Initially, I couldn't see those files since a staff member was using them for his own project—that coffee-table book—but he later generously allowed me full access. For several years of research, then, the BNSIC officials gave me a key to that room and access to the photocopier and trusted me to deal with the archival materials. In later years, after the BNSIC hired an archivist, I continued to consult materials housed there. Those archival sources included correspondence, photographs, donor books, visitor logs, director's notes, and the Mary Memorial Altar donor list, a key source that I'd heard about but couldn't find for ten years. I also found some unpublished donor letters there, and at other archives, and those documents helped me to understand the responses of ordinary devotees as well as the intentions of clerical advocates.

To understand the recent past and the contemporary interpretations—primarily but not only for the study of the Filipino oratory I analyze in chapter 6—I turned to participant observation and semistructured interviews. To uncover information about the ordinary men, women, and children who donated or visited between 1909 and 1959, I used other sources: parish records, school information, death indexes, wills, maps, local newspapers, city directories, and census records. The federal census proved especially valuable. Since I had the names and addresses of many donors and pilgrims recorded in the Shrine's archives, I could search census records for them. As the profiles of more than 250 donors and pilgrims listed in the appendices indicate, I discovered that I could learn a great deal about devotees' ethnic background, native language, neighborhood setting, and economic class. However, these sources did not tell me all I wanted to know—*Why* did devotees donate? *Why* did pilgrims visit?—and the presence of some lay devotees remained impossible to discern, no matter how attentive I was. Some of the faithful did not mail a contribution but gave their dollars or quarters to the local parish, school, or diocese, which passed it on without recording individual contributions. Some of those who cared about the Shrine did not visit on pilgrimage, and some who did visit did not sign the visitor's log.

One of the most interesting—and baffling—entries in the visitor's logbook, an entry on the page for October 28, 1928, illustrates the interpretive challenges. In the two columns where pilgrims recorded name and hometown, below the signature of a pilgrim from South Bend and above that of a devotee from D.C., someone penned in cursive: "Nobody-Nowhere." I'm still not sure what this means. Clearly the visitor didn't want to give her or his name. But why? Was it a slightly embarrassed or ambivalent Protestant tourist who wanted to leave a mark but still remain anonymous? A sign of resistance by a lapsed Catholic who was dragged there by a pious relative? Was it a playful prank by a high school student who wanted to annoy the nun who brought her or to amuse the pious visitors who would sign later that day? We'll never know. It's helpful to keep that entry in mind, however, even if it yields more questions than answers. It reminds us that there's much about the past we can't recover—even if we're sensitive to the ways present-day reactions obscure earlier developments. There were plenty of Nobodys from Nowhere who left no trace at all, not even a baffling entry penned in the visitors' log. Still, as I try to show in the rest of this book, we can discern the presence of many men, women, and children at the Shrine, and being attentive to that presence—as well as to what's absent—can tell us a great deal, including how the Shrine reflected shared values during the era of consolidation and why it now provokes such divergent contemporary responses.[20]

1

☙

Laying Catholicism's Foundation

Clerical Aims and Diverse Devotees, 1909–1959

In a photograph of the 1920 foundation stone ceremony, James Cardinal Gibbons and his clerical brethren preside from their lofty perch on a temporary wooden platform. Thousands of supporters gather nearby to witness the historic founding of an institution, a shrine dedicated to the Virgin Mary, a focus of popular piety for Roman Catholics in the United States and around the world (see fig. 1.1). The clerical concern to build institutions—not only shrines but also parish churches, rectories, monasteries, convents, seminaries, hospitals, parochial schools, and colleges—shaped U.S. Catholicism in the era of consolidation, a time when buildings rose, organizations centralized, and networks strengthened. The story of the planning, fundraising, and construction of the National Shrine of the Immaculate Conception, a node in that consolidating transnational network, is a tale about how multiple motives propelled diverse Catholics to respond to local, national, and transnational influences as they enacted their devotion to the Virgin Mary through donation and—as soon as devotees could make out walls amid the scaffolding—through pilgrimage. I tell that story in this chapter, offering an overview that frames the subsequent chapters by answering four preliminary questions: What does the building look like? How did it get built? What did its promoters want? Who supported it by giving or going? I begin by attending to the building's appearance, its design and size, as well as the planners' understanding of religious architecture and the promoters' strategies for reaching supporters, both the Shrine's donors and users. I also consider why the clergy wanted to build it and how the laity responded. In

Figure 1.1. Cardinal Gibbons, who stands on the on the platform to the right, presides at the ceremony for the laying of the Shrine's foundation stone in 1920.

later chapters, I say more about lay devotees—women (chapter 2), children (chapter 3), and immigrants (chapter 6)—but here I give a broader account, saying something about the varied Roman Catholics who crossed the Shrine's threshold before 1959. Bound by a shared veneration of Mary, I'll try to show, those diverse supporters included laity, nuns, monks, diocesan priests, bishops, and popes.

THE BUILDING'S APPEARANCE

Most visitors to the building first notice its scale. It's big. Covering 77,500 square feet and 459 feet long, it is the largest Roman Catholic worship space in North America and one of the ten largest churches in the world. Organizers have been proud of its imposing scale, repeating these statistics in official publications even before the structure was finished. A "fact sheet" sent to the media in 1953, just as the second major fundraising campaign got under way, also gave other details to wow Catholics and non-Catholics alike. "The general impression created by the completed Shrine will be one of majesty and power," that press release predicted: construction workers would use more than 250,000 cubic feet of stone and granite on the exterior; the walls would require 25 million bricks, and it would have a total capacity of six thousand persons, with seating for thirty-five hundred in the Great Upper Church. It turns out that they needed fewer bricks—only 10 million—but the final structure was as imposing as organizers predicted. To put all this in perspective, the Shrine's area in square feet is smaller than that of the Episcopal Cathedral of St. John the Divine in New York (121,000 square feet) and St. Peter's in Rome (227,069 square feet), Roman Catholicism's international center. The Shrine is not as long as the National Cathedral, the Shrine's Episcopalian competitor across town, but is larger than all other American Catholic centers of worship, including St. Patrick's Cathedral in New York, and larger than the major cathedrals at Chartres and Cologne. Adding to the sense of scale, the Shrine's campanile, or bell tower, stands to the left of the main entrance and rises 329 feet from ground level, lower than the Washington Monument but more than twice the height of another imposing religious structure in D.C.'s cityscape, the Presbyterian's Tower of Faith.[1]

Interpreters have noticed more than the building's scale, however. They have commented on its design, too, and that plan reflected the architect's and the founder's beliefs about the function of ecclesiastical buildings and the relation between Catholicism, modernity, and America. The American Institute of Architects' *Guide to the Architecture of Washington, D.C.*, reported that the Shrine was "very loosely modeled on St. Mark's in Venice." Both Shahan, the founder, and Charles Maginnis, the senior partner in the distinguished Boston architectural firm that drew up the plans, acknowledged their appreciation for that Italian church. During a public lecture, "Byzantine and Romanesque Churches," several years after Maginnis submitted those plans, for example, the lay Catholic architect showed his Boston audience a slide of St. Mark's. But since 1919, when the Shrine's periodical announced Maginnis as the architect, he had emphasized that the BNSIC would not be modeled on any single building and would not employ any single style. It would be "distinctively American." Later promoters of the Shrine also highlighted its distinctiveness—and its complicated relation to medieval Catholicism and American culture. For example, in a 1953 appearance on the long-running Catholic television program *Lamp unto my Feet* (1948–1979), the Archdiocese of Philadelphia's John F. Cardinal O'Hara (1888–1960), a member of the Episcopal Committee for the Shrine, acknowledged the parallels with St. Mark's, a Byzantine basilica consecrated in the eleventh century and modeled on Istanbul's famous Hagia Sophia. Yet, echoing Maginnis's stated intention, the archbishop asserted: "the shrine will bear little or no architectural relationship to any existing church but will be of noble, American design, as benefits its purpose."[2]

But what's an "American" design, and how should Catholic ecclesiastical architecture relate to "modern" American values and styles? More than a decade before their collaboration on the Washington site, the architect, Maginnis, and the church historian, Shahan, had expressed remarkably similar views about Roman Catholic architecture. Both celebrated medieval European architectural traditions, though they rejected unreflective appropriation of medieval traditions as well as uncritical commitment to contemporary cultural trends. They acknowledged, as Maginnis put it, that "the architectural history of the Catholic Church has its dead bones." Both believed, however, that the cathedrals they'd visited as students in Europe were the fullest expressions of Catholic culture and still had relevance for church building in the United States. Their viewpoint might be called eclectic traditionalism or—the related term I already introduced—selective countermodernism. This viewpoint emerged from a shared sense that worship spaces should be both aesthetically pleasing and liturgically appropriate. Shahan argued that "the doctrine of the Blessed Sacrament, of the Real Presence . . . created all the essentials of a Christian church." Maginnis agreed. The "principle of the Divine Presence," the architect suggested, has implications for church architecture, which should evoke a sense of "high dignity" and allow for "the emotional comprehension of the mystery." But that shared conviction did not settle the issue, since several types of sacramental architectural designs—Byzantine, Romanesque, and Gothic— might meet those liturgical and aesthetic needs by providing a longitudinal space for processions and a focus on the altar, where the priest's ritual actions transform ordinary bread into the real presence of the body of Christ. Which ecclesiastical design to choose? Maginnis believed that was an especially difficult decision in the United States, where climatic variation, regional differences, and "ethnical complexity" had precluded the development of a "nationally uniform ecclesiastical style." Therefore, the U.S. cultural condition allowed—even demanded—freedom to experiment by mixing styles to creatively adapt Catholic tradition to modern America. "The traditionalist," Maginnis explained, "makes no claims for the literal relevance of European precedents, but holds to the view that, in the absence of a national vernacular, he is justified in an eclecticism that brings what is best in the past to modern correspondence." That meant, the architect proposed, that dioceses across the country might experiment with regionally distinctive styles.[3]

What did that mean for a national shrine in the nation's capital, a commission that presented distinct challenges? The original designs by another architect had pictured a fourteenth-century French Gothic structure, but, for reasons I'll explain later, Bishop Shahan and the Building Committee decided to abandon those tentative plans. When Maginnis's firm got the job, he proposed an unusual blending of Byzantine and Romanesque elements, a design that fulfilled the Building Committee's wishes and reflected Maginnis's understanding of the architect's task in a cultural context where no style predominated. Even though Maginnis and Shahan cared most that the design incorporated Catholic architectural traditions and met aesthetic and liturgical needs—thereby creating a beautiful space that honored the Virgin Mary and evoked a solemn sense of the divine's mysterious presence—they also acknowledged other factors, including the need for the building to harmonize with Washington's urban

landscape and function as a national center. A number of the Shrine's promoters between 1920 and 1959 praised Maginnis's Byzantine-Romanesque
plan, with its tall tower and prominent dome, as a distinctively American
response to the building's urban environment and unique function—as a
national shrine to the country's patroness in the nation's capital.[4]

Yet over the years, as I've already hinted, responses to Maginnis's
design have varied from breathless praise to biting ridicule. A Washington
journalist praised the Shrine as a "dazzling jewel," while a Catholic scholar
dismissed it as "an architectural monstrosity." Those contemporary
observers did not know about the planners' aims, and the author of the
entry in the American Institute of Architects guidebook to D.C. also
seems to have been unaware of the liturgical interests, aesthetic principles, and cultural assessments that shaped Maginnis's eclectic traditionalism. That entry challenged the claim that the building effectively blends
styles, comparing it with a place and a style that the architect and founder
certainly did not have in mind: "it is ostensibly a combination of the neo-
Byzantine and the neo-Romanesque styles, but the finished structure—
particularly the interior—somehow conveys more than a whiff of 1950s
Beverly Hills Moderne."[5]

THE BUILDING PROCESS: THE BNSIC AND THE BRICK AND MORTAR ERA, 1909–1959

Contemporary reactions to the building's design are worth noting, since
the historian is obliged to consider competing interpretations, but for
understanding the process of planning and construction it's much more
important to note the historical context. The BNSIC was planned and built
during an age of intensified ecclesiastical building. Historians have
described the decades between 1920 and 1960, when the Shrine's exterior
was constructed, as the "great age of Catholic monumentalism" and "the
brick and mortar phase of Catholicism." The "consolidating bishops" of
big cities from Philadelphia to Los Angeles consulted prestigious law firms
and employed successful advertising strategies as they functioned as
business managers coordinating large-scale institution building. Consider
Philadelphia, which was—along with Detroit, Buffalo, and Brooklyn—one
of the urban centers that offered the most support to the BNSIC in the
early years. Philadelphia's Dennis Dougherty (1865–1951), who called himself "God's bricklayer," not only chaired the Shrine's first official Building
Committee starting in 1918 but also managed to transform the landscape
of his archdiocese. During his years of leadership (1918–1951), Archbishop

(later Cardinal) Dougherty oversaw the financing and building of forty-eight new churches, ninety-two new parishes, and eighty-nine new parish schools. Similar building activity occurred in Detroit, Buffalo, Brooklyn, and many other U.S. cities. For example, Brooklyn's brick-and-mortar prelate, Archbishop Thomas E. Molloy (1884–1956), founded 102 parishes during his long episcopate from 1922 to 1956.[6]

Already by 1925, one-quarter of all Catholic churches in Molloy's Brooklyn bore a Marian title, including Immaculate Conception of the Blessed Virgin Mary (1853) and Our Lady of Refuge (1911). That's not surprising, since the brick and mortar period overlapped with "the age of Mary," a period of intensified veneration of the Virgin Mary from the 1850s to the 1950s. Two papal proclamations—Pius IX's declaration of the dogma of the Immaculate Conception (1854) and Pius XII's declaration of a "Marian Year" to celebrate that dogmatic pronouncement's centennial (1954)—marked the period's span, while apparitions and miracles at sites in central and southwestern Europe, from Belgium to Portugal, spread the transnational devotion.[7]

Marian devotion found its way to the United States, too. It had arrived early. In an expression of triumphalist Americanism, U.S. clergy reminded anyone who would listen—Catholic or Protestant—that Columbus, the New World's "discoverer," had venerated Mary, as the Reverend Xavier Macleod noted in his 1866 *History of the Devotion to the Blessed Virgin Mary in North America*. That priest, who even changed the central character in the usual historical narrative as he described "Our Lady's discovery of America," also noted that there had been Marian shrines in territories that became part of the United States since the earliest one at St. Augustine (1565). Macleod's book appeared a dozen years after the pope defined the dogma of the Immaculate Conception and two decades after the U.S. bishops named Mary the national patroness. As Macleod told readers, and the Shrine's promoters often reminded donors and pilgrims, at the Sixth Provincial Council of Baltimore in 1846 the assembled U.S. bishops unanimously voted "to place ourselves, and all entrusted to our charge throughout the United States, under the special patronage of the holy Mother of God, whose immaculate conception is venerated by the piety of the faithful throughout the Catholic Church." Since the United States was still a mission territory, the American hierarchy needed the approval of the Vatican's Sacred Congregation for the Propagation of the Faith, and the blessing of the pope and the approval of the Sacred Congregation arrived the following year.[8]

With that 1847 decree, ecclesiastical leaders on both sides of the Atlantic officially linked Mary Immaculate and the United States, but the doctrine of the Immaculate Conception had a complex history before and after that missive arrived. Historians of medieval and early modern Europe have suggested that the notion that Jesus' mother had been conceived without the stain (*macula*) of original sin—purity was necessary for God to dwell in her—developed in the twelfth century, when it was articulated most fully by two Franciscan theologians, Ramon Lull and Duns Scotus. In his official pronouncement of 1854, however, Pope Pius IX cited scripture and tradition as he insisted that the Church "has ever held as divinely revealed and as contained in the deposit of heavenly revelation this doctrine concerning the original innocence of the august Virgin." Most Catholics agreed and pointed to the mid-nineteenth-century Marian apparitions as experiential verification of the doctrine's veracity. Anticipating Pius IX's declaration of the dogma of the Immaculate Conception, Catherine Labouré had reported that in her 1830 vision of the Virgin she also could discern in gold lettering the prayer "Mary conceived without sin pray for us who have recourse to you," and confirming the 1854 papal declaration of the dogma, at Lourdes in 1858 the Virgin had revealed her identity to Bernadette Soubirous by saying "I am the Immaculate Conception." Sparked by enthusiasm for her miraculous interventions in Europe, devotion to Mary then increased in the United States over the next half century and into the twentieth century.[9]

It was a series of events during the next fifty years, 1909–1959, that finally enshrined Immaculate Mary in the nation's capital. Even if the laity had some influence in the earlier period, during both major stages of the Shrine's planning and construction clergy exerted their authority and—despite their suspicions about the modern world—they enthusiastically employed the latest communication and transportation technology and skillfully adapted the advertising strategies of the consumer culture that emerged in the United States between the 1910s and the 1950s. From the parish priest to Peter's successor, ordained men were central agents in the expanding transnational Catholic institutional network centered in Rome, and the ultramontane devotional culture of consolidated Catholicism reinforced their authority. To some extent that devotional culture continued the hierarchy's earlier efforts to centralize control and standardize practice that had begun with the Council of Trent (1545–1563), but those efforts accelerated and took on slightly new forms by World War I. That resurgent transnational Catholic subculture, "nurtured in the world of Catholic parishes, schools, and associations," promoted Marian devotion and—most important for Washington's National Shrine—advocated "a heightened respect for church authorities ranging from the pope to parish priests."[10]

The First Phase of Building, 1909–1933: Marketing Mary and Mobilizing Women

That shared devotional culture provided the context for clerical-lay interactions at the Shrine in the 1910s and 1920s. Bishop Shahan had the most influence, even if others played important roles. The Reverend Bernard A. McKenna (1875–1960), who left his pastoral work in Philadelphia to serve as Shahan's secretary from 1915 to 1929 and as director of the BNSIC from 1929 to 1933, was the second of the "two master minds of the National Shrine," as one lay devotee described them. Planning would not have even started without the endorsement of Cardinal Gibbons, who sometimes also made fundraising trips and contacted potential donors; and since the Shrine was part of CUA in those years, its board of trustees and the Shrine Building Committee it appointed also had some clout. So did the architects, not only Maginnis, the Shrine's primary designer, but also Frederick Vernon Murphy (1879–1958), Shahan's university colleague and the associate architect, and Maginnis's partners, Timothy F. Walsh (1879–1934) and Eugene F. Kennedy, Jr. (1904–1986). Yet as one of those architects recalled, even though McKenna was an energetic promoter and others had influence, Shahan was the Shrine's "chief source of inspiration."[11]

Even before Shahan arrived in Washington in 1891, the idea of an important Catholic church in the nation's capital had been proposed, and several early supporters had suggested a worship space on the grounds of CUA, which formally opened in 1889. Mary Gwendoline Caldwell, CUA's first major donor, had imagined a campus church, and the first donor to contribute to honor Mary at a national shrine in Washington—more on him later in this chapter—passed on the idea and a founding contribution of $1,000 in 1909. Even before that donation arrived, Shahan had a similar idea. A church historian, Shahan had "a vision of a splendid basilica to the Blessed Virgin" as soon as he walked onto the campus as a young faculty member. Four years later, in 1903, he told the CUA community: "the Catholic Church in Washington should not be without a noble ecclesiastical building on the grounds of the University." It would be, he suggested, "the flower of American Catholic genius" and "a monument visible from far and near." That article hinted at Gothic design—he talked of its "tall and slender spire"—but he remained flexible. In a letter to a lay member of the CUA board in 1910, he outlined a few of his firm desires. The proposed building should have "a great free open space, unbroken by columns," that met liturgical needs, and its ornamentation should depict "the origin and glories of Catholics in the United States." Yet he told the board member that he "would not presume to dictate the style of it." A fundraising brochure, signed and circulated by Shahan the following year, encouraged contributions for "the new chapel of the Catholic University," a Gothic edifice that would seat "about seven hundred persons, i.e., the actual body of professors and students, and a reasonable number of visitors."[12]

During the next few years the plan's scope expanded, and the building's design changed. The idea of a national Marian shrine had emerged clearly by 1913, when Shahan met privately in Rome with Pius X and received his apostolic benediction and personal donation. Fundraising activities accelerated that year, and in January 1914 the first issue of *Salve Regina* appeared. That quarterly publication, which Shahan edited, had the sole aim of soliciting contributions for the Shrine. McKenna oversaw the production and distribution of *Salve Regina* as soon as he arrived in 1915. Soon afterward, circulation increased. By 1917, McKenna and his staff were distributing seventy-five thousand copies every six weeks. The number of devotional letters—many of them with small contributions enclosed—increased, too. In 1914, Shahan had written to McKenna, his former student and future assistant: "I wish I could show you the hundreds of most touching letters I have received, showing that the work is truly popular." That work continued to be popular through the 1920s, although they probably received fewer letters than McKenna estimated in his 1922 log book: the "letters received in the Salve Regina office in the past two years if placed end to end in a straight line, would form a path from Washington, D.C. to Quebec, Canada." But the financially savvy McKenna, who took over most of the day-to-day operations as Shahan turned his attention to the university, did manage to increase contributions. The Shrine had receipts of $2,500 in 1913. That annual figure had increased to almost $32,000 by 1915, the year McKenna assumed his duties. In 1920, when Gibbons presided at the foundation stone ritual, Shrine staff had collected $160,000, and the funds continued to swell until 1933, when McKenna returned to pastoral work in Philadelphia and the Great Depression dampened fundraising efforts at the Shrine—and across America. However, by then the BNSIC had brought in $3.1 million, the buying power of about $50 million today.[13]

That's a lot of money, even if the sum was insufficient to complete the Great Upper Church. How did they manage to raise it? Just as Shahan and McKenna embraced the latest communication and transportation technology—for example, a new green and gold "autotruck" transported the granite foundation stone, and Shahan read aloud a congratulatory cablegram from the pope at that 1920 ceremony—they also applied secular marketing techniques. At a time when a consumer culture was emerging in

America, the Shrine's promoters followed the advertising strategies of the day. "Prior to the emergence of commercial radio in the 1920s and television in the 1940s," one historian of advertising has noted, "the options for marketers were the many forms of print: signs, flyers, direct mail, newspapers, and particularly magazines." Shahan and McKenna tried them all. They circulated *Salve Regina* and sent out collateral print media, including devotional books, coupon booklets, and Christmas cards, which first were distributed in 1921 and came to represent 37 percent of annual contributions by 1927. In return, they promised the consumers of Marian devotion a variety of spiritual services—from vigil candles lit on the Shrine altar to request Mary's intercession to memorial tablets placed on the walls to honor family members.[14]

Like other marketers of the period, the Shrine's promoters targeted women. Because it is a fascinating episode that deserves sustained attention, in the next chapter I focus on their efforts between 1921 and 1928 to mobilize the International Federation of Catholic Alumnae (IFCA) to raise money for the Mary Memorial Altar. In this chapter, I highlight the earlier years, 1911–1918, and the clergy's outreach to the National Organization of Catholic Women (NOCW). Shahan and McKenna collaborated with the NOCW because they realized the first step in marketing was "to identify and understand who the customers were and how to target them," and for both consumer goods and Marian devotion that meant women. In one 1915 advertisement, a publishing company advised marketers that woman's purchasing power extended "far beyond groceries and gowns" and included "many products considered outside her sphere," from automobile tires to men's underwear. In fact, women purchased as much as 85 percent of all manufactured goods, one historian has estimated. Catholic advice manuals reminded boys and men of their own spiritual obligations, but Catholic women were still the primary consumers of devotion in the religious marketplace of the 1910s and 1920s. It made sense, then, that Shahan directed the early fundraising campaigns to female devotees. That 1911 fundraising brochure was titled "An Appeal to Catholic Ladies," and in 1913 Shahan pitched his development plan to the pope as one that targeted American Catholic women. In his apostolic letter to Gibbons approving the Shrine, Pope Pius X repeated the shared assumption, referring to the Shrine as a project that "so many pious Catholic women have undertaken."[15]

The pope's apostolic benediction also specifically mentioned an "association of ladies" that had formed to promote the effort. Shahan had tried to bring women into the fundraising process as early as 1910, as he and Gibbons visited potential female donors in New York City, including one woman who proved to be crucial for the fundraising efforts during the 1910s—Lucy Shattuck Hoffman (1856–1925). With Shahan's encouragement, Hoffman founded the organization the pope later alluded to, the NOCW, and it became the Shrine's major fundraising organization between 1913 and 1918. Even though Shahan and McKenna had some oversight, the NOCW allowed laywomen more opportunity to initiate fundraising activities than at any other time in the Shrine's history. The group's aim, according to its constitution, was "to erect a church in honor of Mary Immaculate on the grounds of the Catholic University at Washington." But Hoffman, one of its leaders, had multiple motives. Her son, Frances Burrall Hoffman, Jr., was an established architect, and she hoped he would get the commission. In 1913, Shahan informed Lucy that he had "expressed his own sympathy with that desire" to the board of trustees but was shrewdly neutral about the choice of architect. He added, offering a veiled suggestion, "there is nothing to prevent your son from presenting a sketch of the proposed building," as long as he did not bill the Shrine. Hoffman's son responded by donating his services, which he valued at $3,500, and creating an architectural plan with a plaster model of Gothic design, which toured the country from New York to San Francisco in 1915.[16]

Meanwhile, the energetic and wealthy Lucy Hoffman—she had six domestic servants—was founding new chapters and raising more money and, in turn, Shahan expressed his appreciation, even if he began to have second thoughts about Hoffman's motives and the organization's autonomy. A 1913 story in the *New York Times* profiled the leadership of two NOCW members, Hoffman and Annie Leary, and quoted Shahan as saying that as soon as the hierarchy had approved the plans for the Shrine "a very generous response came from Catholic women." Later that fall, after Hoffman had hosted a successful fundraiser at the Waldorf-Astoria Hotel, Shahan sent her a personal note of thanks: "I rejoice heartily that all went off well and I send my grateful compliments to yourself and all the good and zealous ladies." Yet signs of troubled relations appeared as early as the following year, when, without consultation, Hoffman announced that she planned fundraising trips to Chicago, Buffalo, and Detroit. In response, the bishop said he had "grave reasons" to avoid starting an organization in Chicago. He approved her Detroit trip, however. Apparently following his directives, Hoffman never did bring Chicago into the fold, but she managed to set up a NOCW chapter in Detroit, as well as in more than a dozen other cities, including Pittsburgh, Indianapolis, and San Francisco.[17]

As one NOCW report noted, by 1915 its members had sent out seven thousand copies of *Salve Regina*, six thousand appeals, forty-five hundred circulars, and a thousand handwritten letters to potential donors. And

Marian devotees responded. A self-described "child of Mary" from Walpole, Massachusetts, mailed a handwritten letter and her small donation; Martin Van Den Berg, a Dutch-American "devotee of the Immaculate Conception of the Blessed Virgin" who served as a justice of the peace in Menominee, Michigan, told the NOCW's Washington representative, Fannie Whelan, he would raise funds; and, a wealthy Catholic wrote from her Fifth Avenue home to fellow New Yorker Hoffman to pass on $10 raised by one of her pious and "zealous" Irish servants.[18]

Yet there are signs that McKenna, whom NOCW members elected "national treasurer" shortly after he assumed his duties at the Shrine, was not thrilled with this decentralized system. Like Shahan, he wanted to coordinate the activity and channel the funds, as his messages published in *Salve Regina* indicate: "the secretary of each chapter," McKenna reminded the female volunteers, "should make a return each quarter of all money received to the national treasurer, Reverend Bernard McKenna." And, he continued, "checks should, for obvious reasons, be sent in immediately." Apparently, some chapters were not relaying the contributions or were holding them too long. McKenna and Shahan also visited the chapters, not only to encourage the volunteers but also to coordinate the efforts. To the casual reader of the Shrine's periodical during the middle of the decade, however, relations seemed cordial—and the clergy seemed genuinely grateful for the NOCW's labor. McKenna printed news about the organization's progress in *Salve Regina*: one 1916 issue, for example, bragged that the Pittsburgh chapter had grown to 417 members and reported that sixty-two women, along with Shahan and McKenna, had attended the New York chapter's meeting.[19]

Only a few years later, the private subterranean fissures widened into a publicly visible break between the lay organization and the Shrine clergy. Surviving documents do not fully reveal the participants' motives, though Hoffman's ambitions for her architect son, the board's decision to change the architectural design, and the clergy's worries about decentralization played a role. Most important, in 1918 CUA's Board of Trustees and the Shrine's Building Committee, which both included Shahan, decided to shift from a Gothic to a Romanesque design and agreed to hire Maginnis and Walsh. That meant Hoffman's son wouldn't be awarded the contract. The clergy, however, apparently chose not to tell the NOCW's leaders. Those women found out when a notice appeared in 1919 in the pages of *Salve Regina*: "Great Architects Obtained," the headline announced. It was not just Hoffman who was angry and hurt. According to the minutes of the June 1919 meeting of the New York chapter, the members were "much surprised" to learn of the decision indirectly, in the Shrine's periodical. They were disappointed, too, in the board's rejection of the Gothic style, which the New York chapter's treasurer called "Our Lady's own architecture." And they felt unappreciated. Members had raised over $50,000, with more than $32,000 of that coming from the New York chapter alone. In response, the members of that chapter "sent in their resignations," and one of the first national Catholic women's organizations abruptly disbanded.[20]

In response to the members' complaints, the Shrine staff printed a few notices praising the defunct NOCW: "the good work of these noble women is deeply appreciated," a 1920 issue assured readers. But the clergy also quickly adjusted to the change and aligned themselves with another women's organization. Shahan asked the IFCA, which had been founded in 1914 for another purpose, to solicit funds. That women's group tried a slightly different strategy but still directed its appeal to women. To supplement those efforts and restore control over fundraising, in 1920 Shahan and McKenna also established a new organization of their own, the National Salve Regina League, which broadened the promotional efforts and targeted other consumers of Marian devotion. The organization welcomed all Catholics, but the Shrine staff also continued to use segmented marketing after the NOCW disbanded. In 1919, Shahan mailed a letter to priests all across the country and, to reach those the mailings had missed, reprinted that letter in *Salve Regina*. In another strategy, in 1921 clerical promoters also encouraged "each Catholic family" to have their names entered on the "National Catholic Family Record," the forerunner of the Shrine's Memorial Hall, in order that "children in the generations to come will have complete knowledge of their ancestors" and devotees could appropriately thank Mary for protecting their homes and favoring their nation. Mary had favored the nation during World War I, many devotees believed, and the Shrine's clerical promoters also appealed to Catholics who had lost family members in that brutal conflict. The foundation stone program booklet, which McKenna sold as a souvenir for a dollar, told supporters that "every Catholic can help" but also suggested that the BNSIC was being constructed "in memory of our soldiers and sailors" who had died during World War I.[21]

Whether or not devotees recognized it as they purchased a copy of that program booklet, the 1920 foundation stone ceremony revealed the complexities of that transitional moment in the building of the National Shrine and the history of American Catholicism. During the Progressive Era of the late nineteenth and early twentieth centuries, laywomen played a more prominent role in many Catholic philanthropic, devotional, and reform organizations, but their role diminished over the next several decades as the centralization of ecclesiastical authority set in. As I've suggested, the centralizing forces started to converge in 1917, when the U.S. archbishops formed themselves into the National Catholic War Council to advance the Church's position and coordinate relief efforts, and its successor organization, the NCWC, even more firmly centralized ecclesiastical activities, placing them firmly under national episcopal control. Here, too, the Shrine reflects national patterns during the era of consolidation. Like other Catholic institutions in the years after World War I, the Shrine's fundraising efforts became more centralized between 1918 and 1920, as laywomen lost some of their former collective power and the newly formed Salve Regina League operated completely under episcopal control. Although some prominent laywomen were in Washington that day, Lucy Hoffman and other Progressive Era leaders of the NOCW were notably absent from the crowd at the foundation stone ceremony in 1920.[22]

That audience reflected the changing role of laywomen, and even the sermon by Bishop (later Archbishop) John T. McNicholas (1877–1950) of Duluth, Minnesota, who bemoaned "the so-called new freedom," functioned as a fulcrum between the old and new. McNicholas repeated the old refrain, sounded as early as the first fundraising booklet in 1911—that the Shrine would be "a monument to the religious fervor of the Catholic women of the United States"—while he simultaneously expressed the mounting clerical anxiety about the changing status of women, who had only won the right to vote that year. So talk about the new freedoms, and the "New Woman," were in the air that afternoon in 1920. However, most Catholic women, including the NOCW's leaders, seemed more worried about anti-Catholicism than gender inequality. Like other Catholics, they remained "largely unpersuaded by the emerging feminist movement and its immediate precursors," so the clerical anxiety seemed somewhat misplaced, even if Catholic nuns had more autonomy than most of their female contemporaries and even if the leaders of laywomen's organization had worked effectively, and sometimes independently, for spiritual causes in the preceding decades. Still McNicholas, an Irish-born Dominican who would go on to leadership positions in the NCWC during the next three decades, left nothing to chance in his sermon. He took the opportunity, at that decisive moment when a new Catholic institution was being founded, to warn: "women are seeking a freedom that is excessive." Whether or not the women gathered around the wooden platform recognized themselves in the bishop's assessment is not clear, but in the decades after that foundation stone ceremony, other women's organizations continued to raise funds and send contributions, though Mary's female devotees would never again have as much room to exert their own agency as they did during the NOCW's ascendancy between 1913 and 1918.[23]

The Second Phase of Building, 1953–1959: Exerting Episcopal Power and Mobilizing Diocesan Resources

"Many Sisters and laity"—though still not Lucy Hoffman—were present a few years later, McKenna recalled, when he and Bishop Shahan each "turned a spadeful of the soil on the spot" to start construction in 1922. The Crypt Church was completed by 1926, and workers finished the rest of the lower level in 1931. But coordinated fundraising and new construction halted during the 1930s and 1940s. When the promotional efforts resumed after World War II, female donors and women's organizations would do more than their share, but the campaign to complete the exterior of the Great Upper Church was more top-down than ever. In his 1903 appeal for a university church, Shahan had suggested "there ought to be...an edifice in which the dignity of our bishops and our priesthood might be worthily enshrined on the occasions of the annual meetings of the Archbishops and Trustees of the University, representing the whole episcopate." When Shahan's dream was realized in 1959, the Shrine's own publicity material also emphasized episcopal presence. "The Shrine exists," one media release asserted, "by the authority of all the Bishops of the United States. They approved its erection; the control and management are their concern." The next page of that press release briefly gestured toward the contributions of lay Catholic organizations, including the Knights of Columbus, who donated $1 million for the tower, and the Catholic Daughters of America, who gave $250,000 for five apsidal altars. But the first page of that official explanation of "Why the Shrine Exists" listed the names of more than three dozen episcopal leaders.[24]

One of them was the late Archbishop John F. Noll of Fort Wayne, Indiana, who had been "a particularly energetic and effective apostle for the National Shrine." His support began early. As a parish priest in Huntington, Indiana, he'd sent his personal donation of $5,000 in the early years, and, as he reminded McKenna in a 1953 letter, Noll also had attended the foundation stone ceremony in 1920. He went on to do as much as anyone to help finish the superstructure, even if, unlike McKenna, he didn't live to see the building's dedication in 1959. In 1912, as anti-Catholicism started to increase in Indiana—a Ku Klux Klan stronghold by the 1920s—Noll had founded a weekly newspaper, *Our Sunday Visitor*, to answer Protestant attacks and fortify Catholic piety, and he later used his position as the paper's editor to promote the Shrine's cause. He asked readers to support the Shrine and passed on $120,000 in contributions to Washington. Noll also became a key figure in postwar efforts to resume construction. In the summer of 1944, Bishop Patrick J. McCormick (1880–1953), rector of CUA, and

Archbishop Michael Joseph Curley (1874–1958), the leader of Baltimore's Catholics, approached Noll. They asked him "to head a committee of Bishops to consider the advisability of completing the National Shrine to Mary Immaculate, and, if they thought favorably, to devise a plan for the raising of funds adequate to complete at least the exterior." In turn, Noll approached his episcopal brethren at their annual meeting in Washington. In face-to-face encounters and exchanges by mail, he solicited the opinions of the nation's bishops in 1945 and 1946 and found wide, though not unanimous, support for the idea of completing the Shrine, though "about 15 percent" had warned that the timing was wrong. America, and the Catholic Church, was expending most of its energy and resources to recover from the effects of the war. Still, on Mother's Day 1947, Noll orchestrated a national fundraising drive that targeted parishes, priests, and nuns, but progress slowed again until 1953. Then came the final push to raise the $8.6 million needed to complete the Great Upper Church. That push came partly because of Noll's insistent campaigning and also from the judicious intervention of the leader of the newly formed Archdiocese of Washington, the Most Reverend Patrick A. O'Boyle. That effort was given extra force by papal encouragement: in 1953 Pius XII urged the faithful to "throng" to Marian shrines during the upcoming Marian year of 1954, as Noll reminded U.S. Catholics, and then sent word of his "heartfelt rejoicing" when he was told that the nation's bishops intended to complete the building.[25]

After the major nationwide campaign resumed in 1953 and construction started again the following year, the Marian year, authority was even more centralized, the clergy's media savvy even more evident, and the new fundraising strategies they employed even more successful. The new campaign was organized by a national episcopal building committee, the Episcopal Committee for the Shrine, which Noll chaired from 1953 until his death in 1956, and, at Noll's urging, that committee had agreed on a new tactic. As in the earlier period, they welcomed laywomen's participation, though always checked by clerical control, but the title of the renewed campaign's first press release predicted: "Children Will Help Provide United States with Great Shrine." As Noll confided to O'Boyle in a 1953 letter, "our greatest need at present" is "to get the school children to start contributing their pennies and nickels." With Noll's public leadership and private advice, and a great deal of behind-the-scenes-work in Washington not only by the Shrine's director, Monsignor Patrick O'Connor, but also by Archbishop O'Boyle and Reverend John B. Roeder, whom Noll appointed to direct the campaign from the Shrine's "Appeals Headquarters," the Committee started the renewed campaign by appealing to the more than two million Catholic school children (see chapter 3). At the same time, the Committee was also pressuring diocesan leaders who oversaw those parochial school systems to contribute: promoters used a carefully organized strategy aimed at bishops and archbishops. Most important, the committee set fundraising quotas—at thirty-seven times each diocese's or archdiocese's required NCWC contribution. Those proportional quotas meant that, for example, large cities like Chicago ($740,000) and New York ($666,000) had sizeable amounts to raise, and smaller dioceses like Charleston ($9,250) and Juneau ($7,400) were asked to send less.[26]

As the surviving correspondence shows, the response from the diocesan leaders was generally positive, but there were a few problems at first. A few bishops, for example the bishop of Portland, Oregon, did not respond to the initial appeal. Some, for example the bishop of Lansing, complained that there were just too many collections, and other dioceses asked for a delay for one reason or another, for example Grand Rapids, whose leader had recently died, and Brooklyn, which was raising funds for its centennial celebration. In a handful of cases, there was very polite resistance. One North Carolina leader, for example, wrote to Noll to protest that their assigned quota amounted to "a per capita allotment of $9," which was, "humanly speaking, impossible to attain." However, an analysis of the final accounting sheet shows that 90.6 percent of dioceses and archdioceses met their quota eventually, though the local enthusiasm for the national campaign still varied. Portland, slow to respond at the start, was one of eight dioceses that never collected its prescribed allotment. Trenton missed its quota by the largest margin (coming in $61,266 short). Chicago contributed $819,324, the highest amount and more than its quota. Some dioceses far exceeded expectations: not only Fort Wayne, Noll's home diocese, but also St. Louis, which collected $92,000 more than the Committee asked.[27]

The diocesan campaign was so successful in places like Chicago and St. Louis, and many other towns, in part because of the Committee's skillful use of all available media—print, radio, and television—both during the start of the effort in 1953 and again as the 1959 dedication approached. Noll's official report to the Committee in January 1954, just after the initial fundraising drive, gives some indication of the marketing campaign's scope and effectiveness. In 1953, he reported to his episcopal colleagues, the staff in Washington had distributed stacks of letters and a variety of collateral print media. "Campaign Headquarters," as he called it, shipped 75,334 appeals posters aimed at adults and 59,252 aimed at children. Following a Protestant philanthropic practice Noll had introduced to Catholics as editor of *Our Sunday Visitor*, that year the staff also mailed an astonishing 13.2 million "collection envelopes." They reached out to the media, too. On behalf of the Shrine, the NCWC's news service distributed twenty-two different stories and features, and more than twenty national Catholic magazines responded by providing coverage. Local diocesan media directors sent out weekly releases to the "secular press." *Time* had assigned a reporter to the story, and they were in conversation with *Life* to do the same. One priest promoted the effort on the National Council of Catholic Men's *Catholic Hour* on the NBC Radio Network, and a prominent church historian from CUA, John Tracy Ellis, added his pitch on CBS Radio's *Church of the Air*. To reach television viewers, the Committee asked for the help of Philadelphia's Cardinal O'Hara and turned to the public face of midcentury Catholicism, Bishop Fulton J. Sheen (1895–1979), who as a recently ordained priest had served as an acolyte for the 1920 ground blessing ceremony. Sheen did a half-hour show, "America's Shrine to Mary," which aired in November 1953 on NBC. The media blitz continued over the next six years and intensified as the dedication date drew near. In 1959, the Committee sent dioceses "broadcasting kits," which included "radio recordings, public service announcements and slides, press releases, news script, and photographs of the Shrine." Besides the usual outreach to print media, promoters also were successful in producing, for a nationwide audience, twenty-three radio and television programs, which reached, they estimated, "a cumulative audience of 100,000,000, through the facilities of 1500 local radio and TV stations." Coverage appeared on all the major radio networks of the time, NBC, CBS, ABC, Mutual, even Voice of America, and TV coverage explained Marian devotion and narrated the history of U.S. Catholicism, including, for example, CBS's four-part series *The American Catholic Story*. Of course, there was also coverage of the November 20 dedication and the associated two days of events, for example on NBC's morning show, *Today* (fig. 1.2).[28]

THE PROMOTERS' AIMS: HOPES AND FEARS

In his description of the morning's two-and-a-half-hour dedication ceremony, the reporter from the *New York Times* gushed about the "imposing new Washington landmark" and the "colorful ceremony rich in ancient pomp and splendor." He noted too, that more than three thousand devotees of Mary had filled the completed Great Upper Church, and that in an overwhelming turnout by the hierarchy "nearly all of the prelates of the church attended," including "about 200 archbishops and bishops" and—since Cardinal O'Hara was too ill to travel—three of the four U.S. cardinals. One of those cardinals, Boston's Richard Cushing (1895–1970), suggested

Figure 1.2. Dedication mass for the Shrine, November 20, 1959.

in his sermon at the evening mass on November 20 that the morning's dedication ceremony had been "overpowering": the "pent-up feelings of America" had found "eloquent" expression in that historic ritual. Also emphasizing the role of sentiment, Archbishop Karl J. Alter (1885–1977) of Cincinnati, who took over the chairmanship of the Episcopal Committee for the Shrine after Noll's death in 1956, proposed in another sermon during that three-day celebration that the superstructure's completion "marks the fulfillment of the cherished hopes of many generations." Some interpreters of religion have noted that religion involves emotion, including humans' "hopes and fears," and the other clergy who played a prominent role during the two major periods of the Shrine's construction expressed varied desires and multiple concerns as they called for donations and explained its function.[29]

Clerical Aspirations

The clergy hoped to build institutions, mobilize women, engage children, contest Protestants, incorporate immigrants, and claim civic space (the crucial aims I analyze in this book's six chapters), and each of these aims was vividly expressed at the foundation ceremony and the dedication ritual. For example, some of their hopes and fears had to do with the nation. Like many Catholics at the time, Shahan, who wrote the program booklet for the 1920 foundation ceremony, feared exclusion from national life and hoped that the Shrine might claim Catholic presence in the civic arena. The souvenir booklet, which included an image of Mary flanked by the Shrine and the Capitol, suggested that the building stood as "a National Memorial to Soldiers and Sailors" (see fig. 5.1). Further, Shahan noted, "our holy religion has not ceased to grow," and "this Great Republic" had prospered, too, and, as "every Catholic man, woman, and child is conscious, it's because of "the protection and intercession of Mary Immaculate." The sermons at the dedication also linked Marian devotion and national identity, including the message by St. Louis's Archbishop Joseph E. Ritter (1892–1967). "It is particularly fitting that this National Shrine in honor of Mary Immaculate should stand here in our national Capital," he told worshipers that fall morning in 1959. "The overriding interests of our citizens, their deepest loyalties, and their patriotic memories are centered here. To commemorate the glories of our nation and the decisive events of our history, many imposing monuments have been erected." But the BNSIC was necessary, too: "To give visible expression . . . to the fullness of our national life, not only civic or secular monuments are needed, but also those which tell the story of our religious hopes and aspirations." Other aspirations surfaced, too, by 1959. The Shrine's clerical advocates hoped to overcome disappointment, create beauty, promote morality, confront modernity, and make transnational connections that proclaimed the site's hemispheric reach and elevated the status of the U.S. Catholic Church in the eyes of Europe and in the view of the Vatican.[30]

Among the most basic emotions at work by 1959, after decades of inactivity, was embarrassment. In 1928, the Shrine's fundraising periodical, *Salve Regina*, had announced that supporters would say novenas to "invoke the aid of Our Blessed Mother" to meet their goal—to finish the superstructure's Great Dome by the following year. That didn't happen, of course, though the building's lower level was finished by 1931 (see fig. 1.3). In the next few years, a Marian statue was added here and a memorial tablet there, but there was little progress after 1933. Some devotees were forgiving about that. One laywoman, a 1937 graduate of nearby Trinity

Figure 1.3. The lower church under construction in 1925; it would be more than three decades before the superstructure was added in 1959.

College, lived to see the superstructure's completion but recalled that when she had worshiped there in the 1930s "the magnificent National Shrine was then below ground, just a basement beginning." But she understood: "it was Depression times and there was no money for building." The architects and clergy were less patient. In the 1940s, Charles Maginnis confided in a letter that it would be "a humiliating tragedy" if it were not completed, and John J. Reilly, the Shrine's director at the time, noted that some had started calling the site "The Hall of Disappointment": it bore "all the ear-marks of frustration" and constituted "a challenge to all the lovers of Mary in the United States." Noll repeated in one appeal what a lay devotee had told him in a letter—that the unfinished building was "a standing reminder of failure." Another cleric, the bishop of Reno, was even more pointed in an article published in *Salve Regina* in 1956: "The Shrine has been long, too long, in building," and "since the '20's it has remained a shapeless bulk of masonry half-buried in the ground."[31]

Yet clergy were not just overcoming embarrassment and confronting dis-appointment. Other motives drove clerical supporters, both as Bishop Shahan and Father McKenna made plans and raised funds during the 1910s and 1920s and during the 1950s as Noll, Alter, and the Episcopal Committee collaborated with the Shrine's fourth and fifth directors—O'Connor (1950–1956) and Monsignor (later Bishop) Thomas J. Grady (1956–1968)—to resume work on "the shapeless bulk of masonry." They also hoped that the new building might have other influences—aesthetic and moral—on American Catholics. Aesthetic aspirations were especially important to a few episcopal leaders, including Bishop Shahan in the founding decades and Archbishop Alter in the later period. In an essay reprinted in *Salve Regina*, "Why We Build Beautiful Churches," Shahan insisted that "the house of God must be a thing of beauty," and in the foundation ceremony booklet he promised that the BNSIC would be "one of the great churches of the world." Alter addressed aesthetic motives in his sermon at the 1959 dedication, too. He acknowledged that some were saying that "great monumental and inspiring churches have become outmoded," but he defended the Shrine on religious grounds, as he launched a polite attack on Protestants. In contrast to the "the puritan austerity of the sixteenth century reformers," buildings like the Shrine "should reflect a sense of awe and reverence so as to create a sympathetic atmosphere for the soul's upward flight to God."[32]

Alter also argued in that sermon that the Shrine's architecture might counter "the drab existence of present day secular life." He hoped that beautiful architecture might provide moral and spiritual uplift. Shahan had made a similar point decades earlier, arguing that "art for art's sake is an impiety," and asserting: "There is no real beauty...when it is separated from what is true and good." Aesthetic, moral, and spiritual motives inter-twine in the creation of sacred art: "the fine arts tend to withdraw man from an excessive devotion to the individual and the transient, the specific and merely useful in life, to fix his gaze upon the eternal verities of the moral life, and to bring him into closer union with his Maker." In short, Shahan and some other leaders hoped that beautiful architecture might be a weapon in the Church's battle against the temptations of modernity. Catholicism was secularity's "only adversary," and, as he told priests in the text of that 1919 fundraising appeal, "the noblest works of ecclesiastical architecture" can relieve Americans "of the intolerable thralldom of a fatal-istic philosophy of materialism, realism, and naturalism." So the Shrine's architecture would aid in the moral development and spiritual formation of Catholics. As the organizers noted, the Shrine would nurture the under-graduates at CUA, the nation's "chief educational center," and would instruct the children, adolescents, and young adults who encountered the lessons chiseled in stone.[33]

Some of the clergy's "hopes and aspirations" were more transnational than national in focus. Noting Columbus's Marian devotion, Shahan suggested that Mary's reach extended throughout the hemisphere. The bishop, who had studied in Canada, made the same point the year before the foundation stone celebration, noting "to our American clergy of the New World Mary is inexpressibly dear, since it is under her guidance and inspiration that they have evangelized both Americas for five hundred years." Focusing on the hemisphere's northern region, one issue of *Salve Regina* made sure that all North American devotees felt welcomed. Its front page headline reported a pattern evident in the archival records—a small proportion of donations and pilgrims came from Central America, the Caribbean, and Canada—but also expressed a clerical desire: "All America to Honor the Blessed Mother of God." Shahan suggested that "Newfoundland to Mexico, Alaska to Puerto Rico, will join in the glorious work of building our first American monument."[34]

In a surprising twist, one of the first to join in that "glorious work" had been Jean Joseph Marie Aboulin, CSB (1841–1931), a French-born parish priest from a Canadian religious order who retained his French citizenship and moved back and forth between Canada and the United States during his long life. He was the first to send a donation and, by some accounts, the first to propose the Shrine, even if similar ideas had been circulating for decades. A member of the Basilian Fathers of Toronto who had served congregations on both sides of the border, Aboulin was working in a Detroit parish in 1909 when he approached a cleric who knew Cardinal Gibbons. That colleague, in turn, passed on the idea and the donation. Shahan and McKenna, the keepers of the Shrine's official memory, celebrated Aboulin's role. In 1922, for example, they printed a recently penned list of Aboulin's "intentions" and described him, now an octogenarian, as "the first to write the late Cardinal Gibbons urging the erection of a National Shrine to Our Blessed Mother."[35]

As builders erected the superstructure in the late 1950s, there were some limited signs of the earlier clerical hope to make the BNSIC a hemispheric religious center. A bishop from Montreal attended the 1959 dedication, as did the bishop of Nassau and the archbishop of Guadalajara, and during that three-day celebration they heard the U.S. hierarchy retell the story of Columbus's Marian devotion, when both Alter and Ritter mentioned that his ship the *Santa Maria* was dedicated to Mary. Ritter, whose diocese, St. Louis, was the first in the United States to establish a foreign mission in Bolivia, also noted that Mary had been "providentially" brought to the Americas by "the French who came by way of the St. Lawrence on the North" and "the Spaniards who came through the South." Yet the messages from the Shrine's pulpit at the height of the Cold War tended to define "America" more narrowly, as the territory within the United States' political borders.[36]

All this was a lot for one building to accomplish, but American prelates expressed still other hopes and fears as they promoted its role in strengthening bonds with the Vatican and competing with other Catholic countries, especially in Europe. The United States had emerged from World War I as an international power, and the American Catholic Church had demonstrated its enduring national loyalty and expanded its ecclesiastical power. The Shrine, clergy hoped, would make this progress manifest. The Shrine's promoters tirelessly reminded Catholics that the Vatican had supported the project at every stage: the foundation stone program book noted that two popes, Pius X and Benedict XV, had "solemnly blessed the great and holy work," and the donation form included in a 1927 issue of Salve Regina assured potential contributors that "this movement has the approval of the Holy See." The sermons at the 1959 dedication noted that approval, too, though the Shrine's supporters updated the number of Peter's successors who had sanctioned the building efforts. In the earlier period that papal sanction had even greater significance. Some U.S. church leaders, including Gibbons and the progressives at CUA, had been shaken in 1896 when the Vatican suddenly removed the university's liberal rector, John Joseph Keane, and again in 1899 when the pope condemned accommodationist "Americanism." Shahan, the university's fourth rector and the Shrine's founder, had been linked with the progressives during the 1890s. An amiable administrator, Shahan tried to avoid ecclesiastical controversies, so he had other reasons to appreciate the Vatican's formal affirmation. It helped with fundraising, of course. It also was required, since the Shrine was formally affiliated with CUA, a pontifical institution, until 1948. For those old enough to remember the Americanist Controversy of the 1890s, however, papal support also was a comforting sign that relations with Rome, the geographical and spiritual center of the Catholic world, were good.[37]

At the same time, the Shrine's construction also asserted U.S. Catholicism's autonomy and, the clergy hoped, elevated its international standing. Shahan had noted the year after the foundation stone was put in place that "every nation has some great National Monument in honor of our Blessed Mother," and when the Shrine was finally completed in 1959, Alter proclaimed: "we can now join the rest of Christendom in the proud possession of a church worthy of the purpose it serves," now that it was joining the other great shrines of the world at "Lourdes, Fatima, Loreto,

Guadalupe." The dedication "marks a significant epoch in the history of the Catholic Church in America," Ritter suggested, and "stands as a majestic and compelling witness" to "the physical and material maturity of the Church in our land." Appealing to the same developmental metaphor, Cardinal Cushing announced from the pulpit on dedication day: "Catholic America...has come of age today." "At long last," he continued, "as proud adolescents we are happy to place in the hands of our Mother our first pay envelope. 'This shrine, dear Mother, is all yours; it is our gift to you.'"[38]

Responding to Clerical Aspirations: Dissent and Consent

Yet not all Catholics saw the Shrine as a "gift," and some favored other causes, even other causes in the capital. Some benefactors preferred to give to nearby Trinity College, the Catholic women's college dedicated in 1900, and some nuns and priests, including CUA's Thomas Edward Shields, were planning the Sisters College to meet the needs of teaching nuns. The Sisters College opened in 1911, using a building owned by the Benedictine Sisters that stood several blocks from CUA's campus, but Shahan, who endorsed the efforts to educate teaching nuns, unwittingly made things harder for the Sisters College fundraisers. In 1914, he returned from Rome with the pope's endorsement and a plan to appeal to the Catholic women of America, but the campaign's timing and strategy was "a death blow to the financing of the Sisters College," as it meant that two distinct institutions in Washington were appealing to Catholic women at the same time. Both projects suffered to some extent, though the new central building of the Sisters College was dedicated in 1916, and, as I've indicated, the Shrine started construction in 1922.[39]

The Sisters College supporters expressed no hostility to the Shrine project, but others vigorously dissented from the effort to construct a monumental shrine in Washington. Non-Catholics occasionally complained. In his biting critique of religion as "a source of income and a shield of Privilege," the socialist writer Upton Sinclair quoted *Salve Regina* when he lambasted attempts to secure donations by appealing to devotees' concern for their deceased relatives' fate: they "see before their eyes the glare of flames, and hear the shrieks of their loved ones writhing in torment through uncounted ages and eternities." Sinclair's hyperbolic tirade made him few friends among his Catholic contemporaries, but some of the devout also had reservations about the Shrine's attempts to raise money. Some Catholics probably just threw away the fundraising appeals they received in the mail. Others who had especially strong feelings took the time to register their dissent. For example, John Gormly of Norristown, Pennsylvania, sent a blunt letter to Father McKenna in 1927 to complain, first, about the mass mailings themselves: "the sending by mail of things to be bought or returned has become such a nuisance" that law enforcement officials should imprison "such people as a public pest." But Gormly had a second, more substantial objection: he was not thrilled with the cause itself. Fundraising should be directed primarily to foreign missions, he told McKenna. "Souls, souls, souls are the only thing of value on this earth." Money should be raised to "redeem" non-Christians, including "Chinese babies," from "spiritual famine." God does not want grand architecture: "shrines, sanctuaries, and cathedrals are as dung in His sight." The Shrine's fundraising appeal, Gormly suggested, was "an insult to God and His Blessed Mother and will get no aid from me while I am sane." Gormly then asked to be removed from the mailing list and reported that he had tossed the Shrine's appeal "into the fire as the devil's propaganda."[40]

Few Catholics—at least those who have a presence in the historical record—seem to have dismissed the fundraising appeals as unconditionally or passionately as Gormly, but even among those who supported the Shrine, some of the clergy's aspirations for it resonated more fully with the faithful than others. On the whole, if the surviving devotional letters and donor records are any indication, lay devotees seemed less concerned to use the new building as a bridge to the Vatican or as a weapon against secularity. When the Great Upper Church was finished, and even during the years when only the lower level's "bulk of masonry" stood on the site, some ordinary Catholics reported they found the architecture and design inspiring, although they were less driven by embarrassment at the construction's slow progress and less inclined to emphasize, as some episcopal leaders had, the significance of aesthetic motives. Perhaps because their gaze focused on the problems of daily life in the home, the workplace, and the neighborhood, where ecclesiastical structures certainly exerted local authority, they also were less likely to be concerned about the American Catholic Church's standing in relation to other Catholic nations in the Americas or Europe, though some of the faithful did express pride that the United States now had its own Lourdes, its own national devotional center. Like the clerical supporters, lay donors and pilgrims seemed to share some worry about Catholicism's position in American life, especially during the intolerant 1920s, and they agreed with the ordained men who emphasized the strategic positioning of the Shrine in the nation's capital. During the founding years and then again after the 1960s, lay supporters also worried about ethnic diversity, or at least about the possible loss of their heritage, and many welcomed opportunities to create links with their ancestral homelands, while also claiming a place at the nation's Shrine, whether by donating family memorial tablets for the walls of the Crypt Church or fundraising for a statue or chapel dedicated to their national patronesses.

Whether their veneration focused on a national patroness or on some other Marian symbol, it was devotion to the Blessed Virgin that bound them together. From prominent episcopal leaders preaching from the Shrine pulpit to the poorest lay follower kneeling in the back pew, it was Mary's aid with the ordinary problems of life and death, devotees' most personal fears and hopes about health, money, and family, that seems to have prompted many clergy and laity to support the Shrine. Shahan's message in the foundation stone program booklet noted "the practical influence of the Mother of God on every faithful Catholic," and in an earlier appeal he'd told the faithful that with a donation a person could "make known to the world in some public enduring way all that he owes to Mary Immaculate... all the vicissitudes of his life even to his hopes of a happy death." Reaffirming that original emphasis in his sermon at the 1959 ceremonies, Ritter explained the primary motivating force behind the building efforts: "Mary's honor is our motive." Unlike Lourdes, Fatima, and Guadalupe, the Washington shrine was not built at a spot where "Our Lady manifested her supernatural favors." No apparitions or miracles established its sacrality. Yet it was still a hallowed site, the archbishop argued, since Mary had helped American devotees in the past and would do so again: the Shrine "represents our gratitude for past favors, and even more an urgent appeal to her powerful intercession for continued protection in the future."[41]

Lay Catholics agreed with the bishops on this point: they, too, felt moved to support the BNSIC because of their devotion to Mary and their gratitude for her intercessory power. Mary Kelly, an unemployed thirty-two-year-old devotee from Massachusetts, wrote to McKenna about health concerns. She lived with her blind widowed mother, an Irish immigrant, in a very modest rental home. Mary reported she had "weak nerves," but most of all she prayed that she would "never go blind." Another devotee, William Smith, wrote to McKenna to pass on two intentions. First, he sent a small donation and asked McKenna whether anything "could be done in the way of burning a candle at the Blessed Mother's Shrine or having a mass said for a non-Catholic friend of mine that the almighty God saw fit to call to him last February." "Her and her husband," William explained, "was good friends of mine." A widower in Bethlehem, Pennsylvania, who lived on an ethnically diverse block with other steelworkers (including men who had migrated from Czechoslovakia, Poland, Hungary, Italy, and Greece) William also worried about the living. He was concerned about what would happen to his only son, John, if he were injured at work. "I sure do need Her protection. I will tell you my dear Father the work that I do down at the Steel Plant is awful dangerous, one slip or one mis-step on my part will mean that I will be a cripple for life or I will be a case for the undertaker...so you can see that I sure do need Her blessing and protection."[42]

THE DIVERSE SUPPORTERS: MANIFESTING PRESENCE BY GIVING AND GOING

Many other U.S. Catholics felt that they needed Mary's "blessing and protection," and those diverse devotees, from popes to paupers, had a presence at the BNSIC from the 1910s to the 1950s as they interacted in a vast Catholic institutional network that stretched from the local—the home, the parish, and the diocese—to the transnational: the Vatican, the Holy Land, and the homeland. The far was brought near in a vivid way as Gibbons blessed the foundation stone, since it contained a stone taken from the Holy Land, "a small block of marble from the Mount Carmel in Palestine, the most ancient of Shrines of Our Blessed Mother." That marble block moved Mary's devotees across time and space to founding events and sacred terrain, and other transtemporal and translocative artifacts established connections with the immigrants' homelands, including the Crypt Church's columns and the ethnic chapels (see chapter 6).[43]

And the edifice linked America and Rome. The year before he received the first donation from Father Aboulin of Detroit, Shahan had celebrated transnational Catholic links in "The Apostolic See," a sermon he delivered at an episcopal consecration. Emphasizing the Vatican's role, he proposed that the U.S. Catholic Church owed to "the successors of Peter its existence, preservation, and progress." The Shrine, in particular, Shahan and other promoters have emphasized, also has owed much to the Vatican. Archbishop John Bonzano, the apostolic delegate to the United States, represented the papacy as he blessed the site on May 16, 1920, and every pope since Pius X has declared his support. Two popes, John Paul II (1979), who named the Shrine a minor basilica, and Benedict XVI (2008), who addressed the U.S. bishops in the Crypt Church, have visited the Shrine. Other pontiffs have made their support tangible in other ways. A high relief on the East Porch memorializes Saint Pius X, who approved the Shrine in 1913 and offered a personal donation of $400. Paul VI and John XXIII donated ritual artifacts, and both gifts—Pope Paul's tiara and Pope John's stole—are on display in the lower church. Two mosaics now placed side by side in the Great Upper Church's chancel were created as papal gifts in the Vatican Mosaic Studio. In

1960, Pius XII and John XXIII presented the Shrine with a mosaic copy of Titian's painting *Assumption of the Virgin*, and three decades earlier Benedict XV commissioned another mosaic to "set an example" and show his support for "this most holy purpose." His successor, Pius XI, fulfilled that promise in 1930 when he sent a copy of Murillo's famous painting *Immaculate Conception*, which adorned the Crypt Church before it was relocated to the Great Upper Church (see fig. 1.4).[44]

Pope Benedict XV made his promise to send the mosaic in a 1919 letter addressed to Gibbons and the U.S. prelates, and bishops have had a major presence at the Shrine, too, by giving and by going—as well as by encouraging donation and pilgrimage among the faithful. Between 1916 and 1920, many ecclesiastical leaders donated and visited. For example, donor books record the names of bishops who gave in those early years, and we can see, randomly selecting contributors from three pages of one book, that episcopal support was strong and was national in scope (see appendix 1.1). Fourteen different states and all regions are represented among the twenty selected donors listed in appendix 1.1, with bishops from Los

Figure 1.4. Shahan (*center*) and McKenna (*back*) pose with lay devotees and two workers. Behind them is the recently uncrated mosaic of Murillo's *Immaculate Conception*, which was shipped from the Vatican Mosaic Studio and arrived on June 17, 1930.

Angeles to Boston and San Antonio to Juneau making personal contributions. Those leaders of the immigrant church—and 65 percent of them were also foreign born—grew up speaking French, German, and Dutch as well as English, and their presence in the donor records show that a wide range of episcopal leaders supported the Shrine, even during the first phase of building (see table 1.1). They also visited, and not only for the foundation stone ceremony in 1920, when two cardinals, eleven archbishops, and fifty-six bishops came to Washington. Even more had visited the site of the future Shrine in 1919—including 90 percent of the donors listed in appendix 1.1—when ninety-one leaders gathered that year for the first of many annual meetings of the U.S. hierarchy on the grounds of CUA. Shahan was at that meeting, of course, and his presence is hard to miss at the Shrine, too, since his tomb is visible to even the most casual pilgrim. Noll, the key figure during the mid-1950s, is memorialized not far away, on a black memorial tablet in the lower level. Even more prominent in the architecture of the Shrine, the U.S. hierarchy also are remembered as major donors for the Great Upper Church's main altar and baldachin and, along with diocesan priests, listed as the primary donors for the Blessed Sacred Chapel.[45]

Those diocesan priests, the "hierarchical middlemen" who have received surprisingly little attention from historians, have had a presence, too, and not only in that chapel. Priests have "shaped and shared" the devotional culture with women religious and laypeople, and many priests have been ordained at the Shrine, although reports vary about how many: *Salve Regina* counted almost three thousand ordinations between 1924 and 1932, and a 1959 press release estimated that the Crypt Church had been the site of only two thousand ceremonies since 1929. In any case, other priests who received holy orders in other churches have visited or donated, too. The first pastor to send a donation on behalf of his parish was Thomas J. Walsh (1873–1952) of Buffalo's St. Joseph's, in 1918, and the following year many priests responded to Shahan's direct appeal by sending in their personal donations, including the twenty randomly selected clerical contributors

Table 1.1. PROFILE OF SELECTED EPISCOPAL DONORS, 1916-1919

Percent foreign born	Number native languages	Percent Irish ancestry	Number of states represented	Percent at 1919 meeting of hierarchy
65%	4	50%	14	90%

Source: "Journal, High Altar Contributions," Archives, BNSIC.

listed in appendix 1.2. An analysis of that list shows that, as with the episcopal donors from the same year, there was a surprising geographical range, with money sent by priests in twelve states and the District of Columbia, including three each from New England, the Mid-Atlantic, and the South, four from the Midwest, and five from the West Coast (table 1.2). Three-quarters of those clerics worked in parishes, and the total included fewer immigrants (40 percent) than among the episcopal donors, as you might expect from the younger cohort, and slightly more men of Irish descent (61 percent). And priests who served in parishes continued to send money and organize pilgrimages after 1919. Patrick J. Doyle (1877–1973), a thirty-two-year-old diocesan priest living in St. Lawrence's rectory with two other priests and a housekeeper in St. Louis, mailed a small personal donation in 1920. Ten years later, Leo J. Krichten (1894–1964), an assistant pastor at St. Patrick's in Harrisburg, Pennsylvania, brought forty members of the Sodality of the Blessed Virgin to the Shrine by Greyhound bus one autumn day. Priests journeyed there in even greater numbers during the 1950s, and, as donor records show, continued to offer personal contributions and organize collective giving.[46]

Almost all women's and men's religious orders active in the United States have had some presence at the Shrine, too. The Sisters of St. Joseph have played especially important roles at every stage of the BNSIC's history, contributing the funds for the first temporary chapel in the 1910s, collecting donations from children for the Mary Memorial Altar in the 1920s, and giving money for thirty-six dome windows in the upper level in the 1950s. The Sisters of St. Joseph and other orders have traveled there, too, although the visitor logs do not reveal all we want to know, since not all pilgrims signed the book and many devotees, especially nuns, provided limited information, for example a "Sister Mary" from Philadelphia and a "Sister Teresa" from New York City who signed the book in the early 1920s. Yet the presence of religious orders is clear (see appendix 1.3). Some women religious signed the book alone—though we cannot say if they visited alone—including Sister Mary Blanche, a daughter of German immigrants who

Table 1.2. SUMMARY PROFILE OF SELECTED CLERICAL DONORS, 1919

Percent parish priests	Number of states represented	Percent foreign born	Percent with known Irish ancestry
75%	12 (and D.C.)	40%	61%

Source: "Journal, High Altar Contributions," Archives, BNSIC.

taught at Immaculate Conception Academy in Davenport, Iowa. Most often, male and female members of religious orders visited in large or small groups—and sometimes one member of the group signed for all of them. Four members of the Sisters of St. Joseph of Carondelet from the College of St. Catharine in St. Paul, Minnesota, signed the visitors book in 1926. Convent records show that those St. Joseph nuns, including the Art Department chair, Sister Marie Teresa Mackey (1867–1952), taught or created art, and that was part of their motive for visiting the almost completed Crypt Church. However, surviving records do not offer any clues about the motives of other religious who traveled there, including Brother Norbert G. Piper, a resident of the Carmelite House of Studies in D.C., who went to the Shrine with his older brother Walter, a switchman on the railroad in Ponca City, Oklahoma, and his sister-in-law and two-year-old niece, Mary Ellen.[47]

The Carmelite Order also donated the Our Lady of Mount Carmel Chapel, while another order, the Jesuits, gave the funds for five small chapels in the western apse of the Great Upper Church, where members of the Society of Jesus, including its founder, Ignatius of Loyola, are honored. Male and female religious, or their convents and monasteries, gave in less public ways, too. The Ursuline Convent in Toledo offered a modest collective contribution in 1954, the Marian year. Nuns, who did most of the heavy lifting in Catholic schools, social service agencies, and hospitals, were dramatically underpaid, but some managed to scrape together a few dollars for a personal donation, too. For example, Sister Mary Teresita, OSM, a Colorado-born daughter of Italian immigrants, joined the Servites and sent money to memorialize a family member in the 1950s. More commonly, nuns sweet-talked or strong-armed donations from the lay Catholics at the institutions where they labored, as did Sister Mary Ludger from Loreto Academy in Santa Fe, New Mexico, who passed on what she had collected in 1919.[48]

By giving and going, lay Catholics had a presence, too. The NOCW and the IFCA were decisive for fundraising efforts in the early years, and many other male and female lay organizations also have been important. In fact, almost every major U.S. Catholic group has had some connection to the Shrine, including the Ladies Auxiliary of the Ancient Order of Hibernians and the Polish Women's Alliance and fraternal organizations like the Catholic Order of Foresters and the Knights of Columbus. Men from a Brooklyn branch of the Knights of Columbus secured bragging rights as the first out-of-town pilgrims, arriving in May 1923, and the national group donated the soaring bell tower, which was dedicated in 1959. The group that began as the women's branch of that organization, the Daughters of Isabella, also visited and donated. In the later fundraising campaign for the Great Upper Church, they donated Ivan Mestrovic's statue *Mary Immaculate with Angels*, which stands on the balcony above the Shrine's central door. In the early years, they funded a chapel in the lower church's north apse and made an annual pilgrimage to celebrate their contribution and express their devotion. McKenna made notes about one of those pilgrimages, on May 29, 1927: "The Daughters of Isabella met in the Crypt Church for their annual Mass celebrated on the Altar of St. Elizabeth in the chapel which the Daughters of Isabella contributed. Father McKenna said the Mass and about 100 of the Daughters received Holy Communion."[49]

Individual laymen and laywomen also sent their dollars or made the trip. The twenty male lay donors from 1919 listed in appendix 1.4 include a much smaller proportion of foreign-born devotees (15 percent) than did the clerical contributors in the same year. Those laymen lived in New England, the Mid-Atlantic, and the Midwest, hailing from eleven different states in those regions. Most of those who sent their money were working-class city dwellers—including a janitor, a machinist, a truck driver, and a saloonkeeper—but George Banchoff, the son of German migrants, worked on his farm in rural New Jersey. The saloonkeeper, John Franey, sent McKenna the largest donation from his modest Philadelphia home, but the record is mute about his motive. Fortunately, other sources give us some sense of why the faithful contributed. In an anonymous letter published in 1918 in *Salve Regina*, one male devotee from D.C. who had sent a small donation made a request: "I am sending herewith our mite for the Shrine of the Immaculate Conception and in so doing I would ask your prayers for Our Lady's Intercession in behalf of my dear wife, that her health may be restored." The next year, a mother sent a small donation and explained her motives in a heartbreaking letter. Like many other lay devotees, she seemed focused on making ends meet and caring for family members, living and dead:

> I am giving this...in memory of my dear, departed husband. He died January 18, leaving me with five small children, the oldest being eleven years and the youngest was ten days old when he died. He died of pneumonia, a fine healthy man and a kind and loving father. I have a hard road ahead of me, but I know God will take care of us. I thank God I am a Catholic; that is my only comfort now. I send the boys to Confession every week. My two oldest are Altar boys, and it was my greatest desire that they should be Priests....I make them visit the Blessed Sacrament every day, and we say the beads every night, unless something prevents us. I hope you will pray for my dear husband. I also lost a beautiful little girl last October. She was only two years old and her name was

Rosary, and she died in the month of the Rosary. My oldest boy was drowned when he was nearly six years old. I have had eight children, five living now. God spare them [and] me. My comfort is that God has them and no one else. I hope this little Trifle will help you in this grand work, and I only wish it was a thousand times more.[50]

Some lay devotees could—and did—give a thousand times more. George Logan Duval (1855–1931), a wealthy New York merchant and fervent Marian devotee, gave to many Catholic causes, from a hospital wing in Valparaiso, Chile, to a chair in Marian theology at CUA. The Shrine's promoters have remembered Duval, however, because he also funded the first chapel constructed outside the Crypt Church, the Chapel of Our Lady of Lourdes, which honors the national patroness of the United States and recalls Mary's miraculous apparition in France. The largest individual benefactor before 1931, however, was an Irish-born contractor from Philadelphia, James J. Ryan (1874–1929), whom Pope Pius X honored by naming him Knight of the Grand Cross of St. Gregory the Great. Like Duval, Ryan was one of the two lay members of the Shrine's Building Committee, and he visited regularly and gave $50,000, which Shahan used to pay for the Crypt's Good Shepherd Chapel. After Ryan mailed the last portion of his promised gift in 1925, McKenna wrote back to him: "your action has been, so to speak, the veritable foundation stone of the whole structure." Ryan had visited the site both before and after Gibbons blessed the foundation stone in 1920, and even more prominent lay Catholics have donated and visited over the years, including the actor Douglas Fairbanks, who signed the visitors' log, and the entertainer Bob Hope, and his wife Delores, who donated the funds for the 1994 Our Lady of Hope Chapel.[51]

Most lay donors and visitors over the years have been less famous, however, and they have hailed from near and far, from many foreign countries and all across the United States. For example, in the 1920s, Sara Ritter traveled a little more than two miles across town to attend mass with her daughter and husband; but John J. Giacoma, a twenty-one-year-old who signed the register just below pilgrims from Los Angeles and Seattle, was more than two thousand miles from his home in Walkerville, Montana (see also appendix 1.3). In the 1950s, a few days before the dedication ceremony, Joseph Puglise, from nearby Arlington, Virginia, sent money for a memorial tablet, and Mary Rose Schwab, a German-American teacher who lived in Healdsburg, California, offered a contribution for the upkeep of the Shrine. In the years of intense fundraising from 1953 to 1959, many other contributors sent their gifts, and those donors were a diverse cross-section of the nation's Catholics, as the Shrine's donor books show. Appendix 1.5, which was constructed by sampling from the donor book for 1953, offers interesting hints about the supporters.[52] If this list is any indication, a surprising proportion (44 percent) were male. It's not surprising to find, however, that three decades after America's gates closed for most immigrants, a much smaller number of the faithful (16 percent) were first-generation Americans than when Gibbons blessed the foundation stone. With the increased distance from the immigrant generations, it is more difficult to trace devotees' ethnic heritage, though their census records indicate that some of the early diversity remained: the list of contributors includes Henry Brown, a black, Louisiana-born Catholic living in Los Angeles, and the other donors in this group claimed not only Irish and German but also Polish, Canadian, Italian, Czech, and Hungarian ancestors. The support also remained national in scope, with twelve states represented in that list of thirty contributors. The Mid-Atlantic region and surrounding states boasted many of the Shrine's supporters, and the Deep South continued to show the least interest during the later period, though Louisiana, Kentucky, and Tennessee had their fair share of donors and pilgrims. Yet during both phases of construction the devotion's geographical range was surprising: attracting donors from California and pilgrims from Montana, the project managed to gain widespread support (see appendices 1.6 and 1.7).[53]

That Montana pilgrim, Giacoma, visited with other adults, and some parents, like Ritter, journeyed with children or adolescents in tow. So did diocesan priests, who led parish pilgrimages, and teaching nuns, who brought students, traveling in tour buses or, worse, riding in dilapidated vehicles owned by the order or the diocese, as they alternately cajoled and threatened their alternately manic and bored charges, appealed to the intercession of the saints, and, perhaps, wondered if the fires of hell they had so vividly described to the kids rivaled the travail of a hot, bumpy journey in June with a bus load of thirteen-year-olds. With more or less travail, some secular groups—like public schools, Boy Scouts, and Scripps National Spelling Bee finalists—also made the trip as part of an excursion to the nation's capital, but the director's "Day Book" and the Shrine's visitors register show that Catholic school groups were among the most regular and numerous visitors. Some came from the Washington area. McKenna's "Day Book" described one visit by children from nearby St. Anthony's: "The First Communion Class of St. Anthony's Parish under the direction of Rev. Dr. Johnson made their First Holy Communion in the Crypt of the Shrine at 8 o'clock.... There were about 180 children in the class. About 1800 people attended the mass, nearly all of whom received Holy Communion." Children also came from surrounding states up and down the East Coast. In May 1930, for example, several thousand students visited from more than fifty-one public and Catholic schools, including, for example, a public school in Spartanburg, South Carolina, and a Catholic school in Camden, New Jersey.[54]

A few months earlier in 1930, a group from Brooklyn's Bishop McDonnell Memorial High School for girls that made the pilgrimage included the school's middle-aged, Brooklyn-born principal, Reverend John F. Ross, and ten nuns—members of the Sisters of St. Dominic, Sisters of Mercy, Sisters of Charity, Daughters of Wisdom, and, Sisters of St. Joseph. The group also included 105 students from the school, which was the largest in Brooklyn in 1930. Young people from Brooklyn and all across the country also contributed. Their parents gave them the money—and sometimes wrote the letters—or they earned the funds, as letters indicate, by crocheting for neighbors or doing odd jobs. However they got the contributions, children sent them with multiple intentions, usually concerns about relatives or success in school. One ten-year-old asked McKenna "to pray for my father, who is deaf" and noted that her father had given her "a pretty locket, which has a Scapular inside"; another elementary school student sent a dollar so he could "get along well in school" and so that his father would "get strong." Children continued to give later, too, during the fundraising campaign that began in 1953. That year, for example, boys and girls from the Civics Club at St. Patrick's parochial school in Weston, West Virginia, sent a few dollars, and so did teens from the Sodality of the Immaculate Conception at Chicago's Notre Dame High School. Thus, children and adolescents, who were sometimes obscured amid the records of adult-centered piety, also had a presence at the Shrine by giving or going.[55]

So the Shrine was not "just about bishops," though the episcopal presence was more decisive between 1953 to 1959 than in the earlier building phase, especially between 1913 and 1918, when the centralization that would shape Catholicism and the Shrine after World War I had not fully taken hold. During both phases, the full force of Catholicism's transnational institutional network could be felt at that site, and the full range of America's Catholics had a presence there, by giving and going, during that brick and mortar period of U.S. Catholicism. That varied presence also was inscribed materially in the Shrine's architecture and ornamentation. It's discernable in the pope's mosaic, the Founder's Chapel, and the diocesan clergy's Blessed Sacrament Chapel. It's there in the Knights of Columbus tower and on the 14,400 marble and granite tablets that line the walls of the lower church and memorialize Mary's diverse devotees—including nuns, monks, laymen, laywomen, children, and families. Even Lucy Hoffman and the NOCW, the Shrine's first fundraising organization, which had a falling out with the clerical promoters—though not with the Virgin Mary—have a presence: in the pages of *Salve Regina*, in the records of the Shrine archives, and even in the stone and brick of the Romanesque Crypt Church, which they didn't like as much as the proposed Gothic structure but, nonetheless, helped to build with their energetic fundraising campaign.[56]

2

⚭

Mobilizing "America's Marys"

Women, Fundraising, and the
Mary Memorial Altar, 1913–1938

Clara Douglas Sheeran, a Brooklyn devotee of Mary and cofounder of the IFCA, was worried. That's clear from the personal letters and published articles she wrote in 1927 and 1928. It was not just that her health was bad—though it was, since she'd suffered a heart attack. She almost seemed more worried that the IFCA wouldn't keep its earlier promise, her promise, to raise $20,000 for the Mary Memorial Altar, the central altar in the Crypt Church (fig. 2.1). So Sheeran and several other IFCA members rededicated themselves to fundraising. These leaders came up with new marketing plans and penned appeals that appeared in the Shrine's *Salve Regina* and the IFCA's *Quarterly Bulletin*: "Let us remember the marble altar which we pledged ourselves to erect at the National Shrine of the Immaculate Conception," Sheeran urged IFCA members in an editorial in the March 1927 issue of the *Bulletin*. Behind the scenes, by posted letters and face-to-face chats—several fundraisers lived in Brooklyn—Sheeran and other members brainstormed about how to raise money for the altar that had became so important to her.[1]

One March 1928 letter to Father Bernard McKenna revealed how much Sheeran had come to cherish both the Mary Memorial Altar and the efforts to raise funds for it. Apparently the Shrine's director also was worried and had written to Sheeran. She responded by assuring him that the IFCA would meet its goal. Then Sheeran noted that she'd been confined to her

Figure 2.1. The Mary Memorial Altar.

bedroom for months as she did some of this planning and the Mary Memorial Altar had become a focus of her devotional life in that most intimate domestic space: "I am to go out for the first time this year on Saturday, if the good Lord continues to help me improve in health. This is my longest illness and really there were times when I felt I would never again lift my head. I used to look at my altar facing my bed where the picture of the Mary Memorial Altar stands and visualize mass at your wonderful shrine." In many ways, of course, the Shrine was Reverend McKenna's, but Sheeran had made it her own, too, especially its Mary Memorial Altar, which had offered her comfort through that long illness.[2]

Despite poor health (in the surviving photographs of the event she looks a bit frail), Sheeran traveled to Washington later that year to see the fulfillment of her promise. On December 8, 1928, the feast of the Immaculate Conception, Sheeran and other women from the IFCA gathered around the visual and liturgical focus of the Crypt Church, the Mary Memorial Altar, a freestanding rectangular block of golden Algerian onyx with a base of Roman Travertine marble. The five-thousand-pound altar had been installed in December 1926, and a presentation ceremony of sorts happened in the fall of the next year. The women hadn't raised all of the $20,000 they'd promised until the end of 1928, however. When they did reach their fundraising goal, the organization's leaders and the Shrine's clergy scheduled a second presentation ceremony in the Crypt Church on December 8. The female pilgrims—and the symbolic scallop shells capping the altar's niches reminded participants it was a pilgrimage site—gathered that afternoon to formally present the altar to the male clergy and, thereby, keep their promise, Sheeran's promise.[3]

Male clergy were well represented at the ceremony. At least nine priests participated. Monsignor Edward A. Pace (1861–1938), the director of the women's organization, gave the address. McKenna offered the introductory remarks. Bishop Thomas J. Shahan, the Shrine's founder and the IFCA's "honorary president," officiated at the benediction of the Blessed Sacrament. Shahan also officially accepted the donation of the altar, an artifact that, as an attentive viewer might have noticed, included images of more men: in the niches along its base stand carved onyx statues of Jesus, Paul, and the twelve disciples.[4]

Women were present, too, however. Some of them participated in the dedication: Chicago's Mary Blake Finan, the IFCA's current president, presided, and the governor of the organization's D.C. chapter, Elizabeth J. Dolan, offered an "Address of Welcome." Sheeran had the honor of giving the "Presentation Speech," just before Bishop Shahan formally accepted the gift. In a later part of the ceremony, the other IFCA cofounder, Sister Mary de Paul Cogan, was one of two women who unveiled the bronze tablet that memorialized the presentation ceremony. Two women from D.C. who raised funds but had no formal role in the 1928 ritual, Mary Bryne O'Toole and Helen Stafford Whitton, also were recognized on the program as the "international chairmen" of the Mary Memorial Altar Fund.

Thousands of other Catholic women were neither entirely absent nor fully present: the American "Marys" who had given $8,000 to the altar campaign from 1919 to 1927 and those who had donated $12,000 more as part of the intensified 1928 fundraising effort that used the newly established Mary's Day Movement as an enticement to give. The fundraising activities for the altar initially exhorted all women named Mary—"the Marys of America"—to each give a dollar to the cause, but as the deadline to meet the IFCA's goal drew near and Sheeran grew more worried, that effort expanded to include all women who had "even remote kinship with the name Mary," including relatives and teachers named Mary. In a plan devised by Sheeran's Brooklyn neighbor, Elizabeth M. Brennan, a portion of the rest of the promised funds came from women and girls who gave to the Altar Fund as part of the movement to celebrate "Mary's Day" on the Saturday before Mother's Day in 1928.[5]

Later that year, "arrangements had been made to run special trains from New York, Maryland, and Virginia to enable friends of the federation to attend the services," but not all the members of the IFCA, or those who donated to their cause, could make it to the altar presentation ceremony that December afternoon. Those donors were not entirely absent either. Religions can imaginatively transport devotees temporally and spatially, and some narratives, artifacts, and practices at the presentation ceremony positioned those absent female donors near the main altar of that darkened Crypt Church. They were remembered in the speeches as participants told stories about the "Marys of America" who gave the funds for the altar. The bronze plaque unveiled that day recalled them, too: its inscription announced that the altar was "representing the Marys of America." Further, the donors' names had been recorded on a "roster" of Marys, and at one moment in the ceremony a priest ritually transported those women and girls from across the country to the altar. As Brennan, the founder of Mary's Day and the major organizer of the 1928 fundraising efforts, recalled in a letter she wrote years later, "as part of the consecration ceremony Dr. Pace, with his own hands, placed underneath the newly consecrated Mary Altar a metal box containing the names" of the female donors. It's not clear why Brennan chose to emphasize that Monsignor Pace, whom she came to see as a friend, had done this "with his own hands." Was that because he'd long served as the clerical leader of the IFCA, so it seemed especially appropriate that he was the ecclesiastical official to have the privilege of placing those names there? Whatever the reason for that emphasis in her narrative, it seems more important, at least for my purposes in this chapter, that a priest, any priest, placed the names of female donors "underneath...the Mary Altar," thereby embedding those names—and, in a sense, positioning those women—within the altar itself, situating them at the center of the ritual space where the male clergy officiate at liturgies.[6]

Whether or not all observers sensed the ritually and materially conjured presence of those absent donors, few could fail to notice the female organizers and male clergy who participated in the presentation rite. One posed photograph unwittingly illustrates, however, the way those women and men interacted in complex ways as they worked to raise funds for the altar (see fig. 2.2). Photographs cannot recover the past, but only provide a positioned glimpse of a single moment, yet it's useful to consider several features of this image: the plaque in the background, the dress of the participants, and the position of the figures.[7]

Note, first, the Mary Memorial Altar plaque on the right wall behind the posed figures. Its inscription suggests that the altar represents Catholic women, but it also goes on to celebrate a priest:

Figure 2.2. Participants in the Mary Memorial Altar presentation ceremony on December 8, 1928.

THE MARY MEMORIAL ALTAR
Representing the Marys of America
Erected in Honor of
MARY IMMACULATE
Patroness of the
International Federation of Catholic Alumnae
To Commemorate
The loving, active, religious leadership
Of their
Honorary President, Rt. Rev. Thos. J. Shahan, D.D.
By the
International Federation of Catholic Alumnae
1915–1928

This tablet commemorates the leadership of a bishop who was instrumental in building the Shrine and overseeing fundraising, but who did less labor in securing donations for the Mary Memorial Altar than most of the women standing near the plaque or identified on the donor list beneath the altar.[8]

Second, notice the contrast in the colors of the participants' dress: most of the ordained men wear lighter hues, while the women have on dark coats and hats, including the black habit of Sister Mary de Paul, who stands on the far right. This contrast between light and dark directs the viewer's attention to the men. Their dress also differs in social function. The men's attire—the vestments of the priesthood—sets them apart from the women, who have no access to ordination and no authority to officiate at the other six Catholic sacraments. Dress, in this case, marks male inclusion and female exclusion. Even though there's no surviving evidence that any of the women present recognized this irony, Sheeran, Brennan, and the others had labored to raise funds for an altar on which they could never say mass. Absent from the altar during the liturgy by church law, they could never ritually summon the "real presence" of the divine through the Eucharist. In that way, the priests' clothing, and especially the liturgical costume of the three primary celebrants on the front row, reaffirms their superior religious rank and concomitant social power.

Finally, the positioning of the figures is revealing. Bishop Shahan, who wears a pointed white mitre that symbolizes episcopal authority and adds height to his image, stands second from the left in the front row. In terms of the image's composition, Shahan seems most central. Not only is he the tallest figure on the front row, but—and this was probably an accident of the photographic staging—he is positioned just beneath the illumination from the electric light behind and above the group. The other clergy join him on the front row, or they stand immediately behind the other priests. The women, however, are either partially obscured by the ecclesiastical officials or, like Sheeran, who stands to the right of the priests and below her friend Sister Mary de Paul, are relegated to the photograph's margins, clustered on the far left or the far right.

This photograph helps us formulate questions about the fundraising for the Mary Memorial Altar. In that era when the devotional culture of consolidated Catholicism emphasized centralized ecclesiastical authority and the culture of Catholic womanhood celebrated Mary's example and prescribed female submission, what was the relationship between the male clergy and the IFCA leaders as they mobilized America's Marys to support this project? To what extent, as in this photograph, were female leaders obscured or marginalized by clerics? If they were obscured in some ways, how did these women work within the "structural constraints"—including their exclusion from ordination—to exert "personal agency"? One feminist scholar has argued that "women are invisible in American Catholic history," both in the Church and in most scholarship about the Church. Did those structural constraints render lay elites and ordinary devotes invisible? To what extent were laywomen present and absent in this fundraising effort— and in the Shrine itself?[9]

Focusing on fundraising for the Mary Memorial Altar, I suggest, provides an illuminating angle of vision on larger questions about the place of women at the Shrine and in the Church. Moving from the first efforts to raise funds for the altar in 1913 to the culmination of those efforts in 1938, in the remainder of this chapter I explore these questions. I argue that in this period before the full clericalization and centralization of Catholic philanthropy, some middle- and upper-class IFCA members living in cities, especially on the East Coast, managed to exert some power and play significant roles, just as Hoffman and the women of the NOCW had done before 1919. Assertively submissive—or submissively assertive—in their relations with the clergy, between 1919 and 1938 the IFCA's leaders rarely challenged priests or bishops, though they certainly prodded them occasionally. At the same time, though they admired Mary's virtuous submission, they were much more than passive subordinates. They led the efforts to raise the money for the Mary Memorial Altar, and focusing on the altar as artifact and metaphor shows how women, both lay elites and ordinary devotees, were absent and present at the Shrine.[10]

CLARA SHEERAN, SISTER MARY DE PAUL COGAN, AND THE IFCA

After the dissolution of the NOCW, other women's groups stepped in to raise funds for the Shrine between 1919 and 1938, including the Ladies Auxiliary of the Ancient Order of Hibernians, the Daughters of Isabella, the Ladies Auxiliary of the Knights of St. John, and the Polish Women's Alliance. Starting in 1919, when Sheeran established the Mary Memorial Altar Fund, the IFCA also played a key role. The IFCA was organized in 1914 by Sheeran and Cogan (later Sister Mary de Paul Cogan, OP), who also served as the group's first two presidents from 1914 to 1920. They lived in Brooklyn's Bay Ridge neighborhood, belonged to the same parish, had known each other since high school, and had attended St. Joseph's College in Emmitsburg, Maryland, where Elizabeth Ann Bayley Seton (1774–1821), the first native-born American saint, established the Sisters of Charity in 1809. Gratitude for their experience at that Catholic college, Cogan said, led them to found the group. How they approached the task reveals a great deal about how members interacted with religious authorities during the years ahead: the women formulated a plan and labored to realize it, but they consistently sought approval from priests, and sometimes nuns, all along the way. Their first act was to seek the endorsement of the leader of the Sisters of Charity, Mother Margaret, so they could use their leadership roles in the Saint Joseph Alumnae Association (Sheeran was regent and Cogan was secretary) as a foundation on which to construct the IFCA's superstructure. With that approval in hand, they then worked on two fronts—first, to contact Catholic alumnae associations (or sodalities, if the school had no alumnae group), appealing to institutions to join the new organization, and second, to contact the Catholic hierarchy, appealing to clergy to formally endorse their initiative. They asked for the blessing of Cardinal Gibbons, inviting him to serve as the organization's first honorary president. They then "called on" or wrote letters to a large number of clerics, including John Murphy Cardinal Farley of New York and William Cardinal O'Connell of Boston, as well as Shahan and Pace at CUA.[11]

All this activity led to the inauguration of the organization on November 27, 1914, when 102 applicants for membership met at the Hotel McAlpin in New York City and left with an organizational structure and a president: "it was my privilege to move," Sheeran recalled, "that Clare I. Cogan be elected by acclamation, the first president of the IFCA." At the next annual meeting, which was held in Chicago, the group adopted a "Constitution and By-Laws," which stated that the organization's member-ship was open to alumnae of all Catholic high schools, colleges, and univer-sities, and each institution could send one delegate to the annual convention. The IFCA's purpose was to uphold "ideals of Catholic Womanhood and to formulate plans for the extension of Catholic education, Catholic litera-ture, and Catholic social work." A separate "department" oversaw activity in each of those arenas, and each department had a leader or "head."[12]

The organization's by-laws granted the IFCA's president considerable powers, and Cogan (1891–1953) campaigned for "modesty" in women's dress, raised funds for nuns' higher education, supported the war effort, and advised bishops about the formation of another major women's orga-nization, the National Council of Catholic Women. Her first public act as president, however, was to remind the female delegates in 1915 that they had placed themselves "under the patronage of Our Lady of the Miraculous Medal." She ended her remarks to applause from the audience by reaffirm-ing the group's ecclesiastical role and its Marian devotion: "I ask you tonight, with the prayer in your hearts that this Association will prove always a handmaid to the Church, to say: 'Oh Mary, conceived without sin, pray for us who have recourse to thee.'"[13]

Cogan, in her own way, also seems to have viewed herself as a "hand-maid to the Church," from her student days with Visitation nuns to her final days as the supervisor of Maryknoll nuns. A granddaughter of Irish immigrants, Cogan was born in Virginia into "a truly Catholic family." That middle-class family—her father was a contractor—moved to an ethnically and linguistically diverse area of Brooklyn, where she lived during her years as IFCA president, from 1914 to 1919. She joined the Foreign Mission Sisters of St. Dominic, commonly known as the Maryknolls, in 1921, and as Sister Mary de Paul dedicated her life to serving those who spoke other languages and embraced other faiths. In 1950 she contracted a terminal illness, and after a long period of suffering, she died in the fall of 1953. She was eulogized by a priest who valorized that suffering—which is "a main instrument in God's established spiritual economy"—but the posthumous tributes from women religious focused more on her life and her virtues. Mother Mary Joseph, the head of the order, remembered Sister de Paul as "docile, happy, generous, [and] faithful." She also reported that Monsignor Pace, the widely esteemed CUA professor, had said once "she was the most brilliant woman he had met in the United States." Most important for her duties with the order and, earlier, her work with the IFCA on behalf of the Shrine, Mother Mary Joseph remembered Cogan as "a superb organizer and administrator."[14]

So was Clara Douglas Sheeran (1876–1957), Cogan's longtime friend and the second president of the organization. A second-generation Irish American, she was born in New York and spent "happy girlhood years" with a "devoted" aunt in Philadelphia, apparently sent there because her mother was blind, though classmates later recalled Sheeran's warm relationship with her father as well. She graduated from St. Joseph's Academy in Maryland in 1894 and returned to Brooklyn. There, in 1916—two years after she started the IFCA—she married James Jerome Sheeran, an electrical contractor. During the 1920s, when she did so much for the Shrine, Sheeran lived with her three sons, adopted daughter, sister, and mother-in-law in one of the most expensive houses in a pluralistic middle-class neighborhood.[15]

Before and after marriage, Sheeran worked as a public school teacher and as a special education instructor for the blind, while she also volunteered for causes close to her heart. Less interested in foreign missions than her friend, before and after her term as IFCA president in 1919–1920, Sheeran labored on some initiatives begun by Cogan, including for modesty in women's dress. Sheeran had her own causes, however. A biographical form she filled out for the St. Joseph's Alumnae Association and a brief autobiographical sketch she wrote for the National Council of Catholic Women offer some clues about what seems to have mattered most to her. She mentioned her work for the St. Joseph's Alumnae Association and her pedagogical efforts, especially for the blind. She listed her graduate training at New York University and Hunter College and her memberships in the Catholic Teachers Association of Brooklyn and the Sight Conservation Association of New York. In the space on the form designated "Travel," she noted "three trips to Europe, including the Seton Pilgrimage to Rome." Sheeran has an enduring place in American Catholic history—and at her death she was hailed in the *New York Times* as "a leader in the Roman Catholic laity"—because she was one of the most active laywomen involved in the canonization of Ann Seton. Sheeran gathered signatures for the petition to make Seton the first native-born saint. Using the third person in her autobiographical sketch, she recalled: "Mrs. Sheeran organized a group of Alumnae known as the Seton Pilgrims who sailed for Rome during the summer of 1931 and presented a petition bearing 153,000 signatures to his Holiness Pope Pius XI."[16]

Both the autobiography and the form mention her activity on behalf of Seton's canonization, but Sheeran also listed among her most important accomplishments her efforts for the IFCA, and especially its campaign to support the Mary Memorial Altar. Sheeran's own accounts, like the posthumous tributes to her by members of Catholic women's organizations, accentuated her roles as cofounder, periodical editor, and leader of efforts to raise funds for the altar. As Sheeran herself noted, she formed a Mary Memorial Altar Fund in 1919: "the president had arranged for a fund to erect the main altar in the Crypt of the National Shrine through the Marys of America." She mentions another crucial element of her legacy on the alumnae form: "As president of IFCA... [I] proposed 'Mary's of America' to raise funds for the Mary Memorial Altar in the National Shrine." It was Sheeran's idea to appeal to the Marys of America in the fundraising campaign, though she was not the first to coin the phrase. That honor goes to an Indiana schoolgirl, who played a role as unwitting collaborator, mythologized donor, and ordinary devotee.[17]

MARY DOWNS AND THE MARYS OF AMERICA

That girl was Mary Downs (1902–1986), who achieved some very minor celebrity in Catholic circles while she was an undergraduate at St. Mary's College for something she had done when she was eleven. As *Salve Regina* noted and some midwestern newspapers boasted, Downs sent a letter and a donation to Bishop Shahan in 1913, in which she suggested that every Mary in America make a donation for a statue of Mary to be added to the National Shrine. She enclosed a small donation, for herself and her mother, who also was named Mary. Shahan responded several days later in a hand-written note. "Your letter of the sixteenth gave me great pleasure," he wrote, "and I think your idea of a statue of the Immaculate Mother of God to be contributed by the Marys of our nation a very fine and practical idea." He promised that he and "the ladies of the Committee"—he meant the NOCW, not the IFCA—"will take it up in due time." He was worried that her plan "might distract [our people's] attention from the all-important idea of the great church itself." Shahan reassured the girl, though: "But we shall cherish your inspiration, dear child, and shall surely take due measures to execute it a little later on."[18]

It took six years for fundraisers to publicly return to Downs's "inspiration," or some modified version of it, as the plan shifted from providing a statue to building a chapel to funding an altar. Sheeran established the Mary Memorial Altar Fund in 1919, and the IFCA membership passed a resolution pledging support in June of that year, as both the Shrine's *Salve Regina* and the IFCA's *Quarterly Bulletin* noted. Shrine fundraisers had been appealing to the Catholic women of America from the start, but the new campaign, which Sheeran formally proposed in a letter to McKenna, appealed to "the Marys of America" to each contribute to the altar. "I herewith propose for your consideration," Sheeran wrote, "that you inaugurate a special drive for the Shrine, appealing to every *Mary* in the land, and everyone whose mother's name was *Mary* (to get the men) to contribute one dollar to Mary's Memorial." McKenna embraced Sheeran's suggestion, just as Shahan had responded warmly to Downs's earlier idea, and the first marketing strategy for the altar's fundraising was set. Even though the Shrine and IFCA periodicals reprinted Sheeran's letter to McKenna in 1927, as they made the final push to fulfill their fundraising promise, the initial credit for the plan to honor "the Marys of America" went to Downs—though Sheeran recounted another origin in her letter to McKenna. Sheeran had recently attended business meetings of Wilson College and Smith College, she reported, and "both of these colleges are using the method of appealing to every Wilson and to every Smith to contribute one dollar." Perhaps because he found the Downs story a more compelling fundraising hook—or his superior, Shahan, did—McKenna retold the story of the young Indiana schoolgirl and reprinted Shahan's 1913 response to Downs in the January 1921 issue of *Salve Regina*, with the title "First to Suggest the Mary Memorial."[19]

In an interesting twist, news of the new initiative for the Mary Memorial Altar reached Downs, then an undergraduate at St. Mary's College in Indiana. She wrote to Shahan in 1920 with a contribution, and he wrote back. He thanked her "in the name of Our Blessed Mother" for her donation. Shahan remembered her, even telling Downs that he'd tried to locate her during his recent trip to Terre Haute, where she had been living when they last had contact. The bishop returned her 1913 letter and mailed an issue of *Salve Regina* and an account of the foundation stone ceremony, which had taken place only a few months earlier. That local-girl-makes-good story, in turn, made its way into newspapers in Indiana, where Downs's family lived and she went to college. The stories noted *Salve Regina*'s reprinting of her earlier letter and the bishop's crediting Downs with the idea. "A few days ago, more than seven years after Mary Downs wrote her first letter," one newspaper reported, "Dr. Shahan notified her that her plan had been adopted and that 10,000 Catholic girls and women named Mary had signified their willingness to join." It also noted the change of plan: "He said the memorial would not be a single statue but that it would be a large marble altar of imposing design and artistic workmanship."[20]

So the narrative of Mary Downs, the midwestern parochial school girl as marketing icon, afforded her a presence in the Shrine's periodical and in some subsequent official representations—including in the published histories and tour guide stories. It's more difficult, though, to distinguish mythologized public narrative from lived personal history. Who was Mary Downs and what was her relation to the Mary Memorial Altar and the Shrine? Using a range of sources—including scrapbooks, family photographs, census records, and taped interviews—it's possible to get some limited sense of the young girl in 1913 and the adult lay devotee (see fig. 2.3). That view is limited in part, however, because she went on to become a middle-class homemaker who was disinclined to self-disclosure, as her sons, who both entered the priesthood, recalled in an interview ten years after her death: "She just did not talk about herself much. She was a very quiet, quiet person."[21]

But we do know something about her. She was born in Indiana into a modest, working-class home—her father was a mill foreman in 1910—and her family seems to have valued Catholic devotion and Irish heritage. Her paternal grandparents were Irish immigrants from County Clare, and her grandfather worked on the railroad all his life. Her father, a devout Catholic whom she credited with encouraging her to write the 1913 letter, celebrated Irish nationalism. In a departure from the standard topics of father-daughter missives, and in a letter Mary valued enough to save, Michael Downs wrote to her at college the day after the signing of the Anglo-Irish Treaty of 1921: "Is your Irish heart full of gladness? . . . If it is my dear, there are two of us that are glad of the news today."[22]

A number of things seemed to gladden her Irish heart, including football and poetry. In 1928, she married a young man, Hubert Ricker, who

Figure 2.3. In this photograph taken around the time she first wrote to the Shrine in 1913, Mary Downs is seated and holding her sister Patricia. Her other siblings, Kathryn and William, stand on either side.

had studied for a year at Notre Dame. He sent her notes about the outcomes of Notre Dame football games while they were courting, and she saved those, including a copy of the 1926 season schedule with the scores penciled in by Ricker. The local newspaper in Lima, Ohio, reported that she traveled to South Bend for the Notre Dame homecoming game that season. Into her later years, she continued to be an avid football fan, always anxious to make sure that her television worked on New Year's Day, so she could watch the "Fighting Irish." Her scrapbook also reveals a gentler, more pensive side. It includes a wistful poetic reflection on the finding and losing of love: "Love, such a gossamer thing it is—but it tears the soul apart!" That handwritten poem, "Just a Memory," apparently was never published, but several of her poems appeared in St. Mary's College periodicals. "Crumbs and Grumbles" was a lighthearted account of Thanksgiving; another poem, "A New Year," observed that, as with our treatment of infants, we greet each new year "with joyful hearts" but are less excited and less attentive as it ages.[23]

A student of music who played the organ at campus events, Downs graduated with honors in 1924. Her senior report card from St. Mary's also indicates that she excelled in religion (earning a grade of 91). Another of her published poems, "Purification," provides a glimpse of her religious views and practices, especially her devotion to Mary:

> O Mother Mary, in whose arms
> The Infant Child was offered
> To His Heavenly Father,
> Take Thou my soul
> Within those self-same arms,
> And make of it a perfect gift.

We cannot know much about her piety at age eleven, but it seems from this poem and other surviving evidence that she continued to venerate Mary throughout her life. Her sons recalled that she prayed the rosary regularly, and at her parish she taught Mexican migrant children, the sons and daughters of itinerant farm workers, about Our Lady of Guadalupe. Photographs of the interior of her home and reports from her relatives indicate that she was surrounded by Marian images: a small image on a Miraculous Medal dangled from her watch; a "Kitchen Madonna," with broom in hand, perched on the window sill near the sink; several statues of the Virgin, including a white porcelain Madonna and Infant given to her by her sons, adorned knickknack shelves and end tables in the living room.[24]

Mrs. Hubert Ricker—as her name appeared on most documents—did have more connections to the Mary Memorial Altar after the 1913 letter, the 1920 donation, and her minor and fleeting public celebrity. She didn't boast of her role in later years, but when pressed she would tell the story of her original letter to Shahan and the fundraising efforts for the Mary Altar. One of her sons, Michael, even said mass on the Altar in 1960, and he reported that the event gave his mother "a special satisfaction." Most important, she even got to visit herself. Eschewing the more usual romantic getaways, Mary and Hubert traveled by train to Washington on their honeymoon in October 1928, one month before the IFCA's formal presentation ceremony. She even saved the baggage tag and ticket receipt in her scrapbook, perhaps signaling how much she valued that trip to see the

Shrine and its altar.[25] As mythologized young icon and proud teen donor—even as adult pilgrim—she'd done what she could to venerate Mary and the Mary Memorial Altar.

ELIZABETH MARABLE BRENNAN AND THE
MARY'S DAY MOVEMENT, 1928–1938

When the IFCA presented the altar to the clergy a month after Mary Downs's honeymoon trip, the organization had kept its promise to donate $20,000, but that last check did not cover the altar's full cost, which was $50,000. At that point, and during the year before the presentation ceremony, another lay Catholic, Elizabeth Marable Brennan (1873–1968), stepped in with another strategy to help raise money.[26]

Little about Elizabeth Marable's early life foreshadowed the important role this "distinguished lay woman" later would play in fundraising for the Mary Memorial Altar—or in promoting many other Catholic causes, from donating a Catholic chapel on a Navajo reservation in Arizona and carrying to Rome tribal petitions for the canonization of Catherine Tekakwitha to organizing the Brooklyn Catholic Big Sisters and giving a New Hampshire island—yes, an island—to the Sisters of Providence. Bessie—the nickname recorded on the 1880 census record—was born in Memphis into a southern Protestant family. Her father, a clerk, supported two children and his mother, who lived with them in Nashville in 1880, when Bessie was seven. That household also included a white "music teacher" and an African-American servant and her one-year-old son. Bessie seemed destined to stay in the South—generations had been born in Tennessee and Kentucky—and remain a Protestant. Tragedy changed all that. Orphaned at age eleven, she ended up in Indianapolis, at St. John's Academy, a Catholic boarding school that was associated with the oldest Catholic parish in that city. She lived at that school, run by the Sisters of Providence, through high school. Even though she cherished those nuns, whom she lived with again in New Hampshire during her final years, she only converted to Roman Catholicism after her marriage in 1897 to Philip A. Brennan, a second-generation Irish Catholic from Brooklyn. Her husband, who also labored for Catholic causes, worked first as a medical doctor and then was admitted to the New York Bar Association in 1901. He went on to become a successful trial lawyer, and that lucrative profession allowed the childless couple to buy the most expensive home in an exclusive—though still multiethnic—Brooklyn neighborhood that bordered Prospect Park. That was where they were living when Philip was elected on the

Democratic ticket to the Supreme Court of the Second Judicial District in 1933.[27]

At that time, while Judge Brennan also was volunteering for Catholic organizations, Elizabeth served as IFCA's president, a post she held from 1930 to 1934 and, by almost any standard, served in energetically. She supported the organization's bureaus of education, literature, and social service and its international committees, including two committees that her friend and Brooklyn neighbor, Clara Sheeran, also held dear: committees for the blind and for the canonization of Mother Seton. During her term, Brennan traveled with Sheeran to carry the petitions for Seton's canonization to the pope and made two other trips to Europe, where she worked to extend the IFCA's transnational reach. Sheeran was impressed by Brennan's leadership, suggesting that her "field service has been unequalled in the history of the IFCA."[28]

But what was most important to Brennan? What do we know about her personal beliefs and practices? Four bound volumes containing copies of her official IFCA correspondence, which she carried with her on one of those transatlantic journeys, offer a portrait of Brennan as a diligent and assertive lay Catholic leader who had formal and casual contact with many laywomen, nuns, and clergy—from parish priests to the pope. Articles in religious periodicals and letters preserved in archives provide more evidence about her private devotion. Two documents seem most illuminating, however: a 1936 pamphlet and a 1924 song. They reveal two primary religious interests—miracles and Mary, two aspects of Catholic devotion that this convert's Protestant extended family and former Tennessee neighbors might have found especially troubling.

Brennan's interest in the miraculous is evident in a thirty-two-page pamphlet she published two years after she stepped down as IFCA president. In *Visits to Theresa Neumann*, Brennan describes her encounters in the Bavarian hills with "a living saint" and "the greatest mystic of our time." Neumann had become paralyzed and blind from an accident, Brennan recounted, and then "was miraculously cured from probably fatal illness through the intervention of St. Thérèse of Lisieux." That healing intervention by the Little Flower of Jesus, as the saint was called, left several marks, however: "The paralysis affected her throat and finally in 1923 she ceased entirely to eat, and since 1927 no liquid has passed her lips," Brennan reported in the 1936 pamphlet. Further, "the Sacred Host remains undissolved within Theresa's breast" between each trip to the communion rail, so her body was a tabernacle for the Real Presence of Jesus. Finally, Theresa also became a stigmatic, one who has bodily signs of the wounds of the crucified Jesus' redemptive suffering: "He has given her the stigmata on her hands and feet. Over her heart is a deep wound from which the blood flows profusely, saturating her white night clothes. Around her brow are the wounds of the crown of thorns, the blood from which soaks through the headcloth she wears. From her eyes, drop by drop, black blood streams, forming two small rivers that blot out her vision and make her an agonizing sight to behold."[29]

Brennan beheld that "agonizing" sight in 1933, while she was still IFCA president, during the first of her three visits to Theresa between July 1933 and October 1934. Brennan always traveled with multiple relics, and she and her husband had picked up more in Rome that year. She showed those sacred artifacts to Theresa and gave her a prized possession, "a little silver locket containing a strand of hair of your beloved Little Flower." In turn, Theresa gave Brennan one of her own rosaries, a mother-of-pearl string of consecrated beads. Those white rosary beads, Brennan claimed, turned out to have been the occasion for a "miraculous manifestation." Three times between July and October 1933, six of the white beads turned red for a short time: "I saw six blood red beads on the third decade, which, of course, is the recitation of the Sorrowful Mysteries, is the decade of the Crown of Thorns, and Theresa has six deep wounds on her hand, representing the Wounds of Our Savior from His Crown of Thorns."[30]

Less miraculous but more important for the history of fundraising for the Mary Memorial Altar, Brennan also showed Theresa, who neither read nor spoke English, IFCA records—the 1932 convention program, a list of the 520 affiliated alumnae associations, and a white and gold Mary's Day booklet. She asked Theresa to pray for the IFCA and even "requested her to repeat after me the words 'Mary's Day' so that I might hear this beloved phrase from her sweet lips." Theresa obliged, and said to Archbishop Nicholas of Serbia, "a dear friend" who was traveling with Brennan and her husband: "Your Excellency, Mrs. Brennan is doing God's work."[31]

Much of Brennan's work, as she emphasized in her encounters with the famous European stigmatic, involved promoting devotion to the Virgin Mary in the United States and around the world. Brennan had a lifelong interest in music—perhaps inspired by the music teacher who lived in her childhood home—and one of her compositions, "Mary's Day Hymn," seems to reflect her own beliefs and practices. This hymn was written in 1924, four years before she inaugurated Mary's Day to promote devotion and raise funds. The theology expressed in the lyrics is familiar, reaffirming that Mary leads devotees to Jesus: "Help us, guide us to Jesus thy Son." Being led to Jesus is important, since that "cross laden" savior brings salvation, though Mary also can intervene and plays her own role in the salvific plan: "Lovingly aid us till Heaven is won."

The use of maternal imagery has a long history in Catholic devotions, and it seems especially strong in this song, whose lyrics repeat the word "mother" twelve times. Mary is not only Jesus' mother, she is everyone's mother. In turn, extending the kinship metaphor, not only is she the "model of Mothers" but also all devotees are her children: "Help all thy children to love thee alway." It's not unusual that a Marian devotee might frame her devotion in these terms, of course, but two things seem noteworthy. First, Brennan employed images about mothers and children very frequently. Second, these familial tropes take on special significance in her case since she was orphaned at eleven, and she and Philip never had any children.

Whether maternal images were as personally significant for Brennan as it appears, it seems certain that she imagined Mary's role as extending to all people and places. The Mary's Day Movement she established in 1928—though she envisioned it earlier—was devoted to Mary under a new title: "Mary, Mother of Mankind." Although this confident organizer did not need much encouragement for this idea, or others, it was a title the famous stigmatic had endorsed, too, Brennan recalled in a letter more than twenty years later: "In 1933, Theresa Neumann, the saintly Mystic of Bavaria, told me this title, except for that of 'Mother of God,' was the most important of all the many titles of Our Lady!" Emphasizing the Virgin's transnational maternal role, her "spiritual motherhood of the human race," Brennan commissioned statues of Mary, Mother of Mankind, in various places—her alma mater in Indiana, Memphis's St. Agnes College, the IFCA's headquarters in New York, and a shrine "memorializing motherhood" in Emmitsburg, Maryland. She dedicated buildings to Mary, Mother of Mankind, too: the chapel she donated to the Navajo school and the convent she gave to the Sisters of Providence.[32]

Brennan also commissioned the Catholic sculptor Harry Eversfield Donohue to make a statue for the lower level of the National Shrine of the Immaculate Conception, and in a letter to the episcopal leader of Baltimore she offered suggestions for its placement: "My hope is that some day when the great edifice is completed 'Mary, Mother of Mankind' may be placed in the center of some large space where her children can circle around her, rather than have her hidden in some niche or corner." Brennan got her wish, and the statue, which was dedicated on May 8, 1938, was placed in the center of the Shrine's lower level in Memorial Hall, where 14,400 tablets of marble and granite are inscribed with the names of benefactors and eight marble foundation piers recall important persons and events in U.S. Catholic history, including the first American bishop, John Carroll, and the founder of the Sisters of Charity, Seton. In an interesting coincidence, the pier celebrating Seton also memorializes Brennan as Mary's Day founder and IFCA president, just to the left of inscriptions honoring Sheeran, Cogan, and other leaders of the IFCA. Only the most attentive contemporary pilgrim might notice the chiseled record of Brennan's accomplishments, though most visitors might discern other features of Memorial Hall, including the "special computer kiosks" that allow the faithful to access the digitized Memorial Registry, a visual and verbal record of family members memorialized by donors. In any case, it is hard to miss the Marian statue Brennan and her husband donated. Memorial Hall is a space that materially and virtually inscribes the presence of laity as well as clergy—on the walls, the pillars, and the computer—but its central image is the statue of Mary, Mother of Mankind, which is surrounded by white votive candles. There are no "kneeling benches," which Brennan requested be placed nearby. Still, as Brennan hoped, occasionally Mary's "children" have gathered there over the years, as when CUA students and women's groups came for novenas during the 1940s and 1950s. Mary's children have assembled near the statue for less formal and less pious occasions, too, as when some fourth-graders from Baltimore's Our Lady of Lourdes School sprawled nearby to complete their teacher's assignment—to sketch the Marian statue—and then asked me to include them in the photograph I took (see fig. 2.4).[33]

Brennan continued to promote Mary's Day for decades after that statue's dedication. In 1952, at age seventy-nine, she donated her Brooklyn home to the Diocese of Brooklyn, which promised to promote the Mary's Day celebration from the luxurious home's lower floors, while the three upper floors would become the Girls Town of Brooklyn. In the same year, when her longtime personal secretary died, Brennan was still drumming up support for Mary's Day. She wrote to the current Shrine director from her quarters in the Convent of Mary, Mother of Mankind, in New Hampshire, citing the endorsement of Theresa Neumann, who had encouraged her to promote Mary's Day for the rest of her life: "For this reason I shall keep on reaching out, through my correspondence, to the far corners of the world, so long as I am able to hold a pen." And that reaching out had its effects: in 1953, Brooklyn's Catholic weekly, the *Tablet*, ran a front-page story about the "founder of Mary's Day." In the accompanying photograph, a grey-haired Brennan poses beside her parlor piano. On top of that instrument, probably the one at which she composed her Marian hymn, stood a small replica of the Washington Shrine's statue of Mary, Mother of Mankind. The caption indicates that the occasion was the silver jubilee of the Mary's Day Movement. It had been fifteen years since the statue had been installed at the BNSIC and since Brennan had used the Mary's Day Movement to help to raise the remaining $30,000 needed for the Mary

Figure 2.4. Children from Our Lady of Lourdes School in Baltimore, Maryland, pose in front of the statue of Mary, Mother of Mankind.

Memorial Altar, and a quarter century since she had proudly watched as the IFCA formally presented the altar to the clergy in 1928.[34]

THE 1928 MARY ALTAR DONOR LIST: A SOCIAL PROFILE OF DEVOTEES

Those fundraising efforts for 1928 are especially illuminating—both for understanding the complex relationship between female lay elites and male clerics and for getting a glimpse of the ordinary women who donated to the altar.

Illuminating hints about the relationship between Brennan and Pace, the IFCA's spiritual director, emerge from two surviving documents—the 1953 article in the *Tablet* and a three-page letter Brennan wrote to the Shrine's director in 1954. The published account notes that Brennan proposed the idea for Mary's Day at the IFCA meeting in the fall of 1927, but that "the popular appeal of the Mary's Day Devotion was questioned by the executive board." In the letter, Brennan explained that Pace and the laywomen on the board worried that her idea "might interfere with the campaign to raise the $20,000 pledged for the Mary Altar." With the board poised to reject Brennan's idea, however, Pace offered a compromise, she recalled later: "Monsignor Pace rose to his feet and said there can be no question as to accepting Mrs. Brennan's plan, which I can see has far reaching possibilities in bringing honor and glory to the Blessed Mother.... My one fear, he continued, is that it... may not prove practical to launch it at once throughout the nation. I advise, therefore, that... we leave it in Mrs. Brennan's hands to prove its practicality." Pace's compromise solution was that Brennan begin with only three IFCA chapters—three regions. A bit stung by the board's reluctance to fully embrace her plan, Brennan decided to abide by the modified strategy. She chose three areas, and later explained: "my choice of areas, naturally, was Tennessee, where I was born; Indiana, where I was educated; and New York, where I lived."[35]

So began the first limited efforts to celebrate Mary's Day on the Saturday before Mother's Day each year—and raise the remaining funds for the Mary Memorial Altar. Those who agreed to honor Mary's Day in 1928 pledged to wear the Miraculous Medal, receive Holy Communion, and intensify Mary's "Mite" though some small sacrifice on that day in May. They also agreed to contribute to the altar: the motto for the first Mary's Day in 1928 was "Mary's Mite on Mary's Day for Mary's Altar." Thousands joined the cause, and Brennan was proud of those donors, especially those who responded to the vigorous fundraising efforts that year:

> From my office in Brooklyn my secretary and I sent out 17,000 invitations to alumnae to join with the three areas in celebrating the first Mary's Day, Saturday, May 12, 1928. A printed slip was enclosed appealing to all to return it to me with name and address and a "Mary Mite" for this first Mary's Day, as an offering to help pay for the Mary Altar! The response in six weeks time was fifteen thousand names and $2,700, chiefly in dimes, quarters, with a few dollar bills.

Brennan reported on the success of her fundraising efforts at the IFCA's next annual meeting in 1928, announcing how much she had raised in a few months. On hearing of her efforts, Brennan recalled, "the remainder of the $12,000 needed to complete the fund was donated by the chapters, from the floor." Although the article in *Salve Regina* only reported the funds raised, Brennan could not resist noting in her letter that she had been right after all, a point she also made in a private exchange with Pace on the conference platform: "After making my report during the 1928 Convention I turned and said to Dr. Pace, who was seated on the platform, 'do you think now, Monsignor, Mary's Day has proven to be practical?' His eyes lighted, and face wreathed in a broad smile, his answer was 'I should say so!'" Brennan, who felt vindicated, reluctantly had gone along with the priest's compromise, and she also had sought the permission of bishops in New York, Tennessee, and Indiana for her efforts to establish Mary's Day and raise funds for the altar. A few years later, in 1937, she also sought—and received—the approval of Pope Pius XI: a letter from the Vatican noted that "the Holy Father has been graciously pleased to bestow his paternal Apostolic Benediction upon the members of the International Mary's Day Committee and upon their intentions and activities."[36]

Those "activities" in 1928 led donors across the country to send some contributions for the Mary Memorial Altar directly to the Shrine: for example, Catherine Murphy, a thirty-nine-year-old transit company clerk living with her sister in a row house in north Philadelphia, designated her donation for the altar. As the Mary's Day pledge cards instructed devotees, however, most other donors sent their contributions directly to Brennan in Brooklyn. Her secretary prepared a typed twenty-five-page list of those donors to the Mary Memorial Altar, "Individual Contributions to Fund of International Federation of Catholic Alumnae for Mary Altar." That list, which recorded donations sent to Brennan for that first Mary's Day, has survived (although it took me years to find it in the BNSIC archives) and allows a glimpse at some of the ordinary devotees who cared enough about Mary and her altar to send a gift. The contributor list includes 1,488 entries, recording donations of $1,964.11 from fourteen organizations and 1,474 individuals. More than 90 percent of the donors were female, and about 13 percent of those were named Mary or some derivative of that name. When I first saw the list I couldn't figure out why the donors primarily came from only a few places, since the rhetoric in Shrine publications and tours has emphasized the *national* scope of the fundraising efforts for the altar. Only when I found Brennan's letter in the archives later did I understand that the contributors' regional distribution was a result of the compromise fundraising strategy Pace had suggested. The majority of donations (1,122) came from the state of New York, with 66 percent from Brennan's Brooklyn. Thirty-six Marian devotees from Indiana contributed and sixteen from Tennessee (see table 2.1).[37]

These numbers do not tell us much about these ordinary Catholics who supported the Mary Memorial Altar, however, so I tried to learn more.

Table 2.1. GEOGRAPHICAL DISTRIBUTION OF
MARY ALTAR DONORS WITH KNOWN LOCATIONS

Region	Number	% total
Brooklyn	847	66.3%
New York (not Brooklyn)	275	21.5%
Midwest	81	6.3%
Mid-Atlantic (not NY)	26	2%
South	20	1.6%
International	16	1.3%
New England	8	.6%
West	5	.4%
Total	1,278	100%

Source: "Individual Contributions to Fund of International Federation of
Catholic Alumnae for Mary Altar," Archives, BNSIC.

Focusing first on the donors from Brooklyn and then on those who lived
beyond its borders, I used federal census records, maps, and parish
information to construct a social profile of these Marian devotees.[38] Some
adult donors were male. One hundred and thirty-five anonymous seminarians from Our Lady of the Lake Seminary in Cleveland, Ohio, sent a
collective contribution to Brennan, and one priest's name appears on the
rolls: Monsignor Timothy A. Hickey (1866–1943). That cleric, the son of
Irish immigrants and graduate of St. John's Seminary, sent $100 he had
collected from parishioners at Brooklyn's St. Brendan's Church, where he
served in 1928. Of the other nine adult male donors who are named, four
were from Brooklyn. One of the Brooklyn devotees was Brennan's husband.
Others were less well off than that prominent physician and attorney. For
example, John F. Brady, a fifty-nine-year-old second-generation Irish
American, managed to make a modest donation even though he was unemployed. Apparently his son, an attorney, supported the family. They lived in
an above-average home on an ethnically diverse working-class block in
Bedford-Stuyvesant that included two households of African Americans
from the South and Catholic and Jewish neighbors who spoke Yiddish,
Spanish, Romanian, Russian, and Polish. A few adult male devotees sent
money from beyond the boundaries of Brooklyn; among them a resident of
the Diocese of Bridgeport: Robert Dunn, a twenty-eight-year-old Scottish
immigrant who graduated from Fordham and worked as a machinist for
the railroad in Greenwich.[39]

Most of those who sent their dollars—and quarters, too—were not adult
men like Brady and Dunn, however. Two twelve-year-old boys from the same

neighborhood in Greenwich, Connecticut, each contributed their coins to the altar: George Higgins, the son of Irish immigrants, and Michael Morano, the grandson of Italian immigrants. Brennan's 1928 contributor list includes hundreds of children (much more on this in the next chapter), and a few of those who sent funds, often on behalf of children, were women religious, like Sister Mary Raphael, RSM, a thirty-two-year-old Sister of Mercy of Anglo-Irish heritage who taught at St. Catherine's Academy in the Bronx.[40]

The Brooklyn Connection

Many of the donors were adult laywomen, however, and a disproportionate number lived in Brooklyn, which locals have called "City of Churches" at least since 1844. At that time, however, the former Algonquin territory and Dutch colony was a city dotted with Protestant steeples: in Brooklyn Heights, for example, the Church of the Assumption of the Blessed Virgin, one of five Catholic parishes in Brooklyn, was surrounded by five Protestant churches. In that neighborhood and across town, Protestants moved confidently through the streets, as they did in 1844 for the annual Sunday School Union Anniversary Day parade, perhaps the most important Protestant public ritual. Catholics didn't join the five thousand parading Protestants, including girls in "white dresses, new hats, and wreaths of orange blossom." When Catholics did venture beyond their enclaves in the middle of the nineteenth century, they sometimes encountered hostility in the streets. There was "riot and bloodshed" in 1854 when the military was called out to quell violence between local Irish immigrants and the Know-Nothings, a political group that openly condemned Catholics. For the next few decades, Protestants continued to exert public power—and ritually enact that clout in the parades—but during the middle of the century more and more immigrants arrived, many of them Irish and German Catholics. After 1880, those Catholics were joined by Scandinavian Protestants and eastern European Jews—as well as Eastern Orthodox Christians from Greece, Russia, and Syria. More Catholics arrived, too, including many from Italy and Poland. By the turn of the century, Catholic presence was undeniable, as one 1902 newspaper story proclaimed: "Heavy Immigration Is Changing the Character of the City." A controversy erupted that year because the Protestant parade began to look "too sectarian." The public event went on as usual, however, even though Brooklyn's heterogeneity was becoming harder and harder to ignore.[41]

It only intensified. Brooklyn's population more than doubled between 1900 and 1940, with the greatest increase (532,000) occurring during the

1920s. By 1928, when Brennan asked her neighbors for donations, Brooklyn—and America—had changed. In that year a Catholic, Alfred E. Smith, was New York's governor and a presidential candidate, and Catholics claimed the largest membership of any denomination in the United States. By then Brooklyn had been consolidated into Greater New York City, and the borough's social and economic landscape had been transformed. One third of Brooklynites were foreign born, and 44 percent were either immigrants or the children of immigrants. Factories buzzed with the labor of more than 166,000 production workers, while tens of thousands more worked as longshoremen, warehousemen, and truckers. Brooklyn workers, both white- and blue-collar, also could commute across town and throughout the other four boroughs, as new bridges and tunnels opened and railways and trolleys improved. The swelling population also moved to the new neighborhoods—Brooklyn led the nation in housing construction in 1923—that formed along the expanding transportation network.[42]

Catholics helped bring about these social and economic changes, and there were concomitant religious shifts, too. By the mid-1920s, Brooklyn's Catholics were more numerous and had more churches than any Protestant denomination: more than 138 Catholic parishes and almost seven hundred thousand members. So in 1928 when ten thousand Protestant children paraded through the streets for the ninety-ninth anniversary of the first Sunday School Union celebration, the power of the local Protestant establishment already had been vigorously contested—and not only because Smith, the Catholic governor and presidential candidate, was invited to review the parade that year. Those streets were no longer just Protestant streets, despite the parade's ritual claim on public space. When Brennan collected funds for the Mary Memorial Altar in 1928, Brooklynites walked Protestant streets, Jewish streets, and Catholic streets. Most interesting of all, many streets, including those where Brennan and many donors lived, were filled with the sounds, sights, and smells of the borough's ethnic, linguistic, and religious diversity.[43]

As Brennan walked those diverse streets to seek funds and opened the donation envelopes delivered to her home, which was down the street from Prospect Park, she found that most of the adult women who gave to the altar contributed a dollar—equivalent to more than $12 today. That was the median donation for the twenty-five women profiled in appendix 2.1. Marie Fox, a widowed stenographer from St. Malachy's parish, gave the most in this group, and Anna Murphy, a single woman from St. Thomas Aquinas parish who worked in a hat factory, gave the least. Like Murphy, nine of the twenty-five women never married, and this selection of donors includes a slightly higher proportion of single women (40 percent) than we might expect, given their proportion in the population (26 percent). With a median age of thirty-eight, these twenty-five Marian devotees, married and single, also were a bit older than the Brooklyn population as a whole. Honoria McLoughlin from Holy Innocents parish was the oldest, at sixty, and Elinor Woods from St. Francis of Assisi was the youngest, at twenty-two.[44]

Woods worked as a newspaper copywriter and lived in one of the more expensive homes in Crown Heights, a neighborhood just across Prospect Park from Brennan. Forty percent of these women worked outside the home, almost double the national average at the time. The reports on the 1930 census analyzed occupations using six categories, from unskilled workers to professionals, and these donors tended to be slightly higher on the occupational scale than we might expect. One was an unskilled worker in a shirt factory; another was a semiskilled factory laborer. The census officials would have classified the occupations of several other donors as "clerks and kindred workers": Mary Doherty was a stenographer, and two were secretaries. Three public school teachers were in the sample but no other professionals, unless we count the newspaper copywriter as a journalist. Either way, this group has a few more professionals than might be expected from the national average for women (11 percent). Some donors were part of the emerging Catholic middle- and upper-middle class and had professional husbands, including Miriam Schmid, whose husband was a lawyer, and Margaret Zimmerman, whose husband was a physician. Both of them also had live-in servants. Zimmerman, who worshiped at Brennan's well-to-do parish, had two maids and a secretary in her home. Other women, including four of the fifteen who reported no occupation, also had household members who were not relatives but boarders they took in to earn money. For example, Rosella McHugh, a thirty-seven-year-old woman married to a machinist who worked in a furniture factory, shared her home with eight others, six of them lodgers—two nurses, two secretaries, and two stenographers.[45]

McHugh and her husband owned their home, as did eighteen of the twenty-five, a proportion that was triple the Brooklyn average. The value of McHugh's home ($14,000) was well above the national median ($4,778) and slightly above Brooklyn's standard ($11,207). It also was higher than the median value for this group of donors, $10,000 (approximately $125,000 today). Some donors couldn't afford a home—or even a radio— for example Melvina Jones, who lived her son, and Florence Miranda, who worked at a factory to help support her mother and two sisters. At the same time, some contributors' homes were worth much more than the local and national average. For example, Elizabeth McCaffrey, a twenty-seven-year-old teacher, lived in her father's $40,000 house in Flatbush with her extended family and two maids of African descent, one from Virginia and one from Barbados. For the seven donors who rented, some lived in luxurious accommodations with a maid, as did Schmid in Brooklyn Heights, but others, like the poorer Catherine Rizzo, paid less than the average Brooklyn renter.[46]

With the exception of Rizzo and a few others, the economic status of these Marian devotees was slightly higher than most Brooklynites and most Americans. The census records also document the ethnic heritage and native language of the donors and their neighbors. Rizzo, who left Italy in 1898, also stands out because she was an immigrant, one of only two out of the twenty-five. She lived on an ethnically and linguistically homogenous street near St. Rita's Church, an Italian-speaking parish in a predominantly Italian neighborhood. Mr. and Mrs. Goldstein, who lived next door, were Jewish immigrants who spoke Hungarian and Yiddish, but the rest of Rizzo's immediate neighbors were Italian immigrants or the children of Italian immigrants. Elinor Woods heard only English on her posh street in Crown Heights, and Margaret Sherry heard seven languages in her Bay Ridge neighborhood. But most of the donors lived on blocks where residents spoke three or four different languages. Overall, in these contributors' neighborhoods, eighteen different languages were spoken. They ranged from Italian, German, and Norwegian to Serbian, Armenian, and Arabic. Sherry, who spoke English at home, was born in Ireland, but Woods and her parents were native New Yorkers, as were seventeen others in the twenty-five, and most of them were second- or third-generation Irish Americans.[47]

Adult Female Donors outside Brooklyn

To raise funds according to the compromise plan—and prove Pace wrong—Brennan also sought donations in her native state, Tennessee, and in Indiana, where she went to Catholic school, and a large proportion of the fifty-two women from those places also were of Irish heritage. Consider the social profile of fifteen of those devotees in appendix 2.2. The ethnic heritage of these contributors was about the same as the Brooklynites', though these women in Indianapolis, South Bend, and Memphis had slightly more expensive homes and a bit less ethnic and linguistic diversity on their streets; nonetheless, Ownie Miller, a native Mississippian whose husband worked for an adding machine company, had immediate neighbors in Memphis who were Catholic and Jewish immigrants, and their mother tongues were German, French, Spanish, Yiddish, and Polish.[48]

Rather than focus on the contributors from just those two states, it seems more helpful to consider a sample of twenty donors from all locations outside Brooklyn (appendix 2.3). Since that sample reflects the approximate proportion from each region, it includes many contributors from New York, the third state in Brennan's fundraising plan, though Marian devotees in other parts of the country did send Brennan contributions. The age of donors outside Brooklyn was slightly lower than within it. The youngest was Clara Schaffler, a nineteen-year-old from Memphis; at fifty-seven, the oldest donor was Margaret Mette, who lived near Shaffler in the same city. Both of Mette's parents were born in Ireland, and about half of the contributors beyond Brooklyn's boundaries were of Irish heritage. Catholics sometimes crossed ethnic lines in marriage, and several contributors claimed dual or multiple ethnic backgrounds, as did Alma Centilivre. Her father was the son of French immigrants, and her mother was the daughter of German immigrants. Only one immigrant, a German, lived on Alma's block in Fort Wayne, Indiana. Since the Manhattan devotees were closer to Ellis Island, the port of entry, it's not surprising that they witnessed the most ethnic and linguistic diversity in their neighborhoods: Anna Malloy, an unmarried secretary who lived with her Irish-born father on East 67th Street, heard nine languages on her block, where about half of the residents were immigrants. She lived next door to a Norwegian immigrant with a Swedish wife. Next to them were the Millers from Germany, the Gyulays from Hungary, and the Akitas from Japan. A few houses farther down the block lived Yiddish-speaking Polish Jews and an Italian Catholic family. Like everyone else on her block, Malloy and her father rented their place, but most of the other donors in this sample owned their homes or lived with relatives who did. The median value of their homes was $10,000, as for the Brooklyn donors, but a few of the contributors were very well off. Loretta Hendrick, a single secretary staying with her mother and siblings in New Rochelle, lived in a very expensive house, worth almost $800,000 today. Like Hendrick, a relatively high proportion of the other non-Brooklyn contributors were employed (60 percent), well above the national average (22 percent), and all of those twelve women were white-collar workers, including three public school teachers and five clerical workers.[49]

A collective portrait of the donors on Brennan's 1928 list emerges from the census records. Part of the emerging Catholic middle class, in general, these women were in their twenties and thirties, were second- or third-generation Americans, and were living in diverse urban neighborhoods, especially in the Mid-Atlantic states. They were more likely to work outside the home than other American women. They were more likely to own their homes, which housed more people than the local and national average and cost as much or more than that average. Vivid biographical details emerge, too. Anna Malloy heard nine languages on her block; Melvina Jones couldn't afford a radio; Rosella McHugh shared her home with six lodgers; both of Margaret Mette's parents were born in Ireland; Marie Fox, a widowed stenographer from St. Malachy's parish, donated thousands of dollars.

All this detail—and the collective social profile—helps us recover some women who have been absent from the historical record, though the sources can't tell us why they donated. Why did Fox, that widowed stenographer, give so much? We'll never know. However, some clues about other female donors' motives can be found in the letters sent to the Shrine. As did those who sent donations in the previous decade, devotees sometimes contributed to the altar to give thanks or to keep a promise. A New York contributor said she sent her relatively large donation "to our dear Lady for favor received," and, using identical language, a woman named Mary sent money as "a small thanksgiving for favors received." If the letters are any indication, America's Marys sought different kinds of "favors," but mostly they wanted to remember the dead and help the living, especially family members. Sometimes they had illness on their minds: one gave "to fulfill a promise I made if my nephew got better." Sometimes it was the dead that prompted their generosity. A California devotee sent "one dollar for my name Mary, and one dollar for a beloved niece—deceased—also named Mary." Another donor sent a check for $100 for a family member named Mary—"in memory of my dear Mother (deceased) that she may receive all the spiritual benefits." Sometimes the desired benefits were not spiritual but material: a contributor sent $5 "in honor of Mary Immaculate, through whose intercession a splendid position was secured by a devout client of hers." That devotee got a job, and credited Mary. Others claimed to get something just as important, even if the spiritual exchange didn't pay the bills. "There are two more 'Marys' who wish to join the list of contributors," wrote one woman, thereby "giving a sense of ownership in the tribute to Catholics in all sections of our Country." For some, it seems, giving meant belonging. It was a way of having a presence at the Shrine. They were attracted by the promise of having their names on the list of donors and being remembered at the altar, Mary's altar, with other Marys across the country.[50]

CONCLUSION

After learning a bit more about these American Marys, including the stenographer Marie Fox and the others on the 1928 donor list, and uncovering a good deal about Mary Downs, the iconic donor, and several women who played major roles in the IFCA's fundraising for the Mary Memorial Altar, we're in a position to return to the questions we asked at the start, including the question to what extent were women present in this fundraising effort—and in the building itself?

We have some sense of the relationship between lay elites and male clergy in the fundraising campaign, and the IFCA's founding document, its "Constitution and By Laws," is illuminating. It mandated that the organization's leadership include an elected president, three vice presidents, two secretaries, a treasurer, and five trustees. Two male members of the clergy joined those dozen women on the Executive Board—the honorary president and the director. Article 1 outlined the duties of the two priests. The honorary presidents Cardinal Gibbons and, later, Bishop Shahan served as the group's "guiding spirit." Apparently trying not to demand too much from this position, the by-laws recognized that the honorary president would serve the Executive Board "as his time and inclination allow." The director's role, assumed by Monsignor Pace during the years the group raised funds for the Mary Altar, was a bit more substantial: he could call meetings of the Advisory Council and propose agenda items for the annual meetings. He also served as liaison with the hierarchy to make sure the IFCA did not unwittingly advocate heterodoxy or heteropraxis. It fell to Pace, the professor of philosophy and psychology at CUA, "to submit to the proper ecclesiastical authority, whenever necessary, any measure contemplated or adopted by the Federation and to inform the Advisory Council concerning the attitude or desires of ecclesiastical authority regarding the policy and action of the Federation." In the fundraising efforts, and much else, the clergy's prescribed roles were as advisor and authorizer, and they seem to have actually performed them. Priests offered their counsel and their blessing.[51]

In the spirit of this prescribed relationship, the clergy continually reminded the lay female leaders of their relative power and respective roles, and lay elites like Sheeran and Brennan continually sought clerical advice and sanction. Recall that in founding the IFCA, Sheeran and Cogan sought the approval of parish priests, bishops, archbishops, cardinals, and the pope himself. In turn, even when the clergy seemed to be offering their blessing or granting women power, ordained men often reminded the organization's leadership about the limits of their authority. For example, the pope offered his blessing of the IFCA, but even in the letters relaying the good news there was always the reminder about the limits of laywomen's authority. For example, Gibbons, the IFCA's first "honorary president," wrote to Sheeran in 1921 to say he was "pleased with the splendid letter of commendation sent by the Holy Father." He ended the brief letter by sending his own "blessing and best wishes," but not without fortifying the barriers that blocked access to formal ecclesiastical power. "The best evidence of [the IFCA's] appreciation of this singular privilege," Gibbons told Sheeran, "will be renewed zeal and activity in all the works proposed by the Hierarchy." So, according to Gibbons, the women were to work zealously, but only for aims proposed by the clergy. In a similar way, a year later the papal secretary of state, Cardinal Pietro Gasparri, wrote on behalf of the pontiff to the Shrine's director, who had transmitted a message "in the name of the IFCA." Gaspari relayed the Apostolic Blessing of His Holiness, who was "deeply appreciative of this proof of filial attachment and humble submission to the direction of the Holy See which the Federation has hastened to offer Him." In the original typed letter, the word *humble* is crossed out and *entire* is handwritten above it. Apparently even "humble" submission was not enough; the clergy asked for the women's "entire" submission.[52]

Sheeran and Brennan, both wearing the traditional black dress and head covering, did genuflect in the papal throne room in 1931 before they presented Pope Pius XI with the twenty-nine volumes of petitions requesting the canonization of Mother Seton, but it seems misleading to say they always offered their "entire" submission to the hierarchy. If the surviving evidence is any indication—and it might not be—Sheeran and Brennan seemed to accept the clergy's roles as advisor and authorizer. Neither of them emulated the New Woman or sided with fellow Brooklyn Catholic Lucy Burns (1879–1966), the prominent suffrage leader. Neither seemed ready, as some Catholic women were decades later, to protest a papal visit to the Shrine by carrying a sign that read "Sexism is a Sin: Repent!" That does not mean, however, that these lay elites didn't sometimes disagree with Shahan, McKenna, and Pace, though usually about fundraising strategies and not doctrinal tenets. Nor does it mean that the advice, even requests, went only in one direction. McKenna politely nudged Sheeran to pay the IFCA's debt, but Sheeran also prodded him to send things to her— the latest donation receipts, the photograph of the dedication, and so on. The phrase "entire submission" also seems misleading in other ways, since it highlights their formal ecclesiastical relationship and implies that interaction was restricted to church rituals or official meetings. It was not. For example, Sheeran mailed McKenna a book she recommended; Brennan invited Pace to "a little holiday over the weekend." Although it's not clear the clergy felt the same way, Sheeran and Brennan saw the Shrine's staff as friends: Brennan thought fondly of Pace, for example, and Sheeran wrote to McKenna about "our long friendship."[53]

"Entire submission" also seems too strong a phrase to characterize their relationship for another reason. As with Sheeran's plan to appeal to the

Marys of America and Brennan's proposal to use the Mary's Day celebration to raise funds, lay elites had some power, at least in one understanding of the term: to a surprising extent, they had the ability to enact decisions by controlling individuals and mobilizing institutions. The IFCA presidents, for example, presided at meetings, allocated budgetary funds, called special meetings of the Executive Board, decided disputes about parliamentary rules, and appointed all committee members. They made and enacted plans. The IFCA's female leaders could—and did—disagree among themselves, and sometimes they displayed the frustration that emerges in most organizations. For example, from the moment Sheeran stepped down as president and through the final months before the altar presentation ceremony in 1928, she showed little confidence in her successor, Mary Finan, especially her ability to meet the promised fundraising goals. "The present incumbent smiles beautifully," Sheeran confided to McKenna in a 1928 letter, "and that is the most charitable thing I can say." We have no surviving record, however, of what charity prevented Sheeran and the other female leaders from saying about the male clergy. Did they have as much affection for Shahan and McKenna as their letters suggest? Did they sometimes roll their eyes when the priest turned his back? We don't know.[54]

What do we know? What can we say about the relationship between laywomen and male clerics in the fundraising efforts for the Mary Memorial Altar? It seems that in many ways the women worked within male-dominated structures to make their presence felt in the fundraising process, and, like many other Catholic women before the 1960s, they had more opportunities for challenging leadership and meaningful work within the Church than they did in the wider culture. Yet their relationship with the priests was complicated. If they were not "entirely submissive," as the Vatican representative had hoped, nor were they entirely assertive. To submit, the dictionary says, is "to place oneself under the control of a person in authority or power" or "to urge or represent with deference." To assert, on the other hand, is "to set free." It is "to lay claim to" or "to maintain the cause of . . . to champion" something. Sheeran and Brennan yielded to the authority of the clergy—as Brennan did when Pace rejected a nationwide appeal for Mary's Day—though they rarely seemed humbly subservient. They actively hatched plans and efficiently executed them, though always with the official sanction of the clergy, or at least with the priests' benign neglect or reluctant approval. Further, Sheeran and Brennan had many good qualities, but humility was not high on their list of virtues. Both women proudly promoted themselves and their endeavors, making sure that published accounts recognized their role in the altar fundraising. For example, one 1928 account in the *Tablet* that Brennan must have written, or had a hand in writing, notwithstanding its title, "Mary's Day Finds Wide Support," made sure to report clerical sanction for Brennan's efforts, quoting effusive letters to her from two bishops, including one from Shahan saying that her plan "meets my full approval." It seems most helpful, then, to characterize these women's relationship with clergy in paradoxical terms: in these fundraising efforts the IFCA's female leaders were submissively assertive or assertively submissive. They championed causes, although usually respectfully and deferentially. They laid claim to some things—including the Mary Memorial Altar—although they did not openly challenge the clergy's ecclesiastical authority.[55]

In a similar way, and just as paradoxically, these female leaders and the ordinary donors were both absent and present in the Shrine itself, including at the altar they claimed. They were absent, as I've suggested, because they were blocked from many roles by the prohibition against women's ordination, including the role of Eucharistic celebrant at the Mary Memorial Altar, and because they were, as in the dedication photograph, often obscured or marginalized in the collective memory preserved in narrative, ritual, and artifact at the Shrine. Although the Shrine's guidebook does mention Brennan, the other leaders and donors remain mostly forgotten. At the same time, the women have a presence in some artifacts and spaces in the Shrine. As I have noted, the names of Sheeran, Cogan, and Brennan appear on the bronze tablet commemorating the Mary Memorial Altar and on one of the marble piers in Memorial Hall, not far from the plaque that also reminds visitors that Brennan donated the statue of Mary, Mother of Mankind. In addition, on the walls of Memorial Hall thousands of names of ordinary female devotees have a place. Sheeran and Cogan also have a presence elsewhere in the Shrine. More than three decades after the 1928 altar dedication ceremony, the IFCA cofounders were memorialized in the rose windows of Great Upper Church's east and west transepts. Thousands of IFCA members donated the funds for those windows, which are decorated with images and symbols of Mary. Both the Shrine's and the IFCA's periodicals reported on the blessing of these prominently placed windows and on the cofounders they celebrated, and the Shrine's current guidebook mentions that the IFCA donated them. The guidebook also recounts the group's formal presentation of the Mary Memorial Altar on December 8, 1928: "More than 30,000 women who held 'even a remote kinship with the name Mary' contributed to or are remembered in this altar." Claims about the number of altar contributors have varied over the years—officials have estimated ten thousand, thirty thousand, and fifty thousand American Marys. Brennan said that she received fifteen thousand names and $2,700 in six weeks, and the 1928 donor list records more than thirteen hundred female contributors and their donations, which amounted to almost $2,000. Whatever the actual number of donors—and I remain unsure—it seems fair to conclude that at least several thousand American women contributed and that some of their names are recorded in the roster of American Marys that Brennan collected and Pace embedded in the altar.

Obscured from the sight of contemporary pilgrims, Shrine officials, and religious historians, those devotees remain absent, almost invisible. Yet, as I've tried to suggest, they are there, too—as dimmed light radiating from the stained glass rose window in the east transept of the Great Upper Church and on the walls of Memorial Hall, the plaque near Mary's statue, and the foundation pier. Most important, they are there beneath the cold marble of the Mary Memorial Altar, a monument to those who collected donations and those who sent them. Obscure devotees like Marie Fox and Melvina Jones and IFCA leaders like Elizabeth Brennan and Clara Sheeran, who kept their promise to raise the funds, all of them have a presence at the Shrine—at least as much of a presence as they could manage as they worked with and without, though hardly ever against, the ordained men who enjoyed ecclesiastical clout.[56]

3

⌘

Engaging Catholic Children

Agency, Prescriptions, and Constraints in the
Catholic Institutional Network, 1920–1959

I t wasn't only adult laywomen and nuns who had their names on the
donor list embedded in the Mary Memorial Altar. Hundreds of those
1928 donors were children and adolescents from Brooklyn Catholic
schools, including St. Thomas Aquinas parochial school and St. Joseph's
Commercial High School, the institutions on the list that raised the most
money. For example, Richard Kasprowicz, an eleven-year-old Polish-
American parochial school student, and Rita O'Brien, a thirteen-year-old
Irish-American student at that girls' commercial high school, appeared
on that donor record. And, as I argue in this chapter, these and other
Catholic young people across the country also had a presence at the Shrine
during the era of consolidation. Exerting limited power as they responded
to the cultural prescriptions and structural constraints imposed by the
Catholic institutional network, young people had a presence by giving or
going in the years before and after the Mary Altar dedication, and again
between 1953 and 1959, when adults intensified efforts to get them to
journey to Washington and, as a 1953 Catholic comic put it, "help finish
the construction of the National Shrine" (fig. 3.1).[1]

Many adults influenced the children's piety in the home, the parish, and
the school. It was probably Richard's mother, a homemaker, or his father, a
Polish immigrant who owned a paint company, who gave Richard the coins
he donated; the pennies Rita contributed also probably came from her

Figure 3.1. "The Shrine That You Can Build." Fundraising appeal to young people in a 1953 Catholic comic book.

mother's purse or from the pocket of her father, an Irish immigrant who earned his living as a watchman. Brooklyn's presiding bishop, Thomas Molloy, also made decisions that directly or indirectly shaped their religious life; for example, he assigned their parish priests. In turn, the children's pastors—William F. McGinnis at Richard's parish, St. Thomas Aquinas, and Charles F. Vitta at Rita's parish, Holy Name—exerted some influence from the pulpit and in the confessional. Yet their influence on the children's piety may have been less than that of the nuns who taught them, even if the pastor's public ceremonial role sometimes made the women religious less visible, if not invisible. For example, in a 1938 photograph of eighth-graders and their pastor at St. Thomas Aquinas School, Richard's alma mater, the teaching nuns are absent (fig. 3.2). The parish priest sits at the center of rows of well-groomed students, but because Brooklyn's Sisters of St. Joseph usually didn't pose for photographs during the first decades of the century, the nuns who actually taught those pupils every day don't appear within the camera's field of vision. To get those eighth-graders to pose so uniformly, however—only one boy in the front row failed to fold his right hand over his left—there must have been at least one nun whispering admonishments off camera. Again laboring beyond the field of vision, it also was the

Figure 3.2. The eighth grade class of St. Thomas Aquinas School in 1938, with Father Joseph C. Curren, McGinnis's successor, seated in the center and, according to the Sisters of St. Joseph's usual practice at the time, with the teaching nuns absent from the photograph.

Sisters of St. Joseph who encouraged and collected Richard's and Rita's contributions for the Shrine's Mary Altar: Sister Mary Oswald Ryan, CSJ, St. Thomas Aquinas's principal, and Sister Teresa Joseph O'Brien, CSJ, the principal at Rita's high school. In Brooklyn and across the United States at that time, being a nun "mostly meant to be inescapably bound to children," and for that reason women religious often were central ecclesiastical agents in local and national efforts to engage Catholic children and youth and to encourage Marian devotion. More specifically, nuns played a decisive role in the efforts to fortify young people's connection to the BNSIC, even if their presence there was sometimes limited and usually mediated by adults.[2]

CHILDREN AND CHILDHOOD: THE 1920s TO THE 1950s

American Childhood

Nuns are missing from that photograph, but some recent scholarship has tried to attend to their presence in U.S. history. Young people, however, are still mostly missing from the history books. As scholars have argued, "children were hidden from historians but in plain view." We've failed to notice them for many reasons—not only because of historians' adult-centered perspectives. Formidable methodological challenges face anyone who tries to recover children's historical presence. To respond to those challenges, I've relied on varied sources. I've looked at advice literature, school textbooks, diocesan curricula, and adult memoirs—all sources that can be helpful in describing the culture of childhood. Since they usually say more about adult values than children's practice, however, I consulted other sources that are still imperfect but allow a glimpse of children themselves: visitor logs, donation lists, devotional letters, school yearbooks, census records, and archived photographs.[3]

Even though the usual methodological challenges remain, some recent scholarship has advanced the historical study of children and adolescents. Specialists in that field assume that young people were "active agents in the evolution of their society" and that childhood is not only a biological stage but "a social and cultural construct that has radically changed over time." From that perspective, there have been many American childhoods: they've varied not only over time but also by region, class, gender, ethnicity, and race. Yet there have been some continuities: there has been recurring "adult panic" about children's well-being, and children inevitably have had less power than adults. Yet the "power relations" between young people and adults changed during what scholars consider the "three overlapping phases" of American childhood, and the period between the Shrine's foundation ceremony and dedication rite falls within the third phase, known as "modern" childhood.[4]

From the 1910s to the 1950s, most American adults viewed young people as "innocent, malleable, fragile creatures who needed to be sheltered from contamination." While that basic view held, subtle but significant changes in adults' idea of childhood occurred over the decades. In 1920, when the Shrine's foundation stone was put in place, and in the preceding years, when parents, priests, and nuns first engaged children at the Shrine during the 1910s, the modern notion of the sheltered child predominated. Young children's clothing changed to reflect the presumption of innocence, and a new commercial children's culture appeared, as store-bought toys replaced homemade ones. Most important, adults decried "the weakening of parental authority, the growth of peer attachments, and the decline of traditional morality." Nonetheless, 1920 was not a time of unconstrained freedom and pampered indulgence for most U.S. children. Certainly middle-class children, even those whose parents were immigrants, could enjoy "new forms of commercial entertainment, including candy stores, ice cream parlors, soda shops, nickelodeons, and, later, movies." But daily life for poor, orphaned, and immigrant children could be hard. By 1920, immigrants and their offspring constituted a significant proportion of the population outside the South: for example, they formed between half and three-quarters of the residents of Boston, Cleveland, Milwaukee, San Francisco, and St. Louis. Many of the immigrants' children—mostly Jews, Buddhists, and Catholics—felt forced by economic circumstances and parental prescriptions to function not only as wage earners but also as "cultural intermediaries," since they usually adapted to U.S. culture and

English language more fully than the adults in their households. Even those children, however, began to participate in the new national youth culture that emerged in the 1920s and 1930s—in part because of new transportation and communication technology, especially cars, telephones, radios, and movies.[5]

By the time of the 1959 dedication, in a period of "outward optimism but inward anxiety," "modern" childhood was at its peak of influence. Some patterns set in the 1920s had only intensified—the presumption of children's innocence, the nationalization of youth culture, and the strength of extrafamilial attachments. Yet some things had changed by the "child-centered" 1950s. There were fewer immigrants and more children. Between 1946 and 1964, 7.5 million infants were born, and the boom's zenith, 1953, coincided with the year the Shrine directed its fundraising campaign at children. Many of the baby boomers' parents, Catholic and non-Catholic, had more real income—even if almost one-third of postwar kids grew up at or near the poverty line—and middle- and working-class American families moved in increasing numbers to ranch-style houses in suburbia. Both in the suburbs and in the cities, "the Cold War emphasis on conformity, sociability, patriotism, and religiosity colored postwar middle-class childhood." But adults noticed that young people sometimes didn't conform. They weren't all as sociable, patriotic, and pious as grown-ups hoped. At the same time, more than ever, many middle-class adults presumed kids were innocent and, if raised properly at home and in school, basically good. As the leading parenting manual, Dr. Benjamin Spock's *Common Sense Book of Baby and Child Care*, put it: "Your baby is born to be a reasonable, friendly human being." To account for the anomalies, midcentury adults proposed various psychological, sociological, or cultural explanations for wayward kids—and corresponding remedies. For all the postwar emphasis on the home, the period actually was a time when extrafamilial institutions— schools, churches, television, and consumer culture—"fostered separate worlds of childhood and youth." That consumption-driven youth culture in postwar America was subdivided further, not only by race, ethnicity, and region but also by gender: boy culture stressed "physical competition, construction, and rough and tumble play," and girl culture valued "love, doll play, relationships, hairdressing, and grooming." Of course, adults worried about what girls and boys might do together when those two subcultures met, and they also expressed concern about other aspects of the postwar culture of childhood, including cars and movies. Although it might now seem odd, "comic books, which sold 100 million copies a month, were a particular source of alarm." In fact, by 1954, the year after the 1953 issue of the Catholic comic *Treasure Chest of Fun and Fact* solicited children's donations for the Shrine (fig. 3.1), thirteen states had passed laws regulating the production and sale of comic books.[6]

Catholic Childhood: The Culture of Authority in the Era of Consolidation

Presumably, U.S. legislators were not worried about pious comics like *Treasure Chest of Fun and Fact*, but Catholic leaders did labor to prevent negative influences on children from popular culture—not only movies and books but also comics. They responded by competing in the same media and warning about secular temptations. For example, the May 1950 issue of *Topix*, another Roman Catholic comic of the period, published a list of "acceptable comics." Not surprisingly, *Treasure Chest* was on that list, which had been prepared by the St. Paul Confraternity of Christian Doctrine and the Catholic Youth Council and approved by *Topix*'s editorial advisory board. The archbishop of Boston, Richard J. Cushing, chaired that board, which included priests, monks, and nuns representing varied institutions and organizations, including Chicago's Catholic school system, the archdiocese of St. Paul, a New Jersey convent, the Catholic Biblical Commission, the leading Jesuit periodical, and the Catholic Press Association.[7]

Like *Treasure Chest*, which called children to donate to the Shrine, *Topix*—and its editorial message and reading advice—revealed adults' concern to form good Catholic boys and girls. In particular, *Topix* endorsed three themes that recurred in the devotional culture of Catholic childhood and shaped children's piety at the Shrine: most of all, this issue of *Topix* encouraged obedience to authority, praised self-sacrifice, and promoted Marian devotion. In the culminating moment of "Daniel and the Devil," a cleric not only exhorts the young protagonist to have the discipline to resist demonic temptations but also tells him that salvation requires submission to ecclesiastical authority: "enter into the Church," the bishop tells the young convert, "that you may join Christ and His saints." In "So Beat the Drums," young readers are reminded of the value of sacrifice, as the young protagonist, an Indian convert who makes the ultimate sacrifice at the hands of the Iroquois, is memorialized by a missionary as "a true martyr" who has earned the "victory of eternal life." The nature of the prescribed sacrifice took slightly different forms: boys were asked to heroically endure, like Jesus, a redemptive suffering, and girls more often were exhorted to enact a more passive self-emptying, so they might become, like Mary, a vessel for the divine. But both variants celebrated the disciplining of desire and the denial of self. In a direct message to young readers of that

May 1950 issue, *Topix*'s editor also reminds them that just because summer is coming doesn't mean there is nothing to do for matters of faith and morals. Emphasizing the fervent Marian devotion of the 1950s, he warns, as Our Lady of Fatima had, that if humanity remains unrepentant, "the entire human race is in for more trouble than it has had so far." That editorial message, "We Can Win," reminds young Catholics "religion is an all-year-round affair." "The Blessed Virgin did not say that men should go to Communion on the first Saturday of every winter month and pray their Rosaries more often just in winter." "Never before," this Cold War editorial continues, "have the battle lines between good and evil been drawn so clearly. And never before has our Blessed Mother told the world so definitely just how we can win that battle for the Divine Son." This comic book published in 1950 illustrates many elements of Catholic piety in the period—not only the endorsement of Marian devotion, clerical authority, and personal sacrifice but also the emphasis on the sacraments and the parish and the worries about pagans and communists; and the advisory board's varied organizational affiliations illustrate how the Church mobilized its vast institutional network to engage young people.[8]

That transnational network's devotional culture was sanctioned by the Vatican, promulgated by the bishops, fortified in the parishes, and transmitted in the schools; moreover, it shaped and sustained Catholic childhood between 1920 and 1959. Adult Catholics in this period worked out their own faith as they promoted young people's "spiritual formation"—their phrase for religious instruction—and "what was formed . . . was the realness and presence of the sacred in the bodies and imagination of children." These adults shared some of the presuppositions of their non-Catholic contemporaries—though Catholics' vivid sense of both the stain of original sin and the purification of sacramental grace was not as widely shared among members of other denominations—and they endorsed, in their own way, the "modern" view of children as (mostly) innocent. Catholics in the consolidated era believed they were living in the "age of Mary," but it was also "the age of children." Adults valued childlike faith—or said they did—and linked Marian devotion with childhood innocence. Children learned that it was young people who had witnessed Marian apparitions at the major shrines in Europe; and adults encouraged young people to cultivate their devotion to Jesus' mother, as special intercessor and guiding presence. Stories and artifacts in the home and the church reminded them of the enduring presence of the saints, including Mary; and a vernacular sacramentalism—preached by mothers in the pews as much as priests in the pulpit—inculcated a hushed reverence for the "real presence" of Jesus, who was really up there on the altar. Since 1910, when the pope lowered the age at which children could receive the Eucharist from eleven to seven, young people in this era had gained more participation in the worship life of the community. With more than a little moral scrupulousness, they also went to confession on Saturdays and communion on Sundays, though only after fasting—a sacrificial practice they wore like a badge of spiritual honor and a marker of Catholic difference. The boys could even get closer to the divine presence, since they could serve as altar boys, thereby playing their role in the luxuriant theatricality of Catholic ecclesiastical culture. With less to do—and less pressure, too—those boys, with female siblings and parents around them, also went to church for Novenas, Stations of the Cross, and Rosaries.[9]

Adults also encouraged children and adolescents to practice their religion with their families at home. With the approval of clergy and the affirmation of the laity, Catholics already had been decorating domestic interiors with mass-produced artifacts before the 1920s. One advice manual, *The Correct Thing for Catholics*, had said it was important "to have a crucifix in every bedroom" and "Catholic engravings or paintings in the parlors as well as in bedrooms." However, the cult of Catholic domesticity intensified after World War II and emerged fully by the 1950s. Catholic families were even instructed to build "A Shrine to Our Lady in Every Home," as the title of one magazine article put it. "Measure approximately 4´6˝ and 6´6˝ up from the floor and mark with a pencil," the instructions began. Producers of Catholic culture also encouraged ritual practice in that sanctified space— and the parish priest might actually have blessed the home during his annual round of households. Many families said a blessing before meals. Most important for the devotional life of young Catholics, in the postwar period, parents were encouraged to pray the rosary at home with the whole family. Promoted tirelessly after 1942 by its founder, Father Patrick Peyton, the "Family Rosary Crusade" was trumpeted as the Catholic answer to the midcentury variant of "adult panic," American parents' shared worries about children and the home. It was meant to be, in Peyton's words, a "self-defense against the temptations" that faced children and the "most effective means of combating the evils that now beset the American home." It's unclear how many families agreed with the movement's motto—"The family that prays together stays together"—or how many actually gathered regularly for prayer, though many certainly did. Whether their own families did or not, many Catholic children got the idea: whether they were kneeling on the living room floor with their parents to recite the Hail Mary, claiming (and reinforcing) clerical power by "playing mass" with siblings in their bedroom, or refusing the chocolate cake on the kitchen table because they were giving up sweets for Lent, the culture of Catholic childhood never took a day off and extended into the deepest recesses of daily life.[10]

SCHOOL CULTURE: STRUCTURES, PRESCRIPTIONS, AND PRACTICES

Inscribed on young bodies in posture, gesture, and affect and imprinted on young minds in doctrine, ethics, and cosmology, that culture took hold especially strongly in those who attended Catholic schools. Cultural prescriptions varied according to ethnicity, class, and region, and were contested in practice by parents and children. Still, to an astonishing extent, especially in urban areas with large Catholic populations, during the first half of the twentieth century a vast Catholic institutional network that was centered on the parish and the school created remarkably self-contained local subcultures. Those subcultures provided children and teens with a coherent and compelling religious world—and a sense of belonging. As a Catholic raised in the 1940s remembered, "everything came to depend on immediate, unquestioning, total acceptance," but the habituated rituals were "hypnotizing" and the worldview was "sophisticated." So that subculture of "total acceptance" set constraints but had enormous appeal: "For though it was an enclosure, we lived there in most pleasant captivity." It was "shared, part of community life." "It was a ghetto, undeniably," that lay Catholic recalled, "but not a bad ghetto to grow up in." In terms of the lived experience of many young Catholics in those totalistic environments, neighbors were classified in terms of binaries that reflected school attendance—neighbors were Catholics or "publics"—just as Catholics' cognitive maps marked space in terms of parish boundaries. Catholics responded to questions about identity not by reporting their street or neighborhood; rather, "I'm from St. Brigit's" (or Holy Name or Immaculate Conception) would have been the most common answer. To be asked about your identity in those subcultures during those years was to be asked about your parish and its school.[11]

Agency and Structure in the Expanding Institutional Network

In the parish and the school, youngsters and grown-ups created those local subcultures together through asymmetrical interactions that allowed children and teens some vernacular creativity, but always within the choices made available to them by the structures of daily life. As I'll show below, they enacted beliefs and values by donation and pilgrimage at the Shrine, even if adults usually mediated giving and going. There also were other opportunities to make choices—small choices. In Brooklyn and elsewhere, students had many devotional and recreational organizations available to them, from Marian societies to basketball teams. In those organizations and at school, children sometimes squeezed through the interstices of institutional structures to make some small difference, even if nuns peered over their shoulders or priests insisted on final approval. Consider an example from one of the Brooklyn schools that funded the Mary Memorial Altar. Virginia Walsh Lane, a graduate of St. Joseph's Commercial High School, remembered the satisfaction she and her classmates had as they produced their yearbook: "We all typed it—stapled it and put a blue paper cover on it. We worked on it all year.... We all added our favorite poems. We were very proud of our year book." The twenty-seven graduates added small flourishes that made it their own. Virginia's classmate, Kathryn Seh, wrote the class's playful "Last Will and Testament," which included phrases the nuns didn't come up with: the students bequeathed "a large pail of brain glue" to next year's entering class, for example. In a move that showed their immersion in American consumer culture, one student matched students' personalities with advertising slogans: like Ivory Soap, Mary McGovern was "99 44/100 percent pure," and Marie Stakem was, like Maxwell House coffee, "good to the last drop." Again making small choices that left their mark, each graduate also listed her favorite song: Kathryn liked the 1927 Hoagy Carmichael jazz number "Star Dust"; Virginia favored the sentimental tune "Drifting," whose lyrics captured the bittersweet moment of transition: "We're drifting, drifting, can't you see we're drifting from the days we knew?"[12]

When those Catholic school students did "drift" off into adulthood, they enjoyed more power to shape their own lives, as least as much as young female clerical workers could wield during the Great Depression. Yet when they had been back at school, institutional structures put in place by adults had constrained their agency. Those structures transmitted an enduring sense of belonging but also set limits on what young people could do. Students could produce yearbooks, pull pranks, pass notes, and—in later decades—almost imperceptibly hike the hems of their school uniforms to playfully enact a micropolitics of self-assertion. But they knew who had most of the power. For Catholic children and adolescents between the 1920s and the 1950s, the structuring patterns of daily life came not only from the consumer culture and the home—and, for immigrants, the homeland—but also from the Church, including the enduring effects of actions taken by Pope Leo XIII (1878–1903) and the American hierarchy decades earlier. In 1884, Rome responded to "complaints and appeals from American Catholics" about many issues, including religious education, by convoking the Third Plenary Council at Baltimore, the first American council initiated by the Vatican. Gibbons, the papal appointment as apostolic delegate to the council, joined with 108 ecclesiastical leaders to issue binding decrees that not only transformed the built environment of American cities, enlarged the role of women religious, and expanded the ecclesiastical network's scope, but also influenced the culture of Catholic childhood for the following six decades. In their document "On the Catholic Instruction of Youth," Gibbons and his clerical brethren sought to counter the influence of Protestantism and invigorate Catholicism by decreeing that "near each church, where it does not exist, a parochial school is to be erected within two years," and priests were to "cherish their schools as the apples of their eyes." The faithful, in turn, had obligations as well. The bishops instructed the laity to "regard the parish school as an essential part of the parish" and proclaimed, "all Catholic parents are bound to send their children to the parochial schools." The hierarchy in Rome and the United States set the constraints and defined the options in other ways, too. For example, Pius X (1903–1914), who lowered the age for First Communion, "wished above all to reinvigorate the religious life of the young," and Pius XI (1922–1939) encouraged youth movements, including the Children of Mary and the Legion of Mary, as part of his concern to endorse "Catholic Action."[13]

Catholic schools, which sponsored some of those youth organizations, had many advocates, including Mary Finan, the IFCA leader who not only raised funds for the Mary Altar but also hoped to realize the goal of "Every Child in Catholic School." Not every Catholic young person attended a Catholic school during that decade, the 1920s, when the parochial school system became more centralized—and Italians were less enthralled with parochial schools than the Irish, Germans, and Poles—but large numbers of young people did get their educational start and spiritual formation at those institutions. In 1926, the NCWC counted almost 2.5 million students enrolled in Catholic institutions at all levels (see fig. 3.3), and "by the middle of the 1960s, when the Catholic parochial school movement had reached its high point, there were more than 4.5 million children in parish elementary schools—fully 12 percent of all the children enrolled in the United States at that time." And more Catholic young people at the time were attending other educational centers in the massive institutional network.[14]

Cultural Prescriptions: Catechisms, Textbooks, and Curricula

Yet while parents, priests, monks, and nuns fortified those institutional structures, catechisms, textbooks, and curricula shaped the culture of Catholic childhood that emerged from the asymmetrical power relations negotiated in that vast network. Again, to understand the ecclesiastical context of the consolidated era, it's necessary to look back to officials

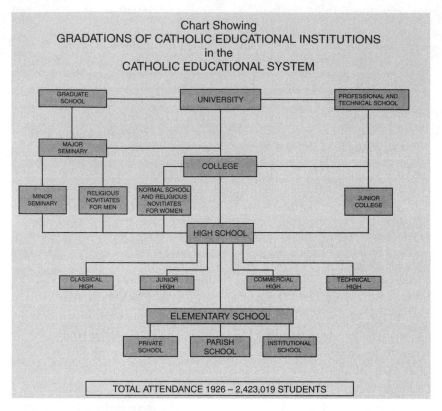

Figure 3.3. Representation of the Catholic Educational Network in 1926 by the National Catholic Welfare Conference.

attending the 1884 Third Plenary Council. Catholic belief and practice needed standardizing, many bishops believed, to bring more coherence and conformity to the devotional flux and plurality prompted by waves of immigration. The catechism mandated by the Council was directed at children, drafted by a Jersey City pastor, edited by an Illinois bishop, and approved by Gibbons, and went on to exert more influence on popular piety between the 1920s and the 1950s than any text, with the possible exception of the daily missals. For children, it was the standard against which belief and action had to be measured. As one historian has noted, "up until the 1960s, the *Baltimore Catechism* remained the staple of the Catholic Sunday School and of children's religious instruction in general."[15]

That catechism, which children memorized and recited in the schools, including many Brooklyn schools, was revised in 1941, but it retained its basic format. The original 1885 edition included 421 questions and answers divided thematically into thirty-seven chapters. It included prayers for the home and the parish, everything from the "Apostle's Creed," recited at every mass, to "The Blessing before Meals," recited at every meal. It also offered a primer of scholastic theology, using phrases schoolchildren would remember for years after they reached adulthood:

Q: Why did God make you?
A: God made me to know Him, to love Him, and to serve Him in this world, and to be happy with Him forever in the next.

It provided further instruction on the nature of God, the sinfulness of humans, the role of Jesus, the path to redemption, the nature of the sacraments, and the obligations of the commandments. Most important for children's donation and pilgrimage at the Washington Shrine, the Baltimore Catechism, like the May 1950 issue of *Topix*, also prescribed deference to authority, control of the self, and devotion to Mary.

The catechism exhorted young readers to "remember that the church is the house of God, where the living God dwells." To aid them in their effort "to be reverent and modest" in the pews, the catechism suggested a "Prayer before Mass" that recognized their limited capacities but still set out challenging obligations, including the duty to stop squirming in the pews: "O my God, I am only a child; help me to be attentive, and to pray with my whole heart during this holy Mass." It also mandated other acts of self-discipline: children should remember that they "can help the souls in Purgatory," the way station between heaven and earth, "by their prayers, fasts, and alms-deeds." Such acts also serve another function, the catechism explained: "The Church commands us to fast and abstain in order that we may mortify our passions and satisfy our sins."[16]

The catechism emphasized, as the wider ultramontane Catholic culture did, the authority of the Church and its leaders. Children were obliged to obey parents, but also "bound to honor and obey our bishops, pastors, magistrates, teachers, and other lawful superiors." The catechism championed a top-down ecclesiology and transmitted a culture of authority. It asked about the meaning of that authority, and teachers drilled children to respond: "By the authority of the Church I mean the right and power which the Pope and the bishops, as the successors of the Apostles, have to teach and to govern the faithful." That uniquely authoritative church is also "universal," the primer reminded them: it "teaches all nations and maintains all truth."[17]

If the catechism established firm limits on right belief, it also promised help for children's devotional life—not only the sacraments but also the angels and the saints. The catechism, in all its editions, included a prayer "to the guardian angel," an important supernatural figure in the sacred cosmos of Catholic children during the first six decades of the twentieth century. The catechism also encouraged Marian devotion. It included hymns to the Virgin ("Hail, Heavenly Queen"), prescribed a morning prayer ("protect me as thy property and possession"), and mandated the Hail Mary as one of five primary prayers children should say when kneeling by the bed at night. The catechism also included questions about Mary in its carefully scripted intergenerational interrogation. After explaining the origin and nature of sin, it asked young readers which one person was free of original sin. And then the answer: "The Blessed Virgin Mary, through the merits of her Divine Son, was preserved free from the guilt of original sin, and this privilege is called her Immaculate Conception."[18]

Mary in her many forms, including that of the Immaculate Conception, also made an appearance in the textbooks used in Catholic schools, including those read by those young Brooklyn donors. *The Catholic Educational Series of Primary Textbooks*, a six-volume textbook series authored by CUA faculty, including Reverend Pace, the IFCA advisor who placed the donors' names beneath the Mary Altar, illustrates the larger patterns. Others connected with the Shrine's history played a role in the series, too. Bishop Shahan encouraged the authors, and Cardinal Gibbons provided the imprimatur. In the first volume, Pace and Thomas Shields, his CUA colleague and coauthor, eased children into the process of spiritual formation. Establishing Marian devotion early, this textbook told first-graders "the Blessed Virgin's heart is full of love and wonder." Later textbooks and manuals tried to cultivate that devotion, too. One 1928 manual for teachers, for example, relayed how to instruct first-graders about the Feast of the Immaculate Conception and explain why everyone goes to mass that day—"because she was always free from sin"—and a 1956 textbook for high school students also noted her feast day and explained, in more advanced idiom, that "Mary was conceived—that is, brought into existence—without any spot or trace of sin on her soul" and was "fully endowed with sanctifying grace."[19]

The other values prescribed by the culture of Catholic childhood, including the emphasis on sacrifice and obedience, also found their way into the textbooks. The presumption of innocence, one feature usually associated with "modern" childhood in America, was qualified a bit in most Catholic textbooks between the 1920s and the 1950s. For example, in 1921 another of Pace's CUA colleagues, Robert MacEachen, published a manual for those teaching first-graders. That manual, which was introduced by

Shahan, suggested that young children have "innocence and simplicity" and "are naturally good and religious." That didn't prevent MacEachen or other Catholic educators from reaffirming the need for disciplining the will, which was vitiated by original sin, and highlighting the value of self-sacrifice. One textbook of the 1950s told high school students: "sacrifice has always been associated with true religion." Another classroom text, written by a nun with graduate training in Thomistic philosophy, proposed that sacrifice is "the supreme expression of man's adoration of God" and directed students to control "the passions" as a means of forming "good habits" and cultivating the virtues.[20]

Among the most important virtues to cultivate, the textbooks proposed, was obedience to authority. The second volume in the series by Pace and Shields, for example, stressed "the obedience of all creatures to God and to all legitimately constituted authority." That theme reappears in an even more strident formulation in a series of textbooks by Reverend Raymond J. Campion that were written, tested, and used in the Brooklyn diocese in the 1920s. Campion's *Religion: A Secondary School Course* told instructors to begin with the local parish, the topic of his first chapter. As the course proceeded, students were to learn not only about the Virgin Mary but also about the sacraments and the mass, which he described as "the center of our devotions." Most striking, however, is the textbook's unconditional celebration of consolidated Catholicism's culture of authority. The author reminded his ninth-grade readers that "the Bishops of the Catholic Church are successors of the Apostles" and that "the Bishop of the diocese then is one of the Apostles, and has the authority which our Lord gave to the Apostles, when He said, "Amen, I say to you, whatsoever you shall bind on earth shall be bound also in heaven." Reinforcing the parish clergy's power, Campion's textbook also asserted: "the priest is another Christ." The textbooks of the 1950s tended to use a corporeal metaphor that had become more important in the preceding decade—the notion that the Church is "the mystical body of Christ"—but that didn't translate into less emphasis on obedience or authority. One textbook, *The Way, the Truth, and the Life*, included a section that emphasized Jesus' obedience and suggested that to avoid "juvenile delinquency," teenagers should practice "the imitation of Christ's obedience" and "obey civil and religious laws."[21]

The curricula of the Catholic schools that the young Brooklyn donors attended expressed many of the same values and reaffirmed the same themes. It was mostly female teachers, more than half of them nuns, who implemented the diocesan curricular policy, and in 1928—the year they contributed to the Shrine—the diocese had a newly revised curriculum, entitled "Course of Study for the Catholic Elementary School." That document required teachers to choose from an approved list of textbooks, which included both the Baltimore Catechism and Campion's *Religion*, and mandated attention to the usual core secular subjects, along with some time devoted to other pursuits like music, drawing, and exercise. The total number of minutes allotted to each subject was similar to that in public schools at the time, although the average urban public school student spent much more time on science and much less on spelling. And, of course, the public school allotted no classroom time to the formal study of religion, while Brooklyn's Catholic elementary schools prescribed almost a half hour per day. Brooklyn's secondary school curricula—both the general course of study and the commercial course—included a comparable range of subjects, including courses in civics and U.S. history to make Catholics good citizens, though there was more study of classical languages, Latin and Greek, in the Catholic institutions. The commercial course, which was the curriculum for the young donors at St. Joseph's in 1928, included other subjects that prepared graduates for clerical labor, including commercial arithmetic, typewriting, shorthand, bookkeeping, and economics. Almost all the Catholic secondary schools in Brooklyn, including St. Joseph's, also taught religion every day for twenty to thirty minutes.[22]

That doesn't mean that religious instruction and devotional participation were limited to those times. The diocesan plan for elementary students also allotted ten minutes daily for opening and closing prayers, and the secondary school students had opportunities for extracurricular activities. Brooklyn's secondary school students at the time listed "mission activities" as their most popular choice—for almost five thousand students at thirteen schools—while the Sodality of the Blessed Virgin, the largest Catholic youth organization in the country, ranked second. At various times during the year, teachers also would lead the students to the church, or to the school grounds, to participate in one ritual or another. May Crownings, which brought together most members of the parish community, could be quite elaborate, as a photograph of one procession at Holy Child in Philadelphia shows (fig. 3.4). With the parents lining the route and the nuns keeping order, girls of varied ages, all of them wearing crisp white dresses and holding bouquets, lead the priest and the boys, who are off camera in this shot, walking stiffly in pressed white shirts, and, like the others in the procession, stepping purposefully toward the statue of the Virgin.[23]

The students at St. Thomas Aquinas and St. Joseph's participated in May Crownings, too. Marie Moringiello, who entered St. Thomas Aquinas School in 1952, recalled the events vividly:

Figure 3.4. May Procession at Holy Child in Philadelphia on May 5, 1940.

There was great Marian devotion. The May Crowning was a big event. The girls were dressed in all different colors, blue, white, pink. If you participated your mother usually dyed one of your dresses to match the color you wanted it to be. Then for a small fee you got a big bow to match the color of your dress with your hair, along with a wreath of greens. It was quite the thing and everyone wanted to participate.

Marie, like a number of other Aquinas students, went on to St. Joseph's for secondary school, and another graduate of St. Joseph's, which had more than a thousands students by 1953, wrote an account of the May Crowning for her yearbook. According to that account, penned by Helen Morton, the "entire student body" assembled in front of the school's outdoor statue of the Virgin to sing "Oh Mary, we crown thee with blossoms today" and to honor their "friend, guide, model."

The procession commenced with eighteen guards of honor, members of the Ave Marie Club, who led the way for the various class presidents who carried fragrant bouquets of baby's breath and pink peonies. The honor of Crowning Our Blessed Lady was given to Eileen McCormick, President of the Ave Maria Club.... As Eileen, resplendent in white, placed a crown of pink rose buds bound with blue satin ribbon upon Our Lady's head each girl sincerely felt that Mary was indeed pleased with the girls of St. Joseph's.[24]

It's helpful to learn that Helen thought "each girl sincerely felt" Mary's approval and that Marie believed "everyone wanted to participate." Those accounts confirm what other sources tell us about children's and teens' devotion in the period, but historians can't be certain that everyone felt as those Marian devotees did. Who, besides Helen, found the May Crownings moving? Who, like Marie, really wanted to go? We do know that those rituals, as well as the devotional organizations, morning prayers, assigned texts, and school curricula, transmitted the cultural prescriptions that the young people responded to as they practiced their piety within the Catholic institutional network, including by giving and going to the Virgin's Washington shrine.

CHILDREN'S PRESENCE AT THE SHRINE: GIVING AND GOING, 1920–1933

As young people sent donations and made pilgrimages to the Shrine, the cultural prescriptions transmitted in catechisms, textbooks, and curricula and enacted ritually in the vast Catholic institutional network of the home, the parish, and the school, constrained but did not determine their interactions with grown-ups and their encounters with the sacred. Catholic childhood, I've tried to suggest, highlighted obedience to authority: the priest is Christ, and other ecclesiastical representatives, including nuns, are not far behind. That subculture prized self-discipline: stop squirming in the pews and imitate the martyrs' ultimate sacrifice or, at least, offer up your insignificant suffering for the poor souls in purgatory. And it promoted Marian devotion: she was without sin, and for Catholic children and their heightened vigilance about sinfulness, next to ingesting Jesus himself in the Eucharist or getting absolution in the confessional, Mary's intercessory power was the best bet for getting the ear of the divine. All of those transmitted prescriptions would be relevant as children and teens, who had little money of their own and no independent means of transportation, interacted with adults who asked them to donate or took them to visit. In a culture of authority, it would be difficult to decline an "invitation" from a nun or priest; in a culture of sacrifice in which contributions were represented as "acts of sacrifice and service," complaining about raising the money or making the journey did little good and, besides, self-discipline is good for you; and in the age of Mary, venerating her could only help in the quest to avoid sin, seek sanctity, and get help for yourself or your family.[25]

Some children dissented from the prescribed values and practices, even the most cherished ones: one Catholic memoirist confessed that as a child she "never felt much affinity for Mary." Yet, as she recognized, she was in the minority. Some of the children who did feel "affinity"—or felt pressured to go along—made donations, and in the decade or so after the foundation stone ceremony, sometimes those young people sent the money themselves. A student from Ohio wrote a letter that explained her contribution: "Enclosed is a dollar for the Shrine of Mary. I am a thirteen-year-old schoolgirl, and have earned it by crocheting. No better use could be made of the money than donating towards a Shrine of the Mother of God." That girl relayed how she got the money, but she didn't mention a motive, besides her devotion to Mary; other young people said a bit more in the notes that accompanied their donations. One Wisconsin "farmer boy" sent a small donation because the Virgin "always gives me what I pray to her for." A "little Chinese girl" from Newark, New Jersey, had converted "a few years ago," and she enclosed her small gift "for my father to become a Catholic." Another letter writer requested something for himself: "I am a little boy 8 years old. Have been sick this winter and hope the Blessed Mother will cure me."[26]

Sometimes children and adolescents sent the donations on behalf of a group of their peers from a Catholic organization or institution. "We have been saving during the past year," a group of "blind and crippled children" at a "home" run by nuns reported as they explained their donation, which they mailed to the Washington shrine "to honor our Dear Heavenly Mother," gain "spiritual benefits" for themselves, and thank "the dear Sisters who devote themselves to our welfare." Young girls associated with an Oregon parish's Sodality noted that they "held a social at our hall, which netted the [enclosed] sum." Sixth-grade members of a Marian society in Missouri got cash by enacting the self-sacrifice adults prescribed: "All through Lent we have been dropping our spending money into a little bank at the foot of Our Blessed Lady's statue. Every nickel and dime means a little act of self-denial." Some fifth- and sixth-graders from Michigan offered up their time and labor: "A few of us boys from All Saints School made up a club . . . to spread love for the Blessed Virgin, but labor conditions are so bad that when we tried to gather some money to send to D.C. we found it was not an easy job to get this much; we did some work for the school, and that helped us pull up to $5." Girls from another school turned to the arts for fundraising: "The senior academic class of our school recently presented a playlet, based on...'Little Women.' At this performance, at which only the pupils were present, we took up a voluntary offering."[27]

Adults in the home, the parish, the asylum, or the school also mailed in gifts on behalf of young people. A New York mother sent her contribution and then passed on another from her child: "My son 7 years old also sends $1 that he may get along well in school and that his father will get strong." Priests, monks, and nuns—especially nuns—also passed on donations collected from young people. Nuns working at a parochial school in Kansas sent money "from the children of St. Anthony's School." Explaining another donation, a nun told the Shrine's director that the enclosed money was "a small tribute of love to Our Immaculate Queen from the children of the fifth, seventh, and eighth grades of St. Mary's School." The nuns at a school in New York asked the students "to bring pennies during the month of May" and then sent them to the Shrine.[28]

St. Thomas Aquinas and St. Joseph Commercial School: A Social Profile of Donors

The Sisters of St. Joseph also collected pennies and nickels at the Brooklyn schools that made the largest donations to the Mary Memorial Altar in 1928: St. Thomas Aquinas and St. Joseph's Commercial High School. Surviving evidence doesn't provide all the information we want about those young donors—for example, why did they give and where did they get the money? Nonetheless, as with the adult contributors to the Altar, we can create a social profile of these young Brooklyn devotees by selecting a sample from the donor list and consulting the federal census records to find biographical information. This approach allows us to recover their presence to some extent.[29]

First, we can see some patterns, even if we don't have a large enough sample to come to sweeping conclusions. As an analysis of appendix 3.1 reveals, the typical young donor from St. Thomas Aquinas was eleven or twelve years old. He or she was a second-generation American with at least some Irish heritage and belonged to a two-parent, blue-collar family of six that spent $50 each month for rent, and lived on an ethnically diverse block whose residents spoke three different languages. That rent was higher than the national average, so most of these donors were not poor, though they lived in larger-than-average working-class households. As appendix 3.2

Table 3.1. STATISTICAL SUMMARY OF SELECTED DONORS:
ST. THOMAS AND ST. JOSEPH

Brooklyn School	Percent second generation	Percent of Irish ancestry	Persons per household (median)	Foreign languages on donors block (median)	Percent home renters
St. Thomas	60%	60%	6	3	57%
St. Joseph	56%	56%	5	3	64%

shows, the households of St. Joseph's donors were slightly smaller, though still bigger than those of most Americans'. Those girls—because they attended high school—were about fourteen, a few years older than the Aquinas students. Otherwise, the profile is similar: the typical St. Joseph's donor also was a second- or third-generation American with some Irish ancestry who was born in New York. She was living in a rented house on an ethnically diverse street, and the donation, and other household expenses, probably came from the weekly pay of a father who worked as a skilled or unskilled laborer.[30]

Second, this sort of dry-as-dust quantitative analysis has another payoff: it can recover flesh-and-blood children, actual distinctive individuals and not just generic collective aggregates. This approach gives us a rich profile of the donors and their social world. So we can learn that among the Aquinas donors, Jeanette Cornely was the youngest, at age nine, and fourteen-year-old Edna Brennan was the oldest (appendix 3.1). Even if the majority had some Irish heritage, there was some ethnic diversity. I already mentioned Richard Kasprowicz's Polish ancestry. Some other young donors had British, Canadian, French, and German roots. Three students, including Gabriel Brillante, heard Italian spoken at home; all their parents had migrated from Italy. Altogether, the Aquinas students' neighbors spoke eleven foreign languages, and Gabriel also had the most people on his block who spoke languages other than English at home: not only Italian but Polish, German, Danish, Estonian, and Lithuanian. The breadwinner in Gabriel's house was his brother, who owned a barbershop, and they had the most expensive home. The poorest in the entire sample was Catherine Murphy. Her Irish-American father, a street sweeper, had eight mouths to feed. Her family's house was the most modest and its monthly rent was cheapest. It's not surprising, then, that this eleven-year-old's contribution was the smallest. Despite her family's economic status, Catherine managed to do well in school: The *Tablet* listed her as one of Aquinas's "Star Pupils."[31]

Some important differences also are apparent among the donors from St. Joseph's (see appendix 3.2). At twelve, Margaret Hamma was the youngest contributor, and seventeen-year-old Veronica Jensen was the oldest. Veronica's father emigrated from Denmark, as did their next-door neighbor, who worked on the docks with Veronica's father. Her mother, however, was a second-generation Irish American. More than half of the other St. Joseph's contributors also had Irish ancestry on at least one side of their family trees, but Veronica's classmates also claimed other nationalities—including Italian, English, Scottish, French, German, and Swiss. Cecelia McCarthy, who had Irish and Italian roots, lived on the most ethnically diverse street. Her neighbors spoke seven languages at home, including Romance languages like Portuguese and Spanish and Scandinavian languages like Norwegian and Swedish. Cecelia's classmates heard fourteen different languages on their streets. For example, Christina Connolly's diverse block in Brooklyn Heights included migrants who grew up speaking Yiddish, Spanish, Swedish, and Chinese. Those young donors' homes were all over Brooklyn—the girls listed in appendix 3.2 are from fifteen neighborhoods and seventeen parishes. Helen Gandolfi, whose father was a policeman, lived in Dyker Heights and went to Sunday mass at St. Ephrem's, one of the new parishes established in the 1920s to nurture Brooklyn's expanding and dispersing Catholic population. Helen's house, which rested on a nice street that included Scandinavian Lutherans as well as Roman Catholics, was more expensive than any of her classmates', while Loretta Zimmerman, whose father drove a coal truck, had the most modest housing, a rental. She was probably one of the poorest of St. Joseph's teen donors. Like Loretta's father, most of the other breadwinners among these working-class families were skilled or unskilled blue-collar workers—bricklayers, fitters, roofers, drivers, electricians, and plumbers—although there were a couple of policemen and one white-collar worker: Helen Gorman's father was a newspaper reporter. By 1930, when she was working as a stenographer, Helen might have had the resources to make her own contribution, but back at St. Joseph's in 1927 at age fourteen, she probably had asked a parent for the donation.[32]

Young Pilgrims at the Shrine during the 1920s

During the 1920s, children and teens also visited the Shrine. Consulting the surviving visitors logs, the notices in *Salve Regina*, the entries in the director's personal record—and again appealing to census records where it's possible—we also can get some sense of their presence in the building.

For example, perhaps in an act of playful transgression, William F. Smith signed the Register of Visitors on page 599, at the end of the logbook and far from all other signatures. Luckily, he added his street address, so, after a great deal of searching, I was able to find biographical information about him. William was born in 1916 and lived in a multigenerational household less than a mile from the Shrine with his mother, Bessie, a telephone operator, and his older brother's young family (see appendix 3.3). Since he didn't include the date, we don't know which day in 1926 or 1927 he visited; but we know he was ten or eleven at the time. In one of the most intriguing traces of children's presence I've found, William also drew a phonograph above his signature and, to identify the music being amplified from its protruding horn, he penned the first lines of a popular song written in 1924 by Abel Baer and Cliff Friend, "June Night." "Just give me a June night, a moonlight, and you," William wrote. The tune's next lines— "with you in my arms with all your charms, the moon above and we'll make love"—reveal that it was a romantic song. Catholic tradition has included some devotees, including mystics like St. John of the Cross, who have used those sorts of metaphors to talk about union with God or devotion to Mary, but surely young William didn't intend that. In fact, his drawing and message neither express affection for Mary nor challenge Marian devotion. What he did have in mind—was it an act of creative self-assertion that playfully appealed to secular entertainment?—we'll never know, though the inked traces of his distinctive presence are unmistakable.[33]

William lived close enough to walk, but we can't be sure if he came alone that day or if an adult escorted him there. The visitor logs from the 1920s, however, show that many other young pilgrims came with their families. For example, as the visitor book from 1926 and 1927 shows, James P. McAndrew, a teenager from Scranton, Pennsylvania, traveled with his older brother. The McLaughlin boys, William and Clement, came from the Bronx with their father, a well-to-do real estate agent. Entire nuclear families, including two families from nearby Maryland, made the pilgrimage together, too. John and Cecelia Urziehart brought their two girls, Rose and Marcella; and, on another day, the Kellys made the short trip from Baltimore with their children, Eileen, Thomas, and William, who was only three at the time (see appendix 3.3).[34]

Pilgrimage wasn't only local or regional, and children didn't arrive only with siblings or parents. Many more children visited in extrafamilial groups. Some came with nonsectarian organizations, like the Boy Scouts and Girl Scouts, as with the Massachusetts scout troops that traveled to Washington in 1930. Protestant, Catholic, and Jewish children also visited with teachers and classmates from public schools: in 1928 about 250 seniors from two

Michigan public high schools journeyed there in June, as part of a class trip to the nation's capital. And, of course, most young people traveled with one organization or another from the Catholic institutional network. Children living in orphanages and asylums visited the BNSIC, usually brought by women religious. Marian devotional organizations had a presence, too. More than fifty Children of Mary traveled from Baltimore with four members of the Sisters of the Holy Cross in the summer of 1925 and came back the following May, when the girls "made a full day retreat" and ran into the Japanese consul's wife, who told them: "I also am a Child of Mary" and said she "was received into the... Sodality in Japan when I was a little girl." Children of all sizes, little and big, also came to the Shrine with classmates from their Catholic schools. About five thousand Catholic children from the parochial schools of the District of Columbia assembled on the grounds for a morning mass and then participated in athletic competitions at CUA's stadium during the 1926 "May Day Games," and, as *Salve Regina* assured readers, "every one of them passed through the National Shrine." Shrine officials also reported that "more than a score of Catholic schools" visited the BNSIC during their trip to Washington in May and June the same year. Guided by several members of the Sisters of the Immaculate Heart of Mary, 120 students from Philadelphia's Catholic Girls High School made a pilgrimage that May, when seven classmates singed the visitor's book on the same page, including Viola Conley, one of four children of a father from Ireland and a mother from Germany.[35]

CHILDREN'S PRESENCE AT THE SHRINE: GIVING AND GOING, 1953–1959

Viola's diocese, and almost every other diocese, participated in ever more centralized and vigorous efforts to encourage young people to send donations and to make pilgrimages during the 1950s, when U.S. bishops set diocesan quotas and reached out to children to do their part.

Adult Appeals and Children's Donations during the 1950s

The clergy had directed early fundraising efforts toward women, and the renewed campaign during the "child-centered" 1950s was careful to appeal to young people. Children might have been innocent—or as innocent as anyone who inherited original sin could be—but they still had their obligations and opportunities to participate in church life. Ecclesiastical officials used many means to reach them. Their parish priest, on orders from his bishop, mentioned the Shrine's fundraising efforts from the pulpit, though it's difficult to know how much the young congregants actually heard or understood. Clergy tried other ways, too. In the title of the first press release issued during the 1953 campaign, the Most Reverend John F. Noll, chairman of the Episcopal Committee for the Shrine, and his colleagues urged the Catholic and non-Catholic media to take notice: "Children Will Help Provide United States with Great Shrine." That press release, which was sent to dioceses to distribute to the print media, claimed that "Catholic parochial school children throughout the country—more than 2,000,000 of them—are making individual gifts to help raise the superstructure of the great National Shrine of the Immaculate Conception in Washington, D.C." It noted: "while the individual contribution will be small, the overall gift of the Catholic school children is expected to be impressive." The fundraising drive was an obligation as well as an opportunity: "it will give millions of growing youngsters a very real connection with one of the most impressive churches ever constructed." To assure readers that the children were behind the efforts, diocesan officials were encouraged to fill in the names of local clergy in the copy of the press release that they sent the media: "The children in this area are more than enthusiastic about the plan," said the Reverend _____, Superintendent of Schools for the Diocese of _____." The document continued by noting that many children "already have seen that portion of the Shrine that is completed" and "all of them have seen pictures of what the great church will be like when it is finished... The children want it to be their Shrine, too, in a very particular way."[36]

As part of that coordinated national media campaign, church officials used media like television, radio, and comics. One of the bishops on the fundraising committee, Philadelphia's John F. O'Hara, appearing on the Catholic half-hour television program *Lamp unto My Feet* on the afternoon of November 29, 1953, noted that "Catholic school children in the United States have been engaged in their own collection of funds for the Shrine" and "boys and girls in our Catholic schools have a very proud record of assisting worthy causes." This new "Children's Collection," he stressed, "gives girls and boys a real and personal opportunity to contribute towards the erection of a great national church building honoring the Mother of God." They have "a very deep affection for the Blessed Virgin" and will find it satisfying to see the church "they really helped to pay for." That theme— that young people could help fund the Shrine—was the central message communicated directly through Catholic comics, too. In the same month the national Children's Collection began, *Treasure Chest of Fun and Fact* published an appeal on page 2, just inside the cover, entitled "The Shrine You Can Build." That page included the architect's black-and-white rendering of the Shrine, and the accompanying text acknowledged to young readers that it might "sound strange" to be asked to build the Shrine, but "the Bishops of our country are asking you to do just that." Then the authorial voice, shifting, continued by noting that "although we will not be able to actually work on it with our hands…we can do a great deal by contributing part of the $8,000,000 that will be necessary to finish it." That message was reinforced in the comic's next issue (see fig. 3.1). With the same title and message as the earlier appeal, it included a two-page entry summarizing the history of Marian devotion in the United States and presenting the building of the BNSIC as its culmination. Children's role is highlighted in this appeal, in which one bishop says to another, "We'll start a building fund and ask our people to contribute generously to it." His fellow bishop responds, "Yes, everyone can help us to finish the shrine—even the school children."[37]

In case the print stories, television interviews, and comic books didn't reach young people, the bishops also extended their efforts even more directly—to teachers and students in the classroom. In 1953, the episcopal committee invited Mary Synon, an important figure in Catholic educational efforts, to write a "handbook for teachers." They distributed eight thousand copies of that handbook, which offered suggestions about how they could incorporate the Shrine's fundraising appeal, and information about Mary, into religion and social studies classes. Leaving little to chance, the manual even offered seventeen specific "suggestions for student activities." To engage kids and win support, for example, the students might "build a shrine in your classroom," "make a script," "make a movie," "make a drawing," or add "a special prayer to other prayers each day for the success of the appeal for the shrine."[38]

Those prayers—and all the coordinated effort—paid off. Children contributed to the cause. And a December 1959 issue of *Treasure Chest*, which included four pages about the Shrine's history and architecture and a back cover that reproduced an image of the completed structure, triumphantly announced to young readers that "the appeal succeeded and this year one of the largest and most splendid religious buildings to be found anywhere in the world was opened." Most contributions went directly to the parish or the diocese and then to Washington. As the donor books archived at the Shrine show, however, some children gave as part of a family effort. Even if a parent wrote and mailed the letter, the Wysocka family from New Jersey, the Galiano family from Missouri, and the Webb family from Texas, for example, all made sure that officials knew their donation represented all of them. As in the earlier period, children also gave as part of a joint effort with peers in Catholic organizations or schools. The girls from the Sodality of the Immaculate Conception at Chicago's Notre Dame High School donated in 1953, and members of the same devotional organization at St. Mary's Academy in Alton, Iowa, sent their contribution the following year. Schools all across the country are represented in the donor books, showing the ways this later fundraising period became even more national in scope. In the months after the U.S. bishops sent their appeal directly to children, young people responded. *Treasure Chest* also included a continuing series, "Civics Clubs in Action," which showed young Catholics how to participate in their communities and help their nation, and these civics clubs mailed money to the Shrine. Other students also responded: for example, the seventh- and eighth-graders at St. Patrick's School in Mauston, Wisconsin, and the fourth-graders at Seattle's St. Joseph's School.[39]

Children and Pilgrimage during the 1950s

Children and teens, or at least the adults who supervised them, also responded to the call to visit the Shrine between 1953 and 1959. In the middle of that period of high activity—both in donations and pilgrimage—Thomas J. Grady, the director who took over from O'Connor in 1956, offered some observations about what it was like in the building, as an active worship space and a busy construction site: "sleepy-eyed school girls coming out of the bus for Mass...the guide's modulated voice, 'seventh largest church in the world'...the honeycomb of scaffolding...the shuffling noise of large groups conducted through the crypt...the clatter of high heels..." Some of that "shuffling" and "clatter" came from families visiting, as in the earlier period. Sometimes those visits were hasty and insignificant. Other times they made a lasting impact. One pilgrim still vividly recalls a family pilgrimage from Leominster, Massachusetts, in 1957, when he was seven years old, just before his First Communion. Here's the story James O'Toole tells, and his third-generation Irish-American parents "reverently told and retold":

> In the summer of 1957, between first and second grade for me, my family took the standard trip to Washington: mom, dad, my two brothers, my sister, and me (the youngest)....Apart from the usual sightseeing, our week in DC included a visit to the Shrine, then very much under construction. I have only the vaguest of mental pictures in my mind, but there must have been kind of program for people to walk around as the thing was being built....In any case, one of the

construction workers gave me (the littlest and cutest one, of course) a piece of stone from the building as a souvenir.... In any event, this became a treasured object in the family, and the tale of its acquisition was told and retold afterward.... It's possible that my mother, now 97, still has it. But for a time it certainly functioned as a relic of "our shrine."[40]

As that Catholic remembered it, the pilgrimage was important because— and he uses language that echoes the press releases—it was about "how little old us" were "connected to [a] great national icon of the faith." But many more pilgrims got "connected" to the Shrine by visiting in larger groups. Members of the Ukrainian Catholic Youth Convention journeyed there in 1955, for example. Some children came as part of a diocesan pilgrimage, as the cover photograph of *Salve Regina* for May 1954, the Marian Year, shows. In that image, pilgrims from the Archdiocese of Baltimore pose with dozens of children, toward the front, and the Shrine's director and a Baltimore priest in the middle of the large crowd in the half-completed interior.[41]

Some of the young pilgrims in that photograph attended Catholic schools, and a 1953 issue of *Salve Regina* had included a posed photograph at the Shrine of the director, then O'Connor, facing two neatly dressed high school students, a boy in a plaid sports coat and tie and a girl in a mid-calf-length skirt. A story below on the same page, titled "Children United to Honor Their Heavenly Mother," echoed the other public proclamations of that year and noted: "many of them have come here on Pilgrimage with their high school classes." Tourist agencies, including Parker Tours of New York and New Jersey, transported some of the student pilgrims. On one day in May 1957, for example, Parker Tours arranged for several buses to bring a large group of students from five different schools in New York, Connecticut, and New Jersey. Sometimes smaller school groups traveled by bus with just their classmates and teachers, as did one group of New York Catholic high school girls and their instructors, who were Ursuline nuns (fig. 3.5).[42]

CONCLUSION

By focusing on young people's pilgrimage and donation to the Shrine we see an important feature of Catholicism in the era of consolidation—the impulse to engage children and teens—and we can detect their presence at that building. Some young devotees' names remain hidden away in the Shrine's archives, in donor books and visitor logs. Some are inscribed on

Figure 3.5. In 1953, students and teachers from an Ursuline school in New York pose with the Shrine's director, Patrick J. O'Connor, with a rendering of the planned superstructure in the background.

the walls of Memorial Hall. Hundreds more, like the young Brooklyn donors Richard Kasprowicz and Rita O'Brien, are inscribed on the donor list embedded in the Mary Memorial Altar. Even their teachers, the Sisters of St. Joseph, have an enduring presence, since in the decade after the dedication that order donated the funds for the main dome's thirty-six windows, which Monsignor Grady promised would "cast shifts of constantly moving color into the center of the Shrine."[43]

Children and teens were rarely at the center, but they were always there, even if authorities more explicitly and more vigorously appealed to young people to donate and visit during the 1950s. In both the early and later periods, however, their presence usually was mediated by adults, and the network's emphasis on Marian devotion, self-sacrifice, and ecclesiastical authority constrained but didn't determine young Catholics' religious practice. We have some intriguing clues about how they enacted creativity and exerted agency within the structures of Catholic childhood. We know, for example, that a thirteen-year-old girl from Ohio donated the money she earned from crocheting and an eleven-year-old boy from D.C. made his mark on the visitors' book by drawing a phonograph and quoting a love song. These examples remind us to be attentive to children's presence, and ask us to consider both how adults reached out to children and how children responded by giving and going.

4

ᴄᐱᴐ

Contesting Protestant Interpretations

The Virgin Mary, the Crypt Church, and the Incorporeal Other, 1913–1932

Writing to the Shrine's director in 1926, as construction continued on the Crypt Church, the chief architect expressed satisfaction about their ongoing efforts. That Catholic layman, Charles Maginnis, noted that "we have tried very hard to achieve something really worthwhile" in the building's design and ornamentation. One of the things the lay and clerical planners—and especially the director, Bishop Thomas Shahan, and his superior, James Cardinal Gibbons—"achieved" in that structure was to offer a response to Protestant interpretations of Roman Catholic belief and practice. As Gibbons had observed in *The Faith of Our Fathers*, an 1876 "exposition and vindication" of Catholicism that had sold 1.4 million copies in eighty-three editions by 1917, "the Catholic Church is persistently misrepresented" and "attacked" in the press and from the pulpit. The attackers mock Marian devotion and key elements of the Church's teaching about her: not only did they challenge the notion of the Immaculate Conception but also "the doctrine of the perpetual virginity of Mary is now combated by Protestants." Like Gibbons, Shahan was sensitive to the Protestant criticisms about Mary, especially to the charge that Marian devotion, so important to Catholics in the era of consolidation, was an inauthentic medieval invention. That church historian countered those interpretations in one book, *The Blessed Virgin in the Catacombs*, by citing evidence about those early burial chambers and arguing that the veneration of Mary was "not a late and artificial, but an early, natural, and organic outgrowth" of early Christianity.[1]

Figure 4.1. This 1926 photograph depicts the Crypt Church's north apse, with its "catacombal" decoration, before the installation of the Mary Altar, which would be dedicated to "Our Lady of the Catacombs."

In turn, Shahan and his assistant, Father Bernard McKenna, imagined the Shrine's lower church as a corrective to those "misrepresentations"—as an architectural rejoinder, a counterargument in stone, glass, clay, and marble (fig. 4.1). To put it differently, and use Gibbons's other guiding metaphor, they wanted to defend themselves, and the Virgin Mary, from Protestant "attacks"—and maybe even establish a site from which they might launch a final victorious blow in that long-standing sectarian battle. Turning from verbal to material expression, then, those Catholic leaders hoped the Shrine's design, and especially the architectural form and symbolic ornamentation of the Crypt Church's interior, which replicated the dark subterranean chambers of the early Christian catacombs, could defend Mary and counter Protestants. They wielded the lower church's "catacombal" design as a weapon, as they tried to combat "misrepresentations" and establish that Marian devotion was authentic and ancient.[2]

These planners, like Catholics before and after them, hoped to contest Protestant interpretations, and in this way, too, the Shrine functioned as a threshold to Catholic America. During the period of consolidation—and before the decline of the Protestant establishment in the 1960s—U.S. Catholics had to make meaning and negotiate power in relation to Protestants. And just as many ordinary lay Catholics, who negotiated daily in the workplace and the streets with their Protestant neighbors, had a presence at the Shrine by giving and going, so, too, the Shrine's clerical planners found that they were able to make their presence felt there—by materially manifesting their own desires in the building itself. Yet Protestants had a presence in the Shrine, too. It was not only the Protestant landscape architects, Olmsted and Olmsted, who recommended where to situate the Shrine on the campus plan, or the many non-Catholics who later visited and donated, like Susanna Fay, the Protestant donor of one of the apsidal altars. Protestants also were always lurking in the Crypt Church's subterranean shadows, as the incorporeal Other against which those clerics had to define themselves and against whom they felt they had to defend their embattled Church.[3]

THE COMPLEXITY OF PROTESTANT ATTITUDES
BEFORE AND AFTER 1913

One art historian has proposed that "the search for meaning—the process that is commonly called 'interpretation'—is a virtually limitless one, which can be terminated only by the atrophy of the individual subject's desire to know." My "desire to know" the Shrine's meaning hasn't "atrophied"—and I hope yours hasn't either—and the search for a building's significance only seems "virtually limitless" if the interpreter either seeks *one* meaning and is predictably frustrated by not finding it or, in the absence of disciplined reflection about what a building is and what it does, if *all* accounts are judged equally plausible. As I already have made clear, I don't think any building, including the Shrine, has a single meaning. Meaning is always multiple and contested, inscribed by users and viewers, as well as by designers and promoters. At the same time, as I noted in the introduction, we can set some limits on interpretation by considering ten factors that seem useful in discerning the converging and diverging meanings of a religious site and the rituals conducted there. In the previous two chapters, I focused on the *donors* and *users*—and on *representations* of the building, in donor letters, comic books and other media. This chapter interprets the Crypt Church as a response to Protestants, and takes other important factors into consideration. It seems crucial to consider what the *makers*, the Shrine's planners and promoters, thought they were doing when they designed and built the Crypt Church, although discerning their expressed intentions hardly settles the matter. The *appearance* of the lower church is important, too—both the choice of Romanesque architectural style and the "immediate impact" of that dark, intimate space on visitors. The clergy, architects, and artists who designed the structure also emphasized its *relation* to other architectural spaces, including Santa Maria Maggiore and the catacombs in Rome.[4]

But the makers' allusions to other spaces and their choices about architectural design only make sense if we also consider the historical *context* in the years before and after 1913, when the Shrine's director traveled to Rome to seek the pope's approval for the project. In recent decades, it's become common for art historians to put art and architecture in "its larger context," especially its social and political context, though "context" is harder to discern than it might first appear. How far in time and space does it extend? In this case, "context" means primarily Protestant-Catholic relations, especially regarding Marian devotion, since the sixteenth century, and especially sectarian relations in the United States, and D.C. in particular, in the years before and after 1913. I will say more later about the longer historical trajectory of interaction, but the most immediate contexts for the clergy's decision to offer an architectural rejoinder to Protestants were national and local. What were the relations between the two faiths in America—and in Washington—and how might that have shaped the planners' aspirations for the building? The short answer: there were some signs of cordial relations by 1913, even tolerance, and some Protestants converted to the faith or had selective attraction, expressing some sympathy for Mary or for the smells and bells, the aesthetics of Catholic art and ritual. Yet there were also clear signs, including in the capital, that Protestant hostility to Catholics had not gone away and that there still was a need to defend the faith in the ongoing sectarian battle.[5]

Protestant Cooperation, Sympathy, and Conversion

In that public struggle, Catholics didn't face a uniform "Protestantism." As Catholics delighted in pointing out, nineteenth- and twentieth-century Protestants disagreed among themselves, even if they shared a historic identity as those "protesting" against the alleged abuses and errors of the Roman Catholic Church. In the same way, there was no single Protestant attitude toward Catholicism: liberal Unitarians and Universalists, on the whole, were less hostile to Catholics than conservative Congregationalists and Presbyterians. Further, there were regional variations, and Protestant attitudes toward Catholics changed over time, with cresting and falling periods of anti-Catholicism, including moments in the 1850s, 1880s, and 1920s when Protestant anxieties spiked, often as Catholic immigration rose.[6]

To be fair, it's important to note that there were places and times when it seemed that the American experiment in religious diversity was working. Consider two local examples. Less than two miles from the Shrine stood an ivy-covered stone chapel built in 1876 to attend to the spiritual needs of residents of the Old Soldiers' Home, which Congress had established a quarter century earlier as "an asylum for old and disabled veterans." Since those veterans claimed different religious affiliations, the original plan had called for a shared chaplaincy, with one Protestant and one Catholic official, and the surviving evidence suggests that ecumenical strategy worked well there. So in 1913, the year Shahan traveled to Rome, Reverend Edward W. Southgate from nearby St. Anthony of Padua Catholic Church shared responsibilities at that military chapel with a local Episcopal clergyman, Reverend H. Allen Griffith. Each Sunday the two conducted separate services in that chapel—with Catholics gathering for worship in the morning and Protestants in the evening. Each denomination buried its own dead. And when the American civic calendar called for public ceremony, as on Memorial Day, the chaplains shared duties, taking turns in alternate years "asking the invocation" at the start of the ceremony and "pronouncing the benediction" at the end. In a similar way, the D.C. press, on the whole, was fair in its coverage of religion around that time, too. For example, in its 1913 story about Easter services, "Anthems of Praise Proclaim Easter Joy Today," the *Washington Post*'s layout was a model of judiciousness. The editor placed the Easter reflections of the Episcopal bishop of Washington on the far left side of the page and those of James Cardinal Gibbons on the far right. Between those two equally sized pastoral messages, at the top and bottom of the page, appeared six other Easter meditations by local pastors, from Congregationalist to Swedenborgian.[7]

Some Protestants did more than just cooperate with Catholics or try to represent them fairly. Some felt an attraction to Roman Catholicism. Some even converted, continuing a practice that had begun in the nineteenth century and had included some of the most prominent U.S. Catholics—Elizabeth Ann Bayley Seton (1774–1821), Orestes Augustus Brownson (1803–1876), and Isaac Thomas Hecker (1819–1888). Other cradle Protestants who never shifted affiliations were—as was Seton—drawn to Catholic art and devotion. That attraction had many sources and took many forms. The nineteenth-century Gothic revival, with its influence on domestic and church architecture, was an ambivalent appropriation of a form associated historically with medieval Catholic Europe. Whether or not they favored the ornate sculptural program and soaring verticality of Chartres Cathedral, some prominent Protestant literary figures expressed some sympathy for Catholicism, in their private lives and in their public work, including Nathaniel Hawthorne, Margaret Fuller, Harriet Beecher Stowe, Henry Adams, and T. S. Eliot. In one of the most surprising developments, those writers and others sympathetically appropriated the Virgin Mary, whom they imagined variously as an empowering feminine divine or as a domestic gender model. Protestants still vigorously disputed various Catholic beliefs about the Virgin in religious magazines: for example, in an article on the Immaculate Conception in the *Methodist Quarterly Review* and another on "Mariolatry" in the *Baptist Review*. But travel books often gave surprisingly positive accounts of the art and architecture of Catholic Europe, and general interest magazines with predominantly Protestant editors, contributors, and readers also turned their attention to Mary. In the second half of the nineteenth century, those periodicals often circulated art, poetry, and fiction that favorably portrayed the Madonna, including in articles and images appearing in *Harper's*, *Hours at Home*, and *Overland*. Some historians even have suggested that the art prints of Mary in homes and schoolrooms and the literary accounts in magazines and travelogues helped to create and sustain the nineteenth-century Protestant preoccupation with motherhood as the defining characteristic of women.[8]

Protestant Presence at the Shrine

One of the travelogues that gushed about European Marian art, *Echoes of Europe* (1860), described the Protestant author's encounter with Murillo's painting of the Immaculate Conception, telling American readers that Murillo's Mary had both a "lofty serenity" and "a holiness." By 1930, both Protestant and Catholic visitors to the BNSIC could encounter that "holiness" themselves, for the Vatican's mosaic workshop had replicated Murillo's painting and shipped the mosaic to the Shrine (fig. 1.3). And some Protestants did visit the BNSIC, even during the early years when workers were constructing the Crypt Church. We'll never know how many Protestants toured the building, however, since many did not sign the visitor logs, and even those who left a signature usually did not indicate their religious affiliation. But we have some hints about Protestant presence there in the early period, including in McKenna's Day Book, his daily journal. That source shows that Protestants visited the Shrine in groups— from Boy Scout troops to public high school classes. *Salve Regina* also printed notice of Protestant visitors, including one note in 1926 suggesting that more and more of them seemed to be making the trip: "Not Catholics alone come to the Crypt to offer their devotions to Our Blessed Mother, but it is a hopeful sign that there is a steadily increasing number of non-Catholics who come to wonder and remain to pray." We do not know what those Protestant visitors actually thought or did at the Shrine, but one woman McKenna encountered there prayed to the Virgin for healing: "Recently a poor sick woman made a journey of 200 miles to Washington that she might come and pray in Our Lady's Church."[9]

The editors of *Salve Regina*—first Shahan and later McKenna—also made efforts to tell readers about other examples of Protestant cooperation, conversion, and sympathy. There is a hint of overeagerness in their attempts to recover historical examples of Protestant affection for Mary and to scan the contemporary landscape for signs of acceptance. One 1916 piece in *Salve Regina*, "A Protestant Tribute," recalls a sixteenth-century British Protestant who wrote a hymn titled "Our Lady's Immaculate Conception," and the lead article of a 1921 issue, "A Protestant Tribute to Mary," took notice of a contemporary Protestant clergyman who had suggested six years earlier that the Virgin was "the first place of all God's creation." The Jesuit who had sent the editors that account added his own note of approval, which they reprinted, too: "Homage more beautiful could not come from the lips of a devout Catholic."[10]

Sometimes "homage" was a preliminary to conversion, and the Shrine clergy also reprinted messages from converts who made pilgrimages or sent donations. In 1922, one devotee sent a dollar and pledged the same annual contribution for five years: "That is if the Lord is willing that I live so long. I am now 66 years of age and only five years a convert, but those five years have been happy ones, and a great comfort." That devotee also added, as many donors did, a note about personal needs: "My brother who is very dear to me is very ill and I am not well. Pray for us both." Two years later, clergy reprinted another letter with the title "A Convert's Praise." A former Protestant had sent a "little gift for our Blessed Mother's Shrine" with her explanation: "I am a convert having been baptized about a year ago, and one of the sweetest and most precious things about my faith is the thought that I have this loving Mother in heaven watching over me. I pray to her constantly and know that she has helped me so many times."[11]

Sometimes Protestants who retained their denominational allegiance but cherished that "loving Mother in heaven" also sent donations. For example, in a 1915 letter to a member of the NOCW, Bishop Shahan reported: "a Protestant gentleman gave me a hundred dollars yesterday." He and McKenna also reprinted excerpts from Protestant donors' letters in *Salve Regina*. In a 1918 missive one wrote: "Although I am what you would call a Non-Catholic, I still have love for the Blessed Lady and am glad to send in my mite ($1) for her honor. She has obtained many blessings for me." A few years later, to mention only one more of many similar communications, the clergy published a note that passed on a contribution from a family member: "Enclosed please find a check for five dollars in honor of the Immaculate Conception. In thanksgiving to Our dear Lady for a great favor granted. This is sent by my mother who is a non-catholic. Kindly remember her in your prayers."[12]

Another Protestant mother, Susanna H. Fay, sent another donation in 1921 that paid for one of the Crypt Church's apsidal chapels venerating her namesake, St. Susanna, a Roman martyr. Fay, an Episcopalian, was born to Irish immigrants in Philadelphia in 1843. She and her husband, Alfred, a salesman who hailed from New England Protestants, lived well. In 1880, the young couple had two female servants living with them and their two young children in their large Philadelphia home on a corner lot just north of downtown Philadelphia. One of those two children, Sigourney, would be remembered at his death in 1919 for a number of reasons. Some Anglo-Catholics would recall his earlier work as an Episcopalian priest and seminary professor, but mostly he would be remembered for the work he did after he converted to Roman Catholicism in 1908. That conversion got the attention of the *New York Times* that year, and, wasting no time, he was ordained as a Roman Catholic priest in the Archdiocese of Baltimore by Cardinal Gibbons in 1910. He went on to assist the influential Gibbons, and over the next nine years he exerted influence of his own. He was a minor presence in the District of Columbia, giving sermons and lectures, and taught briefly at CUA. He had some impact at the Shrine, too, since it was he who suggested the title for its magazine, *Salve Regina*. Beyond the capital, he is also remembered as a major influence on the novelist F. Scott Fitzgerald, whom he encountered while he was serving at a Catholic preparatory school in New Jersey. The novelist gave his clerical mentor literary immortality when he modeled a character, Thayer Darcy, on Fay and dedicated his 1920 novel *This Side of Paradise* to him. At the time of his death, Monsignor Fay had just returned from humanitarian service in Europe, and, as his 1919 obituary in the *New York Times* noted, he had been acting "as a representative of Cardinal Gibbons at the invitation of the Red Cross." A day after he succumbed to pneumonia, an audience of twenty-five hundred Protestant and Catholic women in New York City also remembered him: the members of a civic organization he had addressed previously, it was reported, "rose yesterday morning in Carnegie Hall and stood in silent tribute." His Episcopalian mother saw to it that he had one more posthumous tribute—in the material culture of the BNSIC.[13]

At one level this is just an account of a bond between a mother and her only son, but it's also an interesting example of Protestant presence at the Shrine. It's a narrative that has been recounted since Susanna Fay first promised the funds for the St. Susanna Chapel in 1921. The local newspaper, the *Washington Post*, thought the story of a Protestant gift to a Catholic worship center warranted coverage in 1926. So did the periodical her son named, *Salve Regina*, when it announced to its readers the same year: "Non-Catholic's Gift Is Memorial to Her Son Who Became Priest." William Kennedy's history of the building, published by the Shrine in 1927, repeated the same story. In turn, many Shrine publications by the staff, including Bernard McKenna's 1959 *Memoirs* and Gregory Tucker's 2000 *America's Church*, have noted both Sigourney's conversion and Susanna's donation. Protestants, the narrative affirms, can convert to the faith, and even when they don't, they can still express affection for Mary and make donations to her Shrine.[14]

THE SECTARIAN BATTLEFIELD: THE CONTEXT FOR THE CRYPT CHURCH'S DESIGN

Yet if Protestant-Catholic relations were as rosy as these accounts of Protestant cooperation, conversion, and donation suggest, then there would have been no need for Shahan and Gibbons to respond to Protestant challenges. The most important thing to note about the historical context of the Crypt Church's planning and construction, before and after Shahan's 1913 papal audience, is that Catholics saw signs that anti-Catholicism was alive and well. Shahan was born in the mid-1850s, when anti-Catholic sentiment surged, and he died in the early 1930s, after another wave of public attacks in the 1920s had receded. So that immigrant Catholic witnessed the cresting and falling waves of public hostility to Catholics and immigrants; and even when the tide of controversy was at a low point, he still could sense a steady stream of Protestant anxiety. Many Protestants, he knew, dismissed his faith as spiritually misguided, culturally ambitious, and politically dangerous.[15]

Anti-Catholicism before and after 1913

The emergence of the Know Nothing Party in the 1850s and the reemergence of the Ku Klux Klan in the 1920s symbolize two waves of hostility, and both those anti-Catholic movements reached the nation's capital.

Catholic-Protestant tensions in Washington had erupted earlier in the nineteenth century, including when competing pamphlets disputed whether a local laywoman had been miraculously healed in 1824 at St. Patrick's Catholic Church, which had been founded three decades earlier to serve Catholic stonemasons who were building the White House and the Capitol. The anonymous author of the Protestant pamphlet, a "Friend of Truth," complained that the residents of the nation's capital "have been long exposed to that dominion under which the mental faculties of every true Papist must be enslaved," and three decades later Protestants in the District of Columbia were still worried about Catholicism's local and national influence. Pope Pius IX, who proclaimed the doctrine of the Immaculate Conception, planned to donate a marble block to be added to the Washington Monument, which was then being constructed. One 1852 pamphlet warned about this impending "desecration" of the monument: the gift was a "mortification to nearly every American Protestant who looks upon it" and a dangerous encouragement to "the zealous supporters of the Roman hierarchy...." Calling for public protests, the Protestant author warned about the coming evils: "Yes, fellow citizens, I desire to oppose the approaches, under the garb of friendship, of a Power that will, when it gains the designed and desired ascendency, burn our Bibles, bind our consciences, make slaves of us, and put us to the stake, the rack, or the dungeon, for attempting to exercise the free minds with which a gracious Creator has gifted us." Protests did follow, and the anti-Catholic Know Nothing Party even gained control of the Washington National Monument Society in 1854. That year, the stone donated by the Vatican mysteriously disappeared. Rumors circulated, and the Society offered a $500 reward for its safe return. No one ever claimed the money—or returned the block. In later decades, however, former Know Nothing Party members proudly claimed responsibility for the theft and destruction of the "papist" gift. We can't be sure what happened to that marble block, which was inscribed with the words "Rome to America," but the incident clearly expressed Protestant anxiety about Catholic influence during the 1850s.[16]

Protestant anxiety emerged again with some force in the 1920s, when laborers were building the Shrine's Crypt Church. It was a "decade of ethnic and racial conflicts," and a period when "the noise of conflict" between Anglo-Saxon Protestants and religious outsiders filled the streets. The timing was not a coincidence. Immigration had been bringing more and more Catholics (and Jews) to American shores in the proceeding decades, and "between June and December 1920 more than fifty thousand immigrants arrived each month." By 1920, the number of Roman Catholics had risen to 17,549,324, or about 15 percent of the U.S. population. Protestant anxiety sometimes focused on immigration, and new legal codes expressed that worry, including the Emergency Immigration Act of 1921 and the National Origins Act of 1924, which reflected theories about the supremacy of the Anglo-Saxon race. Despite the long-standing claim by American Protestants that they had nothing against Catholics, that it was just the errors of Catholicism, many Protestants between 1920 and 1928 overtly challenged both Catholics and Catholicism.[17]

In a sleight of hand that fooled no one, some Protestants also attacked Catholics' suspicion of public schools and their desire to build parochial schools, as critics had done in the nineteenth century—and as Hiram Wesley Evans, the imperial wizard of the Knights of the Ku Klux Clan, did in a pamphlet that circulated in the 1920s titled, "The Public School Problem in America." Evans began the tract by advocating "a free public school system" and "rigidly enforced immigrations," but showed his hand two pages later, where he condemned the Vatican's desire to exert church control over the state. Evans demanded, in turn, "in the name and in the interest of democracy, that they be completely separated." Anti-Catholicism erupted again in the 1924 and 1928 elections, as the prospect of a Catholic president brought out the worst in some Protestant observers. Yet in some ways the symbolic peak of publicly expressed anti-Catholicism occurred on September 13, 1926. On that afternoon an unmasked Evans led thousands of Klan supporters, including a young New Jersey woman crowned "Miss 100 Percent America," in a triumphant parade down Pennsylvania Avenue and toward the Washington Monument (fig. 4.2). They were there, spokesmen told the press, to protest Al Smith's rise to national prominence and "the influence of the Catholic Church in American politics." In that parade they were reclaiming civic space for Anglo-Saxon Protestantism, just as the vandals had done in 1854 when they had stolen the pontiff's gift and saved the Washington Monument from "desecration."[18]

Anti-Catholicism in 1913: "A Guerrilla Warfare of Words"

In 1913, the year Shahan formally proposed the Shrine project, anti-Catholicism also went public when "a guerrilla warfare of words" broke out, as the reluctant Catholic combatant, Monsignor William T. Russell (1863–1927) of St. Patrick's Church, described it. The other key figure in that sectarian battle in the local press was the Reverend Randolph Harrison McKim (1842–1920), the rector at the Episcopal Church of the Epiphany. Praised at his death as "an intense, loyal, fighting Christian," over the years this southern evangelical engaged two main opponents—the Yankee army and

Figure 4.2. The KKK parade in Washington, D.C., on September 13, 1926. Hiram Evans, the Imperial Wizard, appears just behind and to the right of the flag bearer.

the Catholic Church. McKim had served the Confederacy on the battlefield, eulogized Robert E. Lee as "an example of Christian faith and conduct," and published *A Soldier's Recollections: Leaves from the Diary of a Young Confederate*. Before and after he assumed his duties in Washington in 1888, McKim also preached and wrote about the errors and dangers of the Catholic faith. So by the time tensions erupted again in 1913, he already had publicly criticized a New York priest in 1879 and addressed an open letter to the pope in 1897. In 1908, he even had taken aim at the most prominent local and national Catholic leader, Cardinal Gibbons, for his triumphalist Americanism. McKim criticized Gibbons's claim that Catholics in Maryland, not New England Protestants, had established America's tradition of religious liberty. Russell, who had served as Gibbon's assistant, knew all this and recalled McKim's earlier attacks when the first shots were fired in the local newspaper in 1913.[19]

As with multigenerational family feuds, both sides raised the old issues—whether or not they were relevant—and combatants could not agree about who or what started the most recent incident. However, the 1913 "warfare of words" had two immediate causes. At the end of the three-month controversy in the pages of the *Washington Post*, McKim wrote a pamphlet in which he claimed he'd delivered a lecture titled "Why We Are Protestants" to a standing-room-only crowd at the New National Theater in December in response to a series of appeals directed at Protestants from the pulpit of St. Patrick's, Russell's Washington congregation. As the local newspaper reported, a prominent Paulist priest, Bertrand Conway (1872–1959), had held a two-week "mission" there in October, with Father Russell also taking part. McKim's response, which repeated rhetoric he'd used in earlier public debates, employed martial imagery to stir his Washington audience—and to mobilize the eighty thousand readers who purchased his pamphlet during the next few months: "The Protestant unity of action is coming. I hear the sound of its advancing feet; I hear from afar off the tramp as of a mighty army marching on to the *Battle Hymn of the Republic*." To make sure that no one misinterpreted this as a call to violence, McKim added, "It is an army of peace; its weapons are not carnal, but spiritual." Four months later, in a new introduction to a book that reprinted his former criticisms, *Romanism in the Light of History*, McKim claimed to resort only to the illuminating power of historical inquiry. He challenged doctrines like papal infallibility and the Immaculate Conception, and defended his impassioned response to Catholics like Gibbons, Conway, and Russell. It was necessary, he wrote in April 1914, because "there is an unmistakable and widespread awakening among American citizens to the peril involved in the...political power of the Roman hierarchy." Besides, the Catholics had started it. In their "avowed purpose 'to make America Catholic,'" the Catholic Church was "displaying at the present time a boldness and aggressiveness greater than ever before in her history in our country. She is forcing the fight. Never have her claims been so arrogant. Never has she so openly set at defiance the public opinion of this Protestant nation."[20]

In their recalibrated Americanism, Catholics disputed the notion that America was a Protestant nation, of course; but in his final rejoinder to McKim, Russell didn't repeat his earlier historical counterarguments. Instead, the pastor of St. Patrick's and future bishop of Charleston indicated that he "refused to enter into a guerrilla warfare of words on theological subjects." He also criticized McKim because his editorials and sermons had "stirred up some nasty ill-feelings among the people who believe in you as a minister of God." So, Russell decided, he wouldn't prolong the exchanges, but he suggested in closing that the real source of outrage was not the Paulist mission but the recent controversy about the Pan American Thanksgiving Day Mass.[21]

Russell was right: McKim was troubled by that mass and had stirred controversy, locally and nationally, by coordinating a protest that fall against the president's attendance at St. Patrick's Church on Thanksgiving. Just before that holiday in 1913, the *Washington Post* informed readers: "Mgr. Russell has arranged for the usual elaborate services Thanksgiving day at St. Patrick's." That was the problem, however, as McKim saw it. The religious event had become *too* elaborate. In 1909, Russell had conceived of the idea of a mass to celebrate hemispheric unity and convinced President William Howard Taft, a Unitarian who had been respectful to Catholics, to attend the service. Taft and his wife, Nellie, came to St. Patrick's each Thanksgiving during his term in office, from 1909 to 1912 (fig. 4.3). The newly elected Woodrow Wilson, who didn't realize what he was getting himself into, did the same in 1913. The protests grew so clamorous that year, however, that no president ever returned to that annual celebration. To a large extent, the tradition stopped because McKim and his Protestant colleagues in the Washington Ministerial Alliance met at a local hotel on

Figure 4.3. Monsignor Russell greets President William Howard Taft and his wife, Nellie, as they arrive to participate in the "elaborate" Pan American Thanksgiving Day Mass in 1912.

November 18, 1913, to pass a resolution complaining about "the presumption of the Roman Catholic press...that the Roman mass is the official celebration of Thanksgiving day in the capital" and "against the attempt to convert our national Thanksgiving day into a Roman Catholic festival." As the press noted, the event got more elaborate each year: Cardinal Gibbons, Bishop Shahan, Monsignor Russell, and their local clerical colleagues were joined at the event by many of the most prominent U.S. government officials and Latin American representatives, all of them wearing formal attire. Puffed with pride, some Catholic periodicals had hinted in 1912 and 1913 that the religious ritual had become a "permanent institution." That was the final blow. To suggest that the celebration of that American holiday could fall into the hands of Roman Catholics was too much to bear. So yielding to the local and national pressure, much of it from McKim himself, President Wilson did not attend another holiday mass at St. Patrick's after 1913.[22]

CATHOLIC ADVANCES IN THE SECTARIAN CONFLICT

Protestants might have won that battle, but the interfaith struggles were far from over. Catholics responded to the hostility, before and after 1913, in varied ways. Some ignored it, either because they actually didn't notice it or because it didn't bother them. Lay Catholics who didn't speak English as their first language, or who rarely ventured beyond their own ethnic subcultures—those unaffected by the "warfare of words" in the *Washington Post*—didn't pay much attention. They were focused more on the hardships of daily life. Others ignored Protestant attacks, when they didn't affect them directly, because many Catholics of the period were, as one historian proposed, "smugly triumphalistic." Just as sure as their Protestant critics were about the eternal fate of their opponents, some Catholics rested confidently in the teaching that there was no salvation outside the Church. They had heard that from the pulpit and learned it as children from the Baltimore Catechism, which prohibited them from "marrying non-Catholics" and taught that "he who knows the Church to be the true Church and remains out of it cannot be saved." Or, as one Catholic high school textbook put it, they knew the Church "fearlessly condemns all those who oppose her or contradict her [and] brands as heretics those who call themselves Christians yet differ in doctrine."[23]

Other Catholics, mostly the lay elite and male clergy, always had one eye on their Protestant antagonists, and tried to avoid making things worse. As a member of the IFCA suggested in 1923, when the KKK had reemerged as a visible force, those Catholic school graduates aimed in all their activities "to show to a world of bigotry, prejudice, and alliteratively captioned societies, the unity, culture, and conservatism of the daughters of Holy Mother Church." Prescriptive literature sometimes provided detailed instructions about how Catholics should behave in public settings, so they would not make interfaith relations worse: "These pages aim," the Catholic author of one advice manual explained, "to be at once a guide for the exterior conduct of Catholics on some of the occasions where there is a liability of annoying mistakes.... In a country where Catholics in certain crude communities are still regarded with suspicion and dislike, and where even in more cultivated centers the clouds yet linger of ignorance and hereditary prejudice, Catholics are doubly bound to bring no reproach on the grand old Church. We are judged not as individuals but as Catholics."[24]

As with some U.S. Jews who also used varied "strategies of survival," including "defense," Catholics who sensed Protestants' harsh judgments directly countered the attacks. Sometimes they did it ritually. For example, devotees of Mary, including a thousand male members of the Knights of Columbus, challenged anti-Catholicism in 1924 when they engaged in a pilgrimage to the BNSIC to express outrage at recent Protestant criticisms of Mary. The *Washington Post* announced to local Protestant readers "Thousands of Catholics Will Visit Shrine Here" and then explained the purpose of their ritual: "Pilgrims to Come as Protest against Questioning of Christ's Virgin Birth."[25]

Bishop Shahan was among the instigators of that ritual protest, and some Catholic clergy also directly responded to Protestants in newspapers, magazines, pamphlets, and books. Shahan and the other clerical apologists for the faith often used a conciliatory tone, however. "With all due respect for my dissenting brethren," Gibbons began one passage in his frequently reprinted book aimed at Protestants. In his "mission" at St. Patrick's Church in October 1913, Father Conway followed the established practice of putting a "Question Box" at the back of the Church and then trying to respectfully answer the questions of Protestants, whom that Paulist missionary generously described as "earnest seekers." In his first public response to McKim, in December 1913, Russell ended by appealing for more cooperation: "Now, my dear Dr. McKim, let me assure you the community expects better things of us than these petty bickerings. Let us betake ourselves of the quiet of our studies and prepare our Christmas sermons on 'Peace, good will to men.'"[26]

But we should not let their conciliatory tone obscure the confidence with which they defended the faith. The clause about "dissenting brethren" I quoted from Gibbons's *Faith of Our Fathers* is followed by another that begins: "truth compels me to say" and ends by leaving no uncertainty about where Gibbons, or the Church, stood on doctrinal matters. And truth, as they understood it, "compelled" Catholic apologists to say many things, since Protestant critics raised many issues, and in their polite but firm rejoinders Catholics employed a variety of rhetorical strategies. They appealed to reason and experience and, at their most effective, even gestured toward their opponents' deeply held beliefs and values, as Gibbons did brilliantly in his defense of the veneration of Mary. He shrewdly appealed to Protestant patriotism, and especially Americans' affection for George Washington. "Heroes and statesmen may receive the highest military and civic honors which a nation can bestow without being suspected of invading the domain of the glory which is due to God...and yet the admirers of Mary's exalted virtues can scarcely celebrate her praises without being accused in certain quarters of Mariolatry." Gibbons went on to point out that all Americans honor Washington's monument, statue, and grave, and set aside a day on the national calendar for him. So how could it be wrong, he asked, for American Catholics also to venerate Mary on her feast day at statues and shrines?[27]

Contesting Historical Narratives

In the same section of his book, Gibbons also used a second rhetorical weapon, one Protestants had wielded in their own attacks. In *Romanism in the Light of History*, for example, McKim suggested the situation demanded "a calm and careful consideration of the claims of the Church of Rome in the light of history," and Gibbons had said the same earlier in *Faith of Our Fathers*, when he encouraged Protestants to "study her history in the pages of truth." In a strategy used primarily by clergy and directed mostly at learned Protestants, Catholic apologists used historical scholarship and challenged Protestants' historical narratives. McKim's 1908 attack on Gibbons had been prompted by Gibbons's triumphalist claims about Catholicism's place in U.S. history, just as Russell's first response to McKim in 1913 had focused almost entirely on historical claims about the American past. At the heart of Protestant identity were a series of historical claims about the illegitimate emergence of the papacy, the corruption of the medieval church, the late invention of Marian devotion, and the need for the Protestant Reformation. Catholic apologists, in turn, contested Protestant claims about European Christian history. In his parish missions and in his 1903 book *The Question Box*, which sprang from his experience answering queries Protestants submitted, Father Conway often dealt with historical questions. He did the same in a later book, *Studies in Church History*, which was "for the most part summaries of important volumes on Church History." He used the latest scholarship to answer questions he received, including "Did Jesus Really found a Church?" and "What proof is there of the Assumption of the Virgin?"[28]

Gibbons had written the preface to Conway's book and, drawing on his experience of serving churches in the South, in *The Faith of Our Fathers*, he also was able to anticipate the questions of his imaginary Protestant readers. That meant, among other things, dealing with Protestant claims about medieval and early modern history. As he turned to the historical origins of Protestantism, he announced he wanted to "calmly survey the field after the din and smoke of battle have passed away . . . and examine the conditions of the old Church after having passed through those deadly conflicts." He went on to discuss "the so-called Reformation of the sixteenth century," but reinterpreted it as a "revolt" and a "schism" and compared it with the "Arian heresy," which had denied the full divinity of Jesus. Like that earlier heresy, he hinted, Protestantism, too, might fade from history: "The extinction of Protestantism would complete the parallel." He took a similar approach when defending Marian devotion. He cited scripture to establish the antiquity of that devotion and noted that "the Catholic is the only Church whose children, generation after generation, from the first to the present century, have pronounced her blessed." "Although the Immaculate Conception was not formulated into a dogma of faith until 1854," Gibbons argued, "it is at least implied in Holy Scripture. It is also in strict harmony with the place which Mary holds in the economy of Redemption, and has virtually received the pious assent of the faithful from the earliest days of the Church."[29]

As a church historian, Shahan also used scholarship about the Christian past as a weapon in the battle with Protestants. He wrote and taught about Christian history at CUA starting in 1889, so it was his job to take the long view. He put the contemporary sectarian battles in historical perspective: in every century since Jesus' death, the gospel "has been open to attack and criticism" and a "defence of the Word of God" has become necessary, as "each generation is impelled and compelled to take up the ancient conflict on new levels and amid new surroundings." Such a defense of the faith was even more necessary at present, he wrote in 1905: "perhaps the cause of our Catholic faith was never more open to its enemies than now." He explained that he meant the attacks by "orthodox Protestantism," which in earlier times had acknowledged some common ground with Catholicism but had become more divisive by the early twentieth century. The required defense of the faith, Shahan proposed, could vary in tone and form. "There is a defence of the Word of God that is harsh and violent, and there is another defence, or rather an illustration, not less admirable or useful, that is gentle and winning." Shahan favored the latter approach, which could employ different ways to reach those in the pews of Catholic churches and those beyond the ecclesiastical threshold. He thought the clergy should launch their defense from "the pulpit" but he believed that historical scholarship also could protect the faith and counter Protestant attacks.[30]

Shahan's own scholarship covered all periods of Christian history. He displayed historical breadth, for example, in his *Outline of Church History*, his essays in *The Middle Ages*, and his editing and writing for the massive *Catholic Encyclopedia*. Like Gibbons, he also offered his own reinterpretations of later church history. Unlike the usual Protestant historical narratives, which placed the Reformation as the end of the medieval period and the start of another, Shahan's story described sixteenth-century Protestantism as a schism from the one true church and suggested that medieval Christianity "closes with the [Catholic] discovery of the New World." But he didn't just offer alternate periodizations. Turning a bit less "gentle and winning," Shahan also criticized the "moral bankruptcy" of both the Reformation and the Enlightenment: "neither the sixteenth nor the eighteenth century fulfilled the brilliant...promises...each made to mankind."[31]

Even though his scholarship spanned all periods, Shahan cared most about the first three centuries of Christianity. He expressed a scholar's delight in learning about the past for its own sake, but he was especially sensitive to the rhetorical uses of the new scholarship about early Christianity in the ongoing interfaith strife. Moreover, having studied in Berlin, Rome, and Paris, he was prepared for battle. He knew the latest European historical and archeological scholarship on early Christianity and showed that erudition in his translation of an important German work, *Patrology: The Lives and Works of the Fathers of the Church*, and in his own work *The Beginnings of Christianity*. That 1904 survey for Catholic readers opened with an explanation of the topic's significance. Using prose as dense and indirect as some of the German and Italian academic writing he cited, Shahan nonetheless made his point clear: the new scholarship challenged Protestantism and buttressed Catholicism. "There are not wanting reasons of a modern and immediate nature which make it henceforth useful and consoling to reflect on the earliest history of the Church," he suggested. He employed the trope of biological evolution that was so popular on both sides of the Atlantic at the time and welcomed "the science of history" for its ability to trace the "origin" and "growth" of Christianity. That new science, including both textual criticism and Roman archeology, analyzed "the books of the New Testament and the primitive elements of the Christian faith." The result of that scholarship, Shahan believed, had been "the steady, consistent disintegration of the original bases of Protestantism."[32]

Gibbons also had mentioned the new scholarship, which started to appear before he wrote the first edition of *Faith of Our Fathers*; and, like Shahan, he was especially encouraged by the new archeology of the early Christian burial places around Rome, the vast network of 340 miles of narrow underground galleries painted with symbols and images: "the catacombs of Rome, to which the faithful alone were admitted, abounded ... in sacred emblems and pious representations, which are preserved even to this day and attest the practice of the early Christian Church." Gibbons alluded to this new scholarship to defend the Catholic use of "sacred images," but Shahan, his clerical colleague, knew that research even better and applied it to a variety of contested issues. Shahan proposed in *The Beginnings of Christianity* and in an earlier book, *The Blessed Virgin of the Catacombs*, that the new textual and archeological evidence fortified Catholic claims about the papacy, for example. Most important for Shahan—and for the design of the Crypt Church—the new scholarship defended Marian devotion against Protestant assaults.[33]

THE CATACOMBS AS "WEAPON" AND THE "CATACOMBAL" DESIGN AS COUNTERATTACK

Observers have nominated different events as the turning point in the history of Catholic claims on public space in Anglo-Saxon Protestant America, and some have considered the 1926 International Eucharistic Congress in Chicago to be one of those moments. A Catholic editorial writer, still aglow with pride after the public pageantry, suggested that the event triumphantly signaled Catholicism's presence. "At Chicago we came—so to speak—out of our holes and corners," he wrote, "out of our catacombs into a blinding light." But Shahan, who attended the proceedings in Chicago that year, had decided much earlier, in consultation with architects and artists, on a different strategy for negotiating publicly with Protestant culture in America. Some Protestant antagonists, like McKim, had proposed that disputants examine competing claims "in the light of history," and Shahan was eager to let "the historical temper of mind" settle things. He used different metaphors, however, as he discussed the historian's task: "As far as the past is concerned, we walk amid shadows and reflections, in an ever deepening twilight." Welcoming the "shadows and reflections," he proposed that Catholics descend again into those subterranean cemeteries—not to keep company with the dead or hide from public view. Rather, as earlier students of Christian history had done, Shahan hoped to use the new research about ancient Christian burial chambers, and especially the wall paintings found there, to defend Mary and fortify Catholicism.[34]

The Protestant habit of using historical narrative to combat Catholic claims goes back to the first decades after the sixteenth-century Reformation. European Protestants tried to show that the Catholic Church accepted beliefs and practices, including the use of images and the veneration of Mary, that were not found among the early Christians. Catholics responded in kind, as with Cesare Baronio's multivolume work *Ecclesiastical History from the Birth of Christ until the Year 1198*, which appeared in twelve volumes between 1588 and 1607. One historian has noted that Baronio's work expressed much more "self-confidence" than previous Catholic apologetic works. That new confidence sprang from the author's conviction that the Catholic view of history, and its material culture and devotional practice, had been vindicated by "the rediscovery of the Christian catacombs of Rome" in 1578. That year, workers in a vineyard outside Rome accidentally found what later turned about to be an ancient underground chamber for Christian burial. This meant Catholics had not just texts but artifacts to use in their interfaith struggles. The wall paintings in the catacombs, which preserved early representations of the Madonna and Child and other saints, "provided Catholic intellectuals with new and rather deadly ammunition," that historian has noted. "Thus such scholars were armed with good evidence to argue that the iconoclasm of the Protestants that had led to the destruction of many a Catholic Church in Northern Europe, was not in the least consistent with the ideas and ideals prevalent among the earliest Christian communities." Catholics could argue that "the veneration of the Virgin Mary was not a recent Catholic invention, but rather it was an original Christian practice that went back to the beginnings of the Christian faith." As one Catholic apologist of the Counter-Reformation phrased it, the catacombs were "arsenals from which to take the weapons to combat heretics, and in particular the iconoclasts, impugners of sacred images."[35]

Catholic apologists received even more "weapons," first in the seventeenth century and again in the nineteenth. A posthumous publication by Antonio Bosio (1575–1629), *Roma Sotterranea*, provided help: a monumental archeological study of the catacombs, it appeared first in Italian in 1634 and later in a Latin translation in 1651. That Catholic scholar's enormous volume, which included illustrations of the wall paintings and analyses of the cemeteries, soon incited responses from Protestants, who sensed what was at stake in these contestations about the past. A nineteenth-century Italian Catholic, Giovanni Battista de Rossi (1822–1894), did even more systematic excavations, and in 1854 he unearthed the so-called crypt of the popes, a finding many Catholics took as supporting their claims about the papacy. More important for Shahan and other Catholics who treasured images and honored Mary, De Rossi, the "founder of the modern scholarly approach to catacomb archeology," also found even more burial chambers with even more images, including a fresco of the Madonna in the Catacomb of St. Priscilla from the late third century (fig. 4.4). When De Rossi, who also worked for the Vatican archives, published his three-volume work *La Roma sotterranea cristiana* (1864–1877), he predicted it would bring "new victories for the truth and for the faith."[36]

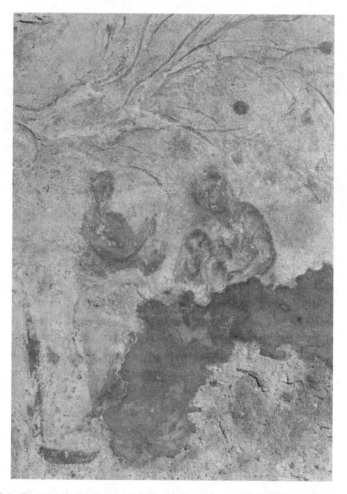

Figure 4.4. Fragment of a Fresco of the Madonna and child, with a prophet. Fresco. 40 x 27 cm. Catacomb of St. Priscilla, Rome.

De Rossi's works appeared in translations, including an English version in 1879, and between 1854 and 1904 notice of his research circulated in American magazines. The new evidence was discussed in general interest periodicals like *Harper's* and the *Atlantic*. Protestant periodicals, including Baptist, Methodist, Lutheran, and Presbyterian magazines, ran stories that reported and assessed the excavations, as with a piece titled "The Catacombs of Rome" in the *Baptist Quarterly*, by Samuel Lunt Caldwell, a professor at Newton Theological Seminary. In another article, "Is There a Science of History?," Caldwell continued to defend historical analysis, as did other Protestants, and they found themselves responding to counteroffensives made by Catholic scholars. Some of those Catholic apologetic writings appeared in magazines like *Catholic World*, which warmly reviewed the first volume of De Rossi's *Roma Sotteranaea* in 1865, and the *American Catholic Quarterly Review*, which published an article titled "The Catacombs of Rome" in 1891.[37]

The next year Shahan published a book-length study, *The Blessed Virgin in the Catacombs*, in which he cited research in German, Italian, and French. He drew heavily on the work of De Rossi, whom Shahan called "the prince of Christian archeologists" and "the Columbus of the Catacombs." In his "discovery" of subterranean Rome, Shahan believed De Rossi had provided the evidence that allowed Catholics to establish "the early origins of the cult of the Blessed Virgin." To persuade readers, Shahan began his 1892 book by alluding to the usual Protestant claims. He noted that most observers seemed to agree that Mary was venerated by the fifth century, when the Council of Ephesus (431 CE) proclaimed her *theotokos*, the Mother of God. The Catholic veneration of Jesus' mother only began then, the Protestant narrative suggests, and then intensified during the corrupt medieval period. Shahan's stated purpose in his study, however, was to use the new scholarship to offer an alternate interpretation. To accomplish that, he reiterated his main argument in his first chapter and the conclusion: "the affectionate veneration of the Virgin Mother of Our Lord is a fact which meets us at the very threshold of Christian history." Chapter 2, "The Catacombs and Their Contents," gave an overview, and much of what he said there would be accepted by specialists today, though scholars now have unearthed at least sixty catacombs, not fifty, and they date some of the images a half century to a century later than either Shahan or De Rossi proposed. Most specialists would agree that representations of the Madonna appear in those ancient subterranean spaces, and Shahan wanted to go even farther and show that "the primitive Roman Christians entertained a profound sentiment of respect and veneration for the Blessed Virgin Mary." So in his next three chapters he considered, in turn, Marian representations on large tombs, gilded glasses, and wall paintings.[38]

Shahan was especially taken by the wall paintings, or frescos, which he called "the embryo of Christian art." Those paintings include many images of Jesus as the Good Shepherd who is worthy of the death of the entombed martyrs, and among the paintings are banquet scenes (*fractio panis*), interpreted by Shahan, and many other Catholics, as eucharistic rituals. One early representation of a banquet scene can be found in the Catacomb of Priscilla, which Shahan rightly described as "one of the oldest of Christian burial places." The ornamentation on its walls includes various early Christian symbols—the anchor, the fish, the peacock—and, as Shahan emphasized, "the earliest and most important" fresco of the Madonna (fig. 4.4). In chapter 5, he lingers over his discussion of that image. First he offers a description. "It represents a female figure seated, and nursing a little child," he notes. "She is dressed as a matron, with pallium and veil. Before her stands a youthful figure holding in his left hand a scroll, and pointing with the right to a star." But who is the standing figure and when was the fresco painted? Shahan proposes that it's the prophet Isaiah and that it alludes to a passage in the Hebrew Bible: "Behold a young woman shall conceive and bear a son, and shall call his name Emmanuel." Some scholars have agreed with Shahan on that point, while most now identify the figure as the Prophet Balaam and point to a passage from Numbers: "a star shall come forth out of Jacob, and a scepter shall rise out of Israel." Either way, the crucial issues for Shahan and his Protestant critics were, first, whether the fresco represented Mary (and most would agree with him "that we are before a painting of the Virgin Mother and the Divine Infant"), and second, how early those images were. On the second crucial point, Shahan concludes that "it is certainly not later than about the middle of the second century," and most scholars today would agree that he only slightly misjudged its antiquity, since the fresco seems to have been created sometime in the third century. Whatever its exact date, Shahan and the scholars he relied on gained ground in the conflict by calling attention to the catacombs: since the material evidence we have about early Christian burial chambers in Rome portray the Madonna and Child, whatever artists actually intended in those images, Marian devotion in some form predated the Council of Ephesus in 431 and, as the Shrine's director claimed, extends back to the first centuries of Christianity.[39]

Moving in Time and Space: The Crypt Church as Roman Catacomb

In his historical study of the catacombs and in his book *The Beginnings of Christianity*, Shahan tried to verbally re-create devotional life during those first Christian centuries, especially early devotion to Mary, but he also expressed his own historical conclusions and theological convictions materially in the architecture of the Crypt Church. In his writings before he sought papal approval for the project, Shahan had suggested that ecclesiastical architecture served two main functions—liturgical and didactic—but, as the interpretations published in *Salve Regina* and other periodicals between 1919 and 1926 reveal, the founder also came to see that it could serve another purpose: architecture, including the Washington Shrine, might have apologetic uses, too. That subterranean church served all three functions, including an apologetic mission. It did so through the names for the lower church and its altar, the relations of the space with other spaces, and the appearance of the interior. Just as the appearance of the interior did, the labels that designers and promoters used—calling the space a "crypt" officially dedicated to "Our Lady of the Catacombs"—evoked Rome's underground burial chambers and other ancient Christian spaces. Most important, the Crypt Church fulfilled its apologetic function, I suggest, in that the experiential impact of the space and the "pictorial theology" of its ornamentation transported visitors to the time and space of the earliest Christian communities, thereby reaffirming Mary's place in the ancient church.[40]

So, for Shahan, ecclesiastical art and architecture could serve a liturgical, didactic, and apologetic function. First, all churches, Shahan suggested more than a decade before he proposed the Shrine, need "a large free space where all could see one another, where all could hear, where access was easy to the Eucharistic table or altar, around which the ministers of the banquet could serve...the celestial food." The basics of ecclesiastical design, Shahan believed, were determined by the sacramental function of the space, and that design and use dated back to the earliest Christian communities. "In other words," Shahan wrote, "the doctrine of the Blessed Sacrament, or the Real Presence...created all the essentials of a Christian church, such as they are found in the catacombs and such as they will exist as long as the religion itself." Those spatial requirements were met, he noted, in each succeeding period in the history of Christian architecture: the "upper room" in a Christian home, the "little chamber of some cemetery where some martyr lay," the "over-ground chapel with its triple apse," the imposing Romanesque basilica, and the majestic Gothic cathedral. And in all those worship spaces, Shahan proposed in another early essay, the "teaching-function" of churches also "has conditioned their architecture." The Church informs the laity of the truths of the faith both from the pulpit and in the vivid "pictorial" language of the building's decoration.[41]

That didactic function overlaps with the third function of religious buildings, the apologetic one, since visual instruction can be directed both to
those already within the fold and to those outside it. From the time the
planners announced the composite Romanesque-Byzantine design in 1920
until workers completed the Crypt Church in 1926, stories in *Salve Regina*
and in daily papers, which mostly repeated information provided by
McKenna and Shahan, noted that apologetic function. One account in the
Shrine's periodical proposed that the lower church would be a "fearless
assertion" of devotion to Mary, and apparently that assertion was directed
both to Catholics, at least to those who needed reassurance about the
authenticity of Marian devotion, and to Protestants, who continued to
challenge Catholic piety. In 1925, just a year before laborers and artists
completed most of the work on the lower church, a headline in *Salve Regina*
announced "Early Church History in Shrine Decorations." The article
pointed out that the adornment of the interior recalled "the early Christians
in the catacombs of Rome" and that the architectural decoration "hoped to
popularize in the new world the labors of the great Catholic scholars of
Rome, such as De Rossi and Wilpert." That view of the building's function
did not emerge only as an afterthought. As early as August 1920, a month
before the foundation stone ceremony and more than two years before
workers poured the first concrete, Shahan already was conveying to devotees the message that the space would not only serve its liturgical functions
and teaching functions but would defend Mary and fortify Catholicism. His
piece in *Salve Regina* of that date, "The Crypt of the National Shrine," noted
that the architecture would combine features of the earliest architectural
styles. "Its high altar will be dedicated to [Mary] under the title of Our Lady
of the Catacombs, and will reproduce striking features of the religious art
of the Catacombs that were often carried over into the Early Romanesque."
Noting that "the earliest and most attractive frescoes of the Catacombs"
represented the Madonna and Child, Shahan proposed that no one could
argue any more with Catholic belief and practice, since those images "witness to the apostolic origin" of Marian devotion and "other elements of
Catholic teaching."[42]

The Impact of the Space

So the building itself "witnessed" to Shahan's convictions, and it did that,
first, by the immediate visual impact of the interior space. The Crypt
Church, which takes up only part of the Shrine's lower level basement, lies
beneath the sanctuary and chancel of the Great Upper Church, supporting

the weight of the Baldachin altar and canopy above. But the Crypt is much shorter in length and lower in height than the massive worship space it supports. The Great Upper Church's interior has, to apply one scholar's terms, a "classic sacramental design." Unlike the "classic evangelical design" favored by many Protestants, with its "auditorium space" for proclamation, its low "symbolic resonance," and its focus on the pulpit where the minister preaches the gospel, the Shrine's upper level has high symbolic resonance, a longitudinal space for procession, and a visual focus on the sacrificial altar where the priest summons the "real presence" in the consecrated host. The immediate impact of the Great Upper Church's long nave (399 feet) and tall dome (159 feet) creates "a dramatic setting for the interplay of transcendence and immanence," as in other sacramental churches. In contrast, the Crypt Church's more intimate surroundings (200 feet long and 23 feet high) emphasize the closeness of the divine, just as the earliest Christian devotional spaces did (fig. 4.5). Those early spaces served their liturgical function, Shahan suggested, by providing an altar for "the celestial food," as well as a sense that "the God of the Christians was no longer far away."[43]

It's the immanence of the sacred that strikes the viewer on first entering the squat Crypt Church, but that liturgical space also serves an apologetic function by evoking parallels with the earliest Christian styles.

Figure 4.5. The Crypt Church.

As you enter, you first might notice the low ceilings and the descending curves of the heavy groin vault, which give the sense of being in a subterranean chamber. If you look up, you see the two domes, each spanning 65 feet. Visually tracing the descending lines, you notice that each dome is made of four rounded Roman arches supported by four ten-ton granite columns. As you look even more closely, you notice the multilayered timbrel vaulting created by Rafael Guastavino, Sr., a Spanish-born architect; the earth tones of those tiles evoke the walls and ceilings of the catacombs, just as the domes and arches recall earlier Roman structures and later Romanesque styles. As your eye travels down the nave, you encounter a freestanding marble altar, the liturgical and visual focus, and your eye comes to rest on three apses arrayed in the space behind it, as in the fifth-century Santa Maria Maggiore in Rome, whose planners' retrospective gaze also had tried to "recapture the architectural style of first- and early-second-century Rome." Each apse, in turn, contains five chapels, and the reredos of those fifteen apsidal chapels each contains a mosaic. Above each chapel is a six- by four-foot stained glass lunette window that allows in a subdued glow of light and color. Visitors who know art historical labels might notice that several periods and styles are evoked in the Crypt Church's architecture, including Romanesque and Byzantine, but the immediate visual impact of the low ceilings, earth-toned tiles, groin vault, and subdued lighting is to re-create the experience of being in a small, dark space. That, of course, is exactly what Shahan and the planners wanted. They wanted to transport visitors to the narrow subterranean burial chambers of Rome.[44]

The Function of the Ornamentation

The ornamentation of the space also transports viewers to the earliest Christian communities in Rome. One *Salve Regina* article about the Crypt Church informed Marian devotees that the overall design "will be Early Romanesque and will embody many distinctive features of that style, by far the oldest of the purely Christian styles" but the images and symbols that decorate that interior "will reproduce . . . the religious art of the Catacombs that were often carried over into the Early Romanesque." Those "catacombal" images and symbols constituted what Shahan and McKenna called the Crypt Church's "pictorial theology," its vivid visual articulations of cherished doctrines about Mary and the Church. That pictorial theology was inscribed in the iconographical scheme found in the apsidal chapel mosaics and windows and on the ceiling tiles and medallions.[45]

All those decorative elements work together in the plan, which offers a theology of salvation history: the symbolism moves counterclockwise from the west apse, associated with "Prophecy," to the north apse, associated with "Promise," and finally to the east apse, associated with "Fulfillment." At first glance, it might seem that such symbolism could be found in any Christian church, Protestant or Catholic, but two recurring emphases in the interior ornamentation mark the scheme as distinctively Catholic and "assertively" apologetic: the centrality of Mary in the history of redemption and the importance of the first centuries of Christian history.[46]

Those points are alluded to in the fifteen lunette windows created by Charles J. Connick (1875–1945), the Boston-based stained glass artist who also made windows for Ralph Adams Cram and other prominent architects. Connick, who believed that stained glass design should harmonize with the surrounding architecture, knew that Catholic tradition taught that Mary, not just Jesus, was foreshadowed in prophecy. The five windows of the west apse reflect that view by portraying prophets (e.g., Moses) and disciples (e.g., John the Baptist) associated with Mary's role and Jesus' birth. So Mary, like Jesus, played her role—as immaculate vessel for the divine—in realizing the promise of salvation history, and that doctrinal point is made manifest in the north apse windows, which show evangelists, apostles, and disciples. Jesus gifted his followers with the divine spirit to guide the ongoing church, but Mary also was figuratively linked with that church by subsequent theologians and therefore was associated with the postresurrection community and the history of her son's church. In turn, the east apse lunette windows depict early church leaders and martyrs.[47]

Martyrs and the first centuries of Christian history also figure prominently in the apsidal mosaics created by Bancel La Farge (1865–1938), the Catholic artist who also designed the main dome mosaic in the Chapel at Washington's Trinity College, and whose brother was an influential Jesuit magazine editor and social activist. The *Washington Post's* art critic called La Farge's mosaics for the Crypt's apsidal altars "among the finest things in ecclesiastical art in America." She praised the way the mosaics "glow with subdued colors." "The background is a dull gold with the figures, Byzantine style, in rich deep colors." The reds, greens, and yellows of the figures stand out, though not too much, against the iconic gold surfaces, and mesh with the earth tones of the Crypt Church's interior. The warm hues add visual interest to the dim recessed altars but without detracting from the immediate impact of the intimate space, and the figures portrayed on the mosaics reinforce the historical claim enacted in the lower church's ornamentation. The north apse's central altar, the Chapel of the Good Shepherd, which displays the Tiffany tabernacle holding the consecrated host, not only serves a liturgical function by securing the Real Presence but also serves an apologetic function by re-creating the art of the Catacomb of Priscilla and the other underground cemeteries as it displays the representation of Jesus that predominated in the early frescoes (see fig. 4.1). In a similar way, the mosaics of the chapels in the west and east apses also explicitly recall the first centuries of Christian history and the subterranean cemeteries where martyrs were entombed: they picture female saints, both cradle Christians and pagan converts, who gave their life for the faith. The mosaics in the east apse include representations of St. Susanna of Rome, the martyr venerated in the chapel donated by Susanna Fay, and St. Lucy, a martyr celebrated by the tradition for aiding the poor during the Diocletianic persecution. The chapels of the west apse memorialize other female martyrs, including two early saints, Felicity and Perpetua, whose *Passion* remains "the oldest surviving Christian material one may attribute to a definite historical woman."[48]

A Protestant "Mary" for the Sectarian Battle: "Catacombal" Ceramics

It was a very different "historical woman," a Protestant artist from the Midwest, who created the tiles and medallions that completed the Crypt Church's interior decoration and most effectively transported viewers to the first centuries, thereby "assertively" defending Marian devotion as authentic and ancient. As that ceramic artist, Mary Chase Stratton (1867–1961), recalled in her unpublished autobiography, Charles Maginnis and Bernard McKenna visited her Michigan home to propose that she use her celebrated "Pewabic" ceramics, with their iridescent glazes, to decorate the Crypt Church. She followed up by visiting Shahan in Washington. At that meeting, Stratton recalled, "it was decided... that the decorative manner should be that of the beginning of the Christian Church, meaning the first four hundred years as demonstrated in the catacombs of Rome." Stratton might have seemed like an odd choice for that apologetic task, since she was a Congregationalist and, as assistant architect Fred Murphy put it, "altogether unfamiliar with Christian signs and symbols." That was why, Murphy proposed, "Bishop Shahan was the chief source of inspiration" for the ceramic decoration. Yet Stratton embraced the challenge, even though she'd worshiped weekly at the Congregationalist Church, attended Sunday School, and, like many other American Protestants, attended a revival at which the preacher exhorted her to evangelize. "One year there was a good deal of religious fervor," Stratton recalled, "the kind of experience that came to be known as 'a revival.'" The revivalist asked everyone to bring one new member to the church next time, so Stratton approached an older man she knew. When he protested "they wouldn't have me because I am a Methodist," the young girl responded by asking "couldn't you be a Methodist and join the Congregationalists too?" She asked because she'd been clandestinely visiting the Methodist Church across the street: "once in a while I slipped over there for an afternoon service." That sort of ecumenical impulse was reinforced by other childhood experiences—both her own pastor and the town's Catholic priest regularly dined with them—and that inclusive inclination intensified and endured in adulthood, as she maintained her Protestant affiliation but befriended Charles Freer and other Americans who had become enamored with Buddhism.[49]

So perhaps it's not surprising—though it's delightfully ironic—that the ecumenical Stratton, who felt "almost speechless awe" for the "wise and tactful" Shahan, and who had affection for "the kindly sisters" who served them during their lunches in Washington, eagerly tried to carry out Shahan's apologetic aims for the Crypt's decoration. She went to great lengths to prepare herself for the task. She read scholarly works on the archeology of the catacombs suggested by Shahan, and she even visited the Roman catacombs. "That I might be personally conversant with these earliest records of Christian embellishment, and gain a spirit of them at first hand, my husband and I decided to go abroad," reported Stratton years later. As she descended into the catacombs, she found herself coming up with ideas for the Crypt Church's ceramic scheme, but the impact also was emotional: "Marked upon the soft surface were inscriptions full of passionate meaning. At various points, the gentle Shepherd with the lamb upon his shoulders was tenderly expressed. Most of all, the catacombal representation of the Blessed Lady as a wide-eyed Virgin, with the earliest conception of the Holy Child upon her lap, was to me very affecting." By the end of that 1926 visit, Stratton had come to understand, and endorse, Shahan's vision, which combined a concern to defend Marian devotion and a desire to foreground Catholic women. As Stratton tells it, "It was the intention and endeavor both in the design and execution of the decoration to retain the archaic quality of the early Christian era. The entire Shrine ideal . . . is one of devotion to the Virgin Mary, and as far as possible the women in scripture are used as themes for decoration, especially stressing the Marys." Both Stratton and Shahan were aware of the irony that it was a Protestant who was commissioned with that task, but both seemed to relish the cross-denominational collaboration: "Once when Bishop Shahan remarked kindly that it was fortuitous they had found a 'Mary' to help in the project, I at once replied from the bottom of my heart, that the marvelous part was the opportunity it gave me to make my ceramic dreams come true."[50]

Once prepared by the lunch conversations with Shahan, her reading in Catholic archeology, and most of all her "affecting" visit to the catacombs, that Protestant Mary felt ready to realize those artistic "dreams": she was ready "to promulgate [the design] in a similar manner an ocean away on another continent." And even if Shahan had shaped the overall scheme, Stratton contributed to the design, too. Accepting the previously established stylistic themes, she added her own interpretation of the "decorative whole of prophesies, promises, and fulfillments, with motives and characters falling into their parts like a proven drama." So "on the train...to Washington to confer with the Bishop, I was able to make a diagram, expressing what was in my mind." Stratton was hesitant to relay her ideas but "secretly" hoped she had become "sufficiently informed" to understand, and creatively implement, Shahan's vision. "It was perhaps one of the proudest moments of my life," she recalled decades later, "when the kindly and most scholarly of men approved" the plan she had sketched on the train.[51]

The decorative plan Shahan inspired and approved took almost seven years to complete, from 1924 to 1931, and included millions of tiles fired using the glowing glazes Stratton had invented. She and the craftsmen she employed made ceramic roundels, panels, and friezes, as well as forty-two ceiling medallions that embellished the Crypt Church along the nave, at the interception of each arch, and around the triple apses. When she began working, the mosaics and lunettes were in place, and so were the earthtone ceiling tiles. Her aesthetic task, as she understood it, was to "enliven some subdued areas." Stratton did that, for example, by installing over two hundred feet of rippling gold and blue ceramic tiles over the lunette windows of each of the fifteen apsidal chapels.[52]

Stratton also took her other tasks seriously, and the prescribed didactic and apologetic aims converged. Shahan had told her again and again that her ceramic embellishments should be a "pictorial theology" that was "legible even to the point of being literary." So she designed and implemented a "legible" decorative plan, complete with twelve scriptural passages, that fit with the overall themes of prophecy, promise, and fulfillment, for example by including ceramic images that figuratively embedded Mary within the long history of salvation, as in the west apse's title medallions that memorialize ancient "types" of Mary—Miriam, Deborah, and Ruth. Most striking, at least to observers who know about Shahan's apologetic aims and Stratton's "affecting" experience in the catacombs, is how many clay symbols and images in the Crypt Church recreate those preserved in Rome's subterranean burial chambers, especially the Catacomb of Priscilla. Stratton created many small tiles, which repeat on different surfaces, and incorporate symbols found in those ancient funerary spaces, including the Chi-Rho symbol, a Greek monogram for Christ, and the peacock, an ancient emblem of immortality. The ceramic medallions of the apses even more explicitly evoke subterranean Rome. Three tiles in the east apse, for example, mirror scenes from the *Virgo Sacra* of Priscilla and represent a virgin consecrated to God, Christ crowning martyrs, and Christ and the saints. A tile panel in the west apse, to offer another example, is adapted from the fresco of the Madonna and Child with the Prophet, which also adorns a wall in the Catacomb of Priscilla. To make the associations with ancient subterranean Rome even more transparent, a tile medallion in the north apse shows Mary with her son, and three lower tiles there depict the Adoration of the Magi, the banquet scene, and the Good Shepherd, each image recalling frescoes from the Catacomb of Priscilla.[53]

CONCLUSION

Like the other symbolic ornamentation in the Crypt Church, and as with the sensual impact of the dark intimate space, those ceramic embellishments visibly manifested clerical desires. Shahan and those who stood with him in the interdenominational conflict—including Maginnis, Gibbons, McKenna, Conway, and Russell—could welcome the Crypt Church's architecture as a satisfying visual rejoinder to Protestant arguments. There in clay, glass, and stone they found a material defense against Protestant attacks. Shahan also managed to recruit Stratton, that midwestern Protestant "Mary," to serve on Catholicism's side in the struggle for the authenticity and antiquity of Marian devotion, but that meant that Stratton, as the creator of the Crypt Church's ceramic ornamentation, also had a visible presence in that subterranean space, which in its immediate impact and its architectural ornamentation simultaneously performed aesthetic, liturgical, didactic, and apologetic functions. Other Protestants had a presence in the lower church, too, as I've tried to suggest, including the converts who visited and contributed and those who, like Susanna Fay, retained their affiliation but expressed some sympathy with Marian devotion. To the extent that Shahan and those he mobilized for the cause remained worried about anti-Catholicism, they unintentionally also ensured that their Protestant opponents, like the racist Evans and the combative McKim, continued to have an immaterial presence there, too. Although no Catholics admitted to sensing their presence, those Protestants continued to haunt that dim underground chamber. Unable to escape their fate as perpetual combatants in interfaith conflict, even in death, Evans and McKim still lurk in the Crypt Church's shadows as the incorporeal Other against which Catholics defined themselves and in relation to whom they practiced their faith, including their beloved but embattled devotion to the Virgin Mary.[54]

5

⌒ᜎᜓ⌒

Claiming Civic Space

The National Shrine, the Subjunctive Mood,

and the Nation's Capital, 1913–1959

D espite the hostility they sometimes encountered from Protestants in the public arena, the clergy—and some lay elites—had hopes for American Catholicism and for the enormous Shrine they were building in the nation's capital. It's not that most rank-and-file lay devotees dissented. They didn't. They just had other things on their mind as they spent their days in domestic spaces and neighborhood streets. Many lay donors and pilgrims focused on making ends meet and caring for relatives, and they worked out much of their religious life in the private spaces of the home, reciting the rosary in the living room, saying night prayers in the bedroom, and whispering requests to Mary in the kitchen. Remember the widower who had sole responsibility for his son and mailed a donation from his modest house to seek Mary's protection because "the work that I do down at the Steel Plant is awful dangerous," and the mother who'd buried a husband and three children and "said the beads every night" with her five surviving sons and daughters in their living room. Like them, most of the faithful who visited and supported the Shrine didn't dare to imagine exerting influence beyond the home and the parish. Some, like Mary Downs, found that a small private act unexpectedly yielded big public consequences; but most lay devotees couldn't hope to do more than that devout mother who told the Shrine's director she sent her "little trifle" to support the clergy's "grand work."[1]

MARY IMMACULATE PATRONESS OF THE UNITED STATES

Figure 5.1. Raphael Pfisterer, OSB, *Mary Immaculate, Patroness of the United States*, ca. 1920, program illustration, 15.5 × 10.5 inches. Program booklet for the Shrine's foundation stone ceremony on September 23, 1920.

And in the years between the Shrine's approval and dedication, the clergy believed there was "grand work" to do. At the Shrine and beyond its threshold, the clergy hoped their efforts would secure Catholicism's public presence. Ecclesiastical leaders not only hoped to contest Protestant interpretations of their faith, but—in a related effort—they also tried to claim civic space (see fig. 5.1). They did so by working locally, regionally, and nationally to assert influence on American politics, culture, society, and economy. A few who ventured into the public arena had direct or indirect links with the Shrine. More important, in this chapter—which focuses on the building's geographical location, exterior design, and cultural function—I argue that its clerical promoters helped to create the American tradition of making religious claims on civic space in the nation's capital, an important but overlooked pattern of public religious practice in the United States. Like the leaders of Protestant, Eastern Orthodox, and Jewish groups, Roman Catholic advocates increasingly focused their attention on Washington, where they asserted their presence through rituals (vigils, processions, pilgrimages, and parades) and architecture (war memorials, the Vatican's embassy, churches, and shrines).[2]

Those efforts to claim civic space in the nation's capital changed over time. That impulse intensified when Congress approved a new (Episcopalian) National Cathedral in 1893. By the 1920s, Washington journalists were commenting on the emerging pattern: the national capital, the press suggested, was becoming "the spiritual capital," and religious competition for civic presence in the District of Columbia continued in the decades ahead. Catholic confidence surged and Protestant hostility declined during both world wars, when Catholics did more than their patriotic share and some Catholic efforts to exert influence and claim presence proved successful. Before 1959, however, Catholics' performative and monumental assertions on civic space in Washington still expressed a wish more than they reported a fact: *if only Catholics were to have a civic presence*. To use grammatical terms, as the British Catholic John Henry Newman did in his *Essay in Aid of a Grammar of Assent*, a study of the "different modes of holding propositions," we can identify a grammar of assertion, distinguishing the different modes of claiming space. Applying the classificatory terms of that invented "grammar," I suggest that during the era of consolidation, U.S. Catholics' public assertions in gesture and stone were expressed in the subjunctive mood rather than the indicative mood. As the dictionary notes, the subjunctive refers to "an action or state as conceived (and not as a fact)" and therefore "expresses a wish, command, exhortation, or a contingent, hypothetical, or prospective event." Catholic leaders were not sure their "wishful" and "prospective" claims on public space would succeed, although to some extent the very act of public assertion created the imagined social reality and, as sociologists might put it, generated "civic social capital." Despite their best efforts, however, American Catholic leaders failed in their attempt to position the Shrine as the nation's central site for civic celebrations: The Washington National Cathedral—or, more formally, the Episcopalian Cathedral Church of St. Peter and St. Paul—won that interdenominational competition. Yet after 1959, Catholic claims on civic space and national memory seemed less like hopeful expressions of desire. Those assertions shifted from the subjunctive to the indicative mood as Roman Catholic influence in American cultural life became more of a reality with the decades' passing. And, as I suggest in this chapter, Catholic monumental architecture, including the Shrine's large polychromatic dome and imposing bell tower, confidently announced its presence in the nation's capital, just as the west transept's "Patroness Windows" and the East Wall's sculpture positioned Mary and her American devotees at the center of U.S. history.[3]

ASSERTING PUBLIC INFLUENCE

Roman Catholics managed to exert some influence on American life during the years the Shrine was planned and constructed. The BNSIC's directors— from McKenna to Grady—didn't initiate that influence, of course, since it was a devotional center without official ties to organizations that ventured into the public sphere. So the connections are mostly indirect. Still, many of the individuals and organizations that shaped the wider culture crossed its threshold, including clerical promoters who led fundraising efforts and presided at major ceremonial occasions as well as lay devotees who sent their contributions or came to worship. Some of those devotees from the era of consolidation even have had an enduring presence there, since they are memorialized in the Shrine's material culture.

Politics and Media: Political Savvy, Wartime Patriotism, and Cultural Vigilance

Catholics exerted influence, first, in electoral politics. The long-term effects of transnational migration and high birth rates afforded Catholics an increasing demographic presence in the United States: they constituted about 13 percent of the U.S. population in 1900, 15 percent by 1913, and 22 percent by 1959. Catholic candidates for elected office, especially in northeastern and midwestern urban areas, took advantage of that. Already by the 1890s, many major U.S. cities had a Catholic mayor or a large proportion of Catholic city council members. Catholics also sought national office, including the presidency, as early as 1872, when Charles O'Connor made the first failed attempt. Governor Al Smith, who visited the Shrine and signed the visitors' log, won the democratic nomination for president in 1928, though it would not be until 1960 that a Roman Catholic would occupy the most prominent site in Washington's civic space, the White House. Before and after John F. Kennedy's election, however, U.S. Catholic leaders, including those linked with the Shrine, had contact with presidents. Cardinal Gibbons was the most well-connected Catholic of his generation. He rubbed elbows with the nation's leaders at many civic and religious events, standing on the podium with President McKinley at the 1899 celebration of Admiral George Dewey's return to Washington, greeting President Wilson at the 1913 Pan American Thanksgiving Mass, and sitting at the right hand of President Taft in 1909 (see fig. 5.2). New York's Francis Cardinal Spellman, who dedicated the Shrine in 1959 and is pictured in an east apse mosaic, was probably the most politically connected episcopal leader of the next generation, and he, too, conversed with presidents. For example, President Johnson, who had visited the Shrine five months earlier to attend his daughter Luci's highly publicized wedding, phoned Spellman in January 1967 to invite him to the White House and discuss the cardinal's recent trip to Vietnam.[4]

As the audiotape of that recorded telephone conversation indicates, the former military vicar for the Armed Forces during World War II responded by telling Johnson that he was "doing a great job" in Vietnam, thereby continuing a tradition of American Catholic leaders fervently supporting patriotic causes, both armed conflicts and ideological battles. This, too, gained them some public influence. Starting in 1917, the bishops' National

Figure 5.2. President Taft *(center)* flanked on his right by James Cardinal Gibbons at the Catholic Summer School of America, Cliff Haven, New York, in 1909.

Catholic War Council effectively coordinated efforts to support the cause at home and abroad, and in 1920 the Shrine's founder, Bishop Shahan, and his superior, Cardinal Gibbons, championed patriotism as they consecrated the new devotional site "in memory of our soldiers and sailors." American Catholics volunteered for duty in World War II, and the U.S. hierarchy again supported that war effort, even if some prelates with Germans in their dioceses felt the need to emphasize the patriotism of all the faithful. For example, John T. McNicholas, who had delivered the sermon at the Shrine's foundation stone ceremony in 1920, was unwavering in his support of World War II, though in a 1942 address he reminded his fellow citizens that German-American Catholics "are not pro-Nazi; they are not even pro-German; they are American and pro-America." In that year, McNicholas and other American bishops associated with the National Catholic Welfare Conference, the Washington-based organization formed in 1919 to continue and expand the bishops' activities, also reaffirmed their patriotic support for World War II: "We ask our people to be united and prepared to make every sacrifice which our government deems necessary for a just and enduring peace through the victory of our armed forces." Typical of the Church's stance during the first six decades of the century, that pastoral letter also condemned "totalitarianism," just as Bishop McNicholas, who repeated the language of Pius XI's 1937 encyclical on the subject, had decried "atheistic communism" in his 1942 address. Other American Catholics did the same in the years ahead, including politicians like Wisconsin's Senator Joseph R. McCarthy, lay intellectuals like William F. Buckley, Jr., and prominent clerics like Cardinal Spellman (fig. 5.3), whose anticommunist fervor remained unmatched and, as his phone conversation with Johnson indicated, continued through the Vietnam era.[5]

Just as Jewish participation in the U.S. military eased hostility and aided acculturation, Catholics' patriotic participation in military campaigns and impassioned support for the ideological battle against communism had other effects, intended and unintended: those efforts challenged long-standing Protestant perceptions about the incompatibility of Roman Catholicism and American democracy, perceptions that sometimes had blocked Catholicism's entrance into civic space. Those Protestant concerns about church-state issues had arisen in the controversy about the papal contribution to the Washington Monument and again in the debate about the Pan American Thanksgiving Mass. In both incidents, Catholic advocates expressed a triumphalist Americanism. Father Russell of Washington's St. Patrick Church emphasized the U.S. Catholic Church's affirmation of religious liberty and representative democracy, just as Gibbons, the Shrine's great supporter, championed "civil and religious liberty" and proposed that

Figure 5.3. Francis J. Spellman, then Military Vicar for the U.S. Armed Forces, posing with Corporal George T. Robinson and other U.S. airmen at a base in Tunisia in 1943.

Catholics originated the idea. In the 1920 foundation stone ceremony program, Shahan praised "the glorious religious liberty of our land," and Archbishop Ritter's sermon at the 1959 dedication interpreted the Shrine as "the expression of the Catholic democracy of the United States." Like Al Smith before him, on the eve of the 1960 election John F. Kennedy explained to a ministerial association: "I believe in an America where the separation of church and state is absolute."[6]

The American who had the most influence on Catholic thinking about church-state relations before and after that election, the "liberal" Jesuit theologian John Courtney Murray (1904–1967) had a material presence at the BNSIC, even though he was "banned" from speaking on CUA's campus in 1963. Because of his influential role in formulating the Second Ecumenical Vatican Council's "Declaration on Religious Freedom," however, he was represented (across from Spellman) on a mosaic in the Great Upper Church's east apse. Like the overwhelming majority of U.S. Catholic leaders between 1945 and 1965, Murray also affirmed the Church's anti-communist position. Some midcentury Protestant critics, like Paul Blanshard, repeated the old accusations and added new ones—that communism and Catholicism had "deadly parallels"—but Catholics' ideological opposition to communism, along with their wartime patriotism, probably did as much to ease Protestant fears and clear a pathway into civic space as all the Catholic apologetic books, sermons, and editorials had done in the preceding century.[7]

Another twentieth-century American Catholic who passionately condemned communism, Fulton J. Sheen, had a presence at the Shrine. He attended the 1920 foundation ceremony and the 1959 dedication celebration—and even broadcast a nationwide television appeal from the Crypt Church in 1953. Sheen's professional accomplishments point to another area of American life, the media, in which Catholics did more than hold their own. They exerted influence by taking advantage of emerging communication technologies and vigilantly assessing the new media's moral value.[8]

They embraced radio and television. A capacity crowd that included congressmen and diplomats filled the Crypt Church on February 12, 1931, to hear Pope Pius XI's broadcast initiating the Vatican's new radio station, and during the 1930s Catholics in Washington could listen regularly to local and national Catholic programs. On Sundays in 1932, for example, radio listeners in the capital could encounter much of America's religious diversity, though African Americans were underrepresented. On December 4 of that year, for example, Washingtonians could hear a Sephardic Jewish rabbi, the Mormon Tabernacle Choir, the Jehovah's Witnesses *Watchtower Service*, and a variety of services and sermons by white mainline Protestant ministers, including Episcopalians broadcasting from the Shrine's greatest rival, the National Cathedral. Catholics in the capital could plant themselves by their radios for three consecutive hours every Sunday. They could listen to Father Charles Coughlin's national broadcast at four o'clock and the local Washington *Catholic Hour* at five, both on ABC, and then at six they could turn to NBC to hear Sheen on *The Catholic Hour*. No American Catholic took advantage of new media, radio, and television more effectively than Sheen, whom Protestant evangelist Billy Graham called "one of the greatest preachers of our century." That popular CUA professor was also probably the most famous priest of his day because of those radio broadcasts, which aired for more than two decades. Sheen's fame only increased when he began his television program *Life Is Worth Living* in 1952. That Tuesday night series included episodes about personal well-being ("You Are Not as Odd as You Think"), social issues ("Teenagers"), and political concerns ("Communism and Russia"). The combination proved successful. Sheen's program ran for five seasons, enjoying more than 5.7 million viewers and becoming "the most widely viewed religious series in TV history." The year after that series ended, 1958, Pope Pius XII declared St. Claire of Assisi the heavenly patron of television. Yet if the Vatican had broadened the criteria for sainthood to include miraculous interventions in emerging media, Sheen might have been on his way to canonization, and America might have had its own native-born patron saint of radio and television.[9]

Movies grew in popularity during the 1920s and 1930s, and Catholics proved influential in that medium, too, though it was their attempts to evaluate film's moral content that afforded them the most cultural clout. Those efforts at moral vigilance—what came to be praised or criticized as "censorship"—had indirect connections to the BNSIC. McNicholas, who had helped celebrate the laying of the foundation stone, was the first leader of the Legion of Decency, the national organization founded in 1934 because, as *Time* put it, "the U.S. Churches have deplored what they call the brazen indecency of U.S. cinema." As *Time* went on to note, the Catholic organization was "embarked on a new crusade, brandishing a new weapon—the boycott." The Legion, which enjoyed high visibility into the 1960s, was still recognized in a 1965 *Time* article as "the only organization of consequence in the U.S. that makes an effective judgment on what is morally in or out of bounds." Screeners for the Legion offered those judgments using four categories—ranging from A1, morally unobjectionable for all, to C, condemned—and those ratings prodded studios and constrained directors. Many Americans, and not only Catholics, took note of the Church's evaluations, including those offered by bishops who spoke at the 1959 dedication ceremonies; earlier, in 1954, Cardinal Ritter denounced *The French Line* and two years later Cardinal Spellman condemned *Baby Doll*.[10]

Other episcopal leaders associated with the Shrine supported the moral scrutiny of popular culture, including Bishop Noll, who created the National Organization for Decent Literature in 1938; it was, however, lay Catholic donors and pilgrims who took the lead in such efforts and continued to be involved after the Legion's founding. The IFCA, which raised funds for the Mary Memorial Altar, had been scrutinizing the new entertainment medium since 1922, eight years before the Motion Picture Producers and Distributors of America devised their Production Code and a dozen years before the Legion began its work. Rita McGoldrick, who also sent a donation for the Mary Altar, chaired the IFCA's Motion Picture Bureau; she and her staff were previewing movies for Hollywood and passing on their evaluations to the industry's president, William Harrison Hays, during the 1920s, when cinema was new and standards were being set. By 1928, "the IFCA was becoming a force in motion pictures." That year they sent out more than two hundred thousand pieces of film literature to more than five thousand groups. The IFCA's movie list appeared in two large city newspapers, and McGoldrick's weekly broadcast of film recommendations could be heard on radio stations in major cities, including New York, St. Louis, and New Orleans. In this way, too, as guardians of popular media, Catholics who had some presence at the Shrine influenced American life.[11]

Society and Economy: Social Service, The New Deal, and the Catholic Worker Movement

On the Waterfront (1954), a film the major studio executives had rejected as too politically controversial, portrayed a socially concerned Catholic priest and probed the problems of the urban working class. By that time, Catholics had been expending a good deal of energy for decades trying to address the social and economic challenges that came with industrialization, immigration, and urbanization. Those reform efforts and remedial services had intensified during the late nineteenth century, although they usually were overseen by Catholics who labored for smaller mediating institutions, including religious orders and diocesan agencies. Starting in 1919, what came to be called the NCWC's Social Action Department tried to centralize social outreach; and, by issuing pamphlets on various topics (including "Unemployment," "Church and Labor," and "Outlines of a Social Service Program for Catholic Agencies"), the clergy tried to prompt and guide social action. By the time Shahan began fundraising for the Crypt Church, Catholics had established an enormous social services system, mostly staffed by women religious, and both the caretakers and the needy who interacted in that vast system also crossed the Shrine's threshold. For example, the orphans from nearby St. Vincent's Home, and the Sisters of Charity who nurtured them, visited regularly. Father McKenna remembered those nuns and the more than one hundred young visitors they brought as "the first pilgrims to the Shrine," since they had come in 1918 to the temporary Salve Regina Chapel, and in subsequent years they often made the short walk to the site, as when Sister Rosalia Malone and a group of communicants visited for First Communion in 1923, as construction was under way (fig. 5.4).[12]

Two of the most important Catholic voices for social and economic justice during the half century when the BNSIC was envisioned and completed were John Ryan and Dorothy Day; both had a presence at the Shrine, though Ryan, who taught at CUA, had opportunities for much more regular attendance. In an interesting coincidence, however, both Day and Ryan visited the Shrine on the feast day of the Immaculate Conception, December 8, only a year apart, and each of those visits to the dark Crypt Church marked milestones in their careers, which focused on shaping American social relations and economic life.

It was on December 8, 1932, that Day said a prayer at the Shrine that, as she remembered it, launched her career as a Catholic social activist. She had been visiting D.C. as a reporter for a Catholic periodical, covering the socialist-sponsored Hunger March, which aimed to secure, among other things, unemployment insurance and retirement pensions for workers. After she finished her work, Day turned her attention to spiritual matters. "When the

Figure 5.4. Father Bernard McKenna and the Sisters of Charity gather with children from the nearby orphanage, St. Vincent's, on May 1, 1923.

demonstration was over and I had finished writing my story, I went to the national shrine at the Catholic University on the Feast of the Immaculate Conception. There I offered up a special prayer which came with tears and with anguish, that some way would open up for me to use what talents I possessed for my fellow workers, for the poor." When she returned to New York she found "heaven's answer." A way "opened up" to help the poor when she met Peter Maurin, who would serve as her collaborator in the Catholic Worker Movement, which she founded in 1933. That movement would establish hospitality houses across the country, agitate against war, and promote economic justice.[13]

The same year Day founded the Catholic Worker Movement, Ryan ritually celebrated a major milestone in his own career in the Crypt Church on the feast day of the Immaculate Conception. Ryan had been honored with a new title—Right Reverend Monsignor—which was, the apostolic delegate's letter indicated, "a well-deserved recognition of your services to the Catholic University and in the fields of Economics and Social Action." So, as Ryan recalled, "on December 8, I was formally 'invested' by [the] Archbishop of Baltimore, with the robes appropriate to my new dignity. The ceremony took place in the National Shrine of the Immaculate Conception at the University." The guest list for the testimonial dinner that night in 1933, like the list of those who attended his seventieth birthday and retirement banquet in 1939, included the movers and shakers of Washington. By 1943, *Time* would honor Ryan with the title "Right Reverend New-Dealer," and President Franklin Roosevelt, who instituted the progressive programs of the New Deal and implemented many social reforms Ryan advocated, sent a congratulatory message that was read aloud at his retirement banquet: "With your voice and pen, you have pleaded the cause of social justice and the right of the individual to happiness through economic security, a living wage, and an opportunity to share in the things that enrich and ennoble human life." Ryan's pleading for social justice had found expression earlier in his drafting of "the Bishop's Program," as it came to be called. Perhaps the most widely influential of the NCWC's Social Action pamphlets, its official title was "Social Reconstruction: A General Review of the Problems and Survey of Remedies," and the Washington-based group circulated that pamphlet in 1919. The document, which presupposed that "the only safeguard of peace is social justice," signaled a Catholic attempt to make claims on—and change—American public life. It included twelve main proposals, among them "minimum wage legislation," "insurance against unemployment, sickness, invalidity, and old age," and "a sixteen-year minimum age limit for working children." As one historian has noted, the proposals "all have now been either wholly or partially translated into fact. Only one, the participation of labor in management and a wider distribution of leadership, has made little progress."[14]

So on December 8, one year apart, two of the most important Catholic voices for social change worshiped at Mary's shrine in Washington, one just starting her work and the other at the peak of his influence at home and abroad.

CLAIMING CIVIC SPACE AND NATIONAL MEMORY IN THE CAPITAL

Roman Catholics also asserted public influence by joining in the spirited competition to establish a presence in the nation's capital: they employed public ritual and built monumental architecture to claim civic space and national memory.

Rituals: Catholic Vigils, Processions, and Parades

Catholic rituals could be more or less visible to other Washingtonians. Some rites held inside Catholic ecclesiastical spaces took on a public character because they were announced in the local press or drew widespread attention by other means. The Pan American Thanksgiving Day Mass at St. Patrick's in 1913 became a public event, even though most of the ritual activity was confined to the church's interior. Eight years later, officials at the BNSIC used the media to try to make a ritual public, even national: a press release Bishop Shahan sent to the *New York Times* in 1921 announced that vigil lights would burn at the Shrine for five days as local Catholics sent "patriotic prayers for the guidance and support of President-elect Harding," and that story noted that the Shrine's founder had called on "all Catholics of the United States to participate in the acts of national devotion" by offering a prayer on Inauguration Day "that God will guide our Chief Executive wisely and well." The Shrine also was the site of a public ritual that even more directly and effectively linked civil servants and the Catholic faith when clergy celebrated the "Red Mass" each year from 1939 to 1952. Named for the red flame that symbolizes the guiding presence of the Holy Spirit, it was a spiritual gathering for legal professionals that marked the opening of Congress and the Supreme Court. The dean of CUA's law school initiated the tradition, which had precedent in Europe and the United States, and from the first mass in 1939 it drew legislators, diplomats, cabinet members, and judges. Supreme Court justice Pierce Butler, the son of Irish Catholic immigrants, came that year, and so did Protestants like the prominent Republican senator Henry Cabot Lodge, Jr., and the Democratic secretary of labor Frances Perkins, the first woman to serve in the cabinet. In 1952, the last year the clergy celebrated the rite there, dignitaries heard a countermodernist sermon that condemned "modern materialism," praised "the Age of Scholasticism," and exhorted the civil servants gathered inside the dark Crypt Church "to restore God's order to the intellectual, moral, and juridical world."[15]

Some rituals spilled out into the streets, even if the devout didn't venture too far from local churches. In 1913, almost two thousand Catholic children from four local parishes processed through the Washington streets for May Day celebrations honoring the Virgin Mary. For example, at Monsignor Russell's parish, St. Patrick's, twenty-five altar boys led six hundred children and youth. The procession included 110 first communicants, the boys wearing white ribbons on their arms and the girls decked out in white dresses and long white veils. Even younger girls, aged four to six, carrying bouquets of wildflowers, surrounded the communicants. Behind them were the older girls from the Children of Mary. At the end of the procession were the Queen of the May, nineteen-year-old Sunday School teacher Regina Fisher, with eighty "maids of honor." All of them marched the short distance down G Street and turned left on Tenth Street into the church, where they sang Marian hymns and crowned the parish's statue of the Virgin. At these May processions,

Catholics didn't venture far from their parishes, but they did in other public performances in the city. In the same year, 1913, congregants from three local parishes commemorated "the sixteenth centenary of freedom in Catholic countries" by participating in an elaborate linked ritual in which congregants prayed together in their own church at four o'clock and then moved on to the other two parishes in the northwest section of the city. So, for example, the fifteen-hundred men, women, and children from St. Patrick's "formed in line and marched to St. Mary's Church on Fifth Street," prayed briefly there, and then walked on to Immaculate Conception Church in what the local paper called "a public demonstration" to affirm religious liberty.[16]

Many more Catholics, from Washington and across the country, took to the streets of the capital in 1924 for another even more visible "public demonstration." President Coolidge stood with America's senior cardinal, the Vatican's delegate, and Bishop Shahan (the event's host) as he spoke to an estimated one hundred thousand Catholics who belonged to the Holy Name Society (fig. 5.5). Coolidge told the crowd that their Society was "performing both a pious and a patriotic service" and reassured them that "civil, political, and religious liberty is the essence of freedom" and "no religious test shall

Figure 5.5. With the Washington Monument in the background, President Calvin Coolidge (*center*) posed with clergy before addressing 100,000 Catholics who attended the Holy Name Society Parade on September 21, 1924.

ever be required" for public office. The crowd, witnesses reported, responded warmly: "triple cheers greeted the every reference by the President to religious freedom, devotion to God and loyalty to country." Earlier in the day the Catholic men assembled on the mall had paraded with banners raised. To the sound of the "blare of trumpets, the shrill lyricism of fifes, and the beating of bass drums," rows of men had marched down Pennsylvania Avenue and toward the grounds north of the Washington Monument, in a multisensorial public performance that one secular newspaper called "a spectacle rarely equaled for impressiveness and picturesqueness" and "perhaps the greatest religious gathering in the history of the United States."[17]

Architecture: "National" Churches in the Nation's Capital

Catholics also competed for civic presence in the capital by erecting monuments and buildings, and to make sense of this multireligious competition it's important to understand the cultural function of the capital in a nation with legally sanctioned separation of church and state. America's civil religion—that (always contested) piety connected with the political arena—has flourished since the 1790s at inaugural addresses, Memorial Day parades, and solemn political occasions. At the same time, the First Amendment's prohibition of a state church and protection of the "free exercise" of religion also has shaped religious life in the United States. Although some denominations (for example, Episcopalians, Congregationalists, and Unitarians) have wielded disproportionate cultural power, federal and state statutes announce the government's commitment to religious toleration. In this political and cultural context, America's faiths have been forced to compete with one another to negotiate power, assert identity, and secure visibility. And the capital's urban landscape has been an important site for these contests. In the United States, a nation with legally sanctioned religious diversity, the capital has taken on special significance. Especially since the early twentieth century, American religious groups have symbolically negotiated cultural power and denominational identity in Washington by constructing national religious centers there.[18]

The idea of constructing national churches in the U.S. capital arose more than two hundred years ago, and the promoters of one of D.C.'s most impressive sacred buildings have suggested that the venerable idea has been architecturally realized in the Episcopal Cathedral Church of St. Peter and Saint Paul, better known as the Washington National Cathedral (fig. 5.6). As the National Cathedral's tourist guidebook proudly declares, the idea of an ecumenical national church in the capital originated with the

Figure 5.6. The Washington National Cathedral or—its official name—Cathedral of St. Peter and St. Paul, 1906–1990.

city's chief designer, French-born architect and civil engineer Pierre Charles L'Enfant. His 1791 plans for Washington called for a church "for national purposes, such as public prayer, thanksgivings, funeral orations…and assigned to the special use of no particular sect or denomination, but equally open to all." In part because some officials had difficulty reconciling the designer's proposal with the First Amendment's separation of church and state, it took another century before federal lawmakers acted on L'Enfant's suggestion. Yet in 1893, Congress granted a charter incorporating the Cathedral Foundation, and in 1907, President Theodore Roosevelt tapped in the foundation stone for the Gothic structure that, as the cathedral's guidebook and pamphlets proclaim, aims to serve as "a house of prayer for all people." And if an Episcopalian house of worship—or any structure affiliated with a single faith—could have sated Americans' desire to symbolically stake out civic space in the nation's capital, that impressive structure might have. Given the American political context, however, it's not surprising that in the years ahead, other faiths would organize resources to take their place in the federal city's landscape.[19]

That symbolically negotiated competition for visibility and clout in the capital that had started with the 1893 plan to build a "national" worship center intensified during the next three decades. The effects of that multi-faith effort peaked between 1925 and 1929, a time when many observers were complaining that secularizing forces were taking hold in the country. It was a time, one scholar has suggested, when a "spiritual depression" set in, several years before the economic depression touched off by the stock market crash of 1929. The first hint that something new was happening in the capital, however, appeared in a story in the *Washington Post* in 1923. Addressing those who had been complaining "of the decay of faith in God in the national capital," the article pointed to recent census evidence to argue that there was a "rising tide of religion" in the country and that Washington was "keeping pace." It was not just that predictions of secularization seemed overstated, however. There was something else going on in Washington, observers suggested. Starting in 1925, the local press started to comment on what observers believed was a noteworthy new pattern. One story published that year noted that Americans "have become accustomed to look upon the National Capital as the fountain-head of governmental authority and political influence...but that Washington is also becoming the religious and spiritual capital of the nation is a fact frequently overlooked." That piece included photographs of the Catholic National Shrine and the Episcopalian National Cathedral, both under construction, and printed images of two already completed Unitarian and Baptist churches. The accompanying text ventured an observation about the practice evident among Catholic, Protestant, and Jewish bodies: "denominations are establishing headquarters in the Capital."[20]

Newspaper accounts during the next few years made the same point, each featuring the National Shrine and the National Cathedral and listing other planned architectural projects. "There is a growing disposition among denominations to build national churches here," a 1927 story reminded local readers. The District of Columbia was home to 112 centers of worship that year, but it was more than just the number of churches and synagogues that caught journalists' attention. "The striking thing about the renaissance of church building in Washington is the national character of the movement," a piece published in 1929 proclaimed. "Nearly all great denominations have seen the fitness of erecting in the Capital of the land a church that will be representative of the denomination as a whole." "Washington is becoming the religious capital of the land," and this emerging pattern, they claimed, was a good thing. That 1929 story in the *Washington Post* declared: "the Nation has decreed it a thing altogether fitting and proper that in this Capital City should be erected magnificent temples to Divinity." A year earlier, another journalist had agreed. She found it praiseworthy that each tradition now hoped "to have its own church close to the nation's heart" and that those faiths thereby "constantly exert their uplifting influence on affairs of State and on the life of the nation as a whole."[21]

The Great Depression slowed the frenzied building pace, but the newly established practice of claiming civic space by constructing worship centers in the capital continued with renewed energy again after World War II. A century after President Roosevelt attended the National Cathedral's foundation stone ritual, eleven Washington, D.C., houses of worship included "national" in their titles, including one non-Christian site, the National Gurdwara. The primary planner behind the effort to build that Sikh temple, which stands only one block from the National Cathedral, explained his reasoning: "We looked at Embassy Row and saw all the religious places and asked ourselves: 'Will the day come that *we'll* have a place on Massachusetts Avenue?' We wanted to be counted among the others."[22]

Other non-Christian communities who wanted to "be counted among the others" built mosques, temples, and synagogues. The newspaper accounts of the late 1920s mentioned the Washington Jewish Community Center on Sixteenth Street, where President Coolidge had attended the foundation stone laying ceremony in 1925, and Jews had had a presence in the city's landscape since the middle of the nineteenth century. The organizers of the oldest Jewish community in the capital, the Washington Hebrew Congregation, had worried about anti-Semitism and secured an "act of incorporation" passed by the Congress and signed by President Franklin Pierce, so its right to exist enjoyed federal sanction. But that congregation, and the others that followed in the District of Columbia before and after 1959, didn't claim "national" status in their title. Neither did most other non-Christian groups, though in 1925 an architect and American supporter of the Baha'i faith, an Iranian tradition founded in 1863, organized an unsuccessful campaign to build in Washington a non-sectarian "National Church and Shrine" where "people of all religious sects meet in harmony and without bias to hold aloft and maintain the moral and spiritual forces of the nation." Four decades later, revised immigration laws would bring advocates for other religions—Hindus, Jains, Muslims, and Buddhists—and they would build impressive structures in the suburbs outside the limits of the District of Columbia, including on "Religion Row" or "Highway to Heaven," a ten-mile stretch along New Hampshire Avenue in Montgomery County that boasts not only twenty-nine Christian churches but also Muslim, Hindu, and Buddhist sites. Asian migrants also would found some worship spaces in the District itself, though their leaders wouldn't claim to represent followers across the nation. Neither did the organizers of the Islamic Center (1949–1957), which was erected by foreign diplomats and American Muslims on Embassy Row after World War II. It had slightly more ambitious aims, though, and, as the mosque's leaders proudly note, federal leaders have crossed its threshold: for example, President Dwight Eisenhower presided at the mosque's dedication, and President George W. Bush visited in 2001, several days after the attacks of September 11. Even if that building, with its stately minaret, remained the most architecturally prominent Muslim site in the capital into the twenty-first century, spokesmen didn't formally claim it was a national center.[23]

Some D.C. Christian churches are noteworthy, even if they also don't include "national" in their title. Several congregations, including the Swedenborgian Church of the Holy City and Metropolitan African Methodist Episcopal Church, function as denominational centers and assert national status in their signs, foundation stones, or publications. Other Washington worship sites don't explicitly declare national denominational status but, because of location, members, or influence, have been prominent in the capital's religious landscape. Three congregations that were among the first to build along Sixteenth Street, which by the early twentieth century became known as "the Street of Churches," fit this pattern: First Baptist, Foundry United Methodist, and St. John's, the neo-classical Episcopalian "church of presidents" just across Lafayette Square from the White House. By tradition, that congregation has set aside pew 54 for the current president, and every chief executive since James Madison has attended services there on occasion, including Barack Obama, who prayed there on the morning of his inauguration.[24]

Some Christian churches whose titles include the term "national" make claims on the public arena. Some of those have centrally located sites, as with two Sixteenth Street churches dedicated in 1930: the neo-Romanesque Universalist National Memorial Church and the neoclassical National City Christian Church, which stands several blocks over on Thomas Circle. Other national churches, for example, the National Presbyterian Church on Nebraska Avenue and Van Ness Street, have less central locations but still manage to make notable claims on civic space. The Presbyterian denomination first designated Covenant First Presbyterian as the "national" church, hoping it would symbolize "the inseparable relationship between true religion and noble patriotism" and promote "the influence of the Presbyterian Church in national life." President Eisenhower and his wife joined, and the congregation had some influence. But more than a decade later, the movement to build a new national church gained momentum, and in the fall of 1969, followers celebrated the dedication of the modern sanctuary, with its adjacent Chapel of the Presidents and 173-foot Tower of Faith, which asserts Presbyterians' presence in Washington.[25]

The Built Environment: Catholic Claims on Civic Space and National Memory

Catholics asserted their presence by constructing monuments and buildings across the urban landscape, including in the Brookland neighborhood surrounding the Shrine. A Roman Catholic Church, St. Patrick's, had been established within the boundaries of the District of Columbia by the end of the eighteenth century, and other parishes followed as transnational migration and regional relocation increased Washington's Catholic population during the next century. By 1923, thirty-one churches dotted the District's landscape, including a parish for Germans (St. Mary Mother of God), another for Italians (Holy Rosary), and three reserved "for the exclusive use of colored people" (St. Augustine's, Holy Redeemer, and Our Lady of Perpetual Help). Residential and ecclesiastical segregation continued thirty years later, though *The Official Catholic Directory* for 1953 no longer listed separate African-American parishes among the capital's thirty-seven Catholic churches.[26]

The District's built environment included more than churches, however. The Apostolic Legation of the Papal State (1938–1939), which was designed by the Shrine's associate architect, Frederick V. Murphy, is a three-story building on Embassy Row that recalls Renaissance Roman palazzos and—as is exemplified by the carving of the papal coat of arms mounted above the entrance—confidently proclaims the Vatican's presence in America's political capital. Dozens of other buildings—schools, rectories, convents, monasteries, orphanages, and hospitals—also signaled Catholic presence, and by the 1950s many of those structures clustered around the Shrine and CUA's campus in the Brookland section of northeastern Washington. That neighborhood had so many Catholic institutions—sixty by 1956—that it came to be called "Little Rome." One of the reasons planners had chosen Washington as the site for the Shrine, a 1921 article in *Salve Regina* explained, was that the city was "our chief Catholic educational center." Its importance only increased over the decades. With the encouragement of Cardinal Gibbons and his episcopal successors, the area around the CUA campus came to house many educational institutions, including Trinity College, which enrolled laywomen, and facilities that trained men and women in religious orders, including the Paulist fathers at St. Paul's College and the nuns at the Catholic Sisters College.[27]

Nuns also came to have a place in the urban landscape beyond the Brookland neighborhood when local and national leaders dedicated a bronze memorial on "one of the most select spots in Washington" to the Nuns of the Battlefield, the women religious who nursed wounded Yankee and Confederate soldiers during the Civil War (fig. 5.7). At the "elaborate" and "dignified" dedication of that monument, Cardinal O'Connell of Boston praised the nuns' "deeds of valor" and promised Catholic patriotism in future American wars. If "our beloved nation" again needs to defend "its sacred institutions," he predicted, Catholic soldiers would again "stand valiantly or die gloriously" and "then too will come out of their cloistered homes another band of ministering angels." The dedication of the memorial to those "ministering angels" occurred on the same weekend in 1924 that members of the Holy Name Society paraded down Pennsylvania Avenue. That parade, and President Coolidge's speech afterward, symbolically staked out civic space, but the Civil War monument, the twenty-first erected in Washington, claimed civic space less figuratively. As one newspaper story emphasized, "the plot on which the monument stands is government

Figure 5.7. Dedication of the Nuns of the Battlefield Memorial on September 20, 1924. Cardinal O'Connell speaks while others look on, including Ellen Jolly, sitting behind him on the podium, and dozens of nuns from the twelve religious orders represented on the bronze monument.

property, and its erection there was authorized by Congress." That six- by nine-foot bronze relief includes life-size figures of twelve nuns, who represent twelve of the twenty-one religious orders that served Civil War soldiers, and organizers sought government approval to place that memorial on a small triangulated piece of land across from St. Matthew's Church and near the intersection of Rhode Island and M streets in northwestern Washington.[28]

The Catholic who unveiled the memorial that day was Ellen Ryan Jolly (1860–1932), chair of the monument committee and the driving force behind its erection, though she attributed the project's success to "the hand of God." As that Rhode Island laywoman noted in her 1927 book, *Nuns of the Battlefield*, she had served as president of the Ladies Auxiliary of the Ancient Order of Hibernians (LAAOH), the women's branch of the Catholic fraternal organization for those of Irish ancestry. Jolly, the daughter of Irish immigrants, had proposed in 1914 that the group sponsor a memorial "in honor of the Sister-Nurses of the Civil War," since a little more than half of those 617 nuns had been of Irish descent. In the intervening ten years, Jolly did the research needed to give the War Department officials what they demanded—"absolute proof of the services rendered by the Sisters." With the help of a Rhode Island congressman and the president of Notre Dame University, Jolly then negotiated with Congress and the Fine Arts Commission, which had to approve the monument's design. With the approvals in hand, the sculptor Jerome Connor (1897–1943) went to work, and the memorial, with its large bronze Angel of Peace and Angel of Patriotism sitting on either side of the stone block, was dedicated on that eventful weekend in 1924.[29]

In a very real way, that monument on federal land claimed civic space, but claims on space also can have implications for assertions about time. Monuments emplace one account of the past while they displace another, just as narratives do. The curriculum and textbooks Catholic students encountered from elementary school through college offered narratives that displaced Protestant accounts and positioned their faith at the center of the story, including the U.S. history textbooks used in Catholic high schools between the 1910s and the 1950s. One 1926 textbook, for example, opened by promising adolescent readers that it would teach them "what the members of our own Catholic Faith have contributed to the growth of our country." Toward that end, in a list entitled "I am Proud of My Faith," the authors included eighteen reasons for such pride, including "a Catholic discovered America" and "liberty of conscience was first established . . . in the Catholic colony of Maryland." In their account of the Civil War, the authors noted: "Catholics on both sides showed devoted loyalty to their causes." Reproducing a photograph of the Nuns of the Battlefield Memorial, the textbook also remembered "the work for the wounded on the field and in the hospitals by devoted Sisters of the many Orders." Those Catholic history texts reached only insiders, however; the advantage of public monuments is that non-Catholic pedestrians and motorists encounter them in daily life, whether they intend to or not. The Nuns of the Battlefield Memorial, then, was important not only because it gave Catholic insiders more ammunition for the battle over public memory. Jolly's 1914 proposal came at a time when many Americans were creating communal memories about the Civil War by either reaffirming or minimizing the sectional divisions between the North and the South, and the monument's significance was that it claimed to tell the story of Americans who had looked beyond those divisions. Still, it's surprising that the effort succeeded: it was led, after all, by a middle-class lay Catholic woman who had been born to Irish immigrants of modest means and who was living in a rented home and working in a hat store. All of those factors—class, ethnicity, gender, and religion—made her success less likely. Yet, in another example of how some lay elites exerted power through women's organizations in the 1910s and 1920s, Jolly managed to gain the official approval of three government bodies—the War Department, Congress, and the Fine Arts Commission. With that approval, and the memorial's 1924 dedication, Catholics challenged the traditional Protestant narrative, which minimized their denomination's role in U.S. history, and attempted to replace that narrative with a material representation that portrayed Catholics as true patriots who looked beyond regional and ideological divisions to seek the nation's common good.[30]

After the dedication of this monument that claimed both political space and communal memory, the crowd walked into nearby St. Matthew's Church, where Bishop Shahan gave the benediction, and that wasn't the only connection with the BNSIC. The monument's sponsoring organization, the Ladies Auxiliary of the Ancient Order of Hibernians, also had a presence at the Shrine. After witnessing the success of their efforts to build that Civil War memorial, Shahan asked them to fund the Shrine's altar to St. Brigid of Ireland, whom Jolly and others called "the Mary of Erin." Ladies Auxiliary members responded generously, and they returned regularly for pilgrimage masses in later years at that altar in the Crypt's east apse. Their former president, Jolly, was among the members who had close ties to the Shrine. She attended the St. Brigid's Altar dedication in 1927, even standing next to Shahan in the group photograph that memorialized that event. The LAAOH also donated ritual objects for that apsidal altar, including a gold chalice decorated with Irish religious and national symbols. The chalice, which Bishop Shahan consecrated in 1928 "as an enduring memorial to the noble service of the Nuns of the Battlefield," had been carried to the Shrine by Jolly. She was among the seventy-five Irish Catholic women who gathered in the Crypt Church to formally present the chalice, another symbol of their pride in their Irish heritage and their appreciation for the "angels of the battlefield."[31]

A NATIONAL SHRINE: SPATIAL AND TEMPORAL ASSERTIONS IN THE SUBJUNCTIVE MOOD

It was that Washington Shrine, which promoters would call "America's Church" by the 1990s, that most fully expressed clerical leaders' and lay elite's desires to transform national memory and claim civic space. In the Shrine's verbal and visual representations, especially the illustration that adorned the foundation stone program booklet, and in the design and ornamentation of the Great Upper Church, planners made subjunctive claims on time and space.[32]

Claiming Time: The Patroness Windows and the East Wall Iconography

The Shrine's interior and exterior ornamentation make controversial claims for Catholic pre-eminence in U.S. history. For example, the "Patroness Windows," located above the nave aisle on the west transept gallery, provide a triumphalist Catholic account of the past by associating national symbols and Marian emblems. Those nine stained glass windows, whose name reminds viewers of Mary Immaculate's role as national patroness, were designed and produced by the studio of Charles J. Connick, whose Boston firm also created the windows adorning the Crypt Church's apsidal altars. Connick, the studio's founder, had passed away by the time workers installed the Patroness Windows in the Great Upper Church four decades later, but the artists in his studio and the bishops who commissioned them still seemed to assume, as Connick did, that "beauty can preach as very few men with bundles of words can preach." Only viewers completely unfamiliar with U.S. history could fail to understand the messages communicated in those windows: Mary protects the nation, and patriotic Catholics celebrate America's past. Each multicolored window includes a representation of a national symbol: the Statue of Liberty, the Alamo, a riverboat, the Great Seal of the United States, the Capitol, the Lincoln Memorial, Washington's Mount Vernon, and Jefferson's Monticello. Uniting Marian devotion and national identity in a retrospective and prospective gaze, above each of those nine patriotic symbols craftsmen placed a large gold crown, signaling Mary Immaculate's protection of the United States. Mary, the windows propose, has been with Americans from the start. She is with them now, and, turning to the subjunctive mood, the stained glass hopefully asserts that the Virgin will continue to guide the nation.[33]

Planners made a similar temporal claim in the iconography of the Great Upper Church's exterior, especially the East Wall's sculptural program. Lay Catholic John De Rosen (1891–1982), the Polish-born muralist who chaired the Shrine's Iconography Committee, shared Connick's conviction: "Art, in the service of the Church," he suggested, "becomes a means of communication at times as powerful as the word spoken from the pulpit." The plan for the East Wall that he and his colleagues proposed in 1955 vividly relayed the lay and clerical planners' message about Catholicism's centrality in American history. As a writer for the archdiocesan newspaper observed four years later, when the east façade was finished, it "is a little shrine in itself to Catholic America."[34]

The plan for that "little shrine" proposed by the Iconography Committee and approved by the bishops was implemented by several artists, including De Rosen, John Angel (1881–1960), the celebrated British sculptor who emigrated to the United States in 1928, and George H. Snowden (1901–1990), the New York–born sculptor who taught art at Yale from 1939 to 1951. The ornamentation of the East Porch, where designers hoped to narrate "the coming of the faith to the United States," includes fourteen scriptural inscriptions, fourteen relief figures, eight symbols, five marble mosaics, and three relief tympana. A relief figure by Snowden, who also created the seven-foot statue of Mary Immaculate atop the canopy on the main altar inside, memorializes Columbus, thereby establishing Catholicism's chronological priority in the New World. One of that mariner's ships was named for Mary, as Catholics emphasized, and her formal connection to the United States also found a place on the east façade. John Angel's relief tympanum, celebrating the bishops' naming of Mary Immaculate as national patroness in 1846, includes five figures. Mary, crowned and enthroned, sits in the center of the group; two kneeling American bishops on either side look upward as they seek her intercession. Another of Snowden's relief tympana, covering the area between the lintel and the arch on the East Porch, depicts the founding of the first British Catholic colony, Maryland, and De Rosen's marble mosaics within the East Porch commemorate other notable events and people, including the founding of the oldest parish at St. Augustine in 1565 and the evangelization by Junipero Serra and Eusebio Kino in the sixteenth and seventeenth centuries.[35]

Claiming Space: The Dome, the Tower, and the Program Illustration

One of the fourteen scriptural passages inscribed on the East Wall proposes that faith is, by definition, an assertion in the subjunctive mood—"faith is the substance of things hoped for"—and, like the leaders of other denominations, many of the Shrine's planners and promoters also "hoped for" a presence in the capital. The scale of the massive building made it difficult to ignore, and promotional literature from the 1920s to the 1950s repeated its impressive dimensions. Yet the Shrine's advocates also hoped that its great dome might recall the federal buildings in Washington, including the Capitol, and that its bell tower might make the site, and Catholicism, more visible.[36]

The bell tower, which officials named the "Knight's Tower" for the fraternal organization that funded it, can be seen from many places in the District of Columbia, just as the architects and promoters hoped (fig. 5.8). In 1957 the Shrine's director, Monsignor Thomas J. Grady, traveled by train to New Haven with Archbishop Patrick A. O'Boyle of Washington to meet the Knights of Columbus's elected leader, Luke E. Hart (1880–1964). The supreme knight, who was born in rural Iowa and became a successful attorney in St. Louis, already had made a name for himself for his role in the movement to add the phrase "under God" to the Pledge of Allegiance. At Hart's urging, the Knights began using the phrase as early as 1951, and, even though some Protestants later claimed it was their idea, most historians suggest that Hart, an anticommunist Marian devotee, was a moving force behind that Cold War campaign designed to use civic performance of the pledge to distinguish God-fearing Americans from Russia's "godless communists." Some government officials also recognized Hart's role. He met with President Eisenhower at the White House in 1953, while the amendment was being proposed, and he received a letter of thanks from the White House the next year, when Congress voted to revise the pledge.[37]

Since their organization's origin, the patriotic members of the Knights of Columbus had defended the faith by emphasizing the nation's Catholic roots, and they also had been early supporters of the Shrine. They processed at the 1920 foundation stone ceremony, and they returned in the succeeding years, including as early as 1923, when members from Brooklyn gathered on the grounds near the construction site for the first official pilgrimage to the Shrine. So perhaps it is not surprising that in 1957 Hart, speaking for more than one million Knights, agreed to contribute a dollar for each member. Given his convictions and his organization's history, it makes sense that when construction ended two years later, Hart praised the "soaring tower" as both "a knightly pledge of loyalty to Our Lady" and

Figure 5.8. National Shrine of the Immaculate Conception.

"a symbol of our country's aspirations." The patriotic members of the Knights had hoped to claim civic space since their organization's inception, and the campanile rising to the left of the Shrine's main entrance did that. It asserted Catholic presence. After the fifty-six bells were added in 1963, the year before Hart died, those within the vicinity could hear the "Virgin Mary bell" (B-flat) strike every hour, and from all over Washington residents and tourists could eye the tower. At 329 feet, it's not as tall as the 555-foot Washington Monument, but, as *Salve Regina* and press releases proudly proclaimed, because of its original elevation from the ground, the tower rises within a few feet of that civic landmark.[38]

From the 1920s to the 1950s, the Shrine's designers and promoters were keenly aware of Washington's civic monuments and federal buildings' architectural style, especially the "domical style" of the U.S. Capitol. They also knew that the Shrine's location in the District of Columbia was crucial for their aim to assert influence and increase visibility, as a piece published in *Salve Regina* a few months after the foundation stone ceremony explained: "Washington is a city of monumental buildings, attracting thousands of visitors annually; the temporary home of our numerous government officials." As the destination for civic tourism and the seat of federal government, Washington was the perfect site for a building with nationalist aspirations. And, as the promoters came to believe, its Great Dome realized those aspirations. The size of the Shrine's dome, which rises above the crossing of the nave and the transepts, makes it visible from a great distance. With a circumference at the base of 280 feet and a height of 237 feet from the ground to the steel cross on its peak, the Shrine's dome is massive, although somewhat lower than the Capitol's (288 feet). The Shrine's polychromatic tiles, which are decorated with five Marian symbols, also draw the viewer's attention.[39]

Yet the dome's claims on civic space depended on more than massive scale and bright colors. There were several reasons that Bishop Shahan and the CUA's trustees settled on a design that featured a dome. The first designs had called for a Gothic structure, but in 1918 the planners rejected that in favor of a composite Byzantine-Romanesque plan. They did this because Gothic structures are expensive to build and slow to complete, and the Episcopalian National Cathedral, already being constructed across town, was Gothic. Archbishop (later Cardinal) John Glennon, Shahan's friend and a CUA trustee, had favored a Romanesque exterior and Byzantine interior for the new archdiocesan cathedral in St. Louis. Glennon also influenced the planners' decision. However, the Byzantine-Romanesque plan also blended best with Washington's built environment. It would complement the government buildings and civic monuments in the cityscape. As one 1922 explanation put it, "the architects . . . concluded that a domical style of architecture would best convey the *national character* of the project." The Shrine's associate architect, CUA's Frederick V. Murphy, had helped to design government buildings as a draftsman in the Supervising Architect's Office in Washington from 1899 to 1905, and the other architects, Maginnis and Walsh, also were sensitive to the proposed building's wider architectural context.[40]

In fact, the preliminary architectural plans by Maginnis and Walsh had envisioned a dome that looked remarkably similar to the U.S. Capitol's, and the designers and some other early promoters hoped the structure would complement that political center. "The Shrine," they wrote, "is by no means to be considered as intended to rival the Capitol; architecturally it complements it, rather; its grandly proportioned mass will be as manifestly ecclesiastical in motive as that of the Capitol is secular." In print and in sermons, promoters made the same point during the two major fundraising and building periods of the 1920s and the 1950s. For example, Cardinal Cushing's

dedication sermon drew attention to the two domes while also acknowledging church-state separation. "Down this broad avenue is another shrine,
another dome," Cushing said from the pulpit, and to those who worried
about Catholicism's public assertions, "let us sincerely and without equivo-
cation declare before all that there can be no rivalry between our patriotic
and spiritual loyalties." A year before the Shrine was dedicated, a Jesuit from
nearby Georgetown University also compared the two buildings: "In
Washington, District of Columbia, two sovereignties have built two capitols.
Our continent-conquering forefathers have built our glorious capitol there;
and our Catholic ecclesiastical fathers have erected our spiritual capitol
there, on the campus of the Catholic University of America, in the glorious
National Shrine of the Immaculate Conception." Readers today might be
more sensitive to the harsh social consequences of gendered language and
westward expansion, and might squirm at the priest's celebration of "our
continent-conquering forefathers;" yet his main message was clear: the
Shrine, with its large dome, stands as the spiritual capitol.[41]

In an image reproduced in the 1920 foundation stone ceremony booklet
(fig. 5.1), the Shrine is rendered as the spiritual capitol that complements
the political capitol; it's portrayed as a site that makes claims on both historical memory and federal space. The Shrine's staff reprinted that illustration in a 1922 issue of *Salve Regina* and again in the 2009 volume celebrating
the fiftieth anniversary of the building's dedication. A Bavarian-born
Benedictine ecclesiastical artist and parish priest, Raphael Pfisterer, OSB
(1877–1942), created it. His ornately decorated, even cluttered, Baroque
image recalls sixteenth-century Venetian paintings of Mary but probably
owes its most direct inspiration to the German artistic traditions of the
Benedictine Order, which Boniface Wimmer founded in the United States
in 1846 with the patronage of Bavaria's King Ludwig I. At a time when
mural painting was being revived in Europe, Ludwig commissioned wall
paintings—some of them emphasizing nationalist themes. Wimmer, the
Benedictine leader in America, also supported the musical and visual arts.
Pfisterer was the next generation in this religious and artistic lineage.
When he created this image as a design for a mural commission, Pfisterer
was pastoring a parish and overseeing the Benedictine Order's Studio of
Christian Art in Manchester, New Hampshire. That studio—and Pfisterer's
representation of the Virgin and the two capitols—continued American
Benedictine artistic traditions of creating spiritual paintings, ritual objects,
and architectural ornamentation.[42]

Some nineteenth-century European murals expressed nationalist themes,
as Pfisterer's image does, but the program booklet image asserts religious
as well as national identity. The artist wasn't identified in the 1920 souvenir;

the caption for the centerfold illustration read only "Mary Immaculate, Patroness of the United States." Shahan had recognized the artist's contribution and thanked that "dear friend and benefactor" in *Salve Regina* earlier that year. However, neither that 1920 article nor another article about the artist published in *Salve Regina* two years later mentioned that his rendering was a study for a mural at St. Francis Xavier Church in Buffalo, New York. Some details about how that image ended up in the program book are missing from the archival record, but Pfisterer seems to have created it early in 1920 and sent it to Charles Maginnis soon afterward. In a return letter dated May 15, 1920, the Shrine's main architect thanked the artist for "the illustration of your design for the Buffalo church, which we find very interesting indeed." Maginnis didn't explain why he used the plural "we," but at some point he showed the painting to his partner, Walsh, and to Shahan and McKenna as well. In any case, all involved found it interesting because Pfisterer's illustration included a representation of the proposed Shrine. Obviously, that artist living in a Benedictine monastery in New Hampshire had been keeping up with the plans to honor Mary in Washington.[43]

His program book illustration depicted Mary as the Immaculate Conception. In that image she hovers in the air with the U.S. Capitol on the viewer's left and the architect's design of the Shrine on the right. Beneath the Virgin is an American flag, which two girls hold aloft. On the left, just beneath the Capitol, a bishop points to Mary; on the right, just beneath the Shrine, a mother looks up reverently. At the bottom of the scene, two indigenous women kneel, one astride a toppled totem, symbolizing their rejection of native traditions and conversion to Christianity. Those young women, pointing to a U.S. map that omits tribal nations' precolonial boundaries, seem to plead for the patroness's protection. That map excludes Alaska and Hawaii, which were U.S. territories in 1920, but the official seals of the forty-eight states frame the elaborate image. National unity is reaffirmed by a ribbon threaded through the emblems of the states and held in an American eagle's beak. Pfisterer's image revises national memory by associating indigenous peoples and Catholic tradition: even America's earliest inhabitants acknowledge the authority of Mary and the Catholic Church, the visual rhetoric proposes. Perhaps as vividly as any public ritual or material expression, this illustration also claims civic space, representing the Shrine as the spiritual parallel to the U.S. Capitol and positioning the Virgin at the nation's political center. The Shrine, with its large dome, stands as the nation's spiritual capitol—a notion that the program booklet's image first announced and that a later composite photograph commissioned by the Episcopalian National Cathedral contested (see fig. 5.9).[44]

Figure 5.9. Commissioned composite photograph of the U.S. Capitol and National Cathedral.

CATHOLICISM AFTER 1959: FROM THE SUBJUNCTIVE
TO THE INDICATIVE MOOD?

Pfisterer painted that image of the Shrine in 1920, and in that decade—when the Holy Name Society members paraded, O'Connell dedicated the Nuns of the Battlefield monument, and McKenna celebrated the Shrine's first mass—Catholic presence in American public life was not secured. Another wave of anti-Catholicism was cresting, and Anglo-Saxon Protestant hostility toward immigrants, including Catholics, was gaining momentum. Many signs—including the nativist immigration act of 1924, the open-air racism of the Klan's Pennsylvania Avenue parade in 1926, and the religious bigotry expressed during Smith's unsuccessful presidential campaign in 1928—reminded Catholics that many of their fellow citizens challenged their presence in the public arena, even their opportunity to enter the country and their right to practice their faith. Catholics did not have proportional representation in Congress. They didn't enjoy the cultural clout of Protestants. They didn't share equally in America's economic bounty. In short, Catholic claims on time and space seemed more hopeful than certain in the 1920s. They were "wishful" assertions in the subjunctive mood.

By the 1959 dedication, assertions of influence had begun to seem somewhat less "wishful," and Catholics' public presence and cultural clout would increase in the next few years, even if anti-Catholicism didn't simply go away. In his dedication day sermon, Cardinal Cushing told the Catholics gathered in the Shrine: "from this day on, the mood is changed." He was not thinking of grammar, but Cushing was right in at least two ways. Around that time, Catholic attitudes had begun to shift, becoming more and more confident. And things changed in a related way, as their claims on civic space and national memory shifted from the subjunctive to the indicative mood, even if the Shrine never displaced the National Cathedral as America's worship space. Decades before promoters trumpeted the Shrine as "America's Church," U.S. Catholicism had stood poised to secure its place in the capital. More Catholics had entered the middle class. In media, sports, and politics they wielded influence. By 1965, Catholics had gained proportional representation in national government: twelve Catholic senators and ninety-one Catholic representatives served in Congress. A symbol of national Catholic presence, John F. Kennedy, had entered the White House four years earlier.[45]

But even Kennedy's victory didn't propel Mary's Shrine, or any Washington Catholic church, to national attention. The congregation with presidential membership usually attracted the media spotlight: that happened, for example, with Eisenhower and First Presbyterian, Johnson and National City, and Carter and First Baptist. But the Shrine was unable to claim the only Catholic president, Kennedy, as a regular. Vice president and future president Harry S. Truman attended a mass at the Shrine in 1945, and two standing presidents visited during the twentieth century—Johnson in 1966 and Gerald R. Ford in 1976. Yet Kennedy's daily appointment books, and all available written and oral sources, indicate that he never visited the nearby Shrine while he was in the White House. Nor could any Washington parish boast of the Kennedy's exclusive allegiance. His wife, Jackie, suggested that Kennedy was "a poor Catholic," and when he did go to mass he alternated among several churches, including St. Stephen's, Holy Trinity, and St. Matthew's, which hosted his state funeral. Further, because of his well-grounded worries about anti-Catholicism, Kennedy withdrew his less than fervent piety to the private sphere, forced by some anti-Catholic opponents to continually reaffirm his commitment to fortify the boundary between church and state. For that reason—and because of his minimal interest in the traditional Marian devotionalism that predominated at the Shrine—it's perhaps not surprising that Kennedy stayed away. But because he did, that worship center with nationalist aspirations missed its chance—or its first chance—to be illumined by the presidency's reflected light.[46]

The result was that even after the political rise of American Catholics, and the post-1960s decline of the national Protestant establishment, centrally located Presbyterian, Methodist, Baptist, Disciples, and Episcopal churches continued to enjoy substantial visibility and influence in the capital. During the twentieth century, two Washington houses of worship seemed especially prominent: the current president's congregation and the Episcopalian National Cathedral, the site of many religious ceremonies with civic significance, including three state funerals (Eisenhower, Reagan, and Ford), one official burial service (Wilson), and seven memorial services for former presidents. By almost any standard, the National Cathedral stood as the most venerated and visible religious structure in Washington by the turn of the twenty-first century and seemed to have won the struggle to serve as a national spiritual center. As one Catholic pilgrim at the Shrine acknowledged, and the staff reluctantly admitted, "Most in D.C. think of the National Cathedral as America's Church."[47]

Yet the BNSIC had gained in visibility after 1959. Catholic Tourists of America and other agencies have been coordinating visits since 1924, but the Shrine didn't appear on most Washington sightseeing tours until later in the century. By 2000, however, the site was attracting about one million annual visitors, more than any religious site in the capital except the National Cathedral. Further, many tourists who never visited the Shrine still noticed it. As the Shrine's director had boasted in 1959, it's visible within a nine-mile radius of metropolitan Washington that includes Maryland and Virginia: "From all these places one can see the shrine. Within the District and from many, many places, even across town, one can see the shrine. The dome and bell tower are definitely on the Washington skyline." Although the staff still worried that the building didn't get the attention it deserved, by the century's end it was more visible than ever. After years of being ignored, it appeared in the American Institute of Architects' architectural guidebook to the city. And the local media took notice. A 1997 story in the *Washington Post* couldn't avoid mentioning its Episcopal counterpart, the National Cathedral, but praised the new lights installed on the Shrine's dome: "Washington night owls may have noticed recently a spectacular new adornment to the city's skyline—the brilliant multicolored dome of the National Shrine of the Immaculate Conception, high on its northeast hill." The reporter continued by noting that the "fabulous dome" had been there for years but the site often had been over-looked. "Though it is every bit as monumental as the Washington National Cathedral—the great Gothic edifice on Wisconsin Avenue—the shrine has always suffered unfairly by comparison." Yet sometimes the comparisons, which had begun in the 1910s, didn't favor either ecclesiastical site. By the end of the century, Washington postcards—another sign of visibility—also started to include the Shrine. One postcard produced in 1993 and sold around town during that decade displayed sixteen Washington buildings and monuments, including the Shrine (fig. 5.10). The Benedictine who cre-ated the foundation stone booklet illustration in 1920 and the Jesuit who compared the National Shrine and the U.S. Capitol in 1958 would have been pleased to see where the photograph of the building was placed on that souvenir of Washington: just above the photograph of the National Cathedral. And in an interesting coincidence—probably an unintended choice by the postcard's designer—the "spiritual capitol" appeared imme-diately beside the "political capitol."[48]

This postcard offers more evidence that by the end of the century the Shrine, and Catholicism, had found a place in the civic landscape. As I've argued in this chapter, Catholics in the era of consolidation asserted influence in electoral politics, communications media, and social policy, and some of those who ventured into the public arena had some presence

Figure 5.10. Postcard. "Washington, D.C." 3 × 5 (1993).

at the Shrine, including Smith, Ryan, and Sheen. The faithful and the clergy also used public ritual and civic monuments to make their presence felt, as with the Holy Name Society parade, the Red Mass, and the Nuns of the Battlefield Memorial. Catholic presence in the built environment of the nation's capital was hard to miss, not only in the churches and schools across the cityscape but also in the dozens of institutions in "Little Rome." Of all the sites in the District of Columbia, none expressed clerical aspirations as clearly as the BNSIC. Even if other ecclesiastical sites, especially the National Cathedral, effectively challenged its claim to be "America's Church," the Catholic sanctuary dedicated to America's patroness, with its polychromatic dome and imposing tower, was as prominent in Washington's religious landscape as any of the other worship spaces that declared denominational centrality or asserted national status. And by prominently positioning the denomination in Washington, I've suggested, the Shrine's clerical promoters helped create an important but unrecognized component of America's public religious practice. In the United States, with its legally sanctioned diversity, faiths have negotiated political power, constructed denominational identity, and secured public visibility by positioning national churches in the nation's capital. More than a century after Congress approved the plan for a national cathedral, the practice of building denominational centers in the District of Columbia had become part of the American way of being religious. Mary's Shrine, then, stands as one of many sacred buildings that, more or less successfully, symbolically claim their place near America's political center.

6

⌒⌀⌒

Incorporating Catholic Immigrants

Diversity, Migration, and the Shrine's Columns
and Chapels, 1913–1997

nternal ethnic and cultural diversity had been the great accomplishment and the persistent challenge of the U.S. Catholic Church since the
mid-nineteenth century, and the Shrine's clerical promoters during the
1910s and 1920s knew that. They knew that claiming civic space in the
capital wasn't their only pressing task. Their challenges began abroad as
well as at home, and they knew it wasn't only transnational flows from the
Vatican that had brought change. Periodic emigrations also had altered the
demographics of American society and the built environment of U.S. cities—and, most important, had transformed the devotional life of both the
recently arrived Catholics, who balanced allegiances to the homeland and
the new land, and the native-born faithful who shared the same pew with
their foreign-born neighbors.

Transnational flows advance and recede, however; and migration wasn't
a steady stream. The Shrine's clerical advocates were aware of the faithful's
diversity throughout the era of consolidation, though they addressed the
challenges more regularly and energetically during the 1910s and 1920s
than during the 1940s and 1950s, and—to again extend the chronological
scope and trace developments after 1959, as I did in chapter 5—here I try
to show how that issue took center stage again as the new immigration
transformed the ecclesiastical community during the post-1960s era of
fragmentation. Those shifts in the clergy's aims make sense, since, as some
historians have argued, "during the period from the middle 1920s to the

Figure 6.1. Our Lady of Peace and Good Voyage Oratory, a space venerated by Filipino Americans and dedicated to the Virgin of Antipolo.

middle 1960s...globalization was at its low ebb." Especially with regard to the flows of people across borders, the years between the restrictive immigration act of 1924 and its revision in 1965 were the exception—in U.S. history and Catholic life. In the first years of the consolidated era, when the Shrine was being planned and the Crypt Church was being constructed, many U.S. residents, including Catholics, were foreign born, though after the mid-1920s there were fewer new migrants arriving on America's shores and entering religious communities.[1]

That doesn't mean the faithful who gathered in Great Upper Church to participate in the BNSIC's dedication were homogenous. They weren't. Nor does it mean the Shrine's planners and promoters ignored the internal diversity of the laity between 1913 and 1959. They didn't, as I try to show in this chapter. Even before the Vatican sanctioned the Pauline view of the church as the "mystical body of Christ" in 1943, ecclesiastical leaders labored earlier in the century to "incorporate" immigrants. They tried to incorporate them into the body politic, making immigrants into good Americans; they tried to incorporate them into Christ's "mystical body," making them good Catholics. And as clergy tried to bring migrants into the Church, they simultaneously worried about the Church's "diversity" and proclaimed its ultimate "unity."[2]

The Shrine's material culture eventually would represent the diversity of peoples and cultures beyond U.S. borders—those who hadn't affirmed the Gospel or joined the Church—but the sanctuary's promoters cared more about ethnic and cultural diversity *within* the U.S. Church and at the Washington Shrine. That diversity meant African-American and Amerindian Catholics, too, and those devotees had some presence at the BNSIC. Most of all, however, diversity meant immigrants. The Shrine's leaders wanted to incorporate the foreign-born into the ecclesiastical body; and, I suggest, this is a final way that devotional center has functioned as a threshold to Catholic America, both during and after the era of consolidation.

In the century's first and last decades, diversity was an important issue for those at the Shrine. By 1919, the founder and architects imagined a site that would welcome "a perpetual chorus of peoples." As the building's promoters saw it, the Crypt Church's columns would represent the faithful's multiple ethnic identities and national allegiances, the diverse "members" of Christ's body. That impulse to acknowledge diversity while also proclaiming unity diminished somewhat after the 1920s, though it never disappeared. It returned with great intensity after the 1960s. The clerical concern to incorporate migrants was materially expressed in the oratories and chapels that began to appear in larger numbers around the time the revised immigration legislation opened America's gates again. Ethnic saints and national Virgins began to be enshrined in those places of prayer after 1964, and both the clergy's desire to include immigrants and immigrants' desire to be included were hard to miss by the end of the century: for example, devotional spaces honoring Marian figures beloved by Asian migrants stood on either side of the Crypt Church's main altar, and one of those sites, the Filipino oratory, included the foundation stone Cardinal Gibbons had blessed in 1920 (fig. 6.1). As I show—by using semistructured interviews as well as textual and visual sources to focus on that Filipino place of prayer—by the 1990s, Asian Catholics had symbolically claimed the foundation stone, and the Shrine's rector, Monsignor Michael J. Bransfield, was emphasizing the pilgrimage center's role in unifying a diverse Church. Resembling the immigrant generation that built the Crypt Church more than the acculturating generation that completed the superstructure, diverse Catholics, including post-1965 immigrants from Asia, Africa, and Latin America, claimed a presence at that national shrine in the nation's capital by the end of the twentieth century.[3]

INCORPORATING IMMIGRANTS INTO THE BODY POLITIC, 1913–1959

American Catholic immigrants were constantly reminded that many of their neighbors didn't welcome them because of their ethnicity and their religion, and those detractors doubted the newcomers could become acculturated citizens. As Protestant nativists such as Samuel Morse and Josiah Strong had done in the nineteenth century, the Klan's leader Hiram W. Evans argued in 1924 that the nation needed "a rigidly enforced immigration" as part of an effort to "re-Americanize," since "this country continues to be flooded by inferior people whose assimilation is impossible." Evans and other Protestants who claimed "Anglo-Saxon" heritage and worried about "race suicide" got their way that year, when Congress limited foreign immigration and the federal government and secular institutions focused their attention on citizenship and acculturation in the first decades of the twentieth century. For example, a 1919 poster designed and circulated by the U.S. government advised immigrants: "To enjoy opportunities, become an American citizen." The color lithograph showed a group of the foreign born looking up toward a large sun whose rays each illustrated one of citizenship's benefits, including "prosperity" and "schools." Catholics, like Jews, were never fully convinced that public school curricula and textbooks were free from Protestant prejudice, but secular educational institutions also advocated a renewed emphasis on "civics." One 1922 civics textbook described that field of study as "the science that treats of citizenship and the relations between citizens and government," and another one published the same year noted the surge of interest: "for the past decade there has been an increasing emphasis placed upon the Civics in our schools."[4]

Catholic institutions also placed an emphasis on inculcating the habits of civic participation as ecclesiastical and educational leaders tried to counter their neighbors' suspicions by doing all they could to incorporate Catholics into the body politic. Looking outward toward the wider society, that form of "public Catholicism" aimed to transform the people in the pews, especially immigrants and their children, who were expected to acculturate and catechize their foreign-born parents. Continuing efforts that predated the turn of the twentieth century, Catholic educators promoted American virtues, such as "industry and application," and taught "lessons of a patriotic and national character." Civics textbooks, courses, and clubs also presented the same "patriotic" messages. By the 1950s, schools sponsored "Civics Clubs," like the group that donated to the Shrine in 1953 from Our Lady of the Lake School in New York, yet as early as the 1920s Catholic schools' curricula included "Civics." In Brooklyn, for example, most Catholic schools in 1929 required the subject, and at St. James Diocesan High School all students, both those enrolled in the "General Course" and in the "Commercial Course," learned about their rights and duties as American citizens. Catholic teachers consulted pedagogical guides, like *Training in Courtesy*, so they could instruct their students in manners, since "a knowledge of social customs and social usages is almost as necessary to a civilized man as knowledge of how to earn a living." Teachers in the Catholic schools assigned civics texts, like Hannah Margaret Harris's *Lessons in Civics for the Six Elementary Grades of City School*, which advised the children of immigrants about what to do on the walk to school and how to act when "visiting public places." Catholic "readers" like the *Elson Reader* for primary schools included chapters on patriotism.[5]

Both that civics text and the elementary reader were used by the Polish-speaking nuns at Toledo's St. Hedwig's School, and that bilingual school, which focused on incorporating Polish children into the body politic, also assigned older students one of the three pamphlets on citizenship issued by the NCWC in 1919 and 1920. The pamphlets were popular, and not only in midwestern cities. Within a year the NCWC had distributed almost one million copies of *The Fundamentals of Citizenship*, and the accompanying workbook, *Civics Catechism on the Rights and Duties of American Citizens*, was translated into fourteen languages by 1927 (fig. 6.2). The workbook and pamphlets tutored upper school children and adult immigrants in the basics of how to be an American. Those texts explained that Jesus had "told men to give obedience to civil rulers, as well as obedience to God." They suggested: "citizenship is our duty to God, fulfilled in our care and solicitude for our country, whose welfare God has placed in our hands." *The Fundamentals of Citizenship* didn't limit its attention to the principles of democracy and the importance of voting. Like the etiquette manuals, schoolroom readers, and civics texts, the NCWC's citizenship guides also instructed immigrants in how to cultivate all sorts of habits—and extinguish others—in order to accelerate acculturation; it included a warning to refrain from "spitting in public places."[6]

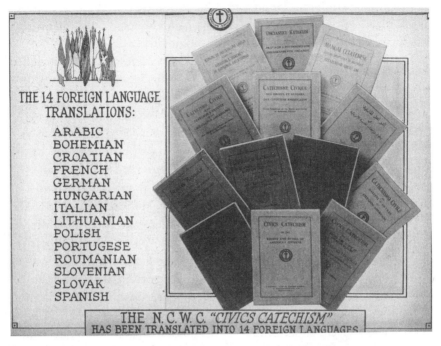

THE 14 FOREIGN LANGUAGE
TRANSLATIONS:

ARABIC
BOHEMIAN
CROATIAN
FRENCH
GERMAN
HUNGARIAN
ITALIAN
LITHUANIAN
POLISH
PORTUGESE
ROUMANIAN
SLOVENIAN
SLOVAK
SPANISH

THE N. C. W. C. "CIVICS CATECHISM"
HAS BEEN TRANSLATED INTO 14 FOREIGN LANGUAGES

Figure 6.2. "Civics Catechism." National Catholic Welfare Conference, 1927. Glass lantern slide, 8 × 10 cm.

INCORPORATING IMMIGRANTS INTO THE
BODY OF CHRIST, 1913–1959

Partly because of the widespread concern about "hygiene" and "cleanliness" in that period and partly because the practice diverged from imagined middle-class norms of acceptable "American" behavior, spiritual advice aimed at immigrants also warned about that impolite habit, spitting. Among the several dozen prohibitions in a 1913 list of "what every Christian-Catholic should remember," for example, immigrants found the same exhortation: the tenth rule was "don't spit on the church floor." That long list also warned the laity about other errors: "don't talk in church;" "don't send your children to non-Catholic schools"; "don't use other languages in your church or around the building." That last rule on the list, which was written in Polish, didn't mean what you might think, however. It didn't require congregants to speak only English. It meant instead that the Polish immigrants in Queens should use only their native language in and near their new ethnically segregated church, and that document illustrates one of the challenges ecclesiastical leaders faced as they tried to incorporate immigrants.

Catholics spoke different languages at home and treasured different devo-tional practices, even if they shared the common experience of hearing Sunday mass in the ecclesiastical universal tongue, Latin.[7]

The fourteen translations of the NCWC's *Civics Catechism*, which included Arabic, Portuguese, and Lithuanian editions, provide clues about the diver-sity of the faithful by the 1920s, but adjusting to ethnic, cultural, and linguistic diversity had long been a challenge for the Catholic Church in the United States. In the colonial period, devotees in New Spain and New France practiced the faith on terrain imagined in very different ways by the inhabitants—as a patchwork of sacred spaces and tribal nations—and the diverse ways of being Catholic in those territories showed the marks of both brutal conquest and intercultural exchange. Further east, in 1815 the Catholic Church in the former British colonies was predominantly an Anglo-American community, but the expansion of the national borders during the nineteenth century changed that, as settlers and migrants of French and Spanish heritage joined Anglo-American Catholics. Then, as every historical survey of U.S. Catholicism has observed, immigration transformed the American Church between 1820 and 1920, when millions of Catholics arrived. First came the Irish and Germans, then Italians, Poles, Mexicans, French Canadians. By 1916, these six communities represented three-quarters of the U.S. Catholic population of more than fifteen million. Several eastern European groups—Slovaks, Czechs, Lithuanians, and Ukrainians—added to the linguistic, cultural, and ethnic diversity. By 1920, these ten main ethnic groups, and several others, spoke twenty-eight lan-guages in parish pews.[8]

Unity remained elusive in such a diverse church. "National parishes," congregations formed along ethnic or national lines, isolated some com-munities from each other, and where ethnically diverse Catholics wor-shiped in the same parish, differences emerged and conflicts erupted, especially as the faithful complained about Irish dominance in the pulpit and petitioned bishops to assign pastors who could hear confessions and give sermons in their own languages. As one historian has noted, diversity presented a formidable challenge: "people of different nationalities were mixed together, and somehow they had to adjust to the American way of life while preserving their own unique heritages. Unity had to be achieved in the midst of diversity. For the Church, this would prove to be a delicate balancing act."[9]

In this more inward-looking form of public Catholicism, devotees in America confronted ecclesiastical diversity, negotiated communal identity, and established modes of interaction in a broader context created by both the theology and practice of the transnational Catholic institutional network and the color-coded hierarchy of values prescribed and enforced in the United States. Some passages in the nation's founding documents, including Thomas Jefferson's famous phrase in the Declaration of Independence "all men are created equal," provided intellectual resources for those who wanted to safeguard the rights of diverse peoples within the national borders, although indigenous tribes displaced from their lands and the descendants of Africans forced into slavery sometimes complained that the phrase, which was coined by a southern slaveholder, only reminded them of the hypocrisy supporting the enduring gap between word and deed. As the twentieth century dawned, some residents in American territories were still ineligible for citizenship. Legal sanctions constrained where they lived and worked, and there was racially motivated exclusion, even violence. Between 1889 and 1918 more than twenty-five hundred African Americans were lynched in the South. In 1919, at least sixty-six African Americans met the same grim fate, and more violence ensued in "race riots" in twenty-six U.S. cities, including in Washington, D.C., on July 19, when a white mob walked the streets and attacked local blacks. The following year, just as "the tribal twenties" got under way, W. E. B. Du Bois published an analysis of the racialized religious identities and practices in America at the time. In that essay, "The Souls of White Folk," that African-American scholar decried the common assumption that "of all the hues of God whiteness alone is inherently and obviously better than brownness or tan." That "religion of whiteness," however, was relatively new; as Du Bois noted, "The discovery of whiteness among the world's peoples is a very modern thing—a nineteenth and twentieth century matter." Informing those "modern" assumptions were racialized evolutionary theories that traced the "origin" and "growth" of "races," from the barbarian to the civilized, from the heathen to the saved.[10]

During the first decades of the era of consolidation, Catholic immigrants made their way in American society and in the Catholic Church in relation to these cultural prescriptions and institutional constraints. "This reconsolidated whiteness," historians have argued, shaped "reactions to the swell of 'new immigrants' to the United States from the 1880s to the 1920s," and some of the newcomers "presented a variety of challenges to operative definitions of whiteness." Sometimes it was difficult to classify Catholic immigrants by the usual measures of racial acceptability, ethnic heritage, and national identity. Some of the complexity arose because of Catholics' ethnic intermarriage, which had increased by the 1920s. In Detroit, for example, between 25 and 40 percent of marriages performed that decade in Catholic churches paired brides and grooms of different national origin and ethnic ancestry, an increase of 300 percent from 1906. But the complexity of classifying migrants in the color scheme was not just because Irish were marrying Germans and Italians were marrying Poles. A Mexican-born Catholic in Chicago in 1928 reported that in her parochial school "the teachers and everyone treated all nationalities alike," but as she recalled her grade school friends of a decade earlier she distinguished between her best friend, "an Italian girl," and "an American girl friend." As she had understood it at eighteen, neither she nor her immigrant friend were "Americans." Her city, Chicago, teemed with ethnic and racial diversity, but in regions with fewer European migrants, especially the South, locals also had a difficult time classifying newcomers. As one Polish priest who served immigrants in Texas recalled, in the late nineteenth century "when they saw a Pole without knowledge of the language, a peasant with no education, these southerners looked upon him as they did upon the blacks, and felt they had the same right to deny him his human rights as they did the blacks." Native-born Protestants, as they did with those eastern European Catholics, sometimes relied on markers of social marginality as much as perceptions of skin color to challenge immigrants' claim to whiteness. Early on, the Irish were linked in the public imagination with African Americans, and various migrants from southern and eastern Europe, including Italian Catholics, were dismissed as "nonwhite." In this cultural context, Catholic immigrants often felt pressured to defend themselves from nativist criticism and institutionalized exclusion by distancing themselves from those ranked lower in America's color-coded social hierarchy, especially citizens who claimed African descent.[11]

The Catholic institutional network, centered in Rome, also constituted part of the wider cultural context that constrained but didn't determine immigrants' reception and response. After all, the Roman Catholic Church offered guidelines about how to think about and respond to *difference*— religious, cultural, linguistic, and ethnic. Religions provide devotees with orienting tropes, with figurative language that orients them in time and space and shapes belief and practice, and Christians have used various tropes—metaphors, similes, and symbols—to represent those within the Christian community and those beyond its boundaries. They have imagined the church—and Jesus' relation to his followers—using pastoral, horticultural, architectural, familial, and corporeal metaphors. The church is a sheepfold, vineyard, temple, mother, bride, and body; in turn, Christ is the shepherd, the vine, the foundation stone, the son, the groom, and the head.[12]

Corporeal metaphors, which were introduced in Pauline epistles and found systematic expression in Pope Pius XII's 1943 encyclical *Mystici Corporis Christi*, were especially important for interpreting difference. The notion of the Roman Catholic Church as "the mystical body of Christ" appeared in the most important ecclesiastical documents issued by the Vatican, including the decrees of the Council of Trent and Vatican I, as well as in the statements of the U.S. episcopal leaders' pastoral letter in 1884, which continued to determine clerical hopes and fears in the era of consolidation. In some of the most influential proclamations about the Church's understanding of non-Catholics, the corporeal metaphor appears in passages delineating who's in the Church and who's not. Ancient ecclesiastical leaders, including Cyprian of Carthage (d. 258), affirmed the theological dictum "Extra Ecclesiam nulla salus" (Outside the church there is no salvation), and Boniface VIII took a similar stand in his 1302 papal bull *Unam Sanctam*. To express that exclusivist theology of religions, Boniface employed the analogy of the body: "we confess with simplicity that outside of her there is neither salvation nor the remission of sins" because the Church "represents one sole mystical body whose Head is Christ." The decrees of the Council of Trent used corporeal images, too, emphasizing papal primacy and sacramental efficacy—especially baptism and the Eucharist—to distinguish "all the faithful, who belong to the body of Christ." Christ's ecclesiastical body includes only those baptized into the faith and in union with Rome, the Council of Trent declared. Vatican I and *Mystici Corporis Christi* concurred. Vatican I reaffirmed that ancient dictum, speaking of "this true catholic faith, outside of which none can be saved" and figuring the Christian community not only as "bride" and "mother" but also as "the mystical body of Christ." In his 1943 encyclical, Pius XII allowed for the possibility of non-Catholics' "unknowing longing" for affiliation but reaffirmed the traditional teaching and used the corporeal simile, noting that "the Church is so constituted that it may be likened to a body," even though some are not included in that organic whole: "actually, only those are to be included as members of the Church who have been baptized and profess the true faith, and who have not been so unfortunate as to separate themselves from the unity of the Body."[13]

The question of whether all non-Catholics are condemned has been debated throughout Catholic history, and some official statements have qualified or softened the usual position in some ways, for example acknowledging that through no fault of their own some people of good conscience have not been effectively evangelized. To remedy that, the devout have been reminded of their obligation to spread the gospel at home and abroad, even though American priests, monks, and nuns have tended to focus on the challenges of incorporating baptized immigrants. In the 1884 pastoral letter issued by the U.S. bishops gathered in Baltimore, James Gibbons and his colleagues were most concerned about how to handle the "increase in the number of our faithful laity." Yet the bishops also felt obliged to note: "there are hundreds of millions of souls in heathen lands to whom the light of the Gospel has not yet been carried." They praised "the heroic labors of our missionaries among heathen nations in every part of the world" and encouraged the cultivation of "the missionary spirit" among the American faithful. "The duties of a Christian," the bishops declared, "begin with his own household and his own parish; but they do not end there." Those in the Church "whose very name is Catholic" must heed the "divine commission": "Go, teach all nations, preach the Gospel to every creature."[14]

That 1884 document mandated, among other things, an annual diocesan collection for missions and established in every parish a branch of the Society for the Propagation of the Faith, which had been founded in France in 1822 and subsequently endorsed by the Vatican. James Anthony Walsh (1867–1936), a parish priest, followed that mandate and directed the archdiocesan missionary effort in Boston starting in 1903. Three years later, Walsh cofounded the Catholic Missions Bureau, and in 1911 left an enduring mark by cofounding the Catholic Foreign Missions Society of America (Maryknoll), which sent its first five evangelists abroad to China in 1917. They, like Walsh, tried to impress on "Orientals" that "the Catholic Church is the church of the world." The foreign missionary effort between the 1920s and the 1950s included women religious, too, and even those who stayed home were invited to think of their everyday labor in the convent as part of the evangelizing effort. One piece of spiritual advice passed on to the Sisters of St. Francis of Assisi in Milwaukee addressed those who felt their assigned duties offered "so few chances of doing anything worthwhile for God." That document, "Missionaries, Sisters All," which appeared in their directory for 1927, encouraged Franciscans to reimagine every space in their environment. After noting the need for missionaries in Africa, China, and India, it proposed that those toiling "in our little kitchen, or classroom, or sewing room" use faith to magically "convert each into a small mission field." "Let the kitchen, for instance, be some poor little village in China, with souls, big souls and little souls, young and old, waiting for spiritual alms." This "strange geography" would move "China into our kitchen, Africa into our classrooms, or Japan into our laundry."[15]

American Catholics who neither traveled to save souls nor consoled themselves with "strange geography" were still able to support the effort to spread the gospel by contributing to the annual mission Sunday collection, and they also could "ransom pagan babies." A French priest who had visited the United States established the Holy Childhood Association in 1843. Just as the Society for the Propagation of the Faith encouraged adults to help reach other adults, this pontifical missionary society gave children a role in the missionary effort. Catholic school children in the United States donated $319,012 between 1893 and 1908, and Holy Childhood Association membership included about seven million Catholic children by 1910. Those efforts to "ransom" children held in the bonds of "paganism" increased during the middle of the century. In 1958, for example, archival records show that the Philadelphia archdiocese collected more than $200,000 for the Society for the Propagation of the Faith on Mission Sunday, and the Holy Childhood Association collected from parochial school children more than $70,000 for "baby ransoms." Some memoirs suggest the enduring psychic influence. One Italian-American Catholic, who donated $5 in 10-cent installments in 1951 to purchase a pagan baby, recalled that she sometimes had doubts. "Maybe they liked their babies pagan. And maybe that was nobody's business." But maybe," she reasoned, "they didn't understand about heaven and hell and purgatory and limbo. Neither did I really, but I decided better safe than sorry." Worries about the children's salvation gripped her: "I was overwhelmed by the power of those five dollars. I had visions of an infant who, by accident of birth, could expect nothing more than hell on earth and not even a chance in heaven. It didn't seem fair. And if five dollars from me could change that agony to ecstasy, I was more than happy to give it."[16]

The spiritually lost also lived closer to home, American Catholic leaders noted, and they sponsored domestic missions to "incorporate" as many of them as possible within the mystical body of Christ. The 1884 pastoral letter also had exhorted the faithful to remember those in the United States who had not yet been evangelized and those who had been baptized but still needed instruction to make them good Catholics, true "members" of the one ecclesiastical body. Gibbons and his episcopal brethren were thinking not only of immigrants but also of indigenous peoples: "Among our own Indian tribes, for whom we have a special responsibility, there are still many thousands in the same darkness of heathenism, and the missions among our thousands of Catholic Indians must equally look to our charity for support." And Gibbons, who had served churches in the South, worried about the spiritual state of Americans of African descent: "moreover, out of the six millions of our colored population there is a very large multitude who stand sorely in need of Christian instruction and missionary labor."[17]

The bishops employed corporeal metaphors as they imagined difference and advised the faithful about how to interact with Africans, Indians, and immigrants. The prelates proclaimed that the U.S. Catholic Church was not "in any...sense exclusive or limited, but an integral part of the one, holy, Catholic, and Apostolic Church of Jesus Christ, which is the Body of Christ, in which there is no distinction of classes and nationalities—in which all are one in Christ Jesus." The Pauline epistle to the Galatians (3:28–29) suggested that "all are one in Christ," and Ephesians (4:15–16) exhorted Christians "to grow up into him who is the head, into Christ, from whom the whole body joined and knit together by every ligament with which it is equipped, as each part is working properly, promotes the body's growth in building itself up in love." Citing and paraphrasing Pauline epistles, the U.S. bishops rejected "narrow, insular, national views" of Christ's body and sanctioned an ecclesiology that held that the Catholic Church was "universal" and "not for any special tribe or tongue." In another letter, published in the year he blessed the Shrine's foundation stone, Gibbons reaffirmed the American hierarchy's earlier views, advocating unity over diversity, homogeneity over heterogeneity. He rejected the request by some Catholics to organize ethnically and racially segregated parishes served by clergy who spoke the same language and claimed the same heritage. Gibbons warned of the "discord"—and increased Protestant hostility— that might arise if he were to assign a bishop to "each of these races, nationalities, tribes, and tongues." The cardinal advocated "Americanization" instead: the various groups—"Indians," "Negroes," and Catholic migrants from "nearly every nation in the world"—"should gradually amalgamate and fuse into one homogenous people," although "without losing the best traits of their race."[18]

Catholic priests, monks, and nuns who shared Gibbons's interest in incorporating American Indians and African Americans into the Body of Christ didn't always challenge racist governmental laws and segregated ecclesiastical practices. They also sometimes unwittingly condescended to the "members" they wanted to unite in the Church's organic whole. At Pope Leo XIII's urging, in 1891 Katherine Drexel (1858–1955) founded the Sisters of the Blessed Sacrament for Indians and Colored People, and for forty-six years Drexel and the nuns of her order staffed schools and hospitals, offering remarkable service to those marginalized Catholics. Yet there could be condescension in the Church's efforts sometimes. John LaFarge, SJ (1880–1963), an advocate of ministry to African Americans, noted that Pope Pius XII had endorsed the efforts: "we confess that we feel a special paternal affection, which is certainly inspired by heaven," the pope said, "for the Negro people dwelling among you." A Hungpapa Lakota who served as a Franciscan nun complained about the Church's history of "paternalism" because "the giver easily dominates the receiver," and for many other Indian and African-American Catholics, that "paternal affection" was part of the problem. For example, Thomas W. Turner (1877–1978), an African-American Catholic layman and Howard University biology professor, founded an organization in 1917 that eventually came to be called Federated Colored Catholics of the United States. LaFarge and other white priests who had belonged to that group and defended African Americans' rights pressed a different agenda—interracial solidarity rather than communal identity—and that led to an institutional split in 1934. The new group, the Catholic Interracial Council, was predominantly white; and, as one historian has observed, "ironically, its energy undercut earlier efforts on the part of black Catholics to organize on their own." Some contemporaries, like Du Bois, put it more harshly. "It is a shame," he proposed on hearing about Turner's displacement and the organization's split, "that 'nigger' haters clothed in its episcopal robes should do to black Americans in exclusion [and] segregation... all that the Ku Klux Klan ever asked."[19]

To make matters worse, many American Catholic institutions were segregated, just as the grid of parish boundaries in urban centers, including Washington and Baltimore, also tended to divide followers not only by neighborhood but also by ancestry. Thomas, like most influential African-American Catholics in the D.C. area, attended the segregated St. Augustine's Church, which stood near an Irish and German parish (St. Paul's) and across town from the future site of the BNSIC. In 1889 St. Augustine's hosted the first meeting of the "National Afro-American Catholic Congress," led by Daniel Rudd (1854–1933), and since 1858 had served as "the mother church of Black Catholics," though it only installed its first African-American pastor in 1991. Turner had no clerical aspirations, but the Josephite Seminary, then in his native Maryland and under Gibbons's jurisdiction, refused admission to African Americans when he was attending college and graduate school during the first decades of the twentieth century, even though ministry to the black community was the order's core mission from its founding in 1893 and even though its missionary magazine, the Colored Harvest, called for "a greater manifestation of justice toward the Negro." Turner also couldn't have joined the Knights of Columbus or attended nearby CUA, whose policy of racial exclusion had become effective, without discussion or documentation, during the years Bishop Shahan, also the Shrine's founder, led the university. Some Catholics, including Katherine Drexel, criticized CUA's policy in the earlier years, and priests and nuns protested racial injustice during the 1950s and 1960s. In 1976, CUA leaders awarded the aged Turner an honorary degree and acknowledged its segregated past, yet the damage had been done: CUA had graduated a "colored" in 1896 but only fully opened its doors to African-American students during the 1930s and only integrated campus facilities, like residential housing and dining halls, in the 1950s.[20]

Immigrants faced obstacles in the American Catholic Church, too, though never as many as Amerindian or African Catholics. Immigrants also got more attention. Dealing daily with the extraordinary linguistic and cultural differences of the Catholic Church between the 1880s and the 1920s, nuns, monks, and diocesan priests spent more energy and time worrying about how to incorporate newcomers. For example, the Italian-born St. Frances Xavier Cabrini (1850–1918) established in 1880 the Missionary Sisters of the Sacred Heart, which energetically attended to the needs of immigrants, mostly Italians, from coast to coast, including New York City's "Little Italy" and Colorado's mining towns. Naturally, the hierarchy worried about immigrants, too. Gibbons's emphasis on the lack of "distinctions" in the "Body of Christ" assumed the presence of millions of the foreign-born, and his 1920 pronouncement was a direct response to Polish immigrants who wanted to emphasize ethnic difference and communal identity. Whether ecclesiastical leaders inclined toward maintaining the newcomers' distinctiveness or toward "fusing" the multitude "into one homogenous people," there was "a preoccupation with immigrants" in the U.S. Catholic Church at least until the end of the 1920s.[21]

Some local studies have shown, however, that heterogeneity persisted up to and after World War II. The diversity was not only among those classified as white, black, yellow, and red in America's color taxonomy. There also was "diversity among and between different white urban dwellers in midcentury America." Ethnic groups that by midcentury had become classified as "white," even though their immigrant ancestors had been represented differently, did not "fuse" as fully as Gibbons had hoped, though the U.S. Catholics who attended the 1959 BNSIC dedication certainly were more acculturated than the participants at the foundation stone ceremony. Then, heterogeneity—and the awareness of difference—intensified again. In the wake of midcentury civil rights movements, African Americans, Latinos, and the indigenous demanded that the U.S. Catholic Church acknowledge their presence. Further, after federal immigration statutes changed and more migrants from Asia, Africa, and Latin America arrived, the U.S. Church again faced the familiar problem of how to interpret difference and incorporate immigrants.[22]

DIVERSITY AT THE SHRINE: "HEATHENS," "INDIANS," AND "NEGROES"

Before and after 1959, all of that diversity—global, national, and local—also had a presence at the BNSIC. For obvious reasons, non-Catholics from other nations did not lend their financial support, but they sometimes visited. Participants at the Third Plenary Council had expressed worries about non-Catholics languishing in "heathen nations," and, as the Shrine's visitor books show, peoples from across the globe and outside the Church had a limited presence at the Shrine between the 1920s and the 1950s. For example, two visitors signed the register in 1928 as "Kong Hi" and "Tongling" from "Chefoo, China." They probably were Mandarin speakers from that northeastern seaport city, now called Yantai, where the traditional blend of Buddhism, Daoism, and Confucianism persisted, despite local Protestant evangelizing.[23]

The diversity of the world's religions and cultures also was represented in the building's ornamentation long before and just after the dedication in 1959. Consider, for example, the mosaic *Descent of the Holy Spirit*. The Shrine's chancel (the area on a church's east end, where the altar is placed) has a dome that is covered with 1.25 million tiles. That large central mosaic spans 3,950 square feet, and the clergy and laity participating in liturgies there can look up to see it. So can the faithful in the first rows of the Great Upper Church (fig. 6.3). As they did for the sculptural program on the east façade that represents the history of U.S. Catholicism, John De Rosen and the Shrine's Iconography Committee established the mosaic's theme—the Holy Spirit. The French artist Max Ingrand (1908–1969) designed and installed the enormous mosaic, which used several scriptural passages and twenty-four images to represent the descent of the Spirit at Pentecost and afterward. Dozens of red "tongues of fire" fall on the dome's golden background. In the central cluster of figures within the mosaic's circle, the presence of the Spirit falls on the Virgin Mary and Jesus' apostles and descends on the other twelve figures there, too: anonymous lay followers and church leaders. More tongues of fire descend toward the figures in the triangular spaces beyond that circle, and the images in those four concave pendentives represent the world's four directions and diverse cultures. As one of the scriptural passages ringing the circle indicates, the designers intended viewers to recall the divine promise "I will pour out my spirit upon all mankind." In this mosaic—installed three years after the Second Vatican Council's decrees softened (but didn't retract) the strongest versions of the Church's exclusivist theology—the Holy Spirit reaches the four corners of the world: Europe, Asia, Africa, and the Americas. A seated figure holding a scroll represents Europe and the classical Mediterranean world. Adorning another corner is a Buddhist monk with shaved head and golden robe. He sits partially cross-legged in front of a stupa containing a relic of the Buddha. Like an exotic nimbus, the long leaves of a palm tree frame the head of a third figure, a proudly erect African "tribesman" who holds an

Figure 6.3. *Descent of the Holy Spirit.* Mosaic in the Great Upper Church.

elephant tusk and, the viewer supposes, practices an indigenous religion. The final pendentive portrays another indigenous person, one from another continent. A longhaired "American Indian," who seems to represent more than one tribe, worldview, and region, sits with a buffalo head from the central plains at his right foot and a southwestern cactus over his left shoulder. At first glance, the mosaic seems rather inclusive. In accord with Catholic theology, it proposes that no one across the globe is without access to the Spirit. That's the good news. For Catholics who care about the eternal fate of their non-Catholic sisters and brothers, however, the bad news is that those four figures are still positioned outside the circle. Even though the Holy Spirit falls on the world's four corners, some remain outside the mystical body of Christ.[24]

To be brought into the Catholic Church as full "members" they would need to hear and accept the gospel, and the interior decoration also celebrates Catholic missionaries and assures viewers that diverse peoples can be evangelized successfully. The Queen of Missions Chapel, for example, includes a Venetian glass mosaic depicting Mary surrounded by peoples from around the world, including Africa, Asia, and the Americas. The Oblates of Mary Immaculate, who have engaged in missionary outreach, donated that chapel, and it portrays Marian devotees with varying hues, clothing, and culture. Those figures represent the places where religious congregations of priests and brothers have preached the gospel, from South Africa to Sweden, from Chile to the Arctic.[25]

The last devotee on the viewer's far left is an American Indian. When Captain John Smith sailed up the Potomac River in 1608 he had encountered thirteen tribes, including the Piscataway, and some members of that tribe later worshiped as Catholics at the Jesuit mission that became St. Ignatius Church in Port Tobacco, Maryland. But "most eventually lost their conscious tribal identities by the turn of the twentieth century," so if any Catholic descendants of those early Indian converts were living in the area at the time the Shrine was founded, they would not have retained any tribal identity. But beyond the metropolitan Washington area, especially in the Far West, the situation was different, and Catholics who claimed tribal identities and those who evangelized them did have a presence at the Shrine by giving and going. A 1920 issue of *Salve Regina* reported that the staff had received "a small donation from the Papago Indians of Arizona," and several years later another issue of that periodical included a photograph of two aboriginal residents of Alaska, with a caption mentioning their donation. In the succeeding decades, Catholic missionaries continued their efforts to incorporate more members into Christ's body. Franciscan missionaries in Arizona, for example, continued their evangelization of the Papagos, the Pimas, and many other tribes in the region, and one friar declared in the late 1940s that "Catholic feasts have supplanted the old pagan ceremonials," although evidence suggests that aboriginal practices endured in a complex mix of influences. By the middle of the century, about one-third of the six thousand Pimas and over half of the six thousand Papagos claimed Catholic identity. Indian Catholic practice, a product of contact, included devotion to Mary, and some of her Arizona devotees sent contributions. For example, in the year that fundraising for the Great Upper Church started again, 1953, Mrs. F. H. Riley, a lay Indian devotee who worked at the Franciscan-operated St. John's Indian Mission in Laveen, Arizona, mailed her own modest gift to Washington (fig. 6.4).[26]

Catholic Native Americans also were among the pilgrims. As Father McKenna's memoir suggests and the Shrine's periodical confirms, in May 1920 "representatives from three important tribes of Montana Indians were in Washington to witness the blessing of the site." Those sources didn't indicate which of Montana's twelve tribal nations attended that

Figure 6.4. Yearbook cover, St. John's Indian School, Laveen, Arizona, where the Shrine's benefactor, Mrs. Riley, worked in 1953.

historic ritual, but the Crow, Salish, and Cheyenne all had Catholic missionary churches and schools by that time. There is evidence that some Native Americans also traveled to the Shrine after that ceremony. For example, on the day after Christmas in 1925, a pilgrim named "Half Moon" signed the visitors' log. Since the recorded address identified only the state, "Colorado," it's difficult to unearth more information. The federal census records and the U.S. Indian census schedules include a possible match in Yuma, Colorado. Several men named "Half Moon" from different tribes (e.g., Nez Perce, Cheyenne, and Wichita) also lived on reservations in other states in earlier years, and one of them might have migrated to Colorado by the 1920s. In any case, even if we cannot be sure about that pilgrim's identity, we know that Indian Catholics came to the Shrine during and after the 1920s, from the spring day when Chickasaw and Choctaw pilgrims visited the almost completed crypt level in 1925 to the summer day in 2007 when more than seven hundred gathered for a mass celebrated by Archbishop Charles Chaput, a member of the Prairie Band Potawatomi tribe and the first American Indian archbishop in U.S. history.[27]

Pilgrims also could notice representations of native peoples and Indian missions in the Shrine's material culture. As you'll recall, Father Raphael Pfisterer's illustration of Mary Immaculate for the 1920 foundation stone program book included three indigenous devotees of Mary (see fig. 5.1). Decorative elements inside the completed lower church did the same. One of the fifty-eight columns installed during the mid-1920s was dedicated to "Our Lady of the Indians," and, as I've noted, a sculpture placed in the lower level four decades later venerated Mary as the Queen of Missions and memorialized indigenous converts as well as those who evangelized them. In 1992, the Bureau of Catholic Indian Missions donated a white marble statue of Catherine Tekakwitha (1656–1680). She was born to a Mohawk father and a Christian Algonquian mother in a village at the eastern extremity of Iroquois country, in land now mapped as New York state; Jesuit missionaries baptized her and, after her premature death, lauded her as an exemplar of spiritual virtue. St. Rose Philippine Duchesne and St. Katherine Drexel, who had established missions to native peoples in the United States, also are remembered in statues that stand nearby in the crypt level.[28]

Drexel, in addition, founded missions to African Americans, who had very limited presence at the Shrine between 1920 and 1959 but increasing visibility by the 1990s. Analyzing the full diversity of devotees, as I've tried to do in this book, means attending to all those who are present. Yet it also means noticing who is absent. During much of the Shrine's history, African Americans apparently were not there very often, except as blue-collar laborers. As photographic evidence suggests, workers who would have been coded as "white" in America's taxonomy held the clerical and skilled laborer positions on the Shrine's staff during the 1920s. All of the eleven workers posing at their posts in the *Salve Regina* office in 1925 were white, as were the twenty-four staff members in the mailroom, filing room, and printing services who posed on and around a truck piled with fundraising items about to be mailed to Marian devotees around the country. There was some ethnic diversity among the "whites" on the support staff; for example, Joseph Rydzynksi, a son of Polish immigrants who was studying at the nearby Franciscan monastery, worked in the Shrine's mailroom translating Polish devotees' letters. But most of the clerical staff were women of Irish ancestry, including Dorothy Rooney and Catharine McGinnis in the mailroom and Bernadette Casey and Anna O'Keefe in the filing room. The contractor in charge of construction for the

Crypt Church was a second-generation Irish American, Charles J. Cassidy, who lived on a racially homogenous street in the District, but he hired local African Americans as semiskilled and unskilled workers. In one photograph taken in 1922, when construction was under way, McKenna and Cassidy stand with twenty-nine laborers, eighteen of whom would have been counted as "black." Other snapshots of work-in-progress taken the following year reveal approximately the same proportions. In one photograph from 1923, of the thirteen workers who pose at the construction site, eight would have been classified as "nonwhite" by the color code of the day (see fig. 6.5).[29]

Some "white" Marian devotees who donated to the building project also supported outreach to African Americans, and there were some Black Catholic benefactors. Nazarino Maisano, a seventeen-year-old son of Italian immigrants, sent a money order from California in 1913, the year fundraising started, and reported that he not only wanted to help with "the shrine to be erected to the honor of the Mother of God" but also that he subscribed to the *Colored Harvest*. African Americans, the spiritual "crop" that missionaries hoped to "harvest," also sometimes contributed to the Shrine. Recall Henry Brown, the Louisiana-born Catholic living in Los Angeles, who mailed a contribution to Washington in 1953 (see appendix 1.5). *Salve Regina* occasionally gestured toward Catholicism in Africa, as it

Figure 6.5. Construction workers posed by the site on September 12, 1923.

did with one 1925 story, "African Devotion to the Blessed Virgin," which argued that recent archeology in North Africa demonstrated the antiquity of veneration of Mary on that continent, but mostly overlooked African-American adherents. In turn, it seems that most African-American Catholics around the country and in D.C. remained more than a little ambivalent about the Shrine. That's not surprising, since they were excluded from the CUA campus until the mid-1930s and residential segregation and ecclesiastical indifference continued even as the local African-American population increased. In 1920, only one-quarter (25.1 percent) of the capital's residents were counted as "black" by census officials, but by 1990 that figure that risen to almost two-thirds (65.8 percent). By the end of the twentieth century, the racial and ethnic composition of the neighborhood surrounding the Shrine had changed. Almost 75 percent of the residents in the Shrine's zip code claimed African-American identity on the census form, and over 16 percent of Washington's five hundred thousand Catholics were African American.[30]

Some of those eighty thousand African-American Catholics in D.C. noticed the lack of African presence in the site's material culture. That omission was addressed on August 30, 1997, when James Cardinal Hickey dedicated the new Our Mother of Africa Chapel, a space donated by the National Black Catholic Congress, the group that had held its first meeting at segregated St. Augustine's. This chapel, which includes a sculpture of a black Madonna and Child, doesn't flinch at the horrors of slavery: an abstract inlay of a seventeenth-century slave ship, the *Henrietta Marie*, adorns the threshold and forces viewers to confront racial injustice immediately on entering the space. Ed Dwight's (1933–) bronze sculptural relief records historical events "from slavery to emancipation" and culminates with two figures emerging from that tragic past to lift their arms to Jesus on the cross. At the chapel's dedication, Hickey acknowledged the Church's errors in its treatment of African Americans and exhorted everyone to "rejoice over the growing African American presence in our family of faith." "We should all stand ready," the cardinal continued, "to welcome back African American Catholics who have been alienated by racial prejudice and indifference." The Shrine's rector, Monsignor Bransfield, agreed. He called the chapel "the missing link" and "one of the most important additions to the shrine in many years." Some leading African-American Catholics welcomed the chapel, too. The chapel's sponsoring bishop, John H. Ricard of Pensacola-Tallahassee, who preached the dedication sermon, suggested it "expresses our values, our hopes, our dreams, our very deepest aspiration, our history." That dedication was scheduled to coincide with the eighth meeting of the National Black Catholic Congress in Baltimore, and the congress's lay executive director, Hilbert Stanley, told a reporter for the diocesan newspaper that "it makes us a real part of this national church." In an interview I conducted with Stanley shortly after the dedication, he elaborated: "the shrine is America's Church and we're as American as anyone else. And if we're going to have diversity expressed at the shrine, then it should include all ethnic groups."[31]

INCORPORATING IMMIGRANTS AT THE SHRINE

The Shrine's planners, all of whom were either immigrants or the sons of immigrants, had hoped to "include all ethnic groups." The Shrine's founders recognized the laity's ethnic heterogeneity, although they didn't always highlight that theme in early fundraising efforts. Shahan, Gibbons, and McKenna focused on regional, class, and gender as much as ethnic inclusiveness as they promoted the building in the early years. It was a project, leaders proposed, for Catholics in every part of the country, from all economic levels, and for women and children as well as men. For example, the first issue of *Salve Regina*, published in January 1914, stressed the shared devotion—especially *women's* devotion—to the nation's official patroness, Mary Immaculate. Even if the early marketing didn't always emphasize the Shrine's role in consolidating ethnic communities, that concern was always in the background as the designers imagined the building's function: the National Shrine was envisioned in 1919 as a "perpetual chorus of peoples," and the tentative plans for the fifteen apsidal altars in Crypt Church had emphasized ethnicity and migration. "Radiating from the high altar were to be fifteen other altars each dedicated to Our Blessed Mother under the invocation of famous national shrines throughout the world." Those chapels venerating Marian figures from places like Mexico, Ireland, and Poland "might be contributed by pious descendants of those races who had carried their particular devotion to Mary to the New World." That intriguing plan for the northern apse never was implemented, though other decorative features of the Shrine, as I'll show, incorporated immigrants' ethnic diversity.[32]

Diversity and the Crypt, 1920–1932: Columns, Foundation Stone, and Memorial Tablets

Immigrants had a presence at the Shrine by giving and going, I've noted throughout this book, but the desire to incorporate immigrant diversity there also found representation in the material culture. The names of Catholics born abroad are embedded in the foundation stone and etched on the walls. As a Shrine publication at the time noted, the foundation stone ceremony "has been practiced for over a thousand years," and, according to Catholic practice, "a cavity is made in the stone in which are placed an attest on parchment recording the act of laying the stone; current coins and also other memoranda are usually inserted." In 1920, Gibbons sprinkled the stone with holy water and inserted the metal container, which contained not only American coins, a Mt. Carmel relic, and a document describing the event but also a list of the persons who had contributed to the recently formed organization of donors, "The Salve Regina League." As far as I can tell, no copy of that donor list has survived; however, analysis of other sources—including the contributor records and donor letters that I matched with census data—suggest that a high proportion of those supporters would have been either immigrants or the children of immigrants. Their presence remains hidden from view, however, even if they found a place in the first and most important artifact in the Shrine. Other immigrants' names are recorded in the archived lists of visitors and donors, as with those who contributed so their loved ones would be remembered in the "National Catholic Family Record": in 1928 Amanda C. Gies from Louisville, Kentucky, sent the suggested donation so that her whole clan, including her father, John, who was born in Germany, might have a place there; so did Bostonian Katherine S. Egan, whose parents, Martin and Bridgit, were born in Ireland. Many immigrants—both Shrine benefactors and those memorialized by loved ones who contributed—also had their names inscribed on the tan marble walls of Memorial Hall in the southern crypt, the vestibule beyond the threshold of the main worship space. As a visitor descends the stairs into the crypt level, for example, the floor-to-ceiling rectangular panels of travertine marble that meet the eye to the left of one stairwell display some of the faithful's European connections: we see the names of the Messall family, who hailed from Germany and lived in Enid, Oklahoma, and of the O'Loughlin family, who came from Ireland and lived in Chicago.[33]

Immigrant diversity also found expression in the northern crypt, including in the columns of the Crypt Church (fig. 6.6). Of the fifty-eight columns, eight are huge granite pillars quarried in South Dakota and Labrador that support the broad vault, but, as McKenna noted in his memoir, "there is a significance attached to each of the fifty smaller columns." Those columns of different colors and from different places—creamy white from Mexico, mica black from Belgium, and soft rose from Italy—were quarried in five continents and represent the Marian shrines

Figure 6.6. The Crypt Church's marble columns, which represent different Marian figures in different nations.

and ethnic identities of Catholic immigrants. Even if the viewer misses the verbal clues at the bases of the columns that identify each one's geographical origin, the alternating hues of the pillars vividly reflect the ethnic diversity of the "members" of Christ's ecclesiastical body. Those colored pillars between the apsidal chapels and near the nave entrances connect Marian devotees to the homeland. One of those pillars, the granite column from Norway dedicated to "Our Lady of Bergen," was an odd choice, since it recalls an image in a Protestant church in a Lutheran country. The dedication refers to the Madonna and Child enshrined in the central panel of the fifteenth-century altar reredos in Bergen's Maria Kirken, which has been a Lutheran church since 1548, as the painting of Martin Luther adorning its side aisle reminds visitors. Even though a Norwegian ambassador who visited the Shrine seemed to appreciate the American Catholics' ecumenical gesture of inclusion, it's not clear that Shahan and Maginnis realized they were unwittingly enshrining Protestantism. Most of the other columns explicitly recall the native piety of foreign-born Catholics, however. By 1926, many immigrant pilgrims could find a marble column that had been dedicated to their national Marian symbol and quarried in their homeland: for example, a gray pillar from Spain, blue from Switzerland, and green from Ireland. But if they did not read the articles about the columns in *Salve Regina* or hear McKenna explain the symbolization—he often spoke to pilgrim groups—visitors might not have noticed these material expressions of inclusion.[34]

Nonetheless, some Marian devotees discovered the pillars' intended meaning and responded warmly to the planners' effort at inclusion. Consider Poles' responses, for example. In 1928, two years after the column dedicated to Our Lady of Czestochowa had been installed in the lower level, *Salve Regina* reported: "many Polish visitors make an extra effort to visit the shrine on account of this memento of the Blessed Virgin in Poland." Other surviving evidence confirms that report. Two years later, a thirty-four-year-old optician, who was living with his Polish-born parents on an ethnically diverse street in Baltimore, wrote to McKenna to inform him "that a large group of the Polish Catholics of this city have requested me to organize a Polish pilgrimage . . . the second Sunday in May." Adding another transnational dimension to the ritual, those lay immigrants and children of immigrants also planned "to bring a choir of Polish singers to render a number of hymns to the Blessed Virgin before and after the Mass." A year later, in 1931, laywomen from the Polish Women's Alliance of America also worshiped in the Crypt Church and then mailed a note to the Shrine's director expressing their gratitude for the column dedicated to Poland's national patroness. In 1931, Polish Catholics could visit the column dedicated to their beloved Virgin—and touch a quarried block of native terrain—and even descend to the subbasement, where McKenna had hung a painting of Our Lady of Czestochowa.[35]

Diversity and the Ethnic Chapels and Oratories, 1964–1997

Four decades later, Polish Catholics could pray in an elaborate chapel in the Great Upper Church that included a brightly colored mosaic of Our Lady of Czestochowa. The early clerical concern to incorporate immigrants and enshrine national saints intensified in the last quarter of the twentieth century, when immigration increased again. The percentage of foreign-born residents in the District of Columbia had been as high as 12.6 percent in 1870, when many European Catholic migrants settled there, but the mid-twentieth-century influx of native-born government workers and the restriction on transnational migration cut that proportion to 4.1 percent by 1970. Then, as in many other places in the United States, by the 1980s the heterogeneity of the local population started to increase again after the revision of federal immigration laws. By 1990, 9.7 percent of the District's residents and nearly 11 percent of Metropolitan Washington's population, which included the suburbs, were immigrants.[36]

Only ten years after the new immigration law, the Shrine's fundraising periodical, *Mary's Shrine*, quoted the planners' 1919 declaration that the site would be "a perpetual chorus of peoples" and affirmed the earlier message: the building would be a place "where all the nationalities that made up the great melting pot would be represented." That piece, which appeared on the eve of America's bicentennial, also called attention to the marble sculpture of Cabrini, the patroness of immigrants, which had been installed in the crypt level a few years earlier. By the 1990s, immigrant presence and ethnic diversity had become a common motif in Shrine communications, and in the messages of Monsignor Bransfield, the Shrine's rector from 1986 to 2005. On the Shrine's website, Bransfield reflected on the meaning of the phrase "America's Church." He suggested that the Shrine's diverse pilgrims "symbolize the Church's catholicity, the Church universal, reaching to nearly every city and village of our vast and ever-expanding globe." And when I interviewed him in his office, Bransfield suggested that the building itself, and especially the sixty-two chapels niched along the walls of the upper and lower churches, symbolized the Catholic Church's ability to hold together ethnic and national diversity. When I asked him about the meaning of the phrase "America's Church," he explained: "It represents the devotion of American Catholics to Our Lady, with an emphasis on the ethnic groups especially. It is a wonderful experience for them that these ethnic groups have expressed their devotion to Mary and their place in American culture." And, he suggested, by having an image enshrined there they found their place in American Catholicism, too. He went on to trumpet the three new ethnic chapels—Filipino, African, and Asian Indian—that would be consecrated in 1997. I then asked for his response to the Catholic educator's dismissal of the Shrine as being "just about bishops." Bransfield implied that he could see the point about *some* sites within the Shrine, but the chapels were different. "You have to distinguish between the church and the chapels," he proposed. "The bishops did build the upper church during the 1950s. But the chapels are a different story. The chapels show that it is a living church." The chapel of Our Lady of Guadalupe is a good example, Bransfield suggested. It "is now one of the most central chapels, because of all the immigrants." He was referring to the large proportion of Latin American immigrants, who then made up about half of all foreign born in the United States and in the capital. Of all newcomers counted in the federal census, more were born in Mexico than in any other nation, over four million in 1990 and almost eight million by the end of that decade; and, as the rector pointed out, at most times of the day, Spanish-speaking pilgrims, often with children and grandparents, knelt in the chapel dedicated to the patroness of Mexico and the Americas (fig. 6.7).[37]

There are other places of prayer in the Shrine: by 2010 bishops had dedicated forty-five chapels and ten oratories. Among the chapels, devotional spaces with an altar, are the fifteen apsidal chapels installed in 1926 in the Crypt Church. To the left of the entrance is the Our Lady of Lourdes Chapel. Dedicated in 1931, that dark small space self-consciously imitates the

Figure 6.7. A Latina devotee kneels in prayer at the Our Lady of Guadalupe Chapel.

famous grotto in southeastern France. The other thirty-nine chapels and oratories have been dedicated since the completion of the exterior in 1959. Religious orders donated a dozen chapels or oratories. Those spaces venerate the orders' founders or patronesses, as with the St. Vincent de Paul Chapel, given by the Vincentians, and the Our Lady of Mount Carmel Chapel, a gift of the Carmelites. Every one of the most popular expressions of Marian devotion is found somewhere in the Shrine, including in mosaics and statues celebrating the apparitions at La Salette and Fatima. And as Bransfield noted, some of the chapels, like those dedicated to Our Lady of Lourdes and the Miraculous Medal, "expressed popular devotion." Taken together, these chapels dedicated to Marian figures and religious orders represent many of the most important institutions and devotions in U.S. Catholic history.[38]

Table 6.1. ETHNIC/NATIONAL CHAPELS AND ORATORIES AT THE SHRINE, 1964–1997

Chapel	Ethnicity	Dedication
Our Lady of Czestochowa Chapel	Polish	1964
Our Mother of Sorrows Chapel	Slovak	1965
Our Lady of Siluva Chapel	Lithuanian	1966
Our Lady of Guadalupe Chapel	Mexican	1967
Our Lady of Bistrica Chapel	Croatian	1970
Our Lady of Brezje Chapel	Slovenian	1971
Byzantine-Ruthenian Chapel	Ukranian	1974
Mary, Queen of Ireland Oratory	Irish	1980
Our Lady of Holy Hostyn Chapel	Czech	1983
Our Lady of Mariazell Chapel	Austrian	1992
Our Lady of Hope Chapel	French	1993
Our Lady of Peace and Good Voyage Oratory	Filipino	1997
Our Lady of Good Health Oratory	Asian Indian	1997
Our Mother of Africa Chapel	African	1997

Reflecting broader patterns in the era of fragmentation, fifteen of the chapels and oratories dedicated between 1964 and 1997 had explicit ethnic or national links and hinted at the diversity of the faithful (see table 6.1).

Most of the Shrine's planners and many of the lay devotees who supported its construction in the 1910s and 1920s claimed Irish ancestry, so it's not surprising that the first space of prayer to explicitly denote an ethnic connection was the St. Brigid of Ireland Chapel (1927). The impulse to mark ethnic identity and national origin in the Shrine's decorative plan, however, grew more intense as identity politics and new immigration transformed American culture during and after the 1960s. The new devotional spaces included monuments to nineteenth-century immigrants—the Polish chapel of Our Lady of Czestochowa (1964) and the Slovenian chapel of Our Lady of Brezje (1971)—while other sites recognized post-1965 migrants—the Asian Indian oratory to Our Lady of Good Health, Vailankanni (1997), and the Our Lady of Peace and Good Voyage Oratory (1997), which celebrates Filipino devotions.[39]

The Filipino Oratory: A Case Study

That aim was clear in the Filipino oratory, and because it's typical of the other ethnic chapels and illustrates larger patterns, I'll discuss it in some detail. To understand the complex meanings devotees inscribed on the Shrine's material culture, especially the oratory, I supplemented archival sources and textual analysis with participant observation and semi-structured interviews. I interviewed dozens of Filipino pilgrims during the year of the oratory's dedication, and one of them, a Manila-born woman who emigrated in 1978, suggested that the Shrine was "for all the peoples of the U.S.A." We spoke on June 7, 1997, when Cardinal James Hickey, the archbishop of Washington, dedicated the Filipino oratory as thirty-five hundred proud Filipinos filled the pews of the Great Upper Church for the mass. This lay devotee came that day to "pay homage to our Virgin," the Virgin of Antipolo, the Filipino patroness who is venerated in the new chapel in the Crypt Church, just to the right of the Mary Memorial Altar.[40]

Even though popes have crowned eleven different Marian statues in the Philippines, and the people have venerated many other regional Virgins, in a formal vote in 1993 the Catholic Bishops Conference of the Philippines chose Our Lady of Antipolo (*Ang Mahal na Birhen ng Antipolo*), for the Washington oratory. The first Spanish governor of the Philippines brought an image of the Virgin Mary to Manila on board *El Almirante* in 1626, and that image began to draw widespread affection among Filipinos in 1648, when that Virgin made the first of her five trading voyages from Manila to Acapulco. Each time, as Filipino Catholics tell the story, she brought the seamen and the ship home safely, and on her last journey (1748), devotees gave the Virgin of Antipolo a new title, Our Lady of Peace and Good Voyage. Since the middle of the eighteenth century, then, the Virgin of Antipolo has been the patroness of travelers, and she continues to attract devotees from all across the Philippines to her church, which the bishops declared the country's national shrine in 1954. Many Filipinos visit that shrine before and after they undertake a long journey; and many Filipino Americans prayed there before they left for the United States. Even if some Filipinos might have chosen another Marian figure for the oratory—and some would have—almost everyone I spoke with endorsed the bishops' decision to enshrine the Virgin of Antipolo in the oratory for Filipino migrants in the United States. As the intercessor for travelers, Our Lady of Peace and Good Voyage seemed a logical, if not unanimous, choice.[41]

Our Lady of Peace and Good Voyage's Washington oratory—the term means a place of prayer—houses a wooden replica of the Virgin of Antipolo that two elderly sisters in the Philippines donated (fig. 6.1). As she does on her altar in the Antipolo church, the dark-faced Virgin stands on a circular pedestal in the D.C. Shrine. Behind that Philippine hardwood pedestal, blue tiles create the illusion of waves, recalling the seas she traveled during her seventeenth- and eighteenth-century voyages. To the statue's left and right are two murals by the Filipino artist Jose V. Blanco (1932–2008) and his seven children. In lush earthy colors, the longer panel to the viewer's left depicts the history of the Virgin of Antipolo; the shorter right panel, which includes recognizably particular Filipino devotees of all ages, recalls the miraculous rescue of the Virgin from the burning town of Antipolo after Japanese soldiers torched it during World War II. So the mural's "folk realism" returns viewers to the nation's past, emphasizing especially the Filipinos' enduring relationship with the patroness of travelers.[42]

This Filipino oratory, one of the Shrine's fifteen ethnic devotional spaces, illustrates how the Shrine made claims to be "America's Church." On the one hand, the Filipino oratory allowed the clergy to proclaim Catholic unity: as Monsignor Bransfield suggested, the building, like the universal Church, holds diversity together. At the same time, the Shrine—and especially the ethnic oratories and chapels—had meaning for the laity. Those devotional spaces allow multiple peoples, like the Filipinos, not only to construct collective identity but also to claim their place in the national ecclesiastical community.

This was clear in a fundraising pamphlet, produced by the Shrine's public relations office, that invited Filipinos to "share in the joy and privilege of building a chapel for Our Lady of Antipolo" by mailing in their tax-deductible contributions. It rehearsed the familiar history of the Virgin of Antipolo and narrated her "journey to the United States." On the back page of the pamphlet, Monsignor Bransfield repeated his claim that the Shrine is "America's Church"; it's important to note this, as it speaks to the clergy's attitude toward the Filipino oratory, as well as the other ethnic chapels. He explained what that meant for donors and visitors: "Pausing in silent prayer at any of the . . . chapels honoring Mary and her role in the history of the ethnic communities represented, one cannot help but be renewed in one's own spirituality and *feel even more central* to the ever-evolving story of faith which we continue to write . . . day by day by our own devotions and works of charity." Note that here, as in other Shrine publications, the clergy suggested that inclusion at the Shrine marks inclusion in the Church. Filipinos should donate to the oratory project, Bransfield proposed, because it would allow them to find their place in American Catholicism. It even could move them, he promised, toward its center. The Filipino oratory's sponsoring bishop (each chapel or oratory must have one), the Most Reverend Alvaro Corrada del Rio, SJ, auxiliary bishop of Washington, made a similar point in his sermon during the dedication ceremony in 1997. He suggested that the oratory represents both Filipino contributions to American Catholicism and American contributions to Filipino Catholics. Most of all, Corrada told the thousands of

Filipinos who had traveled from all across the country to attend the ceremony, the oratory "represents your presence" in the U.S. Church.[43]

And wherever they lived in the United States, the Filipinos I talked with that day confirmed Bishop Corrada's interpretation: the oratory, devotees told me, proclaimed Filipino presence in the American Church. In fact, the oratory project began as a way to announce Filipino presence, as I had learned in an earlier conversation with Tessie Manuel, a Philippine-born devotee of Mary. In October 1991, Tessie was visiting the Shrine when she noticed all the ethnic chapels. "Then I asked," Tessie recalled, "why none of them represented a Filipino Virgin." She decided to try to find a place for the Virgin, and so Filipinos, at the Shrine. Tessie talked with other Filipinos and appealed to clergy, in the United States and the Philippines. On January 11, 1992, Tessie wrote to the Shrine's director to ask for a chapel; Bransfield wrote back the next month. He noted that "the Austrian-Americans had begun fundraising to build a chapel in the last remaining space in the Shrine." Further, even if there were space, the Filipinos would have to meet several conditions: "first of all, there must be evidence of the authenticity of the devotion and its support in the United States; secondly, there must also be evidence that the person or group interested in the project has the necessary funds or the means to raise those funds." He mentioned the standard third condition: "the Shrine requires that a bishop be a member of the chapel committee." Discouraged by Bransfield's cautious response, Tessie told me, she and the other Filipino Catholics decided to persevere anyway.[44]

And it worked. By 1997, when Cardinal Hickey dedicated the oratory, Tessie and others reported that they were proud they had made a place for the nation's Filipinos in the BNSIC—and, in turn, the U.S. Church. And some Filipinos explicitly mentioned the Shrine's role in holding together ethnic diversity. In 1990, the Philippines ranked second only to Mexico as the top sending nation for emigrants, and one middle-aged Filipina, who was born in Pasay City and arrived in the United States in 1989, suggested that the Shrine "is the symbol of the devotion to Mary of the many ethnic groups living in the U.S." Another devotee, a fifty-six-year-old man, suggested that the oratory "represents the Catholic religion from a Filipino perspective." Eduardo D. Caparas, national cochair of the committee that built the devotional space, proposed that the oratory "bears testimony to the strong presence of Filipino Catholics, devotees of Mary, in the United States."[45]

The oratory "bears testimony" to the presence of Filipinos, and other new immigrants, in another tangible way: it claims the foundation stone, the stone with the names of immigrant donors embedded in it, the same one that Gibbons, the leader of the immigrant church, had blessed in 1920.

The Filipino committee met with the Shrine director in 1994 to discuss available sites for the oratory. (Even though Bransfield had told Tessie that none remained in 1992, the Shrine staff managed to find space two years later.) As members of the planning committee recall, Bransfield asked them "to choose between two empty alcoves on either side of the sanctuary of the crypt church, [and] the group unanimously chose the alcove on the right side containing the cornerstone of the Basilica." Caparas, cochair of that committee, told me that choice was "a befitting gesture," since it resonated with his belief that, "we are the cornerstone of democracy and Catholicism back in Asia." Many Filipinos I met, however, noted the symbolic significance of the foundation stone for their position in the United States, not Asia. And it's intriguing to note that the dedication ceremonies of 1997 enshrined new Asian migrants prominently on either side of the Crypt Church's altar: Filipinos venerated their national Virgin in the oratory to the right, and Indians took the remaining site to the left, where they erected the oratory to Our Lady of Good Health at Vailankanni.[46]

Near the Shrine's cavernous subterranean center, where Gibbons had stood decades earlier to bless the foundation stone, recent migrants consecrated their own spaces—Indian and Filipino, but also Catholic and American. The clergy's verbal and material proclamations of ecclesiastical unity were always contested. Architectural and rhetorical proclamations didn't negate all differences or quiet all dissent. Many Asian and Latino/a migrants, and some older immigrant groups, too, said they felt neglected or abandoned by the Catholic Church. As other newcomers had complained in the nineteenth century, those new migrants noted, for example, that the priests couldn't speak their language and the parish couldn't meet their needs. Nonetheless, in the Filipino oratory, and the other ethnic devotional spaces, clerical leaders announced their desire to incorporate diversity, while lay pilgrims claimed their place in the Catholic Church.

"UNITY IN THE BODY OF CHRIST": IMMIGRANT DIVERSITY AT THE SHRINE, 1998–2008

After the 1997 dedication, Filipinos from Metropolitan Washington gathered regularly at their oratory for monthly masses and annual pilgrimages. Two thousand devotees from D.C. and across the country returned for the Tenth Annual National Filipino Pilgrimage; the new rector, Monsignor Walter R. Rossi (2005–), welcomed them, and the archbishop of Manila encouraged them: "witness through your lives the values and virtues of a Catholic Filipino while being away from your homeland." In the decade between 1998 and 2008, the American nation and the U.S. Catholic Church continued to welcome immigrants and confront diversity. At the end of the twentieth century, there were almost thirty million foreign-born residents in the United States, about 11.1 percent of the population, and more than 17 percent of Americans spoke a language other than English at home. That new immigration, mostly from Latin America and Asia, affected regions that experienced little transnational migration during the nineteenth century, including the South, but it also changed the old immigrant centers. Sometimes those changes were surprising. For example, the parishioners at Father McKenna's former Philadelphia congregation, Holy Angels, were 10.2 percent foreign born in 2000, but many of those new neighbors hailed from Asia. By the first decade of the new century, that North Philadelphia church had been designated the archdiocese's Korean parish. The same changes were occurring closer to the Shrine. In the District of Columbia, 12.9 percent of residents—higher than the national average and greater than the 1870 figure—were born outside the United States, and Metropolitan Washington was being called an "immigrant gateway."[47]

As in earlier decades, the Shrine, too, functioned as a "gateway" for immigrants. Between 1998 and 2008, the diverse faithful passed through its doors or found their homeland's devotions represented in its ornamentation. In 1999, the fortieth anniversary of the dedication, Bransfield published a message entitled "Unity through Our Diversity" in Mary's Shrine. Quoting a Pauline epistle (Ephesians 4:15–16), the rector endorsed St. Paul's reflection on the "unity and harmony in the Body of Christ" and praised his view that in that Body, "diverse elements converge to form a united, vibrant whole." Bransfield argued that insight could be "applied to the 'structural church'... and in particular, to the Basilica of the National Shrine of the Immaculate Conception." "As the United States' patronal church," Bransfield observed, the Shrine "has sought to honor and reflect the many devotions Catholics have to our Blessed Mother." Yet that clerical leader's aim was more than just inclusion: it was "to unite these varied and culturally rich faith experiences into a single collected expression of love and trust in Mary and her Son Jesus." That impulse to incorporate diverse peoples into the Body of Christ by gathering multiple ethnic devotions within one building had intensified under Bransfield's leadership, and it continued after Rossi succeeded him in 2005. By 2008, seven more artifacts and spaces venerated national Virgins and marked ethnic identity (table 6.2). Those sites included chapels and oratories honoring immigrant groups that had a major ecclesiastical presence by the early twentieth century, such as the German Chapel of Our Lady of Altötting and the Italian Chapel of Our Lady of Pompei. Other ethnic groups with less visibility in

Table 6.2. ETHNIC/NATIONAL CHAPELS, ORATORIES, AND VOTIVE OFFERINGS, 1998–2008

Chapel/Statue/Mosaic	Ethnicity	Dedication
Our Lady of China Mosaic	Chinese	2002
Our Lady of Altötting Oratory	German (Bavarian)	2005
Our Lady of La Vang Chapel	Vietnamese	2006
Our Lady of Camarin Oratory	Guamanian	2006
Our Lady of Ta' Pinu Oratory	Maltese	2006
Our Lady of Korea at Cana Tympanum	Korean	2007
Our Lady of Pompei Chapel	Italian	2008

the American Catholic Church before the 1970s, including the Chinese, Vietnamese, and Koreans, also gathered for dedication masses at the Shrine between 2002 and 2007.[48]

At the 2007 ceremony dedicating two Korean sculptures, one celebrating Our Lady of Korea at Cana, the archbishop of Seoul added an intriguing twist to the old corporeal metaphors for the ecclesiastical community. In traditional usage, Christ was understood as the body's "head" and the faithful as its "members." Nicholas Cardinal Choeong Jin-Sak asserted: "the National Shrine is the *heart* of the American Catholic Church." In turn, by adding ornamentation to the Shrine, Koreans reminded fellow Catholics that Koreans, too, had their role to play in the organic whole. "It is significant that Korean immigrants have endeavored to dedicate these art pieces here," the cardinal suggested. It "is a sign of the fact that Korean-Americans are no longer outsiders, but have become active members of the American Catholic Church."[49]

As far as I know, no other Catholic has described the Washington Shrine as the "heart" of the Body of Christ, although over the years many others have made a similar point: one of the building's primary functions has been to proclaim unity and confront *difference*—ethnic, linguistic, and cultural diversity. The most fundamental divide was between Catholics and non-Catholics, and although Shrine clergy never emphasized missions, some artifacts represent the unsaved who remained outside Christ's Body, "heathens" abroad, as in the mosaic *Descent of the Spirit*. Members of some Native American tribes, whom clergy sometimes also imagined as "heathens," donated and visited, and a sculpture in the Shrine's Hall of American Saints memorializes an indigenous convert, Catherine Tekakwitha. America's color code marked African Americans as most different—and most marginalized—so it's not surprising that they were mostly absent from the Shrine, except as laborers, until the National Black Catholic

Congress asserted their presence in the 1990s with the installation of the starkly candid but stubbornly hopeful Our Mother of Africa Chapel. Displaced Amerindians and African slaves had been compelled to relocate, but when Catholics have talked about *difference* in the U.S. Church they usually have referred to another kind of migration. Difference has meant the ethnic, linguistic, and cultural diversity of transnational migrants, who might have felt propelled to emigrate by hunger, persecution, or war but who were not "removed" to reservations at gunpoint or shackled on slave ships for the "middle passage." As I've tried to show, those mostly voluntary migrants, and their children, have had a presence at the Shrine by giving and going; and U.S. Catholicism's ethnic diversity and devotional variety found expression in its interior ornamentation. The names of immigrant donors were etched on memorial tablets, and the marble columns quarried in different nations and dedicated to national Virgins transported devotees to the homeland while simultaneously claiming space in the American Catholic Church. The fifteen ethnic chapels and oratories dedicated by 1997, as well as the five installed after that, vividly represented the clergy's desire to incorporate diversity and the laity's concern to gain recognition.

Diverse migrants had secured a place in those devotional spaces, including the Oratory to Our Lady of Peace and Good Voyage, even if they hadn't "fused" into a homogenous whole, as Gibbons had hoped, and even if Bransfield's aim for "America's Church"—that it would create "unity and harmony in the Body of Christ"—might not have been realized as fully as he imagined. Even if corporeal "unity" still eluded an increasingly fragmented U.S. Catholic Church at the start of the twenty-first century, there was no denying the Shrine's leaders' extraordinary efforts to include immigrants. There was no denying, either, that diverse Marian devotees, from Polish visitors to the Crypt Church columns in the early 1930s to Filipino worshipers at their ethnic oratory in the late 1990s, had found meaning in the rituals and artifacts there. Immigrants and their descendants found ritual affirmation and material reassurance. The painted murals, inscribed tablets, polychromatic pillars—and, most of all, the image of their own beloved Mary—allowed some to believe, if only for a moment, that maybe they did have a presence in the Shrine and, so, in the Church. Whether or not the Shrine was the "heart" of the ecclesiastical community, maybe they each had a distinctive role to play, just as each microscopic cell has its function. The Shrine's effusively inclusive material culture proclaimed that despite irresolvable differences and inevitable conflicts, despite the history of racial segregation, missionary paternalism, and pastoral ethnocentrism, maybe all the faithful were, as the clergy promised, integral parts of one organic body.

∽

Conclusion

S
teep granite steps lead visitors to the two tall doors of the Shrine's main entrance, which is framed by a Roman arch and decorated with a sculpted image of the national patroness, Mary Immaculate. Standing there we can mark the passage of time, the historical shifts during the twentieth century, and map the contours of piety, the flows of people, things, and practices. Positioned at that spatial and temporal boundary— glancing up the long nave and turning to face the capital city—we can't see everything, but that threshold provides an illuminating angle of vision, I've tried to argue. Thinking about the history of practice there (devotees' giving and going), and attending to its material culture (the building and its orna- mentation) reveals a good deal about Catholic America in the era of consol- idation—its diverse members, clerical aims, and shared worldview from 1909 to 1959—just as recent developments and contemporary reactions disclose much about the fragmented U.S. Catholic Church that emerged during the half century between the 1959 dedication ceremony and the 2009 Golden Jubilee. Finally, I suggest, positioned at that site we can even learn something about religion and how to study it.[1]

A THRESHOLD TO CATHOLIC AMERICA, 1909–1959

All sorts of Catholics crossed the Shrine's threshold—and some even had an enduring presence in its material culture. Recall some of the pilgrims: the parish priest from Harrisburg who brought a busload of parishioners, the four nuns from St. Paul who came to see the art, the local boy who play- fully sketched the phonograph in the visitors' log. And remember the donors: the indigenous Catholic woman from Arizona, the Irish saloon-keeper from Philadelphia, and the Brooklyn children who supported the Mary Memorial Altar. Their names are embedded in that block of marble, and more of the diverse members of the Body of Christ are hidden from view in the foundation stone and on public display on the crypt level's Memorial Hall. Even non-Catholics had a presence—as "heathens," the target of missions portrayed on mosaics, and as visitors and donors, like Susanna Fay, who gave the funds for an apsidal chapel. And like strident Protestant critics Randolph McKim and Hiram Evans, some were there only as the imagined Other who haunts the dark subterranean space.

There was nothing incorporeal about the ecclesiastical leaders who had a presence at the Shrine before 1959. As the Shrine's founder had imagined in 1903—and as that contemporary liberal Catholic who said it was "just about bishops" complained—it became a site where "the dignity of our bishops and our priesthood might be worthily enshrined on the occasion of the annual meetings." Bishops first gathered on CUA's campus in 1919 and sent their personal donations later that year, though the hierarchy had more influence during the 1950s as shrewd national marketing and demanding diocesan quotas nudged local leaders and lay devotees to contribute and visit. The Founder's Chapel, which entombs Bishop Shahan, symbolizes that undeniable episcopal presence. So that liberal who emphasized the role of bishops had a point. But, like some other contemporary progressive critics, he overlooked another important part of the building's history. Even if it might not have functioned as "America's Church," it made a reasonable claim to be "America's *Catholic* Church" in one important sense: it did attract support from Catholic laity, nuns, monks, and priests from all over the country. Even if some devotees remained anonymous and, therefore, mostly invisible—like the visitor who signed as "Nobody-Nowhere"—and Catholics of color were absent, or only had a presence on the construction crews, it was a place where much of the diversity, and moral complexity, of U.S. Catholic life found vivid expression.[2]

To mention moral complexity—and racial attitudes in the era of consolidation—is to note how the Catholic worldview, and prevailing social attitudes, crossed the Shrine's portal and to suggest that the clergy enjoyed mixed success in realizing their hopes for the building. Those hopes, I've argued, were rooted in a Vatican-centered Thomistic worldview that valued unity, tradition, and authority and affirmed a selective countermodernism and triumphalist Americanism. There was some dissent, even in that period—remember the outraged layman's letter to McKenna—but the Shrine's leaders and supporters agreed about many things, including devotion to Mary. The building they dedicated in 1959 served as a monument to the shared worldview of consolidated Catholicism and the clerical concern to build institutions, mobilize women, engage children, contest Protestants, incorporate immigrants, and claim civic space. In the end, however, they achieved more success with some of those tasks than with others, and even when the clerical promoters managed notable accomplishments, their efforts also sometimes involved personal cost and moral risk.

As with the other impulses discernable at the Shrine, the clergy's efforts to *build institutions* reflected broader patterns during that period. Ecclesiastical leaders managed extraordinary accomplishments, transforming the American landscape, especially but not only cityscapes where immigrants gathered, as they successfully motivated millions to construct a dense and large institutional network that provided generations with a sense of meaning and a feeling of belonging. At times, however, some bishops were less attentive to their pastoral tasks and asked too much of working-class devotees, more than those of modest means had to give, and strained the resources—in time and labor—of lonely parish priests and overworked nuns. That happened at the D.C. Shrine less than in parishes, though the major construction project did demand sacrifices and channel funds. By 1959, no one could call the structure "The Great Disappointment" any more, however. A great deal of the interior ornamentation remained unfinished, but the Shrine's directors—with the decisive support of the Episcopal Committee for the Shrine and U.S. dioceses—managed to complete the superstructure. Contemporary readers will assess this accomplishment differently depending on how much they value grand architecture, appreciate Marian devotion, and like the building's design, but it seems hard to deny the clergy' success in this regard: Catholicism got its massive shrine in Washington.

The fact that some Catholics didn't like the Byzantine-Romanesque design of the completed building is another issue that arises as we try to gauge how successfully the planners realized their goals. The board, with Shahan's endorsement, abandoned the tentative and unofficial Gothic plan for defensible reasons. After all, there was an enormous Gothic Episcopal Cathedral being built across town. Why build another one? And a persuasive logic supported Maginnis's design: in the absence of a single vernacular architectural tradition in America, he reasoned, the architect is free to experiment by mixing features from the past and using them in new ways. Yet the Shrine's planners seem to have underestimated Gothic's ability to secure American popularity and prompt countermodernist nostalgia. Gothic revival was ascendant in the United States from after the Civil War to the Great Depression, and it became "part of the common vocabulary of American urban religious building." For many Americans, Protestant and Catholic, "the

Gothic had come to represent 'what a church should look like.'" In 1919, a lay member of the NOCW called Gothic "Our Lady's own architecture," and Maginnis and Shahan also had great affection for that design and saw it as one of the major triumphs of medieval Catholic culture. That points to another possible reason the design was not universally applauded. It strained against one of the values of the shared worldview of consolidated Catholicism—tradition. That might seem odd to say, since the eventual design appealed to architectural traditions older than Gothic. However, for many Catholics in the 1920s—and in later decades, too—tradition meant Gothic, not Romanesque or Byzantine. By not choosing Gothic, the planners missed an opportunity to most effectively express a particular kind of countermodernism. They missed their chance to reaffirm the glory of the medieval Catholic past and show its applicability in modern America.[3]

Some high-church Protestants of the era relished Gothic's links with medieval Catholicism, while other non-Catholics were much more critical and went to great lengths to explain that it was not really a *Catholic* art form. Roman Catholics noticed this, and some found it amusing, but they were much more concerned by the harsher forms of anti-Catholicism still circulating when the Shrine was being planned and built. As they *contested Protestants*, some Catholics of the era retreated into enclosed subcultures or, worse, replicated their accusers' arrogance as they ignored the best intellectual resources of the regnant Thomism, including its proclamation that everyone moved by the Unmoved Mover could hear the voice of conscience and everyone—even a Protestant critic—is gifted with the natural reason that could lead to God. Shahan and the Shrine's early leaders tended to be conciliatory in their verbal retorts, but their concern to contest Protestants in the Shrine's material culture met with limited success, since the architectural rejoinder expressed in the Crypt Church's ornamentation went mostly unnoticed by Protestant contemporaries. There is little evidence that its "catacombal" theme managed to convince anyone that Marian devotion was authentic and ancient, except perhaps Mary Chase Stratton, the Protestant woman who created the ceramic tiles for the subterranean space. The publicity about the major construction project did get Protestants' attention, however, though it mostly prompted more sectarian rivalry, as other Christian denominations tried to match the impressive efforts of Catholics and Episcopalians. As for Catholics themselves, devotees who read in *Salve Regina* about the ancient representations of Mary in the catacombs and who learned of the clergy's intention to recreate that early Marian history in the Crypt Church's decoration might have found some solace, just as at other sites Catholic efforts to respond to Protestant charges provided a shared identity and a measure of dignity.

Between the 1910s and the 1950s, the clergy were more successful in their effort to *mobilize women*. By linking feminine virtues with Marian ideals, they provided feminine models of excellence, offered women a sense of purpose, and cleared paths for achievement—including meaningful labor for women religious and lay volunteers. By invoking the culture of suffering and prescribing an ethic of submission, however, this devotional culture sometimes also sanctioned the marginalization of women. Still, women's organizations managed to make sizeable contributions during the 1950s, and their role was even more significant earlier. The leaders of some laywomen's organizations (including Lucy Hoffman of the NOCW, Ellen Jolly of the LAAOH, and Clara Sheeran of the IFCA) managed to work with the Shrine's male founder and director to plan and implement development campaigns for a cause they cherished. So the clergy succeeded in mobilizing women to donate to the Shrine, and as the visitor logs and other sources indicate, they also convinced female devotees to go on pilgrimage. Plenty of lay male devotees, like the Building Committee's James J. Ryan, and several men's organizations, especially the Knights of Columbus, had an important presence by giving and going. Yet especially in the 1910s and 1920s, women played a key role in sustaining the effort to honor Mary in Washington.

Children and teens did not usually have the income for donations or the means to travel, and the clergy knew that their participation depended on adults. Still, the promoters sought to *engage children* at the moment when the enormous school system was reaching its peak. *Salve Regina* printed accounts of their donations and pilgrimages during the first phase of building in the 1920s, and Bishop Noll decided that the strategy for finishing the superstructure would begin with the pennies of students in elementary, middle, and high school. Get the children's pennies, he believed, and the adults' dollars will follow. It's difficult to know how to assess the clergy's effectiveness in engaging children and teens, since we cannot fully reconstruct young people's deepest sentiments and guiding motives. If the number of donations and pilgrimages is any measure, however, then those efforts at the Shrine succeeded. Classes sent contributions and schools journeyed by bus. Beyond the Shrine, too, adult efforts to engage children met with some success. We know from the recollections of adults raised in this period that the institutional network provided many young Catholics with a sense of belonging and a coherent worldview that, by championing inherent reason and inherited tradition, countered modernist relativism and, despite some contrary impulses, celebrated the presence of the divine in the world, just as the totalitistic environment of the parish effectively socialized children and adolescents. Yet by emphasizing the authority of the priest and cultivating the virtue of obedience, the devotional culture of consolidated Catholicism sometimes justified excessive coercion and—as Catholics came to realize decades later—set few constraints on clerical misconduct, including the sexual abuse of minors. That culture, as one Catholic historian suggested, had its "dark underside," which started to surface around 1985 and became fully visible by 2002, when the charges of clerical sexual abuse, and the U.S. Catholic Bishops' response, made front-page news.[4]

The clergy's national efforts to *incorporate immigrants* and confront difference—ethnic, cultural, and linguistic—achieved unrivaled diversity, creating an institution that partially embodied American ideals of inclusivity and often lived up to Catholic claims of universality. At its best, it welcomed diverse members into the Mystical Body of Christ. Sometimes, however, the devotional culture of the consolidated Church also perpetuated paternalism, ignored racism, and minimized differences. Sometimes, as one Catholic intellectual has proposed, it yielded to Catholics' "great historical temptation"—to aim for "sameness, making as many people as possible into 'good Catholics'…and in the process failing of catholicity…unity bought at the price of suppressing something of the diversity in the humanity that God created."[5]

At the Shrine, there was both predictable homogeneity and surprising heterogeneity. On the one hand, the Irish presence was undeniable, as it was in parishes from Washington to Boston and in many American dioceses. Almost everyone who played key roles at the Shrine during the early period was either an Irish immigrant or the child of Irish immigrants: the founder (Shahan), his superior (Gibbons), the first director (McKenna), the primary architect (Maginnis), the leading donor (Ryan), the local contractor (Cassidy), and the Building Committee chairman (Dougherty). A high proportion of the donors and pilgrims also claimed Irish descent, as the appendices show. Despite—or because of?—their shared bonds with another homeland, the planners made some efforts to acknowledge ethnic and national diversity, for example, they sought a Polish translator for *Salve Regina*'s office and represented Marian figures from different lands in the Crypt's columns. But diversity meant more than national origin, and during this segregated period African Americans had minimal presence at the Shrine, except as laborers. Even if the site was most important to European Americans who lived in cities in the Northeast and Midwest, many Catholics recognized this national project as their own, the donor records show. It seems that the clergy were right to suppose that Marian devotion crossed ethnic and national lines. In the final assessment, their efforts to incorporate diverse devotees at the Shrine before 1959 had some success: East Coast Irish were dominant and African Americans were excluded, but those who had a presence by giving or going were an exceptionally diverse group—perhaps more plural in ethnicity, origin, region, and language than at any other church in the capital. Further, if we consider the donor lists from the 1920s and 1950s, only a few other American sacred sites in this period—for example, the National Shrine of St. Jude in Chicago and the Miraculous Medal Shrine in Philadelphia—seem to have had the same ethnic variation and national scope.

Because the BNSIC was in the capital, its advocates had an advantage as they tried to attract national attention: other shrines could put "national" in their titles, but this one was positioned at the center of U.S. political power. During this period, which is bookended by Al Smith's failed presidential election campaign and John F. Kennedy's successful one, Roman Catholics were engaged in national efforts to *claim civic space*. As they did so, they overcame their well-earned defensiveness and reached beyond the enclave to the wider culture. By 1959, as one historian put it, American Catholicism had achieved an "uneasy triumph." Catholics made contributions in electoral politics, military campaigns, educational outreach, and communications media and proclaimed a social ethic grounded in a commitment to human dignity that shaped twentieth-century labor practices and political culture. Yet when it went unchecked by traditional Catholic cautions about the vice of hubris, the same impulse also risked the moral danger of blind patriotism—as in the ferocious anticommunism of Joseph McCarthy—or lapsed into self-righteousness, as with some twentieth-century Catholic efforts to censor, and not just shape, popular media in America.[6]

The Shrine's role in this national effort focused on establishing a material presence in the civic space of the nation's capital, and they succeeded in countering Congress's controversial decision to establish a "national" ecumenical church, though one linked with a particular Protestant denomination, by starting a major building project of their own. In that regard, clerical aims were realized. Along with Episcopalians, Catholic planners helped to create an important but unrecognized pattern in American religious life: the shared inclination for faiths to seek their own place, a national center, in the Washington landscape. By the 1920s, church building in the capital became part of how Americans—or at least ecclesiastical leaders—practiced their faith in a land governed by the First Amendment's prohibition against establishment and affirmation of free exercise. Complementing public rituals that also made claims on civic space, like the Thanksgiving Mass and the Holy Name Parade, the Shrine allowed Catholics their place in the capital. One of those important public rituals was held at the Shrine itself from 1939 to 1952: the annual Red Mass, which sought the inspiration of the Holy Spirit for government officials at the opening of Congress and the Supreme Court. Catholic lawmakers, diplomats, and judges and some non-Catholics attended the event during those years. The ritual in 1942, for example, drew about two thousand worshipers and the largest gathering of government officials ever at the BNSIC, including the vice president (Henry A. Wallace), a future president and current senator (Harry S. Truman), the speaker of the house (Sam Rayburn), and six Supreme Court justices (Stone, Douglas, Murphy, Black, Reed, and Byrne). For a time, that ritual succeeded in attracting government officials and public notice.[7]

A publicist for the BNSIC later proposed that with the Red Mass the director, Father John J. Reilly, "had succeeded in asserting the Shrine's relevance to both spiritual and secular concerns." Yet in most ways, the Shrine's advocates' claims on civic space remained in the subjunctive rather than the indicative mood: they expressed a wish more than they described a fact. A standing president had tapped in the National Cathedral's foundation stone in 1907, and other political leaders would have a presence at that worship site in the decades ahead. Standing U.S. presidents did not attend either the foundation stone ceremony at the Shrine in 1920 or the dedication ritual in 1959, however. President Hoover had a good excuse, since he'd been avoiding most pubic appearances after a stroke left him partially paralyzed in October 1919, but the able-bodied President Eisenhower was in Augusta, Georgia, where he played eighteen holes of golf on the Shrine's dedication day in November 1959. Failing to attract the attention of those Presbyterian presidents at those ceremonial occasions was unfortunate, but it's probably even more significant that there were few explicit and direct links between the Shrine and any of the successful Catholic efforts to impact American politics, society, economy, or culture. John Ryan had a presence there, but the Shrine had little to do with the influence he wielded in national politics and social reform. Dorothy Day prayed there, but the Shrine's politics hardly resembled the radical pacifism and voluntary poverty of her Catholic Worker Movement. Members of the IFCA who visited the Shrine and had the major role in funding the Mary Memorial Altar shaped popular culture by evaluating the moral quality of motion pictures, but again the Shrine had little direct connection to that national campaign. The Episcopalian National Cathedral, built in the more fashionable Northwest section of the city, stood only about a half mile closer to the White House, but before 1959 the BNSIC often seemed even more distant than that from the center of political power. The material presence of the Shrine had its influence, and so did the Red Mass, but the promoters had mixed results as they tried to claim civic space, just as they enjoyed both successes and failures as they tried to realize their other hopes for the building.[8]

A THRESHOLD TO CATHOLIC AMERICA, 1959–2009

The sermons at the dedication alternated between the indicative and subjunctive mood—between stating facts and making wishes—but the tone of those ceremonial remarks was appropriately upbeat. We can forgive the Shrine's supporters if they were even more giddy with anticipation of future success when less than two months later, on January 2, 1960, John Fitzgerald Kennedy, a Roman Catholic, officially announced his intention to run for president. The ecclesiastical leaders were aware of both the recent progress the American Catholic Church had made and the lingering signs of religious prejudice. Yet any reasonable observer might have had grounds for hope with the prospect of a Catholic in the White House. Well, for the hopeful, subsequent events brought good news and bad news: Kennedy was elected, but it didn't help the Shrine's cause. It was his Protestant successor, Johnson, who first shined the light of media publicity on the Shrine when he attended his daughter's wedding there in 1966. Kennedy, however, never set foot in the place, and that tells us a good deal about the president's piety, the electorate's expectations, and the transitional moment.

The BNSIC was a monument to the era of consolidated Catholicism, with its triumphalism, countermodernism, and ultramontanism, and that's one reason it's not surprising Kennedy kept his distance and attended three other local parishes. He expressed little personal interest in Marian devotion, which began to decline nationally about the same time, and he was at home in the modern world and in America's political culture. As early as the 1940s some liberals at Georgetown's Holy Trinity, one of the churches he attended, had started referring to the BNSIC as "Abomination of Desolation," in part for its lack of concern with social justice issues, and Kennedy combined a moderate political realism with a liberal social agenda. Most important, at a time when Kennedy and his campaign staff spent a good deal of energy assuring the electorate he wouldn't uncritically yield to episcopal pressure or blindly follow the pope's commands, he needed to distance himself from a site in "Little Rome" associated with Catholic ecclesiastical authority. The BNSIC, after all, had started as the church for America's pontifical university and continued to be the site for bishops' worship during their annual meetings. On the other key issues—modernism and Americanism—Kennedy's stance, as he put it in his famous

Houston speech of 1960, resembled the accommodationist view denounced by papal encyclicals in 1899 and 1907 but (mostly) affirmed by the documents of the Second Vatican Council, which ended in 1965, two years after his death. In other words, the Shrine's consolidated Catholicism couldn't get you elected president in America in 1960, and Kennedy, who inclined toward the "updated" piety he never lived to see implemented, knew it. So his absence from the Shrine discloses a good deal about the era that was passing and the one that was just beginning.[9]

In the era of fragmentation that began soon after the Shrine's 1959 dedication and was still discernable at its 2009 anniversary, the cultural and ecclesiastical context for the earlier clerical aims had changed, and the Shrine's promoters again enjoyed some successes and suffered some failures. The National Cathedral drew more attention as a national worship center, as did St. Matthew's, where Kennedy's funeral mass was celebrated on November 25, 1963; and Washington's archbishop had moved the annual Red Mass a decade earlier. In 2009, attending that rite for legal professionals were five members of the Supreme Court—all but one of the six Catholics on the bench—as well as the Roman Catholic vice president, Joe Biden, and many other government officials. The earlier concern to claim civic space seemed mostly unsuccessful by the jubilee year, but the Shrine's promoters had continued to raise funds to decorate the interior. In recent years, the rector reached out to devotees across the country through the skillful use of contemporary marketing techniques and new communications media, including regular mass e-mails to supporters and a sophisticated website that allows virtual pilgrims to take a tour, memorialize a relative, submit a prayer, or light a candle. The BNSIC's efforts to pay the bills and foster Marian devotion also received a boost in 1990, when the pope elevated it to the status of a basilica, so at a time when U.S. bishops were closing parishes, the impulse to build institutions remained alive at the Shrine. So did the concern to mobilize women and engage children. Women's groups continued to make contributions and make journeys, and children and adolescents continued to arrive by the busload on school trips. Lay men, women, and children also traveled there as part of a well-organized system of diocesan pilgrimages. Women had more presence on the Shrine's altar, assisting the celebrant, though still not as priests. The Shrine reported one million annual visitors by 2009, and it enjoyed some increased success in attracting non-Catholics, as public school teachers and secular tour guides brought a wider range of visitors, though the original apologetic intent of the Crypt Church's ornamentation still seems to have attracted little notice. But immigrants and their descendants noticed increased efforts to reach out to the full range of ethnic and national groups. Those efforts, which began earlier and accelerated after the 1986 appointment of Monsignor Bransfield as director, might stand as the most unqualified success of the half century. African Americans got a chapel—and an apology from Washington's archbishop for the Church's prior racism. Most of the ethnic and national groups who affiliated with Catholicism before and after the revised federal immigration law of 1965 also secured a place in the building. By the jubilee, the chapels and oratories venerating various Virgins, including those cherished by the new immigrants, were attracting more popular piety than anyone might have anticipated when the bishops solemnly processed up the steps at the 1959 dedication.[10]

Positioned at the Shrine's entrance, a number of the most important ecclesiastical shifts and cultural patterns of post-Sixties America come into view—and not just the impact of the new immigration, which is so clearly expressed in the ethnic chapels and oratories dedicated since 1964. The Catholic Church itself had changed before and after *Humanae Vitae* and the Second Vatican Council, whose documents endorsed vernacular liturgies, scriptural study, interreligious dialogue, church-state separation, and a democratic definition of the Church as "the people of God." Outside the Church—and beyond the Shrine's portal—Americans witnessed many social changes. Historians disagree about how much those post-1960s changes had begun decades earlier—just as Catholic scholars disagree about the impact of Vatican II. However, most agree that something changed around midcentury. I've suggested that an era of consolidation gave way to an era of fragmentation, and the Shrine offers a good view of all those changes, as well as of the contemporary ecclesiastical divide between conservatives and liberals and the "culture wars" that dominated politics and divided Americans between 1959 and 2009. Even though the Shrine, which was founded by moderates, seemed more aligned with the right than the left during that half century, it became a contested site where the polarization of the fragmented Church has been evident. Looking down the nave and out the front door, we can see Catholics who aligned themselves with "progressive" causes like women's ordination, gay rights, nuclear disarmament, and antiwar protest as well as those who lamented "the entire 'orientation' of the 'Conciliar Church'" and the rampant immorality of American culture, those with nostalgia for consolidated Catholicism who believe "they have held steady while the world around them has moved."[11]

By 2009, a year after Pope Benedict XVI visited the Crypt Church and confessed his "deep shame" about children's abuse, some lay Catholics and secular journalists were wondering aloud: "Is Liberal Catholicism Dead?" Yet since 1960, the year the Pill was first marketed in the United States and a year after the first American soldiers died in Vietnam, liberal Catholics had some presence, though progressives were most visible when they publicly expressed their dissent inside and outside the Shrine. Consider a few examples. In July 1966, the year that American B-52s first bombed North Vietnam, antiwar protesters gathered outside the Shrine to express their dissent as President Johnson's daughter was married in the Great Upper Church. In 1979, while protesters outside the Shrine carried signs proclaiming "Sexism Is a Sin," inside Sister M. Theresa Kane exhorted Pope John Paul II to consider "the possibility of women being included in all ministries of the church." Then that Sister of Mercy and fifty-two of the five thousand nuns gathered at the BNSIC that fall day stood in silent protest as the pontiff spoke. To mention a final example, when the U.S. bishops met in Washington in 2002 to vote on a new policy designed to confront the heightening sexual abuse crisis, protesters gathered again at the Shrine, to express their outrage about the abuse of children and to raise other concerns, including about gay rights. Three Catholic members of Soulforce, an ecumenical organization founded to change policies on the treatment of gay, lesbian, bisexual, and transgendered Christians, were refused communion at a Shrine mass attended by the American hierarchy on the evening of November 11 and arrested the next morning as they knelt in the lobby of the bishops' hotel, the Grand Hyatt, to again express their dissent and seek the Eucharist. The legal system vindicated those three gay Catholics, however, as Superior Court judge Mildred Edwards, a Catholic who once had defended activist Philip Berrigan, refused to sentence them. She even apologized: "As a member of your church, I ask you to forgive the church." Referring to Catholic teaching about Jesus' "real presence" in the Eucharist and using the corporeal metaphor to invoke their shared ecclesiastical identity, Edwards added: "tremendous violence was done to you, who are the body of Christ, and the body of Christ was denied to you."[12]

For some of Mary's devotees at the Shrine, that incident—including the legal outcome—displayed all that was wrong with postconciliar Catholicism and contemporary American culture. For them, that judge had betrayed Church teachings and overstepped judicial boundaries, just as they thought the U.S. Supreme Court had done in its *Roe v. Wade* decision in 1973. Few of those more conservative Catholics, who have a significant presence at the Shrine, read liberal periodicals like the *National Catholic Reporter*, which printed a sympathetic account of Judge Edward's ruling. As I found in personal interviews and lunchroom conversations at the Shrine, many pilgrims at the turn of the twenty-first century were influenced by the post-1980s surge of apocalyptic Marianism, which focused on apparitions, pilgrimage, and politics. They belonged to organizations like the Legion of Mary and watched Eternal Word Television Network, the conservative

Catholic station that began broadcasting Shrine masses in 1988 and whose website posted "traditional mass resources" as well as television program schedules. Across from the tour desk and near the gift shop, a flat-screen television stayed tuned to this network, which broadcast rosaries, devotions, and masses from many Catholic sites, including the BNSIC. Conservative viewers of this network and others who felt a deep sadness, even an abiding outrage, at the immorality of American culture and the fragmentation of the U.S. Church, found solace as they gathered at the Shrine with like-minded Catholics for various events, including the annual worship service and political rally, which was initiated in 1974 to oppose the practice of abortion and "defend the sanctity of life." In January 2009, thousands of the faithful from across the country attended the "Mass for Life" in the Great Upper Church in the morning and then joined the "March for Life" along the Mall and in front of the U.S. Supreme Court Building. In that way, too, the Shrine was a site that opened out to wider arenas of significance and revealed the fissures in the Catholic Church and American culture.[13]

THRESHOLD TO "RELIGION": METHOD AND THEORY

That vantage also led me to refine my views about how to study religion, especially the history of religious sites. In other words, this project has implications for thinking about method. From the start, I'd identified ten factors to consider in the analysis of architecture, principles I used to guide my research and writing: the building's name, location, appearance, context, relations, representations, makers, donors, users, and functions. At the end of the project those factors still seem useful, but some new insights have emerged for me.

I began with a historical perspective, but I was still unprepared to find how much the building's *context* changed over time. The BNSIC, a site linked with moderate clergy, including Gibbons and CUA faculty who advocated views that led to accusations of accommodationist "Americanism," was widely assumed to be uncompromisingly conservative by the time it celebrated its Golden Jubilee. Modifying a dictum attributed to the Greek philosopher, Heraclitus, we might say: it's impossible to step into the same building twice. Both the viewer and the building change. Even things that seem static, like buildings (the Shrine) and landscapes (Washington), are always in flux, and it's important to attend to those changes by noticing all the traces left on the terrain and following the flows of people, artifacts, institutions, and practices.[14]

But context is geographical as well as historical, and the study of spiritual sites also involves attending to *location*. As I discovered, when researchers follow the flows wherever they lead, often they'll need to extend their study's temporal span and expand its geographical scope. For example, I found that I had to learn about ancient Roman archeology and post Reformation debates about Marian devotion in the catacombs because the design and ornamentation of the Crypt Church makes no sense without that historical context. As with that subterranean worship space, the traces on the landscape might be very recent or quite ancient, and it's helpful to expand and contract the study's historical frame accordingly. In turn, if interpreters follow the flows, the geographical scale of analysis will some-times be larger and sometimes smaller than the nation-state. Even when we study a site that proclaims its "national" status, we shouldn't assume the nation as the default level of analysis, but instead move from the local to the global, or wherever the movements we're tracing take us. For a building shaped by influences from the Vatican in Rome and immigrant homelands abroad, that was important.

It also was important to attend to the building's supporters—*makers*, *donors*, and *users*—and they turned out to be more complex than the pas-sionately polarized contemporary interpretations would suggest. I finished the project even more convinced that to provide the richest representation of a religious site, we need to creatively use a variety of sources to try to recover *all* those who have had a presence, ordinary devotees as well as reli-gious leaders, critics as well as defenders, bricklayers as well as architects, women as well as men, and children as well as adults. I consulted diverse sources—including census records, devotional letters, and donor lists—to try to notice those who were present, while also taking note of those who, for one reason or another, were completely absent or barely visible. Scholars who represent the past, one historian of religion has argued, are obliged "to ask how certain groups were rendered 'invisible'" and then do what they can to bring them into view. So we might ask: Who's there? Who's not there? Who is almost invisible and who lurks in the shadows as the incor-poreal presence of the bitter enemy or the excluded Other? To answer these questions, it also helps to use multiple methods, as I tried to do by combining the social history of ordinary people with the intellectual history of institu-tional elites and, to interpret the recent past and contemporary events, sometimes using approaches borrowed from the qualitative social sciences, including interviews.[15]

As I employed those multiple approaches, I also came to see more clearly the ways that a building's *representations* and *functions* are always medi-ated. Religions are always mediated by transportation and communication technology—note the influence of print and television as well as buses and trains in the Shrine's history. And institutional networks also mediate piety. As I noticed at that site associated with the hierarchy and its authority, religions negotiate power as well as make meaning. All space is marked by the traces of social power wielded by institutions. In the same way, there are no unimpeded flows. The flows—of peoples, artifacts, and practices— are propelled, compelled, and blocked, directed this way and that, by institutions, in this case the transnational network of the Roman Catholic Church. It is important in the study of religious sites to notice this—and so to attend to the ways that power is enacted—and not only the ways that meaning is made.

Attending to both meaning and power, and coming to these insights about method, also got me thinking about broader theoretical questions, and the Shrine also offers a compelling angle of vision on what religion is and how it functions. In an earlier book I offered a theory of religion, an account that emerged from my study of another Catholic shrine. I argued that a religion is a flowing together of currents—some institutionally enforced as "orthodox"—crossing multiple fields, where other religions, other transverse confluences, also cross. Religions cannot be reduced to economic forces, social relations, or political interests, but they always emerge from the swirl of transfluvial currents, as both religious and nonreligious streams propel religious flows. So religions are processes in which institutions channel flows to produce representations (artifacts, rituals, and narratives) that appeal to suprahuman agents (gods, saints, angels) and imagine an ultimate horizon of human life.[16]

If this is what religion is, how does it function? First, religion "intensifies joy and confronts suffering." Religions, which involve feeling as well as thinking, not only interpret and ease suffering—disease, disaster, and death—but also provide ways for humans to imagine and enhance the joys derived from encounters with the natural world and transitions in the lifespan. Religions, in other words, are about enhancing the wonder as much as about wondering about evil. Second, shifting to spatial metaphors, I suggested that religions "make homes and cross boundaries." Religions are about finding one's place (dwelling) and moving across space (crossing). As dwelling, religions are spatial practices that orient humans in time and space, situating devotees in the body, the home, the homeland, and the cosmos. They function, I suggest, as watch and compass. But religions make sense of the nomadic as well as the sedentary in human life and involve another spatial practice—crossing. Religions enable and constrain corporeal, terrestrial, and cosmic crossings. Not only do they mark and traverse the boundaries of the natural terrain, as in pilgrimages to shrines, as well as the limits of embodied life, including illness and death, but they also chart and cross the ultimate horizon, whether that final crossing is imagined as transport or transformation, as attaining enlightenment or ascending to heaven.[17]

This research project on Mary's shrine in Washington confirms and challenges that theory. My earlier suggestion that religion emerges from "the swirl of transfluvial currents"—economic forces, social relations, and political interests—aptly describes what happened at the Shrine. Nonreligious forces (immigration laws, economic depressions, and foreign wars) shaped Catholic piety. Yet even though a visual representation of my theory had placed institutions at its center, analysis of the flows that crossed the Shrine's threshold showed that institutional networks were even more crucial than I'd initially thought. It's impossible to understand piety at the BNSIC without tracing the impact of lay groups, episcopal organizations, parochial schools, religious orders, and the Vatican. I also was right, I think, to note that artifacts are among religion's components, but tangible things—including buildings and images—grounded the religious worlds that twentieth-century Marian devotees inhabited. Artifacts were so significant, it seems to me, that we might even talk about the ways that buildings perform roles and statues exert agency. With only a little exaggeration we might say: things do things. Recognizing their importance, artifacts, like the Mary Altar or the bell tower, might be seen as quasi characters in our narratives of religious life. My earlier claim that religions "intensify joy and confront suffering" is confirmed by my research, too. Donors and pilgrims turned to Mary Immaculate to make ends meet, heal serious illness, and care for family members, living and dead. Only the most cynical interpreter of the donor letters, like the heartbreaking 1919 note from the widow who had buried a husband and three children, could deny the comfort, even joy, Mary's devotees found as they brought her their suffering. Yet my research has made me more alert to the ways that religions also can *cause* suffering. I wept as I read accounts of the sexual abuse of minors, and I felt my face flush with rage as I learned that Thomas W. Turner, that bright African-American Catholic who eventually earned a Ph.D. from Cornell, could not have been admitted to CUA and would not have been welcomed at the Shrine.

I also feel compelled to partially revise my understanding of *crossing* and *dwelling*. My earlier suggestion that religions are about dwelling and situate devotees in the body, the home, the homeland, and the cosmos makes sense of practices at the Shrine, but other spaces—like the neighborhood—seem noteworthy as we try to map the spaces of daily life, and other practices—including public ritual—seem more crucial for marking boundaries and claiming space than I'd supposed when I started the research. Interpreting religious practice as crossing is very helpful in understanding the ways that piety at the Shrine enabled and constrained all sorts of passages—across the life cycle, across the ocean, across the country, and across the boundary between life and death. But I'd privileged certain kinds of terrestrial crossings—pilgrimage and missions—and overlooked donation and the ways that it, too, enacts spiritual crossing. In many traditions, my research at the Shrine has helped me to see more clearly, giving is a highly valued religious practice, whether that is Muslim *zakat*, Christian tithing, or Buddhist *dâna*. Even though I did not begin this project with any interest in donation, I came to see that for many twentieth-century Catholics it was an integral part of religious practice. Giving, I learned, was as important as going.

Attending to both giving and going, I came to see the Shrine as a threshold: a passageway through which consolidated Catholicism crossed, a gateway through which cultural forces flowed, and a portal that opened out to the ever-widening spaces of devotional life, from the home to the cosmos. It was a site that bridged life and death and led—Mary's devotees hoped—to the ultimate horizon, life's farthest reach, where suffering might finally give way to joy, and where, with no more portals to enter or leave, they might finally rest.

APPENDICES

A Social Profile of Selected Pilgrims and Donors, 1916–1959

Appendix 1.1. SELECTED EPISCOPAL DONORS, 1916–1919

Name	Residence	Birthplace and year	Parents' nativity	Ethnicity/ nationality
Rt. Rev. Joseph G. Anderson	Dorchester, MA	Massachusetts (1866)	Massachusetts (father); Canada (mother)	Canadian (mother)
Rt. Rev. Ferdinand Brossart	Covington, KY	Germany (1850)	Germany	German
Rt. Rev. John J. Cantwell	Los Angeles, CA	Ireland (1875)	Ireland	Irish
Rt. Rev. Joseph R. Crimout	Juneau, AK	France (1858)	France	French
Rt. Rev. James Davis	Davenport, IA	Ireland (1852)	Ireland	Irish
Rt. Rev. Arthur J. Drossaerts	San Antonio, TX	Holland (1862)	Holland	Dutch
Rt. Rev. Frederick Eis	Marquette, WI	Germany (1843)	Germany	German
Rt. Rev. Henry Gabriels	Ogdensburg, NY	Belgium (1838)	Belgium	Belgian
Rt. Rev. Edmund F. Gibbons	Albany, NY	New York (1868)	Ireland	Irish
Rt. Rev. Thomas Grace	Sacramento, CA	Ireland (1841)	Ireland	Irish
Rt. Rev. William A. Hickey	Providence, RI	Massachusetts (1869)	Ireland	Irish

(continued)

Appendix 1.1. CONTINUED

Name	Residence	Birthplace and year	Parents' nativity	Ethnicity/ nationality
Rt. Rev. Jules Jeanmard	Lafayette, LA	Louisiana (1879)	Louisiana	French
Rt. Rev. James M. Koudelka	Superior, WI	Austria (1853)	Austria	Austrian
Rt. Rev. Joseph P. Lynch	Dallas, TX	Michigan (1872)	Ireland (father); Canada (mother)	Irish
Rt. Rev. Philip R. McDevitt	Harrisburg, PA	Pennsylvania (1858)	Ireland	Irish
Rt. Rev. John J. O'Connor	South Orange, NJ	New Jersey (1855)	Ireland	Irish
Rt. Rev. Charles J. O'Reilly	Lincoln, NE	Canada (1860)	Ireland	Irish
Rt. Rev. Joseph Schrembs	Toledo, OH	Germany (1866)	Germany	German
Rt. Rev. William Turner	Buffalo, NY	Ireland (1871)	Ireland	Irish
Rt. Rev. Cornelius Van de Ven	Alexandria, LA	Holland (1865)	Holland	Dutch

Source: Journal, High Altar Book, May 1916–March 1926, Archives, BNSIC; *Fourteenth Census of the United States, 1920*.

Appendix 1.2. SELECTED PRIESTS' DONATIONS IN RESPONSE TO
BISHOP SHAHAN'S 1919 LETTER

Name	Residence	Current position	Birthplace and year	Parents' nativity	Ethnicity
Rev. Edmund Burke	Alameda, CA	Curate, Notre Dame Academy	Ireland (1881)	Ireland	Irish
Rev. Daniel Daly	Leavenworth, WA	Parish priest	Ireland (1873)	Ireland	Irish
Rev. Charles Danforth	Peekskill, NY	Assistant pastor, Church of the Assumption	New York (1888)	New York (father); New Jersey (mother)	Unknown
Rev. John P. Doyle	Dighton, MA	Pastor, St. Joseph's	Massachusetts (1878)	Ireland	Irish
Rev. Dominicus Faber	Portland, OR	Rector, St. Vincent's Hospital	Germany (1858)	Germany	German
Rev. John J. Farrell	Boston, MA	Parish priest	Massachusetts (1867)	Ireland	Irish
Rev. Ignatius Fealy	Fort Myer, VA	Chaplain, Army	Missouri (1879)	Ireland (father); Virginia (mother)	Irish
Rev. Thomas J. Fitzgerald	Redlands, CA	Parish priest	Ireland (1857)	Ireland	Irish
Rev. William J. Foley	Hingham, MA	Assistant pastor, St. Paul's	Massachusetts (1883)	Ireland	Irish
Rev. Joseph Frioli	Roanoke, VA	Pastor, St. Andrew's	Virginia (1854)	Italy (father); Ireland (mother)	Irish/ Italian
Rev. Dr. Peter Guilday	Washington, D.C.	Professor, Catholic University of America	Pennsylvania (1885)	Ireland	Irish
Rev. Charles Hickey	Dayton, OH	Parish priest	Ohio (1865)	Ireland	Irish
Rev. Francis Johannes	St. Joseph, MO	Pastor, Immaculate Conception	Bavaria (1875)	Bavaria	German
Rt. Rev. Msgr. Francis Keane	Pittsburgh, PA	Parish priest	Ireland (1851)	Ireland	Irish

(continued)

Appendix 1.2. CONTINUED

Name	Residence	Current position	Birthplace and year	Parents' nativity	Ethnicity
Rev. Frank Kunkel	Menlo Park, CA	Teacher, St. Patrick's Seminary	Maryland (1870)	Germany (father); Delaware (mother)	German
Rev. Edward J. Rengel	Olean, NY	Pastor, St. Mary of the Angels Church	New York (1870)	Alsace-Lorraine	French
Rev. Andrew J. Rinke	Winsted, MN	Pastor, Church of the Holy Trinity	Germany (1873)	Germany	German
Rev. August Schwertner	Toledo, OH	Assistant pastor	Ohio (1871)	Austria (father); Ohio (mother)	Austrian
Rev. Antoine Simon	New Orleans, LA	Pastor, St. Augustine	France (1868)	France	French
Rev. Clarence E. Wheeler	Washington DC	Parish priest	Maryland (1875)	Maryland	Unknown

Source: Journal, High Altar Contributions, Archives, BNSIC; *Fourteenth Census of the United States, 1920.*

Appendix 1.3. SELECTED SHRINE VISITORS, ADULT LAY DEVOTEES AND WOMEN RELIGIOUS, 1925–1927

Name	Residence	Birthplace and year	Relation to head of household	Parents' nativity	Occupation	Neighbors' native languages	Total in household	Value of mortgage/rent
Sister Mary Adelaide	Cincinnati, OH	Ohio (1870)	Lodger	Germany (father); Ohio (mother)	Teacher	Hungarian, French, German	43	N/A
Sister Mary Anna	Syracuse, NY	New Jersey (1893)	Inmate	New Jersey (father); England (mother)	Teacher	German, Polish, Flemish, Italian	67	N/A
Edward Brady	Chicago, IL	Illinois (1889)	Head	Illinois	Realtor	German, Swedish, Danish	4	$90 (rented)
Victoria Brady	Chicago, IL	Illinois (1890)	Wife	Canada	Homemaker; realtor (head)	German, Swedish, Danish	4	$90 (rented)
Margaret Brady	Baltimore, MD	Ireland (1890)	Head	Ireland	Boardinghouse owner	Yiddish, Italian	3	$4,900 (owned)
Sara Brady	Baltimore, MD	Ireland (1894)	Sister	Ireland	Nurse	Yiddish, Italian,	3	$4,900 (owned)
Sister Mary Celestine	Philadelphia, PA	Pennsylvania (1863)	Inmate	Ireland	N/A	Polish	30	N/A
Viola Conley	Philadelphia, PA	Pennsylvania (1909)	Daughter	Pennsylvania	Student; trolley motorman (head)	German, Slovene, Irish	6	Rented
Ann Donnelly	Boston, MA	Scotland (1886)	Wife	Ireland	Homemaker; fireman (head)	Italian	6	$35 (rented)

(continued)

Appendix 1.3. CONTINUED

Name	Residence	Birthplace and year	Relation to head of household	Parents' nativity	Occupation	Neighbors' native languages	Total in household	Value of mortgage/rent
Sister Mary Blanche Forselman	Davenport, IA	Iowa (1870)	Inmate	Germany	Teacher	German, French	42	N/A
Hermina Frey	Louisville, KY	Indiana (1882)	Lodger	Indiana (father); Germany (mother)	Dressmaker	German	5	$10,000 (owned)
Sister Mary James	Philadelphia, PA	Pennsylvania (1890)	Lodger	Pennsylvania	Teacher	English	19	N/A
Celia Keane	Savannah, GA	Georgia (1879)	Daughter	Georgia (father); New York (mother)	Saleswoman	Greek, German	8	Rented
Eleanor Kelly	Philadelphia, PA	Pennsylvania (1908)	Daughter	Ireland	Student; electrician (head)	German	7	Owned
Thomas P. Kelly	Baltimore, MD	Maryland (1875)	Head	Ireland	Superintendent	English	5	$15,000 (owned)
Helen B. Kelly	Baltimore, MD	Maryland (1881)	Wife	Ireland	Homemaker; superintendent (head)	English	5	$15,000 (owned)
Eileen B. Kelly	Baltimore, MD	Maryland (1916)	Daughter	Maryland	None; superintendent (head)	English	5	$15,000 (owned)

Name	Residence	Birthplace and year	Relation to head of household	Parents' nativity	Occupation	Neighbors' native languages	Total in household	Value of mortgage/rent
Thomas P. Kelly, Jr.	Baltimore, MD	Maryland (1919)	Son	Maryland	None; superintendent (head)	English	5	$15,000 (owned)
William J. Kelly	Baltimore, MD	Maryland (1923)	Son	Maryland	None; superintendent (head)	English	5	$15,000 (owned)
Anna Knox	Brooklyn, NY	Ireland (1869)	Wife	Ireland	Homemaker; plumber (head)	Irish, Swedish, Danish, Norwegian	7	Rented
Edna Knox	Brooklyn, NY	New York (1895)	Daughter	London (father); Ireland (mother)	Stenographer	Irish, Swedish, Danish, Norwegian	7	Rented
Margaret Lawlor	Philadelphia, PA	Pennsylvania (1908)	Daughter	Pennsylvania	Student	German, Danish	8	Owned
Helen Loser	Philadelphia, PA	Pennsylvania (1910)	Daughter	Germany (father); Austria (mother)	Student; blacksmith (head)	German, Romanian, Irish	5	Owned
Lillian Madden	Louisville, KY	Kentucky (1899)	Daughter	Kentucky	Bookkeeper	German	4	$15 (rented)
Matthew McAndrew	Scranton, PA	Pennsylvania (1906)	Son	Pennsylvania	Bookkeeper	Italian	4	$10,000 (owned)
James P. McAndrew	Scranton, PA	Pennsylvania (1908)	Son	Pennsylvania	None; investigator (head)	Italian	4	$10,000 (owned)

(continued)

Appendix 1.3. CONTINUED

Name	Residence	Birthplace and year	Relation to head of household	Parents' nativity	Occupation	Neighbors' native languages	Total in household	Value of mortgage/rent
William J. McLaughlin	Bronx, NY	N. Ireland	Head	N. Ireland	Real estate agent	Polish, Yiddish, German	6	$16,000 (owned)
William McLaughlin	Bronx, NY	New York (1910)	Son	N. Ireland	None; real estate agent (head)	Polish, Yiddish, German	6	$16,000 (owned)
Clement McLaughlin	Bronx, NY	New York (1911)	Son	N. Ireland	None; real estate agent (head)	Polish, Yiddish, German	6	$16,000 (owned)
Thomas O'Connor	Peoria, IL	Illinois (1863)	Head	Ireland	Sales manager	German	4	Rented
Edward T. O'Connor	Peoria, IL	Illinois (1896)	Son	Illinois	None; sales manager (head)	German	4	Rented
Harriet S. Riley	New Bedford, MA	Massachusetts (1901)	Stepdaughter	Massachusetts	Teacher	Danish, Portuguese, German	3	$4,500 (owned)
Catharine Robertson	Philadelphia, PA	Canada (1860)	Head	N. Ireland	Homemaker; clerk (daughters)	English	4	$13,000 (owned)
Gertrude Robertson	Philadelphia, PA	Pennsylvania (1881)	Daughter	Canada	Homemaker; clerk (sisters)	English	4	$13,000 (owned)
Rose Saxer	Cleveland, OH	Ohio (1887)	Sister-in-law	Germany	Cashier	German, Finnish, Hungarian	4	Owned
Herbert Showalter	West Bend, WI	Wisconsin (1895)	Head	Wisconsin	Salesman	German	5	$6,000 (owned)

Name	Residence	Birthplace and year	Relation to head of household	Parents' nativity	Occupation	Neighbors' native languages	Total in household	Value of mortgage/rent
John Urziehart	Riverdale, MD	New York (1865)	Head	Irish Free State	Federal government clerk	German	6	$7,000 (owned)
Cecelia Urziehart	Riverdale, MD	New York (1881)	Wife	Irish Free State	Homemaker; federal government clerk (head)	German	6	$7,000 (owned)
Rose Urziehart	Riverdale, MD	Washington, DC (1912)	Daughter	New York	None; federal government clerk (head)	German	6	$7,000 (owned)
Marcella Urziehart	Riverdale, MD	Maryland (1913)	Daughter	New York	None; federal government clerk (head)	German	6	$7,000 (owned)

Source: Register of Visitors, June 1926–August 1927, Archives, BNSIC; *Fourteenth Census of the United States, 1920; Fifteenth Census of the United States, 1930.*

Appendix 1.4. SELECTED LAY MALE DONORS TO THE NATIONAL SHRINE, 1919

Name	Residence	Birthplace and year	Parents' nativity	Occupation	Neighbors' native languages	Total persons in household	Home-ownership
George Banchoff	Lambertville, NJ	New Jersey (1862)	Germany	Farmer	Italian	10	Owned
Michael Barlow, Jr.	Marysville, KS	Ireland (1861)	Ireland	Retired	Bohemian	6	Owned
Philip C. Bok	Reading, OH	Ohio (1878)	Germany	Superintendent	German, Gaelic, Romanian	8	Owned
Michael Campbell	Glenolden, PA	Pennsylvania (1864)	Ireland	Salesman	Armenian	4	Owned
John Cunningham	Bethlehem, PA	Pennsylvania (1875)	Pennsylvania	Merchant	Yiddish, Italian	3	Rented
Daniel Dillon	Butler, PA	Pennsylvania (1850)	Ireland	Butcher	Greek	4	Rented
Harry Ebaugh	Baltimore, MD	Maryland (1882)	Maryland	Salesman	German	3	Rented
John Feuerstein	Cleveland, OH	Ohio (1868)	Germany	Machinist	Magyar, Hungarian, German	5	Owned
John Franey	Philadelphia, PA	Pennsylvania (1877)	Ireland	Saloon keeper	Polish, Lithuanian	2	Owned
Thomas Hogan	Holyoke, MA	Ireland (1883)	Ireland	Paper maker	Gaelic, French, Polish	2	Rented
John L. McCormick	Buffalo, NY	New York (1876)	New York (father); Alsace-Lorraine (mother)	Electrician	English	6	Owned

Name	Residence	Birthplace and year	Parents' nativity	Occupation	Neighbors' native languages	Total persons in household	Home-ownership
Thomas L. McGoldrick	Detroit, MI	Michigan (1881)	Ireland	County clerk	Gaelic, Italian, French, Swedish, Norwegian	5	Owned
John Milliken	Malden, MA	Maine (1844)	Maine	Retired	French	8	Owned
William Mueller	Baltimore, MD	Maryland (1877)	Germany	Merchant	Hebrew, Greek, German, Italian	5	Owned
William Noonan	Lynn, MA	Massachusetts (1896)	Massachusetts	None	English	3	Owned
Thomas J. O'Brien	Hartford, CN	New York (1869)	Ireland	Insurance co. clerk	German	3	Rented
Joseph Redegeld	New York, NY	New York (1867)	Germany	Wholesaler	German	2	Owned
Walter Robinson	Gary, IN	Louisiana (1856)	U.S.	Hospital janitor	French, Swedish, German	74	Rented
John George Schaffer	Terre Haute, IN	Illinois (1873)	Illinois	Teamster	English	8	Rented
William Smithwick	Bristol, CN	Ireland (1881)	Ireland	Charity [illegible]; City Hall	Gaelic, Polish, Swedish, Italian	11	Rented

Source: Donor Book, April 1919–February 1920, Archives, BNSIC; *Fourteenth Census of the United States, 1920.*

Appendix 1.5. SELECTED SHRINE DONORS, 1953

Name(s)	Birthplace and year	Ethnicity	Home/rent value	Occupation (donor and household head)	Neighbors' native languages	Residence	Total in household
James N. Marshall	Pennsylvania, 1930	Unknown	$27.50	Machinist	Italian	Mars, PA	3
Eleanor, Madeline, and Robert McKenna	Pennsylvania, 1899, 1905, 1920 (respectively)	Unknown	$40	Saleslady, saleslady, none; foreman (head)	English, Italian	Uniontown, PA	9
Bernard Piotrowski	Ohio, 1917	Polish	$4,500	None; laborer (head)	Polish, Czech	Cleveland, OH	6
Eva Springer	English Canada, 1896	Canadian	N/A	Homemaker; clerk (head)	Yiddish, English, Spanish, German	New York, NY	2
Dorothy Conway	Ohio, 1924	Unknown	$9,000	None; none (head); other wage earners: salesman, secretary	German, English, Yiddish	Cincinnati, OH	8
Harry Cosgrove	Pennsylvania, 1890	Irish	$21	Shipper	English, Lithuanian	Philadelphia, PA	2
Henry Brown	Louisiana, 1890	Negro	$1,000	Manager	English, Spanish	Los Angeles, CA	2
Mrs. Nellie Anderson	Wisconsin, 1898	German	$15	None; cattle salesman (head)	Norwegian, Danish, Polish, Bohemian	Milwaukee, WI	3
[ ]Nehring	Germany, 1866	German	$1,000	Electrician	German, English, Polish	Schenectady, NY	4
Mary Longeran	Ireland, 1900	Irish	$50	Homemaker; janitor (head)	English, Lithuanian, Dutch	Great Neck, NY	5
Mrs. William Davis (Ella)	Pennsylvania, 1891	Unknown	$3,000	Homemaker; molder (head)	German, English, Italian, Swedish	Ypsilanti, MI	8

Name(s)	Birthplace and year	Ethnicity	Home/rent value	Occupation (donor and household head)	Neighbors' native languages	Residence	Total in household
Mr. and Mrs. McGinn (James and Ella)	Colorado, 1896; Texas, 1900	Unknown	$7	Laborer, homemaker	German, "Jewish," Spanish, Swedish, English	Denver, CO	4
Rev. Martin Neary	Illinois, 1906	Irish	N/A (owned)	None; carpenter (head)	English, German, Gaelic	Chicago, IL	6
Mary C. Moriarty	Pennsylvania, 1904	Irish	$25	Teacher	English, Portuguese, Swedish, German, "Jewish"	New London, CT	5
Mrs. Charles Higgins (Louise)	Pennsylvania, 1907	Unknown	$18	Homemaker; machinist (head)	Czech, Hungarian, German, Italian, Croatian	Pittsburgh, PA	2
Walter E. Swope	Ohio, 1904	Unknown	Lodger (rent not listed); $6,000	Teacher	N/A	Stockport Town, OH	7
Stephen Krajny	Czechoslovakia, 1924	Slovak	$6,000	None; none (head)	Slovak, Hungarian, Lithuanian, Russian, Polish	Cleveland, OH	5
Mrs. George Bissell (Lucille)	New York, 1885	Unknown	$85	None; "aircraft" (head)	German, Russian, Spanish, English	New York, NY	3
Eva M. McTeer	Massachusetts, 1876	Unknown	$30	None; construction (head)	Armenian, English, German, Dutch, Italian	Providence, RI	4
Bertha E. Rawlins	Pennsylvania, 1885	Unknown	$8,000	Homemaker; clerk (head)	English, German	Avalon, PA	6

(continued)

Appendix 1.5. CONTINUED

Name(s)	Birthplace and year	Ethnicity	Home/rent value	Occupation (donor and household head)	Neighbors' native languages	Residence	Total in household
Martha Zoltowski	Michigan, 1896	German	$4,000	Homemaker; laborer (head)	English, Polish	Detroit, MI	8
Mrs. George Schmidt (Emma)	New York, 1892	Unknown	$7,000	Homemaker; accucentrist with Kodak (head)	English, Swedish	Rochester, NY	3
Edward McLaughlin	Massachusetts, 1888	Irish	$6,000	Shoemaker	English, Italian	Holbrook, MA	3
Catherine Regucci	New Jersey, 1922	Italian	$10,000	Homemaker; bookbinder (head)	Russian, Italian, Lithuanian	Tenafly, NJ	7
Rose Renna	New York, 1913	Italian	$20	Homemaker; tailor (head)	Italian, German, "Jewish"	Brooklyn, NY	8
John and Anne Safarik	Nebraska, 1882; Czechoslovakia, 1884	Czech	$12,500	Merchant, homemaker	Czech, German, English, Danish, Dutch	Los Angeles, CA	8
Maude Marlin	Missouri, 1882	Unknown	$5,000	None; none (head)	English, French, Lettish, Polish, Italian	San Francisco, CA	5
William Kinder, Jr.	Ohio, 1926	German, Hungarian	$3,000	Homemaker; laborer (head)	German, Magyar	Elyria, OH	5
Bill Davis	Massachusetts, 1902	Unknown	Boarder (rent not listed)	Printer's helper	Yiddish, Lettish, English, Italian	Everett, MA	6

Name(s)	Birthplace and year	Ethnicity	Home/rent value	Occupation (donor and household head)	Neighbors' native languages	Residence	Total in household
Rev. Sylvester Ronaghan	New York, 1895	Irish	Lodger (rent not listed); $50,000 [head is listed as "pastor"; all others as "lodger/assistant"]	Clergyman	English, German, Lithuanian, Italian	Queens, NY	16
William Durkin	Pennsylvania, 1902	Irish	$4,000	Machinist	English, "Jewish," Swedish	Swissvale, PA	6

Source: Book 42, July 1953 to July 30, 1954, Archives, BNSIC; *Fifteenth Census of the United States, 1930.*

Appendix 1.6. SELECTED SHRINE DONORS, 1954

Name	Birthplace and year	Ethnicity	Home/rental value	Occupation (donor and household head)	Neighbors' native languages	Residence	Total in household
Genevieve and Mary Francis McHale	Illinois, 1902 and 1904	Unknown	$3,500	Secretary, secretary; salesman (head)	English, Russian	Los Angeles, CA	11 (8 lodgers, 3 family members)
Mr. and Mrs. Daniel Iacozza	Italy, 1901 (both)	Italian	$18	Printer	French, German, Italian	Norwich, CT	4
Alice Healy	California, 1885	Irish	$3,000	Librarian	English, Italian, French	San Francisco, CA	2
Stanley Greia	New York, 1913	Polish	$10	Shipping clerk; cutter at a shoe factory (head)	Polish, Ukrainian	Auburn City, NY	5
Humberto Skipwith	Virginia, 1906	Unknown	$1,000	Farmer; farmer (head)	N/A	Tuckahoe District, VA	3
Charles Hoffman	New York, 1899	Unknown	$20	Electrician	Polish, "Jewish," Italian, Greek, English	Little Falls, NY	2
Robert Butler	Kentucky, 1909	Unknown	$8,000	Plumber; salesman (head)	"Irish"	Covington, KY	4
John Buzas	Pennsylvania, 1913	Lithuanian	$40	Bus boy; pipe fitter (head)	Lithuanian, English	Philadelphia, PA	6
Grace Fahy	Minnesota, 1882	Unknown	Hotel Guest	Teacher	English	Minneapolis, MN	15

Name	Birthplace and year	Ethnicity	Home/rental value	Occupation (donor and household head)	Neighbors' native languages	Residence	Total in household
Mr. and Mrs. Joseph Springer	Missouri, 1894	German	$18	Fish monger	Italian	St. Louis, MO	3
Mary F. Fortman	Ohio, 1921	Unknown	$3,500	Homemaker; retail merchant (head)	N/A	Kalida Village, OH	3
Hubert Smith	Michigan, 1888	Unknown	$5,500	Packinghouse owner	Serbian, Finish	Muskegon, MI	10

Source: Book 42, 1953, Archives, BNSIC; *Fifteenth Census of the United States, 1930.*

Appendix 1.7. SELECTED SHRINE DONORS, 1959

Name	Birthplace and year	Ethnicity	Home/rental value	Occupation (donor and household head)	Neighbors' native languages	Residence	Total in household
Paul Karwata	Illinois, 1905	Polish	$7,500	Tailor; dyer (head)	Swiss, Polish, German	Chicago, IL	3
George F. Keating	Wisconsin, 1898	Unknown	$35	Machinist	N/A	Milwaukee, WI	6
Paul F. Prosseda	New York, 1916	Italian	$40	None; carpenter (head)	Italian, Polish	Brooklyn, NY	7
Pauline Utry	Hungary, 1897	Hungarian	$15	Homemaker; laborer (head)	Hungarian, Scotch, German	St. Louis, MO	3
Mary Rose Schwab	California, 1887	Unknown	$5,000	Teacher	German, Italian, English, Irish	Healdsburg, CA	3
Kathleen Roche	Ohio, 1884	Unknown	$30,000	Homemaker; optometrist (head)	N/A	Chillicothe, OH	8
Mrs. Florence Souza	Hawaii, 1902	Unknown	N/A (owns)	Stenographer; bookkeeper (head)	Japanese	Hilo, HI	
Rev. John J. Fee	New York, 1911	Irish	$60	None; bricklayer (head)	German, English, Polish, Lettish, Romanian, Russian	Bronx, NY	3
Mr. George E. Comrad	New York, 1904	Unknown	$50	Pharmacist	English, Welsh	Utica, NY	4
Dolores Hubrik	Los Angeles, 1930	Unknown	$25	Homemaker; meat cutter (head)	Scotch, English, Polish, German, Swedish	San Pedro, CA	3

Source: Book 48, 1959, Archives, BNSIC; *Fifteenth Census of the United States, 1930.*

Appendix 2.1. SELECTED ADULT FEMALE DONORS TO THE MARY ALTAR FROM BROOKLYN, 1928

Name	Birthplace and year	Ethnicity	Home/rental value	Occupation (donor and household head)	Neighbors' native languages[a]	Neighborhood[b]	Parish
Agnes Bowen	Massachusetts (1873)	Unknown[c] (Canadian mother)	$9,500	None (took in 1 boarder; school custodian (husband)	3: English, German, Swedish	Marine Park	St. Thomas Aquinas (1885)
Mary G. Doherty	New York (1904)	Irish	$6,000	Stenographer; detective (father)	3: English, Italian, German	East New York	St. Malachy (1854)
Marie A. Fox	New York (1880)	Irish	$2,200	None (head: took in 2 boarders); printer (son)	3: English, French, German	Prospect Heights	St. Joseph (1850)
Melvina A. Jones	New York (1880)	Irish	$50	None (head); electrician (son)	3: English, German, "Jewish"	Flatbush	St. Jerome (1901)
Frances M. Kelly	New Jersey (1878)	Unknown	$12,000	None; inspector of boats (husband)	6: English, Norwegian, Swedish, Danish, German, Chinese	Bay Ridge	Our Lady of Angels (1891)
Elizabeth McCaffrey	New York (1903)	Irish (father)	$40,000 (2 maids)	Public school teacher; none (father)	2: English, German	Flatbush	Our Lady of Refuge (1911)
Anna K. McGrath	New York (1898)	Irish	$8,000	None; "cardboard" in "office" (husband)	3: English, Italian, Norwegian	Red Hook	St. Agnes (1878)
Rosella McHugh	New York (1891)	Irish	$14,000	None (took in 6 boarders); "mechanic" in furniture industry (husband)	4: English, Russian, Italian, German	Fort Greene	Queen of All Saints (1879)

(continued)

Appendix 2.1. CONTINUED

Name	Birthplace and year	Ethnicity	Home/rental value	Occupation (donor and household head)	Neighbors' native languages[a]	Neighborhood[b]	Parish
Marie McKeever	New York (1885)	Irish	$10,000 (1 servant)	None; heating contractor (husband)	2: English, German	Park Slope	St. Saviour (1905)
Honoria McLoughlin	New York (1870)	Irish	$15,000	None; none (sister)	4: English, Armenian, French, "Jewish"	Flatbush	Holy Innocents (1909)
Jane M. McShane	New York (1874)	Irish	$5,000	None; cablesplicer for telephone co. (son)	2: English, German	Bushwick	Our Lady of Good Counsel (1886)
Florence Miranda	New York (1907)	Italian	$30	"Racker" in shirt factory; none (mother)	4: English, Italian, Swedish, Serbian	East New York	St. Rita's (1913)
Anna Murphy	New York (1887)	Irish	$25,000	"Copyist" in millinery; carpenter (brother-in-law)	4: English, Spanish, Italian, Yiddish	Marine Park	St. Thomas Aquinas (1885)
Katherine L. Noon	New York (1890)	Irish	$25,000	Secretary; none (sister, who took in 4 boarders)	4: English, Norwegian, Arabic, German	Park Slope	St. Saviour (1905)
Catherine Rizzo	Italy (1894)	Italian	$32	"Sales lady" in candy store; "operator" in shoe factory (husband)	4: English, Italian, Hungarian, Yiddish	East New York	St. Rita's (1913)
Miriam V. Schmid	New York (1888)	Irish	$325 (1 maid)	None; lawyer (husband)	3: English, French, German	Brooklyn Heights	St. Charles Borromeo (1849)
Mary Schumann	Massachusetts (1881)	Unknown	$18,000	None; sales manager (husband)	3: English, Arabic, Norwegian	Park Slope	St. Saviour (1905)

Name	Birthplace and year	Ethnicity	Home/rental value	Occupation (donor and household head)	Neighbors' native languages[a]	Neighborhood[b]	Parish
Margaret Shea	New York (1902)	Unknown	$10,000 (1 maid)	Legal secretary; manager at investment firm (brother-in-law)	3: English, "Irish," Yiddish	Midwood	Our Lady Help of Christians (1927)
Margaret Sherry	Ireland (1893)	Irish	$70	None (took in 2 male boarders, Norwegian and Russian); letter carrier (husband)	7: English, Danish, French, Polish, "Jewish," Norwegian, Russian	Bay Ridge	St. Anselm (1922)
Elizabeth R. Sinnott	New York (1894)	Unknown	$9,000	None; president of taxi co. (husband)	5: English, "Irish," German, Yiddish, Swedish	Midwood	Our Lady Help of Christians (1927)
Loretta Teets	Connecticut (1878)	Irish	$60	Housewife; electrician (husband)	4: English, German, French, Russian	East New York	St. Malachy (1854)
Loretta Walsh	New Jersey (1889)	Irish	$18,000	Public school teacher; adjuster (landlord)	5: English, Swedish, German, Armenian, Spanish	Fort Greene	Queen of All Saints (1879)
Margaret C. White	New Jersey (1900)	German/Irish	$16,000	Public school teacher; broker (father)	3: English, German, Italian	Bedford Stuyvesant	Holy Rosary (1889)
Elinor Woods	New York (1908)	Unknown	$25,000	Newspaper copywriter; "deputy" commissioner's office (father)	1: English	Crown Heights	St. Francis of Assisi (1898)

(continued)

Appendix 2.1. CONTINUED

Name	Birthplace and year	Ethnicity	Home/rental value	Occupation (donor and household head)	Neighbors' native languages[a]	Neighborhood[b]	Parish
Margaret Zimmerman	New York (1879)	Irish (father)	$20,000 (2 maids and 1 secretary)	None; physician (husband)	2: English, Swedish	Park Slope	St. Francis Xavier (1886)

a. "Neighbors" here means persons listed on the same page of the federal census in 1930.
b. "Neighborhood" labels are taken from contemporary maps and from the Diocese of Brooklyn's parish directory.
c. "Unknown" means I was unable to determine ethnicity from the 1930 census or earlier census records.
Source: Fifteenth Census of the United States, 1930; "Individual Contributions to Fund of International Federation of Catholic Alumnae for Mary Altar," Archives, BNSIC.

Appendix 2.2. SELECTED ADULT FEMALE DONORS TO THE MARY ALTAR FROM INDIANA AND TENNESSEE, 1928

Name	Birthplace and year	Ethnicity	Home/rental value	Occupation (donor and household head)	Neighbors' native languages	Town	Total in household
Lena Brady	IN (1880)	Irish (father)	$60	Public school teacher	2: English, "Jewish"	Indianapolis, IN	30 (lodger)
Anna Brennan	IN (1905)	Irish (father)	$2,000	Public school teacher	3: English, "Jewish," Polish	Indianapolis, IN	3
Agnes F. Cruse	IN (1883)	Irish	$13,000	Red Cross secretary/ secretary	2: English, German	Indianapolis, IN	5
Celeste R. Dugan	IL (1909)	Irish	$5,500	Clerical work/foreman at chain works	1: English	Indianapolis, IN	5
Margaret Fell	TN (1889)	Unknown	$12,000	None/meat market merchant (brother)	3: English, Italian, Swedish	Memphis, TN	8
Jessie Fellman	OH (1892)	Unknown	$55	None/salesman	2: English, German	Indianapolis, IN	6
Mary Gravel	MA (1880)	German	$12,000	None/superintendent at textile mill	1: English	Signal Mountain, TN	3
Rita Gravel	TN (1915)	German/ Canadian	$12,000	None/superintendent at textile mill	1: English	Signal Mountain, TN	3
Bridget Hagerty	IL (1859)	Irish	$12,000	None	2: English, Swedish	South Bend, IN	3
Ellen Keogan	IN (1877)	Irish	$15,000	None/contractor	1: English	South Bend, IN	5
Clara Langsdale	IN (1863)	German (father)	$50	None/insurance salesman	1: English	Indianapolis, IN	5
Margaret Mette	TN (1869)	Irish	$10,000	None (5 lodgers)/ clerk	1: English	Memphis, TN	8 (5 lodgers)

(continued)

Appendix 2.2. CONTINUED

Name	Birthplace and year	Ethnicity	Home/rental value	Occupation (donor and household head)	Neighbors' native languages	Town	Total in household
Ownie Miller	MS (1887)	Unknown	$65	None/ employee of a retail adding machine co.	6: English, French, Polish, German, Yiddish, Spanish	Memphis, TN	3
Rose Quinn	TN (1882)	Irish	Unknown	Manager of lumber co. / none	2: English, Russian	Memphis, TN	2
Mary Ryan	IN (1910)	Irish	$12,000	Bookkeeper/ salesman	1: English	Indianapolis, IN	3

Source: Fourteenth Census of the United States, 1920; Fifteenth Census of the United States, 1930; "Individual Contributions to Fund of International Federation of Catholic Alumnae for Mary Altar," Archives, BNSIC.

Appendix 2.3. SELECTED ADULT FEMALE DONORS TO THE MARY ALTAR LIVING OUTSIDE BROOKLYN, 1928

Name	Birthplace and year	Ethnicity	Home/rental value	Occupation (donor and household head)	Neighbors' native Languages	Town	Total in household
Margaret Blake	IN (1899)	Unknown*	$8,000	Stenographer/inspector at a shirt factory (aunt) (took in 3 boarders)	3: English, Polish, Hungarian	South Bend, IN	5
Alma L. Centlivre	IN (1902)	German/French	$25,000	none/none (mother)	2: English, German	Fort Wayne, IN	6
Margaret Colgan	NY (1904)	Irish	$10,000	Public school teacher/ mason contractor, owned business	3: English, German, Italian	Buffalo, NY	3
Mary Cotter	NY (1900)	Irish	$8,000	Public school teacher/none (father)	1: English	Buffalo, NY	4
Mary Mahoney Curry	NY (1892)	Irish	$16,500	None/lawyer	2: English, "Jewish"	Hartford, CT	4
Mary Agnes Doolan	NY (1898)	Irish	$4,000	Stenographer/none	3: English, Slovak, German	Bayonne, NJ	4
Emma K. Eder	IN (1882)	German	$8,000	None/abstractor in an abstract office	4: English, Russian, Italian, German	Crown Point, IN	4
Helen K. Garry	CT (1903)	Irish	$7,500	Stenographer/ wholesale agent (father)	3: English, German, Italian	Albany, NY	4

(continued)

Appendix 2.3. CONTINUED

Name	Birthplace and year	Ethnicity	Home/rental value	Occupation (donor and household head)	Neighbors' native Languages	Town	Total in household
Loretta Hendrick	CT (1900)	German/Irish	$60,000	Secretary/none (mother)	2: English, German	New Rochelle, NY	7
Marjorie Kroft	NY (1908)	German/Irish	$50	Student/drug store pharmacist (father)	1: English	Newburgh, NY	4
Frances LaPointe	MI (1904)	French (mother)	$12,000	Public school teacher/ none (father)	4: English, German, Polish, "Jewish"	Toledo, OH	4
Grace B. Leslie	NY (1883)	English	$41,000	None/cotton goods merchant	4: English, German, Hungarian, Polish	Jersey City, NJ	7 (w/ maid and cook)
Anna M. Malloy	NY (1898)	Irish	$80	secretary/none	9: English, Yiddish, Norwegian, Swedish, German, Hungarian, French, Japanese, Italian	New York City (Manhattan)	2
Angela McGratty	NY (1890)	Irish (father)	$50,000	None/university professor (brother-in-law)	6: English, German, French, Polish, Dutch, Yiddish	New York City (Manhattan)	6 (w/ nurse and maid)
Margaret Mette	TN (1869)	Irish	$10,000	None (5 lodgers)/ clerk at water co.	1: English	Memphis, TN	8 (w/ 5 lodgers)
Dorothy Murphy	OH (1889)	German (mother)	$20,000	None/manager	1: English	Lakewood, OH	5

Name	Birthplace and year	Ethnicity	Home/rental value	Occupation (donor and household head)	Neighbors' native Languages	Town	Total in household
Frances B. Paine	MA (1894)	Irish	Rent $5,600/ year	None/treasurer of a lumber company (brother)	8: English, Serbian, Armenian, Norwegian, German, Russian, French, Polish	New York City (Manhattan)	4 (2 servants)
Clara Schaffler	TN (1909)	Swiss (mother)	$22,000	None/president of coal co.	2: English, "Jewish"	Memphis, TN	4
Mary R. Steudle	NY (1899)	German	$9,300	Public school teacher/ none (mother)	4: English, German, Norwegian, Swedish	Buffalo, NY	4
Alice E. Woods	NY (1888)	Irish	$83	Retired (both)	2: English, Italian	Troy, NY	2

" "Unknown" means that the 1930 census only refers to her parents' birth in Indiana, and I was unable to locate Blake in earlier records, where we might see her grandparents' immigration status and ethnic heritage.
Source: Fifteenth Census of the United States, 1930; "Individual Contributions to Fund of International Federation of Catholic Alumnae for Mary Altar," Archives, BNSIC.

Appendix 3.1. SELECTED DONORS FROM BROOKLYN'S ST. THOMAS AQUINAS SCHOOL, 1928

Name	Birthplace and year	Ethnicity	Parents' nativity	Occupation of household head	Neighbors' native languages	Total in household	Home/rental value
Albert Annunziata	NY (1915)	Italian	Italy	Salesman	3: English, Polish, Italian	6	$35
Gabriel Brillante	NY (1916)	Italian	Italy (mother); no father	Barbershop Proprietor (brother)	7: English, Polish, German, Italian, Danish, Estonian, Lithuanian	6	$25,000
Edna Brennan	NY (1913)	Irish (third generation)	New York (no mother)	Ship builder's asstistant	2: English; Italian	7	$45
John Brown	NY (1915)	British/Irish	New York; (England: paternal grandfather, No. Ireland: maternal grandfather)	Carpenter	3: English, Swedish, Italian	4	$9,000
Thelma Casey	NY (1917)	Canadian/Irish	Canada (father); New York (mother)	Brick layer	5: English, Norwegian, Danish, German, Bulgarian	4	$10,000
Jeanette Cornely	NY (1918)	German/Irish	Germany (father); Ireland (mother)	Restaurant manager	2: English, German	5	$5,500
Francis Connors	NY (1917)	British/Irish	England (father); no mother	Street cleaner	3: English, Italian, Polish	6	$30
Jane Dawson	NY (1914)	British/ French (father); German/ Irish (mother)	New York	Insurance broker	6: English, Italian, Irish, German, Swedish, Spanish	5 (1 boarder)	$50

Name	Birthplace and year	Ethnicity	Parents' nativity	Occupation of household head	Neighbors' native languages	Total in household	Home/rental value
James Dorian	NY (1916)	Irish	Ireland	Stableman	1: English	5	$26
Herbert Finch	NY (1916)	Irish	New York	Driver (Laundry)	6: English, Italian, French, German, Swedish, Norwegian	13	$30
Gladys Gruschow	NY (1916)	German/Irish	New York; (Ireland: paternal grandfather, Germany: maternal grandfather)	Plumber	3: English, Italian, German	8	$4,000
James Harley, Jr.	NY (1913)	Canadian/British	New York	Inspector in leather factory	3: English, Italian, Swedish	7	$8,000
Mary Heffernan	NY (1914)	Irish	Ireland	"Oiler" with Gas co.	2: English, Italian	4 (1 nephew)	$25
Richard Kasprowicz	NY (1917)	Polish	Poland (father); New York (mother)	Proprietor of painter company	3: English, Polish, Norwegian	4	$9,000
Paul Martello	NY (1917)	Italian	New York (mother); Italy (father)	Blacksmith	3: English, Italian, Polish	8	$40
Catherine Murphy	NY (1916)	Irish	New York	Sweeper	2: English, German	8	$8
Irene Murphy	NY (1914)	Irish	Ireland	Carpenter	5: English, Italian, Norwegian, Swedish, Danish	9	unknown

(continued)

Appendix 3.1. CONTINUED

Name	Birthplace and year	Ethnicity	Parents' nativity	Occupation of household head	Neighbors' native languages	Total in household	Home/rental value
Margaret O'Brien	NY (1914)	Irish	Ireland	"Utility man" at a bank	3: English, Polish, German	11	$4,500
Loretta Searing	NY (1915)	Unknown	New York (no mother)	Foreman at a garage	4: English, German, Italian, Swedish	4 (1 boarder)	$20
Rita Shea	NY (1914)	Unknown (Canadian)	Canada	Laborer	2: English, Italian	4	$35

Source: Fifteenth Census of the United States, 1930; Fourteenth Census of the United States, 1920; "Individual Contributions to Fund of International Federation of Catholic Alumnae for Mary Altar" Archives, BNSIC.

Appendix 3.2. SELECTED DONORS FROM BROOKLYN'S ST. JOSEPH'S COMMERCIAL SCHOOL, 1928

Name	Birthplace and year	Ethnicity	Parents' nativity	Occupation of household head	Neighbors' native languages	Neighborhood	Parish
Christina Connolly	NY (1913)	Irish	Ireland	Furniture polisher	5: English, Yiddish, Spanish, Chinese, Swedish	Brooklyn Heights	Our Lady of Mercy
Agnes Duffy	NY (1913)	Irish	Ireland (mother); no father	none	4: English, Italian, German, Yiddish	South Brooklyn	St. Agnes
Mary Duggan	NY (1912)	Irish	Ireland	City roads worker (laborer)	4: English, Italian, German, French	Flatbush	Holy Cross
Viola Gallagher	NY (1913)	Irish	Ireland (mother) NY (father)	Chauffer	5: English, Swedish, German, Norwegian, Turkish	Bay Ridge	St. Anselm
Helen Gandolfi	NY (1912)	Italian/English	Italy (paternal grandparents); England (maternal grandfather)	Policeman	4: English, German, Norwegian, Swedish	Dyker Heights	St. Ephrem
Helen Gilfeather	NY (1912)	Irish	Ireland	Waiter	2: English, Italian	Gravesend	Saints Simon and Jude
Helen Gorman	NY (1913)	Scottish/Irish	Scotland (maternal grandfather); Ireland (maternal grandmother); New York (father)	Newspaper reporter	4: English, German, Norwegian, Swedish	Dyker Heights	St. Ephrem
Margaret Hamma	NY (1915)	Unknown	New York	Plumber	3: English, German, 'Bohemian'	Bedford Stuyvesant	Holy Rosary

(continued)

Appendix 3.2. CONTINUED

Name	Birthplace and year	Ethnicity	Parents' nativity	Occupation of household head	Neighbors' native languages	Neighborhood	Parish
Dorothy Hanrahan	NY (1912)	Irish	Ireland	Boarding house keeper	2: English, Spanish	Brooklyn Heights	St. Charles Borromeo
Veronica Jensen	NY (1910)	Danish/Irish	Denmark (father); Ireland (maternal grandparents)	Watchman at the docks	4: English, Italian, Danish, Swedish	Bay Ridge	Our Lady of Perpetual Help
Angeline Keupp	NY (1914)	German	Germany (grandparents)	Bricklayer	3: English, Italian, German	Bushwick	St. Barbara
Marion Kuntzmann	NY (1913)	Swiss/French	Alsace-Lorraine (father); Switzerland (mother)	Roofer	6: English; Swedish, Finnish, German, French, Italian	Bush Terminal	St. Michael
Louise Lanza	NY (1913)	Italian	Italy (mother); no father	(Son) "streetwork"/ "photographs"	3: English, Swedish, Italian	Red Hook	St. Agnes
Dorothy Lyon	NY (1913)	Scottish/Irish	Scotland (father); Ireland (maternal grandparents)	Marble setter	3: English, Italian, Norwegian	Dyker Heights	St. Ephrem
Margaret Maguire	NY (1913)	Irish	Ireland	Fitter	4: English, German, Swedish 'Irish'	Bedford Stuyvesant	St. Ambrose
Mary Maxey	NY (1913)	Irish	New York; (Ireland: paternal grandparents)	None	2: German, English	Prospect Park	Holy Name
Cecelia McCarthy	NY (1914)	Irish/Italian	New York; (Italy: maternal grandfather)	Chauffer	7: English, Italian, French, Portuguese, Spanish, Swedish, Norwegian	Brooklyn Heights	St. Charles Borromeo

Name	Birthplace and year	Ethnicity	Parents' nativity	Occupation of household head	Neighbors' native languages	Neighborhood	Parish
Ellen McCauley	NY (1914)	Irish	Ireland (maternal grandfather)	none	3: English, Swedish, Norwegian	Bush Terminal	St. Michael
Grace Muldoon	NY (1912)	Unknown	New York	Electrician	2: Portuguese, English	Park Slope	St. Francis Xavier
Rita O'Brien	NY (1914)	Irish	Ireland (mother); NY (father); Ireland (paternal grandfather)	Watchman	3: English, Swedish, Danish	Prospect Park	Holy Name
Rosie Olivari	NY (1913)	Italian	Italy	Cook (restaurant)	6: English, Italian, French, Swedish, German, Russian	Fort Greene	Queen of All Saints
Mildred Ryan	NY (1912)	Irish	Mass. (father); no mother; Ireland (paternal grandparents)	"Stat-engineer" (office)	6: English, Danish, Norwegian, German, Swedish, Italian	Bay Ridge	St. Anselm
Anna Strobel	NY (1914)	German	NY (only grandparents listed)	Porter	3: English, Italian, Norwegian	Carroll Gardens	St. Mary Star of the Sea
Kathryn Welch	NY (1911)	Irish/Scottish/ German	CT (father); NY (mother); (grandparents: Ireland, Germany, and Scotland)	Patrolman	2: English, Swedish	Flatbush	Holy Cross
Loretta Zimmerman	NY (1912)	Irish	New York (father); Ireland (maternal grandparents)	"Teamster" (coal industry)	3: English, Italian, Norwegian	Carroll Gardens	St. Mary Star of the Sea

Source: Fifteenth Census of the United States, 1930; Fourteenth Census of the United States, 1920; "Individual Contributions to Fund of International Federation of Catholic Alumnae for Mary Altar," Archives, BNSIC.

Appendix 3.3. SELECTED CHILD AND TEEN VISITORS TO THE NATIONAL SHRINE OF THE IMMACULATE CONCEPTION, 1926–1927

Name	Residence	Birthplace and year	Travelling with	Parents' nativity	Household head's occupation	Neighbors' native languages	Total in household	Value of home/rent
Viola Conley	Philadelphia, PA	Pennsylvania (1909)	Catholic Girls High School	Pennsylvania	Trolley motorman	German, Slovene, Irish	6	Rented
Eleanor Kelly	Philadelphia, PA	Pennsylvania (1908)	Catholic Girls High School	Ireland	Electrician	German	7	Owned
Eileen Kelly	Baltimore, MD	Maryland (1916)	Family	Maryland	Superintendant	English	5	$15,000
Thomas Kelly, Jr.	Baltimore, MD	Maryland (1919)	Family	Maryland	Superintendant	English	5	$15,000
William Kelly	Baltimore, MD	Maryland (1923)	Family	Maryland	Superintendant	English	5	$15,000
Margaret Lawlor	Philadelphia, PA	Pennsylvania (1908)	Catholic Girls High School	Pennsylvania	(Illegible)	German, Danish	8	Owned
Helen Loser	Philadelphia, PA	Pennsylvania (1910)	Catholic Girls High School	Germany (father), Austria (mother)	Blacksmith	German, Romanian, Irish	5	Owned
James McAndrew	Scranton, PA	Pennsylvania (1908)	Brother	Pennsylvania	Investigator	Italian	4	$10,000
William McLaughlin	Bronx, NY	New York (1910)	Father	Northern Ireland	Real estate agent	Polish, Yiddish, German	6	$16,000

Name	Residence	Birthplace and year	Travelling with	Parents' nativity	Household head's occupation	Neighbors' native languages	Total in household	Value of home/rent
Clement McLaughlin	Bronx, NY	New York (1911)	Father	N. Ireland	Real estate agent	Polish, Yiddish, German	6	$16,000
William F. Smith	Washington, DC	Washington, DC (1915)	Unknown	Pennsylvania	Telephone operator (mother)	English	5	$45
Rose Urziehart	Riverdale, MD	Washington DC (1912)	Family	New York	Government clerk	German	6	$7,000
Marcella Urziehart	Riverdale, MD	Maryland (1913)	Family	New York	Government clerk	German	6	$7,000

Source: Register of Visitors to the National Shrine, June 1926–August 1927, Archives, BNSIC; *Fourteenth Census of the United States, 1920; Fifteenth Census of the United States, 1930.*

NOTES

INTRODUCTION

1. I cite structured and semistructured interviews I conducted at the BNSIC here and later, especially in chapter 6. Except in the case of public figures, in order to encourage my interviewees' honesty and protect their anonymity, I kept their identities confidential. In citing these interviews I list only the interview number and/or a pseudonym, interview date, and interviewee's gender, age, and residence. On the BNSIC as "most beautiful": interview no. 19, June 27, 1997, female, age 54, resides N.J. On the Shrine as "neo-ugly": interview no. 38, June 12, 1998, male, age 32, resides Washington, D.C.

2. NCR Today: The Catholic Blog, *National Catholic Reporter*, http://ncronline.org/blogs/ncr-today/welcome-ncr-today (accessed June 28, 2010). *Commonweal*, www.commonwealmagazine.org/ (accessed June 28, 2010). *Soul*, www.wafusa.org/publications/soul/soul.html (accessed June 28, 2010). Eternal Word Television Network (EWTN), www.ewtn.com/ (accessed June 28, 2010). James Carroll, *An American Requiem: God, My Father, and the War That Came between Us* (Boston: Houghton Mifflin, 1996), 93, 155, 141. Carolyn Bell Hughes, "Washington's Little Rome," *Washington Post*, December 9, 1956, p. F3.

3. On Catholic "liberals" and "conservatives" after 1965, see R. Scott Appleby and Mary Jo Weaver, eds., *Being Right: Conservative Catholics in America* (Bloomington: Indiana University Press, 1995); and Mary Jo Weaver, ed., *What's Left?: Liberal American Catholics* (Bloomington: Indiana University Press, 1999).

4. I introduce a new term to describe the Catholicism that predominated in the United States and at the Shrine between 1913 and 1959. Drawing on a word, *consolidation*, that evokes several related developments (centralization, nationalization, standardization, bureaucratization, and modernization), I create and use a historical ideal type. The sociologist Max Weber first self-consciously used "ideal types," or theoretical constructs that function as more or less useful interpretive tools, in the study of religion. He used many in his work—including, for example, "the Protestant ethic." For historians, categories that arise from the study of a particular period and place often prove most useful, and that's how I intend the labels I propose to describe the two historical eras and styles of piety.

Historical ideal types—in this case "consolidated Catholicism" and "fragmented Catholicism"—are formulated by accentuating some features of a particular period in a particular place (e.g., U.S. Catholicism between 1917 and 1959) for a researcher's distinctive purpose. These categories, as I see them, do not perfectly reflect all features of the period; they are more or less useful tools for analysis. In this case, I think these historical ideal types help us analyze what happened before and after 1959. See Max Weber, "Objectivity in the Social Sciences and Social Policy," in *Methodology in the Social Sciences* (New York: Free Press, 1949), 49–112; and Susan Hekman, *Weber: The Ideal Types and Contemporary Social Theory* (Notre Dame: University of Indiana Press, 1983), 38–60. With regard to the first type I use here, *consolidated Catholicism*, the term "consolidate" means "to combine compactly into one mass, body, or connected whole"; *Oxford English Dictionary*, 2nd ed., 1989, OED Online. Oxford University Press, http://dictionary.oed.com. This ideal typical category has some interpretive strength and weaknesses. One of its strengths is that it avoids familiar binary labels (like conservative or progressive). I contrast it here and throughout with *fragmented Catholicism*, a strategic descriptor for the Church after 1959, and especially after 1965, and again that term also emphasizes one feature—internal division. Of course, there was fragmentation before 1959 and consolidation after 1959, and many other things were going on during both periods. Some U.S. historians have used slightly different terms to account for a sensibility that was emerging by 1920, including Robert H. Wiebe, who discussed the "bureaucratic mentality" and a "search for order" in *The Search for Order, 1877–1920* (New York: Hill and Wang, 1967), 293–302. Some historians of Catholicism, including James T. Fisher, in *Communion of Immigrants: A History of Catholics in America* (Oxford: Oxford University Press, 2002), also have used different language to make a similar point: that between 1945 and 1963 Catholicism enjoyed an "uneasy triumph" but seemed more "divided" after 1965 (114–63). I discuss the NCWC in later chapters. The new code of canon law, sometimes called the Pio-Benedictine Code, aimed to create "a clear and orderly collection of all the laws of the Church" for the purpose of "guiding and safeguarding the clergy and the faithful"; *The 1917 or Pio-Benedictine Code of Canon Law*, trans. Edward N. Peters (San Francisco: Ignatius Press, 2001), 21–22 (this English translation has a helpful introduction; the Latin original is *Codex Iuris Canonici Pii X Pontificis Maximi iussu digestus, Benedicti Papae XV auctoritate promulgatus* [Typis Polyglottis Vaticanis, 1917]). That stood as the standard until the 1983 revision. English translations of the encyclicals condemning Americanism and "Modernism" can be found at Papal Encyclicals Online, www.papalencyclicals.net (accessed July 28, 2010): Pope Leo XIII, *Testem Benevolentiae Nostrae*, January 22, 1899; Pope Pius X, *Pascendi Dominici Gregis*, September 8, 1907. See also at the same site Pius X, "The Oath against Modernism," September 1, 1910. On that encyclical's "chilling" effect see James Hennesey, *American Catholics: A History of the Roman Catholic Community in the United States* (New York: Oxford University Press, 1981), 217. For translations of the sixteen documents of Vatican II see Austin Flannery, ed., *Vatican Council II: Constitutions, Decrees, Declarations*, rev. ed. (Northport, NY: Costello, 1996). For a longer history see Guiseppe Alberigo and Joseph Komonchak, eds., *History of Vatican II*, 5 vols. (Maryknoll, NY: Orbis, 1995–2000). My account of the "two parties" is taken from the most accessible short history in English: John W. O'Malley, *What Happened at Vatican II* (Cambridge, MA: Harvard University Press, 2008), 290–313.

5. For Shahan and all those who figure prominently in the story, I give their dates of birth and death at their first mention, as I do here. The previous rector, Reverend Monsignor (later Bishop) Michael Bransfield, used the phrase "America's Church" often in written and oral messages. The coffee table book that his communications director, Gregory W. Tucker, wrote also used that title: *America's Church: The Basilica of the National Shrine of the Immaculate Conception.* Bransfield also used the somewhat more specific phrase "America's Catholic Church." See Michael Bransfield, "The National Shrine: America's Catholic Church," *Mary's Shrine* 54 (spring–summer 1994): 2–3. He started to use the other phrases more often. In the last edition of the guidebook to the Shrine that was published during his tenure, Bransfield's "Welcome" called the Shrine "the patronal church of U.S. Catholics and the nation's preeminent Marian shrine." *Basilica of the National Shrine of the Immaculate Conception: A Guidebook and Personal Tour* (Washington, DC: Progress Printing for the National Shrine of the Immaculate Conception, n.d. [2005]), 2. This and the earlier editions of this guidebook have been of great use to me in my research. I want to thank the contributors, who are listed on p. 77 of the 2005 edition: Jean Bicher, Sister M. Josellen Dajer, SND, Sonia Gonzales, Salvadore Mazzuca, Ph.D., Jane Palladino, Geraldine M. Rohling, Ph.D., and Peter Sonski. The current rector, Reverend Monsignor Walter R. Rossi, JCL, has continued to use Bransfield's phrases. In his "Greetings from the Rector" on the Shrine's Website, Rossi welcomed Internet visitors to "the country's patronal church and its preeminent Marian shrine." Basilica of the National Shrine of the Immaculate Conception, www.nationalshrine.com (accessed July 8, 2007). Those phrases as well as "America's Catholic Church" also were repeated in a later mission statement circulated by the Development Department: "Mission Statement," e-mail, news@bnsic.org to Development mailing list, July 21, 2010.

6. "Presence," *Oxford English Dictionary*, 2nd ed., 1989, OED Online. Robert A. Orsi, *Between Heaven and Earth: The Religious Worlds People Make and the Scholars Who Study Them* (Princeton, NJ: Princeton University Press, 2005), 73.

7. On the saints represented see *Basilica of the National Shrine of the Immaculate Conception: A Guidebook and Personal Tour*, 74–77. This guidebook also mentions these and other representations of Mary in the building, and it describes "Mary's Garden," on the northwest grounds of the site (8). The full title of the Crypt Church's main altar is the "Mary Memorial Altar," which recalls the women named "Mary" (or some variant) that contributed or were remembered by contributors. Throughout the book I sometimes shorten the phrase—to "Mary Altar"—but I am referring to the same altar.

8. On the number of archbishops and bishops, see *MEM*, 70–72. On planning the dedication to coincide with the annual episcopal gathering, see *AC*, 153.

9. On the centralization of Catholic philanthropy in the twentieth century see Mary J. Oates, *The Catholic Philanthropic Tradition in America* (Bloomington: Indiana University Press, 1995).

10. On European developments, see Nicholas Atkin and Frank Tallett, *Priests, Prelates, and People: A History of European Catholicism since 1750* (New York: Oxford University Press, 2003), 129–264. On the United States, I am especially indebted to the summaries in John T. McGreevy, *Catholicism and American Freedom: A History* (New York: Norton, 2003), 12–13; R. Scott Appleby, general introduction to *Creative Fidelity: American Catholic Intellectual Traditions*, ed. R. Scott Appleby, Patricia Byrne, and William J. Portier (Maryknoll, NY: Orbis, 2004), xvii–xxvii; Jay P. Dolan, *In Search of an American Catholicism: A History of Religion and Culture*

in Tension (New York: Oxford University Press, 2002), 47–189; and Philip Gleason, *Contending with Modernity: Catholic Higher Education in the Twentieth Century* (New York: Oxford University Press, 1995), 105–66. Gleason also described the shared neo-scholastic "worldview" between 1919 and 1941 and noted "Catholics' near obsession with order and unity" (118–23). "Triumphalist Americanism" originated earlier, even if it gained clarity and force after 1899. For an earlier example by a prelate connected with the Shrine see the 1876 classic by James Cardinal Gibbons, *The Faith of Our Fathers: A Plain Exposition and Vindication of the Church Founded by Our Lord Jesus Christ*, 11th ed. (Rockford, IL: Tan Books, 1980), 186–203. Shahan was thinking in similar ways by 1910, three years before he proposed the Shrine to Rome, writing to a CUA board member that he hoped the building might be "covered with noble historical frescoes depicting the origin and glories of Catholics in the United States." Thomas J. Shahan to Mr. [Michael] Jenkins, July 28, 1910, Archives, BNSIC.

11. On "progressive" Thomism at CUA see Gleason, *Contending with Modernity*, 110–11. Charles G. Herbermann, Edward A. Pace, Condé R. Pallen, Thomas J. Shahan, and John J. Wynn, eds., *The Catholic Encyclopedia*, 15 vols. (London: R. Appleton, 1907–12), available at www.newadvent.org/cathen/01001a.htm (accessed July 29, 2010). See the entries "Thomism," "Neo-Scholasticism," "Modernism," and *Testem Benevoentiae*. Shahan and Pace had connections with Thomists at the University of Louvain, one of the European centers of neo-scholasticism, and those connections were evident in the choice of contributors: they asked Maurice De Wolf, professor of logic, to write the entry on neo-scholasticism and Arthur Vermeersch, SJ, professor of moral theology and canon law, to discuss modernism. As I'll show, Fulton J. Sheen, professor at CUA, had connections with the Shrine from 1920 to 1959, and he defended Thomist philosophy in his writing and broadcasts. For Sheen's dismissal of the "modern" thinkers I mention see his *Philosophy of Religion: The Impact of Modern Knowledge on Religion* (New York: Appleton-Century-Crofts, 1948), xiv, 54–56, 83–84, 88, 185, 343.

12. Guilday's sermon on November 15, 1916, is excerpted in *MEM*, 15. I called for "translocative" histories that do not presuppose the nation-state as the default unit of analysis and that consider varying scales from the local to the transregional in Thomas A. Tweed, "American Occultism and Japanese Buddhism: Albert J. Edmunds, D. T. Suzuki, and Translocative History," *Japanese Journal of Religious Studies* 32.2 (2005): 249–81. Peter R. D'Agostino advocated a transnational approach, emphasizing the links with Rome, *Rome in America: Transnational Catholic Ideology from the Risorgimento to Fascism* (Chapel Hill: University of North Carolina Press, 2004). A number of U.S. historians also have situated U.S. developments in global history. See Daniel T. Rodgers, *Atlantic Crossings: Social Politics in a Progressive Age* (Cambridge, MA: Harvard University Press, 1998); Eric Rauchway, *Blessed among Nations: How the World Made America* (New York: Hill and Wang, 2006); and Thomas Bender, *A Nation among Nations: America's Place in World History* (New York: Hill and Wang, 2006).

13. My approach revises and extends the methods I employed in my previous work, including Thomas A. Tweed, *Our Lady of the Exile: Diasporic Religion at a Cuban Catholic Shrine in Miami* (New York: Oxford University Press, 1997). I refined that approach as I learned from colleagues in the Visual Culture of American Religions Project (1995–2000) and taught courses on religion and visual culture to students at the University of North Carolina at Chapel Hill and the University of Texas at Austin. My list of ten factors to consider in the interpretation of architecture

draws on insights found in various sources on the study of art and architecture, including S. Brent Plate's "components" that comprise the field of vision, Sylvan Barnet's "basic questions" to ask when interpreting art, Thomas A. Markus's "three domains" to be considered in the interpretation of architecture, and David Morgan and Sally M. Promey's "four operations" by which images participate in religious practice. Morgan also sent me his unpublished list of "Questions to Ask When Looking at Works of Art," which he has used in the undergraduate classroom. I also have learned from many other studies of religious architecture, including Helen Hills, *Invisible City: The Architecture of Devotion in Seventeenth-Century Neapolitan Convents* (New York: Oxford University Press, 2004), Peter W. Williams, *Houses of God: Region, Religion, and Architecture in the United States* (Urbana: University of Illinois Press, 1997), and Richard Kieckhefer, *Theology in Stone: Church Architecture from Byzantium to Berkeley* (New York: Oxford University Press, 2004). S. Brent Plate, ed., *Religion, Art, and Visual Culture: A Cross-cultural Reader* (New York: Palgrave, 2002), 5. Sylvan Barnet, *A Short Guide to Writing about Art*, 9th ed. (Upper Saddle River, NJ: Prentice Hall, 2008). Thomas A. Markus, *Buildings and Power* (London: Routledge, 1993), 3–28. David Morgan and Sally M. Promey, eds., *The Visual Culture of American Religions* (Berkeley: University of California Press, 2001), 2–15. I also refined my thinking by pondering Promey's analysis of "The Public Display of Religion" in their co-edited volume cited above (27–48), and Morgan's analysis of the function of religious images: David Morgan, *The Sacred Gaze, Religious Visual Culture in Theory and Practice* (Berkeley: University of California Press, 2005), 55–74. There he mentions several functions also operative at the Shrine: images, Morgan proposes, order space and time, imagine community, communicate with the divine or transcendent, embody forms of communication with the divine, collaborate with other forms of representation, influence thought and behavior by persuasion or magic, and displace rival images and ideologies (55).

14. I offered an overview of shrines and pilgrimage in Thomas A. Tweed, "Pilgrimage" and "Shrine," in *Contemporary American Religion*, ed. Wade Clark Roof, vol. 2 (New York: Macmillan Reference USA, 2000), 534–36; 674–76. I noted several ways to classify shrines, including by function. I distinguished several types: commemorative, miraculous, found-object, ex voto, imitative, and identity. In terms of that typology, the BNSIC is an "identity" shrine, one that functions to help visitors construct collective identity. In terms of Nolan and Nolan's typology, it is a "devotional" shrine: Mary Lee Nolan and Sidney Nolan, *Christian Pilgrimage in Modern Western Europe* (Chapel Hill: University of North Carolina Press, 1989), 216–90. I'm aware that my definition, which was constructed by comparing multiple religious cases, differs from the Church's in the 1983 Code of Canon Law, can. 1230, "By the term shrine is understood a church or other sacred place to which numerous members of the faithful make pilgrimage for a special reason of piety, with the approval of the local ordinary" (www.vatican.va). I've learned a great deal from Bob Orsi. His rich study of a Catholic shrine in Chicago helped me ask better questions about the site in D.C.: Robert A. Orsi, *Thank You, St. Jude: Women's Devotion to the Patron Saint of Hopeless Causes* (New Haven: Yale University Press, 1996). I also have been thinking about shrines and pilgrimage, and reading anthropological and religious studies and geographical literature on those topics for a long time. In that sense, many other books have shaped my thinking, including John Eade and Michael J. Sallnow, *Contesting the Sacred: The Anthropology of Christian Pilgrimage* (London: Routledge, 1991), Simon Coleman and

John Elsner, *Pilgrimage: Past and Present in World Religions* (Cambridge, MA: Harvard University Press, 1995), Anne Feldhaus, *Connected Places: Region, Pilgrimage, and Geographical Imagination in India* (New York: Palgrave, 2003), Simon Coleman and John Eade, eds., *Reframing Pilgrimage: Cultures in Motion* (London: Routledge, 2004), and Ian Reader's *Making Pilgrimages: Meaning and Practice in Shikoku* (Honolulu: University of Hawai'i Press, 2005).

15. On the U.S. Church's new status in 1908, see John Tracy Ellis, *American Catholicism*, 2nd ed. (Chicago: University of Chicago Press, 1969), 124. Tracy notes that Pope Pius X issued the apostolic constitution, *Sapienti consilio*, which removed the United States from the jurisdiction of the Congregation de Propaganda Fide and declared it was no longer a missionary territory.

16. This account of U.S. history in 1920 distills many things I've learned from many historians, too many to cite. I've benefited especially from David J. Goldberg, *Discontented America: The United States in the 1920s* (Baltimore: Johns Hopkins University Press, 1999); Lynn Dumenil, *The Modern Temper: American Culture and Society in the 1920s* (New York: Hill and Wang, 1995); and Lizabeth Cohen, *Making a New Deal: Industrial Workers in Chicago, 1919–1939* (Cambridge: Cambridge University Press, 1990). On Catholicism in the years before and after 1920 see William M. Halsey, *The Survival of American Innocence: Catholicism in an Era of Disillusionment, 1920–1940* (Notre Dame, IN: University of Notre Dame Press, 1980); Arnold Sparr, *To Promote, Defend, and Redeem: The Catholic Literary Revival and the Cultural Transformation of American Catholicism, 1920–1960* (Westport, CT: Greenwood Press, 1990); Deirdre M. Moloney, *American Catholic Lay Groups and Transatlantic Social Reform in the Progressive Era* (Chapel Hill: University of North Carolina Press, 2002); and Kathleen Sprows Cummings, *New Women of the Old Faith: Gender and American Catholicism in the Progressive Era* (Chapel Hill: University of North Carolina Press, 2009). These books also include insights about the later period, as does Gleason's *Contending with Modernity: Catholic Higher Education in the Twentieth Century*, which is much more synthetic and expansive than its more narrowly framed subtitle suggests.

17. On suburbanization, and a useful "metropolitan approach" that considers the interaction of the urban and the suburban, see Kevin M. Kruse and Thomas J. Sugrue, eds., *The New Suburban History* (Chicago: University of Chicago Press, 2006). The editors' introduction notes the proportion of suburban dwellers in 1960 (7) and the new historiography, which attends to suburbia's ethnic diversity and "class heterogeneity" (8). On the culture of consumption and the consumer movement, I'm thinking especially of Lizabeth Cohen, who used the phrase "consumer's republic" to discuss the vision that won out in the 1950s—"the notion of a Consumer Republic that entrusted the private mass consumption marketplace, supported by government resources, with delivering not only economic prosperity but also loftier social and political ambitions for a more equal, free, and democratic nation": Lizabeth Cohen, *A Consumer's Republic: The Politics of Mass Consumption in Postwar America* (New York: Vintage, 2004), 13. Pope Paul VI, *Humanae Vitae*, July 25, 1968, available at www.vatican.va.

18. My earlier study is Tweed, *Our Lady of the Exile*, and the theory that emerged from that study is Thomas A. Tweed, *Crossing and Dwelling: A Theory of Religion* (Cambridge, MA: Harvard University Press, 2006).

19. *NS. MEM. AC.* Geraldine M. Rohling, *Jubilee 2009: A Photographic History of the Basilica of the National Shrine of the Immaculate Conception* (Washington, DC: Basilica of the National Shrine of the Immaculate Conception, 2009). On the

clerical editing of published letters, I should say that whenever I found both original versions and published versions they have agreed. Shahan and McKenna didn't publish letters that didn't promote the fundraising cause, but as far as I can tell the letters they excerpted accurately represented the letters they received.

20. "Nobody" from "Nowhere": October 28, 1928, Register of Visitors to the National Shrine, September 1927 to May 1930, 184, Archives, BNSIC.

CHAPTER 1

1. The quotation and the architectural details are from "Fact Sheet: Appeal for National Shrine of the Immaculate Conception," 4 pp., box: Appeals, 1953–1954, file: Appeals 1953: Public Relations, Archives, BNSIC. *America's Church*, the book produced by the BNSIC, listed the dimensions of rival churches and reported that the National Cathedral has twenty-five hundred fewer square feet; *AC*, 281. The Website of the National Cathedral listed the Episcopal building's area as 83,012 square feet, which is 5,512 square feet larger than the Shrine's. Washington National Cathedral, "Architectural Facts," www.cathedral.org/ (accessed July 8, 2007). The Shrine's Website was more precise, giving the area of the Great Upper Church (76,396 square feet) and the area of the lower level, including the Crypt Church (129,912 square feet). Using those figures, the BNSIC again seems larger in area. That Website also lists the details about the number of bricks: "Architectural Style," BNSIC, www.nationalshrine.com (accessed July 12, 2007). On the Tower of Faith and the Presbyterian national center see *The National Presbyterian Church: The First Two Hundred Years, 1795–1995* (Washington, DC: National Presbyterian Church, 1996).

2. G. Martin Moeller, Jr., *AIA Guide to the Architecture of Washington, D.C.*, 4th ed. (Baltimore: Johns Hopkins University Press, 2006), 348–49; "Lectures on Church Architecture: Charles D. Maginnis Gives First of Series," *Boston Daily Globe*, December 9, 1925, p. A16; "Interview with Archbishop O'Hara: *Lamp unto My Feet*," November 29 [1953], 3:00–3:30, typescript, 6 pp., box: Appeals, 1953–1954, Archives, BNSIC.

3. Charles D. Maginnis, *Catholic Church Architecture* (Boston: Everett Press, printed for the author, 1906), 26. On Maginnis's "eclecticism" and "traditionalism" see Milda B. Richardson, "Chancel Remodeling: Charles D. Maginnis," in *The Makers of Trinity Church in the City of Boston*, ed. James F. O'Gorman (Amherst: University of Massachusetts Press, 2004), 176–77. Thomas B. Shahan, *The Middle Ages: Sketches and Fragments* (New York: Benziger, 1904), 315–16. See also his essay "Why We Build Beautiful Churches," which appeared in Thomas B. Shahan, *The House of God and Other Addresses and Studies* (New York: Cathedral Library Association, 1905), 51–95. The passage about real presence appeared in Charles D. Maginnis, *Charles Donagh Maginnis, FAIA 1867–1955: A Selection of His Essays and Addresses*, ed. Robert P. Walsh and Andrew W. Roberts (New Haven, CT: privately printed, 1956), 26. That passage was quoted in Thomas J. Grady, "America's Great Tribute to Mary," *American Ecclesiastical Review* 141 (July–December 1959): 221. On the "classical sacramental church" and the other traditions of church design (the "classic evangelical church" and the "modern communal church") see Richard Kieckhefer, *Theology in Stone: Church Architecture from Byzantium to Berkeley* (New York: Oxford University Press, 2004), 11–15. Maginnis, *Catholic Church Architecture*, 26. Maginnis quoted in Richardson, "Chancel Remodeling," 177.

4. On this point see chapter 5, which deals with claims on civic space.

5. The Shrine as "dazzling jewel" is from Denis Barnes, "A Mosaic of Faith: Shrine to the History of Catholic People in America and Tribute to the Almighty," *Washington Times*, January 9, 1997, pp. M4–M6. A Catholic scholar who will remain anonymous—for obvious reasons—told me in 2010 he thought it was an "architectural monstrosity." Moeller, *AIA Guide to the Architecture of Washington, D.C.*, 349.

6. The phrase from James O'Toole about "monumentalism" is quoted in Robert A. Orsi, *Thank You, St. Jude: Women's Devotion to the Patron Saint of Hopeless Causes* (New Haven, CT: Yale University Press, 1996), 15. It's originally from O'Toole, *Militant and Triumphant*, 159, 211, 241. Jay Dolan, *The American Catholic Experience: A History from Colonial Times to the Present* (Notre Dame, IN: University of Notre Dame Press, 1992), 350–51. Patrick W. Carey, *The Roman Catholics* (Westport, CT: Greenwood Press, 1993), 67. On Dougherty see Hugh J. Nolan, "The Native Son," in *The History of the Archdiocese of Philadelphia*, ed. James F. Connelly (Philadelphia: Archdiocese of Philadelphia, 1976), 339–418. On Molloy see The Diocese of Brooklyn, *Diocese of Immigrants: The Brooklyn Catholic Experience, 1853–2003* (Strasbourg, France: editions du Signe for the Diocese of Brooklyn, 2004), 107. On Buffalo, see Thomas Donohue, *History of the Diocese of Buffalo* (Buffalo: Buffalo Catholic, 1929) and the timeline produced by a local sister of St. Francis: Fran Gangloff, *A History of the Diocese of Buffalo* (Buffalo: Diocese of Buffalo, 1995). I'm also grateful to Sister Ann Louise of the Chancery Archives in Buffalo for sending me that document. On Detroit, see Leslie W. Tentler, *Seasons of Grace: A History of the Archdiocese of Detroit* (Detroit, MI: Wayne State University, 1990).

7. James M. O'Toole, *The Faithful: A History of Catholics in America* (Cambridge, MA: Harvard University Press, 2008), 126. *Diocese of Immigrants: The Brooklyn Catholic Experience, 1853–2003*, 229. Barbara Corrado Pope, "Immaculate and Powerful: The Marian Revival in the Nineteenth Century," in *Immaculate and Powerful: The Female in Sacred Image and Social Reality*, ed. Clarissa W. Atkinson, Constance H. Buchanan, and Margaret R. Miles (Boston: Beacon Press, 1985), 173. Mary appeared to young followers in Paris (1830), LaSalette (1846), Lourdes (1858), Pontmain (1871), Fátima (1917), Beauraing (1932), and Banneaux (1933), and shrines followed in those places and elsewhere across Europe.

8. Xavier Donald Macleod, *History of the Devotion to the Blessed Virgin Mary in North America* (New York: Virtue and Yorston, 1866), 1–9, 28–29. Christopher Rengers, *Mary of the Americas: Our Lady of Guadalupe* (New York: Alba House, 1989), 33–37. For a listing of Catholic shrines, including those dedicated to Mary, see Ralph L. and Henry F. Woods, *Pilgrim Places in North America* (New York: Longmans, Green, 1939) and J. Anthony Moran, *Pilgrims' Guide to America: U.S. Catholic Shrines and Centers of Devotion* (Huntington, IN: Our Sunday Visitor, 1992). The latter describes the shrine in St. Augustine (160) and ninety-four other centers devoted to Mary, including fifteen honoring Our Lady of Fatima and twenty-seven venerating Our Lady of Lourdes (223–25).

9. Miri Rubin, *Mother of God: A History of the Virgin Mary* (New Haven, CT: Yale University Press, 2009), 303. Apostolic Constitution of Pius IX, *Ineffabilis Deus, Defining the Dogma of the Immaculate Conception*, December 8, 1854 (Boston: Daughters of St. Paul, n.d.), 4. Many historians have traced the history of the dogma. See Jaroslav Pelikan, *Mary through the Centuries: Her Place in the History of Culture* (New Haven, CT: Yale University Press, 1996), 189–200. On Marian devotion, including the apparitions, see also Sandra Zimdars-Swartz, *Encountering Mary* (New York: Avon, 1992); and Paula M. Kane, "Marian Devotion since 1940:

Continuity or Casualty?," in *Habits of Devotion: Catholic Religious Practice in Twentieth-Century America*, ed. James M. O'Toole (Ithaca, NY: Cornell University Press, 2004), 89–129. The references to Mary, and to the Immaculate Conception as national patroness, were many in the late nineteenth and early twentieth centuries. I mention examples throughout. The Shrine's periodical published many pieces on that theme, including a patriotic poem by a priest who had migrated from Ireland but still associated Mary and America: "She's the Land of Our Lady, now and e'er more": William P. Treacy, "A Hymn to Our Lady: Patroness of the United States," *SR* 7.7 (November 1920): 53. Other devotional periodicals not directly associated with the Shrine sounded the same theme: "Thoughts on Our Patronal Feast," *Ave Maria* 16.24 (n.s.), December 9, 1922, 737–39. See also artifacts, including holy cards. For example, one early to mid-twentieth-century holy card includes a pink image of Mary standing above a map of the United States and pointing with her left hand to a green U.S. Capitol. The title on the reverse side is "Prayer to Mary Immaculate, Patroness of the United States," and the text implores the Virgin to "watch over with a loving smile this blessed land of America." Holy card distributed by Daughters of St. Paul, Cleveland, in Holy Cards, box: "Mary Alone, Full-Length," Marian Library, International Marian Research Institute, University of Dayton, Dayton, Ohio. Art historian Kristin Schwain has proposed that the graphics "suggest an early to mid-twentieth century production date." Kristin Schwain, e-mail to author, January 25, 2000.

10. On "ultramontanism," see Nicholas Atkin and Frank Tallett, *Priests, Prelates, and People: A History of European Catholicism since 1750* (New York: Oxford University Press, 2003), 18, 130–41; John T. McGreevy, *Catholicism and American Freedom: A History* (New York: Norton, 2003), 12–13; Ann Taves, *The Household of Faith: Roman Catholic Devotionalism in Mid-nineteenth-century America* (Notre Dame, IN: University of Notre Dame Press, 1986), 102–6; and Peter R. D'Agostino, *Rome in America: Transnational Catholic Ideology from the Risorgimento to Fascism* (Chapel Hill: University of North Carolina Press, 2004), 24.

11. On "the two master minds" see Clara Douglas Sheeran, "The Completion of the Mary Memorial Altar, *SR* 15.10 (October 1928): 74–75. On Shahan as "the chief source of inspiration" see "Conversation with Mr. Fred V. Murphy, September 9, 1957," box: "Architects," Archives, BNSIC. On McKenna see "Msgr. M'Kenna, 85, Rector, Educator," *New York Times*, June 22, 1960, p. 23.

12. Thomas J. Shahan, "Who Will Build the University Church?," *Catholic University Bulletin* 9.4 (1903): 509–10. Thomas J. Shahan to [Michael] Jenkins, July 28, 1910, correspondence files, Bishop Thomas J. Shahan, Archives, BNSIC. As Kennedy noted, a notice appeared in the Lowell *Courier* on January 29, 1846, announcing that "a magnificent Catholic church is to be built at Washington, something after the style of the cathedrals of the Old World." *NS*, 28. C. Joseph Nuesse, *The Catholic History of America: A Centennial History* (Washington, DC: Catholic University Press of America, 1990), 27–30, 162. On Shahan's vision, see *AC*, 19. On the original Gothic design see "Conversation with Mr. Fred V. Murphy, September 9, 1957," box: "Architects," Archives, BNSIC. On the early period, see *AC*, 13–52; Geraldine M. Rohling, *Jubilee 2009: A Photographic History of the Basilica of the National Shrine of the Immaculate Conception* (Washington, DC: Basilica of the National Shrine of the Immaculate Conception, 2009), 1–35; and Geraldine M. Rohling, "The Early Years," pt. 1 of the History of National Shrine of the Immaculate Conception, at the Website of the BNSIC, www.nationalshrine.com (accessed July 27, 2006).

13. An excerpt of the letter from Thomas J. Shahan to Bernard A. McKenna, which was dated March 2, 1914, was reprinted in *MEM*, 13. The circulation figures appear in "First Public Mass in Honor of the National Shrine," *SR* 5.1 (February 1918): 4. McKenna's estimate about the number of letters is in *MEM*, 123. Doing the calculations, that would mean almost 3.5 million pages of devotional letters, so that estimate seems exaggerated. The report of the accountants, Haskins & Sells of Baltimore, includes the statements from 1913 to 1933, and it is reprinted in *MEM*, 258. My estimate of the number of pages is based on the assumption that each page was eleven inches long and that the approximate distance between Montreal and D.C. is six hundred miles. My calculation of the buying power today is based on several online calculators that use the Consumer Price Index and consider the annual inflation rate over the period—approximately 3.72 percent between 1933 and 2009. In other words, $1 in 1933 was worth approximately $16.05 in 2009. I give these rough estimates just to give some sense of the relative value of the sum collected.

14. On the new "autotruck" see Geraldine M. Rohling, "The Dedication of the Cornerstone," at the Website of the BNSIC, www.nationalshrine.com (accessed July 27, 2006). Daniel Delis Hill, *To the American Woman, 1900–1999* (Columbus: Ohio State University, 2002), vii. Other scholars have emphasized "the striking convergence in these years between novel forms and methods of devotional promotion and the new American advertising industry"; see Robert A. Orsi, *Thank You, St. Jude: Women's Devotion to the Patron Saint of Hopeless Causes* (New Haven, CT: Yale University Press, 1996), 16. On consumer culture see Richard Wightman Fox and T. J. Jackson Lears, eds., *The Culture of Consumption: Critical Essays in American History, 1880–1980* (New York: Pantheon Books, 1983), and Lizabeth Cohen, *A Consumer's Republic: The Politics of Mass Consumption in Postwar America* (New York: Vintage, 2004). Thomas J. Shahan, *An Appeal to Catholic Ladies: The New Chapel of The Catholic University of America* (Washington, DC, 1911), Archives, BNSIC. On the proportion of income from Christmas cards, see *AC*, 47.

15. Hill, *To the American Woman*, vii. Shahan, "Appeal to Catholic Ladies." Apostolic Letter of Pope Pius X to James Cardinal Gibbons, July 8, 1914, reprinted in *NS*, 41.

16. Ibid. On Hoffman, see *AC*, 25; and Rohling, "Early Years." See also "Mrs. F. B. Hoffman Dies, Long Prominent in Society and Charitable Work in New York," *New York Times*, February 9, 1925. "Constitution: National Organization of the Catholic Women in the United States of America," typescript, Archives, BNSIC. For a photograph of the plaster model of the original Gothic design and McKenna's assessment of the role of Hoffman and the NOCW, see *MEM*, 59–60. He suggests that "great credit" must be given to Hoffman and the other leaders of that early women's organization (60). Thomas J. Shahan to Mrs. F. B. Hoffman, November 21, 1913, Archives, BNSIC. On the cost of the architect's donated services, see "Financial Report of the National Organization of Catholic Women of the United States of America, for 1913, 1914, 1915," Thomas J. Shahan Papers, box 7, National Organization of Catholic Women, American Catholic History Research Center and University Archives, the Catholic University of America, Washington, D.C. (hereafter ACUA).

17. Hoffman's census record for 1920 lists one employee and six servants living with her in her home on East Seventy-ninth Street: Lucy Hoffman, U.S. Bureau of the Census, *Fourteenth Census of the United States, 1920*, Manhattan, Assembly District 15, New York, New York; roll T625_1213; p.12B; enumeration district

1087; image 722. "Catholics Plan Shrine: Church on University Grounds in Washington to Be Built by Small Donations," *New York Times*, January 22, 1913. Thomas J. Shahan to Mrs. F. B. Hoffman, November 21, 1913, Archives, BNSIC. That letter and other material is quoted in Cecilia Annette Moore, "Good and Zealous Ladies": The Role of Catholic Women in the Building of the National Shrine of the Immaculate Conception" (M.A. thesis, Department of Religious Studies, University of Virginia, 1991), 41. For a list of fifteen National Organization of Catholic Women chapters see "Director of N.O.C.W. Chapters," *SR* 3.2 (April 1916): 23.

18. "Financial Report of the National Organization of Catholic Women of the United States of America, for 1913, 1914, 1915. Thomas J. Shahan Papers, Series 4, Box 39, Folder 7 (Shrine), ACUA. Anonymous ["A Child of Mary"] to Fannie Whelan, March 18, 1914, Thomas J. Shahan Papers, Series 4, Box 39, Folder 7 (Shrine), ACUA. Martin Van Den Berg to Fannie Whelan, March 3, 1914, Thomas J. Shahan Papers, Series 4, Box 39, Folder 7 (Shrine), National Organization of Catholic Women, ACUA. Natalie Wood [Mrs. J. Walter Wood], to Lucy Hoffman, undated handwritten letter [before 1919], Thomas J. Shahan Papers, Series 4, Box 39, Folder 7 (Shrine), ACUA.

19. For McKenna's message to chapter leaders, see "National Shrine Notes," *SR* 3.3 (October 1916): 37. The information about the Pittsburgh and New York chapters appeared in "N.O.C.W. Chapter News," *SR* 3.2 (April 1916): 26.

20. "Great Architects Obtained," *SR* 6.4 (June 1919): 28. I explain the reasons for changing the architectural design to Byzantine-Romanesque in chapter 5. On the dissolution of the National Organization of Catholic Women see Moore, "Good and Zealous Ladies," 59–66. Some information about the motives for the split is included in "The Founding of the National Shrine," [typescript with handwritten revisions], 5 pp., Shahan Papers, ser. 4, box 39, file 8: Shrine. (I have been unable to identify this document's author or date, so I don't use it in my analysis; it's written in the third person, and it's possible that McKenna, or even Shahan himself, wrote it, though I'm not sure.) This document, despite it's uncertain authorship and date, does offer a plausible interpretation—it asserts a primary cause: the NOCW's leaders "wanted not only to sponsor but even to supervise the building" (3) and, as a handwritten addition in the margin of another passage suggests, wanted "the project to be completely under their supervision" (4).

21. "New York Chapter, N.O.C.W.," *SR* 7.1 (February 1920): 5. The new organization was announced in "Salve Regina—Hail! Holy Queen," *SR* 7.2 (March 1920): 12. Shahan sent his letter to the clergy on July 2, 1919, and it appeared as "A Letter to Priests," *SR* (September 1919): 42, 44. "National Catholic Family Record," *SR* 8.1 (January 1921): 5. [Thomas J. Shahan], "Program," Laying of the Foundation Stone, September 23, 1920, booklet, 8 pp., Archives, BNSIC. On appeals to memorialize the fallen in World War I, see also "To Our Soldiers and Sailors We Dedicate the Month of April," *SR* 8.4 (April 1921): 28.

22. For the official account of the foundation stone ceremony see "Vast Shrine Is Begun," *SR* 7.6 (November 15, 1920): 42, 44; and "Laying of Foundation Stone," *SR* 7.7 (November 1920): 50, 52. Many historians have noticed what Lynn Dumenil called the "increased centralization and bureaucratization of the church and its institutions": Lynn Dumenil, *The Modern Temper: American Culture and Society in the 1920s* (New York: Hill and Wang, 1995), 176. In fact, despite differences in interpretation on other matters, there is much agreement among historians of Catholic philanthropy, education, women, and reform that a centralizing

impulse took hold in many areas of U.S. Catholic life during and after World War I. For example, see Mary J. Oates, *The Catholic Philanthropic Tradition in America* (Bloomington: Indiana University Press, 1995), 94–97, 165; Philip Gleason, *Contending with Modernity: Catholic Higher Education in the Twentieth Century* (New York: Oxford University Press, 1995), 62–72, 131–36; Debra Campbell, "Lay Organization and Activism, 1889–1928," in *Transforming Parish Ministry: The Changing Roles of Catholic Clergy, Laity, and Women Religious*, by Jay P. Dolan, R. Scott Appleby, Patricia Byrne, and Debra Campbell (New York: Crossroad Press, 1990), 211–12. Deirdre M. Moloney, *American Catholic Lay Groups and Transatlantic Social Reform in the Progressive Era* (Chapel Hill: University of North Carolina Press, 2002), 2–3, 7–11, 167–204; Kathleen Sprows Cummings, *New Women of the Old Faith: Gender and Catholicism in the Progressive Era* (Chapel Hill: University of North Carolina Press, 2009), 2–16. I'm indebted to Cummings for the insight that religion trumped gender for Catholic women in this period.

23. McNicholas's sermon: "Calls 'New Freedom' Curse," *SR* 7.6 (September 1920): 42. On McNicholas, an important national figure in the Church before 1950, see Steven M. Avella, "John T. McNicholas in the Age of Practical Thomism," *Records of the American Catholic Historical Society of Philadelphia* 97 (1986): 15–25; and Thomas W. Tifft, "McNicholas, John T.," in *The Encyclopedia of American Catholic History*, ed. Michael Glazier and Thomas J. Shelley (Collegeville, MN: Liturgical Press, 1997), 894–95.

24. *MEM*, 123; Shahan, "Who Will Build the University Church?," 509–10; "Fact Sheet for the National Shrine of the Immaculate Conception," May 15, 1959, typescript, box E-6 (folder: Special Services and Events), Archives, BNSIC.

25. On Noll's contributions, see *MEM*, 62, 245. His letter to McKenna, dated February 16, 1953, is reprinted in *MEM*, 301. The total amount given by *Our Sunday Visitor* readers ($120,000) is verified on the official accounting documents: "Building Fund Receipts to September 20, 1961," box: Appeals 1953–1954, folder: Shrine Appeal—1954, Archives, BNSIC. Noll's recollection of the postwar events is included in his preface to *Proposed National Shrine of the Immaculate Conception*, undated printed appeal, box: Appeals 1953–1954, folder: 1953 Promotional Materials, Archives, BNSIC. Noll mentioned the papal endorsement in an article distributed by the NCWC and published in Brooklyn's diocesan newspaper: "Hope to Finish Marian Shrine: Prelate Is Confident of Success of Appeal during 1954," *Tablet* (Brooklyn) 46.35 (October 17, 1953): 4. Noll reproduced the papal endorsement of the new fundraising campaign in a letter he sent to U.S. bishops and archbishops on November 5, 1953, box: Appeals, 1953–1954, Archives, BNSIC.

26. Episcopal Committee for the Shrine, "Children Will Help Provide United States with Great Shrine," Release Number One, box: Appeals 1953–1954, Archives, BNSIC. John F. Noll to the Most Reverend Patrick A. O'Boyle, October 6, 1953, box: Appeals 1953–1954, Archives, BNSIC. On Roeder's appointment, see the letter he mailed to diocesan leaders, September 18, 1952, copy, box: Appeals, 1953–1954, Archives, BNSIC. On the acceptance of Roeder's appointment by the Shrine's director and the director's promise "to assist him in any way we can," see Right Reverend Monsignor Patrick J. O'Connor, director, to Most Reverend Patrick A. O'Boyle, June 19, 1953, box: Appeals 1953–1954, Archives, BNSIC. Noll and the Committee explained the formula they used to set the quotas in John F. Noll to U.S. bishops ["Your Excellency"], n.d. [1953], box: Appeals 1953–1954, Archives, BNSIC. The diocesan quotas and final payments are listed in

"Building Fund Receipts to September 30, 1961," box: Appeals 1953–1954, Archives, BNSIC.

27. The information about the status of dioceses and archdioceses is helpfully summarized in a document explaining where the fundraising materials had *not* been sent in 1953: Bernard F. Kelly, "Dioceses Not Receiving Appeal Aids," [1953], box: Appeals 1953–1954, Archives, BNSIC. The totals about quotas and final contributions are taken from "Building Fund Receipts to September 30, 1961," box: Appeals 1953–1954, Archives, BNSIC. The letter protesting about the limit came from North Carolina: Vincent G. Taylor, OSB, to the Most Reverend John F. Noll, August 7, 1953, box: Appeals 1953–1954, Archives, BNSIC. In 1924, that ecclesiastical territory was divided into the Diocese of Raleigh, which had jurisdiction over most of the state, and the eight counties of the *abbatia nullius* of Belmont Abbey, which was presided over by the abbot of the Benedictine monastery, not far from Charlotte. In 1944, the Diocese of Belmont Abbey Nullius shrank still further. By the time they sent out the 1953 quota letters, the abbot had responsibility for only one county in a predominantly Protestant state. See Gerald Lewis, "North Carolina, Catholic Church in," in Glazier and Shelley, *Encyclopedia of American Catholic History*, 1056–157.

28. John F. Noll, "Report on the Appeal of The National Shrine of the Immaculate Conception," January 12, 1954, box 5, John F. Noll Papers, University of Notre Dame Archives, Notre Dame, Indiana (hereafter ND). "Report of the National Council of Catholic Men on Radio-Television-Film Promotion for the Dedication of the National Shrine of the Immaculate Conception," box E-6, folder: Special Services and Events, Archives, BNSIC. A photograph of the procession for the ground blessing ritual, with a caption noting Sheen's location, appeared in *MEM*, 5. Sheen had been ordained in 1919 and was studying at CUA, where he earned the S.T.L. and J.C.B. in 1920.

29. John D. Morris, "Catholics Dedicate National Shrine in Washington," *New York Times*, November 21, 1959. "Text of the Sermon Delivered by His Eminence Richard Cardinal Cushing, at Evening Mass on the Day of the Dedication of the National Shrine of the Immaculate Conception, Washington, D.C.," November 20, 1959, press release, box C-2, Archives, BNSIC. "Text of the Sermon Delivered by the Most Reverend Karl J. Alter, at the Solemn Pontifical Mass for Religious in National Shrine of the Immaculate Conception, Washington, D.C.," November 21, 1959, press release, box E-5, Archives, BNSIC. I noted the role of emotion in Thomas A. Tweed, *Crossing and Dwelling: A Theory of Religion* (Cambridge, MA: Harvard University Press, 2006), 68–72. David Hume, who wasn't very sympathetic to religion, also used the phrase "hopes and fears" in his 1757 work *Natural History of Religion*: David Hume, *Dialogues and National History of Religion* (New York: Oxford University Press, 1993), 139–40.

30. [Thomas J. Shahan], "Program," Laying of the Foundation Stone, September 23, 1920, 8 pp., Archives, BNSIC. The middle pages of this booklet open up to reveal an image of the Virgin Mary that was executed by Father Raphael Pfisterer, OSM, probably in 1920, shortly before a larger version appeared on a mural in the left transept altar at St. Francis Xavier Church in Buffalo in 1921. McKenna and Shahan also reproduced that image: "Patroness of the United States," *SR* 9.3 (March 1922): 21. I analyze Pfisterer's image in chapter 5. "Bishop Shahan's Letter to Priests," in *NS*, 56–58. The Most Reverend Joseph E. Ritter, "Text of the Dedication Sermon," November 20, 1959, box E-5, Archives, BNSIC.

31. "Dome Is the Diamond Jubilee Goal, 1854–1929," *SR* 14.9 (September 1928): 67. The memories of the Trinity graduate Mary Louise Tindall Tietien were recorded in a typed document dated October 22, 1997. I'm grateful to her granddaughter, Julie, for giving me a copy. Charles D. Maginnis to the Reverend Thomas F. Coakley, December 17, 1946, Charles Donagh Maginnis Papers, Archives of American Art, Smithsonian Institution, Washington, D.C. John J. Reilly, "Mary's National Shrine: A Statement of Progress," *American Ecclesiastical Review*, 120 (June 1949): 458–62. Monsignor Reilly, then the Shrine's director, noted that a 1947 article in the same periodical had referred to the building as "the hall of disappointment" (458). John F. Noll, "The Laity Are Awaiting the Call," n.d., typescript, Noll Papers, box 5, Archives, ND. Robert J. Dwyer, "U.S. National Shrine Stirs Up Discussion," *SR*, 17 (August 1956): 3.

32. Alter, "Text of Sermon." Thomas J. Shahan, *The House of God and Other Addresses and Studies* (New York: Cathedral Library Association, 1905), 2, 51–96.

33. Alter, "Text of Sermon." Shahan, *House of God*, 2, 7, 42. The comment about matieralism's "only adversary" is from an address Shahan delivered in St. Louis on June 24, 1919, at the sixteenth annual meeting of the Catholic Education Association (now the National Catholic Education Association). It originally was published as "Civilization: Pagan or Christian," *Catholic Educational Bulletin* 16 (1919): 47–53. It was later reprinted as a pamphlet, which I discovered at the American Catholic History Research Center and University Archives. I'm grateful to W. John Shepherd for helping me find the original citation. The passage I quote is from that pamphlet: Thomas J. Shahan, *Civilization: Pagan or Christian*, 9. "Bishop Shahan's Letter to Priests," in *NS*, 56–58. Shahan, the rector, called CUA the "chief educational center": [Thomas J. Shahan], "Program," Laying of the Foundation Stone, September 23, 1920, 8 pp., Archives, BNSIC.

34. Ibid. "Bishop Shahan's Letter to Priests," in *NS*, 56–58. "All America to Honor the Blessed Mother of God," *SR* 15.6 (June 1928): 41.

35. "List of Intentions," *SR* 9.11 (November 1922): 82. On Aboulin see "Aboulin, Jean Joseph Marie," in Robert J. Scollard, *Dictionary of Basilian Biography: Lives of Members of the Congregation of Priests of Saint Basil from Its Beginnings in 1822 to 1968* (Toronto: Basilian Press, 1969). I found biographical information about this donor in Jean Joseph Marie Aboulin, C.S.B., to the Reverend Bernard McKenna, July 30, 1928, Bernard McKenna Papers, box 1, Archives, BNSIC. I also consulted the records of his religious order, the Basilian Fathers of Toronto, and U.S. census records. His name is wrong in the 1920 census (as "Abaulin"): U.S. Bureau of the Census, *Fourteenth Census of the United States, 1920*, Detroit Ward 10, Wayne County, Michigan; roll T625_809; p. 11A; enumeration district 296; image 428.

36. [Press release], November 20, 1959, 5 pp., box E-5, Archives, BNSIC; this document indicates it is to be released on the dedication day and gives the media information about the three-day celebration. The Most Reverend Joseph E. Ritter, "Text of the Dedication Sermon," November 20, 1959, box E-5, Archives, BNSIC. The Most Reverend Karl J. Alter, "Text of Sermon," The Solemn Pontifical Mass for Religious, November 21, 1959, box E-5, Archives, BNSIC.

37. "My Offering to Mary Immaculate," *SR* 14.10 (September 1927): 72. On "Americanism" and "Modernism" and the controversies at CUA see R. Scott Appleby, *"Church and Age Unite!": The Modernist Impulse in American Catholicism* (Notre Dame, IN: University of Notre Dame Press, 1992), 207–8, 215, 222; and C. Joseph Nuesse, *The Catholic University of America: A Centennial History* (Washington, DC: Catholic University of America Press, 1990), 70–87, 147–93.

See also Gerald P. Fogarty, *The Vatican and the American Hierarchy from 1870 to 1965* (Stuttgart: Anton Hiersemann, 1982), 176–94. Fogarty noted that because of their defensiveness about the earlier condemnation of Americanism, the United States clergy "overreacted" to suspicions about modernism, and as a result, "properly speaking, there was no real Modernism in the United States" (191).

38. "Why Washington Was Selected as the Location for the National Shrine of the Immaculate Conception," *SR* 7.3 (March 1921): 21. The Most Reverend Karl J. Alter, "Text of Sermon," The Solemn Pontifical Mass for Religious, November 21, 1959, box E-5, Archives, BNSIC. The Most Reverend Joseph E. Ritter, "Text of the Dedication Sermon," November 20, 1959, box E-5, Archives, BNSIC. His Eminence Richard Cardinal Cushing, "Text of Sermon," Evening Mass (A Pontifical Low Mass), November 20, 1959, box C-2, Archives, BNSIC.

39. Justine Ward, *Thomas Edward Shields: Biologist, Psychologist, Educator* (New York: Scribner's, 1947), 211–13. I'm grateful to Mary J. Oates for alerting me to the fundraising competition between the Shrine and the Sisters College. As Philip Gleason has noted, the Sisters College "paved the way for full coeducation at the Catholic University" since over three thousand women, religious and lay, had attended the Sisters College by 1923, and, more broadly, it "played a key role in legitimating the idea that it was proper for religious women to seek professional training in institutions of higher education." Philip Gleason, *Contending with Modernity: Catholic Higher Education in the Twentieth Century* (New York: Oxford University Press, 1995), 88. On the founding of Trinity College, see Cummings, *New Women of the Old Faith*, 67–87. On the wider topic, see also Tracy Schier and Cynthia Russett, eds., *Catholic Women's Colleges in America* (Baltimore: Johns Hopkins University Press, 2002).

40. Upton Sinclair, *The Profits of Religion: An Essay in Economic Interpretation* (n.p.: Upton Sinclair, 1918), v, 27–28. John Gormly to the Reverend Bernard A. McKenna, March 16, 1927, Bernard A. McKenna Papers, MC-61, Philadelphia Archdiocesan Historical Records Center (hereafter cited as PAHRC).

41. [Thomas J. Shahan], "Program," Laying of the Foundation Stone, September 23, 1920, 8 pp., Archives, BNSIC. "Bishop Shahan's Letter to Priests," in *NS*, 56–58. The Most Reverend Joseph E. Ritter, "Text of the Dedication Sermon," Dedication of the National Shrine of the Immaculate Conception, November 20, 1959, box E-5, Archives, BNSIC.

42. Miss Mary Kelly to the Rev. Bernard A. McKenna, May 12, 1930, Small Collection, Bernard A. McKenna Papers, HM 23, F6, ACUA; William Smith to Rev. Bernard A. McKenna, April 1, 1927, Small Collection, Bernard A. McKenna Papers, HM 23, F3, ACUA. To find biographical details about these two devotees see Mary Kelly, U.S. Bureau of the Census, *Fifteenth Census of the United States, 1930*, Holyoke, Hampton County, Massachusetts; roll 906; p. 3A; enumeration district 161; image 1048.0. William Smith, *Fifteenth Census of the United States, 1930*, Bethlehem, Northampton County, Pennsylvania; roll 2086; p. 10A; enumeration district 30; image 1106.0.

43. The quotation is from *NS*, 78.

44. The quotation from Shahan is taken from Thomas J. Shahan, *The Apostolic See: A Discourse Delivered at the Episcopal Consecration of Rt. Rev. Denis J. O'Connell... in the Cathedral of Baltimore, May 3, 1908* (n.p.: n.p., n. d.), [29 pp.], 17, Reading Room, University of Notre Dame Archives. On the blessing of the site see *NS*, 59. The papal letter is also reprinted in *NS*, 42–43. An issue of Washington's archdiocesan newspaper that celebrated the dedication included an image of the relief of

Saint Pius X (p. 25), along with articles summarizing the Shrine's history and architecture: "The National Shrine of the Immaculate Conception: On Its Day of Dedication" (Washington, DC) *Catholic Standard*, November 20, 1959.

45. For the papal letter see *NS*, 42–43. The names of episcopal donors in appendix 1.1 are from three pages of the folio-sized "Journal, High Altar Contributions," Archives, BNSIC. I compared the list of donors in appendix 1.1 with the list of attendees at the 1919 meeting of the hierarchy. The names of these attendees are recorded in Rt. Rev. Owen B. Corrigan, "List of Prelates Present at the First Annual Meeting of the Hierarchy at the Catholic University of America, Washington, D.C., September 24 and 25, 1919," *Catholic Historical Review* 6.1 (April 1920–January 1921): 200–203.

46. The priests listed in appendix 1.2 and discussed here were found among the donors listed in "Journal, High Altar Contributions," Archives, BNSIC. I refer here to patterns in scholarship. For a few influential pieces about Catholic historiography that, in turn, also include many helpful citations see Jay P. Dolan, "The Immigrants and Their Gods: A New Perspective in American Religious History," *Church History* 57 (March 1988): 61–72; Leslie Woodcock Tentler, "On the Margins: The State of American Catholic History," *American Quarterly* 45.1 (March 1993): 104–27; Patrick W. Carey, *The Roman Catholics* (Westport, CT: Greenwood Press, 1993), 353–61 ("Bibliographic Essay"); Patrick Carey, "Recent American Catholic Historiography: New Directions in Religious History," in *New Directions in American Religious History*, ed. Harry S. Stout and D. G. Hart (New York: Oxford University Press, 1997), 445–61. On parish priests and their place in the hierarchy and in the scholarship see Leslie Woodcock Tentler, "God's Representatives in Our Midst": Toward a History of the Catholic Diocesan Clergy in the United States," *Church History* 67.2 (June 1998): 326–49. The quotation about the priests' role in shaping and sharing the devotional culture is from Orsi, *Thank You, St. Jude*, 18. On the number of ordinations see *MEM*, 244; and Press Release for Dedication Day, October 2, 1959, box C-2: Patrick Cardinal O'Boyle Papers Concerning the Shrine, Archives, BNSIC. No name is included in McKenna's note describing "the first parish to make a contribution to the shrine" in June 1918: *MEM*, 120. I'm grateful to archivists at the Diocese of Buffalo Archives who helped me identify the Buffalo priest, Walsh, who served at St. Joseph's in 1918. I then found biographical information about Walsh using resources made available by the Diocese of Trenton and the Archdiocese of Newark, where he served as bishop and, later, archbishop from 1928 to 1952. *SR* also noted Walsh's promotion to bishop of Trenton: "Right Rev. Thomas J. Walsh, D.D.," *SR* 5.4 (June 15, 1918): 28. See also "Archbishop Walsh Dies at Age of 78," *New York Times*, June 7, 1952, p. 19. I'm grateful to a staff member in the Archdiocese of St. Louis's archives (who wanted to remain anonymous) for helping me to identify the parish (St. Lawrence O'Toole) and later assignments of Father Doyle, who went on to serve as chaplain at St. Mary's Orphanage and Visitation Parish and then pastored Sacred Heart, a small church in Caruthersville, Missouri. I found other information on Doyle, the son of Irish immigrants, in the census records: Patrick J. Doyle, *Fourteenth Census of the United States, 1920*, St. Louis Ward 4, St. Louis, Missouri; roll T625_949; p. 7A; enumeration district 64; image 820. The record of Father Krichten's visit is found in Shrine Day Book, 1929–1930, Archives, BNSIC. The Pennsylvania-born Krichten remained a parish priest, though he moved to St. Joseph's Church in Gettysburg, where he had a long pastorate (1935–1960). I want to thank the archivist of the Diocese of Harrisburg, Linda Itzo, for her help in locating

biographical information about Krichten. The census record adds more details about his life at the time, when he lived with two priests, a maid, and a cook on State Street in Harrisburg. My comments about donors during the 1950s emerge from my analysis of the donor books, including Book 42: July 1953 to July 30, 1954, donor record book (typescript), Book 48: July 1, 1959 to June 30, 1960, donor record book (typescript), both in Archives, BNSIC.

47. The names of Sister Mary, Sister Teresa, Sister Mary Aloysius, Sister Mary Blanche, Sister Mary Celestine are written in Register of Visitors, June 1926–August 1927, Archives, BNSIC. Despite its title, that register actually includes visitors' names from as early as 1922 and as late as 1927. The biographical information I include comes primarily from federal census records for 1920 and 1930. Brother Piper's name was handwritten in the visitor book in 1928: Register of Visitors to the National Shrine, September 1927 to May 1930, 201 and 180, Archives, BNSIC. I found further biographical details about Norbert Piper and his brother in the census records: Norbert G. Piper: *Fifteenth Census of the United States, 1930*, Washington, District of Columbia; roll 302; p. 14A; enumeration district 352; image 844. Walter J. Piper: *Fifteenth Census of the United States, 1930*, Ponca City, Kay County, Oklahoma; roll 1909; p. 8B; enumeration district 33; image 110. The biographical information about Sister Marie Teresa and her colleagues from St. Catherine's is in the order's archives in St. Paul. Sister Marie had studied painting in Italy and had a special fondness for Marian images. "Her love for our Blessed Lady increased," one of her fellow sisters recalled, "with every lovely Madonna she was privileged to paint." The quotation is from an obituary in the archives: "Sister Marie Teresa Mackey, 1867–1952." For help with that obituary and the other biographical information I am indebted to Sister Mary E. Craft, CSJ, Archivist, Sisters of St. Joseph of Carondelet, St. Paul Province, St. Paul.

48. A description of the Jesuit and Carmelite chapels can be found in *GTB*, 49, 52. The donations from the Ursuline Convent and Sister Mary Teresita are recorded in a shrine donor book on May 17 and May 19, 1954: Book 42: July 1953–July 30, 1954, typed donation records, Archives, BNSIC. Tracking down biographical information on Sister Mary Teresita proved very challenging. I found a census record for 1930, when she was teaching at St. John's School in Gilmore City, Iowa: Mary Teresita: *Fifteenth Census of the United States, 1930*, Gilmore City, Pocahontas County, Iowa; roll 673; p. 2A; enumeration district 16; image 175. And archivists from several diocese and religious orders helped with other biographical information about her, including John Treanor at the Archdiocese of Chicago, Dan Burns at the Diocese of Sioux Falls, and Sister Joy, OSM, the Servite archivist at Our Lady of Sorrows Convent in Omaha. The donation of Sister Mary Ludger in 1919 is on p. 24 in Donor Book, April 1919–February 1920 (Record of Contributions to the National Shrine of the Immaculate Conception, book no. 3), Archives, BNSIC. On p. 100 is also the 1919 donation by the Sisters of St. Joseph of Concordia, Kansas, for the temporary Salve Regina Chapel.

49. The information on the pilgrimages by the Knights of Columbus and the Daughters of Isabella is found in *MEM*, 124, 132.

50. The male lay donors listed in appendix 1.4 and discussed here, including George Banchoff and John Francey, are found in Donor Book, April 1919–February 1920, Archives, BNSIC. I found the biographical information about them in the federal census records. The passage from the male donor's letter appeared in "Our Collector's Circle," *SR* 5.2 (March 15, 1918): 14. The woman's letter was published as "Her Only Comfort," *SR* 6.4 (June 15, 1999): 28.

51. On Duvall see "G. L. Duval Is Dead; A Philanthropist," *New York Times*, March 17, 1931. On the conditions of his will, see "G. L. Duval Willed Estate of $944,843; Thirty-Seven Religious and Charitable Institutions to Receive $382,754," *New York Times*, June 9, 1934. On Ryan see *MEM*, 124, 245. See also his obituary, "James J. Ryan Dies; Retired Builder," *New York Times*, November 17, 1929. Bernard A. McKenna to Sir James Ryan, January 22, 1925, James Ryan Papers, MC-39, folder 17, PAHRC. Our Lady of Hope Chapel is profiled in *Basilica of the National Shrine of the Immaculate Conception*, 33. I give the amount of Ryan's contribution ($50,000), which would be more than $600,000 today, because his donation was previously revealed in a published book written by a former director of the shrine: *MEM*, 124, 245. However, officials at the BNSIC asked me not to reveal the specific amount of individual adult contributions recorded in donor books in the archives. With the staff's permission, I do report the amount of some collective children's contributions, which were usually very small. In most cases here and throughout the book when I discuss individual contributions I do not give an exact amount, however, but only a rough indication of the relative size of the donation. This seems to be a strategy that honors the staff's request and protects the privacy of donors while also meeting my obligation to readers to convey some sense of the relative value of what devotees gave, especially when that seems relevant to the point at hand, for example when I want to give some indication of the donor's economic class. For the record of Fairbanks's visit on October 24, 1925, see the entry in Register of Visitors to the National Shrine, 215, Archives, BNSIC.

52. To create this sample, I chose every fiftieth page and every fifth name on each page until I had thirty names.

53. The signatures of Ritter and Giacoma are in the shrine's visitor book in 1928: Register of Visitors to the National Shrine, September 1927 to May 1930, 201, 180, Archives, BNSIC. I used census records to find biographical details: Sara Ritter: *Fifteenth Census of the United States, 1930*, Washington, District of Columbia; roll 304; p. 30A; enumeration district 373; image 60. John J. Giacoma: *Fifteenth Census of the United States, 1930*, Walkerville, Silver Bow, Montana; roll 1261; p. 1B; enumeration district 2; image 972. The donations by Puglise and Schwab are recorded on November 18, 1959: book 48, typed donation records, Archives, BNSIC. The information on Schwab is from the census: Mary R. Schwab: *Fifteenth Census of the United States, 1930*, Healdsburg, Sonoma, California; roll 222; p. 3B; enumeration district 21; image 107. I created the list of donors in appendix 1.5 by randomly selecting names found in Book 42: July 1953 to July 30, 1954, donor record book (typescript), Archives, BNSIC. I then searched for biographical information in the 1930 federal census and other government records.

54. My characterization of visitors is based on a reading of published sources, like *SR* and *MEM*, as well as archival sources such as the director's "Day Books" (the notes McKenna kept about daily activities at the Shrine) and the visitors' logs (the blank books visitors signed). The Boy Scouts (January 1), Spelling Bee competitors (May 30), and public school students all visited in 1930. Information about these visits and the others cited here are from Shrine Day Book, 1929–1930 (Shrine Notes, 1929–1930), Archives, BNSIC. McKenna's account of the St. Anthony's First Holy Communion is in a source with the same name but different contents that started earlier: Shrine Day Book, 1929–1930 (Shrine Notes and Events Starting May 1, 1926), Archives, BNSIC.

55. The visit of the Brooklyn school in March 1930 is recorded in the Shrine Day Book, 1929–1930 (Shrine Notes, 1929–1930), Archives, BNSIC. I found information on the priest who led the Brooklyn school pilgrimage and the nuns who taught there in *The Official Catholic Directory: 1928* (New York: P. J. Kennedy, 1928), 243. Biographical details on Father Ross, who also was assigned to St. Gregory the Great Parish in 1930, are from John K. Sharp, *Priests and Parishes of the Diocese of Brooklyn, 1820–1944* (New York: Roman Catholic Diocese of Brooklyn, 1944), 102. On Brooklyn Catholic schools, including the claim that McDonnell was the largest, is from William A. Maguire, "Catholic Secondary Education in the Diocese of Brooklyn" (Ph.D. diss., Catholic University of America, 1932), 12. The donations from St. Patrick's School and Notre Dame High School recorded on December 29 and 30, 1953, are in Book 42: July 1953 to July 30, 1954, donor record book (typescript), Archives, BNSIC. Children's letters indicating that they earned money by crocheting or school jobs appeared in "Our Collector's Circle," *SR* 8.6 (June 1921): 46; "Thoughts from Far and Near," *SR* 8.4 (April 1921): 26. The letter from the girl with the deaf father appeared in "Suffer Little Children," *SR* 4.3 (May 1917): 20. The young donor's letter about his schoolwork and his father's health was published in "Our Collector's Circle," *SR* 7.2 (March 1920): 14.

56. The number of tablets in Memorial Hall, and this description, is taken from *GTB*, 11. Information about the other mosaics, chapels, and architectural features also can be found in that booklet. I have referred to the Shrine's working undated list of major donors and the statue, chapel, or space they sponsored for my analysis in this chapter, and that document does not mention the National Organization of Catholic Women, since they did not directly sponsor an altar or chapel. See "Donors and Gifts," box: Appeals 1953–1954, folder: Shrine Appeal 1954, Archives, BNSIC, a document that is undated but was almost certainly produced between 1953 and 1959.

CHAPTER 2

1. [Clara Douglas Sheeran], "Editorials," *Quarterly Bulletin of the International Federation of Catholic Alumnae* 10.1 (March 1927): 3. The Shrine's periodical also ran a number of articles in 1927 and 1928 that asked women to donate to the Mary Memorial Altar. One 1927 issue noted the IFCA's original 1919 pledge to raise funds and reprinted a letter by Sheeran that appeared in a 1920 issue and called for "every Mary in the land" to give a dollar. It also reprinted a more recent piece by Helen Stafford Whitton that called for "an intensive campaign to complete this sum," the amount still owed. "Mary Memorial Altar Pledges," *SR* 14.4 (April 1927): 27, 30.

2. Clara Douglas Sheeran (Mrs. James J.) to the Reverend Bernard A. McKenna, March 9, 1928, Archives, BNSIC.

3. One of the surviving photographs is figure 2.2. Another one, reprinted here as figure I.2, offers a better view of Sheeran, who poses with Mary Finan, Bishop Shahan, Helen Stafford Whitton, and the Reverend McKenna (reprinted in *AC*, 63). Many Shrine publications over the years have included a detailed description of the Mary Memorial Altar, and they tend to offer similar historical details and almost identical physical descriptions. For example, see *AC*, 62–63. On the altar installation see "Mary Memorial Altar Placed at Catholic U.," *Washington Post*, January 9, 1927, p. 26. Several sources produced by staff at the Shrine mention that the altar was "formally presented" in November 1927, but don't explain why

there was a second ceremony in December 1928. See *MEM*, 192; *AC*, 63. As proof of their journey and a memento of the trip, pilgrims brought back scallop shells from Santiago de Compostela, Spain, one of the most important medieval Christian pilgrimage sites. The scallop came to be seen as a symbol of pilgrimage. Shahan, a church historian, knew that symbolic meaning. See the entry in the reference work he coedited: Bede Jarrett, "Pilgrimage," in *The Catholic Encyclopedia*, ed. Charles G. Herbermann, Edward A. Pace, Condé B. Pallen, Thomas J. Shahan (New York: Encyclopedia Press, 1913–14). Note that Pace, another priest present at the altar presentation ceremony, also served as coeditor of that reference work.

4. The presentation ceremony program is reprinted in *MEM*, 192. On Edward Aloysius Pace, who had expertise in psychology, education, and philosophy, see William P. Braun, "Monsignor Edward A. Pace, Educator and Philosopher" (Ph.D. diss., Philosophy, Catholic University of America, 1968); Patricia De Ferrari, "Pace, Edward Aloysius," in *The Encyclopedia of American Catholic History*, ed. Michael Glazier and Thomas J. Shelley (Collegeville, MN: Liturgical Press, 1997), 1103–4; and "Mgr. E. A. Pace, Noted Catholic Educator, Dies," *Washington Post*, April 27, 1938, p. X9.

5. Other sources collaborate this claim about the relative proportion of donations for the altar, and Brennan recounted it decades later in an exchange with the Shrine's director: Elizabeth Marable Brennan to [Monsignor Patrick J. O'Connor], December 3, 5, 9, 1954, Archives, BNSIC; Monsignor Patrick J. O'Connor to Mrs. Philip A. Brennan, December 15, 1954, Archives, BNSIC. Clara Douglas Sheeran, "The Mary Memorial in the National Shrine," *SR* 14.9 (September 1927): 66.

6. "Catholic Alumnae to Present Altar," *Washington Post*, December 8, 1928, p. 5. I've made this point about the function of religion in Thomas A. Tweed, *Crossing and Dwelling: A Theory of Religion* (Cambridge, MA: Harvard University Press, 2006). Elizabeth Marable Brennan to [Monsignor Patrick J. O'Connor], December 3, 5, 9, 1954, Archives, BNSIC. Brennan was wrong in calling it a "consecration" ceremony, since the clergy inexplicably forgot to consecrate the whole altar and only corrected this oversight in 1952. Brief notice of the belated consecration of the south portion of the Mary Memorial Altar appeared in *SR*, which noted that the Most Reverend Patrick J. McCormick blessed the altar and that it had been "given by the International Federation of Catholic Alumnae and the Mary's of America": "Altar Consecrated," *SR* (May 1952): 6. The oversight, which also included the failure to bless the whole Crypt Church and its other seventeen altars, is recounted in an internal Shrine memorandum: TJG [Thomas J. Grady], "Memorandum on the Status of the Shrine," November 10, 1959, Archives, BNSIC.

7. For an interesting argument about the promise and the limits of images, including photographs, as historical evidence see Peter Burke, *Eyewitnessing: The Uses of Images as Historical Evidence* (Ithaca, NY: Cornell University Press, 2007). For a different point of view see Alan Trachtenberg, *Reading American Photographs: Images as History: Mathew Brady to Walter Evans* (New York: Hill and Wang, 1989).

8. The proposed inscription for the bronze tablet appeared in *SR* (November 1928): 85. Apparently, the inscription was changed, however. So I reconstructed the content of the actual tablet inscription. A full-page reproduction appeared in *MEM*, 191.

9. In an attempt to explain "women's absence" from historians' accounts of U.S. religious history, Catherine Brekus offers "five suggestions." I refer indirectly to her

fourth proposal: historians "have had difficulty developing models of historical change that take seriously both structural constraints and individual agency." Catherine A. Brekus, editor's introduction to *The Religious History of American Women: Reimagining the Past* (Chapel Hill: University of North Carolina Press, 2007), 8. The quote about invisibility is from Mary Jo Weaver, *New Catholic Women: A Contemporary Challenge to Traditional Religious Authority*, 2nd ed. (Bloomington: Indiana University Press, 1995), 1. There is less scholarship on Catholic womanhood between the 1920s and the 1950s, but the section on nuns (Patricia Byrne, "Part II: In the Parish but Not of It: Sisters") and the laity (Debra Campbell, "Part III: The Struggle to Serve: From the Lay Apostolate to the Ministry Explosion"), both in Jay Dolan, R. Scott Appleby, Patricia Byrne, and Debra Campbell, *Transforming Parish Ministry: The Changing Roles of Catholic Clergy, Laity, and Women Religious* (New York: Crossroad Press, 1989), 111–280, are very helpful. Campbell rightly points out that the period from 1929 to 1959 was "the heyday of Catholic action and the lay apostolate," and lay female devotees during that period did use the language of "Catholic action" in private correspondence and public writing. As she also notes, between 1889 and 1928 there was "a trend toward firmer hierarchical control of lay organizations" (211–12). At the Shrine, laywomen seemed to have the most individual and collective clout before 1928, and especially before 1920. By the 1950s, centralization and clericalization of philanthropy, the giving of time and money, changed things, though laywomen continued to work hard for causes they cared about, including the Shrine.

10. Mary J. Oates, *The Catholic Philanthropic Tradition in America* (Bloomington: Indiana University Press, 1995), 94–97.

11. Cecilia Annette Moore, "'Good and Zealous Ladies': The Role of Catholic Women in Building the National Shrine of the Immaculate Conception" (M.A. thesis, Department of Religious Studies, University of Virginia, 1991), 68. A posthumous tribute is Clara Douglas Sheeran, "In Loving Memory: Sister Mary de Paul Cogan, O.P., Co-Founder of IFCA," photocopy, Sister Mary de Paul file, Maryknoll Mission Archives, Ossining, NY. See also a helpful thesis written by a priest who interviewed Cogan, Sheeran, and other participants: Joseph J. Burns, "The Educational Efforts and Influences of the International Federation of Catholic Alumnae" (M.A. thesis, Catholic University of America, 1937). Sheeran, "In Loving Memory."

12. Sheeran, "In Loving Memory." International Federation of Catholic Alumnae, "Constitution and By-Laws of the International Federation of Catholic Alumnae," [adopted at the convention in Chicago], November 27, 1915, pamphlet, copy in IFCA Collection, ACUA. All quotations or references to the goals and structure of the organization are to this pamphlet.

13. The biographical information here about Cogan has been gleaned from multiple archival and published sources, including "Mary de Paul, 62, Maryknoll Sister," *New York Times*, November 19, 1953; [Clara Douglas Sheeran], "Clare I. Cogan (now Sister Mary de Paul, MM, AM, LLD) Alumnae Association of Saint Joseph's College, Emmitsburg, MD, Co-founder and First President of the IFCA," typescript, Maryknoll Mission Archives; and Clare I. Cogan: U.S. Bureau of the Census, *Fourteenth Census of the United States, 1920*, Brooklyn Assembly District 9, Kings, New York; roll T625_1157; p. 6A; enumeration district 474; image 45. "Stenographic Report of Addresses Made at the Evening Sessions of the First Convention of the International Federation of Catholic Alumnae," November 26, 27, 28, 1915, Chicago," file: First Convention, box 19, IFCA Collection, ACUA.

14. The assessment of Cogan's family is from Mother Mary Joseph to "My dear Sisters All," November 22, 1953, Maryknoll Mission Archives. The information about her ethnic heritage and her family—as well as her neighbors' ethnicity and native languages—is from the census records: *Fourteenth Census of the United States, 1920*, Brooklyn Assembly District 9, Kings, New York; roll T625_1157; p. 6A; enumeration district 474; image 45. Her Brooklyn street, which was only ten blocks from Sheeran's Bay Ridge home and seven blocks from their parish, was diverse. Her most immediate neighbors included not only Polish, Irish, and Italian Catholics but also central and northern European Protestants, and those nearby residents spoke seven different native languages—English, Spanish, Polish, Italian, Dutch, Swedish, and Norwegian. The vast majority of Swedish, Dutch, and Norwegian migrants in Brooklyn and around the country were Protestants, so it's very likely that some of Cogan's neighbors affiliated with one or another Protestant church. Sheeran, "Clare I. Cogan," Maryknoll Mission Archives. Her major contributions to the missionary effort would be the training and supervision of those serving in the mission field. Sister Mary de Paul, who received a Ph.D. from Mount St. Mary's College in 1931, went on to serve the order as secretary general (1931–1937) and dean of Maryknoll Teachers College (1931–1946). From 1947 to 1952, she was regional superior of the Maryknoll sisters and principal of a school in Hawaii. She later wrote about wartime missionaries in the Pacific: Sister Mary de Paul Cogan, *Sisters of Maryknoll through Troubled Waters* (New York: Scribner's, 1947). Her communication with her community after learning of her terminal illness was quoted in Reverend John J. Considine, MM, "Eulogy delivered at Sister Mary de Paul's Funeral," typescript, November 19, 1953, Maryknoll Mission Archives. Mother Mary Joseph to "My dear Sisters All," November 22, 1953, Maryknoll Mission Archives.

15. Anonymous, untitled posthumous tribute to Clara Douglas Sheeran, n.d. [probably July 1957], typescript, 6 pp., Archives, St. Joseph's Provincial House, Emmitsburg, Maryland. Some of the information here and elsewhere in this chapter about Sheeran, her family, and her neighborhood is from census records: Clara Sheeran: U.S. Bureau of the Census, *Fourteenth Census of the United States, 1920*, Brooklyn Assembly District 9, Kings, New York; roll T625_1157; p. 4B; enumeration district 481; image 295. *Fifteenth Census of the United States, 1930*, Brooklyn, Kings, New York; roll 1508; p. 17B; enumeration district 1113; image 36.0.

16. Her work history is listed in several archival and published records, including *Fifteenth Census of the United States, 1930*, Brooklyn, Kings, New York; roll 1508; p. 17B; enumeration district 1113; image 36.0; Alumnae permanent biographical file (Clara Douglas Sheeran), Archives, St. Joseph's Provincial House; "Mrs. J. J. Sheeran, Catholic Leader," *New York Times*, July 18, 1957. Alumnae permanent biographical file (Clara Douglas Sheeran), Archives, St. Joseph's Provincial House. [Clara Douglas Sheeran], "Mrs. James J. Sheeran, LL.D., Alumna of Saint Joseph's College, Emmitsburg, MD, Co-Founder and Second President of the IFCA," 1932, autobiographical profile, typescript, Archives, Maryknoll Mission Archives. The typescript identifies Sheeran as the author in a parenthetical note at the end: "Autobiography written by Clara Douglas Sheeran, at the request of the NCCW in 1932." Alumnae permanent biographical file (Clara Douglas Sheeran), Archives, St. Joseph's Provincial House. "Mrs. J. J. Sheeran, Catholic Leader," *New York Times*, July 18, 1957. [Clara Douglas Sheeran], "Mrs. James J. Sheeran, LL.D., Alumna of Saint Joseph's College, Emmitsburg, MD, Co-Founder and Second

President of the IFCA," 1932, autobiographical profile, typescript, Archives, Maryknoll Mission Archives.

17. Alumnae permanent biographical file (Clara Douglas Sheeran), Archives, St. Joseph's Provincial House.

18. Mary Downs to Thomas J. Shahan, March 16, 1913, handwritten note; Thomas J. Shahan to Mary Downs, March 21, 1913, handwritten note, both in correspondence files, Archives, BNSIC. Downs's son, the Reverend Michael Ricker, sent Shahan's letter to the Shrine after his mother's death: Michael Ricker to Monsignor Murray, July 25, 1986, correspondence file, Archives, BNSIC.

19. Clara Sheeran's letter to McKenna, which I quote, was reprinted in the IFCA's periodical and several years later again in *SR*. The letter also included a history of the IFCA's support, noting its original resolution of support in November 1916 and the second one in June 1919: Mary Byrne O'Toole, "The National Shrine of the Immaculate Conception," *Quarterly Bulletin of the International Federation of Catholic Alumnae*, September 20, 1920; "Mary Memorial Altar Pledges," *SR* 14.4 (April 1927): 27–30. Sheeran's letter was reprinted in "Mary Memorial Altar Pledges," *SR* 14.4 (April 1927): 27–30. Shahan's response to Downs's 1913 letter was reprinted in "First to Suggest the Mary Memorial," *SR* 8.1 (January 1921): 6. The title and content of that piece credited Downs with the strategy of appealing to the Marys of America, but the next page of that issue acknowledged Sheeran's role too, though her plan was to fund a chapel and not a statue, as in Downs's suggestion, or the Mary Memorial Altar, as with the final fundraising plan. The piece reported that it was the idea of the IFCA president, Sheeran, to urge "that every woman named Mary, and everyone whose mother's name was Mary, contribute one dollar towards a memorial chapel to Our Lady in the splendid new Shrine": "A Mary Memorial Chapel: Catholic Women of Our Country Who Are Named Mary Asked to Build Chapel in National Shrine," *SR* 8.1 (January 1921): 7. Apparently that also was the issue of the Shrine periodical that Shahan sent Downs and that her son, Michael, sent back to the Shrine in 1986. Michael Ricker to Monsignor Murray, July 25, 1986, correspondence file, Archives, BNSIC.

20. Thomas J. Shahan to Mary Downs, November 3, 1920, correspondence file, Archives, BNSIC. "Catholic Girls to Contribute: Rector of University of Washington Accepts Plan Suggested by Former Resident," clipping, scrapbook of Mary Ricker, in the possession of Michael Ricker. Her son, Michael Ricker, identified the source as a Terra Haute newspaper in 1920. Since the article mentions that it is "several days" since Shahan wrote to Downs, it probably was published sometime between November 4, 1920, and February 30, 1921, since Shahan's letter was dated November 3, 1920, and Shahan seems to have sent a copy of the January 1921 edition of *SR* to Downs, perhaps in a second mailing. Another clipping, an untitled article by Margaret Lewis with a photograph of Downs, apparently appeared in another newspaper, perhaps early in 1921, since Lewis suggests that Downs's original letter was published in *SR* "last week." Since that reprint was in the January 1921 edition of *SR*, this second newspaper story probably appeared between January and February 1921.

21. The story of Mary Downs has been recounted in some publications produced by the Shrine or by those who have worked for the Shrine, from the earliest to the most recent publications, including *NS*, 135, and *AC*, 62. Over the years, some of the Shrine's official guidebooks and pamphlets have not mentioned Mary Downs: *The National Shrine of the Immaculate Conception: The Main Altar and the Northern Apse of the Crypt* (Washington, DC: Catholic University of America, 1927); and

Guide Book of the Crypt of the National Shrine of the Immaculate Conception, Washington, D.C. (Washington, DC: National Shrine League, 1941). The 2006 guidebook also failed to mention Downs: *Basilica of the National Shrine of the Immaculate Conception: A Guidebook and Personal Tour* (Washington, DC: Basilica of the National Shrine of the Immaculate Conception, n.d.). So did the Website's section "History" and its virtual tour of the crypt level: Basilica of the National Shrine of the Immaculate Conception, www.nationalShrine.com (accessed February 14, 2007). But the 1990 guide did tell Downs's story: Michael P. Warsaw, *The National Shrine of the Immaculate Conception: America's Church* (Washington, DC: National Shrine of the Immaculate Conception, 1990), 6. Downs's story also was recounted in the 1990s by the official guides who took visitors on tours: "National Shrine of the Immaculate Conception: Tour Information for Shrine Guides," [1996], typescript, in author's possession. I've taken the tour myself multiple times over the years and spoken with many tour guides about what they say, including their narrative about the Mary Memorial Altar. My copy of the "Tour Information for Shrine Guides" was given to me in 1996 by a volunteer tour guide. Mary Downs's sons, agreed to (1) respond in writing to twenty-five questions about their mother and her devotion that I submitted to them in a letter dated November 17, 1996, and (2) do a taped-recording of their joint responses to the same questions. My quotations in this chapter are from the taped-recording, unless otherwise noted: audio recording, Michael Ricker and Kevin Ricker, December 8, 1996. It was just an interesting coincidence, they said, that they taped it on the feast of the Immaculate Conception.

22. Information in this section about Mary Downs and her family (relatives' occupation, ethnicity, and so on) has been taken from a number of sources, including census records: *Thirteenth Census of the United States, 1910*, Terre Haute Ward 4, Vigo, Indiana; roll T624_385; p. 6B; enumeration district 155; image 634, *Fifteenth Census of the United States, 1930*, Delphos, Allen, Ohio; roll 1746; p. 5A; enumeration district 10; image 668.0. Michael F. Downs to Mary L. Downs, December 8, 1921. Her son, Michael Ricker, sent me a photocopy of this letter, which was typed on the letterhead stationary of the Hoosier Rolling Mill Company, her father's business. It was found among Mary's personal belongings at her death in 1986. For background on the Anglo-Irish Treaty and its interpretation, see Jason Knirck, *Imagining Ireland's Independence: The Debates over the Anglo-Irish Treaty of 1921* (Lanham, MD: Rowan and Littlefield, 2006).

23. Among the materials Michael and Kevin Ricker gave me was an obituary clipped from a local newspaper, but they had saved no identifying information for this death notice, which mentions the date of her wedding. Mary's scrapbook included the newspaper notice of her wedding: "Miss Mary Louise Downs Will Wed Hubert Ricker This Morning at St. Rose," and in the margin Michael had scribbled a note next to the sentence in it that said Hubert Ricker was a Notre Dame graduate: "Dad took Architecture for a year, but discontinued." That one-sentence notice appeared in "Review of Week in Lima Society," *Lima Sunday News*, November 21, 1926, 1. Mary Downs, "Just a Memory," n.d., typescript, photocopy in author's possession. Mary Downs, "Crumbs and Grumbles," *St. Mary's Chimes* 32.4 (December 1923): 57. Downs also published several other poems in that college periodical, including "Gifts" [30.4 (December 1921], and "Fulfillment" [30.9 (May 1922)]. She published a few pieces of short fiction there too, including "No Room in the Inn" [31.4 (December 1922)], and "St. Valentine's Message" [32.6 (February 1924)]. Downs's poem "A New Year" also was published, though I have been

unable to locate the published version. I have only the copy from her college scrapbook.

24. "Report of Class Work," St. Mary's College, Notre Dame, IN, in author's posses-
sion. A photocopy of this report card, from the third quarter of Mary Downs's senior year in 1924, was sent to me by Michael and Kevin Ricker in 1996. The other information about Downs's academic record and musical performances was retrieved from copies of *St. Mary's Chimes* found in the St. Mary's College Archives: "Certificates for Completing the Elementary Course in the Art Progressive ser. of Music," *St. Mary's Chimes* 29.10 (June 1921): 184; "Graduating Honors," *St. Mary's Chimes* 32.10 (June 1924): 222. The account of a program performed on "St. Cecelia's Feast" indicated that Downs played the organ that fall night: *St. Mary's Chimes* 32.4 (December 1923): 4. Mary Downs, "Purification," *St. Mary's Chimes* 32.6 (February 1924): 93. Michael and Kevin Ricker, audio recording, December 8, 1996. The oral reports about her Marian images came from the same audio recording. The brothers also sent me, at my request, photo-graphs of the interior of their mother's home, including photographs of her living room shelves. The "Kitchen Madonna," usually a white alabaster figurine of the Virgin using a broom to sweep, continues to be sold in Catholic bookstores and online outlets, including the Catholic Company, Catholic Family Catalog, and Aquinas and Moore Catholic Goods. One Website, Heaven Sent Religious Gifts, reminds customers that "She has graced the lives of working women both in and out of the home for years."

25. Michael and Kevin Ricker, audio recording, December 8, 1996. A "Baggage Identification Tag" for Mrs. Hubert Ricker, a "Passenger's Check," and other mementos of the honeymoon trip were found in her belongings at her death. Her sons photocopied these for me; they added a handwritten note: "Mementoes from the Honeymoon trip to Washington, D.C."

26. Many published and unpublished documents mention that the full cost of the Mary Memorial Altar was $50,000. See for example "Altar Built by Those Named 'Mary' Installed," *SR* 14.2 (February 1927): 13.

27. Her obituary called her a "distinguished lay woman" and noted some of her achievements: "Mrs. Elizabeth Brennan, Founder of Mary's Day," *Tablet* (Brooklyn), 60 (August 1968): 9. On the Navajo chapel see "Navajo Chapel Dedicated: Gift of Judge and Mrs. Brennan of Brooklyn Blessed in Arizona," *New York Times*, October 29, 1936. As the article noted, it was "the first church in this country dedicated to 'Mary, Mother of Mankind' under that title." The church was part of St. Michael's Mission on the Navajo Indian reservation, which is not far from Window Rock, Arizona. Brennan mentions her donation of Lady Isle to the nuns in Elizabeth Marable Brennan to [Monsignor Patrick J. O'Connor] no date [1952], Archives, BNSIC: "In 1941, my late beloved husband, Supreme Court Justice Philip A. Brennan, and I gave beautiful 'Belle Isle,' our summer home in Portsmouth, New Hampshire, to the Sisters of Providence of Saint Mary-of-the-Woods, Indiana." I found further information about Lady Isle, as it was renamed for Mary, and Brennan in that order's archives, including "Lady Isle, New Hampshire: Historical Data," typescript, Sisters of Providence Archives, St. Mary-of-the-Woods, Indiana. Their files also include a photocopy of an article about the donation: "New Convent at Lady Isle," *Saint Mary-of-the-Woods Alumnae News*, 1941, 62–63.

28. A comment by Clara Sheeran in a 1932 survey of the IFCA for the National Council of Catholic Women, as quoted in Burns, "Educational Efforts and Influences of the International Federation of Catholic Alumnae," 11.

29. The quotations taken from Brennan's pamphlet on Neumann are, in order of their appearance, from Elizabeth Marable Brennan, *Visits to Theresa Neumann* (New York: Paulist Press, 1936), 4, 3, 6, 7, 12, 8–9, copy in Alphabetical Pamphlet Collection (ALP 004), Archives, ND.

30. Quotations in this paragraph from, in order, Elizabeth Marable Brennan, *Visits to Theresa Neumann* (New York: Paulist Press, 1936), copy in Alphabetical Pamphlet Collection (ALP 004), Archives, ND, 5, 12, 21, 18.

31. Quotations in this paragraph from, in order, Elizabeth Marable Brennan, *Visits to Theresa Neumann* (New York: Paulist Press, 1936), copy in Alphabetical Pamphlet Collection (ALP 004), Archives, ND, 12, 15.

32. Elizabeth Marable Brennan to "Your Excellency," n.d. [1952], Archives, BNSIC. This letter seems to be addressed to the Shrine's director, who was Monsignor Patrick J. O'Connor from 1950 to 1956, in an attempt to gather support for Mary's Day. Using her childhood nickname, Brennan described three of these commissioned statues of Mary, Mother of Mankind, in a letter to the superior of the order that had taught her in high school: Bessie Marable Brennan to Revered Mother Mary Raphael, February 17, 1934, typescript, Archives, Sisters of Providence, St. Mary-of-the-Woods, Indiana.

33. Elizabeth Marable Brennan to the Most Reverend Michael Curley, DD, December 6, 1936, Archives, BNSIC. On Memorial Hall, see *GTB*, 11. For a brief but helpful account of Mary's Day and the statue of Mary, Mother of Mankind, see Geraldine M. Rohling, "From the Archives," *MS* 62.2 (fall 2001): 2. Some appeals to Catholics "to have their relatives, friends, or benefactors commemorated on the walls" referred to this space in the lower church as "the Memorial Chapel," as does one printed appeal preserved in the Shrine's archives. That flier and order form, which circulated sometime between 1929 and 1932, described the tablets' purpose, size, and cost, which ranged from $100 to $1,500: "Memorial Tablets," printed flier and order form, "Memorial Tablets, 1929–32," box D-4, Archives, BNSIC. In later years, the Shrine staff turned to new technology to raise funds and memorialize ordinary Catholics: one flier distributed at the Shrine encouraged visitors to donate $100 to "enroll your loved ones in the National Shrine Registry Program," a computerized record of deceased family members that is "maintained within special computer kiosks located in the National Shrine's Memorial Hall." "Memorial Registry Program," folded flier and order form, Washington, D.C.: Basilica of the National Shrine of the Immaculate Conception, n.d. [2006], copy in author's possession. The marble tablet memorializing Elizabeth Brennan is near the stairs, on the Seton Pier (54E) in Memorial Hall.

34. "Will Celebrate Silver Jubilee of Mary's Day," *Tablet* (Brooklyn) 46.11 (May 2, 1953): 1, 24.

35. Elizabeth Marable Brennan to [Monsignor Patrick J. O'Connor], December 3, 5, 9, 1954, Archives, BNSIC. "Will Celebrate Silver Jubilee of Mary's Day," *Tablet* (Brooklyn) 46.11 (May 2, 1953): 1, 24.

36. The slogan appeared on the pledge card included in *SR* in 1928, the year of the first Mary's Day celebration: "Mary's Altar: Mary's Day Outline and Pledge Card," *SR* 15.5 (May 1928): 39. "Will Celebrate Silver Jubilee of Mary's Day," 24. Elizabeth Marable Brennan to [Monsignor Patrick J. O'Connor], December 3, 5, 9, 1954, Archives, BNSIC.

37. In my construction of this social profile, I tried to represent the range of adult female donors from each region. Since donors from the same neighborhood or institution often appear on the same page, I took no more than four names from

any page. So, for example, when analyzing Brooklyn donors I selected the first name with a Brooklyn address. Some of the twenty-five pages have no Brooklyn addresses; others are filled with them. I then selected every *other* name after that until I had four from that page, if there were that many from Brooklyn. For some entries, the name, address, or donation are incomplete or unclear, however, and some entries do not yield an unambiguous match with the 1920 or 1930 federal census records, which provide a good deal of information about the household and the neighborhood. If an entry on Brennan's list was incomplete or I could not locate the donor in the census records, I went to the next name on the page. After retrieving that preliminary biographical information, I then determined the donor's neighborhood and parish, to get some sense of the local social context. Some of the contributions sent directly to the Shrine in 1928 and designated specifically for the Mary Memorial Altar were handwritten in pen in an untitled, red-spined, folio-sized ledger book with "Journal" printed on the side that I found in the BNSIC's archives. The donations designated for "M.M."/Mary Memorial Altar" included contributions in 1928 from diverse places, including the East Coast and the Midwest: Maria de Rosa from New York City (p. 3); Mary Catherine Lay from Baltimore (p. 4); Mrs. J. F. Shafter from Poseyville, Indiana (p. 4), and Marie Bonchateau from St. Paul, Minnesota (p. 8). Catherine Murphy's donation was listed on p. 4 of this ledger book, and I found the other biographical information I cite here in U.S. Bureau of the Census, *Fifteenth Census of the United States, 1930*, Philadelphia, Pennsylvania; roll 2133; p. 46A; enumeration district 1034; image 597.0. I am grateful to my former research assistants Anne Blankenship and Kate Bowler for their help in finding information about donors on this list.

38. I used several published and online sources, including an 1899 map entitled "The Roman Catholic Churches of Brooklyn, New York," available at Tim Desmond's personal Website, http://mysite.verizon.net/timdesmond/files/churches.htm, formerly located at http://home.earthlink.net/~desmondcorp/tim/churches .htm, and the "Find a Parish" option on the Diocese of Brooklyn's Website: http:// www.dioceseofbrooklyn.org/parish_search.aspx, formerly located at www. dioces-eofbrooklyn.org/cgi-bin/pa_Search.pl. Every selection method has flaws, including this one. For instance, using the 1930 U.S. Census privileges women whose status didn't change between 1928 and 1930, but that census is closest in time to the year they donated, so it seemed most useful. This method, however flawed, allows a limited social profile of the donors. The records themselves contain other flaws, too, as scholars such as Miriam L. King and Diana L. Magnuson have noted: "Perspectives on Historical U.S. Census Undercounts," *Social Science History* 19.4 (winter 1995): 455–66. The Census undercounted or overcounted some persons. According to one estimate, for example, the Census undercounted the national population by 6.7 percent in 1920 and by 5.3 percent in 1930 (458). Certain urban dwellers were more likely to be undercounted, especially boarders, immigrants, watchmen, and transients, and rural dwellers like miners, lumberjacks, and those living in cabins in wooded areas have also been underrepresented (461, 463).

39. The information from the donor list in this paragraph and in the remainder of the chapter is from "Individual Contributions to Fund of International Federation of Catholic Alumnae for Mary Altar (High Altar in Crypt)," Archives, BNSIC. The first page of that donor list also printed the information from the 1928 Mary's Day pledge cards, which included the slogan "Mary's Mite on Mary's Day for Mary's Altar" and the instruction to "tear off and return with offering" to

Mrs. Philip A. Brennan of Brooklyn. The contribution from the seminarians is on p. 7. The one from the Reverend Hickey is on p. 8. Biographical information on Father Hickey, who lived with three other priests, a nun, and a maid, is from the census records: *Fifteenth Census of the United States, 1930* (Washington, DC: National Archives and Records Administration, 1930), Brooklyn, Kings, New York; roll 1498; p. 6A; enumeration district 1316; image 455.0. I found other information—his full name, death date, and seminary training—in John K. Sharp, *Priests and Parishes of the Diocese of Brooklyn, 1820–1944* (New York: Roman Catholic Diocese of Brooklyn, 1944), 57. Dunn's contribution also is on p. 8. Biographical information on Dunn is from *Fifteenth Census of the United States, 1930*, Greenwich, Fairfield, Connecticut; roll 257; p. 9B; enumeration district 134; image 752.0. Brady's donation is on p. 10. Biographical information on Brady is from *Fifteenth Census of the United States, 1930*, Brooklyn, Kings, New York; roll 1527; p. 16B; enumeration district 661; image 395.0.

40. The donations from Higgins and Morano are on p. 8. Biographical information on Higgins is from *Fifteenth Census of the United States, 1930*, Greenwich, Fairfield, Connecticut; roll 257; p. 9B; enumeration district 134; image 752.0. Morano's biographical information is from *Fifteenth Census of the United States, 1930*, Greenwich, Fairfield, Connecticut; roll 257; p. 2A; enumeration district 133; image 707.0. The donation from Sister Raphael is recorded in "Individual Contributions to Fund," p. 1. Biographical details about her are derived from U.S. Bureau of the Census, *Fourteenth Census of the United States, 1920*, Manhattan Assembly District 21, New York, New York; roll T625_1224; p. 14B; enumeration district 1443; image 1000.

41. The first local reference I could find to Brooklyn as "the city of churches" was "City of Churches," *Brooklyn Daily Eagle*, March 6, 1844, 2: "City of Churches. Such, in time, will be the distinctive appellation of Brooklyn," the journalist accurately predicted. On Brooklyn history, including its churches, I also consulted multiple sources—city directories, local newspapers, congregational histories, and census records. I also relied on local histories, including Henry Reed Stiles, *The Civil, Political, and Ecclesiastical History, and Commercial and Industrial Record of the County of Kings and the City of Brooklyn, N.Y., from 1683 to 1884* (New York: W. W. Munsell, 1884). On Assumption Church, and Catholic parishes, see Sharp, *Priests and Parishes of the Diocese of Brooklyn, 1820–1944*; John K. Sharp, *The History of the Diocese of Brooklyn, 1853–1953: The Catholic Church on Long Island* (New York: Fordham University Press, 1954); the Diocese of Brooklyn's online parish directory, www.dioceseofbrooklyn.org (accessed June 3, 2007); "History of Assumption Parish," at the Website of the Church of the Assumption of the Blessed Virgin Mary, www.assumptionparish.net/ (accessed: June 3, 2007); Diocese of Brooklyn, *Diocese of Immigrants: The Brooklyn Catholic Experience, 1853–2003* (Strasbourg, France: Éditions du Signe, 2004). The local newspaper reported that Sunday School teachers—327 women and 273 men—led 4,327 children in the 1844 parade, but Catholic children didn't fill the streets that afternoon. See "Sabbath School Celebrated," *Brooklyn Daily Eagle*, May 29, 1844, 2. On the conflict between Irish Catholics and the Know Nothings see "Riot and Bloodshed!!: A Sabbath in the City of Churches," *Brooklyn Daily Eagle*, June 5, 1854, 2. On the significance of Irish and German Catholics in New York see Jay P. Dolan's *The Immigrant Church: New York's Irish and German Catholics, 1815–1865* (South Bend, IN: University of Notre Dame Press, 1983). On the ways parades negotiate meaning and power see Susan G. Davis, *Parades and Power: Street Theater in*

Nineteenth-Century Philadelphia (Philadelphia: Temple University Press, 1986). "Heavy Immigration Is Changing the Character of the City," *Brooklyn Daily Eagle*, August 17, 1902, 3. That piece focused on changes to Manhattan, but the same transformations were happening in Brooklyn. See "Brooklyn's 'Little Italy,' the Largest in America," *Brooklyn Daily Eagle*, May 20, 1900, 20. The controversy in 1902 began when "an American Mother" complained that the annual parade, which also entailed closing public schools, was too "sectarian" for the emerging diversity. A heated exchange ensued in Board of Education meetings and local periodicals. Lillian Cray, a twenty-eight-year-old Presbyterian Sunday School teacher, understood that some on the Board thought the public parade and the school closing "looked too sectarian," but she suggested that was "a rather one-sided way of putting it." Carrie Legler, a sixteen-year-old Protestant German American, had "heard that the Catholics are against the schools being closed on Anniversary Day" but wondered "why they cannot be closed, that we may parade and raise our banner for the Lord." The problem, of course, was that multireligious Brooklynites raised many banners and were not so certain they worshiped the same Lord. See "An American Mother," letter to the editor, "Against Anniversary Day: 'An American Mother' Points Out Its Unfairness to Those Not Concerned in Parade," *Brooklyn Daily Eagle*, April 27, 1902, 18; "School Children Sad: No Closing for May Walk," *Brooklyn Daily Eagle*, May 22, 1902, 22; "Anniversary Day Secure," *Brooklyn Daily Eagle*, May 29, 1902, 4. The editor announced the paper wouldn't publish the other letters it had received, including those from "A Roman Catholic" and "A Catholic Teacher": "Letters on Anniversary Day," *Brooklyn Daily Eagle*, May 29, 1902, 6. For a sampling of the letters, including those by Cray and Legler, see *Brooklyn Daily Eagle*, May 27, 1902, 6. I found biographical information about Cray and Legler in the federal census records. On the 1902 parade: "Sunday School Union: Reviewed by Governor Odell," *Brooklyn Daily Eagle*, June 7, 1902, 6.

42. Population statistics quoted in David Ment, *The Shaping of a City: A Brief History of Brooklyn* (Brooklyn: Brooklyn Educational and Cultural Alliance, 1979), 68. Statistics on Catholic membership and churches for the nation and for Brooklyn in 1926 are available from U.S. Bureau of the Census, *Religious Bodies: 1926*, vol. 1, *Summary and Detailed Tables* (Washington, DC: Government Printing Office, 1930), 14, 490. For Catholic statistics in 1928, when the Church claimed 19,689,049 members, see *The Official Catholic Directory* (New York: P. J. Kennedy, 1928). I calculated the proportion of immigrants and children of immigrants using 1930 census records, which reported 868,770 foreign-born and 1,126,953 who were either foreign-born or had an immigrant parent among the total Brooklyn population of 2,560,401: *Fifteenth Census of the United States, 1930*. I take the information about the Brooklyn economy and transportation from Ment, *Shaping of a City*, 77. The information about Kings County housing construction is from Elliot Willensky, *When Brooklyn Was the World, 1920–1957* (New York: Harmony Books, 1986), 11.

43. On the number of Catholic members and churches in Brooklyn see *Religious Bodies: 1926*, 490. For a slightly later listing of churches, including Catholic churches, see Historical Records Survey, Work Projects Administration, *Guide to Vital Statistics in the City of New York, Borough of Brooklyn: Churches* (New York: City of New York, 1942). On the 1928 parade see "400 Sunday Schools in Kings Parade," *New York Times*, May 31, 1928. There was controversy that year, too, as some challenged the proposal to ask children marching in the parade to "carry banners and placards with prohibition slogans": "Oppose Dry Placards in

Children's Parade," *New York Times*, June 7, 1928, 17. The parade continued over the years, though participants and visibility decreased: see Evan Barton, "Unknown to Many, Traditional Sunday School Parade Survives," *Brooklyn Daily Eagle*, June 17, 2006, http://www.brooklyneagle.com (accessed June 3, 2007). According to census records, eleven residents on Brennan's street were Irish immigrants, and five languages were spoken—Polish, German, Danish, Slovak, and English: *Fifteenth Census of the United States, 1930*, Brooklyn, Kings, New York; roll 1515; p. 10A; enumeration district 1631; image 485.0. In this paragraph and earlier ones I refer to the "Protestant establishment," a term coined by sociologist E. Digby Baltzell and employed by historian William R. Hutchison. What was happening in Brooklyn, and reflected in the debates about the Anniversary Parade, can be viewed as challenges to the "Protestant establishment." Using slightly different terms, historian Robert Handy argued that there was a "second disestablishment" between 1920 and 1940. However we label the process, the patterns in Brooklyn mirror a larger cultural process whereby Protestants collectively continued to have numerical dominance in many regions of the nation but lost some of their ability to exercise public power, in a process that began in the nineteenth century and culminated during the second half of the twentieth century. E. Digby Batzell, *The Protestant Establishment: Aristocracy and Caste in America* (New Haven, CT: Yale University Press, 1987). William R. Hutchison, ed., *Between the Times: The Travail of the Protestant Establishment in America, 1900– 1960* (Cambridge: Cambridge University Press, 1989). Robert T. Handy, *A Christian America: Protestant Hopes and Historical Realities*, 2nd ed. (New York: Oxford University Press, 1984), 159–84.

44. I drew the information in appendix 2.1 from the first ten pages of Brennan's typed list, selecting four donors from each page. The census records for the women I discuss in this paragraph, all from *Fifteenth Census of the United States, 1930*, Brooklyn, Kings County, NY, are as follows: Marie Fox: roll 1514; p. 1B; enumeration district 111; image 279; Anna Murphy: roll 1495; p. 1A; enumeration district 1874; image 358.0; Honoria Mcloughlin: roll 1538; p. 8A; enumeration district 866; image 269.0; Elinor Woods: roll 1537; p. 72B; enumeration district 857; image 1004.0. The Bureau of Labor Statistics releases data about the Consumer Price Index (CPI), and an online price calculator uses the CPI to compute cost change over time. I used that online tool: "What Is a Dollar Worth?," Reserve Bank of Minneapolis, www.minneapolisfed.org/Research/data/us/calc/ (accessed June 9, 2010). In this section, comparative national and local data is taken from the 1930 federal census. The proportion of single women over 15 years of age in 1930 was 26.4 percent: *Fifteenth Census of the United States, 1930, Population*, vol. 2, *General Report Statistics by Subject* (Washington, DC: U.S. Government Printing Office, 1933), 837. On the age of the Brooklyn population see ibid., 326.

45. The census records for the women I discuss in this paragraph, all from *Fifteenth Census of the United States, 1930*, Brooklyn, Kings County, New York, are as follows: Mary G. Doherty: roll 1540; p. 6A; enumeration district 484; image 607.0; Miriam V. Schmid: roll 1491; p. 20B; enumeration district 906; image 179.0; Margaret Zimmerman: roll 1513; p. 4B; enumeration district 1493; image 137.0; Rosella McHugh: roll 1513; p. 2A; enumeration district 1495; image 763.0. On the national average of women who worked (22 percent)—as opposed to 40 percent for the sample I analyze here—see *Fifteenth Census of the United States, 1930, Abstract of the Fifteenth Census of the United States* (Washington, DC: Government Printing Office, 1933), 305. On the categorization of occupations and the

proportion of working women who were professionals (11 percent), see U.S. Bureau of the Census, *A Social-Economic Grouping of Gainful Workers in Cities of 500,000 or More: 1930* (Washington, DC: Government Printing Office, March 11, 1938), 10. See also *Fifteenth Census of the United States, 1930, Population*, vol. 5, *General Report on Occupations* (Washington, DC: Government Printing Office, 1933). On the economic status of immigrant Catholics in the early twentieth century, see Jay Dolan, *The American Catholic Experience: A History from Colonial Times to the Present* (Notre Dame, IN: University of Notre Dame Press, 1992), 156–57.

46. The census records for the women I discuss in this paragraph, all from *Fifteenth Census of the United States, 1930*, Brooklyn, Kings County, NY, are as follows: Melvina A. Jones: roll 1537; p. 16B; enumeration district 850; image 544.0; Florence Miranda: roll 1540; p. 13A; enumeration district 479; image 401.0; Elizabeth McCaffrey: roll 1537; p. 11A; enumeration district 848; image 431.0; Catherine Rizzo: roll 1541; p. 11A; enumeration district 498; image 48.0. The national median home value and median monthly rental, as well as the figures for Brooklyn, are in *Fifteenth Census of the United States, 1930, Population, vol. VI: Families* (Washington, DC: U.S. Government Printing Office, 1933), 7, 60–61.

47. The information on Margaret Sherry is in *Fifteenth Census of the United States, 1930*, Brooklyn, Kings, New York, roll 1509; p. 7A; enumeration district 1145; image 605.0.

48. The median home value for donors listed in appendix 2 was $12,000, and an average of only two languages was spoken on their blocks. On Ownie Miller: *Fifteenth Census of the United States, 1930*, Memphis, Shelby, Tennessee; roll 2274; p. 5A; enumeration district 54; image 837.0.

49. The census records for the women I discuss in this paragraph, all from *Fifteenth Census of the United States, 1930*, are as follows: Clara Schaffler: Memphis, Shelby, Tennessee; roll 2275; p. 22B; enumeration district 75; image 702.0; Margaret A. Mette: Memphis, Shelby, Tennessee; roll 2275; p. 26A; enumeration district 65; image 258.0; Alma L. Centilivre: Fort Wayne, Allen, Indiana; roll 574; p. 16A; enumeration district 12; image 939.0; Anna M. Malloy: Manhattan, New York, New York: roll 1564; p. 7A; enumeration district 659; image 939.0; Loretta P. Hendrick: New Rochelle, Westchester, New York: roll 1663; p. 4B; enumeration district 266; image 744.0. On the national average of women who worked (22 percent), see *Fifteenth Census of the United States, 1930, Abstract of the Fifteenth Census of the United States*, 305.

50. *SR* didn't continue its "Collector's Circle" or publish excerpts from donor's letters in 1928, but earlier issues did include passages written by donors who specifically directed their funds to the Mary Memorial Chapel or, later, the Mary Memorial Altar. The quotations from donors are taken from *SR*'s "Collector's Circle." In the order of appearance in this paragraph they are *SR* 8.11 (November 1921): 86; *SR* 10.6 (June 1923): 46; *SR* 10.12 (December 1923): 94; *SR* 9.2 (February 1922): 14; *SR* 9.1 (January 1922): 6; *SR* 10.4 (April 1923): 20; *SR* 10.2 (February 1923): 14.

51. IFCA, "Constitution and By-Laws of the International Federation of Catholic Alumnae," pamphlet, IFCA Collection, ACUA.

52. The IFCA published Gibbons's letter to Sheeran: James Cardinal Gibbons to Mrs. Sheeran, February 14, 1921, *International Federation of Catholic Alumnae Quarterly Bulletin* 4.1 (March 1921): 3. P. Cardinal Gaspari to Monsignor Thomas Joseph Shahan, May 15, 1922, box 18, IFCA Collection, ACUA.

53. The details about their visit to the pope are found in "Holy Candidate," *Time*, August 3, 1931. On Burns, see Weaver, *New Catholic Women*, 17–20. On the protest inside and outside the Shrine during Pope John Paul II's 1979 visit, including the banners protestors carried, see George Vecsey, "53 Nuns, after a Night of Prayer, Stand in Silent Protest to Pontiff," *New York Times*, October 8, 1979. Elizabeth Brennan to Dr. Pace, December 2, 1930, IFCA official correspondence, vol. 1, box 3, IFCA Collection, ACUA. In that letter, Brennan also invites Monsignor Ryan, the famous ethicist at CUA. Sheeran's comment about her friendship with the priest is from Clara Sheeran to Rev. Bernard J. McKenna, February 29, 1928, Bernard McKenna Collection, box 1: 1907–1930, Archives, BNSIC.

54. Here I use sociologist Anthony Giddens's definition of "power." See Anthony Giddens, *The Constitution of Society* (Berkeley: University of California Press, 1984), 257. Sheeran's not-so-charitable comment about Finan is from Clara Sheeran to Rev. Bernard J. McKenna, February 29, 1928, Bernard McKenna Collection, box 1: 1907–1930, Archives, BNSIC.

55. I allude here to Kathleen Sprows Cummings's compelling thesis (that before the 1960s, Catholic women had more opportunities within the Church) in *New Women of the Old Faith: Gender and American Catholicism in the Progressive Era* (Chapel Hill: University of North Carolina Press, 2009), 3. "'Mary's Day' Finds Wide Support: Local Plan to Honor Blessed Mother Draws Approbation," *Tablet* (Brooklyn) 20 (May 5, 1928): 3. *Oxford English Dictionary*, 2nd ed., 1989, OED Online, Oxford University Press, http://dictionary.oed.com (accessed June 13, 2007): I refer here to the entries on "submit," "submission," and "submissive," as well those on "assert," "assertion," and "assertive." On the complexities of women's action in male-dominated institutions, Marie Griffith has written insightfully about the paradoxical "power of submission" among conservative Protestant women: Marie R. Griffith, *God's Daughters: Evangelical Women and the Power of Submission* (Berkeley: University of California Press, 1997).

56. "IFCA Rose Windows Blessed in Shrine," *MS* (February 1961): 3. "Dedication Ceremonies at the Shrine," *IFCA Bulletin* 43.2 (March 1961): 1–2. *GTB*, 22.

CHAPTER 3

1. "The Shrine You Can Build," *Treasure Chest of Fun and Fact* 9.6 (November 19, 1953): 2, copy in Archives, ACUA. Richard's and Rita's names appear on pp. 18 and 25 of the list of donors that Elizabeth Brennan prepared and submitted in 1928: "Individual Contributions to Fund of International Federation of Catholic Alumnae for Mary Altar (High Altar in Crypt)," Archives, BNSIC. Demographic information about Richard Kasprowicz, whose last name is misspelled on the donor list as "Kaspur," is from U.S. Bureau of the Census, *Fifteenth Census of the United States, 1930*, Brooklyn, Kings, New York; roll 1516; p. 8A; enumeration district 620; image 17. Information about Rita O'Brien is from U.S. Bureau of the Census, *Fourteenth Census of the United States, 1920*, Brooklyn Assembly District 7, Kings, New York; roll T625_1155; p. 14B; enumeration district 406; image 351. Kasprowicz also appears on Appendix 3.1, while O'Brien is among the selected students on Appendix 3.2. I gesture here toward a central issue in the study of children—agency versus structure: how much did young people create their own world and how much was imposed on them? I address that issue later in the chapter. For a helpful framing of the issue, see Allison James, Chris Jenks, and Alan Prout, *Theorizing Childhood* (Cambridge: Polity Press, 1998), 200–202.

2. I cited other sources for the Diocese of Brooklyn in chapter 2, but on Malloy, who served as bishop from 1922 to 1956, see Diocese of Brooklyn, *Diocese of Immigrants: The Brooklyn Catholic Experience, 1853–2003* (Strasbourg, France: Éditions du Signe, 2004), 89–116. Information here on the parish priests is from, among many other sources, John K. Sharp, *Priests and Parishes of the Diocese of Brooklyn, 1820 to 1944* (Brooklyn, N.Y.: Roman Catholic Diocese of Brooklyn, 1944), 77, 113, 191, 204. It was Sister Edna McKeever, CSJ, the archivist of St. Joseph's Convent in Brentwood, New York, who first told me in a telephone interview on October 18, 2006, that "photographing sisters was not done widely in the order until the 1960s." My vigorous, but unsuccessful, search for photographic evidence of the nuns' activity in Brooklyn confirms her observation. Sister Edna also helped me identify the principals of the two schools, and she confirmed that information in a letter: Sister Edna McKeever, CSJ, to author, November 20, 2006. The quotation about nuns and children is from Robert A. Orsi, *Between Heaven and Earth: The Religious Worlds People Make and the Scholars Who Study Them* (Princeton, NJ: Princeton University Press, 2005), 82.

3. I cite some of the expanding secondary literature on women religious in chapters 1 and 2. On children, see Catherine A. Brekus, "Religion and Childhood Studies," special issue, *Journal of Religion* 86.4 (October 2006). That issue includes a helpful article on Catholic children since the 1960s, Susan Ridgely Bales, "Decentering Sin: First Reconciliation and the Nurturing of Post-Vatican II Catholics" (606–34). Bales also has published a helpful ethnographic study: *When I Was a Child: Children's Interpretations of First Communion* (Chapel Hill: University of North Carolina Press, 2005). The best historical work on the culture of Catholic childhood to appear so far is chapter 3, "Material Children: Making God's Presence Real for Catholic Boys and Girls and for the Adults in Relation to Them," in Orsi, *Between Heaven and Earth*, 73–109, though many other studies of schools and women religious include relevant information. The quotation is from Joseph M. Hawes and N. Ray Hiner, "Hidden in Plain View: The History of Children (and Childhood) in the Twenty-First Century," in *Journal of the History of Childhood and Youth* 1.1 (2008): 43. See also Joseph M. Hawes and N. Ray Hiner, "Reflection on the History of Children and Childhood in the Postmodern Era," in *Major Problems in the History of American Families and Children*, ed. Anya Jabour (New York: Houghton Mifflin, 2005), 23–31.

4. Steven Mintz, *Huck's Raft: A History of American Childhood* (Cambridge, MA: Harvard University Press, 2004), viii, 3. For a slightly different periodization see Karin Calvert, *Children in the House: The Material Culture of Early Childhood, 1600–1900* (Boston: Northeastern University Press, 1992). On parental anxiety, see Peter N. Stearns, *Anxious Parents: A History of Modern Childrearing in America* (New York: New York University Press, 2003).

5. Mintz, *Huck's Raft*, 3–4, 214.

6. Ibid., 293, 275–76, 279, 282, 284, 292. Benjamin Spock, *The Common Sense Book of Baby and Child Care* (New York: Duell, Sloan, and Pearce, 1946), 19. See also Julia Grant, *Raising Baby by the Book: The Education of American Mothers* (New Haven, CT: Yale University Press, 1998). "The Shrine You Can Build," *Treasure Chest of Fun and Fact* 9.7 (December 3, 1953): 18–19, copy in Archives, ACUA.

7. *Topix* 8.29 (May 8, 1950). This was a weekly comic published by the Catechetical Guild Educational Society in St. Paul, Minnesota.

8. Ibid.

9. Orsi, "Material Children," 76, 79. John T. McGreevy, *Catholicism and American Freedom: A History* (New York: Norton, 2003), 12–13. For another helpful account

of ultramontanism, see Nicholas Atkin and Frank Tallett, *Priests, Prelates, and People: A History of European Catholicism since 1750* (New York: Oxford University Press, 2003), 130–41.

10. Lelia Hardin Bugg, *The Correct Thing for Catholics* (New York: Benziger Brothers, 1892), 148. Charles B. Broschart, "A Shrine to Our Lady in Every Home," *Ave Maria*, December 5, 1953, 12–13. The passage from Peyton's remarks is quoted in Richard Gribble, CSC, *American Apostle of the Family Rosary: The Life of Patrick J. Peyton, CSC* (New York: Crossroad, 2005), 41. For a related wartime effort by a Dominican who portrayed Jesus as "our Commander-in-Chief" and Mary as "Queen of Peace," see the pamphlet "by a Dominican Father," *The Rosary Crusade* (New York: National Headquarters of the Holy Name Society), 1943, copy in Catholic Pamphlet Collection, Special Collections, ND.

11. Gary Wills, "Memories of a Catholic Boyhood," in *American Catholic History: A Documentary Reader*, ed. Mark Massa, with Catherine Osborne (New York: New York University Press, 2008), 263–271.

12. The 1933 yearbook of St. Joseph's Commercial School in Brooklyn, which has no title, though other editions in other years were called *The Parmentier*, and no pagination, is in the school archives at St. Joseph's. I am grateful to Sister Eugenia, principal when I visited the school in 2007. She generously allowed me to view and copy the yearbooks and Lane's letter: Virginia Walsh Lane to Sister Eugenia, March 30, 1995, Archives, St. Joseph's School, Brooklyn. In later years, some of St. Joseph's alumnae remembered the school in their legal wills, as did Kathryn M. Cleary, a former stenographer from the class of 1925 who left the school a sizeable portion of her estate. Sister Eugenia also gave me a copy of Cleary's will, which can be found in the principal's official records: Kathryn M. Cleary, Last Will and Testament, May 12, 1986. After dispersing funds to various individuals and groups, including St. Thomas Aquinas School, which she also attended, Cleary's will allocated 20 percent of the remaining estate to St. Joseph's.

13. Atkin and Tallett, *Priests, Prelates, and People*, 162, 204. The quotations from "The Acts and Decrees of the Third Plenary Council of Baltimore" are taken from excerpts in *Creative Fidelity: American Catholic Intellectual Traditions*, ed. R. Scott Appleby, Patricia Byrne, and William L. Portier (Maryknoll, NY: Orbis, 2004), 83–89. On the Council as a response to "complaints and appeals," see Patrick W. Carey, *The Roman Catholics* (Westport, CT: Greenwood Press, 1993), 51. My account of the attendees is taken from Michael J. Roach, "Provincial and Plenary Councils of Baltimore," in *The Encyclopedia of American Catholic History*, ed. Michael Glazier and Thomas J. Shelley (Collegeville, MN: Liturgical Press, 1997), 1175–77. Slightly different statistics are in Peter Guilday, ed., *The National Pastorals of the American Hierarchy, 1792–1919* (Westminster, MD, 1954), 226.

14. The information on Finan is noted in Joseph J. Burns, "The Educational Efforts and Influences of the International Federation of Catholic Alumnae" (M.A. Thesis, CUA, 1937), 10. Mintz notes the "centralization" of Catholic schools in the 1920s: *Huck's Raft*, 205. The statistics about parochial school attendance are in Timothy Walch, *Parish School: American Catholic Parochial Education from Colonial Times to the Present* (New York: Crossroad Press, 1996), 1.

15. On the Baltimore Catechism, and the genre more broadly, see Berard L. Marthaler, *The Catechism Yesterday and Today: The Evolution of a Genre* (Collegeville, MN: Liturgical Press, 1995). As Marthaler notes, Monsignor Januarius de Concilio was the pastor who drafted the catechism, and Bishop John L. Spalding, who retained the copyright, did the final editing. Berard L. Marthaler, "The Baltimore Catechism,"

in Glazier and Shelley, *Encyclopedia of American Catholic History*, 122–23. On the missal, see for example the Reverend Hugo H. Hoever, ed., *Saint Joseph Daily Missal*, rev. ed. (New York: Catholic Book, 1956). The quotation about the catechism's popularity is from Jay P. Dolan, *The American Catholic Experience* (Notre Dame, IN: University of Notre Dame Press, 1992), 391.

16. The quotations and references to the Baltimore Catechism are from a reprint of the 1933 Benziger Brothers edition: *A Catechism of Christian Doctrine Prepared and Enjoined by the Third Plenary Council of Baltimore, No. 2* (Rockford, IL: Tan Books, 1977), Prayer before Mass (77), Question 415 (74), and Question 395 (71).

17. The Brooklyn Catholic schools didn't prescribe any single catechism but allowed the use of either Thomas O'Brien's *My First Catechism* (Cincinnati: Benziger Brothers, 1912) or the Baltimore Catechism. On this see William Leonard Richert, "The Brooklyn Diocesan Curriculum for the Elementary Schools from the Viewpoint of Principles of Curriculum Construction" (M.A. Thesis, CUA, 1930), 42. Marthaler, "Baltimore Catechism." *A Catechism of Christian Doctrine Prepared and Enjoined by the Third Plenary Council of Baltimore, No. 2*, Question 123 (25), Question 128 (25), Question 131 (26).

18. On guardian angels see Orsi, *Heaven and Earth*, 103–6. *A Catechism of Christian Doctrine Prepared and Enjoined by the Third Plenary Council of Baltimore, No. 2*, Morning Prayers (76), Hymns (92), Question 308 (57), Question 50 (13).

19. Edward A. Pace and Thomas E. Shields, *Religion: First Book* (Washington, DC: Catholic Correspondence School, 1908), 82. Roderick MacEachen, *Religion: First Manual*, MacEachen's Course in Religion (New York: Macmillan, 1921), 170. The Reverend Anthony J. Flynn, Sister Vincent Loretto, and Mother Mary Simeon, *The Way, the Truth, and the Life*, bk. 1, Catholic High School Religion Series (New York: W. H. Sadlier, 1956), 266. The Catholic children who attended public school and went to Confraternity of Christian Doctrine classes at the parish received similar messages in their textbooks; for example, see the Reverend Ferdinand C. Falque, *Catholic Truth in Survey: A Textbook for the Use of Confraternity of Christian Doctrine Classes at the Secondary School Level of Learning* (New York: Benziger Brothers, 1937). For an example from the 1950s see the series used in the Archdiocese of Chicago, including the advice for instructors: *Christian Belief: Teacher Manual*, Public High School Religion Course (Chicago: Confraternity of Christian Doctrine, Archdiocese of Chicago, 1959).

20. Pace and Shields, *Religion: First Book*, 91. MacEachen, *Religion: First Manual*, vi, xi. Flynn et al., *Way, Truth, and Life*, bk. 1, 193. Sister Jane Marie Murray, OP, *Growth in His Likeness*, bk. 3, Christian Life Series (Chicago: Fides Publishers Association, 1957), 279. For a biographical account see Mary Kay Ooskdyke, "Jane Marie Murray," in *Encyclopedia of American Catholic History*, 993. See also Mary Kay Ooskdyke, "The Christ Life Series in Religion (1934–35): Liturgy and Experience as Formative Influences in Religious Education," Ph.D. dissertation, Boston College, 1987.

21. Pace and Shields, *Religion*, 89. The Reverend Raymond J. Campion, *Religion: A Secondary School Course: Book One* (New York: William H. Sadlier, 1928), 6–7. Flynn, Loretto, and Simeon, *The Way, the Truth, and the Life*, 39–40, 291.

22. Office of the Diocesan Superintendent, *Course of Study for the Catholic Elementary Schools*, September 1928, Archives, Diocese of Brooklyn. The Superintendent's Office regularly updated the list of approved texts, and those documents also can be found in the archives. For example, see *Approved List of Textbooks for the Catholic Elementary Schools*, Diocese of Brooklyn, Effective September 1949, 5th complete ed. (Brooklyn: Office of the Diocesan Superintendent, 1949), copy in Archives, Diocese of Brooklyn. Comparative statistics about allotment of time for subjects

from "Time Allotments in the Elementary School Subjects," City School Leaflet no. 19, February 1925, Department of the Interior, Bureau of Education, Washington, D.C. Rickert calculated the corresponding information for the Brooklyn Diocese in 1930: Rickert, "Brooklyn Diocesan Curriculum," 37. The numbers are drawn from periods that are five years apart, but they offer some help in placing the Catholic schools in a wider cultural context of education in the United States. On secondary schools, Maguire's survey included information about the time allotted to religion: Maguire, "Catholic Secondary Education in the Diocese of Brooklyn," 59. The Diocese of Brooklyn was one of the largest in the United States, with more than nine hundred thousand parishioners attending almost four hundred churches, including three dozen "national" parishes, most of them Italian, German, and Polish. By 1900, many Brooklyn parishes had established parochial schools, including St. Thomas Aquinas, and the Diocese almost doubled the number of high schools between 1900 and 1930, when there were more than ten thousand students in thirty-eight secondary schools, including commercial high schools like St. Joseph's. In 1928, the year they contributed, all of the 391 students at the girls-only St. Joseph's Commercial School were girls, but the ratio was more balanced at St. Thomas Aquinas elementary school: there were 417 boys and 425 girls. Nine Sisters of St. Joseph worked with eight lay teachers at St. Thomas Aquinas that year, while fourteen nuns from the same order taught at St. Joseph's Commercial School. One survey at that time revealed that the majority of high school instructors, 63 percent, were women. Lay teachers made up about one-quarter of the 495 teachers, and 51 percent were male or female members of religious orders. A little more than half of the teachers in Brooklyn's Catholic secondary schools were nuns. So women, especially nuns, did form a large proportion of the Catholic school teachers—and the proportions were much higher in the elementary schools—though perhaps not enough to simply assume, as many textbook authors did when they routinely used the feminine pronoun "she" in teachers manuals, that the children were interacting only with women in the classroom. For information about the Diocese of Brooklyn's schools, two studies were invaluable: Rickert, "The Brooklyn Diocesan Curriculum," and Maguire, "Catholic Secondary Education in the Diocese of Brooklyn." Maguire did a survey of schools in the Diocese as part of his study, and I take the information in here from that source (4, 31, 13, 25) and from *The Official Catholic Directory* (New York: P. J. Kennedy, 1928), 233–43. On the presuppositions about teachers' gender, in his preface to MacEachen, *Religion: First Manual*, Shahan assumed a female instructor: "*She* engages the children in conversation" (vi); Pace and Shields made the same assumption in *Religion: First Book*: "The resourceful teacher will naturally use her own methods and it is well that *she* be given the fullest freedom in doing so" (96) (my emphases). On the educational institutions established by the Sisters of St. Joseph, I'm indebted to Sister Edna McKeever, Office of the Archives, St. Joseph's Convent, Brentwood, New York, for information she communicated in a letter: Edna M. McKeever, CSJ, to author, November 20, 2006. I also examined bookkeeping records that the school's principal, Sister Eugenia, generously showed me in 2007. The records for the 1920s, which included student names, guardian names, and payments submitted, tracked how much money each enrolled student paid each month, including the students I list on appendix 3.2 and discuss below.

23. Maguire, "Catholic Secondary Education in the Diocese of Brooklyn," 49. On the Sodality of the Blessed Virgin, and its director from 1925 to 1948, Daniel Aloysius Lord, see Arnold Sparr, *To Promote, Defend, and Redeem: The Catholic Literary Revival and the Cultural Transformation of American Catholicism, 1920–1960*

(Westport, CT: Greenwood Press, 1990), 31–50. Another image from the same collection as fig. 3.4—photograph no. 465, Philadelphia Archdiocesan Historical Records Center—offers another glimpse of the procession: three older altar boys in front are joking among themselves; the middle boy carries a crucifix, and the other two boys hold candles. Immediately behind them, three very young boys, dressed in white suits, hold their hands together in a prayerful position. Other boys, partially blocked from view, carry two flags, and in the distance the rest of the procession walks up the paved path. For another account of May Crownings, see Gina Cascone, *Pagan Babies and Other Catholic Memories* (New York: St. Martin's, 1982), 125–30. On memoirs see Elizabeth N. Evasdaughter, *Catholic Girlhood Narratives: The Church and Self-Denial* (Boston: Northeastern University Press, 1996).

24. After my interview with Marie Moringiello Mastromarino, whom I first spoke with in Brooklyn, she continued her recollections via e-mail: Marie Moringiello Mastromarino to author, July 10 (two e-mails), July 11, 2007 (two e-mails). Helen Morton, "May Crowning,"in *The 1942 Parmentier*, yearbook, Archives, St. Joseph's Commercial High School, Brooklyn. The information about the students and nuns at St. Joseph's in 1953 is taken from *The Official Catholic Directory* (New York: P. J. Kennedy, 1953), 284. That volume also reported the numbers of students (485 boys and 447 girls) and instructors (14 Sisters of St. Joseph and 4 lay teachers) in that year, about the same as in the 1920s, though there was a higher proportion of women religious in the classroom (279).

25. The phrase "acts of sacrifice and service" appears on the Mary's Day pledge cards and on the list of donors who gave to the Mary Memorial Altar: "Individual Contributions to Fund of International Federation of Catholic Alumnae for Mary Altar," November 19, 1927, Archives, BNSIC.

26. Martha Manning, *Chasing Grace: Reflections of a Catholic Girl Grown Up* (San Francisco: HarperSanFrancisco, 1996), 141. "Our Collectors Circle," *SR* 8.6 (June 1921): 46. "Collector's Circle," *SR* 9.8 (August 1922): 62.

27. The quotations are from, in order, "Our Collector's Circle," *SR* 6.6 (September 1919): 46. "Collector's Circle," *SR* 11.8 (August 1924): 70. "Mary's Power," *SR* 6.7 (November 1919): 52. "Our Collector's Circle," *SR* 8.6 (June 1921): 46. "Thoughts of Devotion from Far and Near," *SR* 8.2 (February 1921): 14.

28. "Mary's Power," *SR* 6.7 (November 1919): 52. "Our Collector's Circle," *SR* 7.5 (August 1920): 38; "Our Collector's Circle," *SR* 7.2 (March 1920): 14; "Our Collector's Circle," *SR* 8.2 (February 1921): 10; "Our Collector's Circle," *SR* 12.10 (October 1925): 78. "Our Collector's Circle," *SR* 8.5 (August 1920): 38.

29. I created the sample shown in appendix 3.2 by selecting every fifth name on the 1928 donor list, and the federal census records yielded the information tabulated for each name.

30. Here and elsewhere, when I make comparisons with the national average I'm referring to federal census records and the statistical reports that followed. The information about median family size, median value of owned home, and median monthly rental cost can be found in *Fifteenth Census of the United States, 1930*, Vol. 6, *Families* (Washington, DC: Government Printing Office, 1933), 7.

31. Jeanette Cornely: *Fifteenth Census of the United States, 1930*, Brooklyn, Kings, New York; roll 1515; p. 11B; enumeration district 607; image 744.0. Edna Brennan: *Fifteenth Census of the United States, 1930*, Brooklyn, Kings, New York; roll 1515; p. 5A; enumeration district 617; image 1009.0. Alberto Annuziata: *Fifteenth Census of the United States, 1930*, Brooklyn, Kings, New York; roll 1507; p. 7A; enumeration

district 1746; image 377.0. Paul Martello: *Fifteenth Census of the United States, 1930*, Brooklyn, Kings, New York; roll 1507; p. 9B; enumeration district 1094; image 398.0. Gabriel Brilante: *Fifteenth Census of the United States, 1930*, Brooklyn, Kings, New York; roll 1515; p. 2B; enumeration district 606; image 696.0. Catherine Murphy: *Fifteenth Census of the United States, 1930*, Brooklyn, Kings, New York; roll 1515; p. 14A; enumeration district 606; image 719.0. On Catherine Murphy's recognition see "Star Pupils in the Catholic Schools," *Tablet* (Brooklyn), 24 (May 15, 1926), 16. This was the final Honor Roll report for that academic year.

32. Margaret Hamma, *Fourteenth Census of the United States, 1920*, Brooklyn, Kings, New York; roll T625_1151; p. 1B; enumeration district 276; image 926. Veronica Jensen: *Fifteenth Census of the United States, 1930*, Brooklyn, Kings, New York; roll 1505; p. 24B; enumeration district 102B; image 529.0. Cecelia McCarthy: *Fourteenth Census of the United States, 1920*, Brooklyn, Kings, New York; roll T625_1144; p. 3B; enumeration district 35; image 477. Christine Connolly: *Fourteenth Census of the United States, 1920*, Brooklyn, Kings, New York; roll T625_1159; p. 9A; enumeration district 539; image 39. Viola Gallagher: *Fifteenth Census of the United States, 1930*, Brooklyn, Kings, New York; roll 1509; p. 15B; enumeration district 1148; image 714. Helen Gandolfi: *Fifteenth Census of the United States, 1930*, Brooklyn, Kings, New York; roll 1509; p. 6B; enumeration district 1155; image 972.0. Loretta Zimmerman: *Fifteenth Census of the United States, 1930*, Brooklyn, Kings, New York; roll 1506; p. 4B; enumeration district 1052; image 299.0. Helen Gorman: *Fifteenth Census of the United States, 1930*, Brooklyn, Kings, New York; roll 1509; p. 4A; enumeration district 1153; image 883.0.

33. On William Smith's entry, and the other pilgrims I mention, see Register of Visitors to the National Shrine, June 1926 to August 1927, Archives, BNSIC. For this biographical data see William F. Smith: *Fifteenth Census of the United States, 1930*, Washington, District of Columbia, roll 303; p. 8A; enumeration district 357; image 179.0.

34. Register of Visitors to the National Shrine, June 1926 to August 1927, Archives, BNSIC. James P. McAndrew: *Fifteenth Census of the United States, 1930*, Brooklyn, Kings, New York; roll 2048; p. 1A; enumeration district 99; image 139.0. William and Clement McLaughlin: *Fifteenth Census of the United States, 1930*, Brooklyn, Kings, New York; roll 1487; p. 3B; enumeration district 623; image 304.0. Marsella and Rose Urziehart: *Fifteenth Census of the United States, 1930*, Brooklyn, Kings, New York; roll 878; p. 10A; enumeration district 51; image 712.0. Eileen, Thomas, and William Kelly: *Fifteenth Census of the United States, 1930*, Brooklyn, Kings, New York; roll 858; p. 4B; enumeration district 214; image 10.0.

35. On the visits of the Boy Scouts on January 1, 1930, and the Girl Scouts on May 12, 1930, see Mckenna's own records: Shrine Day Book, 1929–1930, Archives, BNSIC. Father McKenna also communicated with the leader of the boys' troop: Hilliard B. Holbrook to Bernard McKenna, January 9, 1930, Boy Scouts of America file, McKenna Collection, Archives, BNSIC. On the Michigan public schools and the Camden Catholic school see "Shrine Notes," *SR* 15.7 (July 1928): 51. McKenna noted the visit of the Children of Mary in his own records: Shrine Day Book, 1929–1930, Archives, BNSIC. That book actually includes references to visits and events starting in 1926. *SR* also described their pilgrimage: "Children of Mary," *SR* 12.8 (August 1925): 60; "Our Children of Mary," *SR* 13.8 (August 1926): 63. On the athletic and spiritual event in 1926 see "May Day Games," *SR* 13.7 (July 1926): 52. For the visit of the students from Girls Catholic High School see both McKenna's Shrine Day Book, 1929–1930, and *SR* 13.6 (June 1926): 46. The

visitor's log also includes evidence of their visit, as I've noted: Register of Visitors to the National Shrine, June 1926 to August 1927, Archives, BNSIC. Viola Conley: *Fourteenth Census of the United States, 1920*, Brooklyn, Kings, New York; roll T625_1633; p. 3A; enumeration district 958; image 365.

36. "Children Will Help Provide United States with Great Shrine," Release Number One, National Shrine of the Immaculate Conception Appeal, folder: Appeals 1953: Public Relations, box: Appeals, 1953–1954, Archives, BNSIC.

37. "Interview with Archbishop O'Hara," *Lamp unto My Feet*, November 29, 1953, p. 6, Archives, BNSIC. "The Shrine You Can Build," *Treasure Chest of Fun and Fact* 9.6, (November 19, 1953): 2, copy in Archives, ACUA. "The Shrine You Can Build," *Treasure Chest of Fun and Fact* 9.7 (November 19, 1953): 18–19, copy in Archives, ACUA.

38. *Handbook for Teachers*, Appeal for National Shrine of the Immaculate Conception, undated pamphlet [1953], 12 pp., copy in folder: "1953 Promotional Materials," box: Appeals, 1953–1954, BNSIC. I found the author of the handbook, and the number of copies distributed, mentioned in John F. Noll, "Report on the Appeal of the National Shrine of the Immaculate Conception," January 12, 1954," John F. Noll Papers, ND. On Synon's important work for the mislabeled Commission on American Citizenship, which produced a three-volume curriculum guide and a series of eight "Faith and Freedom Readers" that were "used in American Catholic elementary schools for more than two decades," see C. Joseph Nuesse, *The Catholic University of America: A Centennial History* (Washington, DC: Catholic University of America Press, 1990), 297–98.

39. "The National Shrine of the Immaculate Conception," *Treasure Chest of Fun and Fact* 15.7 (December 3, 1959): 31–34, 36, copy in Archives, ACUA. The information about donors I cite is from Book 42: July 1953 to July 30, 1954, donor record book (typescript), Archives, BNSIC. All of the donations I mention were sent after the start of the appeal to children in November 1953. An image of the exterior of the Shrine also appears in a November 16, 1971, issue of another comic: the syndicated comic strip *The Phantom*, by Lee Falk and Seymour Berry. As Shrine archivist Dr. Geraldine Rohling noticed in an unpublished note in the archives, "The Shrine appears at what was the entrance to the 'lost city' after it had arisen from its ashes for a 'single night.'"

40. "Shrine Jottings," *SR* 17 (November 1956): 7. The oral history about the pilgrimage is from one face-to-face conversation on April 17, 2007, and from James M. O'Toole to author, e-mails, January 8 and 15, 2008. I am grateful to James O'Toole for generously sharing this family story.

41. "Nation's Pilgrims Visit Shrine," *SR* 15 (May 1954): 1.

42. "Children United to Honor Their Heavenly Mother," *SR* 14 (November 1953): 8. A photograph of the 1957 visitors from the five schools in New York, Connecticut, and New Jersey and the mention of Parker Tours are in *SR* 18.2 (May 1957): 7. The BNSIC archivist, Geraldine Rohling, identified the school and date shown in fig. 3.5.

43. The Right Reverend Monsignor Thomas J. Grady, Director, to Mother M. de Pazzi, Provincial Superior, November 2, 1964, Sisters of St. Joseph, Provincial Archives, West Hartford, Connecticut. I'm grateful to Sister Mary Jane Garry, CSJ, who shared with me many documents about the order's communications with Shrine officials, especially about the dome windows. Those records also show that the nuns who had responsibility for the two Brooklyn schools, the Sisters of St. Joseph in Brentwood, also contributed to those dome windows. On that see the list of the

various communities that contributed, "Memorial Windows—National Shrine of the Immaculate Conception," Sisters of St. Joseph, Provincial Archives, which included payments made as of April 29, 1969, and was sent by the next director, Monsignor William F. McDonough, to Mother de Pazzi, the coordinator of the collection efforts.

CHAPTER 4

1. Charles D. Maginnis to Bishop Thomas J. Shahan, June 29, 1926, Architects correspondence, Archives, BNSIC. In that handwritten letter, the architect was thinking most directly of his recent plans for the altar that would go in the Crypt Church, the one dedicated to Our Lady of the Catacombs. James Cardinal Gibbons, *The Faith of Our Fathers: A Exposition and Vindication of the Church Founded by Our Lord Jesus Christ*, 83rd ed. (1917; reprint, Rockford, IL: Tan Books, 1980) (originally published 1876), xi, 139. Thomas J. Shahan, *The Blessed Virgin in the Catacombs* (Baltimore: John Murphy, 1892), 79.

2. The adjectival use of the term—"catacombal"—appears in several published and unpublished sources, including "Pewabic Tiles to Decorate Crypt in Beautiful Shrine in Washington," *Detroit News*, April 19, 1925. That piece was reprinted in *SR*: "Pewabic Tiles to Decorate Crypt of Beautiful Shrine," *SR* 12.6 (June 1925): 43–48.

3. On the rise and fall of the so-called mainline Protestant establishment, see William R. Hutchison, *Between the Times: The Travail of the Protestant Establishment in America* (Cambridge: Cambridge University Press, 1989).

4. Stephen Bann, "Meaning," in *Critical Terms for Art History*, ed. Robert S. Nelson and Richard Shiff (Chicago: University of Chicago Press, 2003), 128. The useful distinction between a building's "immediate impact," as opposed to the "gradual accumulation of impressions," is discussed by Richard Kieckhefer, who also outlines three primary traditions of church building—the classic sacramental church, the classic evangelical church, and the modern communal church. The BNSIC is an example of the first type, according to his typology. Richard Kieckhefer, *Theology in Stone: Church Architecture from Byzantium to Berkeley* (New York: Oxford University Press, 2004), 10–11. He also refers to Santa Maria Maggiore (11–12), as Shahan also did in his *Blessed Virgin in the Catacombs*, 64–73. The prominent landscape architectural firm Olmsted and Olmsted was hired to review an existing survey of the proposed campus of CUA, and in 1922 John Charles Olmsted (1852–1920) and Frederick Law Olmsted, Jr. (1870–1957) submitted their plans, which included a recommendation about where to place the Shrine. Those plans can be found in two archives: "General Plan for the Catholic University of America—Washington D.C.," April 1, 1922, ser. 5, Olmsted Brothers: Landscape Architects, folder 1, Frederick Law Olmsted Architectural Drawings and Plans, Division of Rare and Manuscript Collections, Cornell University Library, Ithaca, New York; Olmsted Brothers (Landscape Architects), 1917–1922, Thomas J. Shahan Papers, subser. 2.3, box 19, folder 12, Archives, ACUA. The assistant architect, Frederick Murphy, recalled their participation this way: "A preliminary survey of the whole University premises was made by a company named Brown. Immediately afterwards, this survey was studied by a firm of landscape engineers called Olmsted. It was this company that recommended the present site for the National Shrine. Mr. Olmsted was not a Catholic and the Shrine idea did not mean much to him... He thought of it as a large church to be used by all the religious

houses and the University." "Conversation with Mr. Fred V. Murphy, September 9, 1957, Architects: Maginnis, Walsh, and Murphy," Archives, BNSIC.

5. Paul Mattick, Jr., makes the observation about the tendency in the past few decades to consider the social and political context of art in this essay "Context," and Craig Clunas makes the same point about "context" in his essay "Social History of Art," both in Nelson and Shiff, *Critical Terms for Art History*, 112, 465.

6. There is now a large secondary literature about Catholic-Protestant relations and anti-Catholicism in particular. I cite some of those books in later notes. Here are some helpful works: Ray Allen Billington, *The Protestant Crusade, 1800–1860: A Study of the Origins of American Nativism* (New York: Macmillan, 1938); Jenny Franchot, *Roads to Rome: The Antebellum Protestant Encounter with Catholicism* (Berkeley: University of California Press, 1994); Mark Massa, *Anti-Catholicism in America: The Last Acceptable Prejudice* (New York: Crossroad Press, 2003); Philip Jenkins, *The New Anti-Catholicism: The Last Acceptable Prejudice* (New York: Oxford University Press, 2003); Justin Nordstrom, *Danger on the Doorstep: Anti-Catholicism and American Print Culture in the Progressive Era* (Notre Dame, IN: University of Notre Dame Press, 2006). Another provocative work challenges several presuppositions about the history of Roman Catholic traditions in the United States and, most relevant to my interests here, offers a broader claim—that scholarship about U.S. religion also shows "the continuing influence of a 'Protestant imagination'": Michael P. Carroll, *American Catholics in the Protestant Imagination: Rethinking the Academic Study of Religion* (Baltimore: Johns Hopkins University Press, 2007), ix.

7. For an undated historic photograph of the Soldiers' Home Chapel, see "U.S. Soldiers Home, Chapel Rock Creek Church Road and Upshur Street Northwest, Washington, District of Columbia," Library of Congress, Historic Buildings Survey, HABS DC. WASH, 534G. "Open to All Sects: No Denominational Line in the Soldier's Home Chapel," *Washington Post*, December 5, 1903, p. 14. For examples of how the two chaplains alternated duties for Memorial Day services see "Soldiers' Home Exercises," *Washington Post*, May 31, 1910, p. 2; and "Honors to Soldier Dead to Be Paid by Grateful Nation," *Washington Post*, May 30, 1912, p. 5. The coverage of Easter services appeared as "Anthems of Praise Proclaim the Easter Joy Today," *Washington Post*, March 23, 1913, p. 10.

8. On converts, see Patrick Allitt, *Catholic Converts: British and American Intellectuals Turn to Rome* (Ithaca, NY: Cornell University Press, 1997). Every survey of U.S. Catholicism discusses the converts I identify here, and Patrick W. Carey's fine narrative has the advantage that it also includes brief biographical sketches, including entries on the three converts I mention. Patrick W. Carey, *The Roman Catholics* (Westport, CT: Greenwood Press, 1993), 181–83, 236–37, 305–6. For scholarly assessments about Mary in scripture see Raymond Brown, Karl P. Donfried, Joseph A. Fitzmeyer, and John Reumann, eds., *Mary in the New Testament: A Collaborative Assessment by Protestant and Roman Catholic Scholars* (Philadelphia: Fortress Press, 1978). On literary appropriations of Mary by the writers I mention, see John Gatta, *American Madonna: Images of the Divine Woman in Literary Culture* (New York: Oxford University Press, 1997). On the ways fiction had anti-Catholic impulses, see Susan M. Griffin, *Anti-Catholicism and Nineteenth-Century Fiction* (Cambridge: Cambridge University Press, 2004). There is also a relevant dissertation: James Emmett Ryan, "Inventing Catholicism: Nineteenth-Century Literary History and the Contest for American Religion" (Ph.D. diss., University of North Carolina at Chapel Hill, 2000). On domestic furnishings and architecture,

including Protestant appropriations of Gothic design, see Colleen McDannell, *The Christian Home in Victorian America* (Bloomington: Indiana University Press, 1986). On church architecture, see Ryan K. Smith, *Gothic Arches, Latin Crosses: Anti-Catholicism and American Church Designs in the Nineteenth Century* (Chapel Hill: University of North Carolina Press, 2006). I found the magazine articles I cite here in a search of periodical literature from the middle of the nineteenth century to the first decade of the twentieth. I could cite dozens of other examples. H. B. Smith, "Dogma of the Immaculate Conception," *Methodist Quarterly Review* 15.4 (1855): 275. C. E. W. Dobbs, "Mariolatry: The Virgin Mary," *Baptist Review* 3 (1881): 331. A. A. Sewall, "Madonna and Child: A Poem," *Harper's New Monthly Magazine* 90 (1894–95): 14. "Mrs. S. C. Brown, "Virgin Mary," *Hours at Home* 5 (1867): 506. Mary Bell, "Titian's Dream Madonna," *Overland Monthly* 33 (1899): 48. For the insight about the influence of Mary on American gender ideology, I'm indebted to an unpublished paper: Elizabeth Hayes Alvarez, "The Queen of Heaven and the Angel in the House: The Influence of the Catholic Mary on Nineteenth-Century American Gender Ideology," presented at the conference "Religious Identities," Boston College, March 15, 2008. I'm very grateful to the author for sharing that paper with me.

9. E. K. Washington, *Echoes of Europe; Or, Word Pictures of Travel* (Philadelphia: J. Challen & Son, 1860), 641. This travelogue and others are cited and quoted in Alvarez, "Queen of Heaven," 5. "Shrine Notes and Events Starting May 1, 1926," in Shrine Day Book, 1929–1930, Archives, BNSIC. "National Shrine Notes," *SR* 13.4 (April 1926): 31.

10. "A Protestant Tribute," *SR* 3.1 (July 1916): 6. "A Protestant Tribute to Mary," *SR* 8.7 (July 1921): 49.

11. "A Convert," *SR* 9.7 (July 1922): 54. "A Convert's Praise," *SR* 11.7 (July 1924): 62.

12. "Our Collector's Circle," *SR* 5.5 (Aug. 1918): 38. "Non-Catholic Devotion," *SR* 12.11 (November 1925): 87. The local newspaper also noted Protestant donors to Catholic causes. One story reported that twenty-seven Protestants contributed to Catholic institutions: "$500,000,000 for Catholics: Gifts to Church in the United States Reached Half-Billion Mark Last Year," *Washington Post*, January 20, 1913, p. 12.

13. On St. Susanna, who is often linked with Tiburtius because their names appear on the same day in the martyrology, see "Tiburtius and Susanna," in David Hugh Farmer, *The Oxford Dictionary of Saints*, 4th ed. (New York: Oxford University Press, 1997). On Susanna and Sigourney Fay, I consulted newspapers from Washington, Philadelphia, and New York and government documents, including census records, passport applications, ship passenger lists, and (for Sigourney) draft registrations. The information I cite about the family in 1880 is from "Susan H. Fay," U.S. Bureau of the Census, *Tenth Census of the United States, 1880*, Philadelphia, Pennsylvania; roll T9_1188; p. 81.3000; enumeration district 616. F. Scott Fitzgerald, *This Side of Paradise* (New York: Scribner's, 1920). For brief biographical notes see "Sketch of Sigourney W. Fay," *Records of the American Catholic Historical Society* 33.1 (March 1922): 253–54; and Nuesse, *Catholic University of America*, 215. "Mgr. Sigourney W. Fay Dies," *New York Times*, January 11, 1919, p. 13. "Stand in Silent Tribute," *New York Times*, January 12, 1919, p. 25. That civic group was the League for Political Education, which had been founded the previous year. See "New Civic Club Planned," *New York Times*, February 24, 1918. "Changes Religious Faith: The Reverend Sigourney Fay Leaves Episcopal Church for Catholic Body," *New York Times*, May 15, 1908. Many scholars have noted the links

between Fitzgerald and Fay. See Tracy Fessenden, *Culture and Redemption: Religion, the Secular, and American Literature* (Princeton, NJ: Princeton University Press, 2007), 181–212. See also Joan M. Allen, *Candles and Carnival Lights: The Catholic Sensibility of F. Scott Fitzgerald* (New York: New York University Press, 1978); and Steven Frye, "Fitzgerald's Catholicism Revisited: The Eucharistic Element in *The Beautiful and the Damned*," in *F. Scott Fitzgerald: New Perspectives*, ed. Jackson R. Bryer, Alan Margolies, and Ruth Priogozy (Athens: University of Georgia Press, 2000), 63–77.

14. "Chapel at Shrine to Mgr. S. W. Fay Gift of Mother: Non-Catholic Woman Donates Memorial at Catholic U. to Distinguished Son," *Washington Post*, September 5, 1926, p. M9. "Announce Donors of Shrine Altars: Non-Catholic's Gift Is Memorial to Her Son Who Became a Priest," *SR* 13.4 (Apr. 1926): 30. *NS*, 151–53. *AC*, 67. On the same page Tucker also notes that Father Fay suggested the name for *Salve Regina*. *MEM*, 122. *GTB*, 47 (mentions the donation but omits the reference to Mrs. Fay's affiliation).

15. The books cited above about anti-Catholicism trace the rising and falling of hostility, and others have noticed that anti-Catholicism declined after the 1920s: John McGreevy has argued, for example, that "anti-Catholicism directed against Catholic individuals declined sharply after the 1920s, even as more subtle (and often anti-Catholic) prejudice against hierarchy and authority continued to shape American life." John T. McGreevy, *Catholicism and American Freedom: A History* (New York: Norton, 2003), 15.

16. Friend of Truth, *The Washington Miracle Refuted; Or, A Review of the Rev. Mr. Mathews's Pamphlet* (Georgetown, DC: James C. Dunn, Printer, 1824), 3. John F. Weishampel, Sr., *The Pope's Stratagem "Rome to America": An Address to the Protestants of the United States against Placing the Pope's Block of Marble in the Washington Monument* (Philadelphia, 1852), 7. The term "desecration" is used in the "Remarks to the Eighth Edition" (2). Notice of the theft, and the reward, appeared in "The Destruction of the Pope's Block of Marble," *New York Times*, April 7, 1854. Several recollections appeared later, in the 1880s, and for one of several stories that quote an alleged participant in the "vandalism" of the papal gift see "The Pope's Stone: How the Pontiff's Gift Was Stolen and Sunk in the Potomac," *Washington Post*, September 30, 1883, p. 1.

17. David J. Goldberg, *Discontented America: The United States in the 1920s* (Baltimore: Johns Hopkins University Press, 1999), xi, 151, 140–66. Marty E. Marty, *Modern American Religion: The Noise of Conflict, 1919–1941*, vol. 2 (Chicago: University of Chicago Press, 1991). The statistic about the number of U.S. Catholics in 1920 is taken from *The Official Catholic Directory* (New York: P. J. Kennedy, 1920).

18. H. W. Evans, *The Public School Problem in America: Outlining Fully the Policies and the Program of the Knights of Ku Klux Klan toward the Public School System* (Atlanta: KKK, 1924), 5, 13. "Ku Klan Thousands in Colorful Review as Conclave Opens," *Washington Post*, September 14, 1926, pp. 1, 4, 5. The Klan marched in D.C. in 1924 and 1925 too. For example, "Klan Color Guard Precedes Police Escort in Parade," *Washington Post*, August 9, 1925, p. 3. On the brief reemergence of the Klan in the 1920s, see Goldberg, *Discontented America*, 117–39.

19. "Mgr. Russell to the Rev. Dr. McKim," *Washington Post*, December 22, 1913, p. 13. "Randolph H. McKim," *Washington Post*, July 16, 1920, p. 6. Randolph H. McKim, *In Memoriam: A Sermon Preached on the Occasion of Robert E. Lee's Death* (Baltimore: George Lycett, 1870). Randolph H. McKim, *A Soldier's Recollections: Leaves from the Diary of a Young Confederate: With an Oration on the Motives and Aims of the*

Soldiers of the South (New York: Longmans, Green, 1910). Just after the public feud with Russell in 1913, McKim collected and reprinted those older criticisms of Catholicism, including the writings of 1879, 1897, and 1908. See Randolph H. McKim, *Romanism in the Light of History* (New York: Putnam, 1914).

20. The newspaper account of his lecture "Why We Are Protestants" appeared as "Worship in Freedom: Rev. R. H. McKim Makes Plea for Religious Liberty," *Washington Post*, December 15, 1913, p. 2. McKim repeated the martial images in his 1914 book, which he sent to press in April, and in which he included his 1879 series of talks "The Fundamental Principles of Protestantism": McKim, *Romanism*, 20, 163–244. He included his comments about the recent Catholic "aggressiveness" in that book (3). The notice about Bertand Conway's "mission" at St. Patrick's appeared as "Paulist to Open Retreat: Missionary to Conduct Fortnight Services in St. Patrick's Church," *Washington Post*, October 26, 1913, p. ES8. To get a sense of that Paulist priest's attitudes and approach, see Bertrand L. Conway, *The Question Box: Replies to Questions Received on Missions to Non-Catholics* (New York: Catholic Book Exchange, 1903).

21. Russell's final contribution to the debate was "Mgr. Russell to the Rev. Dr. McKim," *Washington Post*, December 22, 1913, p. 13. His earlier response, which included fifteen historical claims that he invited McKim to refute, and a challenge: the Catholic priest would donate $100 to a charity of McKim's choice for each false statement: "Mgr. Wm. T. Russell to Rev. Randoph McKim," *Washington Post*, December 17, 1913, p. 12. The paper also printed a story about Russell's comments: "Catholic Church Is Firm," *Washington Post*, October 13, 1913, p. 14. Another Catholic engaged McKim, too: "Replies to Rev. Dr. McKim: Catholics Here by Right of Discovery Says Francis de Sales Ryan," *Washington Post*, December 16, 1913, p. 11.

22. Notice of the clerical protest first appeared as "Protestant Clergy Protest: Object to 'Official Atmosphere' They Say Attends Thanksgiving Mass," *Washington Post*, November 19, 1913, p. 14. The announcement of the Thanksgiving mass was in "Services in the Churches," *Washington Post*, November 24, 1913, p. 10. The newspaper printed an interview with Russell: "Not 'Official' Mass: Mgr. Russell Gives Purpose of Thanksgiving Service," *Washington Post*, November 24, 1913, p. 14. McKim responded and repeated the resolution and his fear about the holiday becoming "a Roman Catholic festival": "Thanksgiving Day Mass," *Washington Post*, November 26, 1913, p. 10. The Catholic press was effusive in 1913, covering the last event that included a presidential visitor, but the Milwaukee archdiocesan newspaper that had hinted it was official the year before (and had irked Protestants) claimed only that "the Pan American Mass has become an annual event": "The Pan American Mass: Big Men of Nation Attend," *(Milwaukee) Catholic Herald*, November 29, 1913. On this controversy and the participants see James F. Vivian, "The Pan American Mass, 1909–1914: A Rejected Contribution to Thanksgiving Day," *Church History* 51.3 (September 1982): 321–33.

23. Arnold Sparr, *To Promote, Defend, and Redeem: The Catholic Literary Revival and the Cultural Transformation of American Catholicism, 1920–1960* (Westport, CT: Greenwood Press, 1990), 163. The quotations and references to the Baltimore Catechism are from a reprint of the 1933 Benziger Brothers edition: *A Catechism of Christian Doctrine Prepared and Enjoined by the Third Plenary Council of Baltimore, No. 2* (Rockford, IL: Tan Books, 1977), 53 (Question 288), 24 (Question 121). The Reverend Raymond J. Campion, *Religion: A Secondary School Course*, bk. 1 (New York: William H. Sadlier, 1928), 36.

24. Mary Elizabeth Brennan, "Federation Spirit," *Quarterly Bulletin* (IFCA) 6.1 (March 1923): 11. Lelia Hardin Bugg, *The Correct Thing for Catholics* (New York: Benziger Brothers, 1892), 5.

25. On Jews' "four broad strategies of survival"—"geographic mobility and relocation," "erection of Jewish infrastructures," "adaptation to the host environment," and "Jewish defense," see Benny Kraut, "Jewish Survival in Protestant America," in *Minority Faiths and the American Protestant Mainstream*, ed. Jonathan D. Sarna (Urbana: University of Illinois Press, 1998), 15–60. "Thousands of Catholics Will Visit Shrine Here: Pilgrims to Come as Protest against Questioning of Christ's Virgin Birth," *Washington Post*, April 27, 1924, p. ES7. "Pilgrimage to Protest Attack on Virgin Birth: 1,000 Knights of Columbus from New York Area to Visit National Shrine," *Washington Post*, May 18, 1924, p. 19.

26. Gibbons, *Faith of Our Fathers*, 7. Conway, *Question Box*. Bertran L. Conway, *Studies in Church History* (St. Louis: Herder, 1915). On the origin and use of a question box in 1893, and the shifts in evangelizing strategies among Conway and the Paulists, see Paul Robichaud, "Evangelizing America: Transformation in Paulist Mission," *U.S. Catholic Historian* 11.2 (spring 1993): 61–78. "Mgr. Wm. T. Russell to Rev. Randolph McKim," *Washington Post*, December 17, 1913, p. 12.

27. Gibbons, *Faith of Our Fathers*, 7, 149–50.

28. McKim, *Romanism in the Light of History*, 4. Gibbons, *Faith of Our Fathers*, xiv. Conway, *Studies in Church History*, preface.

29. Gibbons, *Faith of Our Fathers*, 46, 47, 146, 141.

30. Thomas J. Shahan, *The House of God and Other Addresses and Studies* (New York: Cathedral Library Association, 1905), 62, 63, 64.

31. Thomas J. Shahan, *Outline of Church History* (Washington, DC: New Century Press, 1902). Thomas J. Shahan, *The Middle Ages: Sketches and Fragments* (New York: Benziger Brothers, 1904), 5. Thomas J. Shahan, *The Beginnings of Christianity* (New York: Benziger Brothers, 1903), 10.

32. Otto Bardenhewer, *Patrology: The Lives and Works of the Fathers of the Church*, trans. Thomas J. Shahan (St. Louis, MO: B. Herder, 1908). Shahan, *Beginnings of Christianity*, 7, 9.

33. The length of the underground network is noted in "Catacombs," in *The Oxford Classical Dictionary*, 3rd ed., ed. Simon Hornblower and Antony Spawforth (Oxford: Oxford University Press, 1996), 302. Of course, neither Gibbons nor Shahan knew of the full extent of the catacombs when they wrote, since there were more excavations in the subsequent years. Gibbons, *Faith of Our Fathers*, 162.

34. James M. Gillis wrote the editorial for *Catholic World* in 1926, and the passage I quote is also found in William M. Halsey, *The Survival of American Innocence: Catholicism in an Era of Disillusionment, 1920–1940* (Notre Dame, IN: University of Notre Dame Press, 1980), 61. McKim, *Romanism in the Light of History*, 4. Shahan, *Middle Ages*, 312.

35. The quotations here are all from L. V. Rutgers, *Subterranean Rome: In Search of the Roots of Christianity in the Catacombs of the Eternal City* (Leuven: Uitgeverij Peeters, 2000), 12, 13. Cesare Baronio, *Annales ecclesiastici*, 12 vols. (Cologne: Sumptibus Ioannis Gymnici & Anonij Hierati, 1609–13). A digital version is available: Baronio Cesare, *Annales ecclesiastici* (Alexandria, VA: Alexander Street Press, 2007).

36. Rutgers, *Subterranean Rome*, 15–25, 35. Antonio Bosio, *Roma sotterranea* (Rome: Lodouico Grigani, 1650). For an English version of De Rossi's work see Giovanni Battista de Rossi, *Roma sotterranea; Or, Some Account of the Roman Catacombs...* (London: Longmans, Green, Reader and Dyer, 1869). For a useful overview in English on the

Catacombs of Priscilla see Maria Santa Maria, *Guide to the Catacombs of Priscilla*, trans. Alice Mulhern (Vatican City: Pontifical Commission for Sacred Archeology, 2007). The account of the image of the Madonna is on pp. 21–24.

37. G. W. Greene, "Visit to the Catacombs of Rome," *Harper's* 10 (1854–55): 577. C. E. Norton, "The Catacombs of Rome," *Atlantic Monthly* 1 (1857–58): 513, 674, 813; vol. 2 (1858): 48, 129. S. L. Caldwell, "The Catacombs of Rome," *Baptist Quarterly* 4 (1870): 275. S. L. Caldwell, "Is There a Science of History?," *Baptist Quarterly* 1 (Jan. 1867): 102–17. W. H. Withrow, "Christian Evidences from the Catacombs," *Methodist Quarterly Review* 31 (1871): 558. "The Catacombs of Rome," *Christian Observer* 62 (1862): 508. "The Catacombs of Rome," *Universalist Quarterly and General Review*, 24, n.s. 4 (1867): 190. J. L. Ferriere, "Inscriptions in the Catacombs," *Mercersberg Review* 19 (1872): 595. J. S. Northcote, "Catacombs: Rossi's *Roma Sotteranea*," *Catholic World* 1 (1865): 414. P. L. Connellan, "Pictorial Art of the Catacombs," *American Catholic Quarterly Review* 29 (1904): 575.

38. Shahan compared De Rossi to Columbus in *Beginnings of Christianity*, 363; he called him "the prince of Christian archeologists" in *Blessed Virgin in the Catacombs*, 7. The other quotations here are from Shahan, *Blessed Virgin in the Catacombs*, 13, 17. On the Council of Ephesus and *theotokos*, see Jaroslav Pelikan, *Mary through the Centuries: Her Place in the History of Culture* (New Haven, CT: Yale University Press, 1996), 55–65. Shahan listed twenty-one sources at the end of his preface, and he mentioned another work, written by a younger friend, that appeared the same year and included information about the Catacomb of Priscilla: Joseph Wilpert, *Die gottgeweihten Jungfrauen in den ersten Jahrhunderten der Kirche* (Freiburg im Breisgau, 1892).

39. The quotations are from, in order, Shahan, *Blessed Virgin in the Catacombs*, 22, 56, 57, 50, 51. On the representation of Jesus as the Good Shepherd and the dating of the Madonna in the Catacomb of Priscilla as "maybe as early as the third century," see Miri Rubin, *Mother of God: A History of the Virgin Mary* (New Haven, CT: Yale University Press, 2009), 25. On the frequency of the portrayal of Jesus as the Good Shepherd see Margaret Miles, who claims that "about 120 catacomb images" represent him that way: Margaret R. Miles, *The Word Made Flesh: A History of Christian Thought* (Malden, MA: Blackwell, 2005), 60. Other specialists who date the Madonna image in the Catacomb of Priscilla as "third century" and "the beginning of the third century" include Rutgers, *Subterranean Rome*, 137, and Santa Maria, *Catacombs of Priscilla*, 23.

40. Shahan and the Shrine's promoters used the phrase "pictorial theology" in several pieces, including "Early Church History in Shrine Decorations," *Washington Post*, January 11, 1925, p. A10.

41. Shahan, *Middle Ages*, 315–16. Shahan, *House of God*, 68.

42. "Crypt Rising for Shrine to Immaculate Conception," *SR* 10.3 (March 1923): 24. "Early Church History in Shrine Decorations," *Washington Post*, January 11, 1925, p. A10. "The Crypt of the National Shrine," *SR* 7.5 (August 1920): 43.

43. Shahan, *Middle Ages*, 315. My descriptions of the architecture here and below are taken from many sources, including my own photographs and observations. The statistics about the dimensions and other details are included in many shrine publications, including *SR* and *GTB*. For example, "Crypt Rising for Shrine to Immaculate Conception," *SR* 10.3 (March 1923): 24. The Shrine's Website also has descriptions of the space, and over the years the staff has written about it. Among the most helpful sources are Thomas J. Grady, "The Crypt Church of the National Shrine of the Immaculate Conception," *American Ecclesiastical Review* 137

(July–December 1957): 400–409; *AC*; and Geraldine M. Rohling, *Jubilee 2009: A Photographic History of the Basilica of the National Shrine of the Immaculate Conception* (Washington, DC: BNSIC, 2009).

44. Kieckhefer, *Theology in Stone*, 11–15, 22–24.
45. "The Crypt of the National Shrine," *SR* 7.5 (August 1920): 43.
46. Grady, "Crypt Church."
47. The Shrine's architect, Charles D. Maginnis, wrote the foreword to the artist's book: Charles J. Connick, *Adventures in Light and Color: An Introduction to the Stained Glass Craft* (New York: Random House, 1937). See also Noreen M. O'Gara, "Charles J. Connick: The Early Years" (M.A. Thesis, Tufts University, 1988).
48. The piece by the art critic is Ada Rainey, "Shrine of the Immaculate Conception Jewelled with Wondrous Works of Art," *Washington Post*, July 26, 1931, p. S6. For biographical information on La Farge see his obituary: "Bancel La Farge, Artist, Is Dead," *New York Times*, August 15, 1938, p. 15. The quotation here is from Maureen A. Tilley, "The Passion of Saints Perpetua and Felicity," in *Religions of Late Antiquity in Practice*, ed. Richard Valantasis (Princeton, NJ: Princeton University Press, 2000), 387.
49. Mary Chase Stratton, "Unpublished Autobiography," "written in the late 1930s," Mary Chase Stratton Papers, reel 593, Archives of American Art, Smithsonian Institution, Washington, D.C., quotations from, in order, 121, 5–6, 3. It was Murphy who said that Shahan was the source of inspiration for the ceramics: "Conversation with Mr. Fred V. Murphy," n.d., Archives, BNSIC. For a brief biographical sketch of Stratton see "Mary Chase Perry," *North American Women Artists of the Twentieth Century: A Biographical Dictionary*, ed. Jules Heller and Nancy G. Heller (London: Taylor and Francis, 1995). On Stratton's ceramic decorations and her visit to Rome see "Shrine Decorations to Copy Catacombs," *Washington Post*, November 2, 1924, p. 16; "Early Church History in Shrine Decorations: Ceramic Work to Depict Theology of Centuries after Christ," *Washington Post*, January 11, 1925, p. A10; "Pewabic Tiles to Decorate Crypt of Beautiful Shrine," *SR* 12.6 (June 1925): 43–48.
50. Murphy noted that Stratton read archeological works suggested by Shahan: "Conversation with Mr. Fred V. Murphy," n.d., Archives, BNSIC. The quotations from Stratton are, in order, from Mary Chase Stratton, "Unpublished Autobiography," n.d. (late 1930s), Mary Chase Stratton Papers, reel 593, Archives of American Art, Smithsonian Institution, 137–38, 121, 133, 139.
51. Ibid., 133, 6, 137.
52. Ibid., 138.
53. On the references to the catacombs in Stratton's plan see Grady, "The Crypt Church," 406–7. On symbols and images in the catacombs, including the early Christian symbols, see Rutgers, *Subterranean Rome*, 134–38, 153–58. See also Rohling, *Jubilee 2009*, 144; and *GTB*, 35–36.
54. Other Protestants also had a visible presence at the Shrine, including a Danish Lutheran observer at Vatican II, Dr. Kristan E. Skydsgaard, who was represented in a mosaic in the east apse of the Great Upper Church. On that mosaic see Rohling, *Jubilee 2009*, 209.

CHAPTER 5

1. I introduced both those lay devotees in chapter 1.
2. Here at the mention of "public" Catholic practice I want to acknowledge my debt to the work of David O'Brien, who offered a helpful typology of three styles of

Catholic public piety or "three distinct understandings of the relationship between Catholicism and American culture, republican, immigrant, and evangelical."
The first two styles were sometimes expressed at the Shrine, the *republican* style's
emphasis on cultural accommodation and the *immigrant* public style, with its
emphasis on Catholic difference and its focus on institutional growth. Here and in
the next chapter I don't refer explicitly to O'Brien's typology. I use instead the
phrase *triumphalist Americanism* to describe the position that emerged after 1899
and predominated at the Shrine. The quotation above is from David O'Brien and
Joseph Bernardin, "Public Catholicism [with Response]," *U.S. Catholic Historian*
8.4 (fall 1989): 89. See David J. O'Brien, *Public Catholicism* (New York: Collier
Macmillan, 1989).

3. John Henry Newman, *An Essay in Aid of a Grammar of Assent* (New York: Catholic
Publication Society, 1870), 1–6. "Subjunctive," *Oxford English Dictionary*, 2nd ed.,
1989, OED Online (accessed November 25, 2009). On "subjunctives" see also
H. W. Fowler, *A Dictionary of Modern English Usage*, 2nd ed. (New York: Oxford
University Press, 1965), 595–98. In my suggestion that ritual and architecture
can create the reality they imagine, I'm applying and extending a variety of reflections about images and rites, including discussions of "performative utterances."
Roy A. Rappaport, for example, notes that rituals can function as "performatives"
in *Ritual and Religion in the Making of Humanity* (Cambridge: Cambridge University
Press, 1999), 113–15. David Morgan notes that images can "imagine community"
in *The Sacred Gaze: Religious Visual Culture in Theory and Practice* (Berkeley:
University of California Press, 2005), 55. The phrase "civic social capital" was
coined by Alex Stepick, Terry Rey, and Sarah J. Mahler to extend the sociological
notion of "social capital" to include ways that religious organizations enable
"social relationships with the broader society." Alex Stepick, Terry Rey, and Sarah
J. Mahler, eds., *Churches and Charity in the Immigrant City: Religion, Immigration,
and Civic Engagement in Miami* (New Brunswick, NJ: Rutgers University Press,
2009), 13–17. I'm suggesting we might talk about *subjunctive social capital*, or civic
social capital in the subjunctive mood.

4. For an example of the Johnson wedding coverage see "The Wedding in Washington,"
Newsweek, August 15, 1966, 17–21. The estimate of Roman Catholics is based on
the membership figures recorded for these years in *The Official Catholic Directory*
(New York: P. J. Kennedy). Some information in this paragraph and the next is
found in Timothy J. Sarbaugh, "Politics and American Catholics," in *The
Encyclopedia of American Catholic History*, ed. Michael Glazier and Thomas
J. Shelley (Collegeville, MN: Liturgical Press, 1997), 1149–51. Photographs of
Gibbons at two of these three events are William H. Rau, photograph, "President
McKinley and Admiral Dewey at the 'Benediction' by Cardinal Gibbons," 1899,
LC-USZ62-90459, and George T. Woodward, photograph, "President Taft,
Governor Hughes, Cardinal Gibbons and other state and church dignitaries at the
Catholic Summer School of America, Cliff Haven, NY," 1909, LC-USZ62-69893,
both in Prints and Photographs Division, Library of Congress. I couldn't find pho-
tographs of Gibbons and the president at the 1913 Pan American Mass, but there
is a surviving image showing Gibbons and Thomas J. Shahan processing, though
we know that Wilson also attended mass that year: Harris & Ewing, photograph,
1913, "Pan American Mass," LC-DIG-hec-01738, Prints and Photographs Division,
Library of Congress. For a photograph of the east apse mosaic with Spellman and
other attendees of Vatican II see Geraldine M. Rohling, *Jubilee 2009: A Photographic
History of the Basilica of the National Shrine of the Immaculate Conception*

(Washington, DC: Basilica of the National Shrine of the Immaculate Conception, 2009), 208–9. For an account of the Vatican II mosaic see "Already History," *Washington Post*, December 17, 1966, p. C9. Lyndon Baines Johnson to Cardinal Francis Spellman, telephone conversation, January 16, 1967, citation no. 11359, tape WH6701.04, program no. 16, Lyndon Baines Johnson Library and Museum, Austin, Texas.

5. Lyndon Baines Johnson to Cardinal Francis Spellman, telephone conversation, January 16, 1967, citation no. 11359, tape WH6701.04, program no. 16, Lyndon Baines Johnson Library and Museum. [Thomas J. Shahan], "Program," Laying of the Foundation Stone, September 23, 1920, booklet, 8 pp., Archives, BNSIC. The address by McNicholas has been published as "Most Rev. John T. McNicholas, Columbus Day Address, 12 October 1942," in *Public Voices: Catholics in the American Context*, ed. Steven M. Avella and Elizabeth McKeown (Maryknoll, NY: Orbis, 1999), 172–75. The bishops' statement: "Victory and Peace," a Statement Issued by the Administrative Board of the National Catholic Welfare Conference, 14 November 1942," 175–77. Pius XI, *Divini Redemptoris* (Encyclical on Atheistic Communism), March 19, 1937, www.vatican.va (accessed November 27, 2009). There are many books about McCarthy, including Donald F. Crosby, *God, Church, and Flag: Senator Joseph R. McCarthy and the Catholic Church, 1950–1957* (Chapel Hill: University of North Carolina Press, 1978). See also Patrick Allitt, "Catholic Anti-Communism," *Crisis* 14 (March 1996): 22–25; and Patrick Allitt, *Catholic Intellectuals and Conservative Politics in America, 1950–1985* (Ithaca, NY: Cornell University Press, 1993).

6. On the controversies about the Washington Monument and the Pan American Mass see chapter 4. On the effects of Jewish military participation see Deborah Dash Moore, *GI Jew: How World War II Changed a Generation* (Cambridge, MA: Harvard University Press, 2004). James Cardinal Gibbons, *The Faith of Our Fathers: An Exposition and Vindication of the Church Founded by Our Lord Jesus Christ* (Rockford, IL: Tan Books, 1980) (originally published 1876), 186–203. [Thomas J. Shahan], "Program," Laying of the Foundation Stone, September 23, 1920, 8 pp., Archives, BNSIC. The Most Reverend Joseph E. Ritter, "Text of the Dedication Sermon," November 20, 1959, box E-5, Archives, BNSIC. John F. Kennedy, "Address of Senator John F. Kennedy to the Greater Houston Ministerial Association," Rice Hotel, Houston, September 12, 1960, John F. Kennedy Presidential Library and Museum, Historical Resources, www.jfklibrary.org/ (accessed November 27, 2009).

7. Jean M. White, "Catholic U. Accused of Censorship for Banning 4 in Lecture Series," *Washington Post*, February 17, 1963, p. B1. Although the charge of "banning" and "censorship" was mentioned on campus and in the press, university officials presented it as something more informal and less harsh. The Graduate Student Council had submitted a list of more than a dozen names of suggested speakers for the Council's lecture series, the newspaper reported, but the vice rector suggested that university officials only had said that they "preferred not to have" four "liberal" speakers, including Murray and Hans Küng. Pope Paul VI, *Dignitatis Humanae* (Declaration on Religious Freedom), www.vatican.va/ (accessed November 27, 2009). Paul Blanshard, *Communism, Democracy, and Catholic Power* (Boston: Beacon Press, 1951), 79, 160, 164, 239.

8. For Sheen's views on communism see Fulton J. Sheen, *Communism and the Conscience of the West* (Indianapolis: Bobbs-Merrill, 1948). On Sheen's broadcast from the Shrine see *AC*, 122.

9. On the papal broadcast see *AC*, 76. For Washington radio programming, I searched the "On the Air Today" section of the local newspaper for that year and other years. The information I cite here is from "On the Air Today," *Washington Post*, December 4, 1932, p. A4. On Sheen see Christopher Owen Lynch, *Selling Catholicism: Bishop Sheen and the Power of Television* (Lexington: University Press of Kentucky, 1998), and Mark S. Massa, *Catholics and American Culture: Fulton Sheen, Dorothy Day, and the Notre Dame Football Team* (New York: Crossroad Press, 1999), 82–101. The quotations about Graham and the number of viewers can be found in Massa, *Catholics and American Culture*, 83. The transcripts of his television episodes, including the ones I mention here, can be found in Fulton J. Sheen, *Life Is Worth Living*, first and second series (Garden City, NY: Garden City Books, 1955). For the declaration of the patron saint of television see "Apostolic Letter Proclaiming St. Claire as Heavenly Patron of Television," August 21, 1958, The Holy See, www.vatican.va (accessed December 12, 2009). Catholics also continued to use print media in the first half of the twentieth century. For a helpful study of books, pamphlets, journals, and especially newspapers during the earlier period see Justin Nordstrom, *Danger on the Doorstep: Anti-Catholicism and American Print Culture in the Progressive Era* (Notre Dame, IN: University of Notre Dame Press, 2006).
10. "Religion: Legion of Decency," *Time*, June 11, 1934. "Roman Catholics: The Changing Legion of Decency," *Time*, December 3, 1965.
11. Archival sources about the IFCA's involvement in the film industry are in IFCA Collection, Archives, ACUA, including materials by and about Rita McGoldrick, who chaired the Motion Picture Department. Her contributions also were noted in Brooklyn's diocesan newspaper's centennial celebrations, since she and her successor both lived there: "Catholic Alumnae Federation," *Brooklyn Diocese Centennial Supplement Tablet* (Brooklyn) 46.37 (October 1953): 115. Her contribution is recorded on p. 5 of "Individual Contributions to Fund of International Federation of Catholic Alumnae for Mary Altar," Archives, BNSIC. On Catholics, censorship, and the IFCA's role see Frank Walsh, *Sin and Censorship: The Catholic Church and the Motion Picture Industry* (New Haven, CT: Yale University Press, 1996), 33–35, 49–52, 134–36. The quotation about the IFCA is from p. 50. Philip Gleason noted the influence of the IFCA in this regard: *Contending with Modernity: Catholic Higher Education in the Twentieth Century* (New York: Oxford University Press, 1995), 271–72. He also noted Noll's work on assessing popular literature in that same section of his book. For the production code, first established in 1930, see Motion Picture Producers and Distributors of America, *A Code to Govern the Making of Motion and Talking Pictures* (n.p.: Motion Picture Producers and Distributors of America, 1934). On representations of Catholicism in film see Colleen McDannell, ed., *Catholics in the Movies* (New York: Oxford University Press, 2008). Although she doesn't mention the role of the IFCA, McDannell points to the ways "Catholics became regulators of popular culture" (15).
12. On that film, and the wider cultural context, see James T. Fisher, *On the Irish Waterfront: The Crusader, the Movie, and the Soul of the Port of New York* (Ithaca, NY: Cornell University Press, 2009). Committee on Special War Activities, NCWC, *Social Reconstruction: A General Review of the Problems and Survey of the Remedies*, Reconstruction Pamphlets, no. 1, January 1919. Committee on Special War Activities, NCWC, *Unemployment*, Reconstruction Pamphlets, no. 3, May 1919. Committee on Special War Activities, NCWC, *Outlines of a Social Service Program for Catholic Agencies*, Reconstruction Pamphlets, no. 7, June 1919. *MEM*, 120.

"Our First Pilgrims," *SR* 5.5 (August 1918): 36. Other notices of the orphans visiting appeared in later issues: "The Children's Prayer," *SR* 11.5 (May 1924): 46. Nuns at St. Vincent's continued to communicate with McKenna. See Sister Marie to Bernard McKenna, May 4, 1930, Bernard McKenna Papers, folder 13, Archives, PAHRC. I found the name of the head of the home, and the women religious who served there and the orphans who lived there, in government documents. On Sister Rosalia Malone, "superioress," see *The Fourteenth Census of the United States, 1920*, Washington, District of Columbia, roll T625_213; p. 1A; enumeration district 349.

13. Dorothy Day, *The Long Loneliness* (New York: HarperCollins, 1997), 166. That memoir appeared in 1952, twenty years after her Shrine visit. Some evidence suggests she met Maurin the day she returned from Washington and saw this as "heaven's answer" to her prayer at the Shrine. On that see William D. Miller, *A Harsh and Dreadful Love: Dorothy Day and the Catholic Worker Movement* (Garden City, NY: Image Books, 1974), 75. For Day's account of the march see Dorothy Day, "Hunger Marchers in Washington," *Commonweal* 48 (December 24, 1932): 277–79. Day knew Ryan's work, just as Ryan followed Day's movement. Ryan wrote to Day in 1941, for example, renewing his subscription to the *Catholic Worker*. Day, in turn, wrote to Ryan requesting a copy of one of his speeches. After receiving it, Day sent a postcard offering her gratitude and expressing her hope that Ryan "keeps shouting till he is heard." Day took her own advice. She's been posthumously celebrated as "an inspired complainer," "God's panhandler," and "a living saint." On Ryan's talk at the Catholic Worker House see Miller, *Harsh and Dreadful Love*, 96–97. John A. Ryan to Dorothy Day, December 10, 1941; Dorothy Day to John A. Ryan, January 19, 1945; Dorothy Day to Eleanor C. Vogel [Ryan's secretary], January 26, 1945; all three in John A. Ryan Papers, box 9, folder 24, Archives, ACUA. Jim Forest, "An Inspired Complainer: Celebrating Dorothy Day's 100th," *Sojourners* 26.4 (November–December 1997): 13. M. Mayer, "God's Panhandler," *Progressive* 45 (February 1981): 14–15. New York's Cardinal John O'Connor mentioned in a homily, in which he advocated starting the process of canonization, that some have called Day "a living saint": Cardinal John O'Connor, "On the Idea of Sainthood and Dorothy Day," *Catholic New York*, November 13, 1997, 13–14. In March 2000, the Vatican approved O'Connor's request to open the Cause for the Beatification and Canonization. With that action, Day was given the title Servant of God. She then needed two posthumous miracles to be named a saint, and in order to assist the canonization process the Guild for Dorothy Day was established.

14. John A. Ryan, *Social Doctrine in Action: A Personal History* (New York: Harper, 1941), 263–65. "Right Reverend New-Dealer," *Time* 59 (January 11, 1943), 60. "It was Father Charles Coughlin who first referred to" Ryan this way, as Christopher J. Kaufman notes: *Patriotism and Fraternalism in the Knights of Columbus: A History of the Fourth Degree* (New York: Crossroad Press, 2001), 83. Ryan also was described as a "prophet of social studies," a "prophet of social justice," and "the Church's pioneering radical." See R. J. Purcell, "John A. Ryan, Prophet of Social Studies," *Studies: An Irish Quarterly Review* 35 (June 1946): 153–46; J. Fitzsimmons, "Monsignor John A. Ryan, Prophet of Social Justice," *Clergy Review* 39 (September 1954): 527–38; W. J. Cunningham, "The Church's Pioneering Radical," *Information* 76 (June 1962): 44–51. Quotations are from, in order, Ryan, *Social Doctrine in Action*, 281, 264, 133. Full account of his birthday and retirement celebration: 277–81. For his work see John A. Ryan, *A Living Wage* (New York: Macmillan,

1906); and John A. Ryan, *Distributive Justice: The Right and Wrong of Our Present Distribution of Wealth* (New York: Macmillan, 1916). Committee on Special War Activities, NCWC, *Social Reconstruction: A General Review of the Problems and Survey of the Remedies*, Reconstruction Pamphlets, no. 1, January 1919. Quotation about social justice: foreword (p. 4) of the original pamphlet, which was signed by four U.S. bishops, including Charleston's William T. Russell, who had been at the center of the Pan American Mass controversy. For an excerpt see John Tracy Ellis, *Documents of American Catholic History*, vol. 2 (Chicago: Henry Regnery, 1967), 589–607. The assessment of the influence of those proposals and their enactment is taken from ibid., 589. The BNSIC staff didn't make agitation for social justice their main business. It was, after all, a shrine. Further, not all Catholic activists and all social causes were celebrated there. Philip Berrigan (1923–2000) was ordained a Josephite priest in the Crypt Church in 1955, but at a "God Day" rally in 1972 a homilist told the three thousand faithful gathered in the upper level that Berrigan, who was then imprisoned for antiwar activities, was an "extremist" who "subverted the common good." Earlier in the century, however, prelates connected with the Shrine had supported Ryan's less confrontational but still controversial approach to social change. Shahan, as university rector, didn't yield to the pressure to silence Ryan, as Ryan noted in his memoir, and Shahan even proudly proclaimed that Pope Pius XI's 1931 encyclical *Quadragesimo Anno*, celebrating and extending the teaching of Leo XIII's influential statement on labor forty years earlier, was "a great vindication for John Ryan." Indirectly, it was vindication for Shahan, too, for supporting Ryan even when it wasn't popular. Ryan, *Social Doctrine*, 223, 242. For Berrigan's recollection of his ordination see Philip Berrigan, with Fred A. Wilcox, *Fighting the Lamb's War; Skirmishes with the American Empire: The Autobiography of Philip Berrigan* (Monroe, ME: Common Courage Press, 1996), 34. On the God's Day sermon and mass see Donald P. Baker, "Berrigan Brothers Attacked," *Washington Post*, September 17, 1972, p. D1. The paper published an editorial praising Philip and Daniel Berrigan as Christ-like and condemning the homilist, Abbot Edmund F. McCaffery, who was "on his way up the episcopal ladder" and "clothed in sumptuous robes, speaking before 3,000 scrubbed and shiny people in the beautiful multi-million-dollar National Shrine of the Immaculate Conception": Joseph C. Murray, "Robes vs. Bars," *Washington Post*, September 22, 1972, p. A27.

15. "Catholics to Offer Prayers for Support of New President," *New York Times*, March 24, 1921. AC, 91–92. "'Red Mass' to Attract Many Notables," *Washington Post*, January 7, 1939, p. 1; "Red Mass Celebrated at Catholic University," *Washington Post*, January 9, 1939, p. 12; "Dignitaries Expected at Red Mass," *Washington Post*, January 12, 1952, p. 8; "Annual Red Mass: Bishop Calls for Moral Restoration," *Washington Post*, January 14, 1952, p. B1. Washington's archbishop, Patrick A. O'Boyle, moved the Red Mass to St. Mathew's in 1953, and the recently founded John Carroll Society (1951), a group of lay Catholic legal professionals, took over the event's planning. They've sponsored it every year since then at St. Mathew's.

16. "Many Keep May Day," *Washington Post*, May 19, 1913, p. 12. For earlier and later May processions see "Children Pay Homage," *Washington Post*, May 25, 1908, p. 2; and "Catholic Churches of District Hold May Processions," *Washington Post*, May 16, 1927, p. 16. On the multiparish ritual see "Jubilee of Catholics: Church Freedom Celebration Will Last until December 8," *Washington Post*, October 6, 1913, p. 3.

17. "Text of President's Address to Holy Name Crusaders," *Washington Post*, September 22, 1924, p. 4. "Coolidge Calls Religious Freedom Ideal of Nation," *Washington Post*, September 22, 1924, p. 1. "Holy Name Society Convention Closes with Solemn Rites," *Washington Post*, September 22, 1924, p. 3. Journalists' estimates of the crowd varied between seventy-five thousand and one hundred thousand. The senior cardinal in fig. 5.5 is William Henry O'Connell (1859–1944) of the Archdiocese of Boston.

18. Civil religion is the set of religious beliefs, myths, symbols, saints, and rituals associated with the political realm. Usually that term is understood to mean the loosely framed faith that arises outside the churches, although in the variant I discuss in this chapter, civil religion in the nation's capital can be denominationally coded. In the modern West, the idea goes back to Jean-Jacques Rousseau, who proposed a widely shared civil religion that might encourage citizens' loyalty to the democratic state. Robert Bellah's 1967 essay "Civil Religion in America," *Daedalus* 96 (winter 1967): 1–21, sparked the scholarly discussion of the topic among scholars of U.S. religion. A great deal of debate followed. Francis D. Lethbridge of the American Institute of Architects has divided the history of the federal city's architecture into four phases: (1) 1791–1850, Late Georgian and Classic Revival; (2) 1850–1900, Romantic Revival; (3) Classic Eclecticism, 1893–1940; (4) 1940–present. It was during the third period that the District of Columbia became an important site for the contest among faiths for public presence. Most of the important national churches, or their functional equivalents, were started or completed during this period, which began with influences from the 1893 Columbian Exposition and the 1901 McMillan Plan. The latter modified and enlarged Pierre Charles L'Enfant's original design for the capital and was named for Senator James McMillan, who chaired the Senate District Committee and appointed a commission to study the plan of the city. For Lethbridge's periodization and discussion of the third period see Francis D. Lethbridge, "The Architecture of Washington, D.C.," in *AIA Guide to the Architecture of Washington, D.C.*, ed. Christopher Weeks, 3d ed. (Baltimore: Johns Hopkins University Press, 1994), 5–6, 12.

19. L'Enfant's description of his plan was included in the manuscript he presented to Congress in December 1791. That plan first appeared publicly in a Philadelphia newspaper: *Dunlop's American Daily Advertiser*, December 26, 1791. See also Papers of Charles L'Enfant, Manuscript Division, Library of Congress. Many books chronicle the planning and history of the District of Columbia, including Kenneth R. Bowling, *The Creation of Washington, D.C.: The Idea and Location of the American Capital* (Washington, DC: George Mason University Press, 1991). See also Weeks, *AIA Guide*; and Pamela Scott and Antoinette J. Lee, *Buildings of the District of Columbia* (New York: Oxford University Press, 1993). On D.C. churches see Williams, *Houses of God*, 72–76. Quotation from the National Cathedral's tourist guidebook from *Washington National Cathedral* (Washington, DC: Washington National Cathedral, 1995), 17. For more on that building, see Richard T. Feller, *Completing Washington Cathedral for Thy Great Glory* (Washington, DC: Washington Cathedral, 1989).

20. On the "spiritual recession" see Robert T. Handy, *A Christian America: Protestant Hopes and Historical Realities*, 2nd ed. (New York: Oxford University Press, 1984), 174–79. Elisabeth Ellicott Poe, "Religious Life in Washington Keeps Pace with Rising Tide of Religion in Nation," *Washington Post*, March 4, 1923, p. 73. Walter

Harris, "Washington Is Fast Becoming Religious Center of United States," *Washington Post*, November 22, 1925, pp. SM1, 10.

21. "Houses of Worship Multiply in Same Ratio as District," *Washington Post*, December 6, 1927, p. F19. Helen Essary, "Washington Becomes a City of Shrines," *New York Times*, April 1, 1928, p. 83. Franklin Littell, "The Capital's Temples to Divinity," *Washington Post*, June 2, 1929, p. SM6.

22. Quotation from Michelle Boorstein, "A Milestone for Sikhs in D.C.," *Washington Post*, February 18, 2006, p. B9. The Jewish community center was mentioned in Harris, "Washington Is Fast Becoming Religious Center of United States," p. SM10. Besides the BNSIC, other D.C. worship spaces with "national" in their titles include National Baptist Memorial Church, National Community Church on Capitol Hill (Assemblies of God), Ukrainian Catholic National Shrine of the Holy Family, National City Christian Church (Disciples of Christ), National Memorial Church of God, Washington National Cathedral, National Presbyterian Church, National Spiritual Science Center, and Universalist National Memorial Church. Three others explicitly call themselves national centers: Church of the Holy City ("the National Swedenborgian Church"), St. Nicholas Orthodox Cathedral ("the National Cathedral of the Orthodox Church in America"), and Metropolitan A.M.E. Church ("the National Cathedral of African Methodism"). Others function as national denominational centers or at some time have claimed to: St. John's Church (Episcopal), First Baptist, Foundry Methodist, Saint Sophia Greek Orthodox Cathedral, and Founding Church of Scientology. Others use "capital" in their titles, including Capital Memorial Seventh-Day Adventist Church and Unity Center of Truth in the Nation's Capital. A few churches outside the federal city's limits publicly claim national status: The National Church of God (Ft. Washington, Maryland), National Apostolic Church (Silver Spring, Maryland), and National Wesleyan Church (Hyattsville, Maryland).

23. Charles Mason Remey, *The National Church and Shrine of the United States of America to Be Built in the City of Washington* (Washington, DC: Organizers of the National Church Foundation, 1927), 41. Anna Minta, "Planning a National Pantheon: Monuments in Washington, D.C. and the Creation of Symbolic Space," in *Public Space and the Ideology of Place in American Culture*, ed. Miles Orvell and Jeffrey L. Meikle (Amsterdam: Rodopi, 2009), 34–35. As traditional religious corridors, like Sixteenth Street, became crowded, new spaces opened where faiths continued (and revised) the tradition of marking metropolitan Washington's landscape. On "Religion Row" or "Highway to Heaven," see Susan Levine, "'A Place for Those Who Pray: Along Montgomery's Highway to Heaven Diverse Acts of Faith," *Washington Post*, August 3, 1997, B1–4. Because these houses of worship are outside the District and few claim national status, they have less significance for understanding the contest for civic space in Washington. Most local interpreters have taken Religion Row as a sign of the new ethnic and religious diversity of the city and the nation. Nonetheless, the congregations' relative proximity to the capital adds some symbolic power. Muslims and Jews already had claimed space within the District's boundaries before the emergence of New Hampshire Avenue as a religious corridor in 1958. For example, Adas Israel Synagogue was built in 1876 at Sixth and G Streets NW, and moved in 1907 to Sixth and I. As I mention here, the Islamic Center of Washington, D.C., opened in 1957 on Massachusetts Avenue's Embassy Row. On local Jewish history see Martin Garfinkle, *The Jewish Community of Washington, D.C.* (Mount Pleasant, SC: Arcadia, 2005), and Laura Cohen Applebaum and Wendy Turman, eds., *Jewish Washington:*

Scrapbook of an American Community (Washington, DC: Washington Book Distributors, 2007). For other resources see the Jewish Historical Society of Greater Washington, www.jhsgw.org/ (accessed December 6, 2009). On a Buddhist temple see "Washington Buddhist Vihara," www.buddhistvihara.com/ (accessed December 6, 2009). On the history of the Islamic Center see Muhammad Abdul-Rauf, *History of the Islamic Center: From Dream to Reality* (Washington, DC: Islamic Center, 1978). On Bush's visit to the Islamic Center see David E. Sanger, "Bin Laden Is Wanted in Attacks, 'Dead or Alive,' President Says," *New York Times*, September 18, 2001, p. A1. As that article points out, the president also attended a memorial service at the National Cathedral the previous week, and Muslim leaders participated, too.

24. St. Nicholas's, the 1962 Russian sanctuary down the street from the National Cathedral, also claims national status: see *St. Nicholas Orthodox Cathedral*, n.d., brochure, St. Nicholas Orthodox Cathedral, Washington, D.C.; and *St. Nicholas Russian Orthodox Church: Fiftieth Anniversary* (brochure) (Washington: St. Nicholas Russian Orthodox Cathedral, 1980). On "the National Cathedral of African Methodism" see "Metropolitan A.M.E. Church: A Brief History," in *Metropolitan African Methodist Episcopal Church*, n.d., pamphlet, 4 pp., Metropolitan A.M.E. Church, Washington, D.C. For the Swedenborgians, see *Church of the Holy City, Washington, D.C.*, n.d., pamphlet, 4 pp., Washington, D.C.: Emmanuel Swedenborg Center for Worship and Study. First Baptist's visibility derived in part from the political prominence of some of its members, who have included presidents Truman and Carter. The same was true of Foundry Methodist (1904), which moved to the center of attention in the 1990s when President Bill Clinton, a Baptist, and his wife Hillary, a Methodist, attended. Edward Hughes Pruden, *Building the House of God: Some Memories* (Washington, DC: First Baptist Church of the City of Washington, D.C., 1986). Homer Calkin, *Castings from the Foundry Mold: A History of Foundry Church, Washington, D.C., 1814–1964* (Nashville: Parthenon Press, 1968). By the early twentieth century, it had become fashionable for denominations to seek a site on Sixteenth Street. The churches on that street included St. John's (1816; 1881–90; 1919); First Baptist Church (1890; 1955); The Church of the Holy City (1896); Foundry Methodist (1904); Church of the Sacred Heart (1923); All Souls Unitarian Church (1924); Universalist National Memorial Church (1930); National Baptist Memorial Church (1933); and Unification Church [Washington Chapel, Church of Jesus Christ of Latter Day Saints] (1933). On the architecture of that corridor see Sue A. Kohler and Jeffrey R. Carson, *Sixteenth Street Architecture*, 2 vols. (Washington, DC: Commission of Fine Arts, 1978–85). See also Williams, *Houses of God*, 72–76.

25. The idea behind National City Christian Church originated with Alexander Campbell but gained momentum only in the early twentieth century. The Indiana limestone building, where President Johnson attended, was designed by John Russell Pope and has the same monumental character as Pope's other Washington projects, such as the Jefferson Memorial. Situated high on a terrace overlooking Thomas Circle, a prominent location in the city, the church's façade—with its Ionic columns and broad steps—demands the attention of motorists and pedestrians. Hilda E. Koontz, *A History of the National City Christian Church* (Washington, DC: Print and Mail, privately printed, 1981), 1. Across Thomas Circle is the older Luther Place Memorial Church (1870), a red sandstone Gothic structure built to offer thanks for the ending of the Civil War. It is less self-consciously national in character (and less imposing) than the Disciples of Christ Church, although as a

centrally located church in the capital it takes on some significance for the denomination's identity and visibility. On this Lutheran church see Scott and Lee, *Buildings of the District of Columbia*, 295. Presbyterians long debated the idea of a national church in Washington. The notion first came before the denomination's General Assembly in 1803, but it wasn't until 1923 that denominational leaders appointed a commission to seriously consider it. Rather than construct a new building, however, the denomination first designated an existing congregation, Covenant First Presbyterian, as "the national Presbyterian church." *The National Presbyterian Church: The First Two Hundred Years, 1795–1995* (Washington, DC: National Presbyterian Church, 1996), 19.

26. William W. Warner, *At Peace with All Their Neighbors: Catholics and Catholicism in the National Capital, 1787–1860* (Washington, DC: Georgetown University Press, 1994), 100–101. *The Official Catholic Directory* (New York: P. J. Kennedy, 1924), 14–29. *Official Catholic Directory*, 1953, 236–43.

27. On Murphy and the Vatican Embassy see Michael V. Murphy and John C. Murphy, "The Architecture of the Vatican Embassy Building, Washington, D.C.," *U.S. Catholic Historian* 12.2 (spring 1994): 131–38. Carolyn Bell Hughes, "Washington's Little Rome," *Washington Post*, December 9, 1956, p. F3. "Why Washington Was Selected as the Location for the National Shrine of the Immaculate Conception," *SR* 7.3 (March 1921): 21.

28. The quotations about the site and the dedication are from Ellen Jolly's letter to the membership of the Ladies Auxiliary of the Ancient Order of Hibernians on the approval of the monument: "Office of Mrs. Ellen Ryan Jolly, L.L.D, National Chairman Nuns' Memorial Committee," January 1919, Ellen Ryan Jolly Papers, Archives, ND. The quotations from O'Connell are in "Memorial to Civil War Nuns Unveiled by Women of A.O.H.," *Washington Post*, September 21, 1924, p. 2. The quotation about the federal land is from "12 Orders of Nuns Shown on Monument," *Washington Post*, September 20, 1924, p. 5. On the monument and dedication see also Kathryn Allamong Jacob, *Testament to Union: Civil War Monuments in Washington, D.C.* (Baltimore: Johns Hopkins University Press, 1998), 125–27; and Rohling, *Jubilee 2009*, 108–9. On the nurses' activities in wider historical context see Christopher Kaufman, *Ministry and Meaning: A Religious History of Catholic Health Care in the United States* (New York: Crossroad Press, 1995), 82–95. Kaufman also notes that twenty-one religious communities nursed the wounded, not twelve, as the planners of the monument had thought (83).

29. The quotation about "the hand of God" is from "Office of Mrs. Ellen Ryan Jolly, L.L.D, National Chairman Nuns' Memorial Committee," January 1919, Ellen Ryan Jolly Papers, Archives, ND. On Jolly's attachment to Irish heritage—(she praised "the music of the Gael" and "Irish tendencies") and her devotion to the Virgin Mary (she was an avid reader of *Ave Maria*) see this letter: Ellen Ryan Jolly to the Rev. Patrick J. Carroll, CSC, [January 31, 1930], Ellen Ryan Jolly Papers, ND. *Nuns of the Battlefield* (Providence, RI: Providence Visitors Press, 1927), viii–ix. For an account of women religious working as nurses published just two years later see Ann Doyle, "Nursing by Religious Orders in the United States," pt. 2, 1841–1870," *American Journal of Nursing* 29.8 (August 1929): 959–69. The Vatican recognized her for her efforts. See "Receives Papal Medal: Dr. Ellen Ryan Jolly Is Honored for Work for Church," *New York Times*, January 5, 1930, p. N4. For biographical information, some other letters and notes can be found in the Ellen Ryan Jolly Papers, Archives, ND. There are discrepancies: the collection guide at the University of Notre Dame Archives lists her birth date as 1868, while the 1920 and 1930

federal census records agree that she was born in Massachusetts in 1860. I use the latter date here. "Ellen R. Jolly," U.S. Bureau of the Census, *Fourteenth Census of the United States, 1920*, Pawtucket, Rhode Island, roll T625_1675; p. 11A; enumeration district 147. "Ellen R. Jolly," U.S. Bureau of the Census, *Fifteenth Census of the United States, 1930*, Pawtucket, Rhode Island, roll 2173; p. 3B; enumeration district 257. The congressman from Rhode Island who introduced the bill and helped Jolly was Ambrose Kennedy, and the president of Notre Dame who supported the cause was the Very Reverend John Cavanaugh, CSC.

30. In my analysis of the function of memorials I'm combining the insights of several traditions of interpretation. On that see James E. Young, "Memory/Monument," in *Critical Terms for Art History*, 2nd ed., ed. Robert S. Nelson and Richard Shiff (Chicago: University of Chicago Press, 2003), 234–47. William J. Kennedy and Sister Mary Joseph, *The United States: A History for the Upper Grades of Catholic Schools* (New York: Benziger Brothers, 1926), vii, v–vi, 468–69. The information on Jolly is from the census records I cite above.

31. Jolly used the phrase "Mary of Erin" in "Office of Mrs. Ellen Ryan Jolly, L.L.D, National Chairman Nuns' Memorial Committee," January 1919, Ellen Ryan Jolly Papers, Archives, ND. "Memorial to Civil War Nuns Unveiled by Women of A.O.H.," *Washington Post*, September 21, 1924, p. 2. For the photograph of Jolly standing with Shahan at the dedication of the St. Brigid's altar and a description of the chalice see Rohling, *Jubilee 2009*, 110–11. On Jolly's role in the presentation see "Shahan Will Dedicate $2,000 Shrine Chalice," *Washington Post*, May 27, 1928, p. M6; and "Special Challice Designed for the National Shrine of the Immaculate Conception, Washington, D.C.," *SR* 15.6 (June 1928): 46.

32. "900 Attend First Mass Celebrated in Catholic Shrine," *Washington Post*, April 21, 1924. That account was reprinted with the same title in *SR* 11.6 (June 1924): 56.

33. For a description of the "Patroness Windows" see *GTB*, 82. I found the quotation from Connick at the Website of the Charles J. Connick Stained Glass Foundation, www.cjconnick.org (accessed December 12, 2009).

34. On the East façade see *GTB*, 9–10. On De Rosen, who sometimes was referred to as Jan Henryk de Rosen, the Iconography Committee he chaired, and the East Wall iconography see *AC*, 134–41. See also Michael Lampen, "John De Rosen: Mural Master," in Grace Cathedral: An Episcopal Church (San Francisco), www.gracecathedral.org/ (accessed December 12, 2009). The quotation from De Rosen is from John De Rosen, "Artist Tells of Meanings Contained in Shrine Mosaic," *Shrine Dedication Day Supplement, (Washington, DC) Catholic Standard*, November 20, 1959, p. 33. Quotation about the "little shrine" on the East Wall, and details about the ornamentation and the sculptors from "The East Wall of the National Shrine of the Immaculate Conception: Five Artists Create Ornaments," *SR* 19.2 (May 1958): 3–7. See also Clarence M. Zens, "Take the Shrine Tour," *Shrine Dedication Day Supplement, (Washington, DC) Catholic Standard*, November 20, 1959, pp. 6–7, 9. On De Rosen's commission for the Chapel of St. Joseph of Arimathea at the National Cathedral see *Washington National Cathedral*, 57–59; and Bernard Kiernan, "Artist Tells How He Built Vast Mosaic, *Washington Post*, October 21, 1959, B1.

35. Biographical information on Snowden was included in "East Wall of the National Shrine of the Immaculate Conception," 3. On Angel see "South Wall of the National Shrine of the Immaculate Conception: Four Sculptors Create Ornaments of the Façade," *SR* 19.1 (February 1958): 3. A biographical profile and archival materials

are in John Angel Papers, Archives of American Art, Smithsonian Institution, Washington, D.C.

36. The scriptural passage is from Hebrews 11:1: "Now faith is the assurance of things hoped for, the conviction of things not seen" (RSV), *The New Oxford Annotated Bible*, ed. Bruce M. Metzger and Roland E. Murphy (New York: Oxford University Press, 1991).

37. On Hart see "Luke Hart, 83, Supreme Knight of Knights of Columbus, Is Dead," *New York Times*, February 20, 1919, p. 64; and "Mass to Be Offered Here on Day of Hart Funeral," *Washington Post*, February 21, 1964, p. E9. On the campanile or Knights Tower, see "K of C to Build Bell Tower Here," *Washington Post*, April 2, 1957, p. B5; "Great Tower Climbs the Sky," *SR* 19.4 (November 1958): 5; *AC*, 148–49; *GTB*, 12–13. On the debate about who proposed the addition of "under God" see James M. Haswell, "Public Wants 'Under God' Put in Pledge," *Washington Post*, May 18, 1954, p. 10; and "Who Placed 'Under God' in the Pledge to the Flag?," *Washington Post*, March 26, 1955, p. 8. For an account of the Knights of Columbus, Hart, and his role in revising the pledge, see Kaufman, *Patriotism and Fraternalism in the Knights of Columbus*, 123–30. I suggest that Hart was "successful." He was financially successful decades earlier, as federal census records show. In 1930, he owned a house in St. Louis valued at $17,500, well above the local and national median, and his worth and stature only grew over the years. "Luke E. Hart," *Fifteenth Census of the United States, 1930*; St. Louis, Missouri; roll 1245; p. 31A; enumeration district 240. For evidence of Hart's meeting with Eisenhower see "The President's Appointment List," *Washington Post*, October 12, 1953, p. 7.

38. On the Knights' origins see Kaufman, *Patriotism and Fraternalism*, 1–21. The Knights, who continued to defend Catholicism from Protestant attacks, were also the targets of much anti-Catholicism, including by the Ku Klux Klan during the 1920s. See Lynn S. Neal, "Christianizing the Klan: Alma White, Branford Clarke, and the Art of Religious Intolerance," *Church History* 78.2 (June 2009): 350–78. Hart's reflections on the tower appeared in a full-page ad the group took out in the diocesan paper's dedication supplement: "The Knight's Tower," (Washington, DC) *Catholic Standard*, November 20, 1959, p. 14. The dimensions appeared in many stories, for example, "Great Tower Climbs the Sky," *SR* 19.4 (November 1958): 5. Those details also were circulated in press releases. For example, "Fact Sheet for the National Shrine of the Immaculate Conceptions," May 15, 1959, typescript, 9 pp., box E-6: Special Services and Events, Archives, BNSIC. The tower's dimensions, as well as information about its fifty-six-bell carillon, are discussed also in *GTB*, 12–13. On the membership totals see "K. of C. Reports Gains: Convention Told 39,433 Rise Puts Members at 1,048,738," *New York Times*, August 21, 1957, p. 16. Local groups traveled to the Shrine in various ways, including by tour buses. On that see the advertisement inviting Brooklyn members to journey to "America's Holy Land": "Pilgrimage to National Shrine, Washington, D.C.," *Tablet* (Brooklyn), 24 (May 15, 1926): 19.

39. "Why Washington Was Selected as the Location for the National Shrine of the Immaculate Conception," *SR* 7.3 (March 1921): 21. "The Dome," *SR* 19.3 (August 1958): 3.

40. The quotation is from Sylvester Baxter, "The National Shrine of the Immaculate Conception, Washington, D.C.," *Architectural Record* 52 (July 1922): 3–15 (my emphasis). Baxter, a Boston journalist, wrote about architecture and knew Maginnis. They both had links with the Boston Architectural Club, for example. So when he reports the architect's intentions, there is reason to think that he was

reflecting what the architect told him. Baxter reproduced Maginnis and Walsh's "preliminary study," with its Capitol-like dome (10). Grady, the director when the Shrine was dedicated, reported that the architectural firm listed three reasons that Maginnis and Shahan chose Byzantine-Romanesque over Gothic, and he noted a fourth: the influence of John Glennon, later Cardinal Glennon of St. Louis, a close friend of both the architect and the founder. Glennon had a "strong preference for Romanesque." Thomas J. Grady, "National Shrine of the Immaculate Conception," *American Ecclesiastical Review* (January–June 1957): 148–49. The first history of the project, which the Shrine published in 1927, offered five reasons they had placed the building in Washington: (1) "Every nation has some great National Monument in honor of our Blessed Mother"; (2) "The City of Washington is our chief Catholic educational center"; (3) "The Catholic University of America was solemnly dedicated by our Bishops to Mary Immaculate as the patroness of Catholic learning"; (4) "To advance the religious education of our student body"; (5) "Washington is a city of monumental buildings, attracting thousands of visitors annually; the temporary home of our numerous government officials" (*NS*, 12–14). On Murphy's early career, as well as his later work, see John C. Murphy, "Frederick V. Murphy: The Catholic Architect as Eclectic Designer and University Professor," *U.S. Catholic Historian* 15.1 (winter 1997): 91–104.

41. Richard Cardinal Cushing, "Text of Sermon Delivered by His Eminence Richard Cardinal Cushing at Evening Mass on the Day of Dedication of the National Shrine of the Immaculate Conception, Washington, D.C.," box C-2, Archives, BNISC. Eugene B. Gallagher, "The Land of the Immaculate Conception," *American Ecclesiastical Review* (December 1958): 380. See also [Thomas J. Shahan], "The National Shrine: Idea, Means, Results," *SR* 1.1 (January 1914): 2.

42. [Thomas J. Shahan], "Program," Laying of the Foundation Stone, September 23, 1920, 8 pp., Archives, BNISC. This program opens up to reveal an image of Mary that was executed by Pfisterer, probably in 1920, shortly before a larger version of it appeared in a mural in the left transept altar at St. Francis Xavier Church in Buffalo in 1921. McKenna and Shahan also reproduced that image, with an accompanying description, in "Patroness of the United States," *SR* 9.3 (March 1922): 21. See also Rohling, *Jubilee 2009*, 19. Just before the foundation stone ceremony, McKenna and Shahan also had publicly thanked the artist: "We are deeply grateful to our dear friend and benefactor, Father Raphael, OSB, who so kindly sent us the picture which is to be used in the Foundation Number of the *Salve Regina*." That notice appeared as "In Gratitude," *SR* 7.5 (August 1920): 36. On the artist see "Fr. Raphael Pfisterer, OSB," biographical information file, Saint Anselm Abbey Archives, Manchester, New Hampshire. I'm very grateful to the archivist, Keith Chevalier, for his help finding information about Father Pfisterer and his work. On Wimmer, see Jerome Oetgen, *An American Abbot: Boniface Wimmer, O.S.B., 1809–1887* (Washington, DC: Catholic University of America Press, 1997). On Benedictine orders and the arts, I learned from Nathan Cochran, OSB, "Benedictine Schools and the Arts," Keynote Address for the Dedication and Blessing of the Delbarton School Visual and Performing Arts Center, Morristown, New Jersey," May 18, 2007. On the European revival of mural painting, and developments in Germany, see Clare A. P. Willsdon, "Mural: Europe, 1810–1930," Grove Art Online, www.oxfordartonline.com (accessed December 14, 2009). I analyzed Pfisterer's image in Thomas A. Tweed, "'America's Church': Roman Catholicism and Civic Space in the Nation's Capital," in *The Visual Culture of American Religions*, ed. David Morgan and Sally M. Promey (Berkeley: University of California Press, 2001),

77–78. Morgan noted the Baroque and Venetian parallels: Morgan, *Sacred Gaze*, 246–47.

43. Raphael [Pfisterer], OSB to Bernard McKenna, April 18, 1930, Bernard McKenna Papers, MC61, Archives, PAHRC. [Thomas J. Shahan], "Program," Laying of the Foundation Stone, September 23, 1920, 8 pp., Archives, BNSIC. "In Gratitude," *SR* 7.5 (August 1920): 36. "Patroness of the United States," *SR* 9.3 (March 1922): 21. As other archival evidence also suggests, that German immigrant embraced American nationalism and valued Marian devotion. A decade after the foundation stone ceremony, Pfisterer was still creating representations of the U.S. patroness and communicating with the Shrine's promoters. In 1930, he sent Father McKenna another image of "Mary Immaculate, Patroness of the United States," one he had recently completed as part of another ecclesiastical commission, and thanked the Shrine's director "for the services you are rendering to our Patroness by erecting to her such a beautiful shrine in Washington."

44. [Thomas J. Shahan], "Program," Laying of the Foundation Stone, September 23, 1920, 8 pp., Archives, BNSIC. Tweed, "'America's Church,'" 77–78. Morgan, *Sacred Gaze*, 246–47.

45. Cushing, "Text of Sermon Delivered at Evening Mass on the Day of the Dedication of the National Shrine of the Immaculate Conception," Archives, BNSIC. On Catholic advances in politics see Patrick W. Carey, *The Roman Catholics* (Westport, CT: Greenwood Press, 1993), 109.

46. Jackie's famous assessment of President Kennedy's piety is quoted in Thomas J. Carty, *Catholic in the White House?: Religion, Politics, and John F. Kennedy's Presidential Campaign* (New York: Palgrave, 2006), 4. On Kennedy see also Lawrence H. Fuchs, *John F. Kennedy and American Catholicism* (New York: Meredith Press, 1967), and Massa, *Catholics and American Culture*, 128–47. On other presidential visits to the Shrine see *AC*, 97, 178–79, 219. "Index to the President's Appointment Books, 1961–63," John F. Kennedy Library, Boston. Kennedy's appointment books indicate that he attended three local Catholic churches— St. Matthew's, St. Stephen's, and Holy Trinity—but never visited the Shrine. I also have failed to find any mention of the Shrine in any autobiographical or bio-graphical material, and oral history confirms the conclusion that he never attended. Sal Mazzuca, who was an altar server at the Shrine and for many years a tour guide there and also served as part of President Kennedy's Secret Service detail for a time, confirmed in an interview the archival sources in the presidential library. He recalls escorting Kennedy to several D.C. churches—"most often Holy Trinity"—and he maintained: "as far as I know, he never went to the National Shrine." Sal Mazzuca, interview with the author, February 20, 1999. For a broader account of the ways religion has shaped the presidency, see the sources in Gastón Espinoza, ed., *Religion and the American Presidency: Commentary and Primary Sources from George Washington to George W. Bush* (New York: Columbia University Press, 2009).

47. On the presidential funerals, and other details about the history of the Episcopalian house of worship, see Washington National Cathedral, History, www.nationalcathedral.org/about/history.shtml (accessed December 19, 2009). The quotation here is from a lay devotee I interviewed: interview no. 37 (Roberta), June 13, 1998, female, age 46, born Alaska, resides Washington, D.C.

48. In 2010, the staff estimated one million visitors, although "this is not unique vis-itors." Jacquelyn Hayes (Director of Communications) to author, e-mail, August 9, 2010. The official Website also suggested the site attracts "nearly one million

people" each year: Basilica of the National Shrine of the Immaculate Conception, www.nationalshrine.com/ (accessed December 19, 2009). Quotation from Thomas J. Grady, "America's Great Tribute to Mary," *American Ecclesiastical Review* 141.4 (July–December 1959): 217. The Shrine first appeared in the American Institute of Architects' guidebook to Washington in 1994: Weeks, *AIA Guide*, 288. Benjamin Forgey, "Letting the Shrine Shine," *Washington Post*, August 24, 1996, style sec., B1, B7.

CHAPTER 6

1. Quotation and point about globalization from Eric Rauchway, *Blessed among Nations: How the World Made America* (New York: Hill and Wang, 2006), 9, 7, 169. I assume the recent "transnational turn," and the emphasis on global flows and cross-oceanic exchanges. Among the important works that imagine a transnational or postnational American studies see Robert A. Gross, "The Transnational Turn: Rediscovering American Studies in a Wider World," *Journal of American Studies* [UK] 34.3 (December 2000): 373–93; and Shelley Fisher Fishkin, "Crossroads of Cultures: The Transnational Turn in American Studies— Presidential Address to the American Studies Association, November 12, 2004," *American Quarterly* [U.S.] 57.1 (March 2005): 17–57. In an article, originally presented as a conference paper in Kyoto, Fishkin has documented and celebrated the turn toward "transnational American Studies": Shelley Fisher Fishkin, "Asian Crossroads/Transnational American Studies," *Japanese Journal of American Studies* [Japan] 17 (2006): 5–52. See the ample citations in Fishkin's article for more bibliographical suggestions. In addition to Norman R. Yetman and David M. Katzman, eds., "Globalization, Transnationalism, and the End of the American Century," special issue, *American Studies* 41 (summer–fall 2000), similar efforts in American studies include: Michael Cowan and Eric Sandeen, "The Internationalization of American Studies," *American Studies Association Newsletter* 17 (December 1994): 12–14; Heinz Ickstadt, "American Studies in an Age of Globalization," *American Quarterly* 54.4 (December 2002): 543–62; John Carlos Rowe, ed., *Post-Nationalist American Studies* (Berkeley: University of California Press, 2000). Thomas Bender led a collaborative effort sponsored by the Organizations of American Historians: the Project on Internationalizing the Study of American History, which brought together seventy-eight scholars in four conferences. That project issued several reports and a collection of essays: Thomas Bender, ed., *Rethinking American History in a Global Age* (Berkeley: University of California Press, 2002). Bender has criticized "narrow parochialism" and called for "a wider cosmopolitanism" in *A Nation among Nations: America's Place in World History* (New York: Hill and Wang, 2006), 3. Some have noted that this "global babble" can go too far and ignore the power of borders: Janet Abu-Lughod coined the phrase "global babble" in "Going beyond Global Babble," in *Culture, Globalization, and the World System*, ed. A. D. King (London: Macmillan), and it was cited in Ulf Hannerz, *Transnational Connections: Culture, People, Places* (London: Routledge, 1996), 18. On global exchanges during the Progressive Era see Daniel T. Rodger, *Atlantic Crossings: Social Politics in a Progressive Age* (Cambridge, MA: Harvard University Press, 1998); and Bender, *Nation among Nations*, 9–10, 246–95. To give one example, Catholic and Protestant social policy proposals circulated across borders during this era: on that see Bender, *Nation among Nations*, 270–74; Rodgers, *Atlantic Crossings*, 63–66, 238, 524; Deirdre M. Moloney, *American Lay Catholic Groups and Transatlantic Social*

Reform in the Progressive Era (Chapel Hill: University of North Carolina Press, 2002). On transnational links with the Vatican see for example Gerald P. Fogarty, *The Vatican and the American Hierarchy from 1870 to 1965* (Stuttgart: Anton Hiersemann, 1982); and Peter R. D'Agostino, *Rome in America: Transnational Catholic Ideology from the Risorgimento to Fascism* (Chapel Hill: University of North Carolina Press, 2004).

2. On "immigration" as a key theme in Catholic history and U.S. religious history see Jay Dolan, "The Immigrants and Their Gods: A New Perspective in American Religious History," *Church History* 57 (March 1988): 61–72. See also Thomas A. Tweed, *Our Lady of the Exile: Diasporic Religion at a Cuban Catholic Shrine in Miami* (New York: Oxford University Press, 1997), 135–38.

3. The 1919 quotation was included in Shawn Perry, "The Perpetual Chorus of Peoples," *MS* 36 (December 1975): n.p. Shahan also used the phrase in the program book for the foundation stone ceremony in 1920: [Thomas J. Shahan], "Program," Laying of the Foundation Stone, September 23, 1920, 8 pp., Archives, BNSIC. A few clarifications about terms might help. First, the current code of canon law (canon 1223) suggests that a chapel is a type of oratory, a place of prayer set aside for worship and the celebration of the Mass, but the staff at the BNSIC has used the terms in slightly different ways. "The term 'chapel'...has been the preferred usage to describe the smaller and/or side places where the Eucharist may be celebrated, i.e., where there is an altar." In turn, an oratory is "a place of prayer without an altar in the National Shrine." Decorative elements such as mosaics, which I mention in table 6.2, would be understood as "votive offerings of art and piety" (canon 1234). These distinctions are made in Geraldine M. Rohling, archivist, "Oratory and Private Chapel," n.d., typescript, Archives, BNSIC. To avoid repeating both terms, I sometimes will refer to both types of spaces as chapels. Second, as for the labels to describe the Shrine's leader, note that Bransfield's title is "rector," not "director," since that is the appropriate usage for the person in charge of a basilica. The Vatican designated the site a "basilica" in 1990.

4. Samuel F. B. Morse, *Foreign Conspiracies against the Liberties of the United States* (New York: Leavitt, Lord, and Co., 1835). Josiah Strong, *Our Country: Its Possible Future and Its Present Crisis*, rev. ed. "based on the census of 1890" (New York: Baker and Taylor for the American Home Missionary Society, 1891) (originally published 1885). H. W. Evans, *The Public School Problem in America: Outlining Fully the Policies and the Program of the Knights of Ku Klux Klan toward the Public School System* (Atlanta: Knights of the Klu Klux Klan, 1924), 5. *To Enjoy American Opportunities Become an American Citizen*, lithograph color poster, 1919, Stanley Industrial Education Poster Service, LOT 8080, LC-USZC4-3808, Prints and Photographs Division, Library of Congress. John B. Howe, *Howe's New Era Civics* (Syracuse, NY: Iroquois, 1922), 9. Sheldon E. Davis and Clarence H. McClure, *Our Government: A Textbook of Civics* (Chicago: Laidlaw Brothers, 1922), v. See also Charles Edgar Finch, *Everyday Civics: Community, State, and Nation* (New York: American Book, 1921).

5. David O'Brien and Joseph Bernardin, "Public Catholicism [with Response]," *U.S. Catholic Historian* 8.4 (fall 1989): 89–95. David J. O'Brien, *Public Catholicism* (New York: Macmillan, 1989). Robert A. Orsi, *Between Heaven and Earth: The Religious Worlds People Make and the Scholars Who Study Them* (Princeton, NJ: Princeton University Press, 2005), 82–85. Richard Gilmour, ed., *The Sixth Reader*, Catholic National Readers (New York: Benziger Brothers, 1877), xiii. The donations by civics clubs are in the records dated December 15 and 30, 1953, Book 42: July 1953

to July 30, 1954, donor record book (typescript), Archives, BNSIC. William P. Maguire, "Catholic Secondary Education in the Diocese of Brooklyn" (Ph.D. diss., Catholic University of America, 1932), 34–38. Sarah E. Miller, "'Send Sisters, Send Polish Sisters': Americanizing Catholic Immigrant Children in the Early Twentieth Century," *Ohio History* 114 (2007): 54–55. Margaret Schallenberger McNaught, *Training in Courtesy: Suggestions for Teaching Good Manners in Elementary School*, U.S. Bureau of Education Bulletin no. 54 (Washington, DC: Government Printing Office, 1918). Hannah Margaret Harris, *Lessons in Civics for the Six Elementary Grades*, U.S. Bureau of Education Bulletin no. 18 (Washington, DC: Government Printing Office, 1920). The passage from Harris is quoted in Miller, "Send Sisters," 55. William H. Elson, *The Elson Reader*, bk. 4 (Chicago: Scott, Foresman, 1920). See also James Baldwin and Ida C. Bender, *Reading with Expression: Fifth Reader* (New York: American Book, 1911).

6. Miller, "Send Sisters," 54. Committee on Special War Activities, NCWC, *The Fundamentals of Citizenship*, Reconstruction Pamphlet, No. 7, June 1919, p. 22. Committee on Special War Activities, NCWC, *A Program for Citizenship*, Reconstruction Pamphlet, No. 5, July 1919, p. 3. The accompanying workbook: Committee on Special War Activities, NCWC, *Civics Catechism on the Rights and Duties of American Citizens*, Reconstruction Pamphlet, No. 13, 1920. See also the other pamphlet on the same topic: Committee on Special War Activities, NCWC, *Speakers' Outline of Talks on Citizenship*, Reconstruction Pamphlet, No. 11, May 1920.

7. "Instructions to Polish Catholics, Maspeth, New York, 1913," in Jeffrey M. Burns, Ellen Skerrett, and Joseph M. White, eds., *Keeping Faith: European and Asian Catholic Immigrants*, American Catholic Identities: A Documentary History (Maryknoll, N.Y.: Orbis, 2000), 144–45. As germ theory replaced environmental explanations for disease, a new emphasis on public health emerged during the Progressive Era, approximately from 1890 to 1920. That concern led to new professions and fields of study, including "sanitary engineering," and found institutional expression, for example, in the Rockefeller Sanitary Commission (1909) and the U.S. Public Health Service (1912). See "Health and Medicine," in *Historical Dictionary of the Progressive Era*, by Catherine Cocks, Peter Halloran, and Alan Lesseroff (Lanham, MD: Scarecrow Press, 2009), 189. The related discourse about "cleanliness" found institutional expression in the Cleanliness Institute (1927). The call to cleanliness sometimes linked purity with Protestantism and uncleanliness with Catholicism, as with Grace T. Hallock, *A Tale of Soap and Water: The Historical Progress of Cleanliness* (New York: Cleanliness Institute, 1928), which proposed that early Catholic leaders "did not encourage bathing" (49). Richard J. Callahan, Jr., Kathryn Lofton, and Chad E. Seales, "Allegories of Progress: Industrial Religion in the United States," *Journal of the American Academy of Religion* 78.1 (March 2010): 20–28. See also Suellen Hoy, *Chasing Dirt: The American Pursuit of Cleanliness* (New York: Oxford University Press, 1996).

8. Jay P. Dolan, *The American Catholic Experience: A History from Colonial Times to the Present* (Notre Dame, IN: University of Notre Dame Press, 1992), 2, 128–57. There is a rich and ever expanding literature on the U.S. Catholic Church's struggles with ethnic diversity; more books have appeared than I can cite here. Among the most important earlier studies see Jay P. Dolan, *The Immigrant Church: New York's Irish and German Catholics, 1815–1865* (Baltimore: Johns Hopkins University Press, 1975); Dolores Lipak, *Immigrants and Their Church* (New York: Macmillan, 1989); Robert A. Orsi, *The Madonna of 115th Street: Faith and Community in Italian Harlem*

(New Haven, CT: Yale University Press, 1985); James S. Olson, *Catholic Immigrants in America* (Chicago: Nelson-Hall, 1987); Ana Maria Diaz-Stevens, *Oxcart Catholicism on Fifth Avenue: The Impact of the Puerto Rican Migration upon the Archdiocese of New York* (Notre Dame, IN: Notre Dame University Press, 1993).

9. Dolan, *American Catholic Experience*, 127.

10. W. E. B. Du Bois, *Darkwater: Voices from Within the Veil* (New York: Harcourt, Brace, and Howe, 1920), 29–31. I am grateful to Edward J. Blum for pointing out the significance of Du Bois's essay "The Souls of White Folk" and discussing its wider context. See Edward J. Blum, *W. E. B. Du Bois, American Prophet* (Philadelphia: University of Pennsylvania Press, 2007); and Edward J. Blum, *Reforging the White Republic: Race, Religion, and American Nationalism, 1865–1898* (Baton Rouge: Louisiana State University Press, 2005). On the violence in the North and the South and the number of lynchings see National Association for the Advancement of Colored People, *Thirty Years of Lynching in the United States, 1889–1918* (New York: NAACP, 1919). See also David J. Goldberg, *Discontented America: The United States in the 1920s* (Baltimore: Johns Hopkins University Press, 1999), 89–116.

11. Quotations here from, in order, Edward J. Blum, contribution to "American Religion and 'Whiteness'" forum, *Religion and American Culture* 19.1 (winter 2009): 7; Judith Weisenfeld, contribution to ibid., 32; "Mexican Immigrants in the Midwest: Statement of a Chicago Resident, 1928," in *¡Presente!: U.S. Latino Catholics from Colonial Origins to the Present*, ed. Timothy Matovina and Gerald E. Poyo, *American Catholic Identities: A Documentary History* (Maryknoll, NY: Orbis, 2000), 108–9; "The Polish: Panna Maria, Texas, 1866–1870," in Burns et al., *Keeping Faith*, 140. On intermarriages in Detroit see Mathew Pehl, "The Remaking of the Catholic Working Class: Detroit, 1919–1945," *Religion and American Culture* 19.1 (winter 2009): 41. On immigrants and race see also Noel Ignatiev, *How the Irish Became White* (New York: Routledge, 1995); John T. McGreevy, *Parish Boundaries: The Catholic Encounter with Race in the Twentieth-Century Urban North* (Chicago: University of Chicago Press, 1996). Robert A. Orsi, "The Religious Boundaries of an In-between People: Street Feste and the Problem of the Dark-Skinned Other in Italian Harlem, 1920–1990," in *Gods of the City: Religion and the American Urban Landscape*, ed. Robert A. Orsi (Bloomington: Indiana University Press, 1999), 257–88; and Elizabeth McAlister, "The Madonna of 115th Street Revisited: Vodou and Haitian Catholicism in the Age of Transnationalism," in *Gatherings in Diaspora: Religious Communities and the New Immigrants*, ed. R. Stephen Warner and Judith G. Wittner (Philadelphia: Temple University Press, 1998), 123–60.

12. On tropes see Thomas A. Tweed, *Crossing and Dwelling: A Theory of Religion* (Cambridge: Harvard University Press, 2006), 67–68, 177. On figurative language for the church, including the "body of Christ," see *Catechism of the Catholic Church* (New York: Doubleday, 1995), 215–17, 226–31.

13. Pope Pius XII, *Mystici Corporis Christi* (1943), www.vatican.va (accessed January 15, 2010). Norman E. Tanner, ed., *Decrees of the Ecumenical Councils* (Washington, DC: Georgetown University Press, 1990). The thirty-one-page document from the 1884 council was printed with separate pagination at the end of James Gibbons, "Pastoral Letter of the Bishops and Archbishops of the United States Assembled in the Third Plenary Council of Baltimore, to the Clergy and Laity of Their Charge," in *The Memorial Volume: A History of the Third Plenary Council of Baltimore, November 9–December 7, 1884* (Baltimore: Baltimore Publishing Co., 1885). On ecclesiology since Vatican I see Richard P. McBrien, *The Church: The Evolution of Catholicism*

(New York: HarperCollins, 2008), 118–352. For McBrien's useful account of "the mystical body of Christ" see 122–25. Boniface VIII, *Unam Sanctam* (1302), available at the Website of the Fordham University Center for Medieval Studies, Internet Medieval Sourcebook, www. fordham.edu/halsall/source/b8-unam.html (accessed January 16, 2010). Tanner, *Decrees of the Ecumenical Councils*. Pope Pius XII, *Mystici Corporis Christi*. A very helpful overview of Catholic thinking on the subject is Francis X. Clooney, "Salvation outside the Church," in *The Harper Collins Encyclopedia of Catholicism*, ed. Richard P. McBrien (San Francisco: HarperCollins, 1995), 1159–60. See also McBrien, *The Church*, 121–23, 126–29. For another later use of corporeal images see National Conference of Catholic Bishops, *Heritage and Hope: Evangelization in the United States*, Pastoral Letter on the Fifth Centenary of Evangelization in the Americas (Washington, DC: National Conference of Catholic Bishops, 1990). I am indebted to Mark Massa, who points out the theological "loophole" of "implicit desire" and notes the range of interpretations of the binding phrase "extra Ecclesia nulla salus." Mark S. Massa, *Catholics and American Culture: Fulton Sheen, Dorothy Day, and the Notre Dame Football Team* (New York: Crossroad Press, 1999), 21–37. The Vatican's English version of Pius XII's encyclical translates the Latin phrase *inscio desidero* as "unconscious desire and longing"; I render it here as "unknowing longing" because the term "unconscious" has specific meanings that might mislead contemporary readers.

14. Gibbons, "Pastoral Letter of the Bishops and Archbishops of the United States," 2, 30.
15. James Anthony Walsh, *In the Orient: The Account of a Journey to Catholic Mission Fields in Japan, Korea, Manchuria, China, Indo-China, and the Philippines* (Ossining, NY: Catholic Foreign Missionary Society of America, 1919), 18. "A Geography of Prayer, 1927," in *Prayer and Practice in the American Catholic Community*, ed. Joseph P. Chinnici and Angelyn Dries, American Catholic Identities: A Documentary History (Maryknoll, NY: Orbis, 2000), 130–33.
16. Gina Cascone, *Pagan Babies and Other Catholic Memories* (New York: St. Martin's Press, 1982), 64, 63. See also Michael Moore, *Downsize This* (New York: Crown, 1996), 76. The statistics about donations and members between 1893 and 1910 are from John Williams, "Holy Childhood Association," in *The Catholic Encyclopedia*, vol. 7 (New York: Robert Appleton, 1910), available at the Website of Kevin Knight, www.newadvent.org/cathen/07399a.htm (accessed January 16, 2010). The Philadelphia data is from Martin J. McDonough and John C. Kavanagh, *A Confidential Report of All Funds Received at the Office of the Society for the Propagation of the Faith, Archdiocese of Philadelphia: Report on Parish Returns for Calendar Year 1958 and Report on School Returns for School Year 1958–1959*, box 57: Society for the Propagation of the Faith, Archives, PAHRC.
17. Gibbons, "Pastoral Letter of the Bishops and Archbishops of the United States," 30.
18. "The Letter of Paul to the Galatians" (3:28–29) and "The Letter of Paul to the Ephesians" (4:15–16), *The New Oxford Annotated Bible*, ed. Bruce Metzger and Roland E. Murphy (New York: Oxford University Press, 1991). Gibbons, "Pastoral Letter of the Bishops and Archbishops of the United States," 8. James Gibbons, "Response of the American Hierarchy, 1920," in Burns et al., *Keeping Faith*, 162.
19. Pius XII was quoted in John LaFarge, "The Catholic Viewpoint on Race Relations," in *American Catholic History: A Documentary Reader*, ed. Mark Massa, with Catherine Osborne (New York: New York University Press, 2008), 72. Marie Therese Archambault, "Native Americans and Evangelization," in *Native and*

Christian: Indigenous Voices on Religious Identity in the United States, ed. James Treat (New York: Routledge, 1996), 147. Du Bois quoted in McGreevy, *Parish Boundaries*, 35. On African-American Catholic history see Cyprian Davis, *The History of Black Catholics in the United States* (New York: Crossroad Press, 1990); Diana L. Hayes and Cyprian Davis, eds., *Taking Down Our Harps: Black Catholics in the United States* (Maryknoll, NY: Orbis Books, 1998); Cyprian Davis and Jamie T. Phelps, eds., *Stamped with the Image of God: African Americans as God's Image in Black*, American Catholic Identities Series (Maryknoll, NY: Orbis Books, 2003).

20. McGreevy, *Parish Boundaries*. Morris J. MacGregor, *The Emergence of a Black Catholic Community: St. Augustine's in Washington* (Washington, DC: Catholic University of America Press, 1999). "Editorial Comments," *Colored Harvest* 31.5 (October–November 1943): n.p. See also "American Josephites, 1893–1943: On the Colored Missions," jubilee issue, *Colored Harvest*, 31.2 (1943). On CUA's segregation in admission and facilities see John Tracy Ellis, *American Catholicism*, 2nd ed. (Chicago: University of Chicago Press, 1969), 148; C. Joseph Nuese, *The Catholic University: A Centennial History* (Washington, DC: Catholic University of America Press, 1990), 321–22, 344–45. Amy Koehlinger, *The New Nuns: Racial Justice and Religious Reform in the 1960s* (Cambridge, MA: Harvard University Press, 2007).

21. Gibbons, "Pastoral Letter of the Bishops and Archbishops of the United States," 30. D. W. Brogan quoted in Ellis, *American Catholicism*, 149.

22. Joshua M. Zeitz, *White Ethnic New York: Jews, Catholics, and the Shaping of Postwar Politics* (Chapel Hill: University of North Carolina Press, 2007), 2–8. Burns et al., *Keeping Faith*, a collection of primary sources devoted to immigration, also notes that the period after 1924 witnessed both "the persistence and transcendence of ethnicity." Burns et al., Part 4, "After 1924: The Persistence and Transcendence of Ethnicity," in Burns et al., *Keeping Faith*, 209–28. The signature from "Half Moon" is dated December 26, 1925, in Register of Visitors to the National Shrine, September 1927 to May 1930, 238, Archives, BNSIC.

23. The signatures of Kong Hi and Tongling are dated October 21, 1928, in Register of Visitors to the National Shrine, September 1927 to May 1930, 180, Archives, BNSIC.

24. *AC*, 194–95. *GTB*, 102. For the official position on the status of "non-Christians," including citations to the relevant documents of Vatican II, as well as early church councils and leaders, see *Catechism of the Catholic Church*, 241–47. For an accessible overview see Lucien Richard, *What Are They Saying about Christ and World Religions?* (New York: Paulist Press, 1981).

25. *GTB*, 24. Raymond A. Prybis, OMI, "Oblates of Mary Immaculate (O.M.I.)," in *The Encyclopedia of American Catholic History*, ed. Michael Glazier and Thomas J. Shelley (Collegeville, MN: Liturgical Press, 1997), 1063–64.

26. Gibbons, "Pastoral Letter of the Bishops and Archbishops of the United States," 30. Doug Herman, "Native Washington," *AAG Newsletter*, January 2010, 6. "From Our Catholic Indians of Arizona," *SR* 7.4 (June 1920): 28. The caption of the photograph begins "Our Friends from Alaska...": *SR* 14.9 (September 1927): 72. The information and quotations I cite here about Arizona missions are from Christopher Vecsey, *On the Padres' Trail* (Notre Dame, IN: University of Notre Dame Press, 1996), 106–18. Mrs. F. H. Riley, December 30, 1953, Book 42: July 1953 to July 30, 1954, donor record book (typescript), Archives, BNSIC. Because she didn't list her full name, I've been unable to be sure about which of the multiple

women named Riley contributed, though it seems almost certain the benefactor claimed a tribal identity. The donation record indicates that she was married and worked at St. John's Mission, and she might have worked at the boarding school there. As the federal records show, there were a number of girls and women named Riley associated with tribal nations in Arizona and affiliated at some point with St. John's Indian School in Laveen. The students at the mission school came from many southwestern tribes, including the Pimas, Papagos, Apache, Navajos, and Hopi. Some women named Riley at St. John's were White Mountain Apache: as the 1968 yearbook indicates, Sister Pascalita, a former St. John's student who had become a Franciscan nun, had responsibility for elementary students at the school. She was "a sister of Mary Riley," and both women had lived in Whitewater, Arizona, near Fort Apache (22). The photograph in the illustration and this information about the Riley sisters is in *St. John's Indian School, Laveen, Arizona*, pamphlet no. 8, R9791, Special Collections, University of Arizona, Tucson.

27. "Indians Visit the Shrine," *SR* 7.4 (June 1920): 27. *MEM*, 121, 128. Montana Office of Public Instruction, *Montana Indians: Their History and Location* (Helena: Montana Office of Public Instruction, Division of Indian Education, 2009). "Half Moon's" signature on the visitor book is dated December 26, 1925, in Register of Visitors to the National Shrine, September 1927 to May 1930, 238, Archives, BNSIC. Jacob Buckenmeyer, "Tekawitha Conference Mass at National Shrine," *MS* 68.2 (fall–winter 2007): 7.

28. *GTB*, 24, 25, 28, 34. A good deal has been written about Tekawitha. See for example Allan Greer, *Mohawk Saint: Catherine Tekawitha and the Jesuits* (New York: Oxford University Press, 2006); Christopher Vecsey, *The Paths of Kateri's Kin* (Notre Dame, IN: University of Notre Dame Press, 1997), 96–108.

29. Several of the photographs I refer to here are reprinted in Geraldine M. Rohling, *Jubilee 2009: A Photographic History of the Basilica of the National Shrine of the Immaculate Conception* (Washington, DC: Basilica of the National Shrine of the Immaculate Conception, 2009), 39, 46, and *AC*, 54–55. The list of employees in the Salve Regina Office was printed in *MEM*, 250. Where I could find links I matched federal census records with the names on the list of employees in the Office and the name of the head of the local construction company, and for the Polish translator, Joseph Rydzynksi, and the construction company leader, C. J. Cassidy, those records are: C. J. Cassidy: U.S. Bureau of the Census, *Fifteenth Census of the United States, 1930* (Washington, DC: National Archives and Records Administration, 1930), Washington, District of Columbia, roll 302; p. 324; enumeration district 350. Joseph Rudzinski [sic]: *Fifteenth Census of the United States, 1930* (Washington, DC: National Archives and Records Administration, 1930), Washington, District of Columbia, roll 302; p. 1A; enumeration district 351.

30. Nazarino Maisano to Miss Whelan, September 11, 1913, Thomas J. Shahan Papers, box 7, Archives, ACUA. Nazarino A. Maisano: U.S. Bureau of the Census, *Fourteenth Census of the United States, 1920*, Menlo Park, San Mateo, California; roll T625_145; p. 1A; enumeration district 76. Maisano was a seminarian in 1920 and, as the next census showed, a parish priest in Livermore by 1930. "African Devotion to the Blessed Virgin," *SR* 12.12 (December 1925): 94. The population statistics I cite are from the Bureau of the Census. The analysis of race in D.C. is from Campbell Gibson and Kay Jung, "Historical Census Statistics on Population Totals by Race, 1790 to 1990, and by Hispanic Origin, 1970 to 1990, for the United States Regions, Divisions, and States," working paper series no. 56, September 2002, table 23, U.S. Census Bureau, Population Division, www.census.gov/population/ (accessed

February 4, 2010). U.S. Census Bureau, "Race Alone or in Combination, 2000," geographic area 20017, summary FILE 1, www.census.gov/population/ (accessed February 4, 2010). James Cardinal Hickey, "Witnessing to African-American Faith," (Washington, DC) *Catholic Standard*, August 28, 1997, n.p.

31. Donald Martin Reynolds, *A Celebration of Love and Freedom Expressed in Art and Architecture: The Meaning of the Sculpture Program in Our Mother of Africa Chapel* (1997), 4 pp. (document available at the Shrine before and during the dedication program), in possession of the author. *GTB*, 61–62. Hickey, "Witnessing to African-American Faith." Nancy Hartnagel, "Mother of Africa Chapel at Shrine Will Be Dedicated on Saturday," (Washington, DC) *Catholic Standard*, August 28, 1997, p. 13. Hilbert Stanley, interview with the author, September 11, 1997. The dedication ceremony also was broadcast live on Eternal Word Television Network on August 30, 1997; I watched the videotape of that broadcast again before I wrote this chapter.

32. *SR* 1.1 (January 1914). The original plan for the chapels is in *MEM*, 89. There is a vast scholarly literature on religion and the new immigrants, for example, Peter Kivisto, "Religion and the New Immigrants," in *A Future for Religion?: New Paradigms for Social Analysis*, ed. William H. Swatos, Jr. (Newbury Park, CA: Sage, 1993), 92–108; R. Stephen Warner and Judith G. Wittner, eds., *Gatherings in Diaspora: Religious Communities and the New Immigration* (Philadelphia: Temple University Press, 1998); Diana L. Eck, *A New Religious America: How a "Christian Country" Has Now Become the World's Most Religiously Diverse Nation* (New York: HarperSanFrancisco, 2001); Fred Kniss and Paul D. Numrich, *Sacred Assemblies and Civic Engagement: How Religion Matters for America's Newest Immigrants* (New Brunswick, NJ: Rutgers University Press, 2007); Michael W. Foley and Dean R. Hoge, *Religion and the New Immigrants: How Faith Communities Form Our Newest Citizens* (New York: Oxford University Press, 2007).

33. The quotation about the foundation stone is from "Details of Laying the Foundation Stone," in *NS*, 10. On the metal container in the foundation stone I also consulted Gerre M. Rohling, "The Dedication of the Cornerstone" (2006), posted to the BNSIC Website, www.nationalshrine.com (accessed September 16, 2006). Amanda Gies, membership application, National Catholic Family Record [1928], Archives, BNSIC. Katherine S. Egan, membership application, National Catholic Family Record, September 30, 1928, Archives, BNSIC. I searched the federal census records to find information about these and other family donors. The information about the Messall family, for example, can be found in Arthur G. Messall: *Fifteenth Census of the United States, 1930*, Logan, Oklahoma; roll 1912; p. 4B; enumeration district 29. The photograph of the memorial tablets I refer to here is reprinted in *AC*, 78.

34. *MEM*, 111–12. Thomas J. Grady, "The Crypt Church of the National Shrine of the Immaculate Conception," *American Ecclesiastical Review* 137 (July–December 1957): 408. *GTB*, 38. "Seven Columns for Catholic Shrine," *Washington Post*, November 22, 1923, p. 10. Cecilia Annette Moore, "'Good and Zealous Ladies': The Role of Catholic Women in Building the National Shrine of the Immaculate Conception" (M.A. Thesis, Department of Religious Studies, University of Virginia, 1991), 87. H. E. Lidén, *Mariakirken i Bergen* (Bergen, Norway: Association of Norwegian Ancient Monuments Conservation, n.d [2009]), 16 pp. The Norwegian ambassador visited the Washington Shrine on other occasions, too, but notice of one visit appeared in *SR*: "On March 4 the Norwegian Ambassador, Mr. Steen, and his wife, Madame Steen, paid a visit to the Crypt of the Shrine," *SR* 13.4 (April 1926): 31.

35. The notice of the Polish pilgrims is from "Shrine Notes," *SR* 15.8 (August 1928): 62. Peter F. Rydzyuski to the Reverend Bernard McKenna, March 7, 1930, Bernard McKenna Papers, MC61, Archives, PAHRC. Moore, "'Good and Zealous Ladies,'" 88. I found information about the Pole from Baltimore in Peter F. Rydzyuski: *Fifteenth Census of the United States, 1930*, Baltimore, Maryland; roll 848; p. 7B; enumeration district 528.

36. Campbell Gibson and Emily Lennon: U.S. Bureau of the Census, Population Division, Table 22, "Nativity of the Population for Urban Places Ever among the 50 Largest Urban Places since 1870: 1850 to 1990," July 9, 2008, www.census.gov/population/ (accessed February 4, 2010).

37. Shawn Perry, "The Perpetual Chorus of Peoples," *MS* 36 (December 1975): n.p. Michael J. Bransfield, interview with author, June 5, 1997, BNSIC, Washington, D.C. Since Monsignor Bransfield is no longer rector, the earlier messages on the Website have changed, but they were posted at www.nationalshrine.com (accessed June 5, 1998.)

38. Michael J. Bransfield, interview with author, June 5, 1997, BNSIC, Washington, D.C.

39. For information on the chapels and oratories see *GTB*. Between 1927 and 1997, devotees negotiated ethnic identity in some artifacts outside the chapels and oratories, too. For example, on September 4, 1977, a white marble statue of Cuba's national patroness, Our Lady of Charity, was blessed and was pedestaled in the chancel of the Great Upper Church. *GTB*, 97.

40. Interview no. 10, June 7, 1998, female, age not given, born Manila, arrived United States 1978, resides Piscataway, New Jersey. For published accounts of the dedication ceremony see Gerard Perseghin, "Filipino Catholics Celebrate Dedication of Shrine's Newest Oratory," (Washington, DC) *Catholic Standard*, June 12, 1997, p. 3; and "Our Lady of Peace and Good Voyage, Antipolo," *MS* 58.2 (fall–winter 1997–98), 5. See also the ninety-six-page booklet distributed to the crowd at the dedication mass: *Oratory of Our Lady of Peace and Good Voyage* (n.p.: n.p. [printed by the BNSIC], n.d. [1997]).

41. The results of the vote of the Catholic Bishops' Conference of the Philippines are preserved in a letter (photocopy in author's possession): Nestor C. Carino, Secretary General of the Catholic Bishops' Conference of the Philippines, to Filipino Marian Shrine Project, c/o the Most Reverend Alvaro Corrada, SJ, February 22, 1993. As this letter indicates, the sixty-two voters in the plenary assembly expressed their preferences for Our Lady of Peace and Good Voyage in Antipolo (thirty-three votes). Other Filipino Virgins also received votes, however: Our Lady of Barangay (twenty-two), Our Lady of Penafrancia (four), Our Lady of the Rosary of Manaoag (three). On Filipino Catholicism and the Virgin of Antipolo see Monina A. Mercado, *Antipolo: A Shrine to Our Lady* (Manila: Kyodo, 1980). The volume produced by the Journeying with Mary Foundation, associated with the Antipolo Shrine Project, also includes useful historical background: Noemi M. Castillo and Rev. Michael G. Kyte, eds., *Journeying with Mary* (San Francisco: Printout for the Journeying with Mary Foundation, 1996). On Filipino American religion see the following studies, which focus on San Francisco and Houston, respectively: Joaquín Jay Gonzalez III, *Filipino American Faith in Action: Immigration, Religion, and Civic Engagement* (New York: New York University Press, 2009); and Stephen Michael Cherry, "Breaking the Bread, Sharing the Wine: Religion as Culture and Community in the Civic Life of Filipino-Americans" (Ph.D. diss., University of Texas at Austin, 2008).

42. The oratory statue was donated by Pacita Mota and Socorro Mota, and their official letter to Cardinal Jaime Sin, dated October 10, 1994, and indicating their intention to give the image to the Antipolo Shrine Project in the United States, is reprinted in Castillo and Kyte, *Journeying with Mary*, 29. The main architects for the project, Saeed Noorbakhsh and Vernon Geisel, worked for Leo A. Daly, a Washington, D.C., architectural firm selected by Bransfield and the BNSIC staff. Two Filipino architects also were involved: Francisco T. Manosa and Cecilia Silayan-Hofilena of Francisco T. Manosa and Partners of Manila. The Filipino firm designed the circular pedestal, which is made from native materials, including indigenous hardwood and coconut shells. On the design and construction of the oratory and murals see Castillo and Kyte, *Journeying with Mary*, 71–81. "Jose Blanco, Angono Folk Muralist, Dies, 76," *Philippine Daily Inquirer*, August 15, 2008, http://services.inquirer.net (accessed February 4, 2010).

43. *Share in the Joy and Privilege of Building a Chapel for Our Lady of Antipolo*, brochure (Washington, DC: National Shrine of the Immaculate Conception, n.d.) (my emphasis). Author's fieldnotes, Filipino Oratory Dedication Ceremony, June 7, 1997. Bishop Corrada's quotation also was included in Perseghin, "Filipino Catholics," 3.

44. Teresita (Tessie) Manuel and Migs Cruz, members of the Antipolo Shrine Committee, interview with author, June 5, 1997, BNSIC. Monsignor Michael J. Bransfield to Miss Teresita A. Manuel, February 7, 1992, Archives, BNSIC.

45. Interview no. 46, June 21, 1998, female, age forty-four, born Pasay City, Philippines, arrived United States 1989, resides Fairfax Station, Virginia. Interview no. 24, June 13, 1998, male, age fifty-six, born Leyte, Philippines, resides Aldelphi, Maryland. Eduardo D. Caparas, National Co-Chair, Antipolo Shrine Project Committee, "Message," in *Oratory of Our Lady of Peace and Good Voyage* [8].

46. Castillo and Kyte, eds., *Journeying with Mary*, 25–26. Eduardo D. Caparas, national cochair, Antipolo Shrine Project, interview with author, June 7, 1997, BNSIC. On the dedication of the Asian Indian chapel see "Oratory of Our Lady of Good Health, Vailankanni," *MS* 58.2 (fall–winter 1997–98), 4–5. See also the 129-page souvenir booklet distributed to the almost five thousand pilgrims who attended: *Our Lady of Good Health, Vailankanni, at the National Shrine*, Souvenir of Dedication, August 16, 1997. For several studies of Asian-American Catholic traditions see "Asian American Catholics," special issue, *U.S. Catholic Historian* 18.1 (winter 2000).

47. "Tenth Annual National Filipino Pilgrimage," *MS* 68.2 (fall–winter 2007): n.p. The profile of Holy Angels Parish is from the online profiles: Archdiocese of Philadelphia, Philadelphia–North Vicariate, www.archdiocese.phl.org/parishes/ (accessed January 30, 2010). U.S. Census Bureau, Population Division, table 14, "Foreign Born Population by Historical Section and Subsection of the United States, 1850 to 1990," www.census.gov/population (accessed January 28, 2010). Gibson and Jung, "Historical Census Statistics on Population Totals by Race, 1790 to 1990, and by Hispanic Origin, 1970 to 1990, for the United States Regions, Divisions, and States," working paper series no. 56, September 2002, table 23. Several helpful studies by social scientists note the rise of new immigration in the area, though most ignore or deemphasize the District's late nineteenth-century foreign-born presence. See Elizabeth Chacko, "Washington, D.C.: From Biracial City to Multiethnic Gateway," in *Migrants in the Metropolis: The Rise of Immigrant Gateway Cities*, ed. Marie Price and Lisa Benton-Short (Syracuse, NY: Syracuse

University Press, 2008), 203–25. Marie Price et al., "The World Settles In: Washington, D.C. as an Immigrant Gateway," *Urban Geography* 26.1 (2005): 61–83. Marie Price, "Metropolitan Washington: A Restless Immigrant Landscape," *AAG Newsletter* 44.9 (2009): 1, 6–7.

48. Michael J. Bransfield, "Unity through Our Diversity: 40 Years since Its Dedication, the National Shrine Still Furthers Catholic Harmony in America," *MS* 60.1 (spring–summer 1999): 2. For an account of the Italian chapel's ceremony see "Our Lady of Pompei Chapel Dedicated," *MS* 70.1 (spring–summer 2009): 3.

49. "Korean Bas-Reliefs Dedicated," *MS* 69.1 (spring–summer 2008): 5.

CONCLUSION

1. "Threshold," *Oxford English Dictionary*, 2nd ed., 1989, OED Online.

2. Thomas J. Shahan, "Who Will Build the University Church?," *Catholic University Bulletin* 9.4 (October 1903): 509–10.

3. Peter W. Williams, "The Iconography of the American City: Or, a Gothic Tale of Modern Times," *Church History* 68.2 (June 1999): 377.

4. Mark J. Massa, SJ, *Anti-Catholicism in America: The Last Acceptable Prejudice* (New York: Crossroad, 2003), 166. See also John T. McGreevy, *Catholicism and American Freedom: A History* (New York and London: W.W. Norton, 2003), 289–93. On the 1985 Louisiana case that drew attention when a court convicted a priest who abused more than one hundred boys, see Jason Berry, *Lead Us Not Into Temptation: Catholic Priests and the Sexual Abuse of Children* (New York: Doubleday, 1992). The Boston case intensified public scrutiny in 2002 in the United States, just as attention around the world spiked again in 2010, when the media reported more cases of abuse and concealment. The U.S. bishops commissioned a scholarly study: Karen Terry et al., prepared by the John Jay College of Criminal Justice, *The Nature and Scope of the Problem of Sexual Abuse of Minors by Catholic Priests and Deacons in the United States* (Washington, DC: USCCB, 2004). The report is available at http://www.usccb.org/nrb/johnjaystudy/ (accessed July 8, 2010). It documented 10,667 individuals making accusations and 4,392 priests accused of abuse between 1950 and 2002. The problem, it concluded, "affects more than 95% of dioceses and approximately 60% of religious communities." For the bishops' response, see United States Conference of Catholic Bishops, *Promise to Protect and Pledge to Heal: Charter for the Protection of Children and Young People: Essential Norms, Statement of Episcopal Commitment*, revised June 2005 (Washington, DC: USCCB, 2005). See also a lay response: Diane Knight, Chair, National Review Board of the USCCB, "Ten Things Victim/Survivors Taught Us," May 14, 2010, USCCB News Release, www.usccb.org (accessed June 30, 2010). As an historian writing about young pilgrims after the revelations of 2002, I struggled with how to deal with this sensitive and divisive issue. Most of all, I tried to meet the historian's obligation to be fair. That meant, I decided, I should neither unfairly taint ecclesiastical officials with the suspicion of abuse nor overlook the issue. "We shudder from horror," one survivor has proposed, but "for the sake of our children, we must fight this temptation—the temptation to turn away...." David Clohessy's Speech at the USCCB Meeting in Dallas, TX, June 13, 2002, http://www.bishop-accountability.org (accessed July 5, 2010). Fighting both the impulse to turn away and to unjustly condemn, I felt obliged to pose a question that was as painful to ask as it was difficult to answer: were all the young people on all the overnight journeys to the Shrine free from harm? Since clerical personnel records

were inaccessible to me, to try to answer this question I consulted newspaper stories and public documents from legal and ecclesiastical cases that dealt with accusations concerning the period from 1920 to 1959. I found no direct evidence of minors who claimed they suffered abuse during field trips that included a pilgrimage to the Shrine. I found only three documents that suggest possible clerical misconduct during trips to Washington, though none of those specify that the young people went to the Shrine during their multi-day visit. So we can reach no firm conclusions, but these three sources also do not offer reassurance that all young pilgrims before 1959 were free from harm when they stayed in area hotels. First, one accuser has said that during the late 1950s a Cleveland priest, Reverend James Viall, was guilty of sexual misconduct during a trip to Washington. When he was thirteen, he and Father Viall "stayed in the same room," and "the priest threw his arms and legs over the young boy as he began to breathe heavily as they lay in bed together." Second, a signed testimony by a credible accuser in the case against the Reverend Lawrence C. Murphy, who worked at Milwaukee's St. John's School for the Deaf, reports that "during my senior Trip to New York City and Washington, D.C. for a week, Fr. Murphy played with me in the hotel bedroom a few times." Finally, a chilling letter was written in 1948 by Joseph P. Gausch (1917–1999), an alleged abuser then serving a Philadelphia parish, to Charles L. G. Knapp, another priest. By the time of his death, Gausch had been accused of molesting more than ten boys, with incidents starting as early as 1946, and in his boastful missive to Knapp about their respective "escapades" with children and adolescents, he reported, "I am still foaming from this afternoon's experience . . . the closest approximation to an old fashioned roll that I have had in years." Gausch also refers to Knapp's last letter, which obviously had hinted about his own sexual encounters with boys during a recent trip to Washington in May of 1948. "Don't have to tell you I await full details of that pilgrimage to the nation's capital," Gausch wrote in response. "That hotel *must* have been something. More when I see you? Puh-leeeze . . ." Like the other two documents, that letter doesn't state that Father Knapp and his charges visited the BNSIC during their trip, though such a visit also can't be ruled out, since he described the travel as "pilgrimage," that archdiocese had close ties to the Shrine, and the incident occurred in May, a month of heightened devotion to Mary. David Briggs, "Accused Priest's Parish Defends Him Fiercely," *Plain Dealer* [Cleveland, OH], September 3, 2002. The anonymous statement dated May 15, 1974, from a former student at St. John's School for the Deaf is from Milwaukee Archdiocesan Files concerning the Reverend Lawrence C. Murphy and has been made available online: "Account by male survivor . . . ," 1974-05-15, # 00407, Abuse Reports in Milwaukee Archdiocesan Files, http://www.bishop-accountability.org/assign/Murphy_Lawrence_C.htm (accessed July 5, 2010). On the Philadelphia case, see *Report of the Grand Jury*, In the Court of Common Pleas, First Judicial District of Pennsylvania, Criminal Trial Division, Misc. No. 03–00–239, September 17, 2003. On Gausch's case, and the charges against him, see pages 117–24. Gausch's letter, which was dated May 25, 1948, is included in the Appendix, "Selected Documents" (D-6).

5. Charles Taylor, "A Catholic Modernity?," in *A Catholic Modernity?: Charles Taylor's Marianist Award Lecture*, ed. James L. Heft (New York: Oxford University Press, 1999), 14.

6. James T. Fisher, *Communion of Immigrants: A History of Catholics in America* (New York: Oxford University Press, 2002), 114.

7. "School of Law Sponsors Legal Mass Sunday," *Washington Post*, January 17, 1942, p. 6. *AC*, 91–92.

8. *AC*, 91. There is no record of an invitation to the foundation stone ceremony in *The Papers of Woodrow Wilson*, ed. Arthur S. Link, 69 vols. (Princeton, NJ: Princeton University Press, 1966–94). There also is no record of any activity by President Wilson on the date of the ceremony in 1920 in the diary kept by the White House head usher, Ike Hoover. I am grateful to staff at the Woodrow Wilson Presidential Library, especially Danna Faulds and Linda MacNeil, for helping me confirm this. Eisenhower worked for two hours and then played golf briefly in the morning and then again from 12:59–3:45 p.m. Presidential Appointment Books, November 20, 1959, Papers of Dwight D. Eisenhower as President, 1953–61, Dwight D. Eisenhower Presidential Library and Museum, Abilene, KS. That library also contains a file of materials that include the Shrine's invitation and cover letter, the "statement" they hoped he would issue, his noncommittal response, and the documents concerning the final decision to not attend and not issue a statement: "1-EE District of Columbia, November, 1959," box 490, president's personal file, Dwight D. Eisenhower Records as President, White House central files, 1953–61, Dwight D. Eisenhower Presidential Library and Museum. I am grateful to Chris Abraham, archivist at the library, for his assistance.

9. A Catholic familiar with Trinity Church told me this story about the phrase "Abomination of Desolation" but asked that I not reveal his identity or say any more about the context, so I follow his wishes. John F. Kennedy's "Address to Southern Baptist Leaders" has been reprinted often, including in *American Catholic History: A Documentary Reader*, ed. Mark Massa with Catherine Osborne (New York: New York University, 2008), 160–63. Paula Kane has noted the decline of Marian devotion after Vatican II, but also its "resurgence . . . in the 1980s centered on apparitions, apocalyptic warnings, and pilgrimages." Paula M. Kane, "Marian Devotion since 1940: Continuity or Casualty?," in *Habits of Devotion: Catholic Religious Practice in Twentieth-Century America*, ed. James M. O'Toole (Ithaca, NY: Cornell University Press, 2004), 90.

10. One mass e-mail sent in 2009, for example, invited devotees to "Light a Candle" in someone's honor and provided a link to a space at the Shrine's website where they could type a petition and make a donation: Basilica of the National Shrine of the Immaculate Conception (news@bnsic.org) to the author, May 28, 2009, e-mail, copy in author's possession. For a Catholic account of the 2009 Red Mass, see Mark Zimmerman, "At Red Mass, Cardinal DiNardo Encourages Those in Legal Profession to Be Guided by Holy Spirit," *My Catholic Standard* (Archdiocese of Washington), October 6, 2009, www.cathstan.org (accessed August 2, 2010). For an account that emphasizes the controversy surrounding the ritual see Tony Mauro, "Red Mass in D.C. Draws Six Justices, Vice President," The BLT: The Blog of Legal Times, October 4, 2009, http://legaltimes.typepad.com (accessed July 5, 2010). An undated press release on the BNSIC Website in 2010 claimed it "receives an estimated one million visitors annually": "Backgrounder: Overview of Shrine History, Significance, and Current Status," Media Contact, www.nationalshrine .com (accessed August 8, 2010).

11. The quotation criticizing Vatican II is from a forty-page pamphlet that challenged the liturgical changes: Michael Davies, *The New Mass* (Saint Paul, MN: Remnant, 1977), 28. The second quotation is from Mary Jo Weaver, "Introduction: Who Are the Conservative Catholics?," in *Being Right: Conservative Catholics in America*, ed. Mary Jo Weaver and R. Scott Appleby (Bloomington: Indiana University Press, 1995), 2.

12. David Van Biema, "Is Liberal Catholicism Dead?," *Time*, May 3, 2008. Leslie Woodcock Tentler, *Catholics and Contraception: An American History* (Ithaca, NY: Cornell University Press, 2004), 137. "Vietnam Policy Protest Set for Luci Johnson Wedding," *New York Times*, July 19, 1966, p. 3. George Vecsey, "53 Nuns, after a Night of Prayer, Stand in Silent Protest to Pontiff," *New York Times*, October 8, 1979, pp. A1, B7. Joe Feuerherd, "Gay Catholics Denied Communion Found Guilty," *National Catholic Reporter*, February 14, 2003, NCR Online, www.natcath.com/ (accessed February 16, 2010). Several incidents at the Shrine in later decades directly focused attention there on the sexual abuse issue. A Washington journalist, for instance, wondered "whether censorship is still in effect" when the Shrine's staff removed a book about Boston's sexual abuse case from its bookstore shelves and cancelled a book signing by its Roman Catholic author, a former editor of Boston's archdiocesan newspaper. Two years later, leaders of the Survivors Network of those Abused by Priests (SNAP) criticized the choice of a Colombian cardinal as celebrant for a scheduled Latin Mass there because he had been condemned for his handling of a famous case of clerical misconduct. When the Survivors Network publicly challenged that choice, saying "it rubs salt in the wounds of victims," the Maryland-based liturgical organization sponsoring the mass responded to the pressure and replaced the celebrant. So this major ecclesiastical controversy was openly addressed at the Shrine in later years. John Holusha and Ian Fisher, "Pope Begins U.S. Visit; Says He Is Ashamed of Sex Scandal," *New York Times*, April 16, 2008. Chaz Muth, "Oklahoma Bishop to Celebrate Solemn High Mass at National Shrine," Catholic News Service, April 22, 2010, www.catholicnews.com (accessed June 25, 2010). Julia Duin, "Catholic Book Raises Furor," *Washington Times*, September 25, 2008, www.washingtontimes.com (June 20, 2010). The book that stirred controversy was Philip F. Lawler, *The Faithful Departed: The Collapse of Boston's Catholic Culture* (New York: Encounter Books, 2008).

13. Feuerherd, "Gay Catholics Denied Communion Found Guilty." For the program listings and "traditional mass resources" see EWTN: Global Network, the station's Website, www.ewtn.com/ (accessed February 16, 2010). Information about the 2009 and 2010 "Mass for Life" circulated in many media, including e-mails sent to donors and visitors listed on the mailing list at the BNSIC: "Annual March for Life," e-mail, BNSIC, January 15, 2010; "Defend the Sanctity of Life," e-mail, BNSIC, January 30, 2010. On the worldview of twentieth-century Marian devotees, including those in Marian organizations, see Sandra L. Zimdars-Swartz, "The Marian Revival in American Catholicism: Focal Points and Features of the New Marian Enthusiasm," in Weaver and Appleby, *Being Right*, 213–40.

14. G. S. Kirk, ed. and trans, *Heraclitus: The Cosmic Fragments* (Cambridge: Cambridge University Press, 1954), 381, 14. Kirk suggests that the famous saying that it's impossible to step into the same river twice is probably not authentic. Heraclitus's understanding is better represented in fragment 12: "Upon those who step into the same rivers different and again different waters flow" (367).

15. Charles H. Long, "Civil Rights—Civil Religion: Visible People and Invisible Religion," in *American Civil Religion*, ed. Russell E. Richey and Donald G. Jones (New York: Harper and Row, 1974), 213, 218.

16. Thomas A. Tweed, *Crossing and Dwelling: A Theory of Religion* (Cambridge, MA: Harvard University Press, 2006), 54–79. My definition: "religions are confluences of organic-cultural flows that intensify joy and confront suffering by drawing on human and suprahuman forces to make home and cross boundaries" (54).

17. 69–73, 73–77, 80–163.

ILLUSTRATION CREDITS

Figure I.1.　Photograph reproduced in cooperation with and by permission of the Basilica of the National Shrine of the Immaculate Conception, Washington, D.C. (BNSIC). Photograph by the author, 2007.

Figure I.2.　Photograph reproduced in cooperation with and by permission of the BNSIC.

Figure I.3.　Photograph reproduced in cooperation with and by permission of the BNSIC. Photograph by the author, 2007.

Figure 1.1.　Photograph reproduced in cooperation with and by permission of the BNSIC.

Figure 1.2.　Courtesy Philadelphia Archdiocesan Historical Records Center (PAHRC); reproduced in cooperation with and permission of the BNSIC.

Figure 1.3.　Courtesy PAHRC; reproduced in cooperation with and permission of the BNSIC.

Figure 1.4.　Courtesy PAHRC; reproduced in cooperation with and permission of the BNSIC.

Figure 2.1.　Photograph reproduced in cooperation with and by permission of the BNSIC.

Figure 2.2.　Photograph reproduced in cooperation with and by permission of the BNSIC.

Figure 2.3.　Courtesy Father J. Michael Ricker.

Figure 2.4.　Photograph reproduced in cooperation with and by permission of the BNSIC. Photograph by the author, November 20, 2006.

Figure 3.1.　The Treasure Chest of Fun and Fact Collection, The American Catholic History Research Center and University Archives, The Catholic University of America, Washington, D.C.

Figure 3.2.　Courtesy Archives, Diocese of Brooklyn.

Figure 3.3.　The National Catholic Welfare Conference, Lantern Slide Collection, The American Catholic History Research Center and University Archives, The Catholic University of America, Washington, D.C.

Figure 3.4.　Courtesy PAHRC.

Figure 3.5.　Photograph reproduced in cooperation with and by permission of the BNSIC.

Figure 4.1.　Courtesy PAHRC; reproduced in cooperation with and by permission of the BNSIC.

Figure 4.2.　Courtesy Library of Congress.

Figure 4.3.　Courtesy Library of Congress.

Figure 4.4.　By permission of Scala/Art Resource.

Figure 4.5.　Photograph reproduced in cooperation with and by permission of the BNSIC. Photograph by Geraldine M. Rohling.

Figure 5.1.　Photograph reproduced in cooperation with and by permission of the BNSIC; and courtesy of Saint Anselm Abbey, Manchester, New Hampshire.

Figure 5.2.　Photograph by George T. Woodward. Courtesy Library of Congress.

Figure 5.3.　Photograph by Nick Parrino. United States Office of War Information. Courtesy Library of Congress.

Figure 5.4.　Photograph reproduced in cooperation with and by permission of the BNSIC.

Figure 5.5.　Courtesy Library of Congress.

Figure 5.6.　Photograph by Donovan Marks, courtesy of the Washington National Cathedral.

Figure 5.7.　Courtesy Library of Congress.

Figure 5.8.　Courtesy Library of Congress; reproduced in cooperation with and by permission of the BNSIC.

Figure 5.9　Photograph by Theodor Horydczak. Theodor Horydczak Collection, Library of Congress.

Figure 5.10.　Photographs © 1993 by Werner J. Bertsch.

Figure 6.1.　Photograph reproduced in cooperation with and by permission of the BNSIC. Photograph by Geraldine M. Rohling

Figure 6.2. The National Catholic Welfare Conference, Lantern Slide Collection, The American Catholic History Research Center and University Archives, The Catholic University of America, Washington, D.C.

Figure 6.3. Photograph reproduced in cooperation with and by permission of the BNSIC.

Figure 6.4. By permission of Special Collections, University of Arizona Library.

Figure 6.5. Courtesy PAHRC; reproduced in cooperation with and by permission of the BNSIC.

Figure 6.6. Photograph reproduced in cooperation with and by permission of the BNSIC.

Figure 6.7. Photograph reproduced in cooperation with and by permission of the BNSIC. Photograph by the author, 2007.

ACKNOWLEDGMENTS

Now that I've finished this book I hope to return to the Shrine's threshold, the central door of the Great Upper Church, to again look down the nave and out toward the city. On that visit, however, I won't have to walk down to the archives or prepare for an interview. That, I admit, will be a relief, since I've been working on this book for a while. Many books take a long time. This one, which was conceived on my first visit to the Shrine in 1993 and pursued during two periods of research and writing—1995–2000 and 2004–2010—has taken longer than most. It took so long for all sorts of boring reasons. I'll spare you the long version—you're welcome—but let's just say there were distractions and obstacles. I was finishing other books. I had administrative duties, serving as Department Chair and Associate Dean during some of those years. Most of all, I couldn't find some key sources. I'd decided to write about the Shrine during my first visit to the Mary Memorial Altar in 1993, when the promise of recovering the presence of those ordinary lay devotees—the thousands of "American Marys"—hooked me. It was only in early 2005 that I got my hands on the list of donors I'd wanted to see. My geeky delight in that discovery—and the support of lots of institutions and people—helped me finish this.

I began research in 1995 and gave my first public presentation the following year, as part of a collaborative research project on the Visual Culture of American Religions that was organized by David Morgan and Sally Promey. I'm grateful to them and our other collaborators, who also visited the Shrine with me. They offered insightful reactions and sage suggestions, and some campus audiences also asked questions that helped me refine my argument, including scholars and students at Valparaiso University, Duke University, Yale University, and the University of Bergen.

Bergen's Institute for Archeology, History, Cultural Studies, and Religion kindly invited me to be a research fellow and provided a collegial environment during my stay in fall 2009—a period during which much of the writing was done. The University of Texas at Austin funded a release from teaching so I could finish the project. My dean, Randy L. Diehl, and department chair, Martha Newman, helped more than I can say, and so did the generous support of the Shive, Lindsay, and Gray Professorship in the History of Christianity and the Darrel K. Royal Regents Professorship in Ethics and American Society. But institutional support started earlier and included an early travel grant from Notre Dame's Cushwa Center and similar support from the Visual Culture of American Religions Project and the University of North Carolina at Chapel Hill, which awarded me a University Research Council Grant and a fellowship from the Institute for the Humanities. At the University of North Carolina, I also received funding from the William McNeil Faculty Excellence Fund and the Zachary Smith Distinguished Professorship.

All that support, I'm happy to say, led to publications. Some portions of chapter 5 appeared in "'America's Church': Roman Catholicism and Civic Space in the Nation's Capital," in *Visual Culture of American Religions*, eds. David Morgan and Sally Promey (Berkeley: University of California Press, 2001): 129–57. Portions of chapter 6 also were published earlier as "Proclaiming Catholic Inclusiveness: Ethnic Diversity and Ecclesiastical Unity at the National Shrine of the Immaculate Conception," *U.S. Catholic Historian* 18 (winter 2000): 1–18. I am grateful for the permission to use this material.

As I was writing I also received help from students at the University of North Carolina, Duke University, and the University of Texas. Students at UNC and Duke who enrolled in my undergraduate and graduate courses on Roman Catholicism in America gave me their reactions to drafts of some chapters. Other graduate students served as my research assistants along the way: Anne Blankenship and Ilyse Morgenstein-Fuerst at UNC, Kate Bowler at Duke, and William Richter, Charlotte Howell, and Ashley Squires at UT Austin. Ashley helped during the project's final year, and Charlotte provided aid while the manuscript was in press. I owe each of them, and all my assistants, so much.

I also owe a great deal to the scholars who took time to offer comments on my writing, from the first proposal to the full manuscript. It is not their fault if I have made errors of fact or judgment, but I remain moved by their willingness to give this project their attention. Those who read the book proposal include the late Peter D'Agostino, Jay Dolan, Philip Gleason, Timothy Matovina, John McGreevy, Robert Orsi, Leslie Tentler, Grant

Wacker, and Annabel Wharton. Other scholars commented on one or more chapters, or helped in other crucial ways, including Catherine Brekus, Patricia Byrne, Kathleen Sprows Cummings, Erika Doss, James Fisher, Alison Frazier, Helen Hills, Paula Kane, Kathryn Lofton, David Morgan, Martha Newman, Mary Oates, Sally Promey, Susan Ridgely, Geraldine Rohling, Chad Seales, Michael Stausberg, Peter Williams, and Jeff Wilson. Some read the whole manuscript and improved the book in many ways, especially Scott Appleby, Julie Byrne, Mark Massa, James O'Toole, and Ann Taves. So did the staff at Oxford University Press, including Gwen Colvin and Jessica Ryan. My editor, Cynthia Read, was unconditionally supportive, as she was when we worked together on my earlier book, *Our Lady of the Exile*.

I also incurred an unusual number of debts to archivists across the country. Most important, first Gregory Tucker, director of communications, and later Geraldine M. Rohling, archivist, allowed me access to the records at the Basilica of the National Shrine of the Immaculate Conception. Dr. Rohling also gave me permission to use various archival sources, including photographs. I couldn't have done this project without their help. Others at the Shrine, including the Reverend Monsignor (now Bishop) Michael J. Bransfield and the Reverend Monsignor Walter R. Rossi, also spoke with me and supported the project. Many tour guides, security guards, cafeteria workers, gift shop personnel, and receptionists were kinder than they had to be, and I'm especially grateful to Sal Mazzuca, tour guide and Shrine enthusiast, who was the one person there I spoke with from the start to the end of the project. His support meant a lot to me. Lindy Bowman, Director of Development, and Jacquelyn Hayes, Director of Communications, also answered my annoying questions.

I reserved the most annoying questions for archivists elsewhere, who helped me find obscure sources about lay devotees, nuns, monks, and priests. Those archivists included Timothy J. Meagher and his extraordinary colleagues at the American Catholic History Research Center and University Archive at Catholic University; Shawn Weldon at the Philadelphia Archdiocesan Historical Research Center; William Kevin Cawley at the University of Notre Dame Archives; Joseph Coen at the Diocese of Brooklyn Archives; and the Reverend Johann G. Roten, SM, and several staff members at the Marian Library at the University of Dayton. Staff members at many other archives and libraries also helped, and I mention some of them in the notes. But that long list includes staff at the Archives of American Art, Brooklyn Historical Society, the Archdiocese of Boston, the Archdiocese of Chicago, the Archdiocese of Milwaukee, the Archdiocese of St. Louis, the Archdiocese of Newark, the Emmitsburg Province of the Daughters of

Charity, the Diocese of Buffalo, the Diocese of Harrisburg, the Diocese of Phoenix, the Diocese of Trenton, the Library of Congress, the Maryland Province of the Society of Jesus, St. Anselm's Abbey, and St. Mary's College. Women religious who work to preserve the history of religious orders consistently stunned me by their generosity. I cannot name them all—a computer glitch erased my list of those who helped—but I fondly remember aid from nuns associated with the Sisters of Saint Joseph in New York, Kansas, Connecticut, Maryland, and Minnesota: Sister Edna McKeever, CSJ; Sister Barbara Baer, CSJ; Sister Bernadine Pachta, CSJ; Sister Mary Jane Garry, CSJ; Sister Mary E. Craft, CSJ. Other women religious who helped included Sister Alice Wengryzynek, MM, of the Maryknoll Mission Archives; Sister Mary Angelica, CSSF, and Sister Ann Louise, SSMN, in the Diocese of Buffalo; and Sister Marie Esther Siversten, SP, of the Sisters of Providence of Saint Mary-of-the-Woods Archives.

My appreciation for the labor of women religious began in Philadelphia, where I was taught by nuns from three orders: The Society of the Sacred Heart (RSCJ), Missionary Sisters of the Sacred Heart (MSC), and Sisters of the Holy Family of Nazareth (CSFN). Some of those nuns, I suspect, wouldn't like my acknowledgments so far, since I've left out the supernatural intercessors they taught me to remember. Born in the Marian Year, I was tutored by nuns and nurtured by relatives who fervently expressed the consolidated era's devotion to Jesus' mother. They'd have an alternate explanation for how I was able to finish this challenging long-term project: it was the guiding intervention of the saints, especially Mary.

As an historian, I'll leave it to others to decide about the role of supernatural beings in human affairs, but I'm acutely aware of those in my extended family, living and dead, who helped. My children, Kevin and Bryn, patiently asked about this project and put up with detours to the Shrine during family trips. My wife, Margaret McNamee, who also learned from Sacred Heart nuns, was the first reader of each chapter and my constant conversation partner throughout the project. Like many of the Shrine's early supporters, both of my grandmothers, Anna Dougherty Tweed (1895–1963) and Gertrude Fitzmaurice Wurster (1895–1978), were the daughters of Catholic immigrants and raised their children and practiced their faith during the era of consolidation. I dedicate this book to my maternal grandmother, whose friends called her Gertie, because she raised me during my middle school years. From the age of twelve until I went off to graduate school, my aged grandmother was one of my best friends. As I now realize, her stories provoked my historical curiosity. Like other women of her generation, she saw extraordinary changes in secular society and American Catholicism and told me what it was like to encounter the first automobiles, radios, and movies and how it felt to live through World War I, the Great Depression, and the Cold War. Gertie, whose parish was only about 3.5 miles from Bernard McKenna's, was more than my beloved caretaker and cross-generational companion, she was my walking archive.

I never got to ask if she supported or visited the Shrine, though certainly many of my Philadelphia Catholic relatives did: I had six aunts and almost sixty cousins. My experience in that extended family and that institutional network helped as I tried to make sense of the history of the Washington Shrine, even if I don't recall knowing about the building when I was young. My childhood provided a useful perspective, though. Growing up I stood at the transition between the two eras I discuss in this book. I remember one moment vividly, the day when one of the changes of Vatican II was about to be implemented at the local level for the first time. I was an altar boy at St. Katherine of Siena Parish, and before one Sunday mass Father Doyle handed us a sheet of paper with dialogue typed on it. Dressed in our white and red liturgical costumes, we stood open-mouthed staring at each other and the unfamiliar words on the page. Father sensed our confusion and gave a terse explanation before we stepped onto the altar: "The mass is in English today, boys." I recall my first thought, which was predictably pragmatic and embarrassingly self-centered: *I just learned the Latin and now they're changing it?* I now see, however, that as we processed out and stood on the altar in the unsuspecting silence, awaiting Father Doyle's first words in the vernacular, we were poised between the era of consolidation and the era of fragmentation. I didn't realize the moment's significance then, yet that vantage—and my contacts with adults of the earlier generation— helped later as I tried to understand the worldview and practices of Catholics during the years they planned and built Mary's Shrine in Washington. I suspect that my interpretation of that site will elicit diverse responses. I'd be pleased, however, if readers who remember the era that's passed find that Catholic world represented fairly.

INDEX

abortion, 6, 240–41

Aboulin, Jean Joseph Marie, 44, 296n35

absence, 9, 64–65, 92, 94, 230, 242. *See also* presence

accommodationist Americanism, 6, 13, 45, 238, 241

Adams, Henry, 128

Adolescents, 44, 46, 56–57, 73, 93, 96, 100–102, 107, 110–11, 113–15, 119–21, 164, 168, 178, 212, 233, 238. *See also* childhood; children

advertising and marketing, 28, 30–31, 34, 38–39, 117, 238, 332n9

Africa, 195, 206–7, 209, 212–13

missionaries in, 202

Our Mother of, 213

African-American Catholics, 194, 204–6, 213–14

African Americans, 81, 175, 199, 200, 226–27, 234–35

and chapel at the Shrine, 17, 213, 218, 220, 227, 239, 244

exclusion and absence of, 205, 211, 213, 226, 234, 235

missions to, 203, 204, 211

and radio, 164

in Washington, D.C., 16, 176, 199, 205, 213

as workers at Shrine, 211–12, 212*f*

age. *See also* adolescents; children

of donors, 86, 113

for receiving Eucharist/communion, 99–100, 103

agency, 35, 64,101–3, 121, 244, 303n9, 314n1. *See also* structure

"age of Mary," 27, 99

altar boys, 100, 365

Alaska, 38, 44, 51, 209

Alter, Karl J., 40, 43, 44, 45–46

America. *See* Hemisphere, Western; Latin America; United States

American childhood, 95–98

American Institute of Architects, 24, 26, 189

Americanism, 6, 7

accommodationist, 6, 13, 45, 238, 241

papal condemnation of, 6, 13–14, 45, 241

triumphalist, 7, 12–13, 27, 134, 139, 162, 180, 230, 286n10, 330n2

Americanist Controversy of 1890s, 45

Americanization, 204

The American Catholic Story (TV show), 39

Americas, 44–45. *See also* Canada; Hemisphere, Western; Latin America; Mexico; United States

"America's Catholic Church," BNSIC as, 8, 230, 285n5

America's Church (Tucker), 131, 285n5

"America's Church," BNSIC as, 8, 180–91, 214, 218, 222, 227, 230, 285n5

America's Marys. *See* Marys of America

"America's Patronal Church," BNSIC as, 8, 285n5

America's Shrine to Mary (TV show), 39

Angel, John, 181

Anglo-Saxon supremacy, 133, 195

anti-Catholicism, 17, 35–36, 127, 131–37, 187–88, 232, 323n7

and apologetic function, of BNSIC
    architecture, 146–55
  before and after 1913, 131–33
  in Brooklyn, 82
  Catholic responses to, 137–46
  in Indiana, 36
  KKK and, 36, 131, 133, 134f, 137–38,
    187, 340n38
  in 1913, as guerilla warfare of words,
    133–37
  rise and fall of, 126–27, 187–89,
    325n15
  in Washington, D.C., 131–37, 134f
Apostolic Legation of the Papal State, 176
"The Apostolic See" sermon
    (Shahan), 49
"An Appeal to Catholic Ladies," 31
appearance
  of BNSIC, 3–4, 16–17, 22, 23–26,
    231–32
  of Crypt Church, 126, 146–55
apsidal altars, 36, 125, 150, 151, 180, 214
Aquinas, Thomas (saint), 6, 12, 13, 14
Archdiocese of Philadelphia, 19
architecture. See also shrines
  of BNSIC, 3–5, 16–17, 24–26, 32–33,
    43–44, 124, 126, 184, 231–32,
    293n20, 322n4, 340n40
  of Crypt Church, 123, 147–51, 155
  functions of, 147–49, 152, 155, 242
  interpretation of, 125
  liturgy and, 25, 147–49, 152
  McKenna on, 43, 124
  Shahan on, 24–25
  ten factors in study of, 16–19,
    125–26, 241–42, 286n13
  types of, 25, 149, 159, 289n3
archival sources, 19–20
Arizona, 73, 209–10, 230
art, 43, 126. See also mosaics; murals;
    paintings; sculptures; statues
artifacts. See also art; architecture;
    clothing; comics; material culture;
    monuments; pictorial theology;
    photographs; print media; war
    memorials
  analysis of, 19, 243–44
  holy cards, 291n9
  mass-produced, 100
  transtemporal, 49

Asia, 6, 207, 209, 224
Asian Catholics, 194–95, 218, 220–24
Asian immigrants, 175, 194, 206, 224,
    225
Asian Indian Catholics, 218, 220
Assumption of the Virgin (Titian), 50
Austrian Catholics, 220, 223
authority. See also National Catholic
    Welfare Conference;
    ultramontanism
  catechism on, 105
  centralization of, 6, 34–35, 37, 64, 166
  children and, 105, 107, 110–11, 121,
    233–34
  of clergy and bishops, 17, 28, 36, 47,
    64, 90–91, 105, 186
  culture of, 98–100, 105, 230, 243
  in era of consolidation, 6, 14, 64,
    98–100, 107, 230
  governmental, 173
  of papacy, 6, 12, 237
  parental, 96
  textbooks on, 107
  women and, 88, 90–91

baby boomers, 97
Baha'is, 174
Baltimore, 27, 37, 76–78, 102, 115–16,
    120, 130, 167, 201, 205, 213, 217
Baltimore Catechism, 104–6, 108, 137,
    316n15. See also catechisms
Baltzell, E. Digby, 312n43
Banchoff, George, 54
baptism, 201
Baptists, 128, 145, 173, 175, 188, 189
Baronio, Cesare, 143
Basilica of the National Shrine of the
    Immaculate Conception (BNSIC),
    4f.
  African Americans as workers at,
    211–12, 212f
  as "America's Catholic Church," 8,
    230, 285n5
  as "America's Church," 8, 218, 222,
    285n5
  as "America's Patronal Church," 8,
    285n5
  as "just about bishops," 5, 218, 230
  as monument to consolidated
    Catholicism, 7, 231, 237

as "spiritual Rorschach test," 5
appearance of, 5,17, 22, 23–26,
   231–32
architecture of, 3–5, 16–17, 24–26,
   32–33, 43–44, 124, 126, 184,
   231–32, 293n20, 322n4, 340n40
Building Committee for, 25, 29
building process (1909–1959), 26–28
children at, 110–22
claim to civic space, 7, 19, 235–37
clerical aspirations for, 41–49
comparisons to other buildings, 5, 18,
   23–24, 126, 159, 173, 183–86,
   187f, 189–90, 231, 236, 238
dedication of, 10, 17, 36, 39–40, 40f,
   43, 44, 45, 46, 97, 163–65, 188,
   193, 206–7, 236–37, 239
diversity at, 12, 15, 49–58, 206–14,
   224–27, 234–35, 238–39
first phase of building (1909–1933),
   29–35
founders of, 8, 13, 24, 214, 230,
   286n10
golden jubilee of, 185, 229, 238–39,
   241
guidebooks for, 91, 171–72, 285n5,
   285n7, 305n21
history of, 5–21, 131
incorporating immigrants at, 214–24
location of, 7, 16, 47, 176, 183–84,
   242, 341n40
material culture of, 19, 194, 211, 213,
   221, 227
meanings and functions of, 18–19,
   125–26
name of, 16
New York Times on, 39
planning and construction of, 8, 22,
   24–39, 41–44, 42f, 46, 123–25,
   231–32
promoters' aims for, 39–49
responses to, 3–4, 47, 231–32
second phase of building
   (1953–1959), 36–39
spiritual and aesthetic concerns and,
   8, 15, 43
as threshold, 7, 15, 18, 124, 160, 166,
   194, 229–41, 245
tours of, 70, 80, 119–20, 238,
   306n21

Washington National Cathedral *vs.*, 5,
   18, 23, 173, 184, 188–90, 236,
   289n1
website for, 218, 238, 241, 289n1,
   328n43, 355n10
Baxter, Sylvester, 340n40
The Beginnings of Christianity (Shahan),
   141, 146–47
bell tower, 24, 36, 53, 182–83
belonging, sense of, 87, 101–2, 231
Benedict XV (pope), 45, 50
Benedict XVI (pope), 15, 49, 239
Berrigan, Philip, 240, 334n14
Biden, Joe, 238
birth control, 6, 17, 239
bishops
   in Baltimore, 201–2
   BNSIC and, 5, 8, 10, 12, 23, 36–39,
      49–51, 57, 117–18, 165, 218,
      230, 243
   Catholic Bishops Conference of the
      Philippines, 221
   Conference of Catholic Bishops,
      United States, 5
   consolidating, 26
   and NCWC, 6, 35, 162
   and Vatican II, 6
   on Virgin Mary, 7, 27, 181
   in Washington, 10, 49, 51, 230, 240
black Madonna and Child, sculpture of,
   213
Blanco, Jose V., 222
Blanshard, Paul, 163
Blessed Sacred Chapel, 51
The Blessed Virgin in the Catacombs
   (Shahan), 123, 142, 145–46
Blue Army (of Fatima), 3
BNSIC. *See* Basilica of the National
   Shrine of the Immaculate
   Conception
body of Christ
   church as, 12, 107, 194, 201,
      203, 234
   incorporating immigrants into,
      197–206, 234
   unity in, 224–27
body politic, immigrants' incorporation
   into, 194, 195–96
Boniface VIII (pope), 201
Bonzano, John, 49

Bosio, Antonio, 143

Boston, 24, 39, 51, 66, 96, 98, 151, 177, 180, 202, 215, 234

Boy Scouts, 56, 115, 128, 320n35

Brady, John F., 81

Bransfield, Michael, 344n3
  on "America's Church," 218, 222, 285n5
  diversity and, 194–95, 213, 219, 223–24, 225

Brekus, Catherine, 302n9

Brennan, Edna, 113

Brennan, Elizabeth M.
  background of, 73–74, 307n27
  Mary Memorial Altar and, 61–62, 64, 73–78, 83, 85–86, 92, 302n6
  Mary's Day Movement and, 61, 73–78, 79–80, 90–91, 308n32
  Pace and, 79–80, 90
  relationship with male clerics, 88–91

Brennan, Philip A., 73–74, 76

"brick and mortar era" (1909–1959), 26–28

Brillante, Gabriel, 113

Brooklyn, 38, 82–85. See also St. Joseph's Commercial School; St. Thomas Aquinas School
  adult female donors to Mary Altar, living outside, 85–87, 271–73
  adult female donors to Mary Altar from, 265–68
  anti-Catholicism in, 82
  Catholic Big Sisters in, 73
  Catholic churches in, 27
  as "City of Churches," 82, 310n41
  donors from St. Thomas Aquinas School, 93–94, 95f, 112–14, 113t, 274–76
  Girls Town of, 77
  history of, 82–83, 310n41, 311nn42–43
  immigrants in, 82–83, 85, 311n42, 312n43
  Protestants in, 82–83, 312n43
  support from, 26–27, 59, 80–85, 93–95, 112–14, 230
  visitors from, 53, 57, 182, 301n55

Brown, Henry, 56, 212

Brownson, Orestes Augustus, 127

Buckley, William F., Jr., 162

Buddhism, 16, 96, 153, 174–75, 207, 245

Buffalo, 26–27, 32, 186

built environment, 176–80. See also landscape

Bureau of Catholic Indian Missions, 211

Burns, Lucy, 89

Bush, George W., 175

Butler, Pierce, 169

Byzantine-Romanesque, 3, 321

cablegrams, 30

Cabrini, St. Frances Xavier, 206, 218

Caldwell, Mary Gwendoline, 29

Caldwell, Samuel Lunt, 145

California, 55, 56, 87, 212

Campbell, Debra, 303n9

Campion, Raymond J., 107, 108

Canada, 30, 44

canon law, 6, 284n4

canonization
  and Day, 333n13
  of Seton, 68, 74, 89
  of Tekakwitha, 73

Caparas, Eduardo D., 223–24

capital, U.S. See also Washington, D.C.
  civic space in, 168–80, 235–37
  denominational centers in, 18, 175, 191, 336n22
  Jews in, 174
  national churches in, 171–76, 335n18, 336n22, 337nn24–25
  and spiritual capital, 159, 173, 189
  Washington Post on, 173, 174, 189–90

capitol, spiritual, 185–86, 190

Capitol, U.S., 18, 183–86, 187f
  composite with National Cathedral, 187f
  parallels with Shrine's Great Dome, 182–84

Caribbean, 44. See also Hemisphere, Western

Carmelite Order, 53, 219

Carroll, James, 5

Carroll, John, 76

Casey, Bernadette, 211

Cassidy, Charles J., 212

catacombal ceramics, 152–55

"catacombal" decoration, of Crypt Church, 124, 124f, 150, 152–55, 232

catacombs, 142–55
  of St. Priscilla (Rome), 144–46, 144*f*,
    152, 154–55
  Virgin Mary and, 143–46, 144*f*, 148,
    232
catechisms, 103–6, 108, 137, 316n15,
  317n15
Cathedral Church of St. Peter and
    St. Paul. *See* Washington National
    Cathedral
Cathedral Foundation, 172
Catholics. *See also specific ethnic groups*
  of color, 230
  immigrant, 132–33, 192–206,
    214–27
  non-Catholics and, 17, 35–36, 127,
    131–37, 187–88, 201, 206–7, 226,
    230, 232, 238
  number of, 132, 160, 198
  Protestants' relations with, 103,
    123–56, 162–64, 187–89, 232,
    324n12
  public influence of, 160–68
  on radio, 14, 38, 39, 117, 164, 165
  and sectarian conflict, 137–39
  on television, 14, 19, 24, 38, 39, 117,
    118, 164, 240, 241, 243
Catholic Bishops Conference of the
    Philippines, 221
Catholic childhood, 98–100, 110, 121
Catholic Daughters of America, 36
Catholic Encyclopedia, 13, 141
Catholic Foreign Missions Society of
    America, 202
Catholic Hour (radio show), 39, 164
Catholic institutional network, 244
    See also schools
  engaging children and, 93–122
  resources of, 17
Catholic Interracial Council, 205
Catholicism, Roman. *See also*
    anti-Catholicism; consolidated
    Catholicism; fragmented
    Catholicism
  centralization of, 6, 7, 22, 28, 34–35,
    57, 293n22
  conservative *vs.* progressive, 4, 5, 6,
    239–41
  consolidated, 6, 15, 28, 231, 238,
    284n4

fragmented, 5, 6, 238, 284n4
  history of, 5–7, 12–14, 17, 39, 64–65,
    139–43, 178–81, 283n4, 302n9,
    323n6
  institutional networks of, 6, 17, 22,
    28, 49, 57, 93, 99, 101–3, 104,
    110, 116, 121, 200, 231, 233,
    243–44
  media and, 14, 38–39, 164–65
  after 1959, 7, 187–91, 224–27,
    237–41
  public, 195–96, 198
  secularity and., 43, 47
  transnationalism and, 6, 16, 22,
    27–28, 49, 57, 192
  worldview of (1909–1959), 6–7, 12,
    14–15, 101, 229–33
Catholic Missions Bureau, 202
Catholic Order of Foresters, 53
Catholic schools, 12, 93–95, 95*f*, 101–10,
    104*f*, 195–96, 318n22
*The Catholic Educational Series of Primary
    Textbooks* (CUA), 106
Catholic University of America (CUA), 3,
    7, 13, 14, 19, 29, 33, 36, 39, 46, 55,
    66–67, 77, 88, 116, 130, 140, 164,
    166, 169, 176, 184
  affiliation with, 29, 33, 45
  *The Catholic Educational Series of
    Primary Textbooks* and, 106
  as "chief educational center," 43
  and the hierarchy, 51, 230
  moderate and progressive views and,
    13, 45, 241
  as pontifical university, 7, 45, 237, 242
  racism and, 205, 213, 244
  speaker controversy and, 163
Catholic Worker Movement, 167–68,
    236. *See also* Dorothy Day
Catholic Youth Council, 98
censorship, 165, 356n12. *See also* movies
Centilivre, Alma, 86
ceramics, catacombal, 152–55
chapels, 194. *See also* oratories
  definition of, 344n3
  ethnic, diversity and, 217–20, 220*t*,
    225, 226*t*, 227, 239
  Founder's, 10, 11*f*, 230
  of the Good Shepherd, 55, 151–52
  of Our Lady of Altötting, 225

chapels (*continued*)
   Our Lady of Brezje, 220
   Our Lady of Czestochowa, 217, 220
   of Our Lady of Guadalupe, 218, 219*f*
   Our Lady of Hope, 55
   of Our Lady of Lourdes, 55, 218–19
   Our Lady of Mount Carmel, 53
   of Our Lady of Pompei, 225
   Our Mother of Africa, 16, 213–14
   Queen of Missions Chapel, 208–9
   St. Brigid of Ireland, 220
   St. Vincent de Paul, 219
Chaput, Charles, 211
Charleston, 38, 135
Chartres Cathedral, 13, 23, 128
Chicago, 32, 38, 57, 61, 66, 98, 119, 142, 200, 215, 235
childhood, 95–100, 106, 110, 121
children. *See also* age; orphans; schools
   absence of, in scholarship, 95
   adults' influence on, 93–96, 99–100, 233–34
   at BNSIC, 110–22
   childhood from 1920s to 1950s, 95–100
   donations from, 10, 37–38, 52, 81–82, 110–22
   engaging, 93–122, 233
   ethnicity of, 112–14
   families and, 100, 115, 118–20
   identity and, 101
   immigrants and, 96–97
   Marian devotion and, 98–99, 106, 110, 116
   media and, 117–18
   mothers and, 76
   nuns and, 94–95
   from Our Lady of Lourdes School, 77, 78*f*
   pilgrimages and, 114–16, 119–20
   presumed innocence of, 96–97, 99, 106–7
   sacrifice and, 98–99, 106–7, 111
   sexual abuse of, 234, 239–40, 244, 353n4, 356n12
   as visitors, 10, 56–57, 166, 167*f*, 280–81
China, 47, 202, 207
Chinese Catholics, 111, 226
Choeong Jin-Sak, Nicholas Cardinal, 226

Christ, metaphors for, 200–201. *See also* body of Christ
Christianity, history of, 139–43, 146–47
Christ in Majesty mosaic, 10
church
   as body of Christ, 12, 107, 194, 201, 203, 234
   metaphors for, 107, 200
   national, in U.S. capital, 171–76, 335n18, 336n22, 337nn24–25
   as "people of God," 12, 239
church-state separation, 13, 134, 162–63, 170–72, 178, 185, 189
citizenship, 195–96, 197*f*, 199
civics, 195–96
Civics Catechism on the Rights and Duties of American Citizens (NCWC), 196, 197*f*, 198
Civics Clubs, 57, 119, 196
civic social capital, subjunctive, 159, 330n3
civic space, 157–91
   BNSIC's claim to, 7, 19, 235–37
   and monumental and performative assertions in indicative mood, 159, 187–91
   and monumental and performative assertions in subjunctive mood, 159, 180–87, 236–37
   in U.S. capital, 168–80, 235–37
civil religion, 171, 335n18
civil rights movement, 17, 206
Civil War, 177–80
class, of devotees, 17, 20, 54, 65, 67, 70, 81, 84, 86, 96, 97, 101, 112–13, 166, 179, 188, 197, 204, 214, 231
cleanliness, 197, 345n7
Cleary, Kathryn, 316n12
Cleveland, 81, 96, 354n4
Clergy. *See also* authority; bishops; priests
   authority of, 90–91
   fundraising by, 116–17
clerical aspirations, for BNSIC, 7, 39–46
   responding to, 46–49
clerical donors, 52, 52*f*
clerical marriage, 6
clerics, male, relationship between women and, 78–79, 88–91
Clinton, Bill, 337n24

Clinton, Hillary, 337n24
clothing/dress
    at Catholic procession, 108–109, 169
    and girl culture, 97
    at Mary Altar presentation ceremony,
        63–64
    modesty in, 66, 67
    at Protestant parade, 82
    of shrine pilgrims, 120
    at Vatican visit, 89
    of Virgin Mary, 146
Cogan, Mary de Paul
    background of, 66–67, 304n14
    Mary Memorial Altar and, 61, 64,
        65–67, 91
    New York Times on, 68
Cold War, 45, 182
color code, U.S., 199, 200, 212, 226
    See also ethnicity; race; racism
Colored Harvest, 205, 212
Columbus, Christopher, 27, 44, 181
columns/pillars
    of Crypt Church, 194, 215–17, 216f,
        227
    dedicated to Our Lady of the Indians,
        211
comics
    The Phantom, 321n39
    "The Shrine You Can Build," 93,
        94f, 118
    Topix, 98–99
    Treasure Chest of Fun and Fact, 97–98,
        117–19
*Common Sense Book of Baby and Child
    Care* (Spock), 97
Commonweal, 4, 166
communion. *See* Eucharist/communion
communism, 162–64
Conference of Catholic Bishops,
    United States, 5
Congregationalists, 126, 127, 152, 153, 171
Congress, opening of, 169, 236
Connecticut, 82, 120
Connick, Charles J., 151, 180
Connolly, Christina, 114
Connor, Jerome, 178
conservative *vs.* progressive Catholicism,
    4, 6, 239–41
consolidated Catholicism, 6–7, 12, 17,
    28, 64, 99, 107, 193, 231, 284n4

six clerical interests characterizing,
    15, 231–37
worldview of, 12, 14–15, 101, 229–33
consolidation, era of, 6, 11, 237
    authority in, 64, 98–100, 107
    definition of, 283n4
    institution building during, 22
consumption and consumer movement,
    28, 97, 288n17. *See also*
    advertising and marketing
context, 126. *See also* historical context
contraception. *See* birth control; the Pill
Conway, Bertrand, 135, 138, 139–40
Coolidge, Calvin, 170–71, 170f,
    174, 177
Cornely, Jeanette, 113
corporeal metaphors, 107, 200–201,
    203–4, 226, 240
Corrada del Rio, Alvaro, 222–23
The Correct Thing for Catholics, 100
Coughlin, Charles, 164
Council of Ephesus, 145, 146
Council of Trent, 28, 201
countermodernism, 6–7, 13–14, 25, 230,
    232, 237. *See also* modernism
    selective, 12–14, 25
Cray, Lillian, 311n41
Croatian Catholics, 220
crossing and dwelling, 18, 243–45
Crypt Church, 123–56, 149f. *See also*
    Mary Memorial Altar; memorial
    tablets
    appearance of, 126
    architecture of, 123, 147–51, 155
    as catacomb, 146–48
    "catacombal" decoration of, 124,
        124f, 150, 152–55, 232
    columns/pillars of, 194, 215–17,
        216f, 227
    completion of, 36
    design of, context for, 131–37
    diversity and, 214–17
    memorial tablets for, 48, 215, 227
    ornamentation of, 147, 150–52, 232
    Salve Regina on, 148, 150
    space of, 148–50
CUA. *See* Catholic University of America
Curley, Michael Joseph, 37
Curren, Joseph C., 95f
curricula, 107–10, 195–96

Cushing, Richard, 39–40, 46, 98, 184–85, 188
Cyprian of Carthage, 201
Czech Catholics, 48, 56, 198, 220

"Daniel and the Devil," 98
Daughters of Isabella, 53–54, 65
Day, Dorothy, 15, 166–68, 236, 333n13
Day Book, McKenna's, 56–57, 128–29
Declaration of Independence, 199
"Declaration on Religious Freedom" (Vatican II), 163
de Concilio, Januarius, 316n14
De Rosen, John, 181, 207
De Rossi, Giovanni, 143–45
Descent of the Holy Spirit mosaic, 207–8, 208f, 226
Detroit, 11, 26–27, 32
devotional letters, 30, 47, 292n13
devotional organizations, 101–2, 119
devotional shrines, 16, 287n14
Dewey, George, 161
De Wolf, Maurice, 286n11
didactic function, of architecture, 147–48
difference, 226–27
diocesan resources, episcopal power and, 36–39
Disciples of Christ, 188–89, 237
diversity, 6–7, 47–48, 192–227. See also ethnicity; immigrants; immigration laws
    at BNSIC, 49–58, 206–14, 224–27, 234–35, 238–39
    Bransfield and, 194–95, 213, 219, 223–24, 225
    Crypt Church and, 214–17
    of donors, 49–58, 229–30
    ethnic chapels and oratories and, 217–20, 220t, 225, 226t, 227, 239
    foundation stone ceremony and, 215
    occupations and, 211–12, 212f
    religious, 164, 171, 174–75, 336n23
    Salve Regina and, 209, 211–13, 214, 217
    unity and, 194, 198, 204, 222, 224–27
Doherty, Mary, 84
Dolan, Elizabeth J., 61

donation. See also donors; fundraising; Mary Memorial Altar; philanthropy
    as religious practice, 18, 245
    for bell tower, 36, 53
    from children, 81–82, 110–22
    from Jews, 81, 85
    men and, 53–55, 81–82, 256–57
    from priests, 51–52, 249–50
    women and, 12, 17, 31–35, 46, 53–54, 82–87
Donohue, Harry Eversfield, 76
donor letters, 244
    in Salve Regina, 19, 30, 54–55
donor lists, 20. See also Mary Memorial Altar
donors, 18, 125, 242, 300n51. See also fundraising, appendices (this volume)
    adult female, to Mary Altar, from Brooklyn, 265–68
    adult female, to Mary Altar, living outside Brooklyn, 85–87, 271–73
    age of, 86, 113
    classes of, 84, 86, 112–13
    clerical, 52, 52f
    diversity of, 49–58, 229–30, 235
    episcopal (1916–1919), 50–51, 51t, 247–48, 298n45
    geographical distribution of pilgrims and, 7, 44, 50, 54, 56, 80, 81, 86, 308n37
    homes of, 84–85, 86, 113–14
    lay male (1919), 256–57
    motives of, 87
    occupations of, 84, 86, 113–14
    selected (1953), 56, 258–61
    selected (1954), 262–63
    selected (1959), 264
    social profile of, 78–87, 112–14, 113t, 247–81
    from St. Joseph's Commercial School, 93–95, 112–14, 113t, 277–79
    from St. Thomas Aquinas School, 93–94, 95f, 112–14, 113t, 274–76
Dougherty, Dennis, 26–27
Downs, Mary, 68–70, 71f, 157
    background of, 70–73, 306n21, 306n23, 307nn24–25
    Marys of America and, 68–73, 305nn19–21
    poems by, 71–72, 306n23

Doyle, Patrick J., 52, 298n46
Drexel, Katherine (saint), 204, 211
Du Bois, W. E. B., 199, 205
Duchesne, Rose Philippine (saint), 211
Dunn, Robert, 81
Duval, George Logan, 55
Dwight, Ed, 213

Eastern Orthodoxy, 82, 159
East Porch, mosaics within, 181
East Wall
    iconography, 180–81
    scriptural passages on, 182
Ecclesiastical History from the Birth of
        Christ until the Year 1198 (Baronio),
        143
ecclesiastical unity, 7
ecclesiology, 12, 194. *See also* body of
        Christ; canon law; church
eclectic traditionalism, 25, 26
economy, society and, 166–68, 334n14
education. *See* school culture; schools
Edwards, Mildred, 240
Egan, Katherine S., 215
Eisenhower, Dwight, 175, 182, 188, 189,
        236, 355n8
Eliot, T. S., 128
Ellis, John Tracy, 39
Elson Reader, 196
e-mails, 238, 355n10
Embassy Row, 175, 176
Emergency Immigration Act of 1921,
        133
Episcopal Committee for the Shrine, 231
    aims for BNSIC and, 43
    on fundraising quotas, 12, 37–38
episcopal donors (1916–1919), 50–51,
        51t, 247–48, 298n45
Episcopalians, 130, 164, 171, 175,
        232, 235. *See also* Randlolph
        McKim; Washington National
        Cathedral
Episcopalian Cathedral Church of
        St. Peter and St. Paul, 159, 171
    See also Washington National
        Cathedral
Essay in Aid of a Grammar Assent
        (Newman), 159
Eternal Word Television Network, 4,
        241–42

ethnicity. *See also* diversity; *specific*
        ethnicities
    of children, 112–14
    ethnic chapels and oratories, 217–20,
        220t, 225, 226t, 227, 239
    ethnic intermarriage, 199–200
    ethnic saints, 194
Eucharist/communion, 201
    age for receiving, 99–100, 103
    presence through, 64
evangelicals, 6, 133
Evans, Hiram Wesley, 133, 134f, 155–56,
        195, 230

Fairbanks, Douglas, 55
faith, 182
The Faith of Our Fathers (Gibbons), 123,
        138–40, 142
families
    children and, 100, 115, 118–20
    immigrant, 215
Farley, John Murphy Cardinal, 66
Fay, Sigourney, 130–31
Fay, Susanna, 125, 130–31, 155, 230
Federated Colored Catholics of the
        United States, 205
feminism, 6, 35, 239–40
Filipino Catholics, 4, 5, 7, 17, 193, 194,
        221–24, 227
Filipino oratory, 20, 193f, 194, 220–24,
        351n41
Filipino Virgins, 351n41
Finan, Mary, 61, 90, 103, 301n3
First Amendment, 171, 172, 235
First Vatican Council. *See* Vatican I
Fisher, Regina, 169
Fitzgerald, F. Scott, 130
Ford, Gerald R., 188, 189
Fort Wayne, 36, 38, 86
foundation stone ceremony, 10
    diversity and, 215
    Gibbons and, 8, 17, 22, 23f, 30, 49,
        55, 215
    program booklet for, 34, 41, 43, 45,
        48, 158f, 163, 185–86, 211,
        295n30, 341n42
Founder's Chapel, 10, 11f, 230
Fox, Marie, 83, 87, 92
fragmentation, era of, 6–7, 192, 238,
        284n4

fragmented Catholicism, 6–7, 192, 220, 227, 229, 238–41, 284n4

Franey, John, 54

fraternal organizations, 53, 178, 182

Freer, Charles, 153

French Catholics, 44, 45, 51, 85–86, 113–14, 198, 202, 220

Fresco of the Madonna and Child, 144–46, 144*f*

Fuller, Margaret, 128

Fundamentals of Citizenship (NCWC), 196

fundraising. *See also* donations; donors
  by clergy, 116–17
  during first phase of building, 30–35
  for Great Upper Church, 36, 37, 51, 53–54
  letters, 289n19
  McKenna and, 47, 55
  quotas, 12, 37–38, 294n26, 295n27
  responses to, 46–49, 297n39
  Salve Regina and, 32–34, 54, 59, 69, 80, 233
  during second phase of building, 36–39
  women, Mary Memorial Altar and, 59–92, 301n1, 305n19

Gandolfi, Helen, 114

Gausch, Joseph P., 354n4

gay rights, 240. *See also* homosexuality

gender. *See also* feminism; men; nuns; women
  immigrants and, 214
  liturgy and, 62, 64

gender equality, 35

gender roles, 19, 97, 128

geographical distribution of donors and pilgrims, 7, 44, 50, 54, 56, 80, 81, 86, 308n37. *See also specific cities and states and the Appendices (this volume)*

German Catholics, 51–52, 54–56, 82, 85–86, 103, 113–14, 116, 162, 176, 185, 198, 205, 215, 200, 225–26

Giacoma, John J., 55, 56

Gibbons, James Cardinal, 10, 13
  on Americanization, 204
  The Faith of Our Fathers, 123, 138–40, 142

during first phase of building, 29–32

foundation stone ceremony and, 8, 17, 22, 23*f*, 30, 49, 55, 215

IFCA and, 66, 88–89

McKim on, 134

on missions, 202, 203

Taft, W., and, 161, 161*f*

Third Plenary Council at Baltimore and, 102–3, 104

Gies, Amanda C., 215

Girl Scouts, 115

Girls Town of Brooklyn, 77

giving. *See* donation

Gleason, Philip, 286n10, 297n39

Glennon, John, 184, 341n40

Goldstein, Mr. and Mrs., 85

going. *See* pilgrimage

Good Shepherd Chapel, 55, 151–52

Gorman, Helen, 114

Gormly, John, 47

Gothic, 5, 13, 25, 29–30, 34, 127, 147, 172, 184, 231–32

Grady, Thomas J., 10, 43, 119, 182

Graham, Billy, 164

Grand Rapids, 38

Great Depression, 8, 30, 102, 174, 244

Great Dome, 5, 17, 182–85
  Capitol, U.S., parallels with, 182–84
  superstructure of, 41
  windows for, 52, 121, 321n43

Great Upper Church
  completion of, 47
  construction of, 8
  design of, 149
  fundraising for, 36, 37, 51, 53–54
  Patroness Windows and East Wall iconography of, 180–81
  presence at, 9–10
  rose windows of, 91, 92

Griffith, H. Allen, 127

Guamian Catholics, 226

guardian angel, 106

Guastavino, Rafael, Sr., 150

Guide to the Architecture of Washington, D.C. (American Institute of Architects), 24, 26, 189

Guilday, Peter K., 14

Hall of American Saints, 226

Hamma, Margaret, 114

Handy, Robert, 312n43
Harris, Hannah Margaret, 196
Harrisburg, 52, 229
Hart, Luke E., 182–83, 340n37
Hawthorne, Nathaniel, 128
Hays, William Harrison, 165
heathens, 207, 226, 230. *See also*
    missionaries; missions
Hecker, Isaac Thomas, 127
Hemisphere, Western, 13
Hendrick, Loretta, 86
Heraclitus, 241
Hickey, James Cardinal, 213, 221, 223
Hickey, Timothy A., 81, 310n39
Higgins, George, 82
Hinduism, 16, 174–75
historical context, 17, 26, 126, 241–42
    for design of Crypt Church, 131–37
historical narratives, contesting,
    139–42, 143
histories, translocative, 15, 286n12
*History of the Devotion to the Blessed
    Virgin Mary in North America*
    (Macleod), 27
Hoffman, Frances Burrall, Jr., 32
Hoffman, Lucy Shattuck, 32–33, 58,
    292n17
Holy Angels (Philadelphia), 225
holy cards, 291n9
Holy Child Church (Philadelphia), 108,
    109f
Holy Childhood Association, 202–3
Holy Name Society parade, 170–71,
    170f, 177, 235, 335n17
Holy Trinity Church, 237
homes, of donors, 84–85, 86, 113–14
homosexuality, 6, 239, 240
Hoover, Herbert, 236
Hope, Bob, 55
Hope, Delores, 55
hopes and fears, 7, 14, 201
    clerical, 39–46
    lay, 46–49
Houston, 238
Humanae Vitae, 17, 239
Hume, David, 295n29
Hunger March, 166

iconography, East Wall, 180–81
Iconography Committee, 181, 207

ideal types, 283n4. *See also* consolidated
    Catholicism; fragmented
    Catholicism
identity, 101
IFCA. *See* International Federation of
    Catholic Alumnae
Ignatius of Loyola, 53
Immaculate Conception
    apparition of, 28
    doctrine of, 8, 27–28, 132, 140, 151
    feast of, 60, 106, 166–67
    Protestant interpretations of, 123,
        128–29, 135
    as U.S. national patroness, 7, 26–27,
        55, 158, 160, 180–81, 186, 191,
        211, 214, 229, 291n9
Immaculate Conception (Murillo), 50,
    50f, 128
immigrant public style, 330n2
immigrants. *See also specific ethnicities*
    in Brooklyn, 82–83, 85, 311n42,
        312n43
    Catholic, 132–33
    children and, 96–97
    as donors, 81–82, 85–87
    families, 215
    gender and, 214
    languages and, 198, 225
    number in U.S., 225
immigrants, incorporating, 192–227, 234
    at BNSIC, 214–24
    into body of Christ, 197–206, 234
    into body politic, 194, 195–96
immigration laws, 6, 133, 187, 193, 195,
    244
    revised, 17, 174, 206, 217, 239
incorporeal Other, 125, 156
India, 202. *See also* Asian Indians
Indiana, 32, 36, 68–70, 76, 79–80,
    85–86, 269–70
Indianapolis, 32, 73, 85
Indians, 194–204, 206, 208–11, 210f,
    227, 349n26
    as donors and pilgrims, 209–11
    as heathens, 226
    missionaries and, 98, 203, 211, 226
    represented in comic, 98
    represented in mosaic, 208–9
    Shrine column honoring, 211,
    statue honoring, 211

indicative mood, 159, 188, 236, 237
  See also subjunctive mood
Ingrand, Max, 207
institution building, 22, 26–27, 231
institutional networks. See Catholicism;
  institutional networks
International Eucharistic Congress in
  Chicago (1926), 142
International Federation of Catholic
  Alumnae (IFCA), 31, 34
  by-laws of, 66, 88
  Gibbons and, 66, 88–89
  Mary Memorial Altar and, 59–62,
    65–69, 73–74, 77–79, 88–92, 301n1
  on movies, 165
  Pace and, 66, 88
  Shahan and, 66, 88, 90, 91
interpretation, 125
interviews, at BNSIC, 3–4, 20, 194, 214,
  218, 220–24, 283n1
Irish. See also specific individuals
  Catholics, 33, 35, 48, 51–52, 55–56,
    67, 70–71, 73, 81–82, 85–86,
    93–94, 103, 112–14, 119, 169,
    178–80, 205, 211–12, 220, 234
  immigrants, 51–52, 70–71, 82, 85,
    86, 103, 112, 113, 178, 198, 200,
    234–35
  nationalism, 70
  predominance of, 17, 198, 211, 220,
    234–35
  race and, 200
Islam, 16. See also Muslims; mosques
Islamic Center, 175
Italy, 24. See also Rome
Italian Catholics, 53, 56, 82, 85–86, 103,
  113–14, 176, 198, 200, 203, 206,
  212, 225–26

Jains, 174
Jefferson, Thomas, 199
Jehovah's Witnesses, 164
Jensen, Veronica, 114
Jesuits (Society of Jesus), 53
Jesus, Paul, and twelve disciples, statues
  of, 61
Jews
  In Brooklyn, 83, 85
  and Catholics and Protestants, 6,
    162, 195

donations from, 81, 85
immigration of, 82, 85, 96, 132
in Manhattan, 86
in Memphis, 85
on radio, 164
at the Shrine, 115
strategies of survival for, 138,
  327n25
in U.S. capital, 159, 173, 174
John Carroll Society, 334n15
John Paul II (pope), 4, 15, 49, 240
  protests at visit of, 89, 314n53
Johnson, Luci, 161, 237, 240
Johnson, Lyndon Baines, 161, 162, 188,
  237, 240, 337n25
John XXIII (pope)
  support from, 49–50
  Vatican II and, 6
Jolly, Ellen Ryan, 177f, 178–80, 338n29
Jones, Melvina, 84, 87, 92
"June Night" (song), 115
Juneau, 38, 51

Kane, Sister M. Theresa, 240
Kansas, 112
Kasprowicz, Richard, 93–94, 113, 121
Keane, John Joseph, 45
Kelly, Mary, 48
Kennedy, Eugene F., Jr., 29
Kennedy, Jackie, 188
Kennedy, John F., 160, 163, 188–89,
  235, 237–38, 342n46
Kennedy, William, 131
Kino, Eusebio, 181
kinship, as metaphor, 76
KKK. See Ku Klux Klan
Knapp, Charles L. G., 354n4
Knights of Columbus, 36, 53, 138,
  182–83
Knight's Tower, 182. See also bell tower
Know Nothing Party, 82, 131–32
Korean Catholics, 225–26
Korean sculptures, 226
Krichten, Leo J., 52, 298n46
Ku Klux Klan (KKK), 36, 131, 133, 134f,
  137–38, 187, 340n38

LAAOH. See Ladies Auxiliary of the
  Ancient Order of Hibernians
Labouré, Catherine, 28

Ladies Auxiliary of the Ancient Order of Hibernians (LAAOH), 53, 65, 178, 179
Ladies Auxiliary of the Knights of St. John, 65
Lady Isle, 307n27
La Farge, Bancel, 151
LaFarge, John, 204–5
laity, 12, 14, 28, 36, 48, 77, 103, 147, 194, 197, 202, 214, 222, 227, 230. *See also* lay elite
Lamp unto my Feet (TV program), 24, 117
landscape, *See also* architecture; built environment; "Little Rome"; monuments; Washington, D.C.
   civic, 190, 235
   interpretation of, 242
   religious, 171–76, 191, 231
   urban, 3, 25–26, 83, 171, 173, 241
Lane, Virginia Walsh, 102
languages, immigrants and, 198, 225
Latter Day Saints (Mormons), 164
Latin America, 6, 137, 195, 206, 218, 225
lay elite, 12, 65, 78, 88–90, 137, 157, 179–80
Leary, Annie, 32
Legion of Decency, 165
Legion of Mary, 103, 240
Legler, Carrie, 311n41
L'Enfant, Pierre Charles, 172
Leo XIII (pope), 102, 204, 334n14
Lessons in Civics for the Six Elementary Grades of City School (Harris), 196
Life Is Worth Living (TV show), 164
Lithuanian Catholics, 113, 198, 220
Little Flower of Jesus (saint), 74–75
"Little Rome" (Washington, D.C.), 5, 176, 191, 237
liturgy
   architecture and, 25, 147–49, 152
   gender and, 62, 64
location, of BNSIC, 7, 16, 47, 176, 183–84, 242, 341n40
Lodge, Henry Cabot, Jr., 169
Los Angeles, 26, 51, 55, 56, 212
Ludwig I (king of Bavaria), 185
Lull, Ramon, 28
Lutherans, 114, 145, 216

MacEachen, Robert, 106–7
Macleod, Xavier, 27
Madison, James, 175
magazines
   advertising in, 31, 39
   on catacombs, 145
   and missions to African Americans, 205
   on Virgin Mary, 100, 128
Maginnis, Charles Donagh, 13
   as architect, 8–9, 24–26, 29, 42, 123, 152, 184, 186, 231, 341n40
   on presence, 8–9
Maisano, Nazarino, 212
makers, 18, 125, 242. *See also* bishops; clergy; Maginnis, Charles Donagh; priests; Shahan, Thomas
male clerics, relationship between women and, 78–79, 88–91
Malloy, Anna, 86, 87
Malone, Rosalia, 166
Maltese Catholics, 226
Manuel, Tessie, 223
"March for Life," 241
Marian apparitions, 5, 27, 55
Marian devotion, 3, 12, 31, 48, 57–58, 157. *See also* art; artifacts; Mary Memorial Altar; May Crownings; May Day Processions; ritual; Virgin Mary
   apparitions and, 5, 28, 99, 240
   children and, 98–99, 106, 109–10, 116
   church names and, 27
   Columbus', 27, 44, 181
   consolidated Catholicism and, 27, 28, 48, 99, 121, 189
   consumers of, 34
   countermodernism and, 14
   feminine virtues and, 233
   history of, 27–28, 44–45, 118, 240, 290nn8–9
   hymns and, 75, 77, 106, 129, 169, 217
   national identity and, 41, 180
   organizations and, 101, 111, 116
   Protestant criticism of, 123–24, 139, 148, 242
   and spiritual services, 41
   transnationalism and, 22, 27, 215–16, 234

Marian images, 72, 77, 91, 128, 145–46, 180, 184, 194, 219, 221, 307n24. *See also* catacombs
Marian shrines, 16, 18, 27, 30, 37, 215
Marian statues, 41, 76, 77, 78*f*, 91, 181, 221–22, 352n42
Marian Year, 8, 27, 37, 53, 120
marriage
  clerical, 6
  ethnic intermarriage, 199–200
Mary. *See* Virgin Mary
Mary Blanche, Sister, 52–53
Mary de Paul, Sister. *See* Cogan, Mary de Paul
Mary Immaculate with Angels statue (Mestrovic), 54
Mary Joseph, Mother, 67
Maryknolls, 67
Maryland, 13, 62, 65, 67, 76, 78, 115, 134, 178, 181, 189, 205, 209
Mary Memorial Altar (Mary Altar), 60*f*, 285n7. *See also specific individuals*
  adult female donors to, from Brooklyn, 265–68
  adult female donors to, from Indiana and Tennessee, 85–86, 269–70
  adult female donors to, living outside Brooklyn, 85–87, 271–73
  consecration of, 302n6
  cost of, 73
  dedication of, 9*f*, 61, 91
  description of, 60–61
  donations for, 31, 52, 265–73
  donor list for, 20, 78–87, 81*t*, 91–92, 93, 112, 121, 308n37, 309nn38–39, 319n29
  installation of, 8, 60
  plaque for, 61, 62–64, 91, 302n8
  presentation ceremony for, 60–64, 63*f*, 91, 301n3
  scallop shells on, 61, 302n3
  women, fundraising and, 59–92, 301n1, 305n19
Mary Memorial Altar Fund, 61, 65, 68, 69
Mary's Day, 61
  motto for, 79
  pledge cards, 80, 309n39, 319n25
"Mary's Day Hymn" (Brennan, E.), 75–76
Mary's Day Movement, 61, 73–78, 79–80, 90–91, 308n32

Marys of America, 61–62, 64, 91–92
  donation motives for, 87
  Downs, Mary, and, 68–73, 305nn19–21
  Sheeran and, 69
Mary's Shrine, 19, 217–18, 225. *See also Salve Regina*
Mary Teresita, Sister, 53, 299n48
mass, 8, 106
  "for Life," 241
  Pan American Thanksgiving Day, 136–37, 136*f*, 161, 162, 169, 235, 326n22
  Red, 169, 236, 238, 334n15
material culture, of BNSIC, 19, 194, 211, 213, 221, 227. *See also* artifacts
Maurin, Peter, 167
May Crownings, 108–10, 109*f*, 319n23
May Day processions, 169–70
McAndrew, James P., 115
McCaffery, Edmund F., 334n14
McCaffrey, Elizabeth, 84–85
McCarthy, Cecelia, 114
McCarthy, Joseph R., 162, 235
McCormick, Patrick J., 36–37, 302n6
McGinnis, Catharine, 211
McGinnis, William F., 94
McGoldrick, Rita, 165, 332n11
McHugh, Rosella, 84, 87
McKenna, Bernard
  on BNSIC construction and architecture, 43, 124, 215–16
  on Crypt Church, 152
  Day Book of, 56–57, 128–29
  during first phase of building, 29–34, 36, 212
  fundraising and, 47, 55
  Mary Memorial Altar and, 9*f*, 59–61, 69, 301n3
  Memoirs, 131, 209, 215
  with Murillo's *Immaculate Conception*, 50*f*
  Philadelphia parish of, 225
  during second phase of building, 36
  Sheeran, C., and, 89–90
  at Shrine's first mass, 187
  visitors and, 54, 56–57, 129, 166, 167*f*, 209, 216–17
McKim, Randolph Harrison, 133–37, 138, 139, 155–56, 230

McKinley, William, 161
McLoughlin, Honoria, 84
McMillan Plan, 335n18
McNicholas, John T., 35, 162, 165
media. *See also* advertising and
     marketing; cablegrams; comics;
     e-mails; magazines; movies; print
     media; radio; technology;
     television; web sites
  Catholicism and, 14, 38–39, 164–65
  children and, 117–18
  Noll and, 117, 165
  politics and, 160–65
memoirs, 19, 95, 111, 203, 209, 333n13
Memoirs (McKenna), 131, 209, 215
Memphis, 73, 76, 85, 86
Memorial Hall
  description of, 77
  names in, 10, 76, 91, 120–21, 215,
     230
  names on walls of, 215, 230
  National Catholic Family Record as
     forerunner of, 34
  special computer kiosks in, 77,
     308n33
Memorial Registry, 77, 308n33
memorial tablets, 31, 41, 48, 308n33
  for Crypt Church, 48, 215, 227
  Noll on, 51
men. *See also* clergy; Knights of
     Columbus; laity; priests
  donations and, 53–55, 56, 81–82,
     233, 256–57
  lay male donors (1919), 256–57
  lay organizations and, 53, 138
  in religious orders, 53
  relationship between male clerics and
     women, 78–79, 88–91
Mestrovic, Ivan, 54
Methodists, 128, 145, 153, 175, 189
Mette, Margaret, 86, 87
Mexican Catholics, 72, 198, 200, 214,
     215, 218, 220, 223
Mexico, 44, 214–15, 218, 223
Michigan, 111–12
The Middle Ages, 141
Miller, Ownie, 85
Milwaukee, 96, 202, 326n22, 354n4
miracles, 74–75
Miranda, Florence, 84

missionaries, 98, 202–3, 208–10
  U.S. as missionary territory, 16, 27,
     288n15
Missionary Sisters of the Sacred Heart,
     206
missions, 47, 67, 139, 202–3, 211, 245
modern childhood, 96–97, 106
modernism, 6, 13–14, 237. *See also*
     countermodernism
modernity, 13–14, 24, 41, 43
Molloy, Thomas E., 27, 94
Montana, 55–56, 209
monuments, 41, 45. *See also* war
     memorials; Washington
     Monument
  and assertions on space and time,
     159, 176–80, 191
  the BNSIC and, 7, 29, 35, 44, 190,
     231–32, 237
  civic, 41, 139, 183–84
mood
  indicative, 159, 188, 236, 237
  subjunctive, 159, 180–82, 188, 236,
     237
moral risks, of consolidated Catholicism,
     230–37
Morano, Michael, 82
Moringiello, Marie, 108–10
Morse, Samuel, 195
Morton, Helen, 109–10
mosaics, 13, 151–52, 161, 219, 226
  Christ in Majesty, 10
  In Crypt Church, 150–52, 230
  Descent of the Holy Spirit, 207–8, 208f,
     226
  within East Porch, 181
  in Upper Church, 163, 217
  from Vatican Mosaic Studio, 49, 50f,
     128
mosques, 174–75
mothers and motherhood, 76, 128
Mother Theresa, 15
motives, of donors, 87. *See also* agency;
     hopes and fears; structure
movies, censorship of, 165, 166
murals, 185–86, 222, 227
Murillo's *Immaculate Conception*, 50, 50f,
     128
Murphy, Anna, 83
Murphy, Catherine, 80, 113

Murphy, Frederick, 29, 152, 176, 184, 322n4

Murphy, Lawrence C., 354n4

Murray, John Courtney, 163

music, 75, 77, 102, 106, 115, 129, 169, 217

Muslims, 174–75

Mystici Corporis Christi (Pius XII), 200–201

names
  of BNSIC, 16
  of devotees in Memorial Hall, 10, 76, 91, 120–21, 215, 230

National Afro-American Catholic Congress, 205

National Black Catholic Congress, 213, 226–27

National Cathedral. *See* Washington National Cathedral

National Catholic Family Record, 34, 215

National Catholic Reporter, 4, 240

National Catholic War Council, 35, 161–62

National Catholic Welfare Conference (NCWC)
  citizenship and, 196
  Civics Catechism, 196, 197f, 198
  contributions to, 38
  education and, 103
  formation of, 6, 35
  news service of, 39
  Social Action Department of, 166, 168

national churches, in capital, U.S., 171–76, 335n18, 336n22, 337nn24–25

National Council of Catholic Men, 39

National Council of Catholic Women, 66, 67

nationalism, 70, 185–86, 342n43
  See also Americanism

national memory, 168–80

National Organization for Decent Literature, 165

National Organization of Catholic Women (NOCW)
  disbanding of, 34, 293n20
  during first phase of building, 32–35
  Hoffman, L., and, 32–33, 58
  New York Times on, 32

National Origins Act of 1924, 133, 187

National Shrine of the Immaculate Conception. *See* Basilica of the National Shrine of the Immaculate Conception

national symbols, U.S., 180–81

national unity, 186

national Virgins, 194

Native Americans. *See* Indians

NCWC. *See* National Catholic Welfare Conference

neighborhoods, religious practice and, 20, 47, 85, 86, 101, 157, 176, 244

neo-scholasticism, 12–13, 169, 286nn10–11. *See also* Thomism

Neumann, Theresa, 74–75, 76, 77

New Deal, 168

Newman, John Henry, 159

New Jersey, 54, 57, 98, 111, 118, 120, 130, 133

New Mexico, 53

New Orleans, 165

New York (state), 38, 80, 86

New York City, 31–34, 38, 165

New York Times
  on BNSIC, 39
  on Cogan, 68
  on Fay, Sigourney, 130
  on NOCW, 32

Nicholas of Serbia, Archbishop, 75

NOCW. *See* National Organization of Catholic Women

Noll, John F., 10
  construction of Shrine and, 42–43
  media and, 117, 165
  on memorial tablet, 51
  during second phase of building, 36–38

non-Catholics, 201, 206–7, 226, 230, 238. *See also specific religions and denominations*

North Carolina, 38

nuns. *See also specific religious orders, schools, and individuals*
  absence of, 94–95
  autonomy of, 35
  dissent and, 12, 205, 240
  Catholic worldview and, 12
  children and, 94–95
  fundraising and, 37, 53, 93, 95, 112

institutional network and, 103, 110, 166, 201
labor of, 53, 94, 108, 166, 177, 196, 204, 231
monument to, 177
Sister's College and, 46
Ursuline, 53, 120, 121*f*
as visitors, 52–53, 56–57
Nuns of the Battlefield (Jolly), 178
Nuns of the Battlefield Memorial, 177–80, 177*f*

Obama, Barack, 175
Oblates of Mary Immaculate, 209
O'Boyle, Patrick, 10, 37, 182
O'Brien, David, 330n2
O'Brien, Rita, 93–94, 121
O'Brien, Teresa Joseph, 95
occupations. *See also* class
   of donors, 84, 86, 113–14
   ethnic diversity and, 211–12, 212*f*
O'Connell, William Henry, 66, 170*f*, 177, 177*f*, 187
O'Connor, Charles, 160
O'Connor, John, 333n13
O'Connor, Patrick, 37, 43, 121*f*
The Official Catholic Directory, 176
O'Hara, John F., 24, 39, 117
Ohio, 81
O'Keefe, Anna, 211
Old Soldiers' Home, 127
Olmstead, Frederick Law, Jr., 125
Olmstead, John Charles, 125
"On the Catholic Instruction of Youth" (Third Plenary Council at Baltimore), 103
oratories, 194
   definition of, 344n3
   ethnic, diversity and, 217–20, 220*t*, 225, 226*t*, 227, 239
   Filipino, 20, 193*f*, 194, 220–24, 351n41
ordinations
   of priests, 51
   of women, prohibition against, 64, 91
Oregon, 111
original sin, 99, 106
ornamentation, of Crypt Church, 147, 150–52, 232
orphans, 17, 73, 96, 116, 166–67, 176

Orsi, Robert, 287n14, 315n3
O'Toole, James, 119–20
O'Toole, Mary Bryne, 61
Our Lady of Altötting Chapel, 225
Our Lady of Antipolo, 221–22
Our Lady of Bergen, 216
Our Lady of Brezje Chapel, 220
Our Lady of Charity statue, 351n39
Our Lady of Czestochowa Chapel, 217, 220
Our Lady of Good Health, Vailankanni, 220, 224
Our Lady of Guadalupe Chapel, 218, 219*f*
Our Lady of Hope Chapel, 55
Our Lady of Korea at Cana, 226
Our Lady of Lourdes Chapel, 55, 218–19
Our Lady of Lourdes School, children from, 77, 78*f*
Our Lady of Mount Carmel Chapel, 53, 219
Our Lady of Peace and Good Voyage Oratory, 193*f*, 220, 227. *See also* Filipino oratory
Our Lady of Pompeii Chapel, 225
"Our Lady of the Catacombs," 124, 147
Our Lady of the Indians, 211
Our Mother of Africa Chapel, 16, 213–14
Our Sunday Visitor (newspaper), 36, 38
Outline of Church History (Shahan), 141

Pace, Edward A., 13, 61, 302n4
   Brennan, Elizabeth, and, 79–80, 90
   on Cogan, 67
   IFCA and, 66, 88
   Mary Memorial Altar and, 61, 62, 302n3
   modernism and, 13
   textbooks and, 106, 107
   Thomism and, 286n11
paintings, 50, 50*f*, 128. *See also* art; murals
Pan American Thanksgiving Day Mass, 136–37, 136*f*, 161, 162, 169, 235, 326n22
papacy. *See also* Rome; ultramontanism; Vatican; *specific individuals*
   authority of, 6, 12
   and condemnation of Americanism, 6, 13–14

papacy (*continued*)
    defense of, 142, 144
    Protestant criticism of, 139
    support from, 45, 49–50
parades
    Holy Name Society, 170–71, 170*f*,
        177, 235, 335n17
    Sunday School Union Anniversary
        Day, 82–83, 310n41, 311n43
parishes, identity and, 101
parochial schools, 103, 116
paternalism, 204, 227, 234
patriotism, 13, 97, 139, 160–65, 235
        See also Americanism; nationalism
Patroness Windows, 180–81
Pauline epistles, 200, 204, 225
Paul VI (pope), 49
"people of God," church as, 12, 239
Perkins, Frances, 169
Peyton, Patrick, 100
Pfisterer, Raphael, 185–86, 211, 341n42,
        342n43
The Phantom (comic), 321n38
Philadelphia, 19, 24, 26–27, 29, 30, 39,
        52, 54, 55, 67, 80, 108, 109, 116,
        117, 130, 203, 225, 235, 354n4
philanthropy, 65, 245, 303n9. *See also*
        donations; fundraising
Philippines. *See* Filipino Catholics;
        Filipino oratory
photographs, 20, 39, 70, 96, 328n43
    as historical evidence, 62, 72, 302n7
    nuns absence in, 94
pictorial theology, 147, 150, 154
Pierce, Franklin, 174
pilgrimage, 10–11, 22, 50, 61, 159, 243,
        245, 287n14. *See also* visitors
    children and, 110–11, 114–16,
        119–20, 238
    families and, 115
    as protest, 138
    and religious orders, 52–53
    and lay organizations, 53–54
    to Rome, 68
    shrines and, 16
    Tenth Annual National Filipino, 224
    women and, 61–62, 179, 233, 238
pilgrims. *See also* appendices (this volume);
        visitors
    first at BNSIC, 166,182

geographical distribution of donors
        and, 7, 44, 50, 54, 56, 80, 81, 86,
        308n37
    on *Salve Regina* cover, 120
    social profile of, 247–81
    types of, 229
    in visitors' logbook, 20–21
the Pill, 239. *See also* birth control;
        Humanae Vitae
Pio-Benedictine Code, 284n4
Piper, Norbert G., 53
Pittsburgh, 32, 33
Pius IX (pope), 8, 27–28, 132
Pius X (pope)
    on age for communion, 103
    relief of, 49
    Sapienti consilio, 288n15
    Shahan and, 8, 30
    support from, 45, 49, 55
    on women, 31
Pius XI (pope), 50
    on communism, 162
    Quadragesimo Anno, 334n14
    on radio, 164
    Seton and, 89
Pius XII (pope), 204
    on Marian Year, 27, 37
    Mystici Corporis Christi, 200–201
    on St. Claire of Assisi, 164
    support from, 50
Polish Catholics, 53, 56, 65, 85, 93, 103,
        181, 196–98, 200, 206, 211,
        216–17, 220, 227, 234
Polish immigrants, 197
Polish Women's Alliance, 53, 65
politics, 13, 17, 188–89, 235–37
        See also Americanism; civil
        religion; Kennedy, John F.;
        presidents; Pan American Mass;
        Red Mass, war
    Catholic rituals and, 168–71
    Catholic wartime patriotism and
        anti-communism and, 161–62
    church-state relations and, 13, 133,
        162–63
    "culture wars" and, 239
    electoral, 160–161, 237–38
    identity, 220
    JFK's absence from BNSIC and,
        188–89, 237–38

micro, 102
    social justice and, 166–68
    Virgin Mary and, 12, 240
Pope, John Russell, 337n25
popular culture, 98, 165, 236
Portland, Oregon, 38
postcard, Washington, D.C., 190, 190f
power, 96, 243
    definition of, 314n54
    episcopal, diocesan resources and,
        36–39
    meaning and, 243
Presbyterians, 24, 126, 145, 175, 176,
    188, 189, 236
presence, 8–10, 15, 17
    definition of, 8
    through Eucharist, 64
    by giving and going, 49–58, 110–20,
        227, 229
    incorporeal, 9, 125, 156, 230, 242
    real, doctrine of, 8–9, 25, 64, 74, 99,
        147, 149, 152, 240
    as theme for writing Catholic
        history, 9
    types of, 8–9, 21
presidents, U.S., 136, 160–61, 174–75,
    188–89, 337n24. *See also specific*
    presidents
priests
    donations from, 51–52, 249–50
    as hierarchical middlemen, 51
    as isolated, 231
    ordinations of, 51
    parish, 10, 28, 52, 74
print media, 31, 38–39, 117, 332n9
    See also comics; magazines
processions, 159, 168
    May Crownings, 108–10, 109f,
        319n23
    May Day, 169–70
Progressive Era, 34–35
progressive *vs.* conservative Catholicism,
    4, 6, 239–41
progressive websites, 4
Protestant establishment, 83, 189,
    312n43
Protestant Reformation, 139–40, 141
Protestants. *See also particular*
    denominations
    in Brooklyn, 82–83, 312n43

Catholics' relations with, 103,
    123–56, 162–64, 187–89, 232,
    324n12
    complexity of attitudes before and
        after 1913, 125–31
    cooperation, sympathy and
        conversion of, 126–28
    historical narratives of, 139–42, 143
    and Pan American mass controversy,
        136
    Salve Regina and, 128–29, 131
    Seton's conversion from
        Protestantism, 127
    Shahan on, 123–24, 131, 232
    on Virgin Mary, 123–24, 128–29,
        140, 142
    as visitors, 128–31
    Washington Post and, 127, 131, 136,
        138
public Catholicism, 195–96, 198, 330n2
public schools, 108, 115–16, 133, 195
Puerto Rico, 44
Puglise, Joseph, 55

Quadragesimo Anno (Pius XI), 334n14
Quarterly Bulletin (IFCA), 59, 69
Queen of Missions Chapel, 208–9
question box, 138
The Question Box (Conway), 139–40

race
    Anglo-Saxon, 133, 195
    childhood, youth, and, 96–97
    discord and, 204
    evolutionary theories and, 199
    Marian devotion and, 214
    U.S. color code and, 199, 200, 212,
        226
    whiteness and, 199–200, 206, 211
race riots, 199
racism, 204, 234, 239. *See also* Ku Klux
    Klan
    Anglo-Saxon supremacy and, 133,
        195
    CUA and, 205, 213
radio, 39, 164
Reagan, Ronald, 189
real presence, doctrine of, 8–9, 25, 64,
    74, 99, 147, 149, 152, 240
recreational organizations, 101–2

Red Mass, 169, 236, 238, 334n15
regions. *See* geographical distribution of
  donors and pilgrims
Reilly, John J., 42, 236
relief, of Pius X, 49
religion
  as translocative and transtemporal, 49
  civil, 171, 335n18
  crossing and dwelling in, 18, 243–45
  theory of, 18, 241–45
Religion: A Secondary School Course
  (Campion), 107, 108
"Religion Row," 174–75, 336n23
religious ceremonies, at Washington
  National Cathedral, 189
religious diversity, 164, 171, 174–75,
  336n23
religious liberty, 134, 162–63, 170
religious orders, 52–53, 219, 251–55,
  299nn47–48
representations, 18, 125, 242
republican style, 330n2
Ricard, John H., 213
Ricker, Hubert, 70–71
Richer, Kevin, 306n21
Ricker, Michael, 306n21
Ricker, Mrs. Hubert. *See* Downs, Mary
Riley, Mrs. F. H., 209, 210f, 349n26
Ritter, Joseph E., 41, 44, 46, 48, 165
ritual, 159, 168–71, 235–36. *See also*
  baptism; Eucharist; liturgy; mass;
  Pan American Thanksgiving Day
  Mass; parades; pilgrimages;
  processions; Red Mass; rosary; vigils
Rizzo, Catherine, 85
Robinson, George T., 163f
Roeder, John B., 37
Roe v. Wade, 240
La Roma sotterranea cristiana (De Rossi),
  144–45
Roman Catholicism. *See* Catholicism
Romanism in the Light of History
  (McKim), 135, 139
Roma Sotterranea (Bosio), 143
Rome. *See also* Vatican
  importance of, 12
  relations with, 45, 49, 102–3, 242
Rooney, Dorothy, 211
Roosevelt, Franklin, 168
Roosevelt, Theodore, 172

rosary, praying, 100
Ross, John F., 57
Rossi, Walter R., 224, 225, 285n5
Rousseau, Jean-Jacques, 335n18
Rudd, Daniel, 205
Russell, William T., 133–39, 136f, 162–63
Ryan, James J., 55, 233, 300n51
Ryan, John, 15, 166–68, 236, 333n13,
  334n14
Ryan, Mary Oswald, 95
Rydzynski, Joseph, 211

Sacred Congregation for the Propagation
  of the Faith, 27
sacrifice, children and, 98–99, 106–7, 111
saints. *See also* canonization; *specific
  saints*
  and *Christ in Majesty* mosaic, 10
  ethnic, 194
St. Augustine, 27, 181
St. Augustine's Church, 205, 213
St. Brigid of Ireland Chapel, 220
St. Brigid's Altar, 179
St. Claire of Assisi, 164
St. Ignatius Church (Maryland), 209
St. Joseph Alumnae Association, 66
St. Joseph's Commercial School, 318n22
  donors from, 93–95, 112–14, 113t,
    277–79
  May Crownings at, 108–10
  yearbook for, 102, 316n12
St. Louis, 38, 96, 165
St. Mark's (Venice), 24
St. Matthew's Church (Washington,
  D.C.), 238
St. Patrick's Church (Washington, D.C.),
  132, 136, 137, 169, 176
St. Priscilla (Rome), Catacomb of,
  144–46, 144f, 152, 154–55
St. Paul Confraternity of Christian
  Doctrine, 98
St. Thomas Aquinas School, 318n22
  donors from, 93–94, 95f, 112–14,
    113t, 274–76
  May Crownings at, 108–10
St. Vincent de Paul Chapel, 219
St. Vincent's Home, 166, 167f
Salve Regina
  clerical aspirations and, 41–46
  on Crypt Church, 148, 150

diversity and, 209, 211–13, 214, 217
donor letters in, 19, 30, 54–55
fundraising and, 32–34, 54, 59, 69,
 80, 233
pilgrims on cover of, 120
Protestants and, 128–29, 131
on Washington, D.C., 176, 184
Salve Regina League, 34, 35, 215
San Antonio, 51
San Francisco, 32, 96
Santa Fe, 53
Santa Maria Maggiore (Rome), 126, 150
Sapienti consilio (Pius X), 288n15
scale
 of analysis, 242
 local, national, and transnational, 15,
 286n12
Schaffler, Clara, 86
Schmid, Miriam, 84
school culture, 101–10
schools. *See also* teachers; *specific schools*
 agency and structure in, 101–3
 catechisms and, 103–6, 316n15,
 317n17
 Catholic, 12, 93–95, 95*f*, 101–10,
 104*f*, 195–96, 318n22
 curricula in, 107–10, 195–96
 identity and, 101
 parochial, 103, 116
 public, 108, 115–16, 133, 195
 textbooks in, 106–8, 178–79,
 195–96, 317n19
 visitors from, 56–57, 77, 78*f*, 115–16,
 120, 121*f*, 301n55
Schwab, Mary Rose, 55
Scotus, Duns, 28
scriptural passages
 in *Descent of the Holy Spirit* mosaic,
 207
 on East Wall, 182
sculpture, 8
 of black Madonna and Child, 213
 of Cabrini, 218
 East Wall, 160
 of Mary Immaculate, 54, 181
 of Tekawitha, 211, 226
 Korean, 226
 of Mary as Queen of Missions, 211
Seattle, 55, 119
Second Vatican Council. *See* Vatican II

secularity, Catholicism and., 43, 47
segregation, 197, 205, 213, 234. *See also*
 race; racism
Seh, Kathryn, 102
selective countermodernism, 7, 12–14,
 25, 230, 237
separation of church and state, 13, 163,
 171, 172, 185, 189
September 11, 2001 terrorist attacks, 175
Serra, Junipero, 181
Seton, Elizabeth Ann Bayley (saint), 65,
 76–77
 canonization of, 68, 74, 89
 conversion from Protestantism, 127
sexual abuse, of children, 234, 239–40,
 244, 353n4, 356n12
Shahan, Thomas J.
 "The Apostolic See" sermon, 49
 on architecture, 24–25
 The Beginnings of Christianity, 141,
 146–47
 The Blessed Virgin in the Catacombs,
 123, 142, 145–46
 catacombal ceramics and, 152–54
 clerical aspirations and, 41, 43–46
 death of, 8
 during first phase of building, 29–34,
 36
 foundation stone booklet and, 48,
 163
 as founder of BNSIC, 8, 13, 24, 230,
 286n10
 on history of Christianity, 140–43,
 146–47
 IFCA and, 66, 88, 90, 91
 Mary Memorial Altar and, 9*f*, 61, 64,
 68–70, 72, 301n3
 modernism and, 13, 24, 45
 with Murillo's *Immaculate Conception*,
 50*f*
 Pius X and, 8, 30
 priests' donations, in response to
 1919 letter by, 51–52, 249–50
 on Protestants, 123–24, 131, 155,
 232
 sarcophagus/tomb of, 10, 11*f*, 51,
 230
 Thomism and, 13, 286n11
 triumphalist Americanism of, 13, 24, 45
 on Virgin Mary, 153

Sheen, Fulton, 15, 39, 164, 286n11
Sheeran, Clara
  biographical information for, 67–68
  fundraising for Mary Memorial
    Altar and, 59–61, 64, 65, 68, 69,
    90, 92
  after Mary Altar dedication, 9f,
    301n3
  McKenna and, 89–90
  relationship with male clerics, 88–91
Sheeran, James Jerome, 67
Sherry, Margaret, 85
Shields, Thomas Edward, 46, 106–7
Shrine. *See* Basilica of the National
  Shrine of the Immaculate
  Conception
shrines, 45–46
  definition of, 16
  Marian, 16, 18, 27, 30, 37, 215
  pilgrimages and, 16
  types of, 16, 287n14
"The Shrine You Can Build" (comic), 93,
  94f, 118
Sikhs, 174
Sinclair, Upton, 46
Sisters College, 46, 297n39
Sisters of Charity, 65–66, 166, 167f
Sisters of Providence, 73, 76, 307n27
Sisters of St. Joseph, 53, 94–95, 112,
  315n2
  Great Dome windows funded by, 52,
    121, 321n43
Sisters of the Blessed Sacrament for
  Indians and Colored People, 204
slavery, 199, 213
Slovakian Catholics, 48, 198, 220
Slovenian Catholics, 220
Smith, Alfred E., 83, 133, 160, 187, 235
Smith, John, 209
Smith, William, 48–49
Smith, William F., 115
Snowden, George H., 181
"So Beat the Drums," 98
social capital, 159, 330n3. *See also* civic
  space
social profile of pilgrims and donors,
  78–87, 112–14, 113t, 247–81
society, economy and, 166–68, 334n14
Society for the Propagation of the Faith,
  202–3

Sodality of the Blessed Virgin, 52, 108
*A Soldier's Recollections: Leaves from the
  Diary of a Young Confederate*
  (McKim), 134
Soubirous, Bernadette, 28
Soulforce, 240
"The Souls of the White Folk" (Du Bois),
  199
South Bend, 20, 71, 85
South Carolina, 57
Southgate, Edward W., 127
space, 146–50, 157. *See also* built
  environment; civic space;
  landscape; religion
Spalding, John L., 316n14
Spellman, Francis Cardinal, 161, 162,
  163f, 164
spiritual capitol, 185–86, 190
spiritual formation, 99, 106
Spock, Benjamin, 97
stained-glass windows, 150, 151,
  180–81
Stanly, Hilbert, 214
statues. *See also* sculpture
  of Jesus, Paul, and twelve disciples,
    61
  Marian, 41, 76, 77, 78f, 91, 181, 221,
    352n42
  Our Lady of Charity, 351n39
  of Tekakwitha, 211
stigmatic, 74–75, 76
Stowe, Harriet Beecher, 128
strategies of survival, for Jews, 138,
  327n25
Stratton, Mary Chase, 152–55, 232
Strong, Josiah, 195
structure, 47, 90, 101–3, 121, 314n1
  See also agency
Studies in Church History (Conway), 140
subjunctive mood, 159, 180–82, 188,
  236, 237
submission, of women, 64, 65, 89–91,
  314n55
suburbanization, 17, 288n17
Sunday School Union Anniversary Day
  parade, 82–83, 310n41, 311n43
Supreme Court, 169, 236, 238, 240
Survivors Network of those Abused by
  Priests, 356n12
Susanna (saint), 130

Swedenborgians, 127, 175
Synon, Mary, 118, 321n38

Tablet (Catholic weekly), 77, 79, 90–91
Taft, Nellie, 136, 136*f*
Taft, William Howard, 136, 136*f*, 161, 161*f*
teachers, 107–8, 118, 196, 318n22
technology, communication and travel,
    14, 28, 30, 97, 240–43
Tekakwitha, Catherine (saint), 226
    canonization of, 73
    statue of, 211
television, 24, 39, 117, 164, 241–42
temples, 174
Tennessee, 56, 73, 79, 80, 85, 269–70
Tenth Annual National Filipino
    Pilgrimage, 224
Texas, 51, 118, 200
textbooks, 106–8, 178–79, 195–96, 317n19
Theological College, 3
Third Plenary Council at Baltimore,
    102–3, 104, 207
Thomism, 6, 14, 230, 232, 286n11
    See also Aquinas, Thomas;
    consolidated Catholicism,
    worldview of; neo-scholasticism
threshold, BNSIC as, 7, 15, 18, 124, 194,
    229, 245
Titian's *Assumption of the Virgin*, 50
Topix (comic), 98–99
tourists, 120, 189
Training in Courtesy, 196
translocative histories, 15, 286n12
transnationalism. *See also* Catholicism,
    institutional network of
    Catholicism and, 6, 16, 22, 27–28, 49,
    57, 192
    and the "transnational turn," 343n1
transtemporal artifacts, 49
travel books, 128
Treasure Chest of Fun and Fact (comic),
    97–98, 117–19
Trinity College, 46, 151, 176–77
triumphalist Americanism, 12–13, 27,
    286n10, 330n2
tropes, 200. *See also* body of Christ;
    ecclesiology
Truman, Harry S., 188
Tucker, Gregory W., 131, 285n5
Turner, Thomas W., 204–5, 244

Ukrainian Catholics, 220
ultramontanism, 6, 12, 28, 105, 237
Unam Sanctam (Boniface VIII), 201
Unitarians, 126, 171
United States (U.S.). *See also* capital, U.S.;
    presidents, U.S.
    color code of, 199, 200, 212, 226
    issues dividing, 6
    as missionary territory, 16, 27,
        288n15
    national symbols of, 180–81
    number of immigrants in, 225
    Virgin Mary as patroness of, 7, 27,
        180–81, 342n43
    after World War I, 45
unity
    in body of Christ, 224–27
    diversity and, 194, 198, 204, 222,
        224–27
    ecclesiastical, 7
    national, 186
Universalists, 126, 175
University of Notre Dame, 19
Ursuline nuns, 53, 120, 121*f*
U.S. *See* United States
users, 18, 125, 242

Van Den Berg, Martin, 33
Vatican. 6, 7, 12, 41, 45, 47, 49, 80,
    90, 99, 102, 132–33, 164, 170,
    176, 194, 201, 230, 242, 244
    See also papacy; Rome;
    ultramontanism
    embassy in D.C., 159, 176
    Mosaic Studio, 49, 50*f*, 128
    Sacred Congregation for the
        Propagation of the Faith, 27
Vatican I, 201, 244
Vatican II, 12, 207, 238, 239,
    355n9
    as "updating," 6, 238
    "Declaration on Religious
        Freedom," 163
    John XXIII and, 6
Vermeersch, Arthur, 286n11
Viall, James, 354n4
Vietnamese Catholics, 226
Vietnam War, 17, 161, 162, 239–40
vigils, 31, 169
Vincentians, 219

Virgin Mary. See also "age of Mary";
    Immaculate Conception; Marian
    devotion; Marian images; Marian
    shrines; Marian statues; Marian Year
    apparitions of, 5, 16, 27–28, 48, 55,
        99, 219, 240
    catacombs and, 143–46, 144f, 148,
        232
    doctrine of Immaculate Conception,
        27–28
    May Day processions for, 169–70
    as patroness of U.S., 7, 27, 180–81,
        342n43
    Protestants on, 123–24, 128–29, 140,
        142
    sculpture of, as Queen of Missions,
        211
    Shahan on, 153
Virgin Mary bell, 183
Virgin of Antipolo, 221–22
Virginia, 55, 62, 67, 85, 189
visitors. See also pilgrimages; pilgrims
    adult lay devotees and women
        religious (1925–1927), 251–55
    children as, 56–57, 166, 167f, 280–81
    McKenna and, 56–57, 166, 167f
    number of, 189, 238
    nuns as, 52–53, 57
    Protestants as, 128–31
    religious orders and, 52–53, 251–55,
        299nn47–48
    from schools, 56–57, 77, 78f, 115–16,
        120, 121f, 301n55
visitor's logs, 20–21, 114–15
Visits to Theresa Neumann (Brennan, E.),
    74–75
visual culture. See artifacts; media
Vitta, Charles F., 94

Walsh, James Anthony, 202
Walsh, Thomas J., 51, 184, 298n46
Walsh, Timothy F., 29
war. See also specific wars
    and the BNSIC, 244
    Catholic patriotism and, 160–62
    and Jews, 162
    memorials, 159, 177–79
    protests against, 239, 240
    and reduced Protestant nativism, 159
Washington, D.C. See also capital, U.S.

African Americans in, 16, 199,
    205, 213
anti-Catholicism in, 131–37, 134f
diversity in, 217, 225
politics and media in, 160–65
postcard of, 190, 190f
race riots in, 199
Salve Regina on, 176, 184
Sixteenth Street as "the Street of
    Churches," 175, 336n23, 337n24
Washington, George, 139
Washington Monument, 132, 133, 162,
    183
Washington National Cathedral, 159,
    171–73, 172f
    BNSIC and, 5, 18, 23, 173, 184,
        188–90, 236, 238, 289n1
    composite with U.S. Capitol, 187f
    religious ceremonies at, 189
Washington Post
    Protestants and, 127, 131, 136, 138
    on U.S. capital, 173, 174, 189–90
The Way, the Truth, and the Life, 107
Weber, Max, 283n4
websites
    for BNSIC, 218, 238, 241, 289n1,
        328n43, 355n10
    conservative, 4
    progressive, 4
West Virginia, 57
Whelan, Fannie, 33
whiteness, 199–200, 206, 211. See also
    race
Whitton, Helen Stafford, 61, 301n3
Wilson, Woodrow, 136, 137, 161, 189,
    355n8
Wimmer, Boniface, 185
windows
    for Great Dome, 52, 121, 321n43
    Patroness, 180–81
    rose, of Great Upper Church, 91, 92
    stained-glass, 150, 151, 180–81
womanhood, 64, 66
women, 233. See also feminism; nuns
    absence of, in scholarship, 302n
    adult female donors to Mary Altar
        from Brooklyn, 265–68
    adult female donors to Mary Altar
        from Indiana and Tennessee,
        85–86, 269–70

adult female donors to Mary Altar
   living outside Brooklyn, 85–87,
   271–73
as assertively submissive, 64, 65,
   89–91, 314n55
donations and, 12, 17, 31–35, 46,
   53–54, 82–87
Mary Memorial Altar, fundraising
   and, 59–92, 301n1, 305n19
ordination of, prohibition against, 64, 91
Pius X on, 31
relationship between male clerics
   and, 78–79, 88–91

women religious. *See also* nuns; *and
   specific religious orders*
   donations from, 82
   as visitors, 251–55
Woods, Elinor, 84, 85
World War I, 34, 45
World War II, 8, 36, 161–63, 163*f*

youth. *See* childhood; children
youth movements, 103

Zimmerman, Loretta, 114
Zimmerman, Margaret, 84